THE BEST PLAYS OF 1944-45

THE BEST PLAYS
OF 1944-45

AND THE
YEAR BOOK OF THE DRAMA
IN AMERICA

EDITED BY
BURNS MANTLE

ARNO PRESS
A New York Times Company
New York – 1975

THE BEST PLAYS OF 1944-45

Photo by George Karger, Pix Inc.

"A BELL FOR ADANO"

Tina—The torrone is not very good. . . .
Tomasino—She is right. The torrone is like glue. No invitation.
Joppolo—Please tell your wife I will be very glad to come.

(Fredric March, Margo, Alexander Granach)

THE BEST PLAYS
OF 1944-45

AND THE
YEAR BOOK OF THE DRAMA
IN AMERICA

EDITED BY
BURNS MANTLE

With Illustrations

DODD, MEAD AND COMPANY
NEW YORK - - - 1946

INTRODUCTION

THERE was little promise at the end of our third wartime theatre year that much could be expected of the fourth year, which would be that of 1944-45, through which we have just passed. I, your editor, had dutifully pointed out that during such lamentable crises as those developed by a world war, "inspirations falter and routines fail" in the theatre, but I did hold to sufficient courage to predict that some good was bound to come from the overall adventure.

It has. And, in the theatre, much more promptly than the most optimistic of showmen expected. The entertainments, musical and dramatic, that were brought to the Broadway market this season of 1944-45 are generally admitted to be the most satisfying list of plays produced the last decade.

While most of the war plays submitted last season were disappointing, at least three of those produced this year were splendidly stimulating. Paul Osborn's "A Bell for Adano," stemming from John Hersey's prize-winning novel of the same title, was, I believe, the most important of the three. It presented with reasonable conviction situations arising in the invaded countries of Europe that had to be handled with tact and intelligence if the American way of life, and the ideal of liberty for which America was, and is, prepared to fight and to die, is to prevail. Perceptibly strengthened by the incisive performance of Fredric March as the brusquely reluctant but honestly consistent idealist, Major Joppolo, "A Bell for Adano" humanized Army directives and Army directors.

Capt. John Patrick's "The Hasty Heart," approaching the war through the experiences of a volunteer in the American Field Service, recorded individual character virtues and reactions that were both lightly amusing and profoundly moving. And Rose Franken's "Soldier's Wife" intelligently anticipated certain domestic problems that are bound, either directly to invade or indirectly to bear upon those years of readjustment that lie immediately ahead of us.

The reaching out for new forms, the development of novel patterns, in the writing and staging of drama also made definite progress this year. John Van Druten's treatment of such char-

v

acter values and scraps of story as he took from Kathryn Forbes' novel, "Mama's Bank Account," with which he built and vitalized "I Remember Mama," did the theatre a real service, emphasized by the fine performances of Mady Christians and Oscar Homolka.

John Marquand and George Kaufman's treatment of the incidental material they took from Mr. Marquand's novel, "The Late George Apley," added a fine dignity and several excellent individual characterizations to the season's record, headed by the understanding performance of Leo G. Carroll in the name part.

Tennessee Williams' "memory play," "The Glass Menagerie," which enjoyed stirring adventures as a popular favorite in both Chicago and New York, was helped greatly by the uncannily perfect performance of Laurette Taylor. This factor both the author and the dramatic critics, the comedy's most enthusiastic admirers, were quick to admit.

The touch of fantasy that Mary Chase wrote into "Harvey," in her creation of the invisible "pooka," or huge white rabbit that accompanied the amiably bibulous hero through the comedy, sounded a new note in character creation. It will, I fear, be taken up by less inventive writers. If this happens it is earnestly to be hoped that Mrs. Chase's imitators will also bring back to the theatre other comedians of such high individual talent as that of Frank Fay, who, overnight, made the hero of "Harvey" his very own.

There is substantial drama in Philip Yordan's "Anna Lucasta," which was taken over by the American Negro Theatre after the author had written it with a Polish family background. It happens to be the type of human adventure drama that could be played by any race and in any language, but we are bound to believe that the transitional changes made for the Negro Theatre by Harry Wagstaffe Gribble, and the exceptional performances by the Negro actors, had much to do with the success of "Anna Lucasta" in New York.

Philip Barry also felt the trend toward fanciful drama when he wrote "Foolish Notion." Whether or not he had Tallulah Bankhead in mind for the leading role, that of a wife who is about to remarry following the reported disappearance of her husband in the European war theatre, that actress was unquestionably most helpful in establishing the popularity of the play.

Norman Krasna's "Dear Ruth" might fairly be described as a bit of high, and also highly improbable, farce. It strains the probabilities in the cause of a mounting laughter that follows the complications of the plot. The Krasna mission is to entertain audiences, let who will question either the methods he employs or the familiar story he retells.

This is the twenty-sixth volume of "The Best Plays," consecutively published since the season of 1919-20—the twenty-eighth volume if we count the 1899-1909 and 1909-1919 volumes which, with the helpful collaboration of Garrison P. Sherwood, were later added. Two of the digests in this issue, those of "Foolish Notion" and "Harvey," have been made by John Chapman. Your editor, having retired from active play reviewing after forty-five years' service devoted to that profession, felt that this theatre yearbook should continue to have an active representative in the front line of play reviewers. Mr. Chapman, drama critic of the *New York Daily News* and dramatic correspondent of the N. Y. News-Chicago Tribune Syndicate, has agreed to serve as a watchful observer in the field.

Again the editor's thanks to his persistently and consistently loyal readers is heartfelt and expansive.

B. M.

Forest Hills, L. I., 1945

CONTENTS

ILLUSTRATIONS

THE BEST PLAYS OF 1944-45

THE SEASON IN NEW YORK

THERE is always a good deal of talk along the Broadway curbs and in the play producers' offices about the help the moneyed interests of Hollywood have been, and still are, to the better drama and the struggling dramatists of this theatrical capital. There was more of such talk this year than for sometime, due doubtless to the fact that the Broadway theatre has been doing a booming wartime business at its box-offices—a booming business in which the Hollywood moneyed interests shared generously.

According to a *New York Times* statistician, Hollywood producers advanced something like $4,000,000 for twenty-eight Broadway scripts this season, buying up such promising long-run plums as "I Remember Mama," "Life with Father" and "The Voice of the Turtle," and then salving their consciences, if any, or at least balancing their budgets, by taking on such unpromising short-run unpredictables as "The Visitor," "Odds on Mrs. Oakley," and "Violet," not to mention "Oh, Brother," "Sheppey" and "But Not Goodbye."

In any event the commercial tie-in as between the picture-makers and the legitimate play producers is stronger than it has ever been before, and likewise more sanely and co-operatively satisfying than before.

This statement may reasonably be written into the record, despite the fact that one day recently Burton Rascoe of the *New York World-Telegram* counted something like thirty-nine failures among forty recent attempts by Hollywood playwrights to make the Broadway grade. He may have been thinking of the James Gow-Arnold d'Usseau "Tomorrow the World" of last season as the single success, or it may have been Norman Krasna's "Dear Ruth," which threatens to outplay them all. And he evidently did not admit Louis Solomon and Harold Buchman's "Snafu," which got 158 performances.

It is also true (quite painfully true this season) that the picture stars who decide from time to time to come back to Broadway to re-establish themselves as legitimate actors of definite talent have given frequent proof that they have sharpened neither their wits nor their gifts in Hollywood. Billie Burke tried it. Mary Astor tried it. Miriam Hopkins tried it. Gloria Swanson tried it. Carol Landis tried. Richard Arlen, Roscoe Karns, Hugh Herbert, Franchot Tone tried, and flivvered when they did not actually flop.

Still I repeat, as between the Hollywood and Broadway show sectors, this season has been more co-operatively satisfying than any other of recent recording. Scenario-writing and picture-acting do undoubtedly take the edge off more talent than they put an edge on. And it certainly behooves both writers and actors not to get too much of either without an occasional stimulating change to the other. But in end results there is every reason why acting for the screen drama and writing for the screen drama should help to develop and advance the careers of all practitioners of the histrionic and associate arts.

It was a season of exorbitantly high prices in the theatre. First nights for which orchestra seats sold for $12 and $8 were common, and the regular admission scale for the more popular musical plays remained fixed at a $6 top.

It was a season in which the players, as loyal to the war effort as though they had been drafted into Army or Navy, gave unsparingly of their time to make benefit shows popular and successful. Hundreds of the profession made the journey to both the European and South Pacific fronts to cheer the fighting men. The record, not of their sacrifices, but of their loyal interest in and devotion to their troubled country, will brighten the pages of actor history for years to come.

It was a season in which the musical comedy flourished beyond normal expectations. "Bloomer Girl," "On the Town," "Up in Central Park" and "Carousel" were added to "Oklahoma," which had run through the previous season and is still immensely popular. Each one of these added hits was sold at a premium through the season. "Sing Out, Sweet Land," a cavalcade of American folk music, held on for a hundred and one performances. Two efforts were made to capitalize Gilbert-Sullivan patterns, both utilizing "H.M.S. Pinafore" music. One, "Hollywood Pinafore," with Victor Moore and William Gaxton co-starred, was ambitiously conceived by George S. Kaufman. The other, "Memphis Bound," featured a colored showboat performance of "Pinafore." Both failed. Two other expensive failures included adaptations of "Rain," retitled "Sadie Thompson," and "The Firebrand," billed as "The Firebrand of Florence."

And so we come to the factual record of the season. Picking up the production of new plays and important revivals in mid-June, 1944, we discover that there were three Summer plays tried out in June and July. One, "Love on Leave," written by A. B. Shiffrin, was a seven-performance failure; one, Agatha Christie's "Ten Little Indians," was an all-season success, still running when this record was compiled a year later, and one was a happy revival, "Hats Off to Ice," which continues to turn a profit for the Rockefeller-built Center Theatre, located, properly enough, at the edge of that tourist mecca, Rockefeller Center.

Mrs. Christie's "Ten Little Indians" was tricky as all get out, and very popular with mystery story fans. Ten more or less mysterious individuals were mysteriously summoned to an island off the Devonshire coast in England. Arrived there, they were mysteriously informed, by way of a concealed radio, that each of them had been responsible for one or more deaths and would have to pay. One by one they were "knocked off," as gangster terminology has it. Each time one disappeared an Indian figurine toppled off a mantel in the living room of the mysterious house which serves as a setting for the play. When only the hero and heroine were left Mrs. Christie decided to call it an evening and the play ended.

"Icetravaganzas," as they have come to be called, have become a fixture at the Center as definitely as the old-time Hippodrome shows became a fixture at the Hipp. "Hats Off to Ice" had a fine cast of skaters, headed by the comedian Freddie Trenkler and the supremely graceful figure skater, Carol Lynne. Queen Sonja Henie is still a principal stock holder in the ice show business.

In August the fun began. There were eight productions, three of them failures, two of them successful, three of them freakish box office hits. The outstanding successes were "Song of Norway" and "Anna Lucasta," the first a musicalized autobiography of the composer, Edvard Grieg, the second a fairly stark drama of Negro family life in a small industrial town in Pennsylvania. Both ran through the season and were still popular a year later.

The box office hits were, as you might expect, heavy with sex appeal of a kind—Mae West's "Catherine Was Great," which defied a critical drubbing to run for 191 performances, and continue profitably so long as Miss West cared to play it on tour, and a little something in one-piece flesh displays called "School for Brides," thought up by Frank Gill Jr. and George Carleton Brown.

Elisabeth Bergner, who had practically worn herself out the

season before playing the popular melodrama, Martin Vale's "The Two Mrs. Carrolls," came dutifully back to work after a six-week vacation and added another couple hundred performances to the play's record. Then she, too, went touring.

The most satisfying event of the Summer, and the most significant, in a way, was the continuing success of the New York City Center of Music and Drama. At least this was a satisfying success so far as its dramatic features were concerned. Neither the ballet nor the symphony orchestra engagements did too well, though both developed loyal and sizable publics. The revived operas and the popular-priced extension runs of Broadway hits, however, were consistently successful, proving beyond question that a civic theatre can be a self-supporting addition to the social and cultural life of any city, without hurt to its commercial competitors. The drama ranged through Helen Hayes' engagement in "Harriet" and a revival of "Little Women" for the holidays, to three weeks of the Paul Robeson "Othello" and eight performances of Eva LeGallienne's revival of Chekhov's "The Cherry Orchard."

Lou Holtz held a vaudeville bill together under the title of "Star Time" for 120 performances. An interesting failure of the early Fall was a wartime drama called "Men to the Sea," written by a newspaperman, Herbert Kubly. It posed the wartime problems of four or five service men's wives quartered economically in a Brooklyn rooming house. Their devastating loneliness beats at the defenses of the faithful wives, but only one or two are beaten down. A dramatic climax, shown in two parts, revealed the wives and their friends and neighbors indulging in an alcoholic drinking party, while their men were being shot up on a destroyer in the South Pacific.

Two of the earlier hits were Rose Franken's "Soldier's Wife," which is a part of this record, and "Bloomer Girl," an attractive period piece having to do with the hoopskirt and bloomer girl rebellion of the 1860s. With music by Harold Arlen and lyrics by E. Y. Harburg, ballets by Agnes De Mille and a grand assortment of billowing costumes by Miles White, "Bloomer Girl" easily challenged the earlier popularity of the champ, "Oklahoma!", and later held its own fairly well against "Up in Central Park" and "Carousel."

Another October success was John Van Druten's "I Remember Mama," taken from Kathryn Forbes' short stories, published as "Mama's Bank Account." From the date of its opening until it was withdrawn for the vacation weeks of Summer, "I Remember

Mama" was in steady demand, with nary a seat going unsold.

The amusing returned-soldier comedy, "Snafu," written by Louis Solomon and Harold Buchman and produced by George Abbott, as noted, almost made the outstanding hit list. Its freakish title, adapted from the Army "situation normal, all fouled up," and the strong competition of a veritable hit parade, held it back. This was the story of a youthful soldier. He had lied about his age and, at his mother's request, was sent home by his colonel, even though his Army record was well above average.

It was in late October that Miriam Hopkins and Victor Jory came East to co-star in Samson Raphaelson's "The Perfect Marriage." The picture stars were both a hit and a draw with their publics, but Mr. Raphaelson's comedy was voted a little on the obvious side. Ninety-two performances and it was withdrawn.

Ethel Barrymore's luck did not hold through the successor she chose to follow "The Corn Is Green." This was a piece that had been adapted by L. Bush-Fekete and Mary Helen Fay from a Franz Werfel original and was called "Embezzled Heaven." The story had to do with a middle-aged cook who financed a nephew's education with the understanding that he was to study for the priesthood. Her heart was all but broken when the boy turned out to be a crook, though she was comforted by a pilgrimage to Rome and an audience with an understanding Pope. Miss Barrymore suffered a severe illness during her engagement and was kept from the stage for several weeks.

"Harvey," the surprise Pulitzer prize of the season, arrived the first day of November. The second day of November the "Harvey" box office began selling seats for three months ahead and the pace never slackened after that. This fantastic comedy, written by Mary Chase of Denver, Colorado, brought Frank Fay back to Broadway after his long career in vaudeville and the night clubs, as is reported more fully elsewhere.

Otherwise November was more notable for its misses than its hits. Ilka Chase tried a dramatization of her best-selling novel, "In Bed We Cry," and failed. Howard Dietz and Rouben Mamoulian tried, and failed, with an elaborate musicalized version (score by Vernon Duke) of the Colton-Randolph "Rain," which they called "Sadie Thompson." Laurence Stallings, after a protracted absence, came back with a soldier hero's adventure in the South Seas called "The Streets Are Guarded." This got only 24 performances, though it certainly deserved more.

A richly staged operetta, financed by Lorraine Manville Dresselhuys to the tune of $200,000, by report, and called "Rhapsody," got 13 performances and died on its expensive back. An unusually interesting and well-played comedy called "The Man Who Had All the Luck," written by Arthur Miller, was mistakenly withdrawn, it seemed to this writer, after only 4 performances. It was at least worth a three-week chance to find itself and its public.

Only a single hit was revealed to balance this sad list of failures. This was John P. Marquand and George S. Kaufman's dramatization of Mr. Marquand's successful novel, "The Late George Apley." The dramatists used little more than an episode or two from the novel, but succeeded admirably in reproducing the story's dignity and flavor, and were definitely aided by the performances of a splendid dramatic company headed by Leo G. Carroll. Janet Beecher, Margaret Dale and Percy Waram were his chief associates.

The holiday list proved a happy one. Happy, at least, in spots. Paul Osborn's adaptation of "A Bell for Adano," taken from John Hersey's novel of the same title (which afterward won the Pulitzer award as the best American novel of the year), came to Broadway on December 6. It was immediately acclaimed the best war play of the year, and never suffered the loss of its pre-eminence in this category. Its success is a part of this record.

The night following, December 7, the handsome Ziegfeld Theatre, which the venturesome Billy Rose had bought and refurbished, was opened with probably the most extravagantly heralded spectacle ever brought to the Broadway area. Starting with the engagement of Beatrice Lillie, when and if she could get away from her war work in England, Mr. Rose announced stars of magnitude by the dozen, engaged expensive scene and costume designers, employed Cole Porter to write the songs, Igor Stravinsky to do a score of ballet music for a corps to be headed by Alicia Markova and Anton Dolin, tops in their field; took on Bert Lahr for low comedy, George Kaufman and Moss Hart for high comedy material and a Benny Goodman ensemble for jive and such. Then, to top the extravagance of his billing, Mr. Rose announced that opening night seats would cost $24 each in the orchestra circle, with champagne to be served during intermission. "Seven Lively Arts" was the title chosen for the entertainment.

Well, it was a big night. Wartime influences held the sartorial first-night display to modest extremes, but there was a veritable flood of newly pressed tuxedos and feminine dinner ensembles for the first time since Pearl Harbor. Champagne flowed as promised, though there was something less than a river of it. The star-studded program also lived up to its promise, completely so in names, but not in entertainment. Miss Lillie, in fact, was the heroine who saved the show and a good part of the Rose investment. By opening night this had mounted to something more than $350,000. Thanks to the pre-opening sale of several hundred thousand dollars' worth of seats to organized theatre parties, "Seven Lively Arts" played through to May 12. It was followed by a "Concert Varieties" vaudeville of good quality.

Norman Krasna's "Dear Ruth," which ran the year out and played well into the Summer, also winning a place in this volume, was a mid-December entrant. So was the newest Olsen and Johnson gag circus, "Laffing Room Only." The O.J. pattern in shows has been pretty well worked out since "Hellzapoppin" gave it its first impetus in 1938, but there seems to be an almost inexhaustible public that likes it—counting the buyers who come to Broadway to be amused, plus those townsfolk whose ambition it is to keep the buyers happy and receptive.

Putting a part of their "Oklahoma!" and Robeson "Othello" profits back into the business, the Theatre Guild presented a "Salute to American Folk and Popular Music," arranged and staged by Walter Kerr and Leon Leonidoff and called "Sing Out, Sweet Land." The story had its beginnings in Puritan America, with the hero in the stocks singing a hymn, "Who Is the Man?" Before the evening was completed there were scenes and choruses given to "Frankie and Johnnie" and "Casey Jones," and likewise a sprinkling of the jitterbug harmonies of the jive age. Alfred Drake, who started with "Oklahoma!", and Burl Ives, a balladist of the night clubs, headed the cast and there were those who counted the evening among the most happily nostalgic of the season. Unhappily there were not enough of them to carry "Swing Out, Sweet Land" past March.

A second completely modernized musical was called "On the Town." It grew out of a ballet number written by Jerome Robbins called "Fancy Free," and related the adventure of three sailor men on leave from the Brooklyn Navy Yard who were seeing New York for the first time. The book was staged by George Abbott, and though it leaned heavily on dance and ballet features, it immediately caught the interest of the younger dance crowd and ran happily through the season and well into the Summer. Betty Comden and Adolph Green wrote the book and had parts in the cast; Leonard Bernstein wrote the music and Sono Osato and Nancy Walker were featured performers.

"Trio," a legitimate and an effectively dramatic treatment of the unhealthy subject of Lesbianism, adapted by Dorothy Baker and her husband from Mrs. Baker's novel, ran fitfully for sixty-odd performances before New York's License Commissioner took cognizance of the protests of church folk and associate moralists. Then the Commissioner refused the Belasco Theatre a renewal of its license until the offending play was withdrawn. There were a few court skirmishes, but the morality forces finally won. "Trio" was through. Unusually fine performances by Lydia St. Clair, Lois Wheeler and Richard Widmark were features of the engagement.

The second best war play of the season, and the best of the original war plays ("A Bell for Adano" being an adaptation from the Hersey novel), was Capt. John Patrick's "The Hasty Heart," as more fully appears in later pages of this record. This drama skillfully melded tragedy and humor, for all that combination of factors may sound impossible. It told of a dour Scot who had six weeks to live and found great spiritual satisfactions in friendships that were literally forced upon him during that period.

Two actresses of the cinema, and one of the stage, suffered severe shocks to their respective egos early in the new year. The beauteous and well-poised Mary Astor decided to try legitimate again, after years in Hollywood. She came to Broadway in a flimsy little comedy called "Many Happy Returns." It was written by the usually capable Clare Kummer ("A Successful Calamity," "Good Gracious, Annabelle," etc.) and something must have happened to it after it left the Kummer studio. Three performances and it was gone.

Gloria Swanson, determined to act again after something like thirteen years before the cameras, practiced assiduously out of town for a Broadway return in Harold Kennedy's "A Goose for the Gander." There was a scattering of smart lines and the Swanson performance was quite equal to such demands as were made upon it. But the "Goose" was a deader after 20 performances. Or even before.

Diana Barrymore, Jack's pretty and ambitious daughter, who had also been having a try at the trick stages of Hollywood, teamed up with her husband, Bramwell Fletcher, for a tour of the back country in the dramatic version of Daphne Du Maurier's "Rebecca," to be followed by a Broadway run. The tour was highly successful from a box office standpoint, but the Broadway run was mighty short—20 performances and no more. Miss Barrymore, however, was able to read some very nicely worded notices regarding her potentialities. She also probably found some satisfaction in the knowledge that her cousin, Ethel Barry-more Colt, also had failed to achieve the Broadway success she (and doubtless her mother) had dreamed for her. There is still time for both the girls.

Another study in farce comedy sexology, "Good Night, Ladies," which had managed to stick in Chicago for upwards of a full year, was brought East in mid-January with the optimistic hope that it would duplicate its Western box office triumphs. Nothing of the sort happened. "School for Brides" had already skimmed the cream from the burlesque public's support, and "Good Night, Ladies" got only 78 showings. This, incidentally, was Cyrus Wood's rewritten version of Avery Hopwood's "Ladies' Night," a farce which Al Woods produced in 1920.

An interesting revival about this time was that of Shakespeare's "The Tempest," which Margaret Webster staged, following suggestions by Eva LeGallienne, who had at one time intended doing the revival for herself. With the ballet beauty, Vera Zorina, playing a highly decorative Ariel and the Negro star, Canada Lee, making himself hoarse and forbidding as Caliban, and with a splendid reading of Prospero by Arnold Moss, "The Tempest" excited considerable stir and continued for 100 performances.

Dorothy and Herbert Fields had taken the amusing Currier and Ives prints of life in New York in the 1870s as their background for a story of the Boss Tweed grafters and their robber deals. "Up in Central Park" was their title. Sigmund Romberg wrote the score and a large, talented and gaily costumed company was organized by Michael Todd for the presentation. The combination proved one of the happiest events of the year and one of the most successful. A *New York Times* news reporter, played by Wilbur Evans, and a *Harper's Weekly* cartoonist, Thomas Nast, were the heroes of the Tweed exposé. A new prima donna from Chicago, Maureen Cannon, played and sang the role of the heroine most attractively. Not to be outdone by his competitor, Champagne Billy Rose, Mr. Todd gave an after-theatre party at the Casino in Central Park after the "Up in Central Park" opening, entertaining some 700 friends and first-nighters with all manner of liquid refreshments, and champagne as well.

Several times during the season it was remarked by the critics that it would be a pleasant change for them if the plays they were invited to see could be as good as the acting. Like many similar critical observations this one was inspired by a discovery that agreeable personalities, plus a modicum of acting ability, can do more to make a theatre evening bearable than heavy-handed plots and philosophies submitted by the playwrights. "Hope for the Best" was an obvious but earnestly written comedy about a newspaper columnist who wanted to trade his popularity as a folksy writer for a reputation as a political prophet and guide. The chief parts were played by Franchot Tone, a popular young man on both stage and screen, and Jane Wyatt, an actress of social background whose personal charm is potent. William McCleery, newspaperman, was the author, convinced that he had at least a minor message for honest folk. Mr. Tone put his heart and a part of his income into "Hope for the Best," and, with Miss Wyatt's appeal, kept the comedy going for 117 performances, thus making many more playgoers happy than the critics dreamed possible.

"One-Man Show" was less fortunate, though the more important play of the two. Written by Ruth Goodman and Augustus Goetz with impressive earnestness, "One-Man Show" posed the problem of a father and daughter ruled by so strong an admiration and appeal for each other that the girl's interest in other men was minimized. The father's impulse was to encourage her in that detachment. He broke up a couple of potential matings, but along came an understanding young politician who, falling in love with the girl, was able to break the father's influence. The triangle was intelligently represented by Frank Conroy as the father, Constance Cummings as the daughter and John Archer the politician, but "One-Man Show" was withdrawn after 36 performances.

Another comedy temporarily kept from the storehouse by the attractions of its players was "The Overtons," written by Vincent Lawrence. Mr. Lawrence might truthfully be described as the most promising of American playwrights, inasmuch as he has been most promising the longest of any. He misses scoring hits by the narrowest of margins. Again the idea around which "The Overtons" was written offered possibilities. The Overtons had happily trusted each other in marriage for eight years. Then a shapely charmer was observed undressing in Mr. O.'s boathouse and Mrs. O. was ready to rush off to Reno. Mr. O., his pride hurt and his interest in the disrobing lady being nothing to speak of, refused to explain—at least until after the final curtain, when it was promised that he would. Arlene Francis, who had done so well with the role of the Soviet sniper in "The Doughgirls," and Jack Whiting, one of the bouncingest and most likable of musical comedy juveniles, assisted by Glenda Farrell (she contributed the strip)—these three kept "The Overtons" going for 151 performances, which was long after several better plays had closed.

The last third of the season was variously enlivened. It was in March that Tallulah Bankhead arrived with Philip Barry's "Foolish Notion." This one, as frequently happens with the Barry output ("Tomorrow and Tomorrow," "The Animal Kingdom," "Here Come the Clowns," etc.), presented a novel idea in plot and was intelligently treated in the writing and staging—virtues which are more fully discussed in other pages of this yearbook.

It was in March, too, that a poetic and in many respects a fascinating fantasy, "Dark of the Moon," arrived. Written by two gifted young Southerners, Howard Richardson and William Berney, elaborately and generously cast by the Messrs. Shubert, who produced it, "Dark of the Moon" found an appreciative public. Fred Stone's youngest daughter, Carol, played the legendary heroine, Barbara Allen. Her opposite in the role of a witch boy was Richard Hart, a promising juvenile discovered when the play was first done in Summer stock. With the aid of a Conjur Woman, the witch boy became human long enough to woo and wed Barbara, on the promise that if she were untrue to her vows within a year he would return to the witch tribe and never again forsake his kind. Barbara's Christian kin, working upon her emotions at a religious revival, prevailed upon her to forget her marriage vows in the cause of breaking the witch spell. Thus she loses her husband and later her life.

George Kelly ("The Show-off," "Craig's Wife," etc.) came back to Broadway after many too many seasons and brought a new play, "The Deep Mrs. Sykes," with him. It was voted a superior play by most of its critics, and found a determinedly loyal public. But it was never quite strong enough to support the burden of its somewhat heavy treatment of its theme—"There are egotist women, and they say they're much deadlier than the male; because their egotism usually passes for mere feminine jealousy." Mrs. Sykes' intuition told her that her husband was having an affair with a pianist, but she was wrong. It was her married son. Mrs. Sykes' suspicions caused a lot of trouble.

One of the better of the lighter comedies based on the Second World War was Luther Davis's "Kiss Them for Me." Three pals in the crew of an airplane carrier in the South Pacific find themselves in San Francisco on a four-day leave. They hire a hotel suite and announce their intention of devoting the four days to liquor, women and a juke box. Complications begin developing almost immediately. At the end of three acts the boys are awfully glad to start back for the comparatively peaceful life of fighting men. Two of the flyers were played by Dennis King,

Jr., son of Dennis, Sr., who has achieved success in both operetta and the drama, and Richard Widmark, a rapidly advancing leading man with a stock company past.

A costly failure of this period was a musicalized setting of Edwin Justus Mayer's "The Firebrand," a glamorized comedy hit of the middle nineteen twenties. Melville Cooper, the English comedian, proved the only redeeming attraction of "The Firebrand of Florence," and he wasn't enough.

Katharine Cornell, having played forty weeks with "The Barretts of Wimpole Street" in Europe, and finding her soldier audiences wildly enthused, decided to give Broadway another peek at the play which was so sensational a success for her in 1931. Her judgment was sound. "The Barretts" added another 88 enthusiastically acclaimed performances to her record.

As a five-star final event for March, Eddie Dowling and Louis Singer brought in "The Glass Menagerie," with Laurette Taylor as its star. This Tennessee Williams play, which developed into a sensational success in Chicago, was brought to New York with the deliberate intention of calling it to the attention of the prize play judges before they made their awards for the season. Its reward was the capture of the New York Drama Critics' Circle plaque as the best play by an American author to be produced on Broadway the season of 1944-45. A digest of the play is included in this record.

Following the sensational success of their musicalized version of Lynn Riggs' "Green Grow the Lilacs," which they called "Oklahoma!", Richard Rodgers and Oscar Hammerstein 2d decided to try again with Franz Molnar's "Liliom" as their working foundation. "Carousel" was the result, and again their success was sweeping. "Carousel" follows the "Liliom" story with fair consistency. The locale is changed to the New England of 1873. The hero becomes Billy Bigelow, Summer park barker; the heroine is Julie Jordan, the small-town girl who flirts with him. When Billy learns that Julie is to have a baby he takes part in a holdup, hoping to get money enough to educate his offspring properly. Caught by the police, Billy kills himself, spends fifteen years in Purgatory, gets to Heaven's gates, is sent back to earth to redeem his soul with one good deed, is angered by his daughter's refusal to accept the star he has brought her and goes back to Purgatory.

Two superior late-season dramas were Edward Chodorov's "Common Ground" and Elsa Shelley's "Foxhole in the Parlor." Mr. Chodorov, still fighting the reactionary fascist forces and influences that had engaged his earnest attention in "Decision" the

season before, wrote of a U.S.O. unit composed of assorted entertainers. When their plane crashed near Naples, before the Allies
had moved in, the actors fell into the hands of the Nazis. They
were given the choice of going on as entertainers, working the
Nazi front and spreading anti-American propaganda, or accepting
a death verdict and being shot—all except the comedian of the
troupe, who was Jewish. He was sent to a concentration camp.
Though they were all children of foreign-born parents, the actors
decided to continue loyal to America and die rather than submit
to the Nazi terms.

Miss Shelley's "Foxhole in the Parlor" sought to emphasize the
problem of those mental cases returned from the war who find it
difficult to achieve a rational readjustment. Dennis Patterson, a
sensitive pianist, unnerved by his experiences with death and de-
struction, rebels when a tough-minded and misunderstanding sister
seeks to take him back to the mid-West with her in place of letting him stay with sympathetic friends in Greenwich Village. The
sister is about to have Dennis committed to an institution when
he is given a new hold on life, and what he conceives to be his
mission, by a United States Senator on his way as a delegate to
the Peace Conference in San Francisco.

Both the Chodorov "Common Ground" and Miss Shelley's
"Foxhole" were effective dramatic preachments, earnestly written,
and with stimulating character values. But both were a little on
the depressing side and not too successful in a popular sense.
Many self-styled open-minded playgoers prefer to take their
propaganda as propaganda and lose interest when it is disguised
as theatre entertainment.

The show world has been a little "Pinafore" conscious ever
since the "Hot Mikado" was jazzed into a success in 1939-40.
This season two attempts were made to capitalize the Gilbert-
Sullivan story of the Queen's Navee. One, the more dignified
of the two, called "Hollywood Pinafore," was written as to book
by George S. Kaufman, the most successful satirist of his day, and
handsomely staged by Max Gordon, his most confident sponsor.
"Hollywood Pinafore" was not jazzy enough for the average theatre patron and not consistently clever enough to overcome the
prejudices of loyal Savoyards—not even with the Messrs. Victor
Moore and William Gaxton as its chief comedians. Fifty-two
performances and it was gone.

The second "Pinafore" venture was a jazzed framework provided by Albert Barker and Sally Benson, with additional music
by Don Walker and Clay Warnick. In this one a troupe of Negro

entertainers, en route to Memphis on the showboat *Calliboga Queen,* give a performance of "Pinafore" to raise money to get their showboat off a sandbar on which she is stuck. The fact that Bill Robinson, the popular tap-dance champion, was the leader of this troupe helped "Memphis Bound" considerably, but not enough to hold it past 28 performances.

It was the best season financially that Broadway has enjoyed since the boom years of the late nineteen twenties. It was also the most satisfying season artistically that this theatre capital has known in a decade. There being plenty of money available, much of it advanced by Hollywood promoters, the external adornments of the productions were rich and often handsome. This would include the scenic investiture and the costume displays.

The statistical *Variety* counted eighty-three new plays, of which twenty-four were credited as being hits. That ten or twelve of these were placed in the "smash hit" category probably means something more significant than that their receipts at the box office toppled previous box office records, but we don't really think it does. It was just an unusually good season because there was a good deal of wartime money to spend on the theatre as well as on other luxuries.

The fact that there were fifty-nine failures, fourteen holdover favorites from the previous season and six revivals of first importance can also mean whatever you care to make of it.

THE SEASON IN CHICAGO

By Claudia Cassidy

Drama Editor of the *Chicago Tribune*

AMONG other things, the Chicago theatrical season of 1944-45 was the one in which theatregoers practically fought in the streets without taking the trouble to build barricades. The question, succinctly, was this: Was or was not the second largest city in the country getting a fair theatrical deal? One side was inclined to compromise about it, emitting weak cries that if we didn't take what we could get we might get nothing. The opposition retorted that compared to most of our fare, nothing was something.

Variety, meanwhile, piled up ammunition for the recalcitrant by discovering that during the season Chicago spent nearly five and a half million dollars in eight theatres. Producers with a roving eye in our direction are invited to observe what shows skimmed the cream of that cash outlay.

The Theatre Guild sent us a brilliant duplication of "Oklahoma!" that in 60 solid weeks took in $1,800,000, of which $961,000 spilled into the 31 weeks of the 1944-45 season. When this company was yanked out of the Erlanger in the face of capacity business we were told it would return in the Fall. It will. In the Fall of 1946.

Alfred de Liagre Jr. and John Van Druten gave us a version of "The Voice of the Turtle" second only in date of opening, and kept it fresh. In the 35 weeks it had played by June 1, the intake ran to $673,600. "Kiss and Tell," a favorite here for 89 weeks, piled up $411,800 for the 33 weeks of the past season. "Winged Victory," at the Civic Opera House, which seats 3,600, rang up $275,000 in five weeks for Army emergency relief. "The Glass Menagerie" opened here cold the night after Christmas, 1944, in zero weather and against the handicap of low spirits due to the Battle of the Bulge. Yet for its 13 weeks at the little Civic Theatre, *Variety* gives it $188,300. The point of all this is that if certain producers are cheating Chicago, they also are cheating their own bank accounts—or Uncle Sam's.

However, to work. After a steady upclimb for four seasons, Chicago's playgoing took a negligible dip in 1944-45, chiefly because the supply of plays ran out long before the season ended.

17

The long-run record for the 1944-45 season belongs to "The Voice of the Turtle," which was just settling into its stride with the 35 weeks at the break of the season. K. T. Stevens and Hugh Marlowe promptly signed new contracts to finish the run here and move on to Hollywood in due time, but Betty Lawford soon turned the comedienne's role over to Vivian Vance, just back from overseas in "Over 21."

But the long-run record as a conversation piece belongs to "The Glass Menagerie," which the town took to its heart and parted with reluctantly when Tennessee Williams' play hurried to New York in time to slip under the deadline for the Critics' Circle prize—and win it. Some people, including the astute editor of this tome, suspect that we were a bit daft about this play, and no doubt they are right. We aren't arguing that it is the greatest play ever written. We do contend that it opened here fresh and new and shining, and that it did more for playgoing in Chicago than Broadway might suspect, though Broadway has outdistanced us in exhibitions of delight. Don't think us too wistful if we re-iterate we saw it first. The impact of the play itself, of Eddie Dowling's direction, Jo Mielziner's production, Paul Bowles's music, Laurette Taylor's incredibly exciting performance—these things hit us without warning. John Mason Brown wrote much later that he wished he could have seen the play without the build-up. We did.

But how about some statistics? The Harris, which hit the jack-pot last year with a solid 52 weeks of "Kiss and Tell," again was the busiest theatre in town, with 51 weeks of playgoing. That same comedy accounted for 14, 8 went to Ruth Gordon's "Over 21," 23 to a special Chicago company of "Ten Little Indians," headed by Robert Warwick, and 6, at the season's end, to our own troupe of "Dear Ruth," which now looks like a fixture.

The Selwyn and Erlanger tied for second place, with 49 weeks each. The Selwyn had one holdover week of "Rebecca," two of an unhappy version of "Let's Face It," with Benny Rubin in the Danny Kaye part, 11 of Zasu Pitts in "Ramshackle Inn" and 35 of "The Voice of the Turtle." In Miss Pitts's cast, quite un-noticed in the clutter of a creaky whodunit, was one John Richard Basehart. If he turns out to be Richard Basehart of "The Hasty Heart," we will blame it on the lighting.

The Erlanger had 31 holdover weeks of "Oklahoma!", six of Helen Hayes in "Harriet," three of "The Searching Wind," with most of the original cast except for Henry Barnard in Montgomery Clift's role, two of a "Rosalinda" whose charm had faded, six of the Paul Robeson "Othello" and one, as the season ended, of a charming troupe of "Life with Father," headed by Carl Benton Reid and Betty Linley, which settled down for the Summer.

The Blackstone's 36 weeks were due to 4 of Katherine Dunham's "Tropical Revue," 5 of Gloria Swanson's "A Goose for the Gander," which blew up in a storm of litigation, 3 each for the bawdy "Early to Bed," the disappointing because so often miscast revival of "The Cherry Orchard," and a return of "The Student Prince," 7 of a bedraggled version of "Star and Garter" with Willie Howard in the Bobby Clark part ("I'm *Willie* the Roué from Reading, Pa."), 8 of "Chicken Every Sunday," and 3, as the season ended, of "Jacobowsky and the Colonel," still with Louis Calhern and Oscar Karlweis. Mr. Karlweis, a true trouper, played right through the engagement before succumbing to a heart attack, and he was still hospitalized when the company dispersed.

The Studebaker's 36 weeks included 19 of "Kiss and Tell," 2 each of a slightly revised "Tropical Revue," the revived "A Connecticut Yankee," an unfortunate restaging of "Personal Appearance" for Gladys George, and the tag end of "Ten Little Indians," plus 5 for a return engagement of "Over 21" (in this one Miss Gordon's leading men included Clinton Sundberg, Harvey Stephens and Philip Ober) and four for Mae West's "Catherine Was Great," best appreciated by that lady's own term, the connoissewer.

The Civic Opera House, stagestruck by the fantastic grosses possible in such a large though theatrically unsatisfactory auditorium, tossed out its concert clients, had a feud with the union of theatrical managers and press agents, and managed 32 weeks of theatre, plus, of course, opera, ballet and other items. "Winged Victory" had 5 weeks, "One Touch of Venus" lasted 4, with Mary Martin a gallant though appalled exclamation point on the distant stage, and 2 engagements of "The Merry Widow," 1 with Jan Kiepura and Marta Eggerth, ran up 10 weeks. "Blossom Time" held out for 3, and there were 2 weeks each of "Rose Marie," "The New Moon" and "Wildflower," and 1 week of a rundown "Porgy and Bess," limping in from the road. Late in the Spring of 1945 another series of operettas opened, but "Mme. Du Barry" lasted 2 weeks and "Countess Maritza" had run 1 week at the end of this compilation. Soon the whole project collapsed for lack of public interest in poor productions.

The little Civic Theatre had 27 weeks of playgoing, 13 of them due to "The Glass Menagerie," which rescued the house after 8 weeks of "School for Brides," 2 of a revival of "That's a Laff," once known as "Laff That Off," and 4 of a Taylor Holmes farce called "Sleep No More." The rehabilitated Great Northern, which may get Shubert vaudeville if the plan goes through, was lighted for 19 weeks. Five went to a holdover of "Uncle Harry," with Luther Adler, and 2 each went to "It's High Time," "Wallflower" and a return of "The Waltz King," which had failed here the first time. There were 4 weeks of "Two in a Bed," the season's lowest ebb in taste, and 4 of "Sing Out, Sweet Land!", which could have stayed far longer once the town was captivated by Burl Ives.

An orphan in this tabulation is "Alaskan Stampede," which remodeled the Coliseum for a gold rush musical on ice that turned out to be cold storage turkey. In the Yiddish group were Jacob Ben-Ami's "Miracle of the Warsaw Ghetto," and pieces called "The Little Queen," "Shulamith," "A Song of New Russia," "Good News" and "Nathan Takes a Wife." Most of the titles meant something quite different in Yiddish and were hastily improvised for English-speaking reporters, so don't let them fool you.

So much for the past. What of the future? The Shuberts have acquired the long-abandoned Majestic and it will be the New Shubert when it reopens in the splendors of new seats, new lighting, air conditioning and décor of ivory, rose and gold. Billy Rose may make it a season for "Carmen Jones" at the Erlanger. John Wildberg has leased the Civic for a year with options for "Anna Lucasta." Eddie Dowling struck gold and would like to do some more prospecting. Time was when he planned a repertory season and subscribers had their check books out. Maybe he still does. Chicago hopes so.

THE SEASON IN SAN FRANCISCO

BY FRED JOHNSON

Drama Editor of the San Francisco *Call-Bulletin*

SAN FRANCISCO'S otherwise unexciting theatrical year ended with its biggest show to date, the United Nations World Security Conference, holding the municipal Opera House stage with a "name" cast headed by such stars as Stettinius, Eden, Molotov and Truman.

But the legitimate theatre's competition still was on the excessively profitable side, with international delegates joining the local and military throngs in search of amusement and filling to capacity the houses that offered even fair entertainment.

No official stage divertissements for the Conference had developed beyond the rumors that Billy Rose, Mike Todd or the Shuberts had been dreaming up something on the spectacular order. As expected, nothing came of these projects, with the result that a newly named United Nations Theatre catered only to motion picture audiences, with another movie house devoted to conference newsreels and documentaries.

Touring attractions booked within the Conference period were accounted fortunate in being assured of even more generous patronage than the bustling war embarkation port had afforded in the previous months.

The initial honor in entertainment of the delegates went to Helen Hayes as the star of "Harriet," doing 5 weeks of capacity business. Following her in the same Geary Theatre and for the same period was Gladys George in a revival of "Rain," giving a satisfying characterization as Sadie Thompson, with staging and direction by Kent Thurber of the original production and with Victor Kilian of Hollywood in the role of Rev. Davidson.

A new musical comedy called "Watch Out, Angel"—the commercial agent of which had failed to heed its titular warning—was a coast-built production that ventured its première before a semi-distinguished clientele, with Hollywoodian David Allison as producer, author of its original story, and collaborator on its book. A youthful cast, remindful of those juvenile zealots in the more successful "Meet the People," was reinforced by the comedy finesse of veterans Lester Allen, Donald Kerr, Parker Gee and film comedian Lucien Littlefield, with unpretentious choreography by Aida Broadbent.

The critics were unanimous in their blasting of the total outcome in all departments, although the visiting Walter Winchell voted its chorines as beauteous as any he had seen in his Broadway rounds. This verdict, however, was insufficient in prolonging the show's engagement to more than a thinly patronized 3½ weeks.

The season, and the peak of its musical entertainment, was yet to be closed, as usual, with the San Francisco and Los Angeles Light Opera Association's repertoire, which had ended the previous year with the gift to Broadway of its most successful production, "Song of Norway."

The Spring season, now to be extended well into Summer, was opened with Victor Herbert's "The Red Mill," its book revised for the first time by Milton Lazarus and through consent of Mrs. Herbert, and additional lyrics by Forman Brown. The remodeled operetta met with high favor and a fortnight's capacity business before its Los Angeles opening. Under comedian Billy Gilbert's direction, its cast featured the comedy team of Eddie Foy Jr. and Lee Dixon, Nancy Kenyon, Dorothy Stone, Charles Collins and Morton Bowe.

A "Desert Song" more opulent than any previously seen on this coast was the succeeding attraction for a full month, with film actor Sterling Holloway serving both as director and chief comedian. Production and singing principals were of high caliber, the cast engaging, among others, Metropolitan barytone Walter Cassel, Dorothy Sarnoff, Vera Marshe, Edward Dew and Clarissa, a show-stopping dancer in the role of Azuri.

The light opera season was to be extended through August with the engagements of Billy Rose's touring "Carmen Jones" and a revival of "Rose Marie."

A surprise achievement in home production was the five months' Winter run of Gilbert and Sullivan repertoire by the local Savoy Opera Company in a music hall which once had been a church and later a night club. An expert cast of Savoyards under Reginald Travers' direction presented "The Mikado," "Pirates of Penzance," "H.M.S. Pinafore," "Ruddigore" and "Patience" for long engagements, and then repeated the list, its final offering extending even into the rival engagement of R. H. Burnsides' touring Gilbert and Sullivan company, which played for two successful weeks in a downtown theatre.

The gaiety and charm of the local performances were inspired in part by the enthusiasm of old-guard Gilbert and Sullivan followers, for the accomplishment of players also employed in other callings and by the intimacy and hominess of their playhouse.

The season's record run of 10 weeks, ironically if not surprising, was marked up by "Good Night, Ladies," which rowdy farce had its première in San Francisco 3 years ago, with an engagement of 5 weeks before it went on to Chicago for its sensational stay of virtually 2 years.

Nearest to its mark were the runs of "Blithe Spirit," "Othello," with its Broadway cast headed by Paul Robeson, and "Three Is a Family," all for 6 weeks and to excellent patronage, "Othello" drawing capacity.

Within one week of such profitable returns was the engagement of Zasu Pitts in "Ramshackle Inn." "A Doll's House," featuring Francis Lederer, Philip Merivale and the Australian Dale Melbourne at the start of a cross-country tour, was rewarded with an almost sell-out response by the Ibsen cultists. But, as a token of the varied theatrical taste and urge for amusement at the moment, Magician Dante was just as well rewarded.

"Blithe Spirit," which had been cut short in its run the previous season, made up for this by returning with a new cast headed by Violet Heming, Reginald Denny, Lillian Harvey and Renie Riano. After being forced from its tenure of the Curran Theatre it was moved next door to the Geary for a total of 6 weeks.

As had happened before, Paul Small premièred in San Francisco two of his vaudeville exhibits in the same season. His "Star Time," featuring Lou Holtz, Benny Fields and the dancing DeMarcos, was a fairly successful Summer offering of more than a month, followed in January by "Fun Time," with Martha Raye, Smith and Dale and again the DeMarcos. In the latter show was an apparent need of a Holtz or a George Jessel for carrying the proceedings through on a wave of comedy.

Returning comedies, always assured of both new and old audiences, were "Life with Father," teaming Carl Benton Reid and Betty Linley, and "Kiss and Tell," with Lila Lee. Less successful was the reprise of "The Waltz King" musical, starring Richard Bonelli and Margit Bokor, and worse was the response to S. Hurok's New York City Opera Company offering, "The Gypsy Baron," and a Shubert production of "The Merry Widow," with Nancy Kenyon in the title role. For the latter, business went cellarward after a capacity opening.

Theron Bamberger's "Tomorrow the World" exploration of Nazi youth was presented before slim audiences, despite the sensitive acting of Paul McGrath, Edith Atwater and Dickie Tyler. Thus its reception was no better than that encountered the season before by "Watch on the Rhine." A morning round table conducted in the theatre by scientific and other experts dealt with the play's problems and profundities, with more interest to audience listeners than was aroused in the public generally by published reports of the discussion or by the play itself.

No season here being complete without its mediocre coast, or Hollywood production, the year's offerings in this quarter were mercifully reduced to two. One was a new play by Richard Goddard, "No Traveler Returns," set in India and dealing with sinister intrigues and superstitions. The stars, Bela Lugosi and Ian Keith, strove vainly against its almost immediate demise. The other enterprise was a Louis Macloon revival of "Petticoat Fever," still new to San Francisco. Incompetently acted and produced, it was soon closed.

Two musicals were presented on the Opera House stage. Under the California Operetta Festival's banner was "The Merry Widow," starring Jan Kiepura, whose singing won more approval than his playing of Prince Danilo. Replacing Marta Eggerth for the engagement was Wilma Spence, a competent former San Franciscan, in the Sonia role, with Melville Cooper as Popoff.

In the same house, S. Hurok presented Cheryl Crawford's production of "Porgy and Bess," which proved to be better suited to a more intimate theatre. This should not have been the case for the Army Air Force's presentation of Moss Hart's "Winged Victory." But that production lost by comparison with the preceding "This Is the Army" spectacle.

The Shipstads and Johnson "Ice Follies" returned for its 7th local visit as the Summer's most universally popular entertainment. Theatre Arts Colony remained the only active little theatre and the University of California acting forces staged a commendable production of Berthold Brecht's "The Private Life of the Master Race."

THE SEASON IN SOUTHERN CALIFORNIA

By Edwin Schallert

Drama Editor of the *Los Angeles Times*

EVERYTHING was forward-looking during the theatrical season of 1944-45 in Southern California. It had to be, because the record was so hopelessly meager and disappointing. Only a few times was there any substantial lifting of the depression in quality to be discerned. The clouds were chiefly dissipated in the professional sphere by "Othello," with Paul Robeson, the remarkable Jose Ferrer in his Iago role, and Uta Hagen; by Helen Hayes in "Harriet," principally because it starred Helen Hayes; by "Winged Victory" with its original company, and "Carmen Jones" as a light opera event. With these, practically all that was truly notable began and ended.

Of newer New York shows "School for Brides," a weak offering, and "Trio" were given toward the end of the season. "Tomorrow the World" was well staged early, as was "Three Is a Family." "Ten Little Indians" was seen with a company headed by Robert Warwick. "A Doll's House," with Francis Lederer, Philip Merivale, Jane Darwell, Lyle Talbot and Dale Melbourne played a short engagement. One may also mention Gilbert and Sullivan repertoire, not as inviting as previously; "Ramshackle Inn," with Zasu Pitts, and return of "Blithe Spirit," with cast including Reginald Denny, Lillian Harvey, Mona Barrie and Renie Riano.

There were plenty of other plays of sorts, mostly revivals and second and third engagements—mostly, too, with inferior casts, and there were a few efforts at Coast productions, one of the best being "Guest in the House," staged with comparatively little fanfare at the Beaux Arts Theatre.

Onward go, as always, "The Drunkard," the "Turnabout," "The Blackouts," with Ken Murray; the quaint Padua Hills Theatre, with its unique Latin-American spell, the Summer-time Pilgrimage Play. The night clubs, like Earl Carroll's and Florentine Gardens, do a profitable wartime business because of their revues, and others are being added. Attempts are occasionally made to present vaudeville with fair success.

But of good solid theatre there is little of tangible import. As for many years, the Pasadena Community Playhouse has to be relied on to contribute to the sounder chronicle.

Those of us who remember the better days of the stage, which haven't been enjoyed since the late—now very late—gay twenties often wonder when the show world may come to life again—what, more pertinently, may bring it to life. We are aware, naturally, that it needs some moneyed individual or individuals to draw the curtains aside on a new day, and that this protagonist must have a real flair for creation. No prophet has arisen yet, though some very capable men eye the situation now and again, and during the closing months of the season this was one of the most hopeful auguries for the future.

It seemed that during May and June of 1945 the idea of doing something about the show business in Southern California struck fire in several different places. In each instance, the individual who felt the impulse would doubtless be capable of carrying through.

John Wildberg, producer of "Anna Lucasta" and "Memphis Bound," is one who believes a new pioneering effort in the "mañana" area might bear fruit. His Maplewood, N. J., experience inspired him with the idea that it might be a pleasant challenge to try to do something about restoring the stage to a happier estate in Los Angeles.

William Liebling, representative for "The Glass Menagerie" interests, projected the thought of organizing a Coast company for that play, and expressed the belief that there should be a permanent theatre for new productions, and that it should be situate in Beverly Hills.

Lawrence Langner came West about the end of the season with designs for "Oklahoma!" sponsored by the American Theatre Society and the New York Theatre Guild, which expect to extend their efforts to various cities East and West, other attractions also to be proffered.

Civic repertoire projects were being much discussed, and the hope was to mature these into something tangible. At the close of the season, however, there was nothing too tangible about it all, with the possible exception of the Theatre Guild proposal.

What faces all producers who aim at expansion of the theatre is the question of theatres. Availability of showhouses is gradually being reduced. The Music Box during the year lost its identity as a footlight center, even as El Capitan on Hollywood Boulevard was eliminated some time ago. Both now are picture establishments. That does not look like stage progress, needless to say.

Construction of new houses was out of the question because of the war, and there was almost no incentive, considering that even those now existing are dark a good part of the time. The Biltmore, naturally, holds forth with road attractions most consecutively. Paul Small took over the Mayan during the year, and presented the vaudeville type of entertainment. Late in the season "School for Brides" moved in. The Belasco housed occasional shows.

These three theatres might take care of the temporary needs, though it is agreed that new playhouses in other locations will have to meet the requirements of any such theatrical future as is seen in the dreams of those who believe there can be a stage-conscious Los Angeles. The believers about this, incidentally, are often offset by the skeptics.

Besides the larger theatres, there are others either built or adapted to footlight uses like the Musart, Beaux Arts, Film City Playhouse, Playtime, which assume to house more or less professional enterprises. The Actors Laboratory Theatre and the Vanguard are new additions, besides the various "show-case" and so-called little theatres that have previously existed.

The Actors Lab was responsible for some genuine events, like the performance of "Yellow Jack" by members of the "Winged Victory" company; "Noah," "Volpone" and one-acters given with casts drawn from the Hollywood personnel.

"Volpone" was quite distinguished with J. Edward Bromberg, Norman Lloyd, Ruth Nelson, Hugo Haas, Phoebe Brand, Rhys Williams, Houseley Stevenson, Ian Wolfe, Lloyd Bridges and others. Morris Carnovsky was the director, and Mordecai Gorelik designed costumes and settings. This helped materially the sense of accomplishment with the natively splendid resources that exist in Hollywood, and may portend an era of such better endeavor.

The Vanguard Stage, with a 100-seat house, is designated as a professional co-operative activity operating under the jurisdiction of Actors Equity, and had an ambitious 1945 Summer program including "Beyond the Horizon," "Goodbye Again," "Blind Alley," "Snafu" and "Thunder Rock." "Decision" was one of their regular season presentations that attained marked distinction.

The Bliss-Hayden, Callboard, Geller Workshop continue to function with both new plays and familiar presentations. They are showcases for new talent, watched by the film studios, along with others. "Black Savannah" given at the Jewel Box, and written by Norbert Faulkner and Samuel R. Goulding, was headed for the professional stage as a vehicle for Anna Sten, the Russian actress. "The Lady Who Came to Stay" pleased at the Rainbow Theatre.

Pasadena Community, as usual, covered plenty of territory. Most ambitious was the production of "Immortal," by Alexei Arbuzov and Alexander Gladkov, for the first time in America. This was a modern example of the Soviet drama, dealing with the war, and originally put forth in Russia for the men in its armed forces. While it fell short of complete approval, its vitality and strength were not to be denied.

The Community Playhouse gave "Get Away, Old Man" by William Saroyan as a first performance on the Coast—also "Suds in Your Eye" by Jack Kirkland and Muriel Laswell, and also did well by "The Skin of Our Teeth," Thornton Wilder's prize-winning achievement. Arresting was the staging of "Stairs to the Roof" by Tennessee Williams at the Playbox, Gilmor Brown himself taking part in that. It was not done in the larger theatre, although it well might be.

"Uncle Harry," "The Corn Is Green," "A Highland Fling," "The Great Big Doorstep," "Biography," "Is Life Worth Living?" by Lennox Robinson, "My Dear Children," with John Carradine in the John Barrymore role; "Mrs. January and Mr. Ex" by Zoe Akins, "Spring Again," "The Barker," "Junior Miss," "Janie," "Little Women" were in the repertoire, besides "King Lear," with Morris Ankrum in the title part. The Summer season of 1944 was dedicated to the plays of the late Sidney Howard, and the 11th Annual Midsummer Drama Festival of 1945 to eight great living American playwrights.

Light opera continues a mainstay in Los Angeles in proving that people do really like to go to the theatre, and will pay a price. The Los Angeles Civic Light Opera Association, apart from sponsoring "Carmen Jones," vouchsafed only those works which had been given previously, like "Desert Song," "The Red Mill" and "Rose Marie," but in each instance it was a more highly embellished and modernized version that was seen. This helped to keep attendance at the peak. But no "Song of Norway" emerged from this particular series.

"The Merry Widow" was twice performed during the theatrical year, once in the stylized version with Jan Kiepura and Marta Eggerth. The Gilbert and Sullivan repertoire included only one novelty in "The Sorcerer."

Katherine Dunham's "Tropical Revue," a dancing event, was a hit. "Porgy and Bess" was successfully offered. Ethel Waters appeared in "Rhapsody in Rhythm," and there were one or two other colored revues.

Plays that saw the light, but generally did not last long, included "Family Man," "Lady Chatterley's Lover," "Dr. Lincoln's Attic," "Ladies Room," "The Donovan Affair," "Wait for Me, Darling," "The Fighting Littles," "Lisa Kalitina," Russian adaptation; "Too Many Sarongs," "Strange Destiny," "Strange Love Story," "Let's Marry," "Home on the Range," "The Sultan and the Merchant," "African Cavalcade," "Cavalcade of Youth," "It's in the Air." Some of these were with music. Noel Coward's "Fallen Angels" was briefly presented with Doris Lloyd, Jessica Turner and Frank Hilliard.

Freak hits were "A Honey in the Hay" at the Musart and "Anybody's Girl," with Betty Rowland, at the Beaux Arts. They had runs not unlike the earlier "Maid in the Ozarks."

"Personal Appearance" was staged with Louise Allbritton in the Gladys George role, and war veterans in the cast, designed to help the veterans in their resumption of the civilian estate. "Kiss and Tell," "Life with Father," "Petticoat Fever," "Good Night, Ladies," "White Cargo" and "The Waltz King" were repeated. Short Shakespearean adaptations were given under the heading of "The Dream and the Shrew." "A Night in Mexico" was rated well as a Latin-American entertainment.

"Adrift in New York," old melodrama, came to life at the Pirate's Den for laugh purposes, as did "The Blackguard" again. "Fun Time," as vaudeville, had Martha Raye, Smith and Dale, Renee DeMarco and Dean Murphy. Ruth Draper and Virginia Sale did their one-woman shows. Dante performed magic.

Veritably a hodge-podge goes under the "caption" of theatre in Southern California, and the list can extend even farther through show-case and little theatre efforts, comprising brand-new and familiar plays quite endlessly. It isn't so much that Southern California lacks the incentive to do and to create—as why should it with all the talent that is present—but rather that everything is in such a chaotic state.

A BELL FOR ADANO

A Drama in Three Acts

BY PAUL OSBORN

(A dramatization of the novel by John Hersey)

"A BELL FOR ADANO" reached the Broadway stage practically on the third anniversary of the tragedy of Pearl Harbor. It was produced at the Cort Theatre the evening of December 6, 1944, and in the newspaper issues of anniversary day it was heralded as much the best of the plays to come out of the Second World War up to and including that date. With Fredric March as its star the play ran through the season to a succession of capacity audiences.

"A Bell for Adano" was so definite a success, in fact, and proved so well able to stand on its own foundation as a human drama with a wartime background, that all rumored attempts to connect it with any specific incident or any specific personality of the war were quickly and effectively brushed aside.

Thus the rumor that Mr. Hersey, as a war correspondent on the ground, had rushed to his typewriter to record the high-tempered outbreak of a colorful American General during an invasion was discounted, both when it was first mentioned, and again when it was later revived as an explanation of why the play was first chosen for a command performance in Washington honoring the President's birthday ball, and later replaced by "Dear Ruth." It was, explained the promoters, too heavy a production to transport to the Capital for a single performance.

Nor was the fact that Mr. Osborn had in his first draft employed the character of such a high-tempered militarist, and afterward reduced him to "an off-stage noise," ever held against either the play or the military.

The fact that "A Bell for Adano" presents not only a timely but definitely post-war theme was duly appreciated by its reviewers. This, wrote Burton Rascoe in his *New York World-Telegram* review, includes the problem "of first learning for ourselves what democracy, freedom and justice mean. They are not merely principles but principles in action—in all things, big and

little. Many Americans who think they know what democracy
is, don't."

The choice of Fredric March for the role of Major Joppolo was
a happy one. The actor had returned but a few months before
from a tour of the American front line European camps, where
his observation of the fighting doughboys and the officers directing
them was both keenly observant and understandingly sympathetic.

"On that trip I came to have the greatest admiration for the
average run of our G.I.'s," March later told Interviewer Helen
Ormsbee. "They were gentle, and not very talkative. Most of
all they had a feeling of comradeship. They were a real brother-
hood. As for General Eisenhower, what a man he is! I met him
in North Africa. Why, he is a sort of super-Joppolo. He really
believes we are fighting to make things better for people, and he
has such wonderful enthusiasm. 'When you talk to the men,' he
told me, 'they'll listen to you because they don't have to. Won't
you say something about how we allies must all stick together?' "

It is bright midday in July, 1943, when we first enter the office
of the former Mayor of Adano, Sicily. The office is in City Hall
and is a huge room with a very high ceiling. "The room is so
typically Italian," declares the author, "that anyone would know
at a glance where he was."

At the back of the room tall French windows open onto a balcony which is over the street. Practically in the center of the
room "is a massive desk of wood, ornate and heavy. It is covered
with maps and aerial photos. Behind it is a large throne-like
chair. . . . In one corner of the room is a white, stone statue of
a saint which, at the moment, has a piece of American signal corps
wire wound around her neck on its way from the nearest French
window to a desk."

A section of a smaller office is visible at the audience-left, a
work room plainly furnished with a table, a few chairs and several
filing cabinets.

We find the main room empty. It remains empty for several
minutes. The French doors are closed, but the hot mid-day sun
manages to filter in in a collection of bright rays. Presently the
hall doors slowly open and Maj. Victor Joppolo comes wonderingly into the room. "He is a man of medium height, dark skin,
mustache. The most prominent expression on his face is one of
intensity and seriousness, although there is also a latent cheerful-
ness. He is about thirty-five, wears the uniform of an American

Major and carries a brief-case. Behind him is Sergt. Leonard Borth, M.P."

The Sergeant, an upstanding soldier in his late twenties, follows his Major into the room and both men are suddenly stopped dead in their tracks as they gaze about them in awe and amazement. They find both the size and appearance of the room startling.

"Should have brought our roller skates," muses Joppolo, testing the marble floor.

"These Fascist boys sure did themselves right," agrees Borth.

As he drops his brief-case on the desk, Joppolo notices the aerial maps. He also traces the signal wire from the French window to the neck of the saint's statue—

"There's been a field telephone here," Borth tells him. "Some of our boys must have used this as a command post during the invasion this morning. Hiya!" This would be his salute to the lady of stone.

Joppolo turns to swing open the French windows and have a look from the balcony. It is Borth's opinion, respectfully stated, that the Major should not permit himself to become sentimental about this job, which is simply to clean up the streets of the town. But the Major has a different idea.

"Look, Borth, remember that dead Sicilian woman in the alley as we came up just now? Shot this morning in the invasion?"

"Yeah."

"You think she was an enemy of ours? Nuts! Why, my grandmother must have been like her. She came from a little Italian town like this near Florence. Those aren't the ones we're against. It's this bunch of crooks that were here in the City Hall."

"Careful, Major. Now *you're* in the City Hall! Maybe you'll turn out to be a crook."

"That's nothing to kid about, Borth!" The Major's tone is sharp.

"Yes, sir."

They add a bit of rummaging to their investigations. Sergt. Borth is delighted with the completeness of the files he finds in the work room. "Nothing emptied—names, names, names—everybody in Adano—all their records—this will make my job easy."

Another Borth idea. These rooms would be a perfect set-up for Capt. Purvis, in charge of M.P. here. With that idea Major Joppolo agrees heartily. Let the Captain be told.

In one of the larger rooms Sergt. Borth suddenly discovers

the lurking figure of a man. Going for his gun he orders the man into the office. A moment later "a small Italian with a shiny linen coat, with his collar buttoned up but no tie," appears. "He is frightened and yet determined, coming in hesitantly giving them the Fascist salute."

This is Zito Giovanni. He keeps repeating: "Welcome to Americans! Live Roosevelt! I always hated Fascists! Welcome to Americans! Live Roosevelt!"

Zito, by his own nervous confession, has long been known as an anti-Fascist, though he has continued to work in the City Hall as Usher for the Mayor. Getting Zito's name, Sergt. Borth soon has the facts from the files.

"Usher, I love the truth," says Maj. Joppolo, sternly. "If you lie to me you will be in very serious trouble. Do not lie to me. If you were a Fascist, you were a Fascist. There is no need to lie."

There is a moment's pause, then Zito answers, simply: "One had to eat, one had to earn a living. I have six children."

"That I can understand. So, you were a Fascist. Very well, now you will have to learn to live in a democracy. You will be my usher."

Now Zito is all excitement, again blessing Roosevelt and giving the Fascist salute rapidly. It is a moment before Joppolo can convince him that a simple shake of the hand is democracy's greeting.

"What condition is the town in? Has it been bad here?"

"We have been bombed and bombed. For three days we have not had bread. The stink of the dead is very bad. Some people are sick because the drivers of the water carts have been afraid to get water for several days, because of the planes along the road. And our bell is gone."

"Your bell?" Joppolo is puzzled.

"Yes, Mister Major. It was seven hundred years old. It rang with a good tone, each quarter hour. Mussolini took it."

"Oh, yeah?"

"He took it to make rifle barrels. The town was very angry when we lost our bell. Only two weeks before you came. Why didn't you come sooner?"

"Where was this bell?"

"Up there. The whole building tingled when it rang."

"Well, there's nothing we can do about that now. Zito, I want to speak to the priest of this town. Will you get him for me?"

Zito would be glad to fetch the priest, but which one? In

Adano there are thirteen churches and in some two or three priests. He agrees finally that probably Father Pensovecchio of San Angelo is the best.

With another burst of salutes and handshakes Zito is gone. Maj. Joppolo has found his way to his desk and eased himself a little gingerly into the big chair. The picture amuses Borth—

"How does it feel, sitting there, Duce?" Borth is grinning.

"Oh, I don't know!" The Major is a little embarrassed. "There is so much to do I hardly know where to begin."

He has reached into his brief-case for a collection of papers. "Listen," he says, as he begins to read: " 'Instructions to Civil Affairs Officers. First day. Enter the city with the first column. Place guards and seize all records. Place all food warehouses, enemy food dumps, wholesale food concerns and other major food stocks under guard.' " He looks up and mutters, softly: "And there's not even any bread!"

There are pages and pages of instructions on what to guard— foundries, machine shops, refrigeration plants—

"They must have thought we were invading Chicago," suggests Borth. "Just clean up the streets, Major." And Borth goes grinning in search of Capt. Purvis.

Maj. Joppolo is thoughtful for a moment. Then he takes a small notebook from his pocket, turns a page and begins to read softly to himself—" 'Notes to Joppolo from Joppolo: Don't let the red tape get you down. Always be accessible to the public. Don't play favorites. Don't lose your temper. When plans fall down, improvise.' "

After another thoughtful moment or two Joppolo slowly picks up the sheaf of instructions, tears them in two and drops them into the waste basket. Now he hits the desk a resounding whack. With this he seems suddenly to come to life. From his brief-case he takes a British flag and goes with it to the balcony. As he starts to raise the flag over the center window there is a murmur of voices from below. A group of citizens is calling attention to the flag: "Hey, look!" "The flag!" "The English flag!"

Joppolo comes back into the room to get an American flag. That goes up next, with even louder comments outside. Joppolo looks out and waves to the crowd, happily: "Good morning, good morning!" he calls.

As he comes back to his desk there is a knock on his door. Ribaudo Giuseppe is the caller. "He is the typical Italian we are used to." He smiles at Joppolo as he walks in confidently, with his hands in his pockets.

Giuseppe has noticed the flags. The war, he concludes, is over in Adano. Giuseppe is from Cleveland, Ohio. He has been in Adano three years. He could, he feels, do a good job for Maj. Joppolo.

"I'm a good American," declares Giuseppe. "I hate these Fascisti. I could do a good job for you."

"If you're such a good American, why did you leave the States?"

"They kick me out."

It had been a little matter of a passport that had got Giuseppe into trouble. He didn't have one. He got into the United States through the influence of plenty smart friends in Cleveland and Buffalo.

This truth-telling gets Giuseppe the job. He can be a help, decides Joppolo, with the people. What does Giuseppe think Adano needs most?

Well, Giuseppe could go for a movie, but, right now he is willing to settle for something more substantial—

"Food, a boss," says Giuseppe. "Three days a lot-a people no eat nothing. Everyone been-a scared. Bakers don't work, nobody sell-a pasta, water don't come in-a carts, fishermen don't-a fish."

"They don't?"

"They-a scared too—and Tomasino, he tell them-a not to."

"Who is Tomasino?"

"He a crazy old fisherman, a boss. He hate-a the Fascisti, a crooks, and he tell all the fishermen the Americans will be crooks, too. He hate-a the Americans."

Before the Major can make any decision regarding Tomasino, the fisherman, he has two other callers. These are excitable citizens, Cacopardo and Craxi, both about 60 years old and both well-dressed. They are full of "advices," and each tries to get his advice in first. Joppolo listens to them as best he can. He realizes, with Craxi, that the people are hungry and he is eager to help. He also hears with interest Cacopardo's plea that what the people need most is the return of their bell. The bell was of their spirit. But neither Cacopardo nor Craxi has anything practical to suggest. . . .

Capt. Purvis of the M.P.'s has had a look at the inner offices and found they will suit his purposes admirably. The Captain also reports re-routing truck convoys so they by-pass Adano, and thus get through without delay.

Again Maj. Joppolo tries to dismiss the persistent Cacopardo and Craxi, but they are still determined to put over their message—

"But the bell, Mister Major—the bell will give life back to the people! When it spoke, it spoke to us, and our fathers spoke to us," pleads Cacopardo.

"No, it was because it rang the time of day," insists Craxi.

"No, it was the *tone* of the bell! It soothed all the people of this town!"

"It was its history."

"It told us when to do things, such as eating!"

"No, it had a tone for everybody—"

They are both yelling at the same time. Joppolo finally suppresses them with a stern demand for quiet. "I've heard all I want to about the bell! There are more important things to be done here! If anyone says the word bell again in this office—"

There is a knock at the door. Zito has brought Father Pensovecchio. The priest is "gray-haired and dignified. As he approaches Joppolo, he makes a motion with his right hand that could be interpreted as a blessing or as a Fascist salute. There is a murmur of greeting."

"Thank you for coming, Father," Maj. Joppolo is saying. "I am Major Victor Joppolo, of the United States Army, senior civil affairs officer for the town of Adano."

"I know." Father Pensovecchio's smile is understanding.

"I represent the AMG—Allied Military Government of Occupied Territory."

"Welcome to Adano, Major."

"Thank you. I have been trying to get the ideas of various people as to what's the first thing to be done for the town. I know the people are hungry—the streets must be cleaned up—there are so many things—"

"Yes, there are many things. Also of the gravest importance, Major, is the matter of the bell."

There is a sudden pause and a quick silence as the group watches to see what Joppolo is going to do. He grins a little sheepishly at Borth as he turns to the others—

"Yes—I—I have heard something about the bell."

"You see, this bell was the center of the town," Father Pensovecchio continues. "Even we in the churches depended on this bell more than on our own. At noon on the Sabbath, when all the bells in town rang at once, this bell rose above all the others and that was the one you listened to. The bell regulated and gave meaning to the life in this town."

"I thank you all very much for your advice," says Joppolo, suddenly very brisk and businesslike. "I will keep the bell in mind. Now I wish to speak alone with Father Pensovecchio."

With the others gone, Maj. Joppolo is quick to make clear his wishes to Father Pensovecchio. The facts, says Joppolo, are that the Americans have invaded Adano; that the enemy has been pushed back and that there is apparently little chance of a counter-attack. He has, reports the Major, walked through Adano. He has noted the filth and poverty. He understands the people have been without food for three days. He is eager to change all that. But to do so he must have the good will of the people, because they are the ones who will have to do it.

"I have been told you are the best priest in Adano. Therefore, I should like to ask a favor of you. But please feel perfectly free to refuse me if you wish."

"I will not refuse you," answers Father Pensovecchio quietly.

Maj. Joppolo would like to have Father Pensovecchio tell the people, in his own way, about the Americans and about the proclamations that are about to be posted. These should be read. He would like to have it explained that the Americans are different from Fascists, which will mean that there will be some changes in Adano that will have to be adhered to.

As Father Pensovecchio starts toward the balcony Maj. Joppolo stops him hesitantly. "Father," he says, speaking slowly, "I assure you that the Americans want to bring only good to this town. But, as in every nation, there are some bad men in America. It is possible that some Americans who come here will do bad things. If they do, I can tell you that most of the Americans will be just as ashamed of those things as you are annoyed by them."

"I think we will understand weakness in your men just as we try to understand it in our own."

Father Pensovecchio has stepped out upon the balcony and signaled for the attention of the crowd. Everything that is done in this world, he tells them, is done by God.. God has given them bread and God gave them the sun. And now God has given them deliverance from their oppressors. But, no matter who they may have as authorities, they must obey the law, exactly as it is written in the proclamations—

"If you remember, we were told that Americans attacked priests and attacked and killed women," Father Pensovecchio continues. "But right here now is an American, an American in charge of Adano. He is not attacking priests, he is not killing women. I have talked with him and I feel that he is here with only one idea—to feed you, to clothe you, to make you free. Do you know what he said to me? He said, 'I want to make Adano shine!' Because of this man, I believe that Americans are going to be my friends. You must believe the same thing, my children."

As Father Pensovecchio comes in from the balcony Maj. Joppolo thanks him for his speech. For a moment after the priest leaves them Joppolo stands deep in thought. Then he suddenly seems to wake up—

"All right, what are we waiting for? Let's get started!" His tone is angry as he turns on them all.

"Okay, Duce!" snaps Borth.

"Oh, Capt. Purvis, find out where the powerhouse is, put all the public utilities in order, and we've got to get these proclamations posted."

There is a good deal of activity stirred up in both rooms as Capt. Purvis's men start setting his office in order and Borth and Giuseppe put things to rights around Maj. Joppolo's desk. The curtain falls.

Five days later, Maj. Joppolo's office is fairly crowded with excited natives in the midst of a dispute. From what is heard of it the dispute concerns the authority of one Gargano, Chief of the Carabinieri. Gargano is a tall, gangly man given to excited gestures.

Three women: Marguerita, "a large-framed, formidable woman, dressed in black"; Carmelina, "a peasant woman, also in black," and Laura Sofia, "a thin, kittenish spinster, dressed a little more gaily than the others," are, it appears, no longer impressed, either by the uniform or the authority of the Chief of Carabinieri. He may have been Fascist chief; he is not Democracy chief.

Gargano, for his part, threatens to prove that he still is Chief by putting the women under arrest. They are still defying him shrilly to go on and try it when Maj. Joppolo strides into the room and demands to know what the row is all about.

They all fall back from the Major like guilty school children, but finally try to explain. Gargano, it appears, exercising his prerogative as Chief of Carabinieri, had pushed his way to the head of the line in front of Zapulla's bread shop. At least Gargano would have pushed his way in if Carmelina had not refused to be pushed out. So Gargano had arrested Carmelina and now charges her with having disturbed the peace and questioned authority.

Joppolo questions them individually. Who are they? Why are they there? What do they think should be done in this case?

"Carmelina should not be severely punished," ventures Marguerita, in the name of justice. "Even if this man is still Chief of Carabinieri, we think he has no right to push himself to the head of the line before women who have been waiting for hours."

Now Joppolo has come to Tina, the daughter of Tomasino, the fisherman. It is evident that he is immediately attracted to her. She is there, Tina explains, only because she was in the line and followed the crowd.

"You charge this woman with disturbing the peace and questioning authority," says Joppolo, pointing to Carmelina and facing the Chief of Carabinieri.

"Yes, Mister Major."

"I sentence you to one day in jail," says Joppolo, turning to Carmelina, and quickly adds: "The sentence is suspended. You may go—"

Those in the room are taken by surprise. This surely is a new kind of justice. They are muttering among themselves as they slowly leave the room.

As Tina reaches the door Maj. Joppolo calls her back. He would talk with her about her father. Her father, he understands, does not like Americans.

"He does not know them well, Mister Major," Tina would explain. "And he has always hated the men who were in this building."

"I am anxious to start the fishermen going out again. I would like very much to talk to your father. I wonder if you couldn't explain to him that the men who are now in this building are perhaps different from the men that were here before."

"I could explain to him—how Carmelina was not put into jail even though she defied the Chief of Carabinieri, Mister Major. I could tell him there was justice in this building today."

"Yes—well—just try to get him to come and see me if you can."

"Yes, Mister Major."

"Thank you— That's all, then—"

But Tina is hesitant about taking her dismissal. She would like to tell the Major something. She knows he does not like to be lied to. She had lied a little. She had not been standing in line with the others. She was on the street and just followed the crowd. She had wanted to see what the American Major was like—

For a moment Tina and Joppolo stare at each other. Then she departs hurriedly, and the Major turns abruptly to Gargano, covering a slight embarrassment with the severity of his tone—

"Gargano! In the case that has just come up, the woman— this Carmelina—is right. You are wrong."

"Me?"

"You have no right to push yourself to the head of the line. I did not agree with her just now because if I had you would no longer have any authority over the people and I wish to keep you in office because I think you will learn the right way to do things. If anything like this should ever happen again, you will no longer be Chief of Carabinieri. You understand?"

"Yes, Mister Major."

Maj. Joppolo has summoned the town's officials. Zito has brought them in and they stand arrayed before the Major, taking their positions with great dignity but appearing a little comic in their appearance and gravity. Mayor Bellanco, Minister of Finance D'Arpa, Volunteer Health Officer Spinnato—each ready with his report.

Maj. Joppolo has summoned them, he explains, that he may talk with them and perhaps explain a little more fully just what he meant when he told them on their appointment that hereafter Adano was to be run as a Democracy. Either some of them are forgetting, or perhaps they did not understand—

"One of the main things about a Democracy is that the men of the Government are no longer masters of the people," says Joppolo, leaning toward them. "They are servants of the people, elected by the people, paid by the people with their taxes. Therefore, you are now the servants of the people of Adano. I, too, am their servant. When I go to buy bread, I'll take my place at the end of the line and wait my turn. Now, if I find any of you are not willing to act in this way, I shall remove you from office. Just remember that you are now the servants—not the rulers—of the people of Adano. And watch—you may find that this thing will make you happier than you have ever been in your lives. You may find that—"

Suddenly the sound of a motor car is heard as it grinds to a stop outside City Hall. This is followed by the "coarse, brutal tones of a voice, obviously American, shouting in anger" amid a din of police whistles—

The Voice—Goddam your cart, get off the road! Blow your horn, Middleton, blow that bastard off the road! I've had enough of these damn water carts. (*A horn blows many times. Suddenly, apprehensive,* JOPPOLO *hurries over to the balcony and looks out.*) What are they trying to do? Stop the invasion? Come on, get out of the way there.

JOPPOLO (*as* BORTH *comes in*)—What's the matter? What's going on down there?

BORTH—General Marvin—

JOPPOLO—General Marvin! What's he doing here?

BORTH—Just passing through. One of the water carts is in his way and he can't get by, the streets are so narrow. He's sore as hell.

JOPPOLO—What the hell's he coming through here for? Why didn't he take the by-pass?

BORTH—God knows.

THE VOICE (*more angry*)—Get that cart out of there! What do these Italians think they're doing? Trying to stop a truck convoy with a bunch of wooden carts?

JOPPOLO (*to* BORTH)—Is there a truck convoy?

BORTH—Naw, just his car.

THE VOICE—Throw that cart off the road. Turn it over in the gutter. (JOPPOLO *and* BORTH *turn quickly to look out.*)

BORTH—My God, he's going to turn that cart over in the gutter with the driver in it.

THE VOICE—Just turn the whole goddam thing over. Come on, get it over with.

JOPPOLO (*suddenly turning into the room, grabbing his cap from the desk and starting for the door; furious*)—He can't do this!

BORTH (*catching his arm*)—Wait a minute, Major! Don't tangle with General Marvin. He'll murder you. This is an M.P. job! (*As* JOPPOLO *has shaken off* BORTH'S *hand and started to the door, raging, there is a sudden noise outside. There is the sound of a cart being turned over, there is shouting from the indignant bystanders, and dominating all, the shrill, frantic braying of a mule.*) They've turned the whole thing over. Listen to that mule—

THE VOICE—That's better! Serve them damn well right, trying to stop the invasion! Middleton, shoot that goddam mule!!

JOPPOLO (*furious*)—Shoot the mule— Hey, wait a minute— (*He is breathing hard. He starts for the door,* BORTH *hurrying after him. Suddenly comes another terrified scream from the mule.*)

BORTH (*rapidly*)—Listen, Major, take it easy! Don't talk back to him! (JOPPOLO *hurries out*, BORTH *after him. The noise continues outside.*)

THE VOICE—Well, Middleton—?

MIDDLETON'S VOICE—Do you think it's wise, sir?

THE VOICE (*furious*)—What's that? What's that you say?

MIDDLETON'S VOICE—I say, do you think it's wise, sir?

THE VOICE (*screaming*)—Dammit, Middleton, you want a court-martial? You trying to stop the goddam invasion, too? Shoot that mule! (*There is a moment's pause. The mule is screaming. Then three shots ring out. The screaming suddenly stops.*) Got to teach these people a lesson! Who's in charge of this town, anyway?

JOPPOLO'S VOICE (*angry, but controlled*)—I am, sir. Major Victor Joppolo.

MARVIN'S VOICE—Dammit, Major, these Italian carts are holding up the whole invasion.

JOPPOLO'S VOICE—The invasion is finished in this town, sir. We are trying to reconstruct.

MARVIN'S VOICE—Reconstruct? What the hell has that got to do with it? There's a war going on. These streets have got to be kept open.

JOPPOLO'S VOICE—But no troops are going through here now, sir. The water is vital to the town, General.

MARVIN'S VOICE (*screaming*)—*I'm* going through here now! The carts got in *my* way! You keep those carts out of this town!

JOPPOLO'S VOICE—But, General—

MARVIN'S VOICE—Dammit, you hear what I say? You keep those carts out of this town!

JOPPOLO'S VOICE—Yes, sir, I will attend to it right away.

MARVIN'S VOICE—Adano's the name of this town. Remember that, Middleton.

MIDDLETON'S VOICE—Yes, sir.

MARVIN'S VOICE—And what was that Major's name again?

MIDDLETON'S VOICE—Joppolo, sir.

MARVIN'S VOICE—Joppolo! Don't forget that name, either, Middleton. Well, come on, let's get out of here! (*The sound of a motor starting.*) We got a goddam war to fight.

Adano's council of officials has moved back into the room, gesticulating and muttering excitedly. "Why did he shoot the mule?" "His cart is destroyed!" "It was Oleranto's mule!"

Joppolo, coming slowly through the door, stands watching the officials. When they face him he speaks to them, quietly: "I consider it my duty to tell you everything that happens in this town," he says. "We do not want this town to be a place of mystery and suspicion. In a Democracy, one of the most important things is for everybody to know as much as possible about what is going on. (*He takes a deep breath.*) The American authorities have decided that because of military necessity, it will no longer be possible for mule carts to come into the streets of Adano."

"But, Mister Major—no carts? But how do we—?"

"It is because of military necessity." He is looking at them unhappily. "I am sorry. That's all."

As the order is passed on to Capt. Purvis, the officials stand, staring and speechless. The carts are to be stopped at the bridge on the east and at the sulphur refinery on the west.

"I want you to know that I am not happy at this occurrence," Joppolo says, as he dismisses them. "I'll do everything in my power to have this unjust order revoked."

They are all smiles again and straggle through the door calling back their thanks. "Yes, Mister Major!" "Kiss your hand, Mister Major!"

As the last of the officials disappears Borth starts lightly to sing—

" 'Where do we go from here, boys, oh, where do we go from here?' "

Joppolo looks up. His face is flushed with anger. He smites the desk with his fist, tensely—

"The son-of-a-bitch! The lousy son-of-a-bitch!"

Maj. Joppolo and Borth are looking steadily at each other. The curtain falls.

Two days later Joppolo is seated at his desk, busy with his papers. The doors to the balcony are open and a soft Summer light comes through the windows.

Giuseppe is sitting on the couch, shining Joppolo's shoes and softly singing "This is the Army, Mr. Jones." It isn't Giuseppe's song but his own restlessness that presently stirs Joppolo into action. There is something that has been worrying him: Do they have natural blondes in that part of the country? He asks Giuseppe.

Giuseppe grins broadly. He is glad the boss has a pair of eyes in his head after all. Giuseppe, with any encouragement at all, could fix something for the boss, and he can't understand the boss's anger when he suggests it. Yes, in the north blondes are natural. In Adano, not so natural.

To get back to the date: Giuseppe can understand that the boss is lonesome. It is a hell of a long way from the Bronx, U.S.A., to Adano, Sicily. Joppolo is again firm. All he wants of Giuseppe is for him to finish the shoes and then help him to get in touch with Tomasino, the fisherman.

"I have asked to have him come and see me, but he hasn't," explains Joppolo. "The town is getting in bad shape for food since we haven't been able to bring in the carts. We've *got* to get the fishermen going out again. I'm going to get permission from the Navy and I want that Tomasino to come and see me."

Giuseppe will do what he can with that crazy old man, that Tomasino. But he can't promise anything—except that Tomasino has a beautiful daughter, Tina. Joppolo's mounting anger follows Giuseppe out of the office.

Capt. Purvis has come to report. He has been all over hell looking for something to haul water in. No jeeps. Not even any gas trucks. Yet, insists Joppolo, they've got to find some way to get food and water into the town.

"Hell, it's not your fault, Major," comforts Purvis. "Your neck's not out. All you got to do is to send in your report that Marvin ordered the carts to stay out—and let the GHQ worry about it. You're in the clear."

It is Purvis's idea that Joppolo takes things entirely too seriously. What he should do is to relax a little. What about the two of them going out and getting drunk? Let Giuseppe fix them up with a couple of those Italian babes—Joppolo could do the translating—

It's a good idea, but Joppolo has a council meeting—so not tonight. Joppolo is back at his desk. Purvis has gone out through his own office, waving a hand disgustedly at the pile of incoming mail he hasn't found time to get through.

The appearance of Zito in Maj. Joppolo's office reminds the Major of the bell problem. He has been thinking about that. Even if he could get them a bell, it wouldn't want to be just any bell. It would want to mean something. Maybe they could get a Liberty Bell for Adano. What is a Liberty Bell, Zito would know.

"Well, it's bronze, I think," explains the Major. "It has a large crack near the bottom from its age. And it says on it: 'Proclaim Liberty throughout all the land, to all the inhabitants thereof.' "

"The words are good. How is the tone?"

"That would depend on the replica."

"Now about this crack. How old is this bell?"

"Oh—nearly two hundred years old, I guess."

"And it has a crack!" Zito is greatly surprised. "A new bell like that should not crack. Our bell was seven hundred years old but it had no crack. Couldn't you get us a Liberty Bell without a crack?"

"But without the crack it wouldn't be a Liberty Bell."

"Then I think Adano would not like this Liberty Bell. Adano would not like to have a crack, I am sure."

"Yeah, I was afraid of that."

There is a knock at the door. Outside the three men who drive Adano's water carts are waiting to see Maj. Joppolo. The Major is for sending them away. They have their orders and there is nothing more to be said about it. But he reconsiders. Let the men come in.

The cart drivers file in. "They are evidently poor but respected. They each have on an old clean coat and they clutch old cloth caps in their hands. They are ill-at-ease. One is about sixty, furrowed skin, *Afronti Pietro;* another, more timid than the others, is *Erba Carlo;* the other is fat, rather handsome, his hair plastered down with grease, *Basile Giovanni."*

There is nothing that can be done about the carts, Maj. Joppolo warns them. The order has been given and it is a military necessity. But he will hear what they have to say.

Afronti Pietro is the first. He would point out to Mister Major that his (Afronti's) cart is different. It has two wooden wheels, and they sing. Some people call it squeaking, but it isn't. To Afronti it is singing. And these are not Fascisti songs.

"One day last Summer I drove my cart all the way to Gioia de Monti," relates Afronti, "and all the way the wheels sang a song which was also a prophecy. Do you wish to hear this song, Mister Major?"

"No, I don't."

With this encouragement Afronti unbuttons his coat, holds his cap out at arm's length and sings in a very loud voice, but with no particular tune—

" 'The Americans are coming here, Signor Afronti. The Americans are very, very just men, especially with regard to carts.' "

There is a moment's silence as Afronti finishes his song, then Joppolo says sharply: "Don't joke with me, old man. If you have something reasonable to say, do so. Come to the point."

"The music has stopped," shouts Afronti. "There is no more music." They shut him up and Afronti returns to his seat.

Erba Carlo is the next to speak. He is frightened and has a time telling the Major what it is he would like to say: That his water cart is a good cart; dirty on the outside, maybe, but clean on the inside. There is a great thirst in Adano, and how can he help if his cart is kept the other side of the bridge? Also, one proclamation says the people should keep clean with water; how can they do that if the carts cannot come through?

Now it is the turn of Basile Giovanni. The fat one has much to say and is eager to say it. The worst of all the things about the carts is the food, insists Basile, and (*Patting his belly.*) is he not one who can talk of food understandingly? There are those who suffer in Adano. One Galioto is so thin it is easy to count the teeth of his mouth when his lips are closed. "The nine children of Raffaela have big bellies, but their bellies are big only with the gas of hunger," reports Basile.

He pauses for a moment. The Major's irritation has disappeared. He bids Basile continue.

"You have not seen my cart, have you, Mister Major?" asks Basile.

"I may have—I have seen many of them."

"But you would not forget mine if you had seen it. It has four scenes painted on it—from the Holy Word and they are all concerned with eating. There is the miracle of the loaves and fishes. There is the Last Supper. There is the widow's jar which never emptied no matter how much food she took out. There is the wedding at Cana where the water turned to wine. And all of the people in these pictures are fat people, because mine is the cart for food. I do not think it is sacrilegious that even Jesus himself is fat on my cart. (JOPPOLO *says nothing, but just listens.*) But now how can I put between the shafts my fat horse, whose name is General Eisenhower, in honor of our deliverer, and put my fat self on the seat and drive around with my pictures of fat and holy people—when the people of Adano are starving? This fills me with shame. (*Again he pauses. We see* JOPPOLO *is very thoughtful.*) There is nothing in all the proclamations which says Americans came to Adano in order to make people die of hunger—to die of thirst, is there? Thank you, Mister Major."

The three cartmen regard the Major gravely as he passes his hand wearily over his face. "I want you to know," he says to them, "I have been doing everything in my power to bring food and water to the people of Adano without making use of the carts."

THREE CARTMEN—But the carts, Mister Major! Yes, the carts! They are the only way to bring food and water to Adano!

JOPPOLO (*looking at them soberly*)—You don't seem to understand. I am powerless to let these carts back into Adano. The order to keep them out was given by a General of the United States Army. I am only a Major. To countermand a superior officer's order—well, that cannot be done.

THREE CARTMEN (*going to* JOPPOLO)—But the food, Mister Major— The children are hungry— What are we to do?

BORTH (*softly*)—That's a tough one, Duce.

JOPPOLO (*after a moment; coming suddenly to a decision*)— Goddam it! (*He rises abruptly and strides to* PURVIS'S *office, calling*) Purvis! (PURVIS *enters the small office.*) I want you to remove your guards from the bridge and the sulphur works and start letting the carts back into the town.

PURVIS (*shocked*)—What's that, sir?

JOPPOLO (*angrily*)—You heard me! Goddam it! (*He turns to the cartmen.*) All right, go ahead—start bringing your carts back into town!

BASILE—Uh?

JOPPOLO—The food carts, the water carts, all the carts!

THREE CARTMEN (*hurrying off happily*)—Yes, Mister Major— Thank you, Mister Major—

PURVIS—But you can't countermand—

JOPPOLO (*angry and excited*)—Who says I can't?

PURVIS—If General Marvin— Jesus, if—

JOPPOLO (*pacing excitedly*)—General Marvin has ruined everything we've done here! The town is dying— We're not here to kill people!

PURVIS—It's a hell of a chance you're taking, Major.

JOPPOLO—Don't tell me what chances I'm taking! I know them better than you do!

PURVIS—I wish you'd think it over.

JOPPOLO (*deadly serious*)—Purvis, I order you, on my authority, to start letting the carts back into the town, beginning now. I take absolute and complete responsibility.

PURVIS (*straightening up*)—Yes, sir.

Purvis has gone back to his office. Outside a crowd is shouting. The curtain falls.

ACT II

A few days later Maj. Joppolo's office is empty, but Capt. Purvis is at his desk in his office, nursing his head in his hands. The Captain, as he confesses to his aide, Schultz, was "buzzed" the night before—buzzed on "Dago Red," and the result is terrible. That Dago Red— It's murder, admits Schultz.

Capt. Purvis's problem of the moment is finding a way to stop an expanding black market and control inflation. He has decided to send in a request putting the town off limits for all troops.

"Is it the men's fault, sir?" Schultz is quick to ask.

"Who the hell's fault do you think it is?"

"I don't know, sir. I thought it was just some left-over Fascist graft."

"It's the G.I.'s fault mostly. They're too damn generous. My God, they give away everything they've got: candy, C-rations, cigarettes— They don't understand Italian, so when they go into a place to buy something, they don't know how much they're being charged and they wind up paying just what they pay back in the States. You know that barber across the street? He gets three lire for a haircut, three lire—that's three cents. Our men walk in, give him fifty cents and a tip. Last week he cleaned up five hundred lire in one morning. And now the bastard's sitting over there and won't even cut *my* hair."

There is a phone call for Capt. Purvis. Evidently from a Lieutenant who had made one of the party the night before. The Lieutenant isn't feeling very good, either. Maj. Joppolo? "He probably feels like a million dollars, the bastard," complains Purvis. "What's the matter with that guy? Why won't he get plastered once in a while?"

Joppolo, ventures Purvis, would probably be okay if he wasn't so damned serious— "Always talking about Democracy like it was his mother." And there's another thing, too. "He's going to get me in a hell of a lot of trouble," predicts Purvis. "About letting those carts back into town. I been thinking about it. If Marvin ever hears about those carts my neck's going to be out a mile. Huh?—Well, I'm the guy who had to let them back in. Sure I'm supposed to co-operate with Joppolo. But don't forget I'm still responsible to M.P. Headquarters in Algiers. You know what I think I ought to do? Get out a report on it. Say that General Marvin ordered us to keep the carts out of town, that

Joppolo countermanded the order.—Why the hell not? Why should I burn for Joppolo?"

Capt. Purvis has no sooner hung up than Giuseppe bursts into Maj. Joppolo's office looking for help. A crowd outside has spotted the former Mayor of Adano, one Nasta, and is threatening to tear him apart. Giuseppe shares the opinion of the crowd that Mayor Nasta is a bastard, but still he thinks the Captain should come. . . .

In Capt. Purvis's office his aides, Schultz and Trapani, are discussing the episodes of the carts and Joppolo's countermanding of Gen. Marvin's order. It is Trapani's opinion that Joppolo did exactly what he should have done.

"Oh, yeah!" Schultz disagrees. "And who do you think you are? What do you think this man's army would be like if everybody went around countermanding orders? Anyway, Purvis is going to make out a report on it and send it in."

"What do you mean?" Trapani is dumbfounded. "Christ, he can't do that! If Marvin should ever see it—"

The racket outside interrupts him. Suddenly the doors into Joppolo's office burst open and Purvis, Borth and several M.P.'s, with an angry crowd pressing them, bring a frightened and sniveling Mayor Nasta into the room. "Save me! Save me! Don't let them get me!" Nasta is muttering.

Purvis shakes the sniveling out of him. Borth and Giuseppe try to get rid of the crowd. Nasta is under arrest, Borth tells them. The Mister Major will take care of Nasta. Let them get out—

They manage to get the doors shut. Nasta is still whining. "What are you going to do with me?" he pleads. "If you are going to shoot me tell me first. Don't shoot me from behind!"

"That's the way he used to do," sneers Zito.

They herd the pleading Nasta, who feels safer now that he has discovered they are Americans, into the next room, with an M.P. to guard him.

"I hope to God nobody else comes down from the hills today," sighs Purvis, nursing his head. Then suddenly he spies Trapani and is angrily reminded of something he wanted to do. He wanted to send a report to Lieut.-Col. W. W. Morris of the 49th Division respecting the subject of mule carts in the town of Adano— Let Trapani take this down—

" '(1) On July 19, orders were received from General Marvin, 49th Division, to keep all mule carts out of town of Adano. Guards were posted at bridge over Rosse River and at Caco-

Caco—how the hell do you pronounce it—Refinery. Order carried out. (2) On July 21, guards were removed on order of Major Victor Joppolo, Civil Affairs Officer, town of Adano, and carts were allowed back into town.' "

"Make that out, Trapani, and send it to G-one of the Division," concludes Purvis. With that he leaves them.

Trapani is unhappy. Schultz is indifferent. "You can't blame Purvis for trying to cover himself," says Schultz.

"Gen. Marvin'll never be back here, and if he is he wouldn't notice the carts. But once you get it on paper, it's just a sure way to ruin the Major."

"Well, hell, Marvin'll never see that report, anyway."

Trapani has an idea. As he is writing he adds to the Purvis report. He reads to Schultz what he has added. " '—guards were removed on order of Major Victor Joppolo—because carts were essential to town and town was in bad shape without same.' What do you think, if I stick that in? Think that last part might make it sound better for the Major?"

"What's the difference? They can't get you on it."

"I hate to see a guy get into trouble when he's trying to do right."

Joppolo is back. They bring Nasta before him. The ex-Mayor has recovered some part of his nerve. He has come down from the hills, he says, to help the Americans. Joppolo is amazed that after nine years of graft and keeping the people down, Nasta should think that he can help. True, there are others in office who can be recognized as Fascists, Joppolo admits, but they have proved themselves trustworthy. They were not willing Fascists.

Nor was Nasta, so Nasta insists. If he could be Mayor again— Or, maybe, if not Mayor—"Perhaps I would accept something less than Mayor," suggests Nasta.

"Oh, you would!" explodes Joppolo. "Look, you seem to think the Americans are complete fools. Well, maybe we are! Maybe we ought to throw you in jail or shoot you without a trial —but it just happens we don't do things that way. You'll get your trial in time—you'll pay for every crime you've committed against the people of Adano. God knows there're enough of them."

By the time Borth has produced from the files the Nasta record of graft and double dealing, and read it to the unhappy man, he is thoroughly subdued—

"You'll get your trial, all right—but in the meantime you want something to do. All right, I have something. You are to report every morning to Sergt. Borth of the American Army. That is all you have to do each day."

"You mean that Nasta has become a common probationer? Oh—please be generous with me. Give me some work to do."

"Generous?" Joppolo's voice rings with anger. "In the name of God, what do you expect? You report to Borth every morning. The rest of the day you may go about the town and mingle with the crowd."

The thought of what the crowd may do to him sends Nasta into a new fever of fear, but there is nothing he can do about it. He is to report each morning to Sergt. Borth and repent his sins. If the first sin he would like to repent should happen to be the fact that he is Nasta, that would show very good taste, suggests Borth.

Giuseppe reports many activities. First he is much pleased that Maj. Joppolo has favored the council by having his picture taken. To Joppolo this was a silly waste of time. Next, he is sorry the Major has not been able to do anything about a bell for Adano. The people keep asking about that. Finally, Giuseppe would like to report that he has dutifully reported to the little blonde, Tina, that the Major is lonesome and would like to go out with her—

"You're crazy! I never told you any such thing!" Joppolo is visibly disturbed.

"Oh, yes, a boss, you tell me the other day you want to see-a Tina's old man."

"Giuseppe, I want to see Tina's father because I want to start the fishermen going out again. That's all there is to it. Now, get out of here."

Before he goes Giuseppe has further announcements to make. Tomasino is waiting to see the boss. No, no—Giuseppe had not told Tomasino that the boss wanted to go out with his daughter. He had just told him the boss wanted to see him. And, besides Tomasino, there is someone else waiting—the blonde-a Tina! Giuseppe had fixed it up good—

"Good God! You didn't tell her to come here?"

"Sure, a boss."

"Goddam it, Giuseppe, what's got into you? What did you say to her?"

"I tell her the truth like you always want me to. I tell her you-a like her very much and that you want to make a date."

"Damn you! I wish you'd—" Joppolo is very upset. "Well, I can't see her. I haven't got anything to say to her. Tell her it was all a mistake—tell her—I don't care what you tell her—but get rid of her—"

"You-a embarrassed, a boss?"

"Well, what the hell do you think?" The Major is shouting.

"She's not-a embarrassed! She's a very nice girl but she's not-a embarrassed."

"She's not?" Suddenly the picture is changed for Joppolo.

"No, a boss. She's-a glad. She like you the first time she-a saw you."

"She did?" Joppolo is thoughtful.

"Yes-a, boss. Just like you like-a her— And she is the one who made the old man come. She told him if he didn't come, she would make her finger nails all red like they do in the movies."

The Joppolo impatience increases. Giuseppe has, he charges, got him all balled up. Well, let him send in Tomasino, the fisherman. And then let him go to the Navy office and ask Lieut. Livingston to get up there as quickly as possible.

Joppolo, nervous and fidgety, prepares to receive Tomasino. The fisherman is an old man, and suggestively defiant. He stands for a moment, morosely observing the Major. Then he speaks—

"All right, man of authority, arrest me!"

"Arrest you? I'm not going to arrest you, Tomasino."

"All right then, shoot me, go ahead and shoot me."

"I'm not going to shoot you, either. Where'd you get that idea? I asked you to come here to talk to you."

"Men in this building do not talk to people. They arrest them or they shoot them."

"Maybe that's the way it used to be, but it isn't any longer. Sit down, Tomasino."

Tomasino doesn't see why he should sit down, and Joppolo, his irritation mounting, bids him do as he will. All he (Joppolo) wants of Tomasino is that he should organize the fishing. The people of Adano are hungry. They must have fish. Still, Tomasino refuses to go fishing.

"Now, listen to me!" shouts Joppolo, angrily. "I've heard about you! You've got some crazy idea that we're trying to cheat you! Well, we're not! Now I'm not going to argue with you! I want you to get enough fishermen together for five or six boats and get out there and start fishing!"

And who, Tomasino asks, is to be the protector of these fishermen? To whom are they to pay tribute? They have always paid tribute to someone. Or suffered. And how much extra tax must they pay on the gross weight of their catch? There will be no extra tax, Joppolo assures him.

"Wait—wait a moment," protests the surprised Tomasino. "No protection, no tribute, no special tax— You are making fun of me, American."

"Why should I make fun of you? Look, Tomasino, I'm asking *you* to be the head of the fishermen in Adano. I want to have a fisherman over the fishermen."

"You want a fisherman over the fishermen?"

"Yes, of course. What's wrong with that?"

"May I sit down now, American?"

"Certainly, Tomasino."

There is, agrees Tomasino, justice in the idea, but he could not take charge. That would make him a man of authority. He would be the thing he has hated all his life.

"Look, Tomasino, you mustn't judge all men of authority by those you have known. You don't have to be like them, Tomasino. The real authority lies in the people themselves. Your job is to find out what's best for them and to see that they get it."

"It seems too good. I feel there is a trick."

"There is no trick. It is men like you, Tomasino, who can make this thing a success."

"American," Tomasino is saying, a moment later, "I am beginning to think that you are different from the others. And if that is so—it will be a good thing in this town. I will be the head of the fishermen for Adano."

"Good! That's good, Tomasino!" Joppolo is genuinely delighted. "Now all we've got to do is to get permission from the Navy."

Lieut. Livingston is quite young, "rather a college boy still," and at the moment rather cool. Maj. Joppolo explains to him about the fishing, and about Tomasino's agreeing to take charge. All they want from the Navy is six charts showing the location of the mine fields.

Lieut. Livingston is afraid nothing can be done. It isn't easy to get permission—

"You mean you'd have to go running to the Admirals for a little thing like this?" . . . "Listen, Lieutenant— For Christ's sake, this town is hungry. It needs fish. Hell's bells, are we in this war together or aren't we? What's biting you?"

"Perhaps if you had got in touch with me earlier—"

"All right, so you're sore! Listen, Lieutenant, unless you give permission for these men to go out, I'm going to send a separate letter naming each person who dies of hunger in this town to your commanding officer, and in each letter I'm going to say it's your fault."

For a moment the Lieutenant looks at Joppolo intently. There is no doubting that the Major means what he says—

"Well—er—um—maybe we could work something out—"

"You're damn right we could. I want you to have those six charts made up and I want them ready day after tomorrow. Is that clear?"

"Yes, sir."

Now everything is fine. Tomasino is very happy at the chance to go fishing again. Joppolo is greatly relieved. Even the Lieutenant begins to thaw, as Joppolo concedes a point—

"Look, Livingston," says Joppolo, "I—I'm afraid I was kind of abrupt just now. I'm sorry. The fact is, I was so damn anxious —and this old guy had been so damned obstinate—it never occurred to me I was treading on the Navy's toes—I guess I'm a rather single-minded guy. I should have asked your permission first, of course."

Livingston is quick to agree to forget the whole thing. He won't mind having a bit of fish himself. G-rations can get pretty terrible. He agrees, too, that getting fish again will be a fine thing for the people's morale. Livingston knows how important morale can be. It can make all the difference between a winning and a losing team. He knows that, because at Yale he was on the crew for three years. That's how he got into the Navy. Told them that he had had experience with small boats—

"Look, Major," Livingston is saying, "I've organized a little club down by the harbor. Took over a little house just for a place to drop in at—got hold of some Scotch, just a few cases— How about dropping in and having a drink with us some time?"

"Well, that's damn nice of you, Lieutenant. I've half a mind to take you up on that some time, if you're really serious."

The Major is afraid he will not be able to come tomorrow night—until he happens to notice the letter about the bell on his desk. That gives him a new thought—

"Say, look, Livingston— You have a lot of bells in the Navy, don't you?"

"Bells?"

"Yeah—on boats, I mean. Every boat has to have a nice loud bell, doesn't it?"

"Hell, yes, the Navy's full of bells."

"Yeah, that's what I thought— Look, I was thinking, maybe I could drop in tomorrow night after all."

"Swell! You'll like the fellows. Nice bunch of boys. Well, I'll be seein' you then, Major."

"Yeah, I'll be seein' you, Lieutenant."

Livingston has gone. Joppolo moves slowly over to the window. It is late in the day and he is very tired. As he stands at the window Trapani appears in Capt. Purvis's office. He has the pink slip bearing the report of the water cart order in his hand. Schultz sticks his head in the door with the suggestion: Why doesn't he (Trapani) let the report get lost among the other papers that Purvis hasn't gone over? It might be there for years. So Trapani buries the slip deep in the disorderly pile.

Tina has come quietly through the door to Joppolo's office. At first she does not see the Major at the window. When she does she speaks to him hesitantly. She has come to tell him that, until today, she has not seen her father smile since just before Mussolini came into power. She is quite happy that the Major has made her father smile again.

She would go then, but Joppolo stops her, although he supposes, hesitantly, that she is in a hurry to get home. When she assures him she is not he thinks perhaps she would like to have a look at Adano from the balcony. It's very beautiful—

"You know, my mother and father were from a little town in Italy, just like this one."

"Really, Mister Major?"

"Yes. When I first got off the boat here in Sicily, I felt a little as though I were coming home."

"You like it here in Adano, then?"

"Yes—very much—I think—maybe—I've never been so happy in my life."

Where does he come from in America? Tina would know. From the Bronx, he tells her. That's a part of New York. Is the Bronx beautiful? He thinks it may be—for his parents. In Italy they were just poor peasants. In the Bronx his mother has a washing machine and his father has a good job. But for Joppolo it is different. He grew up in America and he wanted something more.

Tina, too, knows what it is to be restless. It was because she was not satisfied that she had dyed her hair blonde. She wanted to change herself some way—

"I was tired of being just Tina, 'Tomasino's daughter, Tina,'" she explains. "That's all I've heard all my life— There are so many wonderful things to do. I felt if I could only get away from

Adano I— But I couldn't—so I dyed my hair instead. (JOPPOLO
smiles.) You must have had a wonderful life, Mister Major."

JOPPOLO—I'd hardly say that, Tina.

TINA—Did you go to one of those big American colleges? Like
you see in the movies? Everyone is so beautiful in them. Did
you, Mister Major?

JOPPOLO—No, not exactly. I went to school until I was sixteen,
then I had to go to work. My first job was a clerk in a grocery
store at $12 a week.

TINA—How much is that?

JOPPOLO—Twelve hundred lire.

TINA—Twelve hundred— You were rich by the time you were
sixteen!

JOPPOLO—No, Tina, twelve hundred lire is all right for Adano—

TINA—All right!

JOPPOLO—But it's not so much in the States.

TINA—You mean everyone is rich in the Bronx?

JOPPOLO—Well, I wouldn't say everyone, Tina. Anyhow, a few
years later I got a job in the City Government, as a clerk in the
Department of Taxation. Then later on, the examinations came
up for advancement and my mother-in-law told me I should try
to pass them.

TINA—Your mother-in-law? You are married?

JOPPOLO—Yes, Tina.

TINA—She is pretty, the wife?

JOPPOLO—Yes, she is very pretty, at least she seems so to me.
I miss her very much.

TINA (*nodding slowly*)—Yes. Major? How long do you
think the war will go on—here on Italian soil?

JOPPOLO (*carelessly*)—Oh, I don't know, Tina. A couple of
months or so, I guess.

TINA—And how long do you think it will be before our Italian
prisoners of war are released?

JOPPOLO (*suddenly suspicious*)—Why? Have you someone
who has been captured?

TINA—I don't know whether he has been captured or killed or
what. I would like to ask you—Giorgio and I were going to be
married—could you find out for me whether he is a prisoner?

JOPPOLO—I can't do anything about that, I'm afraid. That
isn't my business. I'm a Civil Affairs Officer.

TINA—Please help me, Mister Major. You see, Giorgio—he
was more like my brother— He was going to be a musician—

he hated killing—it's so awful to think of him in some prisoners' camp.

JOPPOLO—I'm afraid you've made a mistake, Tina.

TINA—I don't understand, Mister Major.

JOPPOLO—If your reason for coming here was so that I could find your sweetheart for you, I much prefer that you had told me—

TINA—Don't—don't, Mister Major—

JOPPOLO—If it is business you have to do with me, you can come here during hours and frankly state your case. You don't have to pretend anything.

TINA (*hurt; starting for the door*)—Yes, Mister Major. (*She turns.*) I did not come here to ask you about Giorgio, Mister Major. I did not even think of him until you mentioned your wife. (*There is a moment's pause as* JOPPOLO *gets this. She is looking at him gravely.*) Sometimes women can be lonely, too.

Joppolo, realizing that he has been rude to her, comes to Tina to take her by the two arms and to apologize. She is quick to forgive. And glad to hear now that there is a good chance the Italian prisoners will be released. There will be Adano men among them, but whether or not Giorgio will be one of these the Major has no way of knowing.

Again Tina is about to go when Tomasino, her father, appears suddenly in the doorway. He has come with a message from his wife, who is a very difficult woman. Mrs. Tomasino has insisted that, if Tomasino is to be head of the fishermen, then Mister Major must come to their house and help eat some torrone which Tina has made.

It is not very good torrone, Tina is quick to insist, but Major Joppolo is not discouraged. He will be very glad to come.

Tomasino and Tina have gone. Joppolo stands looking after them as Capt. Purvis comes into his office. A quick look in the mirror convinces Joppolo that he needs a shave. Quite jauntily he goes for his hat. Passing the door he catches sight of Purvis—

"Hi, Purvis," he calls. "Why don't you go home? Day's over."

"That's the trouble," grumbles Purvis. "Got plenty to keep you busy during the day—but what the hell do you do at night in this dump?"

"Looks to me like you had enough to do," says Joppolo, picking up some of the papers from the file. "Why don't you clean up this incoming file? You'll get snowed under. Well, good night."

Purvis is in front of the file trying to make a decision. He takes a coin from his pocket and flops it. He loses. "Two out of three," he mutters, flipping the coin again. The curtain falls.

It is early morning, a week later. Tina is arranging a bowl of wild flowers on Maj. Joppolo's desk, but runs into the next room quickly when she hears someone in Capt. Purvis's office.

The Purvis visitor is Trapani. He has brought the mail. Suddenly remembering the pink slip he is hoping Purvis will not find, he searches for it among the papers. When he finds it he buries it a little deeper.

Presently Maj. Joppolo appears, followed by a very excited and angry Cacopardo. "You Americans think you are civilized!" Cacopardo is yelling. "You think you are doing us a favor by coming to our shores! You Americans are no better than the Germans!"

"All right, old man. Take it easy," Joppolo is saying.

The Major goes directly to Purvis's office and summons the Captain. When Purvis comes Joppolo angrily demands to know what the hell's the matter with the M.P. Can't he handle his men or what?

"They are barbarians," cries the wailing Cacopardo. "They are savages! The Americans are liars!"

Purvis is ready to resent this but Joppolo stops him. "He's got a right to be sore," he says. "He was good enough to lend us his house to billet some of your men in and last night they wrecked it. They tore it apart."

"What I have lost I can never get back. They smashed my terra cotta head that was one by Florentine Camilliani in the 16th Century."

"They broke damn near every work of art in the house," Joppolo confirms. "He had a valuable collection. I want you to find out who busted up that stuff and have them in my office in half an hour."

"Yes, sir. I didn't know anything about it. I'll have them here, sir."

Cacopardo is still muttering and weeping as Joppolo assures him that from now on nothing like what has happened will ever happen again in Adano. . . .

Lieut. Livingston is on the phone. He has good news about the bell. The story is a bit complicated to get over the phone, but Joppolo finally pieces it together. It seems that a guy named Toot Dowling, who substituted for Livingston on the football

team at Yale, is now skipper on the *Corelli*. And Toot, who was
a lousy football player, but is probably a good skipper, has a bell.
A bell that has some significance, too, seeing it figured in the
First World War and ties in Italy with America in 1917.

Joppolo is visibly excited by the news. When he gets up from
the phone he discovers Sergt. Borth grinning broadly. Now
Joppolo has called a little wildly for Giuseppe and Zito and
passes on to them the news about the possibility of their getting
a bell—

"It's off a United States destroyer called the *Corelli*—named
after a fellow who commanded a destroyer in the last war," explains Joppolo. "He was on convoy duty in the North Atlantic
one day, November 12, 1917, and a bad storm came up. One of
the ships—an Italian freighter—broke down and started to
founder. It was very dangerous to get close to the freighter in a
storm like that but Corelli did it and he got all the Italians off.
(*He looks at them hopefully.*) There's a meaning in that, don't
you think? The bell has been in both wars and it's kind of American and Italian at the same time."

Yes, Zito thinks there is meaning in such a bell. Now, if it has
a good tone, and there is not a crack in it, Zito is sure it will be a
good bell for Adano.

Giuseppe, too, is pleased. "You fixin' things in Adano fine,
a-boss," beams Giuseppe. "Everybody love you, a-boss."

"Well, that's fine."

"Zito love you, a-boss. *I* love you, a-boss!"

"All right, that's enough, Giuseppe. Get back to your work."

"Yes, boss. And *Tina* love you, a-boss."

"Get out of here!" And Giuseppe disappears.

Tina comes timidly back into the office. She explains about the
wild flowers. The hills are covered with them and she had gathered hers early. She felt so good when she woke up—

"I know what it is," she explains. "It's because there is a new
air in Adano. It's sharp and clean. It makes people smile."

"That's good."

"You don't know what it was like before," Tina goes on.
"We were always afraid. But now, it's so wonderful—to wake up
in the morning, to walk down the streets, to meet your friends
and laugh with them. Listen to our radios, to talk about anything
in the world we want to. I am so happy, Mister Major—"

"I'm rather happy too, Tina. I have been away from home
many months now. In America are those whom I love. I have
missed them terribly. I have been very lonely. But now to have

you bring me flowers like this, to be able to come to your home
the way I have, to be a part of it. I can't tell you how much it's
helped that loneliness, Tina."

"Has it, Mister Major?"

They are looking searchingly at each other. It is plain to be
seen that Tina is in love. Joppolo has taken a step toward her
and she is waiting—

"Tina—I—you don't know how much it's meant to me."

"I was not sure."

"You're very sweet."

For a moment it looks as though he would take her in his arms.
Then from the distance there comes the sound of voices singing.
Tina turns away, listening, an expression of fear on her face.

"It's our war prisoners—they are coming home," she says,
slowly. As he steps away from her she adds: "I'd forgotten.
I must go over."

"Yes, of course," he says.

Sergt. Borth is back. He has been over to the Square where the
prisoners are coming in. "There's a bunch of women over there,
crowded up alongside the building, not saying a word—just staring," reports Borth. "Then when the guys break ranks, *they* just
stand there staring at the women. And then the women start to
run for them—looking into every guy's face—yelling their guy's
name. The guys don't run because they know their woman's
there—but the women aren't so sure. Some of them know damn
well he's not there, but they run anyway, just to be in on it. I'd
say your chances in Adano on getting your man back are three to
one—against—"

Maj. Joppolo thinks perhaps he will go over. . . .

Capt. Purvis has come back to his office. He is plainly in a bad
humor, and the sight of the accumulation of papers on his desk
doesn't help. He starts going through them. His eye falls on the
pink slip. He glances over it and calls lustily for Trapani.

What's the meaning of the report's still being there? Why
wasn't it sent to G-one of the Division, as he had ordered? And
what is this addition: " '. . . *because carts were essential to town
and town was in bad shape without same?' "*

"Did I tell you to say that?" demands the irate Purvis.

"No, sir. I just thought that was the case, sir."

"Oh, you did? Goddam it, I dictated that just the way I
wanted it. What the hell are you—a soldier or a poet?"

"Yes, sir."

"Copy that over and leave out that last. And show it to me when it's finished."

"Yes, sir."

Purvis has stormed out. A moment later Sergt. Borth appears. Trapani tells him what has happened. Borth accepts the situation lightly, but with determination. Let Trapani go ahead and copy the order, and let him give it to him to mail. He'll see that it doesn't get to Marvin.

But Borth should know that Trapani can't do that. If anything slipped up so that the order didn't get to G-one Division Trapani would be in trouble—

"Look, Trapani, I want that order after Purvis has okayed it, see?" The Sergeant has suddenly become very quiet and tough.

"Oh, you do?" Trapani is tough, too. But before anything happens Borth backs away. "Okay, you win!" he says.

Trapani softens. "Well, I don't want to get the Major in Dutch any more than you, but—"

There is a pause, then Borth, looking away, says softly: "Listen, Trapani, you don't know that guy the way I do—you don't know what he is in this town. All you can see is that he's cleaned up the street, he's given the people food. (*He pauses for a moment.*) But there are a hell of a lot more important things than just cleaning up the alleys. Christ! He's made these people want to *live* again—he's put their breath right back into their very goddamned mouths—and he's done it all alone. If anything happened to that guy, this town would go right back to the way it was before we came. (*He pauses a moment, then adds quietly.*) And of course it don't mean anything to you, but I got a great feeling about that guy. He's somebody. He's put his heart and soul and all his guts into this town. It's his. And if he had to leave it, he'd be leaving his heart and his soul and all his guts right here behind him."

Trapani is unhappy. He thinks perhaps he can at least let Borth have a look at the order after it has been okayed by Purvis.

Three M.P.'s—Munroe, Schultz and Pollack—arrive to give Maj. Joppolo their version of the brawl in Cacopardo's house the night before. Schultz thinks he should do all the talking. And they should be careful not to let the Major know that what they did they were doing for him—

"We jumped the gun," Schultz reminds them. "He doesn't know anything about that report. Chances are, it will never go through.—Besides, it was a corny idea to try to get him a present anyway. Who ever heard of an enlisted man getting a Major a going-away present?"

"It seemed like a swell idea last night."

"And there were so many beautiful going-away presents in that house—"

"I shouldn't have told you guys anything about that report." Schultz is regretful.

"Of course," says Munroe, turning to Pollack, "if you hadn't got so drunk and knocked that cabinet over—"

"Oh, yeah? Who was it climbed up after that glass swan in the bowl?"

"Forget it. It's over," orders Schultz.

Capt. Purvis is back. Trapani has finished the report on the water carts. This time, decides Purvis, he will personally see to its mailing. Sergt. Borth's plot has failed.

Maj. Joppolo, back from the Square, is ready to hear the explanations of the rioters. They are quick to confess. They are the guilty ones. They didn't mean any harm. They just got drunk. They were having a kind of roughhouse—

"Look," says Joppolo. "I know we can't be expected to take this thing as hard as the people who have had their whole lives and countries ruined by it—but for God's sake, can't we at least realize we're not at a ball game? You know what that old man said? He said Americans are barbarians, that they're savages, that the Americans are worse than the Germans. You men have given that guy a good start toward hating America for the rest of his life."

Has any of them been out north of town recently? No. If they had been they would have seen a little cemetery there with a white fence around it. It is an American cemetery. It was the idea of the people of Adano. They maintain the cemetery and every Sunday they take flowers there to decorate the graves of American soldiers—boys just like them. "The people are just beginning to like us—to trust us— And you, for Christ's sake, break up a guy's house! Whatever you get from Capt. Purvis —thirty days or thirty months—it won't make up for what you did. That's all. You're dismissed."

The three men shift uneasily and then start out. Joppolo stops them. He touches the Major's insignia on his collar—

"Look, forget this for a moment," he says. "If we're going to get anywhere on this thing, it's going to take every man we got, trying to figure the right thing to do. We got a tough job ahead of us. But we can lick it. In our Army we've got damn near every race in Europe:—no other country in the world has so many men who speak the language of the countries we've got to invade, whose parents have come from there. And that's our chance, because until there's something stable in Europe, our Armies will have to stay here—and it won't be any plans put down on paper that's going to guarantee whether we can lick the job. Only our men can guarantee it—only you and me and the rest of us here. And just as good as we can make things over here, that's just how good they'll be at home. What you guys do today may have a lot to do with what your kids, and their kids, will be doing for years to come. For God's sake, let's grab this chance to bring some sort of sense and decency and hope into the world again. It all depends just how good we can be."

The curtain falls.

ACT III

A few days later Capt. Purvis is lying on a couch in his office when Sergt. Borth approaches him with a request. Borth asks to be transferred. He would, if he could, like to go with Maj. Joppolo.

Joppolo leaving? That's a surprise to Purvis. Where's he going?

"He has been ordered to Algiers for reassignment," reports Borth. "He's been kicked out, sir."

"Kicked out? What the hell do you mean? He's the best man we've got here."

"Yes, sir. This came in the mail this morning. I happened to find it. Would you care to read it, sir?"

"Go ahead."

"It's addressed to the Major. 'One. You are authorized to proceed by first available transportation to A.F.H.G., Algiers, via port of Vincinimare. Two. Reassignment of station will be made by A.F.H.Q. Three. Reason for this order is that Major Victor Joppolo did willfully and without consultation countermand orders issued by General Marvin, 49th Division, re-entry of mule carts into town of Adano.' The order is signed by General Marvin."

Borth is eyeing the completely flabbergasted Purvis steadily. "Jesus Christ!" mutters Purvis.

"Yes, sir. Some son-of-a-bitch must have reported him, sir."

Purvis looks up at Borth slowly. The Sergeant's gaze is still steady.

"Why do you say that?" demands the Captain. "Maybe somebody on Marvin's staff drove through—noticed the carts were back in town—and sent in the report."

"Yes, sir."

Purvis is plainly unhappy. He wishes there were something they could do, but there doesn't appear to be. What is Borth going to do with the order—

"As soon as I have the guts I'm going to give it to him, sir," says the Sergeant.

Maj. Joppolo has come in with Giuseppe. "Brisk and active and cheerful," he is feeling fine. He will be ready to receive the Council, which Giuseppe has reported as waiting, in a very few minutes.

Now Zito has rushed in, all excitement. The bell has arrived. It's in a crate outside. It took ten sailors to get it off the truck. Already the people are gathering to see it, and Guzzo, the bell-ringer, is coming to try the tone.

Joppolo is on the balcony verifying the report. Borth has come in and stands unhappily watching him. Joppolo, all excitement, is beside himself with pleasure. He finds his hat and is for rushing down the stairs. For a second Borth would stop him. Then he lets him go and promises to follow.

After Joppolo has disappeared Borth takes the order from his pocket, slowly unfolds it, and spreads it out on the desk. "So long, Duce!" he says softly with a little gesture of farewell.

From the inner room the Council files in—Bellanco, D'Arpa, Gargano, Craxi and Spinnato. Craxi carries an easel and a portrait, covered with a black cloth.

They arrange themselves at points of vantage and, under Ballanco's direction, go through a sort of rehearsal of presentation. It is a fine time, they agree, to give Mister Major the portrait the same day the bell arrives.

Now, Joppolo followed by a part of the crowd, has come in and greeted them, a little apprehensively when he notes their serious faces. He will be with them in a minute, but first he would like to telephone the Engineers about hanging the bell. There is, they assure him, plenty of time for that.

It is while Joppolo has Major Harvey on the phone, and is happy to learn that the Engineers will be able to take care of the bell the next day that he glances down at his desk and sees the order of his dismissal. He picks it up and reads it slowly. *The life seems to leave his face as he looks at the paper in complete blankness.*

He turns to the Council. "Maj. Harvey said they will do the best they can, and it might be up so we could ring it later this afternoon. Now, if you don't mind—"

"We have something we wish to give you, Mister Major," beams Ballanco.

"We want to give the Mister Major—a Mister Major," sniggers D'Arpa.

Gargano goes to the portrait and unveils it. Now he will know why they wanted him to have his picture taken.

"Mister Major, we have had this portrait painted to give you because we wish to show you that—"

Ballanco's speech sticks in his throat. The others would help him out.

"What the Mister Mayor wishes to say is that the eyes—the eyes of the portrait are honest," says Gargano.

"In the chin there is strength," adds D'Arpa.

"In the fix of the hair there is neatness," contributes Craxi.

"In the cheeks there is a sympathetic warmth," a recovering Ballanco puts in.

"And you can see in the picture that that man wishes that every person in the town of Adano should be happy," concludes Gargano.

Joppolo tries to thank them, but he is too confused to speak. He turns abruptly and walks out on the balcony. At a sign from Bellanco the Council and the people file slowly out of the office. Only Tina is left. She is worried. Something plainly is wrong.

"You were so happy a few moments ago. What is it?"

Joppolo stands looking at her dismally. All the heartbreak that he feels suddenly breaks him. He clutches her.

"Oh, Tina!"

"Tell me, Mister Major."

With an effort Joppolo gets hold of himself. "I'm sorry. Good-by, Tina."

"Why do you say good-by? We will see you tonight?"

"Yes, Tina—tonight—"

Slowly she turns and goes out the door. Joppolo stands looking after her. As he turns back to his desk his eye rests for a moment on the portrait. He has picked up the order and stands reading it again. His hand slowly drops to the desk.

The curtain falls.

A few hours later the sun has come low into Joppolo's office. His things are packed and are being carried out by the M.P.'s. The Major puts the last of his papers in his brief-case. Borth is standing by.

"The jeep will take me to Vincinimare and the boat for Algiers will leave in the morning," says Joppolo. "I don't want to say any good-bys. I don't know whether I could. That's why I wanted to wait until they'd all gone home."

"I wish I could go with you, sir."

"I wish you could. But it's no good, even if we could arrange it. You're needed here. Borth, try to help whoever takes my place here to do a good job for Adano."

"He'd better be good. Adano needs a man who can understand it. Adano needs you, Major."

"Well—it's too late to talk about that. (*He pauses a moment. Picking up another paper to put in his brief-case.*) I wonder how Marvin ever found out about the carts."

"I don't suppose it would make any difference if we knew."

"No, I just wondered. Well, I guess that's the works."

On the desk Tina has left a scarf. Joppolo starts to give it to Borth, changes his mind and puts it in his brief-case.

As he starts for the door the Major turns for a last look around. "Well, anyway, we gave them a good start here, didn't we, Borth?"

"We sure did, Duce."

Joppolo has started briskly out the door. Suddenly a clear, loud, vibrant tone fills the air. It is the bell and it rings with great clarity and power. It stops Joppolo in his tracks. He looks up to where the sound is coming from. Then turns to Borth, listening. The bell fills the whole room, the whole audience. Slowly a broad smile comes to Joppolo's face.

"Listen!" exclaims Joppolo, proudly. "It shakes the whole damned building!"

The voices of an excited crowd can be heard. Joppolo goes abruptly out the door, followed by Borth. The bell does not stop. It rings on and on, full and vibrant.

THE CURTAIN FALLS

I REMEMBER MAMA

A Comedy in Two Acts

BY JOHN VAN DRUTEN

(Adapted from Kathryn Forbes's, "Mama's Bank Account")

"I REMEMBER MAMA" has been a good deal of a family
affair from the first. It is related that Kathryn Forbes's volume
of short stories, "Mama's Bank Account," was first read by Mary
Rodgers, who is the Richard Rodgerses' oldest daughter. Mary,
being charmed, advised her mother to read it. Mrs. Rodgers,
similarly enthused, called it to the attention of Mrs. Oscar Hammerstein, 2d, who in turn insisted that her husband should read
it. Whereupon practically everybody in the two families insisted
that something should be done about making a play out of
"Mama's Bank Account."

Now the Messrs. Rodgers and Hammerstein, having acquired
comfortable bank surpluses, despite the income tax, were already
drawing handsome royalties from the amazingly successful "Oklahoma!", and other stage creations as well, and were not exactly
excited by the thought of adding another venture to their list.
Besides, words and music were their particular specialty. But—
If the play were written, they decided, they would like to have
a hand in its production. Almost before they knew it the producing firm of Rodgers & Hammerstein was formed.

Next, John Van Druten was approached. Would he, or would
he not, be interested in making the adaptation? Mr. Van Druten
thought that would depend greatly on how well he liked the
story. He, too, was basking contentedly in the sunshine of the
success his own "The Voice of the Turtle" had brought him, and
was not too eager about taking on another writing job immediately. However, he read "Mama's Bank Account" and admitted
he liked the story a lot. The signing of contracts then became a
mere matter of form.

When it came to casting the play, Mr. Van Druten allowed
that there was one actress he would like to see play Mama, but
he had no idea she would be willing to do so. She was, he said,
too young to be seriously considering character parts and, anyway, her successes had mostly been scored in serious drama and

the classics. Her name was Mady Christians.

Thereupon Mr. Rodgers, smiling with satisfaction, reached in his desk and drew forth a letter from Mady Christians advising that he really should read "Mama's Bank Account" and see if he didn't agree a play should be made from it. Also if a play ever were made from it, would he please recommend her for the titular role? He had had the letter from Miss Christians, said he, before he and Mr. Hammerstein had any idea that what did happen was going to happen.

And so the play was written. Taken to New Haven and to Boston to see what audiences thought of it, it was brought finally to the Music Box in New York. After its opening, October 10, 1944, the reviews being rather on the ecstatic side, the demand for seats was steadily exciting. Here at last was the perfect play for the escapist. Not a suggestion of war or the results of war. True, there had been three equally un-warlike entertainments before it that had bounded quickly into the hit class—"Song of Norway," "Anna Lucasta" and "Bloomer Girl"—and one so lightly touched with war's echoes as to belong in an un-warlike category, that being "Soldier's Wife." But none of these had the same persuasive promise of a pleasantly undisturbing evening in the theatre as "I Remember Mama." Its rewards were immediate and continued through the season.

The setting for "I Remember Mama" is divided into three parts. At either side of the main stage, which is elevated the height of two steps from the stage floor, there are small turntable stages on which short connective scenes are played. When the turntables are in use, the main stage is cut off by traveler curtains. As each scene is completed on either turntable it is "revolved out."

As we enter the scene a light is focused on the right turntable stage (to the audience's left). Katrin is discovered sitting at a desk facing the audience. She is smoking a cigarette as she writes. Katrin is a small person, capable of looking like a child in her teens as well as a young woman in her early twenties. When we meet her she has her blonde hair done in a modern "up" style, which can easily be loosened and permitted to fall to shoulder length.

For a moment or two Katrin continues to write. Presently she takes up her manuscript and begins to read aloud: "For as long as I could remember the house on Steiner Street had become home. Papa and Mama had both been born in Norway, but they came to San Francisco because Mama's sisters were here. All of us were born here. Nels, the oldest and the only boy—my sister Christine—and the littlest sister, Dagmar. (*She puts down her manuscript and looks out front.*) It's funny but when I look back, I always see Nels and Christine and myself looking almost as we do today. I guess that's because the people you see all the time stay the same age in her head. Dagmar's different. She was always the baby—so I see her as a baby. Even Mama—it's funny, but I always see Mama as around forty. She couldn't *always* have been forty. (*She puts out her cigarette, picks up the manuscript and starts to read again.*) Besides us, there was our boarder, Mr. Hyde. Mr. Hyde was an Englishman who had once been an actor, and Mama was very impressed by his flowery talk and courtly manners. He used to read aloud to us in the evenings. But first and foremost, I remember Mama."

The curtains have parted, revealing the kitchen of the house on Steiner Street. It is a comfortably furnished kitchen, with doors leading to a pantry and to other sections of the house. A third door is in the outside wall (to the audience's right) and leads to the back porch, which can be seen, and which is generally used as an entry-door. Back of the house Telegraph Hill rises in perspective high above the house and is lined with streets and other houses. The kitchen is simply furnished, with stove and china cabinet and with a table at center which is used for meals as well as the family's social gatherings.

"I remember that every Saturday night Mama would sit down by the kitchen table and count out the money Papa brought home in the little envelope—" Katrin's voice comes softly out of the shadows as the turntable stage disappears and the kitchen comes fully into view.

Mama, looking around forty, is emptying the envelope of its silver dollars and smaller coins. Papa, looking a little older than Mama, stands above her.

"You call the children, Lars," says Mama. "Is good they should know about money." Her speech is slightly rather than heavily accented.

The children are called—Nels, Christine and Katrin. Katrin must be called the loudest, instructs Mama, because she is probably in the "study" she has made out of the attic under the roof. Katrin is hoping to be an author. She will be wanting to write stories, and books, perhaps, like those that Mr. Hyde reads to the family.

Dagmar, the youngest, "a plump child of about eight," has

emerged from the pantry with an alley cat in her arms. Elizabeth is the cat's name—Dagmar's beautiful Elizabeth, who, if she does look a bit scarred, only fights for her honor—the honor of being the bravest cat in all San Francisco. Elizabeth, to Dagmar, is a Viking cat—and as beautiful as the dawn—the dawn Mr. Hyde reads about.

Presently Mr. Hyde appears in person—on his way out. "He is a slightly seedy, long-haired man in his fifties. Rather of the old-fashioned English laddie actor type."

"You go out, Mr. Hyde?" inquires Mama.

"For a few minutes only, dear Madam. To buy myself a modicum of that tawny weed, tobacco, that I lust after, as Ben Jonson says. I shall be back in time for our nightly reading."

Mama now adds her voice, sharply, to the calling of the children. Katrin steps up from her "study" to join the group. Her hair is now hanging to her shoulders and she is seen wearing a skirt that is quite short.

Nels is a tall, strapping fellow, "old enough to look 18 or 19 or 15 or 16, according to his dress or demeanor. Now he is about 16." Christine is a pretty child in her early, and important teens.

When all except Dagmar, who is softly crooning to the brave Elizabeth, have found their places at table Mama begins the division of Papa's pay envelope. A pile of silver dollars, "for the landlord," is pushed from one to the other down the table. Another pile is "for the grocer." A half dollar is set aside for the half-soling of Katrin's shoes. And a dime for a new notebook for Christine.

Soon the apportionment is finished for this week. Or would be if Nels did not introduce a problem. Nels will be graduating from grammar school next month, and if he should go on to High —that's going to cost money. "Carfare, clothes, notebooks, things I'll really need," explains Nels. He has it all down. Mama and Papa draw closer together to examine this paper.

"Get the *Little Bank*, Christine," directs Mama, and Christine brings a small box from the dresser.

Katrin has moved down to the front of the kitchen, where a couple of steps lead up from the turntable stage. She is sitting on the top step, looking straight ahead of her and seeing herself again in the present—

"The Little Bank! That was the most important thing in the whole house," reports Katrin. "It was a box we used to keep for emergencies—like the time when Dagmar had croup and Papa had to get medicine to put in the steam kettle. I can *smell* that medicine now! The things that came out of the Little Bank! Mama was always going to buy herself a warm coat out of it, when there was enough, only there never was."

Mama has gone carefully over the contents of the Little Bank. There is not much left. "We give to the dentist, you remember? And for your roller skates?" Nels remembers. He remembers Mama's coat, too, but she is quick to insist that she can get that another time. No, there's not enough for Nels to go to High. Unless they should go to the Big Bank—and they don't want to do that.

Nels thinks he might work in Dillon's grocery store after school. That would add something, Mama and Papa figure, but not enough. Papa thinks he might give up his tobacco. Mama reluctantly figures that in. Still not enough. Christine offers to take care of the Maxwell children Friday nights. More figuring, followed by a triumphant ejaculation from Mama. "Is good! Is enough! We do not have to go to the Bank."

Dagmar is a little curious about the Bank. Why does Mama never seem to want to go there?

"Because," Christine explains, "if we went to the bank all the time there'd be no money left there. And then, if we couldn't pay our rent, they'd turn us out, like Mrs. Jensen down the street." Mama promptly discourages the Bank quiz.

Aunt Trina, "a timid, mouse-like little woman of about 40," has appeared at the back door. The children are afraid the knock may herald the approach of all their aunts and would escape. But it is only Trina. And she has come to have a personal talk with Mama.

When the children have gone, and their father, Trina blushingly tries to get to the errand that brought her. She must tell Marta that she wants to get married. Mama is lightly suspicious.

"You mean . . . you want to get married, or there is someone you want to marry?"

"There's someone I want to marry."

"Does he want to marry you?"

"He says he does."

"Trina! Is wonderful!" Mama is quite delighted.

The prospective bridegroom, Trina continues, is Mr. Thorkelsen, from the Funeral Parlor. He is not very handsome, nor very tall, but Trina loves him. What she wants now is that Marta shall tell the others—Jenny and Sigrid—and Uncle Chris.

Mama agrees to tell Jenny and Sigrid. Nor will they laugh at Trina, as Trina fears. Mama promises that. But Uncle Chris

—Uncle Chris is the head of the family. Always it is the husband who must talk to the head of the family—

"Yes. I know, but . . . well, Uncle Chris is so very frightening," protests Trina. "He's so big and black, and he shouts so. And Mr. Thorkelsen is . . . well, kind of timid, really."

"But, Trina, if he is to be your husband, he must learn not to be timid. You don't want husband should be timid. *You* are timid. Is not good when *both* are timid. (*Then firmly.*) No! Jenny and Sigrid I speak to, but Mr. Thorkelsen must go to Uncle Chris."

Aunt Jenny and Aunt Sigrid come down the street and stop for a moment before the door. Jenny, "a domineering woman in her fifties," waits impatiently for Sigrid, who is "whining and complaining," to get her breath after the climb up the hill.

Jenny and Sigrid have come in search of Trina, who has unaccountably disappeared. Trina, Mama admits, has been here. She had come to talk about something—about marriage, in fact. Trina wants to get married—

"That's no news," snorts Jenny. "Of course she wants to get married. Every old maid wants to get married."

"There is someone who wants to marry Trina."

"Who'd want to marry Trina?"

"Mr. Thorkelsen."

"Peter Thorkelsen? Little Peter?" She gestures a midget.

"He is not so little."

"He's hardly bigger than my Arne—and Arne is not ten yet."

"So he is hardly bigger than your Arne. Does every husband have to be a big man?"

"Trina's making it up. That happens with old maids, when they get to Trina's age."

"No, Jenny—it is true. Mr. Thorkelsen wants to marry Trina."

Trina, Mama admits, is there. She will be coming in in a minute, and they are not to laugh at her.

"If you laugh at Trina I will tell her of the time before your wedding when your husband try to run away."

This bit of family history is news to Sigrid, and rather amusing.

"It does not matter, Sigrid," cautions Mama. "Jenny will not laugh at Trina now. Nor will you! For if *you* laugh at her, I will tell of your wedding night with Ole, when you cry all the time, and he bring you home to Mother."

"This I do *not* know!" chortles Papa.

"Is no need you should know. I do not tell these stories for spite—only so they do not laugh at Trina. Call her, Lars. You like more coffee, Jenny? Sigrid?"

Mr. Hyde has come in and been introduced, escaping to his room as soon as possible. He does not look to Jenny like a boarder who can be depended on for rent, but Mama is satisfied. Mr. Hyde is a gentleman and he reads to them aloud—"from Longfellow and Dickens, and Fenimore Kipling."

Trina has come shyly back into the group and is immediately pounced upon by the exacting Jenny. Why had she told her marriage plans to Marta first? What kind of a living does Mr. Thorkelsen make? He probably thinks Trina will have a dowry like girls in the old country, suggests Sigrid, which gives Trina an idea. Why shouldn't she have a dowry, if Mr. Thorkelsen can get one out of Uncle Chris? Uncle Chris, explodes Jenny, would be more likely to eat Peter.

"Maybe Uncle Chris will tell him some family stories," suggests Mama, with meaning. "He knows many, does Uncle Chris." And this puts an end to the aunts' nagging of Trina.

The children are called to say good-by to Jenny and Sigrid. They come joyfully as soon as they hear that their aunts are leaving. Dagmar is still lugging Elizabeth. That, insists Aunt Jenny, is a very silly name for a cat.

"It's a very silly name for *that* cat," admits Nels. "It's a Tom." Nels knows.

"We should call him Uncle Elizabeth," suggests Papa, and Dagmar is delighted to compromise.

The aunts have gone, and Mr. Hyde has appeared with his book. Mr. Hyde, Mama explains to Trina, has been reading to them *The Tales from Two Cities*—a beautiful story, but sad. Trina thinks she would like to stay for that. She likes sad stories.

"Tonight I would like to finish it," says Mr. Hyde, as the family gathers around the table. "I will go on from where we left off." And he begins to read.

" 'In the black prison of the Conciergerie, the doomed of the day awaited their fate. They were in number as the weeks of the year. Fifty-two were to roll that afternoon on the life-tide of the City to the boundless, everlasting sea. . . .' "

The lights slowly fade, leaving only Mr. Hyde and Katrin plainly visible. "I don't think I shall ever forget that night," muses Katrin. "It was almost midnight when he came to the end, and none of us had noticed."

" 'It is a far, far better thing that I do than I have ever done;

it is a far, far better rest that I go to than I have ever known.'
The End."

Mr. Hyde closes the book. The lights fade on the family and
come up slowly on the turntable stage. Katrin moves slowly down
to her desk—

"I wrote in my diary that night before I went to bed," she is
saying, as she picks up the manuscript and reads: " 'Tonight
Mr. Hyde finished *The Tale of Two Cities*. The closing chapters
are indeed superb. How beautiful a thing is self-sacrifice. I
wish there were someone I could die for.' "

There have been other stories, Katrin remembers—"Treasure
Island" and "The Hound of the Baskervilles." Poetry, too, like
"The Lady of the Lake" and "Rime of the Ancient Mariner."
They were all so interested in the readings you couldn't keep
any of them away. A good thing, too. The readings kept Nels
home nights. He was home the night the gang at the corner
broke into Mr. Dillon's store—

"There were many nights I couldn't sleep for the way he had
set my imagination dancing," Katrin continues, again referring to
her diary. " 'What a wonderful thing is literature, transporting
us to realms unknown.' " She is talking to herself now—

"And all the time my school teacher kept telling me that I
ought to write about things I knew. I did write a piece for her
once about Uncle Chris, and she said it wasn't nice to write like
that about a member of one's own family. Papa called Mama's
Uncle Chris a black Norwegian, because of his dark hair and
fierce mustache, but there were others in the family who claimed
that he was black in a different way. The Aunts, for example."

The light has faded on Katrin and come up on the second turntable. The scene represents a corner of Jenny's kitchen. Jenny
is rolling pastry and Trina is crocheting—

JENNY—Black! I'll say he's black. Black in his heart. Cursing and swearing. . . .

TRINA—Marta says that's only because it hurts him to walk.

JENNY—Rubbish! I know all about his limp and the accident
back in the old country—but has anyone ever heard him complain? Marta's always making excuses for him.

TRINA—I know . . . but he is good to the children. All those
oranges he's always sending them. . . .

JENNY—Oranges! What good are oranges? Turn 'em yellow.
They're the only things he's ever been known to give away, anyway. He's got other uses for his money.

TRINA—What do you mean?

JENNY—Bottles! And that woman he lives with!

TRINA—He *says* she's his housekeeper.

JENNY—Well, he couldn't very well come right out and call her what she is, could he? Though *I* will one of these days. And to his face, too.

SIGRID (*coming through the curtains and crossing to* JENNY *and* TRINA)—Jenny. Trina. What do you think? What do you think Uncle Chris has done now?

TRINA—What?

JENNY—Tell us.

SIGRID—You know my little Arne's knee—that fall he had two months ago? The man at the drugstore said it was only a bruise, but today it was hurting him again, so I left him home when I went to do the marketing. I asked Mrs. Schultz next door to keep an eye on him, and who should turn up not ten minutes after I'd gone, but Uncle Chris. And what do you think?

JENNY—Well, tell us, if you're going to. Don't keep *asking* us.

SIGRID—He took one look at Arne's knee, bundled him into that rattletrap old automobile of his, and rushed him straight off to the hospital. I've just come from there . . . and what do you think? They've operated! They've got him in plaster of Paris!

JENNY—Without consulting you?

SIGRID—It seems the doctor is a friend of his . . . that's why he did it. No, this time he's gone too far. To put a child of Arne's age through all that pain! They wouldn't even let me *see* Arne. I'm going to tell Uncle Chris exactly what I think of him. . . .

JENNY—That's right.

SIGRID—I'm going to tell him right now. (*Weakening a little.*) Come with me, Jenny.

JENNY—Well, I . . . No, I can't leave my baking.

SIGRID—You must, Jenny. We must stand together. You come, too, Trina, and ask about your dowry. *Make* him give it to you.

TRINA—Oh, but . . . Marta said Mr. Thorkelsen should do that. . . .

JENNY—Well, then, go and get Mr. Thorkelsen. Go down to the mortuary and get him now. Sigrid's quite right. We girls have got to stand together!

The lights have dimmed. Katrin is at her desk again. "Nobody knew where Uncle Chris lived," she is recounting. "That was part of the mystery about him." However, Uncle Chris did very well, roaming up and down the country, buying and selling farms and ranches, selling at a profit and coming occasionally into the city, roaring and stamping into the house.

Again the lights are dimming and the sounds of "a very old and noisy Ford car changing gears is heard." As the curtains part to reveal the kitchen scene Uncle Chris's antique car is seen standing in the street. A woman is seated beside the empty driver's seat and Uncle Chris, "an elderly, powerful, swarthy man with a limp," is knocking at the back door. In the kitchen Nels and Christine are cowering, too scared to answer.

Presently Uncle Chris, finding the door on the latch, barges into the kitchen demanding to know why no one answers his call. Nels and Christine stammer excuses and Katrin, walking up the steps, comes into the scene.

They have grown, the children have. Uncle Chris can tell by looking at them, but he also lines them up against the wall where he had previously recorded their heights. Now he misses Dagmar. Where is "de leetle one"? Dagmar, Katrin explains, is ill. Mama and Doctor are with her now. It is her ear. She has had a bad earache for two days.

The report disturbs Uncle Chris. He would be sure that it is a goot doctor Mama has sent for. He is about to go to Dagmar's room when Mama and Dr. Johnson appear. The Doctor is alarmed. They must get the child to the hospital at once. It is probable they will have to operate.

"What is with the child?" Uncle Chris demands of the Doctor.

"I'm afraid it is a mastoid."

"Ah . . . then you operate immediately."

"That's what I said."

Mama has brought out the Little Bank and poured its contents on the table. "Doctor, is enough?" she asks, anxiously. "Is enough without we go to the Bank? My husband is a carpenter. Make good money."

"If there is need of money, *I* pay," cuts in Uncle Chris.

"It'll be all right. We'll take her to the Clinic. You pay what you can afford."

"Goot! Goot! I have a patient there already," puts in Uncle Chris. "My nephew, Arne. They operate this morning on his knee."

"Are you a physician, sir?" It is plain Dr. Johnson does not like Uncle Chris.

"I am a better physician than most doctors. Nels, there, my

other nephew, he become doctor when he grow up."

"Oh, indeed . . . very interesting. Well, now, if you will have the child at the Clinic in . . . shall we say, an hour's time. . . ."

"The child will be at the Clinic in *ten minutes'* time. I haf my automobile."

"I can hardly make arrangements in ten minutes."

"*I* make arrangements. I know doctors."

"Uncle Chris, Dr. Johnson arrange. He is good doctor."

Mama must take command now. It is kind of Uncle Chris to be interested, but there are some things he is not to do. He is not to see Dagmar now. He frightens her. He frightens everyone —all the children. And the girls, Jenny, Sigrid and Trina. Only Mama he doesn't frighten—

"So Nels and I get Dagmar," Mama concludes, facing the puzzled but momentarily subdued Uncle Chris. "You drive us to hospital in your automobile, but you do not frighten Dagmar. And you leave Doctor alone. Dr. Johnson is *fine* doctor. You come with me, Nels. You carry Dagmar."

Uncle Chris can't understand it. Why should the children be frightened of him? He is pleased when Katrin and Christine both admit that they don't like the Aunts very well, either—

"Is goot," agrees Uncle Chris, with a great roar of laughter. "Jenny, bossy. Sigrid, whining. Is true! But your mama, she is different. And she cook good. The Aunts, they cannot cook at all. Only you do not tell your mama we have talked of them so. It is a secret, for us. Then you cannot be frightened of me any more . . . when we have secret. I tell you my secret, too. *I* do not like the Aunts. And so that they do not bother me, I frighten them and shout at them. You I do not shout at if you are goot children, and clean your teeth goot, and eat your oranges."

The posse of Aunts has reappeared, accompanied by Mr. Thorkelsen, "a terrified little man." As they approach the door to Mama's house they notice Uncle Chris's automobile—and the woman sitting in it. There is a tossing of heads, particularly Jenny's head. There is only one thing to do, according to Jenny. They should all cut the offending stranger. Following Jenny's example they sweep past the automobile and into the house.

Sigrid, announces Jenny, has something to say to Uncle Chris. Sigrid starts to prove it, but Uncle Chris is too occupied to listen. He is taking Dagmar to the hospital, and if they get in his way he will throw them out. Sigrid and Jenny, he repeats, brutally, are a couple of old fools.

Nels has brought Dagmar from the house and put her in the car. Uncle Chris gets into the driver's seat. In the house Sigrid would stop Mama. She shouldn't think of riding in the car with that woman.

"So it will kill me or Dagmar if we sit in the automobile with her?" demands Mama. "I have see her. She looks nice woman."

She bundles herself into the rear seat with Dagmar. Uncle Chris backs the car out into the street.

Jenny organizes the pursuit. Let the girls stop gaping and follow her. Jenny has pushed Sigrid out of the door, grabbed Mr. Thorkelsen and is dragging him after her, while Trina follows meekly behind. The curtains close.

Three hours later Katrin and Christine are sitting in a kind of closet room where the children's sports things are kept. Glasses of milk and a plate of cookies are before them. Christine is worried because they have not heard from Mama, but Katrin can think of what is happening only in terms of a story: "The sisters sat huddled in the empty house, waiting for the verdict that was to spell life or death to the little family."

Christine is disgusted, but Katrin can't help it. "I'm not heartless," insists Katrin. "I do have feeling for them. I can't help it if it goes into words like that. Everything does with me. But it doesn't mean that I don't feel it. And I think we *ought* to eat. I think Mama would want us to."

The lights fade as the girls start to eat their lunch. On the central stage the curtains part to reveal a Hospital Corridor. The elevator is at back. Alongside the elevator is a small closet in which are kept brooms, mops, pails, etc. The reception desk at which the nurse is sitting is at one side. Back of it the corridor stretches away in darkness. Across the corridor is a bench on which Mama and Nels are sitting, holding hands. Near by the three Aunts are haranguing Uncle Chris, while Mr. Thorkelsen looks on from a discreet distance.

Uncle Chris hasn't met Mr. Thorkelsen, and Peter is brought forward to be introduced. Still Uncle Chris is not impressed. But before he can escape, Jenny has pushed Mr. Thorkelsen forward to bring up the matter of Trina's dowry.

"Well, there . . . there was a little something else," ventures the little man, timidly. "You see, Trina mentioned . . . well,

in the old country it was always usual . . . and, after all, we
do all come from the old country. . . ."

"What is it? What you want?" snaps Uncle Chris.

"Well, it's a question of Trina's . . . well, not to mince matters . . . her dowry."

"Ah. Her dowry. Trina wants a dowry. She is forty-two
years old. . . . And it is not enough that she gets a husband.
She must have dowry."

"PLEASE!" The nurse is banging on her desk. "Would you
mind going and discussing your family matters somewhere else?
This is a hospital! Not a marriage bureau!"

"You come into waiting room," suggests Uncle Chris to Mr.
Thorkelsen. "I talk to you about dowry."

Now the Aunts turn to Mama. Mama has been looking and
listening for the Doctor. It is now two hours. But she will go
on waiting. She wishes they would go away and leave her and
Nels there to wait. The Aunts agree to go next door and get
coffee. Trina will be back for Uncle Chris and Peter.

A scrubwoman has come down the corridor and put her mop
and pail in the closet. Presently the elevator door opens and
Dr. Johnson in white, followed by an orderly, hurries down the
corridor. Mama starts to intercept them. A moment later Dr.
Johnson reappears wearing his coat and hat. He recognizes
Mama.

Dagmar, the Doctor reports, has come through the operation
beautifully. She is now sleeping off the anesthetic. No, Mama
can't see her—that's the rule—no visitors for twenty-four hours.
"You shall see her tomorrow," the Doctor promises.

"Tomorrow? But, Doctor, she is so little. When she wakes
she will be frightened."

"The nurses will take care of her. Excellent care. You
needn't worry. You see, for the first twenty-four hours, clinic
patients aren't allowed to see visitors. The wards must be kept
quiet."

"I will not make a sound."

"I'm very sorry. Tomorrow. And now— Good afternoon."

The Doctor has gone. Mama stands staring after him a moment and then goes resolutely to the nurse's desk. Dagmar
Hansen, reports the nurse, consulting her files, is in Ward A,
which is down the hall. But she cannot be seen. No, not even
for a minute. It's against the rules.

Mama stands staring before her. Nels touches her arm. "We

must think of some way," she says to him, as they walk away. "If I do not see her today how will I know that all is well with her? What can I tell Papa when he comes home from work?"

"The nurses will look after her, Mama. Would you like to come next door for some coffee?"

"We go home. We have coffee at home. But I must see Dagmar today."

The curtains close as they start away.

A glimpse of Uncle Chris and Mr. Thorkelsen finds them in conference in the waiting room. The situation, Uncle Chris is saying, comes down to this: Mr. Thorkelsen loves Trina; he wants to marry Trina; he is able to support Trina. Then, why does he want a dowry?

Mr. Thorkelsen had never thought of it like that. Neither does he know whether he would still want to marry Trina, even if she had no dowry.

"You don't know?" thunders Uncle Chris. "You think I let Trina marry a man who will not take her without dowry? . . . What kind of a man would that be?"

"Well, not a very nice kind of man," admits Mr. Thorkelsen, helplessly.

"And are you that kind of man?"

". . . I don't think so."

"Then you don't want dowry?"

"No. . . . No, I guess I don't."

"Goot. Goot. You are a goot man. I like you. I give you my blessing. And I send you vedding present. I send you box of oranges."

Uncle Chris is violently shaking Mr. Thorkelsen's hand as the lights fade.

Mama and Nels have arrived back in the kitchen. Mama is still visibly disturbed. Christine and Katrin are quickly aware that something is wrong. Mama will not admit it. The Doctor has said that Dagmar is fine, she tells them. No, she could not see Dagmar. It was a rule of the hospital.

Now Mama has decided upon something. She will scrub the floor. What if she had just scrubbed it yesterday?

"Comes a time when you've got to get down on your knees," says Mama, getting to work. Suddenly, though she has paid little attention to the pleading of the children, she stops scrubbing.

"I think of something!" Mama is sitting back on her heels. "I think I think of something!"

The curtains shut the kitchen from view.

From the left turntable (at the audience's right) comes the booming voice of Uncle Chris. "Ten t'ousand Svedes vent t'rough de veeds at de battle of Coppenhagen," lustily sings Uncle Chris. "Ten t'ousand Svedes vent t'rough de veeds chasing vun Nor-vegian!"

The lights reveal a corner of a hospital room. In bed is Arne, a child of about 8, and sitting near the bed is his singing Uncle.

Arne is having a little trouble. The pain is pretty steady. Arne wonders if it has to be that way. Uncle Chris wouldn't know. But if it is very bad he thinks Arne might try a few swear words. Does he know any? Arne doesn't—not any real ones—

"Then I'll tell you two fine vons to use when de pain is bad. Are 'Damn' and 'Damittohell.' You say them?"

"N-now?"

"No, not now. Ven de pain comes again. You say them then. They help plenty. I know. I haf pain, too. I say them all the time. And if the pain is *very* bad, you say, 'Goddamittohell.' But only if is *very* bad."

Uncle Chris thinks perhaps if he sings a little more Arne can go to sleep. Arne thinks so, too—if Uncle Chris will sing something a little quieter. Uncle Chris starts a Norwegian lullaby, but he doesn't get far before Arne cries out in pain: "Oo—oo—oh, *damn*. Damn. Damittohell!"

"Goot! It helps—eh?"

"Yes—yes." Arne is pleasantly surprised.

"Then you sleep some!" Arne closes his eyes. Uncle Chris takes a drink from his flask. He is fixing Arne's pillow as the lights fade.

Back in the hospital corridor Mama is glad to find that there is a different nurse on duty. Katrin is with Mama and quite apprehensive. For her part, Mama is both confident and determined. Leaving her hat and coat with Katrin on the bench, she goes to the broom closet and takes out a pail and a wet mop. Catching the nurse's eye as she gets down on her knees in front of the desk Mama smiles.

"Very dirty floors," observes Mama, brightly.

"Yes. I'm glad they've finally decided to clean them. Aren't you working late?"

"Floors need cleaning," mutters Mama, lowering her head and starting to crawl toward the corridor. She is still scrubbing as she disappears.

On the bench Katrin is passing the time improvising a poem. "The Hospital" is to be the title, and the text begins:

> " 'She waited, fearful, in the hall
> And held her bated breath—' "

"Breath—yes, that'll rhyme with death—"

> " 'She waited fearful in the hall
> And held her bated breath.
> She trembled at the least footfall,
> And kept her mind on death—' "

Katrin finds a piece of paper and a pencil in her pocket and scribbles out her poem, slowly adding to it line by line. She makes progress until she has her little sister dying. That gives her pause—

"I don't want her to die," Katrin tells herself, "and yet when Mama said she was all right, I was almost—well, almost disappointed. It wasn't exciting any more. Maybe Christine's right, and I haven't any heart. How awful. The girl without a heart. That'd be a nice title for a story, 'The girl without a heart sat in a hospital corridor' " . . .

The lights come up and Uncle Chris comes from the corridor back of the nurse's desk. "He wears his hat and is more than a little drunk." He is also surprised to find Katrin. What is she doing there? And where is Mama? How did Mama get in to see Dagmar? Where, in fact, is Dagmar?

Katrin is not equal to answering satisfactorily, so Uncle Chris goes to the nurse. In what room is his great-niece, Dagmar Hansen? . . . Yes, he knows all about the visitors' rule, but he still wants to know what room she is in.

The nurse refuses to tell him. And, furthermore, if it happens that he is Mr. Halvorsen—Christopher Halvorsen—then she cannot tell him anything at all. On whose orders? On Dr. Johnson's orders—

"There's a special note here: 'Patient's Uncle, Mr. Halvorsen, not to be admitted or given information under any circumstances.' "

For a moment Uncle Chris is stunned. Then, with a hearty "Goddamittohell!" he strides away from the desk. He would console himself with his flask, but finds it to be empty. Mama reappears triumphantly from the corridor. She puts the mop and pail back in the closet, and thanks the nurse.

"Uncle Chris, Dagmar is fine," Mama reports.

"You see her? You see Dagmar?"

"Sure." Mama has taken her hat from Katrin and started to put it on. "Is fine hospital. But such floors! A mop is never good. Floors should be scrubbed with a brush. We go home. Uncle Chris, you come with us? I make coffee."

"Pah! Vat good is coffee? I go get drink."

He gets drunk, Uncle Chris would have them know, because he likes to. But the next minute he has recanted—

"No, is not true," he confesses, his mood changing. "You know is not true. I do not like to get drunk at all. But I do not like to come home with you either. (*Growing slightly maudlin.*) You have family. Is fine thing. You do not know how fine. Katrin, one day when you grow up, maybe you know what a fine thing family is. I haf no family."

"But, Uncle Chris, Mama's always said you were the *head* of the family."

"Sure. Sure. I am head of the family, but I haf no family. So I go get drunk. You understand, Marta?"

"Sure, Uncle Chris. You go get drunk. But," she adds sharply, "don't you feel sorry for yourself!"

Uncle Chris strides away, boisterously singing the song of "Ten T'ousand Svedes." Mama watches him go and then puts on her coat.

"Is fine man," she assures Katrin. "Has fine ideas about family. I can tell Papa now that Dagmar is fine. She wake while I am with her. I explain rules to her. She will not expect us now until tomorrow afternoon."

"You won't try and see her again before that?"

"No. That would be against the rules! Come. We go home."

The curtain falls.

ACT II

Katrin is again at her desk, reading from her script. "It wasn't very often that I could get Mama to talk—about herself, or her life in the old country, or what she felt about things. You had to catch her unawares, or when she had nothing to do, which was very, very seldom. I don't think I can ever remember seeing Mama unoccupied."

She has put down the manuscript and is staring out into the room as she recalls one occasion on which Mama was sociable. It was the day before Dagmar came home from the hospital. Mama had taken Katrin to a drugstore and bought her an ice cream soda. "It was kind of a special treat—a moment in my life that I'll always remember, quite apart from the soda, which was *wonderful*," reports Katrin.

It was while they were sitting at a small table in the drugstore, Mama drinking coffee and Katrin her soda, that Mama got to talking about the old country. Katrin asked her if she had ever wanted to go back to Norway.

"I like to go back once to look, maybe," Mama admitted. "To see the mountains and the fjords. I like to show them once to you all. When Dagmar is big, maybe we all go back once . . . one Summer . . . like tourists. But that is how it would be, I would be tourist there now. There is no one I would know any more. And maybe we see the little house where Papa and I live when we first marry."

It was during this talk, too, that Katrin asked Mama if her life had been hard. "No life is easy all the time," Mama had answered. "It is not meant to be."

"But . . . rich people . . . aren't their lives easy?"

"I don't know, Katrin. I have never known rich people. But I see them sometimes in stores and in the streets, and they do not *look* as if they were easy."

"Wouldn't you like to be rich?"

"I would like to be rich the way I would like to be ten feet high. Would be good for some things—bad for others."

No, Mama had not come to America to get rich. She had come because the rest of the family were here. It is good for families to be together. After her children had been born here Mama had become an American citizen. But not to get rich.

Soon Mama decided that they had talked enough and the party was over. Next day, Mama reminded Katrin, Dagmar would be coming home and they must be ready for her. For one thing they must see that Uncle Elizabeth is surely home. Katrin should see to that. Uncle Elizabeth should be kept in the house all day until Dagmar got there. . . .

The curtains have parted again on the kitchen scene. Mama, Papa and Dagmar are just coming in the door, and the first sound to greet them is the howling of a cat, evidently in pain. "It's Uncle Elizabeth welcoming me home!" exclaims Dagmar.

"That's his song of welcome!"

Uncle Elizabeth is in the pantry, but before Dagmar goes to him they must tell her the bad news. Uncle Elizabeth is sick. He had been in a fight the night before and he came home very sick indeed. Nels has been doctoring him, dressing his wounds with boric acid, but that hasn't done much good. It would be better if Dagmar did not see Uncle Elizabeth right away.

Dagmar will not be stopped. She rushes into the pantry. There is another howl from the cat. Dagmar comes running back in tears. Whatever had happened to Uncle Elizabeth? Dagmar had tried to pick him up. A cut over his eye was bleeding. It was awful!

Mama thinks it would be better, perhaps, if poor Uncle Elizabeth were to go to sleep and never wake up, but Dagmar can't think of that.

"I think he die anyway," puts in Papa. "Nels try to make him well. But I do not think he can."

"Mama can," insists Dagmar. "Mama can do everything."

There is another howl from Uncle Elizabeth. Dagmar is clutching her mother agonizedly. "Make him live, Mama! Make him well again! Please!"

"We see. Let us see how he gets through the night," agrees Mama, comfortingly.

But after Dagmar has gone to bed, and Uncle Elizabeth's howls continue, it is agreed that Nels should go to the drugstore for chloroform. It is the only thing.

"I know," agrees Mama, after a struggle. "But poor Dagmar. It is sad homecoming for her. And she has been so good in hospital. Never once she cry." And then, pulling herself together: "I get her supper," she announces. Uncle Elizabeth's cries follow Mama into the pantry. . . .

Mr. Hyde is leaving. He tiptoes into the kitchen, ready for the street. He would tiptoe out, leaving a letter on the dresser, but Papa looks up from his paper and sees him.

"A letter I received this morning necessitates my departure," explains Mr. Hyde. "My immediate departure."

"Is true?" Mama, coming from the pantry with Dagmar's tray, is surprised and saddened.

"Alas, dear Madam, yes. 'Tis true, 'tis pity. And pity 'tis, 'tis true. You will find here . . . (*He presents the letter*) my check for all I owe you, and a note expressing my profoundest thanks for all your most kind hospitality."

"Was wonderful man," declares Mama, after Mr. Hyde has

gone, and she is opening his letter. "Is too bad."

The check is for a hundred and ten dollars, and that is good. Now they can pay the Doctor everything. And buy Mama the warm coat, too. Papa will go right away to get the money. But before he goes he will read Mr. Hyde's letter—

" 'Dear Friends: I find myself compelled to take a somewhat hasty departure from this house of happiness,' " reads Papa—

"Is beautiful letter," interrupts Mama—

" 'I am leaving you my library for the children . . .' "

That is wonderful news. Papa must go right away and bring the books in. Soon he is back with "The Pickwick Papers," "The Complete Shakespeare," "Alice in Wonderland," "The Oxford Book of Verse," "The Last of the Mohicans," "Ivanhoe." . . .

"We were right in the middle of that," Christine remembers.

"Nels can finish it," promises Mama. "He can read to us now in the evenings. He has fine voice, too, like Mr. Hyde."

The chloroforming of Uncle Elizabeth presents a problem. Nobody knows how to go about it. Mama finally decides the best way will be to soak a sponge with chloroform, put it in a box with Uncle Elizabeth and cover the box and the cat over with blankets.

In the midst of the arrangements Aunt Jenny arrives in a state of considerable excitement. She has just heard something about Mr. Hyde. Mr. Kruper, the restaurant man, had cashed a check for fifty dollars for Mr. Hyde and when he sent it promptly to the bank he discovered that Mr. Hyde did not even have an account there. If Mr. Hyde has paid Mama with a check, that probably is no good either.

"Your Mr. Hyde was a crook," declares Aunt Jenny, with a good deal of warmth, "just as I always thought he was, for all his reading and fine ways. Mr. Kruper said he's been cashing them all over the neighborhood. (MAMA *stands quite still without answering.*) How much did he owe you? Plenty, I'll bet. (*Still no answer.*) Eh? Marta, I said I bet he owed you plenty. Didn't he?"

"No. No, he owed us nothing," answers Mama, her hand touching the books caressingly.

"How much was that check for?" demands Jenny.

"It does not matter. He pay with better things than money," says Mama, tearing the check across and putting the pieces in the fire.

"I told you right in the beginning that you shouldn't trust him.

"I REMEMBER MAMA"

"Comes a time when you've got to get down on your knees," says Mama, getting to work. Suddenly she stops scrubbing. "I think of something . . . I think I think of something," she mutters.

(*Mady Christians*)

But you were so sure . . . just like you always are. Mr. Hyde was a gentleman. A gentleman! I bet it must have been a hundred dollars that he rooked you of. Wasn't it?"

"Jenny, I cannot talk now. Maybe you don't have things to do. I have."

"What? What have *you* got to do that's so important?"

"I have to chloroform a cat."

The next morning Mama is setting the table for breakfast when Dagmar bursts into the room. Her good mornings said, Dagmar is all excitement about Uncle Elizabeth. Is he all well again? She has disappeared into the pantry before they can stop her— and before Mama can tell her what she had planned to tell. Not that the cat had died by itself, as Papa suggests. That would be a lie. But—

"What a funny, funny smell," Dagmar can be heard exclaiming in the pantry. And then, in a softer voice she is heard to add: "Good morning, my darling, my darling Elizabeth!"

Mama and Papa stand stricken. The next minute Dagmar appears, carrying Uncle Elizabeth under her arm, tail end forward. The cat is wrapped in an old shirt, its head covered—

"My goodness, you put enough blankets on him!" says Dagmar. "Did you think he'd catch cold?"

Mama is horror-stricken. "Dagmar, you must not . . ." She stops suddenly. Uncle Elizabeth's tail is unquestionably twitching. "Dagmar, let me see . . . let me see that cat."

As Mama pulls the shirt from Uncle Elizabeth's head it is plain to be seen he is quite well.

Dagmar is overjoyed. "He's well! Oh, Mama, I *knew* you'd fix him!"

"Is a miracle!" stammers Mama, as Dagmar runs out to tell Nels.

"You cannot have used enough chloroform," says Papa. "You just give him a good sleep, and that cures him. We re-christen the cat Lazarus."

The curtains have closed on the kitchen when Christine and Katrin come swinging down the street from school. They are in school clothes. Christine is carrying her books. Katrin is reciting and trying to memorize the "Quality of Mercy" speech from "The Merchant of Venice."

Christine is quite disgusted. All Katrin can think of, all she (Christine) has heard for weeks, is talk of the school play and

Katrin's graduation. Katrin has been so wrapped up in this, charges Christine, that she hasn't given even a thought to what's been happening at home. She probably doesn't even remember that for four weeks Papa hasn't worked a day because of the strike. All Katrin thinks of is the presents she is hoping to get.

Two other schoolgirls, Madeline and Dorothy, come along. They, too, are discussing graduation and presents. Thyra Walsh's family is going to add seven pearls to her string. Madeline is going to get an onyx ring with a diamond in it.

What's Katrin going to get? Well, Katrin isn't sure, but she thinks she is going to get a pink celluloid dresser set—the one that Dorothy's father has been showing in the window of his drugstore.

Oooo . . . Dorothy remembers that set. She had tried to get her father to give it to her out of stock, but he said it was too expensive.

As soon as Madeline and Dorothy have gone, Christine is quick to challenge Katrin's story of the dresser set. She isn't either going to get it, however much she may have hinted. Christine knows what Katrin is going to get. She's going to get Mama's brooch—her *solje*—

"You mean that old silver thing she wears that belonged to Grandmother?" Katrin is disgusted. "What would I want an old thing like that for?"

"It's an heirloom. Mama thinks a lot of it."

"Well, then, she ought to keep it. You don't really mean that's *all* they're going to give me?"

"What more do you want?"

"I want the dresser set. My goodness, if Mama doesn't realize what's a suitable present . . . why, it's practically the most important time in a girl's life, when she graduates."

"And you say you're not selfish!"

"It's not selfishness."

"Well, I don't know what else you'd call it. With Papa not working, we need every penny we can lay our hands on. Even the Little Bank's empty. But you'll devil Mama into giving you the dresser set somehow. So why talk about it? I'm going home."

Christine has gone. Katrin sits on the step. Her mouth is set and stubborn. She is staring straight ahead of her—

"Christine was right. I got the dresser set. They gave it to me just before supper on graduation night. Papa could not attend the exercises because there was a strike meeting to decide about going back to work. I was so excited that night, I could hardly eat, and the present took the last remnants of my appetite clean away."

Back in the kitchen, Papa, Mama and Dagmar are just finishing supper. Christine is clearing the table. Excitement is mounting over the graduation exercises. Presently Jenny and Trina have arrived and Mama would get everyone started.

Katrin is proud of her graduation present and proudly shows it to Aunt Jenny. Jenny, however, is not impressed. She had thought it was to be Mama's *solje*—

"She is too young to appreciate that," Mama is quick to explain. "She like something more gay . . . more modern."

Mama isn't wearing her *solje,* either. Jenny is quick to notice that.

"No. I do not wear it tonight," snaps Mama, as she tries to herd them all toward the door.

Trina decides to stay with Papa for a little, until Peter Thorkelsen comes. Mama goes on with Jenny and Dagmar. Outside, Nels and Christine wait for Katrin, who is gathering up her dresser set to take with her.

"Oh, bringing your cheap trash with you to show off?" sneers Christine when Katrin appears with the box.

"It's not trash. It's beautiful. You're just jealous."

CHRISTINE—I told you you'd devil Mama into giving it to you.

KATRIN—I didn't. I didn't devil her at all. I just showed it to her in Mr. Schiller's window. . . .

CHRISTINE—And made her go and sell her brooch that her very own mother gave her.

KATRIN—What?

NELS—Chris . . . you weren't supposed to tell that!

CHRISTINE—I don't care. I think she ought to know.

KATRIN—Is that true? Did Mama—Nels—?

NELS—Well, yes, as a matter of fact, she did. Now, come on.

KATRIN—No, no, I don't believe it. I'm going to ask Papa.

NELS—You haven't time.

KATRIN—I don't care. (*She rushes back and dashes into the kitchen.*) Papa—Papa—Christine says— Papa, did Mama sell her brooch to give me this?

PAPA—Christine should not have told you that.

KATRIN—It's true, then?

PAPA—She did not sell it. She traded it to Mr. Schiller for your present.

KATRIN (*near tears*)—Oh, but she shouldn't . . . I never meant . . .

PAPA—Look, Katrin. You wanted the present. Mama wanted your happiness; she wanted it more than she wanted the brooch.

KATRIN—But I never meant her to do *that*. (*Crying.*) She *loved* it so. It was all she had of Grandmother's.

PAPA—She always meant it for you, Katrin. And you must not cry. You have your play to act.

KATRIN (*sobbing*)—I don't want to act in it now.

PAPA—But you must. Your audience is waiting.

KATRIN—I don't care.

PAPA—But you must care. Tonight you are not Katrin any longer. You are an actress. And an actress must act, whatever she is feeling. There is a saying—what is it—

TRINA (*brightly*)—The mails must go through!

PAPA—No, no. The show must go on. So you stop crying, and you go and act your play. We talk of this later. Afterwards.

KATRIN (*pulling herself together*)—All right. I'll go.

When Katrin arrives at the school she is emotionally upset. She finds Madeline and Dorothy dressing for the play. She will hurry with her own dressing because she is late, but she wants to see Dorothy's father right after the exercises. She must see him. Dorothy must tell him not to leave until Katrin has seen him. It's very important.

Later that night, in the kitchen, Mama and Papa are drinking coffee and reviewing the situation as it stands. "I am worried about her, Lars," she is saying. "When it was over, I see her talking with Mr. Schiller—and she goes to take off her costume and Nels tells me that he will bring her home. But it is long time, and is late for her to be out. And in the play, Lars, she was not good. I have heard her practice it here, and she was good, but tonight, no. It was as if . . . as if she was thinking of something else all the time."

Papa can explain that. He tells Mama of Katrin's finding out about the brooch. Christine had told her. Now Mama must call Christine and sternly demand from her an explanation.

"I hated the smug way she was acting over that dresser set," admits Christine, a little defiantly.

"Is no excuse. You make her unhappy. You make her not good in the play."

"Well, she made *you* unhappy, giving up your brooch for her selfishness."

"Is not your business. I choose to give my brooch. Is not for you to judge. And you know I do not want you to tell. I am angry with you, Christine."

"I'm sorry. But I'm not sorry I told," says Christine, going back to the pantry.

"Christine is the stubborn one," says Papa.

Now Nels and Katrin are back from school. For a moment they stand outside the house while Katrin gathers courage to do what she has decided to do. Nels pats her encouragingly on the shoulder.

Entering the kitchen Katrin goes directly to her mother. "Mama . . . here is your brooch," she says, handing it to her. "I'm sorry I was so bad in the play. I'll go and help Christine with the dishes." She turns and goes quickly into the pantry.

Mama is unwrapping the brooch. "Mr. Schiller give it back to her?" she asks.

"We went to his house to get it," explains Nels. "He didn't want to. He was planning to give it to his wife for her birthday. But Katrin begged and begged him. She even offered to go and work in his store during her vacation if he'd give it back."

"And what did Mr. Schiller say?"

"He said that wasn't necessary. But he gave her a job all the same. She's going to work for him, afternoons, for three dollars a week."

"And the dresser set—she gave that back?"

"Yes. She was awful upset, Mama. It was kinda hard for her to do. She's a good kid."

"Nels is the kind one," says Papa.

Mama, calling Katrin from the pantry, hands her the brooch. "It is your graduation present," she says simply. "I put it on for you."

Katrin is near to tears. "I'll wear it always. I'll keep it forever," she mumbles.

"Christine should not have told you."

"I'm glad she did. Now."

"I'm glad too," says Papa, eager to have a part in the ceremony. It is time now, he adds, for Katrin to have her first cup of coffee. She is their grown-up daughter. He fills a cup and hands it to her, Mama nodding approval. But Katrin cannot drink it. She takes the cup, lifts it, and then thrusts it back at Papa and rushes from the room.

"Katrin is the dramatic one," says Papa. "Is too bad. Her first cup of coffee and she does not drink it."

"It would not have been good for her, so late at night."

"And you, Marta, you are the practical one."

"You drink the coffee, Lars. We do not want to waste it."

In a corner of Jenny's parlor Trina is at the telephone. Peter Thorkelsen is calling. It is Peter's idea that he and Trina have waited long enough to hear from Uncle Chris. They should get out their wedding invitations right away and go ahead with the marriage. "Peter can be very masterful, sometimes," Trina explains to Jenny. ". . . when he is alone with me."

Presently the phone rings again. This time it is Marta. She is calling from a wall telephone booth. Before her Marta holds a telegram which she would read to Jenny. It says if they want to see Uncle Chris they will have to come without delay. It is from a place called Ukiah, north of San Francisco, and it may be from *that woman*—Marta wouldn't know.

Jenny is of a mind not to go. She doesn't believe Uncle Chris is dying. He is too mean to die—ever.

Marta refuses to argue. There is no time for that. There is a train at 11 o'clock. The trip takes four hours. Jenny can tell Sigrid.

"Four hours by train, and maybe have to stay all night," fusses Jenny. "All that expense to watch a wicked old man die of the D.T.'s."

"I know . . . but . . . there is his will . . ." ventures Sigrid, who has just come in.

"Huh, even supposing he's anything to leave—you know who he'd leave it *to*, don't you?"

"Yes. But all the same, he's dying now, and blood is thicker than water. Especially when it's Norwegian. I'm going. I shall take Arne with me. Uncle Chris was always fond of children."

"I agree with Sigrid," agrees Trina. "I think we *should* go."

Whatever the rest of them do, Jenny is certain that Trina should *not* go. The idea of her meeting a woman like that—and Trina not married—

"Nonsense," protests Trina. "I've never met a woman like that. Maybe I'll never get another chance. Besides, if he's going to change his will, there's still my dowry, remember. Do you think we should take Peter?"

"Peter Thorkelsen? Whatever for?"

"Well, after all, I mean . . . I mean, his profession. . . ."

"Trina, you always were a fool. Anyone would know the last person a dying man wants to see is an undertaker!"

For a moment the lights are out. Presently out of the blackness Katrin appears. She is standing on the steps, wearing her school hat.

"When Mama said I was to go with her, I was excited and I was frightened," Katrin is saying. "It was exciting to take sandwiches for the train, almost as though we were going on a picnic. But I was scared at the idea of seeing death, though I told myself that if I was going to be a writer, I had to experience everything. But all the same, I hoped it would be all over when we got there." (*She starts to walk up the steps.*) "It was afternoon when we arrived. We asked at the station for the Halvorsen ranch, and it seemed to me that the man looked at us strangely. Uncle Chris was obviously considered an odd character. The ranch was about three miles from the town; a derelict, rambling old place. There was long grass, and tall trees, and a smell of honeysuckle. We made quite a cavalcade, walking up from the gate."

Mama, Jenny, Trina, Sigrid and Arne appear at the side, behind Katrin. The curtains part and The Woman, pleasantly, simply dressed and calm in manner, steps toward them.

"How is he? Is he—?" asks Mama.

"Come in, won't you?" asks The Woman, with grave self-possession, holding the curtain aside for them. "The Aunts walk stiffly past her, Sigrid clutching Arne and shielding him from contact with The Woman."

When the curtains are drawn, Uncle Chris's bedroom is revealed, Uncle Chris propped up on pillows in a large double bed. The room is simple and shabby. There is a stand by the side of the bed with a pitcher of water on it. The afternoon sun filters through a window and falls on the bed. Mama is at one side of the bed, Jenny at the other, with the rest of the family ranged below the window. The Woman is not present.

Uncle Chris holds a glass in his hand. He wants a drink, but not of water. Mama and Jenny would talk him out of that notion, but he is persistent. He knows that they know he is dying. They can't fool him. And he doesn't want them there.

"Get out! Get out!" he shouts at Jenny, sitting upright. "I don't vant you here. Get out!"

"Oh, very well," snaps Jenny. "Very well. We'll be outside on the porch if you want us."

"That is where I want you—on the porch!"

As they are leaving he sees Arne and calls to him. How is the knee? Can Arne walk goot? Can he run? Arne circles the room to prove that he can do both. Sigrid, proud of her son's performance, comes back to remind Uncle Chris that Arne has always been very fond of him. Uncle Chris is not impressed—

"I tell you all to get out! Except Marta! And Katrin! Katrin and I have secret. You remember, Katrin?"

"Yes, Uncle Chris."

Now Uncle Chris would have his drink. "Ve cannot vaste vat is left in the bottle," he argues, against Mama's protest. "You do not drink it . . . who vill drink it ven I am gone? Vat harm can it do . . . now? I die anyway. . . . You gif it to me."

Mama mixes a drink of whiskey and water and takes it to him. She sits on the bed beside him and he leans back against her arm and the pillows.

"Marta, I haf never made a vill," he says. "Was never enough money. But you sell this ranch. It will not bring moch. I haf not had it long enough. And there is mortgage. Big mortgage. But it leave a little. Maybe two, tree hundred dollars. You gif to Yessie."

"Yessie?"

UNCLE CHRIS—Yessie Brown. My housekeeper. No, vy I call her that to you? You understand. She is my voman. Twelve years she has been my voman. My vife, only I cannot marry her. She has husband alive somevere. She was trained nurse, but she get sick and I bring her to the country to get well again. There will be no money for you, Marta. Alvays I vanted there should be money to make Nels doctor. But there vere other things . . . qvick things. And now there is no time to make more. There is no money, but you make Nels doctor, all the same. You like?

MAMA—Sure, Uncle Chris. It is what Lars and I have always wanted for him. To help people who suffer. . . .

UNCLE CHRIS—Is the greatest thing in the vorld. It is to have a little of God in you. Alvays I vanted to be doctor myself. Is the only thing I haf ever vanted. Nels must do it for me.

MAMA—He will, Uncle Chris.

UNCLE CHRIS—Is good. (*He strokes her hand.*) You are the good one. I am glad you come, *Lille Ven.* (*He moves his head restlessly.*) Where is Yessie?

MAMA—I think she wait outside.

UNCLE CHRIS—You do not mind if she is here?

MAMA—Of course not, Uncle Chris.

UNCLE CHRIS—You call her. I like you both be here. (MAMA *goes with a quick glance at* KATRIN. UNCLE CHRIS *signs* KATRIN *to come closer. She sits on the chair beside the bed.*) Katrin, your Mama write me you drink coffee now? (*She nods. He looks at her affectionately.*) Katrin, who will be writer. . . . You are not frightened of me now?

KATRIN—No, Uncle Chris.

UNCLE CHRIS—One day maybe you write story about Uncle Chris. If you remember.

KATRIN (*whispering*)—I'll remember. (MAMA *returns with* The Woman. *They come to the side of his bed.*)

UNCLE CHRIS (*obviously exhausted and in pain*)—I like you both stay with me . . . now . . . I think best maybe now Katrin go away. Good-by, Katrin. (*Then he repeats it in Norwegian.*) Farvell, Katrin.

KATRIN—Good-by, Uncle Chris.

UNCLE CHRIS—You say it in Norwegian, like I do.

KATRIN (*in Norwegian*)—Farvell, Onkel Chris. (*She slips out in tears.*)

UNCLE CHRIS—Yessie! Maybe I should introduce you to each other. Yessie, this is my niece, Marta. The only one of my nieces I can stand. Marta, this is Yessie, who haf give me much happiness. . . . (*The two women shake hands.*)

MAMA—I am very glad to meet you.

JESSIE—I am, too.

UNCLE CHRIS (*as they shake hands*)—Is goot. And now you gif me von more drink. You haf drink with me . . . both of you. That vay ve finish the bottle. Yes? (JESSIE *and* MAMA *look at each other.*)

MAMA—Sure, Uncle Chris.

UNCLE CHRIS—Goot. Yessie, you get best glasses. (*With a chuckle to* MAMA.) Yessie does not like to drink, but this is special occasion. (JESSIE *gets three glasses from a wall shelf.*) Vat is the time?

MAMA—It is about half past four, Uncle Chris.

UNCLE CHRIS—The sun comes around this side of the house in afternoon. You draw curtains a little maybe. Is strong for my eyes. (MAMA *goes over and draws the curtain over the window. The stage darkens.* JESSIE *pours three drinks, filling two of the glasses with water. She is about to put water in the third when* UNCLE CHRIS *stops her.*) No, no, I take it now vithout

vater. Alvays the last drink without water. Is Norwegian custom. (*To* MAMA, *with a smile.*) True? (JESSIE *sits on the bed
beside him, about to feed his drink to him, but he pushes her
aside.*) No. No. I do not need you feed it to me. I can drink
myself. (*He takes the glass from her.*) Gif Marta her glass.
(JESSIE *hands a glass to* MAMA. *The two women stand on either
side of the bed, holding their glasses.*) So. . . . Skoal!

JESSIE (*clinking glasses with him*)—Skoal!

MAMA (*doing likewise*)—Skoal!

They all three drink. The lights fade. The curtains close.

The three Aunts are sitting on the porch. Trina and Sigrid
are fighting gnats. Jenny is dozing. Presently Mama comes to
tell them that Uncle Chris has gone.

"Did he . . . say anything about a will?" asks the now wake-
ful Jenny, more gently than is her wont.

"There is no will."

"Well, then, that means . . . we're his nearest relatives . . ."

"There is no money either."

There is, however, a notebook from which Mama is ready to
read to them—

"You know how Uncle Chris was lame . . . how he walked
always with a limp," she begins. "It was his one thought . . .
lame people. He would have liked to be doctor to help them.
Instead, he help them other ways. I read you the last page . . .
'Joseph Spinelli. Four years old. Tubercular left leg. Three
hundred thirty-seven dollars, eighteen cents. Walks now. Esta
Jensen. Nine years. Club-foot. Two hundred seventeen dollars,
fifty cents. Walks now. Arne Solfeldt. . . .' "

"*My* Arne?" Sigrid is startled.

" 'Nine years. Fractured kneecap. Four hundred forty-two
dollars, sixteen cents.' "

Arne and Katrin come running in from the yard. Arne stops,
"awed by the solemnity of the group."

"It does not tell the end about Arne," says Mama. "I like to
write 'walks now.' Yes?"

"Yes," agrees a very subdued Sigrid.

The Woman appears between the curtains. "You can go in and
see him now, if you want," she says.

Jenny, Trina, Sigrid and Arne go in through the curtains.
Mama, Katrin and Jessie are left.

"I'm moving down to the hotel for tonight . . . so that you
can all stay," says Jessie, starting back into the house.

"Wait," Mama calls. "What will you do now . . . after he is buried? You have no money? (JESSIE *shakes her head.*) Where you live?"

"I'll find a room somewhere. I'll probably go back to nursing."

"You like to come to San Francisco for a little? To our house? We have room. Plenty room."

"That's very kind of you, but . . ."

"I like to have you. You come for a little as our guest. When you get work you can be our boarder."

"I don't know why you should bother. . . ." Jessie is awkwardly grateful.

"You were good to Uncle Chris."

Mama has turned to Katrin. She would like Katrin to come with her to see Uncle Chris—

"I like you see him. You need not be frightened. He looks . . . happy and at peace. I like you to know what death looks like . . . then you are not frightened of it, ever."

Mama's arm is around Katrin as she leads her gently through the curtains.

Some months later Trina and Mr. Thorkelsen are sitting on a park bench. Trina stops gently pushing a baby carriage back and forth to coo over the occupant. "Who's the most beautiful Norwegian baby in San Francisco?" she asks. "Who's going to be three months old tomorrow? Little Christopher Thorkelsen."

On closer inspection Trina is ready to assert that the baby is beginning to look a little like Uncle Chris. He has something of the same firmness about the mouth—though, of course, he could get that from his father.

The baby has fallen asleep, and as Trina turns to pay some attention to Peter an idea strikes him. Next Thursday will be their anniversary. Why shouldn't they give a party? It is time Trina was taking her place in society, after a year of mourning, and having a baby, and all. It should be an evening party—"a soiree,"—with perhaps ten people representing Norwegian society. Peter had not thought of including Jenny and Sigrid, but of course if Trina thinks best— They shall come as guests, however, like everyone else. Trina shall have a waitress to help her in the kitchen. When Trina protests that a waitress might suggest a certain ostentation, Peter tries a little nervously to explain—

"Trina, there's something I would like to say. I've never been very good at expressing myself or my . . . well . . . *deeper* feelings—but I want you to know that I'm not only very fond of you, but very . . . well . . . very *proud* of you as well, and I want you to have the best of everything, as far as it's in my power to give it to you. (*As a climax.*) I want you to have a waitress!"

"Yes, Peter."

They are holding hands as the lights fade.

The kitchen has been slightly changed through the years; smartened and refurnished. Mama and Papa and Dagmar all look a little older and when Nels comes in with the evening paper he is wearing long trousers and looking all of his seventeen years. He has picked up a letter for Katrin on his way in. The writing looks strangely like Katrin's own hand.

"She gets too many like that," says Mama. "I think they are stories she send to the magazines."

And so it proves. Katrin opens the envelope to find one of her manuscripts and the usual rejection slip. But the receipt of these help her to a decision: She is not going to go to college. When they ask her why, she answers that it would be a waste of time and money. She had made this last story a test. It is the best she has written and it has come back at least ten times.

"What kind of a story is it?" asks Nels.

"Oh . . . It's a story about a painter, who's a genius, and he goes blind."

"Sounds like 'The Light That Failed.' "

"Well, what's wrong with that?"

"Nothing. Nothing. . . ."

"Besides, it's not like that. My painter gets better. He had an operation and recovers his sight, and paints better than ever before."

"Is good," decides Mama.

"No, it isn't. It's rotten. But it's the best I can do."

Mama thinks if there were someone they could ask about Katrin's stories, that might help. In the evening paper Papa has just noticed a headline—"Woman writer tells key to literary success." A lady called Florence Dana Moorhead, and, from her picture, a fat lady.

Katrin takes the paper from him and reads: " 'Florence Dana Moorhead, celebrated novelist and short story writer . . . blah-blah-blah . . . interviewed today in her suite at the Fairmont . . . blah-blah-blah . . . pronounced sincerity the one essential quality for success as a writer.' (*Throwing aside the paper.*) A lot of help that is."

Still, Mama thinks maybe if Katrin could send this lady her stories—it might be good.

After Katrin has gone to her room to read the want ads in search of a job, Mama would have Nels read her more about Mrs. Moorhead. " 'Apart from literature, Mrs. Moorhead's main interest in life is gastronomy,' " reads Nels.

"The stars?"

"No—eating. 'A brilliant cook herself, she says that she would as soon turn out a good soufflé as a short story, or find a new recipe as she would a first edition.' "

Mama has reached for the paper. "A kind face," she mutters, as the lights fade.

In the lobby of the Fairmont Hotel there is a couch against a pillar with a palm tree behind it. An orchestra is playing softly nearby. Mama is sitting on the couch carefully observing such guests of the hotel as pass.

Presently a bellboy comes through paging "Miss Moorhead." A stout, dressy, good-natured, middle-aged woman stops him, takes the telegram and tips him. Mama rises from the couch and would speak with her. Miss Moorhead is willing to listen, but not for long. And when she hears that it is about Mama's daughter, who wants to be a writer, she is even less inclined to accept the interruption.

"I wait two hours here for you to come in," says Mama, a little pleadingly. "Please, if I may talk to you for one, two minutes. That is all."

"Of course, but I think I'd better tell you that if you want me to read your daughter's stories, it's no use. I'm very sorry, but I've had to make a rule never to read anyone's unpublished material."

Mama nods and then goes on. "It said in the paper you like to collect recipes . . . for eating."

"Yes, I do. I've written several books on cooking."

"I, too, am interested in gastronomy. I am a good cook. Norvegian. I make good Norwegian dishes, Lutefisk. And Kjödboller. That is meat balls with sauce."

"Yes, I know, I've eaten them in Christiania."

"I have a special recipe for Kjödboller . . . my mother give me. She was best cook I ever knew. Never have I told this recipe, not even to my own sisters, because they are not good cooks."

"Oh?" Miss Moorhead is smiling.

"But . . . if you let me talk to you . . . I give it to you.
I promise it is good recipe."

"Well, that seems fair enough. Let's sit down."

In her bag Mama has brought twelve of Katrin's stories. If
Miss Moorhead could read maybe just one . . . "To know if
someone is good cook you do not need to eat a whole dinner,"
admits Mama, and a moment later she adds: "I could write it
out for you. And . . . while I write you could read?"

"All right," laughs Miss Moorhead, "you win. Come upstairs
to my apartment."

They have started for the elevator. "Maybe if you would read
two stories, I could write the recipe for Lutefisk as well," Mama
is saying as they disappear and the lights fade.

Katrin is again at her desk. "When Mama came back, I was
sitting with my diary, which I called my Journal now, writing a
tragic farewell to my art. It was very seldom that Mama came
to the attic, thinking that a writer needed privacy, and I was
surprised to see her standing in the doorway."

Mama had come back to tell Katrin of the visit to Miss Moorhead and what Miss Moorhead had said. She had read five of
Katrin's stories and she said that they were not good. But there
was something else she said, if Katrin will listen—

MAMA—She says you write now only because of what you have
read in other books, and that no one can write good until they
have felt what they write about. That for years she write bad
stories about people in the olden times, until one day she remember something that happen in her own town . . . something that
only she could know and understand . . . and she feels she must
tell it . . . and that is how she write her first good story. She
says you must write more of things you know. . . .

KATRIN—That's what my teacher always told me at school.

MAMA—Maybe your teacher was right. I do not know if I
explain good what Miss Moorhead means, but while she talks I
think I understand. Your story about the painter who is blind
. . . that is because . . . forgive me if I speak plain, my Katrin,
but it is important to you . . . because you are the dramatic
one, as Papa has said . . . and you think it would feel good to be
a painter and be blind and not complain. But never have you
imagined how it would really be. Is it true?

KATRIN—Yes, I . . . I guess it's true.

MAMA—But she say you are to go on writing. That you have

the gift. And that when you have written story that is real and true . . . Then you send it to someone whose name she gives me. It is her agent—and say she recommend you. Here. No, that is recipe she give me for goulash as her grandmother make it. . . . Here. . . . It helps. Katrin, what I have told you?

KATRIN (*subdued again*)—Yes, I . . . I guess it helps. Some. But what have *I* got to write about? I haven't seen anything, or been anywhere. . . .

MAMA—Could you write about San Francisco, maybe? Is fine city. Miss Moorhead write about her home town.

KATRIN—Yes, I know. But you've got to have a central character or something. She writes about her grandfather . . . He was a wonderful old man.

MAMA—Could you write maybe about Papa?

KATRIN—Papa?

MAMA—Papa is fine man. Is wonderful man.

KATRIN—Yes, I know, but . . .

MAMA (*rising*)—I must go fix supper. Is late. Papa will be home. (*She goes up the steps to the curtains, and then turns back.*) I like you should write about Papa. (*She goes inside.*)

KATRIN (*going back to her seat behind the desk*)—Papa. Yes, but what's he ever done? What's ever happened to *any* of us? Except being poor and having illnesses, like the time when Dagmar went to hospital and Mama . . . (*The idea hits her like a flash.*) Oh . . . oh . . . (*Pause—then she becomes the* KATRIN *of today.*) And that was how it was born . . . suddenly in a flash . . . the story of Mama and the hospital . . . and first of all the stories. I wrote it . . . oh, quite soon after that. I didn't tell Mama or any of them. But I sent it to Miss Moorhead's agent. It was a long time before I heard anything . . . and then one evening the letter came. (*She takes an envelope from the desk in front of her.*) For a moment I couldn't believe it. Then I went rushing into the kitchen, shouting. . . ."

The turntable stage has revolved out and the curtains have parted to reveal Mama, Papa, Christine and Nels gathered around the table.

"Mama . . . Mama . . . I've sold a story!" Katrin is shouting as she rushes into the scene.

Katrin tells them then of the letter that had come from Miss Moorhead's agent, with a check for five hundred dollars. What will she do with so much money? Well, first she will buy Mama her warm coat. And then they'll put the rest in the bank. Mama can take the check down town to the bank tomorrow.

But Mama has to confess that there is no bank account; that there never has been a bank account. She had told them a lie—

"Is not good for little ones to be afraid . . . to not feel secure," says Mama, trying to explain. "But now . . . with five hundred dollar . . . I think I can tell."

Katrin is deeply moved by Mama's confession, but before she can speak Mama has another idea. Katrin shall read them the story—all of them. She will call Dagmar. Dagmar can leave her rabbits long enough to hear.

"What is it called, the story?" asks Mama, as she rejoins the family group.

"It's called 'Mama and the Hospital,' " says Katrin. Yes, Katrin knows what Mama had said about her writing about Papa, but this is the way the story had come out. And Katrin begins to read—

" 'For as long as I could remember, the house on Steiner Street had been home. All of us were born there. Nels, the oldest and the only boy . . . (NELS *looks up, astonished to be in a story.*) my sister, Christine . . . and the littlest sister, Dagmar. . . .' "

DAGMAR—Am I in the story?

MAMA—Hush, Dagmar. We are all in the story.

KATRIN—"But first and foremost, I remember Mama. (*The lights begin to dim and the curtain slowly to fall. As it descends, we hear her voice continuing.*) I remember that every Saturday night Mama would sit down by the kitchen table and count out the money Papa had brought home in the little envelope. . . ."

THE CURTAIN FALLS

THE HASTY HEART

A Comedy Drama in Three Acts

BY JOHN PATRICK

THE author of "The Hasty Heart" was on his way home from the Burma front when he wrote this play, most of it on shipboard. He had been serving with the American Field Service, had been promoted to a captaincy and had been attached to the British Army. Arrived here with a manuscript with which he had considerable trouble topping the censorship hurdles—not because of any objection the officials might have to what he had written and described, but because of the time they might take in coming to a decision—he found that there was but one other war play being presented on Broadway. That was the John Hersey-Paul Osborn "A Bell for Adano."

Capt. Patrick did not, however, look upon "The Hasty Heart" as a war play. It had a war background, true, but its action occurs pretty far back from both front lines and the usually forbidding atmosphere engendered by active and booming combat. This fact, he thought, should save it from a playgoer's natural war-play prejudice.

He also realized he had another hurdle to overcome in the fact that his play was really a comedy supported by definite overtones of tragedy. Most play producers are frankly frightened by any suggestion of tragedy in a play script. But again he reasoned that while tragedy did stalk his chief character, that character's adventures and the fellows who helped him through them, were definitely conceived in the spirit of true comedy. He was fortunate, too, in finding producers (the Messrs. Lindsay and Crouse of "Life with Father" and "Arsenic and Old Lace") who, though they prefer those shows that create laughter and a happy glow, are also susceptible to the appeal of honest sentiment and convincing human reactions.

Nor was it easy for the producers to cast "The Hasty Heart." They had trouble finding a young actor who could convincingly produce a deep Scotch burr without appearing ridiculous. Again luck favored the enterprise. A young man named Richard Basehart, with little Broadway experience, had, it was discovered, been studying a Scotch accent which he had frankly adopted from that of William Fyffe, a motion picture actor of Scottish roles, in order to play the Earl of Bothwell in a stock company production of "Mary of Scotland."

So all things worked together for the good of "The Hasty Heart." The play reached production in early January. Its reception by the reviewers was restrained but favorable. Audience response was a bit slow in developing, but once the fear of being saddened was dissipated by word of mouth reports, the Patrick play had an extremely happy run through to the end of the season.

As we move into the action of "The Hasty Heart" we find ourselves facing the interior of the convalescent ward of a British General Hospital in the rear of the Assam-Burma front. The ward is located in a hut, the thatched roof of which slopes toward the back. There are windows through which glimpses of the jungle and the roofs of outlying buildings may be seen.

Inside the ward there are six hospital beds with their heads against the rear wall, a side table alongside each bed. From a bamboo pole that stretches from side to side of the hut overhead six mosquito nettings are hung, attached to six rings suspended over the beds. There are loops of tape to hold the netting when it is not in use, and rolled up to the ring to which it is attached.

Each of the beds is fully equipped with sheets, pillows, blankets, etc. At the moment five of them are occupied by five sleeping convalescents, their nettings tucked in neatly around the mattresses. The hut is in darkness except for such light as seeps in through the bamboo matting, below the doors and around the edges of the shutters. A lantern hangs from the bamboo pole. It can be raised or lowered by a rope attached to the side wall. Now it is lit, but its rays make only a feeble showing in the early morning light. Presently an orderly arrives, sweeps the ward with his flashlight, lowers and extinguishes the lantern and calls lustily to the sleeping patients.

"Wake up! Wake up! . . . Rise and shine! . . . Hurry on—get up!" He is pulling out the mosquito netting from the foot of the beds as he passes them. "Get washed and get your kit together. All patients are going to be evacuated!"

The first man stirring is Yank, who sticks a tousled head out from under his netting, rubs the back of his neck, reaches for his slippers and protests the irritating cheeriness of the service chanticler.

Yank "is in his early thirties, more wholesome than handsome; with a manner more relaxed than lazy." When excited he suffers a slight speech impediment. Yank doesn't consider the evacuation call of the orderly very funny. "Try and think up something different tomorrow," he advises. "Evacuated! Ha—ha—Haw!"

But the Orderly has his own ideas. "Come on—come on!" he shouts. "The hospital's burning down! The monsoons have started! There's an air raid! There's an earthquake!" And as a final plea: "For Gawd's sake, wake up! I'm half an hour late!"

Slowly the ward and its occupants come to life. The five patients are "Digger," an Australian, about 35; "Tommy," an Englishman and "exceedingly fat"; "Yank," the American; "Kiwi," a tall New Zealander, his left arm in a plaster cast "held in the air by a reticulated wire support braced against his hip," and "Blossom," a tremendous Basuto, with "large puffed lips and a bullet-shaped cranium."

Digger, Tommy and Kiwi are "lying patients." The Orderly has already gone to the washroom to fetch basins of warm water for them to wash in. Yank and Blossom are "up-patients" and are herded into the washroom as soon as the Orderly can manage it. Blossom speaks no English, but has learned to answer to the name the others have given him.

There is a good deal of good-natured kidding among them. Much of it is directed at Tommy's snoring. How Tommy can give so perfect an imitation of the mating call of a hippopotamus without waking himself is a mystery to Yank.

The Orderly has brought in a stack of mugs and a bucket of steaming tea. Yank distributes the mugs and Blossom pours the tea. It isn't very good tea, to hear them talk about it, but they all drink it. The breakfast that follows is also a bit on the depressing side—soy link sausage.

"They do everything with a soy bean but make it taste like food," gripes Digger.

Kiwi has a little trouble eating with his one free arm, but he is full of hope. "The Medical Officer said he'd chisel me out of this derrick next week," says Kiwi.

"Ha—you'll be in it a year," announces Digger.

"You was bad shot up when you came in 'ere. I'd say two years," adds Tommy.

"Nope—a man takes a lot of killing," announces Kiwi. "You

shoot an animal and it dies.—You shoot a man—and if there's only part of him left—he gets well. He takes a lot of killing."

Tommy agrees, but Digger doubts Tommy's authority—seeing that he was only wounded by a sandfly. This is a slur Tommy is quick to deny. He was wounded, he admits with a chuckle, while he was asleep. A hot piece of shrapnel plowed into his tender flesh—while he was lying on his stomach.

"The M.O. must have probed up to his elbows," ventures Digger.

"I wrote me old lady I was wounded leading me regiment into battle," giggles Tommy.

The talk turns to the empty sixth bed. Who, the boys wonder, will they get in there? A Canadian, most likely, thinks Kiwi, seeing the R.C.A.F. has moved in up the road. And he'll probably be Irish.

"We 'aven't 'ad a Scot in 'ere for a long time," Tommy reminds them.

"God, I hope we don't get a Scot," hopes Yank.

"Don't ya get along with Scots?"

"I do not. And I d-d-don't know anyone who does. Except another Scot."

"Sister's a Scot," Kiwi reminds him. But Yank is quick to deny this reference to the nurse in charge of their ward. Sister used to live in Scotland, Yank explains, while she was teaching school, but after a year of it she had a nervous breakdown. For that matter Yank himself is of Scottish descent. Which explains a lot—

"I hate all Scots," declares Yank. "You should have known my G-g-grandfather Angus. There were only two infallible beings to his way of thinking: Angus McDonald and God. Sometimes God was wrong but never Grandfather Angus."

"Did you have to live with him?" Kiwi asks.

"When my folks died, he took over the supervision of my soul."

Among Grandfather Angus' other corrections, Yank recalls, was that of making his young grandson stop and recite the books of the Bible whenever he started to lose his temper. Yank can still remember them, from Genesis and Exodus right through to Zechariah and Malachi.

" 'E must have been a fearful man, your grandfather," agrees Tommy.

"And if you tried to argue with him—you know what he'd do?"

"Play your hide?"

"He'd take his damned bag-pipe out and sit playing it. God—

how I learned to hate a bag-pipe. No wonder the Scots always march when they play them. They're trying to get away from the sound."

Blossom has come through the outside door and stands stiffly at attention as he holds it open. A moment later he is followed into the room by Sister Margaret. "She is about twenty-one. She wears two 'pips' on each shoulder of her neat white uniform. She has an easy, assured manner with the men. Her eyes are dark and expressive—giving an impression of inner amusement."

With hearty "Good Mornings" for the group, Sister Margaret passes on through to her office.

"If it were humanly possible for me to get rid of my Scottish blood—I'd d-d-donate it all to the Red Cross," Yank proclaims, stepping out of the washroom, waving his toothbrush.

"You're going to run your blood pressure up—if you don't have a care," advises Kiwi.

"And what's this about the Scots?" Nurse Margaret would know. She has come from her office with a tray of thermometers, charts, etc.

" 'E don't like 'em," explains Tommy.

"Then you don't understand them. They say God broke the mold after he made the Scot."

"I'm s-s-sure He did—right over the Scot's head."

Now starts the second phase of the morning routine. Temperatures have to be taken and pulses counted for the records. Beds have to be made. Nurse Margaret goes about her job with business-like efficiency and is not to be diverted by their gentle and affectionate raillery.

"Ah—Sister—ya make the morning lovely," Digger tells her.

"We was just saying—you're our favorite sister, Sister," adds Tommy.

"I wish I could say the same about you," answers Margaret, ripping the sheets from Yank's bed and throwing them on the floor. "As patients, you're the most untidy and disrespectful lot it's ever been my misfortune to get."

"Ya wound me, Sister." This from Digger.

"You can't mean us," protests Kiwi.

"I certainly do. And I'll be delighted to see the last of you."

"You need some leave, Sister," ventures Tommy. "The matron works you too hard."

"The poor matron has nothing to do with it," snaps Margaret, taking her tray to Blossom and preparing to start with him for the temperatures. "It's you—it's a good thing I once taught in a kindergarten or I couldn't cope with you."

When she gets to Kiwi she gently massages his shoulder and finds it better. When she comes to Tommy she meets his complaint that he isn't comfortable with a quick retort—

"This is a British Military Hospital—you're not *supposed* to be comfortable."

"But I'm a dying man. Don't you run your wards for dying men?"

She takes the thermometer out of his mouth and jots down his temperature on his chart. "You know perfectly well," she says, "that we run the wards so Colonels can inspect them—so be still."

"Ah—what would Old Cobwebs say if he heard such talk?" cautions Digger.

She is taking Yank's pulse. "You will please show a little more respect for our superior officer. You will not refer to Cobwebs . . . to the *Colonel* as Old Cobwebs."

Margaret finds that Yank's fever is up, but he insists that that is because she is holding his wrist. Just the same, she predicts, the M.O. is going to put him on plasma-quinn to get all the malaria out of his system.

Digger's back isn't doing too well. He is sure a bit of a rub would help.

" 'E only wants to be rubbed because I gets rubbed—jealous of me every move," protests Tommy.

There's no time at the moment for a massage, but Nurse Margaret promises to attend to the two of them later. Soon she is through taking temperatures. Blossom is the last. She thinks at first that the big Basuto has swallowed the thermometer, but he hasn't. He just has put the whole thing in his mouth.

Margaret is trying to straighten up the room for inspection when Yank is seized with a small case of jitters. At the window he has seen "Cobwebs" coming, but he can't get the message out until Margaret has broken his stuttering by giving him a smart slap on the cheek.

It's early for inspection, but there is "Cobwebs" approaching the ward. With a muffled scream that everyone should hide his kit, and a wild scramble to get the ward in order, Margaret and Yank manage to make the place presentable before they snap to attention as the Colonel enters. "He is tall, tired and stooped. He is not particularly formidable looking . . . He wears a bush jacket with his stethoscope hanging from his neck."

After the formal "Good Mornings," the Colonel bids them carry on. Although he is early, he is pleased to note that they keep a very orderly ward. He has come to talk to Sister Margaret's patients, he explains, having heard that they are exceedingly congenial.

"They're the most tidy, respectful, pleasant group of men it's ever been my fortune to get, sir," answers Margaret, promptly.

Hearing that there is an extra bed in the ward the Colonel has decided to transfer a patient of his own to this ward.

"It's a case that calls for the co-operation of the whole ward," he explains. "May I have everyone's attention for a moment. I came here this morning to enlist your help. . . . I'm putting a patient of mine in here with you. I did an emergency operation on this man. Took a bit of shrapnel out of him—had to remove his kidney. He's about recovered. I think you can help him."

YANK—May I ask how, sir?

COLONEL—By keeping him—contented. He's anxious to get back to his regiment—but I can't discharge him from the hospital. It's out of the question.

MARGARET—Did you say, sir, that the patient had recovered from his operation?

COLONEL—Quite. In a few days he'll be fully recovered—from the operation. This man has one kidney left. Ordinarily that would carry him through life. We've discovered, unfortunately, that it's defective. It will do the work of two—for a time—a limited time.

YANK—What happens then, sir?

COLONEL—The kidney collapses—ceases to function. He begins to poison himself—uremic poisoning. And that's the inevitable end.

MARGARET—Does the patient know this, sir?

COLONEL—I've decided against telling him. He has no family —no ties. Worry won't help him. So while he's well and waiting —I'm placing him in here because—well—it seems to me that a man should have friends around him when he dies.

KIWI—How long has this man got, sir?

COLONEL—At the most—six weeks.

TOMMY—Nothing can 'elp him, sir?

COLONEL—The only help anyone can give him now, will come from you.

YANK—And he thinks he's well, sir?

COLONEL—In a sense—he is. But it would be criminal to release him just to collapse up forward. Do what you can to keep him contented—and happy.

YANK—Yes, sir.
DIGGER—We'll do our best, sir.
TOMMY—'E won't learn nothing from us, sir.
KIWI—And we'll jolly him along.
MARGARET—These are good men—you can rely on them, Colonel.
COLONEL—Thank you. Damned unfortunate. Carry on.

The Colonel decides to omit inspection and has left. There is a lot of work to do. While Margaret takes on the rubbing of Tommy and Digger, Yank pulls the screens around Kiwi's bed and gives him his bath.

They have all been a little sobered by the Colonel's talk and the thought of the unhappy patient coming in. Kiwi wonders if Yank would want to know it if he were going to die.

"I'm going to d-d-die. Some d-d-day," Yank answers him. "And I'd prefer to let God surprise me."

"Now, why can't a bloke live without a kidney?" Digger wants to know. He is indicating Tommy. "He gets along all right without a brain."

Tommy is squirming. "Turn over and get your backsides rubbed," orders Nurse Margaret.

Digger and Tommy have had their daily fight with flyswatters, as small boys might fight with pillows, and have jumped back into bed when they hear Margaret coming from her office. She has her arms full of sheets and pillow cases. She knows what they have been up to, too, and threatens to take their swatters away from them and let the flies eat them, if she ever catches them at that sort of thing again—

"Get your needlework out and try doing something constructive for a change," orders Margaret. "All of you."

Soon Blossom, the Basuto, is stringing beads. Digger has got out his knitting, which is pink and blue. Tommy is doing a bit of embroidery—a doily with blue flowers. Kiwi has a job of needlework, which Margaret brings in in a stand. They are all busy and there is a good deal of joking about their work when the Orderly appears, followed by the new patient, who is carrying a kit on his shoulder and a set of bagpipes in a green bag in his hand. He would not let the Orderly touch either of them.

The newcomer "has on a bathrobe and convalescent blues over his whites. He is a slight young man of about twenty. He seems smaller than a soldier should. His rebellious hair inclines in all directions. He has blue eyes that are as metallic and sharp as rapiers. His dark good looks are somewhat marred by the unrelenting jut of his jaw. He evinces no interest in his surroundings."

Margaret makes the first advance, but not with great success. "I'm Sister Margaret," she says. "I don't believe the Colonel told me your name." There is complete silence. Margaret reads from the report the Orderly has handed her. " 'Sgt. Lachlen McLachlen.' Are you a Scot?"

The Scottish burr is thick when Lachie answers. "I'd hardly be gaen the name of a Scot if I were nae a Scot ma'self."

"Oh, I don't know. Quite a few parents give their children Scottish names—because they like them."

"It fools nae one. Parading under false pretenses."

"Oh, I doubt if it's a deliberate plot against the Scots. Now the Colonel said you could sit up if you wanted to—or get into bed and rest. Just as you like."

"I'll sit and think a bit."

"Is there anything you want?"

"I dinna like to hae things done for me."

"Don't you? I love to have things done for me."

"Aye—ye may. Not I."

"Well, sing out if you need anything. I'll take your reports into the office and glance at them."

With this Margaret returns to her office, leaving a deep and complete silence behind her. The men continue industriously with their sewing. Yank is the first to make a second advance. He offers a cigarette, but the Scot prefers to smoke his own. He never accepts presents, he says, because he has no wish to put himself in any man's debt.

Digger also has a try. He addresses McLachlen as "Jock" and is promptly informed that that is not the newcomer's name. All Scots are Jock to him, Digger explains, just as all Aussies are Diggers, all New Zealanders Kiwis, all Englishmen Tommies and all Yanks Yank.

"I'm no damned Yank. I come from Georgia," snaps Yank.

"If ye must address me, ye'll use ma' proper name," says McLachlen. But he decides to answer to the "Lachie" they have adopted.

"What regiment are you with, Lachie?" Yank is trying again.

"Why do ye ask?"

"I was j-j-just curious. I thought I might know somebody in your regiment."

"Are ye a Scot?"

"My G-g-grandfather was."

"I think it unlikely ye'd find yur grandfather in ma' regiment."

Yank's temper snaps at this. "I k-k-know where my grandfather is—he's in the family plot where he belongs. But I happen to drive an ambulance and I get to k-k-know lots of regiments. I thought we might have friends in common."

"Most unlikely. I dinna make friends freely."

"You d-d-don't make friends—period."

Lachie puffs at his cigarette. Then he puts it out on his shoe and carefully puts the stub in his pocket. He is unpacking his shaving things and putting them in his bed table when Kiwi tosses a book onto his bed. Lachie tosses it back. He puts no value on books. "Buuks are a waste of a thinking man's time," he says. Nor is he sure he could be interested even in a Bible.

"It's got some damn good poetry in it," promises Yank.

"I poot nae value on poetry, sacred or otherwise," answers Lachie.

"L-l-look— We're a nice friendly bunch in here. If you don't like books or stories—it's all right with us."

"It would hae tae be."

Yank has gone to the side of Lachie's bed and proffered a bar of chocolate. Lachie isn't interested.

"G-g-grandfather Angus r-r-rides again!" proclaims a disgusted Yank.

The talk turns to travel. And what does Lachie think of the homelands of his new friends? Not much. New Zealand, he tells Kiwi, is a heathen land and he leaves heathen lands to the missionaries. Nor does he think much of Tommy's British Empire —an Empire that acquired its colonies, not by conquering them with soldiers—

"Ye conquered them wi' missionaries, no less," charges Lachie, as Tommy writhes. "Ye send yur preachers tae the land ye've got yur 'e's on. Ye teach the simple heathen tae pray—and once ye've got him kneeling doon—ye hoist the English flag o'er him."

As for Australia, which is "Gawd's country" to Digger, "I'm nae impressed by a land that produces naught more sensible than a great jumping rat," says Lachie.

"A Kangaroo ain't a rat," shouts Digger, angrily.

"And New Zealand isn't any heathen land," adds Kiwi.

"And wot represents ye?" Lachie demands, turning to Kiwi. "The kiwi. A bird wi' nae wings. A bird that canna fly."

Yank is highly amused. He is smiling smugly as he turns to Kiwi and Digger. "Well—I guess he's told you off," he says. "You won't find any kangaroos in America—or birds that can't fly."

"Ah, America! The land of Mickey Moose," says Lachie, with both compassion and pity. "The land of plenty—and ye live oot of tin cans and ten cent stores. Ye've as many varieties of churches as ye have pickles—but ye poot yur faith intae vitamins and Roosevelt."

"You're speaking from a warehouse of ignorance," snaps Yank, who is really sore.

"Aye—am I? I sailed from Glasgow—a city of which ye've nae doot heard—when I were twelve. I worked one God-forsaken Winter in yur great New York. I've examined ye at close range and I dinna care fur yur breed. Nothing pursonal."

"B-b-buster, you and I are going to have trouble getting together," concludes Yank.

Nurse Margaret is back, and eager to learn how they have all been getting on. They're practically b-b-buddies, Yank assures her, sarcastically. Margaret is glad to hear that—but the next minute she is disillusioned. Lachie has threatened to rattle Yank's jaw with his fist, and Yank announces that with just one more crack from Lachie he'll stop lend-lease.

It is Margaret who finds a subject in which Lachie is truly interested. That would be Scotland. When he discovers that she has taught school—and such darling children—in his native Ayreshire he is greatly pleased, though he tries hard not to show it.

He's a Cameron Highlander, too, Lachie admits, and that thrills Margaret. That would mean that he wears the Errach tartan. It might, admits Lachie. And did he bring his kilt with him? The boys would love to see Lachie in his kilt, wouldn't they?

"I can h-h-hardly wait," admits Yank.

"Oh—with your cap cocked over one eye—and your kilt swishing as you walk down the street, you must be the proudest man in the world." Margaret is thrilled by the picture.

"I dinna hae a kilt," admits Lachie, after a moment's silence.

"Oh, but you must have a kilt."

"I dinna moost at all."

"But you belong to the Camerons, and you're allowed to wear one—what sort of Scot are you, Lachlen?"

"We're required tae pay fur a kilt ourselves. And there's a great cost tae a proper kilt."

"Oh—you're not issued a kilt?"

"We're issued naught but battle dress."

"Well, if I were in your regiment, I'd buy myself the finest to be had—no matter what the cost."

"Being a woman—ye wuid. I poot ma' money tae better use. It's a question of values."

It's true, Lachie admits, that he has saved much of his pay. But he has invested it in the land. It's a bit of a farm in Ayrshire that is his delight. He'll not return to Scotland "wi' naught but my wounds to show for ma' time." Nor will he take from his farm funds money for a kilt.

"Are you buying your farm to share with someone?" Kiwi asks.

"I share wi' nae one."

"You're going to live on your farm—all by yourself?" Margaret is incredulous.

"Aye."

"And you won't be lonely?"

"I've ne'er been lonely in ma' life."

"Well—you seem to know what you want," concludes Margaret.

For minutes after Margaret has returned to her office the boys work industriously at their knitting. Then, one by one, they turn to look at Lachie, who is gazing out the window. Finally Yank makes another try at friendliness by requesting an answer to just one question: What is Lachie griped about?

"When a guy is friendly to you—why can't you be pleasant?"

"Were ye being friendly?"

"Didn't you g-g-guess?"

"Ye shuid hae told me. I cuid have saved ye time and trouble. I dinna need companionship. I put nae value on the human animal. I dinna like tae hae ma freedom nibbled intae."

"Then just what do you put a value on?"

"I knew ye'd presume tae ask a second question. (*He turns to look up at* YANK *and speaks with angry insistence.*) If ye'd used yur God gaen wits, ye wuid nae ask. I value ma' privacy. Do ye mind?"

"You can have it!" announces Yank, his temper rising.

With that Yank gets a screen, and motions to Blossom to get another. They set them up around Lachie's bed, shutting the dour one off from the ward and the audience.

"You can stay in your private world—and h-h-hug yourself to death. As far as we're concerned, Brother, you w-w-won't exist."

"If ye dinna mind, I'm nae yur brother," announces Lachie, popping up behind the screen.

"Who's got a dull razor? I think I'll cut my throat," sighs Yank, as Lachie disappears again behind the screen.

"Sister's going to take a poor view of that," thinks Tommy, indicating the screens.

But Yank is unimpressed. "I'm just giving him what he asked for," says he.

Gradually the group composes itself restfully. Suddenly the first wailing notes of a bagpipe are heard. Below his screen Lachie's foot can be seen keeping time to the music.

Yank is sitting bolt upright on his bed. "What's that?" he demands. The next minute he is standing on his bed peering over the screen. "It's bagpipes!" he announces. And then, grabbing his sides, he continues through gritting teeth—

"Genesis, Exodus, Leviticus, Numbers, D-d-deuteronomy, Joshua, Judges. . . ."

The curtain falls.

ACT II

Two weeks later the convalescents are variously disposed about their ward. Blossom, the Basuto, is strumming a native, guitar-like instrument and indulging in a sort of chant. Kiwi and Digger are both up-patients now. Kiwi is sitting on Yank's bed, fanning himself with a flyswatter and Digger is lying full length on his bed, idly swatting flies. Tommy is braced against his back-rest, writing a letter, and Yank is sprawled out on his bed on his stomach, looking very bored.

Presently Sister Margaret appears with a cheerful greeting and the mail. That stirs them. There are letters for all of them except Lachie. He, busily polishing his shoes, is neither surprised nor disappointed. Margaret, however, is a little concerned—

"Haven't you told your friends where you are?" she asks.

"I've many friends," boasts Lachie. "Many carefully chosen individuals in Doon Foot, Ayrshire, Glasgow, Rosemarkey, Edinborough and oother places and they all know my views. I dinna hae to write aboot them."

"But don't you miss not hearing from home?"

"Aye—there's mooch I miss. But ye may have heard—there's a war going on."

"Yes—I heard. The man I'd hoped to marry was killed at Crete. I've heard about the war."

"Aye—then ye know."

"And I know it's good to know what's happening back in blighty."

"Ma' knowing will nae change things."

"It might."

Margaret would like to know if there isn't something special she can fix for tiffin. Some particular dish. But the Scot is immediately suspicious—

"I've noticed, Sister, that ye seek tae do me favors. I dinna ken yur motive boot I think it only fair tae warn ye—I've nae place fur marriage in ma' plans."

"How very kind of you to tell me."

"Aye."

"But I assure you that I have no plans to snare you."

"It would nae be the furst time in ma' life."

Neither her explanation that she was merely trying to be thoughtful nor her flaring anger, impresses Lachie—

"I'm sorry I can nae be a weak character tae yur liking," says he.

"So am I," answers Margaret with spirit, "because I've a weakness for weakness. It's something I can understand."

She has gone quickly to her office, but is back in a minute, and in full control of her emotions. "I'm sorry I was cross with you," she says to Lachie.

"I dinna notice the tantrums of women," says he. A second later when she begs him please to be human, and asks again if there is nothing she can get him, he calmly announces: "I'm content wi' ma' lot." With that Margaret leaves him and turns to the others.

Yank is happy with his letter. It's perfect! Digger is excited. He's a baby. At least his wife has! And she's named it after him.

Tommy wishes he could have a baby, but the best he can get is news that his wife has made 'im a bloody 'ero in their town. After she had described his wounds, the citizens of Tommy's village had not only given him a public dinner, but had named a pudding after him—

"Gawd! I'll bet it's heavy!" bets Digger.

"Bless their 'earts—they've made me immortal with raisins. Oh, dear, oh, dear, the silly fools. 'The Percival 'awkins Puffed Wheat Pudding.' "

Everyone is laughing but Lachie. He is more than a little disgusted with them, and with the whole letter writing custom—

"Have ye any idea of the tons of paper that's wasted writing of news that cuid well wait? Hae ye considered the fortune in stamps that cuid be spent on food instead? Do ye ken how many ships and planes it takes tae deliver the latters of millions of giddy females alone?"

"Why don't you run the world for a change and give God a rest?" Digger asks.

"Ye're guilty of criminal waste—ye and yur woman. (*Looks at them all.*) And ye sit there pleased as cats."

"D-d-do us a favor and don't show us the error of our ways, will you?"

"Ah—it's yur consciences trooble ye—nae I."

"All right then! It's my conscience."

Lachie has reached for his bagpipe, hanging at the head of his bed, and prepares to play—

"Oh, God—give him asthma!" prays Yank.

Before there is more than a wheeze from the pipes, Margaret is back with word that the Colonel wants to see Lachie right away. Something about an x-ray. Lachie will go, though he has no use for the Colonel, great surgeon though he be.

"Sister, is he really going to die?" demands Yank, the moment Lachie is out of hearing. "Because, if he isn't I'm going to k-k-kill him."

MARGARET—What a dreadful thing to say. I'm ashamed of you.

KIWI—You don't have to live with him.

DIGGER—That joker's got a spite on the whole world.

YANK—He's got a p-p-porcupine disposition. You c-c-can't touch him.

MARGARET—Have you tried to *know* him?

YANK—To k-k-know him is to loathe him.

MARGARET—Why don't you try to like him?

TOMMY—'E don't like us first. 'E's a terrible stern man, 'e is.

MARGARET—Then why do you antagonize him!

DIGGER—Antagonize him!

YANK—Th-th-that does it!

MARGARET—Listen to me. That boy was not sent in here to make things pleasant for you. He was sent to you for help. That was a compliment.

YANK—Or a ch-challenge.

MARGARET—All right—a challenge. It's a poor show when men run from a challenge. I admit I lose patience too, but we mustn't stop trying.

DIGGER—He'd be miserable if he was happy, Sister.

YANK—If there was only *one* thing about him you could like.

MARGARET—It isn't important whether you like him or not. And whether Lachie is a hero or not—doesn't matter. He's a human being on leave from suffering. How unworthy of you to criticize him. *You're* going to get well.

TOMMY—'E resists you.

MARGARET—His opinions aren't the same as ours. Does that make him an enemy?

TOMMY—It makes 'im 'ard to talk to.

MARGARET—It isn't often that you have an opportunity to make a man grateful he'd spent the last weeks of his life with you. I'm ashamed of you, indeed.

TOMMY—We're no good. Me that was wounded in me behind. (DIGGER *sniggers—and even* MARGARET *has to smile.*)

MARGARET—Well—you've a chance to redeem yourselves to-day. (*Turns to* YANK.) Yank, go into my office—there's a big parcel. Will you please bring it in here. Today's his birthday.

KIWI—His birthday?

MARGARET—I checked on his admittance card.

DIGGER—Are we going to give 'im a ruddy birthday party?

MARGARET—Don't you want to help?

YANK—All right, we'll try once more. (*He goes for box.*)

TOMMY—Did you get 'im a cake?

MARGARET—I thought of a haggis to be piped in—but who could make a haggis here? (YANK *is back with box.*)

TOMMY—Oh, I do like presents, I do.

MARGARET—I've a kilt here.

KIWI—A kilt!

MARGARET (*untying the box*)—And everything that goes with it. I checked with his regiment and ordered it from Calcutta. And it got here on time—thanks to the R.A.F.

They are not going to let Margaret pay for all these things, announces Yank. That was her intention, though she wanted them to give Lachie the presents. It will be all right if they all want to chip in, as Kiwi suggests. That would be fine.

They will, decides Digger, go over the price list and each of them pick out the thing he can afford. He (Digger) will give Lachie the brogues. Tommy will give him the belt. Kiwi, at Margaret's suggestion, draws the spats, stockings and supporters.

"Does anyone object to my giving him the jacket and the

"THE HASTY HEART"

Margaret—Oh, you wretched, stubborn little man. Why must I love you?

Lachie—Please—you confuse me. Do ye—or don't ye?

(Richard Basehart, Anne Burr)

kilt?" asks Yank. "After all, I dislike him more than the rest of you."

"I think that would be splendid," beams Margaret. "I hoped you would."

It takes a lot of pantomime to make Blossom understand that he is to give the cap Margaret hands him to Lachie. Blossom thinks it is for him to wear, with the ribbon hanging over his eyes. But he finally understands.

Margaret's gift is the sporran. " 'E keeps his small change in it," Tommy explains to a curious Kiwi. "M-mixed up with fish-hooks," adds Yank.

"And that's the last of it," announces Margaret. The box is empty.

"Everything? Didn't you forget something very important?" Yank is curious. "Underneath the k-kilts—don't they wear some sort of fancy-pants?"

"Didn't you know?" Tommy beckons to Yank to come close. The two whisper, Tommy making a small circle with his hand, then a gesture of lifting and finally "a gesture of negation." Yank can't believe it—

"Nothing?" he demands, incredulously.

"Nothing," announces Tommy smugly.

"A bit drafty, I think." This from Digger.

"Well, there's nothing else to wear in the box," insists Margaret.

"Maybe they left it out," suggests Kiwi.

"S-sure. It's indecent to be that drafty," insists Yank.

"It's not indecent—it's thrifty," thinks Tommy.

The doubt and curiosity regarding the undergarments that may or may not go with a kilt starts a wild bit of betting. Digger is sure there is some sort of diaper. Kiwi is willing to lay two pounds he's wrong. Yank would like to bet Kiwi is wrong. Digger backs Yank. Tommy is betting they're both wrong. Margaret will have nothing to do with such silly, vulgar business. She puts the box on Yank's bed and they have their tiffin while they wait for Lachie.

"Sister, I was just th-thinking—what if he refuses to take the presents! We're sticking our necks out." Yank is anxious.

"Yes—remember he said he never accepted presents," remembers Kiwi.

"Oh, he won't refuse them," Margaret assures them. "He can't. It's his birthday."

"I p-p-promise you, Sister, if he tosses these presents back at us, I'm going to b-beat him to death with his bagpipe."

And then Lachie comes. He walks straight to his bed without speaking, sees his tiffin plate, picks it up and starts eating. Margaret signals to Digger to start the gift-bearing. Digger gets out the shoes and walks over to Lachie—

"Heard it was your birthday, Lachie," he says. "Thought ya might be able to use a pair of brogues. Congratulations."

Lachie stops eating, the spoon halfway to his mouth, then resumes without a word. Digger withdraws a little awkwardly.

Tommy is next. "Made in Scotland—it says—'appy birthday." He puts the belt alongside the shoes. Lachie chews slowly, but does not look up.

Kiwi gets the next signal from Sister. He advances with his presents. "You can't wear brogues without stockings," he says; "you get corns. And you can't wear stockings without supporters, you'll break your neck. The best of luck to you."

Kiwi has dropped his presents without ceremony on the bed. Margaret manages to get Blossom to put the cap with the other things. Then she takes over the sporran and adds it to the collection—

"Sorry we weren't able to have a haggis for you, Lachlen," she says. "You're gathering quite a collection. G'bless."

As she walks away she motions to Yank. Lachie is still silent. Yank gets out the jacket and kilt, lays them over his arm and walks over to Lachie. The others have stopped eating to see what happens.

"All the b-best to you, Lachie," says Yank, laying the jacket on the top of the pile and spreading the kilt over all. As Yank goes back to his bed, Margaret whispers to Tommy. Tommy clears his throat and begins to sing—

" 'Appy birthday to you, 'Appy birthday to you—"

Margaret and the others join in. Blossom, catching the spirit, starts clapping his hands in native rhythm.

"Happy birthday, dear Lachlen. Happy birthday to you."

Silence greets the song; "a flat, wet silence. They look at each other, self-consciously—"

"Genesis, Exodus, Leviticus, Numbers—" begins Yank. Margaret is quick to put a restraining hand on his shoulder.

Now Lachie has risen. He clears his throat. "I wuid hae a word wi' ye," he begins, swallowing hard. "I dinna understand ye. I dinna understand ma' self. You've done a thing that numbs my brain. (*His hand closes over the kilt.*) Nae mon in

all ma' life befur gae me tu'pence fur naught. I'd nae hae remembered it was ma' birthday if ye'd nae said sae. *But* . . .
Hae I the right tae take yur kilt? The taking lays a claim on
me and I've naught tae pay ye back. (*He looks back at the kilt,
troubled.*) I moost nae make a mistake. They say that sorrow
is born in the hasty h'ert. Now, I've nae wish tae invite sorrow.
So ma' problem . . ."

"Oh, do be quiet, Lachie."

"I moost explain ma' feeling. Now, ma' problem . . ."

"You don't have to explain anything. For once in your life
be hasty and risk a mistake."

"Boot I . . ."

Before he can say more Margaret sticks a thermometer in his
mouth. "Keep your mouth shut and let your heart talk," she
orders. "When a Scot makes a fool of himself he makes a grand
one."

Margaret has gently pushed Lachie and he sits on his bed. "Is
'e going to take 'em, Sister?" demands an excited Tommy.

"Of course he is. There was no other thought in his mind.
You were searching for a dignified way to thank them, weren't
you?"

Lachie nods agreement. Yank has swung around on his bed
and is facing Lachie, begging him to "Put 'em on!" Promptly
the others join in until the requests become a kind of chorus.
There's a bet to be settled—

"Do you or don't you wear something under the kilt?" Yank
puts the question.

Slowly Lachie takes the thermometer out of his mouth. "Ma
friends," he begins, "I deeply regret ye've asked—fur I can nae
tell ye. It's the one question nae Scot will answer rightly."

Lachie's decision is final. They keep up their begging, but to
no avail—

"I'll wear ma' kilt when the occasion is fitting. I'll put on ma'
kilt the day I return to ma' regiment—nae befur."

With this Lachie folds up his kilt and puts it back in the
box. When the boys appeal to Margaret to stop him she sides
with Lachie. It's his birthday—he can do whatever pleases him.

"Thank ye fur ma' gifts. I'll nae soon forget this day." There
is no doubting the Scot's sincerity.

"Is the p-party over?" stutters Yank.

"Is there moor to dew?"

"No—no—th-that's all—I guess," wails Yank. "A perfect

Scottish birthday party!"

Lachie puts the lid on the box and shoves the box under the bed. Then he picks up his plate and resumes eating.

"Now, is there anything I can do for you before I go?" Margaret asks him.

"Naught. I'm most content."

"That's good."

After Margaret has gone back to the office Lachie continues with his tiffin for a moment. The others, he notes, are doing a variety of things. He looks at them and then walks slowly over to the door and looks out. Coming back he goes first for a look out of the window. Then he comes back to speak to Digger. There's a weird tropical bird in the banyan tree, Lachie reports. It's a crow, says Digger.

Taking a package of cigarettes out of his pocket, Lachie offers one to Digger, who takes it with a short "Thanks." Lachie offers one to Tommy. Another to Kiwi. Finally he reaches Yank, still sitting on the side of his bed with his feet swinging.

"Would ye care fur a cigarette?" asks Lachie.

Yank looks a bit amazed, but takes the cigarette without comment. Before he can reach for a match Lachie has struck a light for him, which adds to Yank's surprise.

"May I sit doon?" asks Lachie, indicating the end of Yank's bed.

Yank nods. Lachie sits. Yank is looking at him, curiously, smilingly. As he turns around Yank's back touches Lachie. They are back to back as Yank straightens up. Their arms rise simultaneously as they both take a puff. Yank is smiling. Lachie is contented. The curtain falls.

It is evening, a few days later. The boys are preparing for bed; letting down and tucking in their mosquito nets; taking turns at the washroom with toothbrushes and towels.

All but Lachie. And Kiwi. Kiwi is sitting on his bed. Lachie is standing over him, lecturing—

"And ye may remember, Kiwi, whin a humble member of the House asked Parliament fur thru'pence tae be added tae the auld age Pension. And wot happens?" Kiwi would rise, if he could, but Lachie pushes him back. "Ye would hae thought the Governmint was beng asked tae throw away the Crown jewels. Thru'pence, mind ye. Their Lordships leaps tae their feet— like Jack-in-the-boxes."

It is while Lachie is illustrating with his hands the rising of their Lordships that Kiwi manages to get to his feet—

"That's very interesting, Lachie, but let's finish it tomorrow," proposes Kiwi.

But Lachie has no idea of stopping. When Kiwi escapes into the washroom the lecturer turns on Yank. Yank is also loath to listen—

"Look—Buster—you've been talking steadily for a week," he says, with an affectionate pat of Lachie's shoulder. "Why don't you play your bagpipe?"

Yank manages to elude the conclusion of Lachie's argument, but Tommy gets it. Has Tommy any idea how much the Government is spending daily to prosecute the war? Tommy is sure it must be a fearful amount—

"Over a million pounds! A million pounds!" declaims Lachie. "And who are these magicians that gits money whir none was?" He is pointing an indisputable finger at Tommy. "The eky-nomists!"

"The who?"

"The eky-nomists!"

"Are they on our side?"

"And whir dew they git the money? They up and prints it."

"Then why don't they print more and increase me pay?"

"The more they prints—the less it's worth—that's why I advise ye—follow ma' example and poot your money in the land. Ye cannot print land."

"I'll put mine into my stomach. Beer!" giggles Tommy, ducking into the washroom.

For a moment Lachie is stopped. Then he spies Blossom fixing Kiwi's bed. In a minute he is facing Basuto, who listens confusedly.

"Dew ye realize wot it costs tae train each soldier poot intae the field?" demands Lachie. "Ten thousand pounds apiece! Now, if ye gave each mon of both sides just half of that—ye'd stop the war in two minutes and cut yur national debt in half!"

The arrival of Margaret rescues Blossom. Her order is "Lights out in ten minutes." Anything more that Lachie may have to say he can save until the next day. As he sits on his bed Margaret notices how weary he looks and is a little anxious. Lachie admits that he has not felt altogether fit—

"I've a wee weariness," he says. "Ma' hands sweat a bit and ma' feet seem swollen."

"You've been walking around the ward too much. And talking too much."

A man must walk and talk a bit, Lachie insists. But he does admit that maybe he hasn't been sleeping too well. It's probably because he has a problem to settle—

"May I help?" Margaret asks.

"Weel," Lachie answers, without looking at her, "it's nae easy fur a mon of ma' strong character tae admit he might have blundered. I'm nae wot ye think I am, Sister."

MARGARET—Are you sure you know what I think?

LACHIE—Ye probably think me wise and shrewd. Ye probably think I've the proper value on all ma' problems. Ye probably think there's naught confuses me.

MARGARET—Is that what I think?

LACHIE (*looking up at her*)—Aye. Ye see, Sister, I've nae always liked the human race. I'd nae love or respect fur any mon. I'd nae faith in the guidness of people. And whin the war came, it did nae help.

MARGARET—But you told me you had many friends in Scotland.

LACHIE—I lied. How cuid I? I'd nae education. Being purr as a church mouse, I'd nae money to squander. I'd naught tae interest or offer. A mon canna take wi' out gaen, too.

MARGARET—Why not?

LACHIE—A mon's pride.

MARGARET—But humility's a virtue, too.

LACHIE (*turning away from her*)—Boot nae a strong one. In ma' life befur, nae one ever liked me, and there was nae one I liked. Boot, I've changed.

MARGARET—Gracious—I'd hate to think it took a war to change you, Lachie.

LACHIE—Aye—boot it's true. I did nae ken a mon cuid be yur friend and want nothing frae ye. And now I've twenty-one years tae make up fur. I've got tae dew ma' share of the helping.

MARGARET—Lachie—if you've found a new set of values—don't feel that you must rush out and pay for them.

LACHIE—But it's like repentance, Sister. Ye've no idea how it grows inside me. I've a terrible need tae help.

MARGARET—Well, you've—ample time. When the lights are out, I'm going to bring you back something warm to drink. It'll put you to sleep.

LACHIE—If it's nae trouble tae ye.

MARGARET—No trouble at all. I'll have Yank give you your massage.

Tommy is back from the washroom and ready for bed. Before he turns in Lachie has a suggestion to make. Has Tommy a job waiting for him at home? Well, Tommy's old lady is his job. Her father owns a pub. But, insists Lachie, working for relations is no good—

"As ye ken, I've a bit of land in Scotland and it occurred to me that ye might like a place tae visit and rest a bit. There'd always be tobacco tae smoke and bread tae eat and a guid chair of yur own tae sit and talk in."

"Thank you for the offer, Lachie, but if I ever get away from me old lady—it will have to be farther than Scotland."

It is while Yank is rubbing him that Lachie repeats his offer. "Yank. As ye know, I've a wee hoose in Scotland. I was thinking that whin the war is done—if ye've no place tae go tae but America— Ye cuid come and live in ma hoose as long as ye wanted."

"Thanks, Buster, but when that time comes, I'm headed straight home."

No, Yank admits, he has no occupation to return to, but he has his gal. And he's pretty much in love with her. Yank is expecting that Old Cobwebs will sign his papers tomorrow and the next day he will be on his way.

"It'll nae be the same wi' ye gone," mutters Lachie, looking steadily at Yank. "Most likely I'll never hear of ye agaen."

"When I get married, I'll send you a tinted picture of Niagara Falls."

"And I'll send ye a photo of ma' hoose in Scotland."

"Send me a picture of yourself in that damned kilt. Looks like it's the only way I'll ever see it."

"Ye're sure tomorrow will be yur last day wi' us?"

"Unless Old Cobwebs changes his mind."

"I was planning on wearing ma' kilt the day I went back tae ma' regiment. But if ye liked . . ."

Yank stops rubbing. "Buster—you don't mean you might change your mind?"

"I was thinking—if ye poot a value on it—I cuid wear ma' kilt in yur honor instead."

"Look—Lachie—wear it for me tomorrow and I'll take your picture. I just got two new rolls of film from h-home."

"Dew ye ken—I've never had ma' photo took?" Lachie is a little excited.

"Then we'll take it tomorrow."

"Aye—I'll wear ma' kilt. But ye'll hae tae let me pay fur the film."

The rubbing's over. Yank is ready "to hit the sack," and turn out his light. Digger and Kiwi are in from the washroom, also ready to turn in. Neither can make it, however, before Lachie has invited them to take advantage of his ownership of the wee hoose in Scotland. But Digger has his own plans. He is going to collect his kid and his darling and carry them back to Australia as fast as he can make it. "Gawd! Australia!" sighs Digger. "When I think of it I get a toothache in my heart."

As for Kiwi, once he gets back to New Zealand, nothing will ever get him away again.

There is no one left now but Blossom. Lachie starts toward the Basuto's bed, but changes his mind—

"Naw—they'd nae understand ye in Scotland," he mutters.

He is giving Kiwi's netting and Yank's netting an extra tuck in when Margaret comes back with a warm drink to make him sleep better.

Lachie is still full of the adventure of having found so many friends. The fact that, of their own will, they have promised to write to him from all over the world is wonderful. "No matter where I go agaen in ma' life—I'm nae alone," he says.

So conscious is Lachie of the great blessing that has come to him, he feels that he must certainly do something about it. To owe so much is a great torment to him—

"If it's the guidness in ma' fellowman I've wronged—weel—I cuid turn ma' farm intae a place tae go fur wounded lads wi' nae home of their own."

"Slowly, Lachlen. Remember, 'Sorrow's born in the Hasty Heart.' "

LACHIE—I'm nae hasty. I know ma' duty. I cuid nae be a preacher—I know naught aboot God. And I'm nae so sure I owe ma' friends tae God: I did nae praying.

MARGARET—You simply can't stand being indebted, can you?

LACHIE—I can nae write a buuk. I've nae schooling. I've only ma' wish tae help—and ma' two hands—and ma' land tae gi' away.

MARGARET—Lachie—if you would only— (*She decides to make sure the others are asleep.*) Wait a minute. (*She uses flash-*

light on other beds, then returns to him.) Lachie, instead of things you own—why don't you share yourself with your fellow-man? We'd be much richer. I know that I am—for the things you've shared with me already.

LACHIE—Ye can nae mean me, Sister.

MARGARET—But I do. As a human being, I don't suppose I have any real—oh—individuality. I'm the people I've met. I'm a mixture of everything I've read and seen. I've stolen a virtue here—and a weakness there. I'm everyone I ever loved.

LACHIE—And ye've taken something frae me?

MARGARET—Without your knowing it.

LACHIE—Do ye know something, Sister? If I'd nae stopped ma' bit of shrapnel, I'd nae hae known I cuid be sae content wi' ma'self. I had tae be hurt tae learn.

MARGARET—No—I don't think you *had* to be hurt. But there was good in it.

LACHIE (*pondering*)—Dew ye suppose the world wuid be a healthier place if moor people were sick?

MARGARET—Gracious—I don't know. . . . And now you must sleep.

LACHIE—I'll nae sleep this nicht. Ah, where are the words tae free ma' heart?

MARGARET—Have you been as happy with us, Lachie, as you've ever been in your life?

LACHIE—I think—I've shared a moment wi' Kings.

MARGARET—Good night, Lachie.

LACHIE (*stopping her*)—Sister Margaret—dew ye ken ye've gaen me something too—wi'out yur knowing it?

MARGARET—What, Lachie?

LACHIE—I'm nae sure wot it is. But it's something I ne'er had befur—something that makes me know when ye leave the room even whin I can nae see ye go.

MARGARET (*putting her hand on his shoulder*)—That's very sweet.

LACHIE (*pressing her hand to his cheek*)—Ah—ye lovely, lovely angel.

MARGARET—You shouldn't have done that.

LACHIE (*anxious and grateful*)—Aye—I'd nae right.

MARGARET (*looking down at his upturned face and cupping it in her hands*)—No right at all.

She turns and leaves him. He rises to watch her go and when she has gone he goes quickly to get his bagpipe. He sits on the

end of his bed and starts to blow up the pipe. Then he realizes
his friends are asleep. Gently he folds up the bagpipe and tiptoes to return it to its hook.

The curtain falls.

ACT III

The following afternoon Nurse Margaret has lined the boys
up and is about to snap a camera at them. They are grouped at
the foot of Tommy's bed. Blossom has been posed in back,
next to Kiwi. They're the tall ones. In front is Tommy and
next to him Lachie, wearing his kilt. Yank and Digger are at
the other side of Lachie.

They are a grim lot, and Margaret is having a hard time trying
to get a pleasant look out of them. If Lachie can't smile a little
more—"I'm nae a cinema star," protests the Scot—perhaps he
can frown a little less. She finally has to take Tommy out of the
line and let him kneel on the bed to get them into a more compact group. With a final warning that now is the time to smile,
she counts three for a time exposure, and the picture is taken.

Lachie is about to retire back of the screens around his bed to
put his kilt away when Margaret pleads for a single picture of
him. She has all the others. But Lachie is not for a solo picture.
He could "nae face it alone." But when there is a chorus of
pleas from the others he finally agrees.

Margaret poses Lachie near the foot of Yank's bed. The
others are variously grouped out of range. While Lachie is trying to think of something to do with his hands, and Margaret is
trying to get him in a favorable position, Tommy gets an idea.
Reaching for the flyswatter, and crawling over Yank's bed, he
tries to lift the back of Lachie's kilt. The question of what a
Scot wears underneath may now be settled once for all. The
others watch the maneuver with mounting interest. Margaret is
forced at one time to order Tommy out of the picture, but he
manages to wiggle back.

With Lachie posed, his arms crossed, but nary a smile on his
face, Margaret finally is forced to snap what she can get.

"You're t-t-terrific!" protests a laughing Yank.

"I thought ye were ma' friends," pouts Lachie.

"I'm sorry, Lachie, but a mad Scot in a kilt is t-t-terrific," and
Yank's laughter increases.

Lachie starts again for the screen, but the others call him back.
They want to have another look at the kilt. Can't he walk
around a bit? He can. He marches to the door, turns sharply

and marches back again. Every time he passes the bed on which Tommy, or Kiwi, or Digger is sitting one of them reaches out and tries to get a quick look under the skirts of the kilt. This failing, they flatter Lachie into making quick turns, that they may see how gracefully the kilt swishes. And what would happen if he had to whirl? Lachie is just starting to whirl when Margaret comes back.

Some of them, orders Margaret, will have to go over to Ward C and bring back a bath-tub. Yank is a volunteer, but Lachie asks him to wait. There's something Lachie wants to know. When was it that Yank first knew that he wanted to get married? It was the first time he kissed his gal, Yank frankly confesses—

"If a guid girl kisses ye—it's an encouraging sign, is it nawt?" Lachie is quite earnest.

"Good or bad, it's encouraging any way you look at it."

"And something happens that ye can nae explain away?"

"Oh, I could explain it all right—but it doesn't help."

"I think I'd like to wed. I think."

"Aren't you sure?"

"Aye—that's ma' problem. Do ye think I've a right tae ask a lass tae be ma' wife? Now—wi' things like they are? (YANK *does not answer.*) Why do you hesitate?"

"What do you mean by—'with things like they are'?"

"Weel, if I was to wed now, I'd hae tae return tae ma' regiment. Wuid that be fair tae ma' bride?"

"L-l-look, B-buster—you mean—" Yank is pointing to the door of Margaret's office.

"Aye. Bonnie Sister Margaret."

"B-but you can't."

"She's nae married."

"L-look, Lachie—everybody falls in love with his nurse—it's natural. I'll bet every patient that's been in this ward has fallen in love with Sister Margaret, for a while. She l-looks after us and she's g-good to us. But that doesn't mean she loves us. You might be making a mistake to think it means anything else."

"Aye—that's why I wanted your advice. You're a fellow-scot. (YANK *turns in amazement.*) Did ye ever hear of Sister Margaret kissing a patient?"

"Well, she hasn't k-k-kissed me."

"Then if she kissed a man of her own free will, it wuid mean she meant tae—encourage him?"

"Did she kiss you?"

"Aye."

"Oh."

Again Yank hesitates, and protests. Lachie should know that women often kiss men they have no thought of marrying. If Margaret had kissed him it probably meant something, but—

"I lay awake the whole night wondering how ma' fortune cuid be saw great. Still—I've nae wish tae make a fool of ma' self."

Finally Yank gives in. If Lachie insists on proposing, hell, let him go ahead. This is as good a time as any. A moment later, when Margaret comes in with medicine for Lachie, Yank takes Blossom out to clear the ward for romance.

Lachie doesn't want the Medical Officer's pills that Margaret has brought, though he gulps them to please Margaret, but he does want to talk. He has a proposal of marriage to make and he thinks perhaps Margaret had better be seated while he makes it.

"I told you once that I had na plans fur marriage in ma' future," Lachie begins. "Ye may recall—"

"Vividly."

LACHIE—Weel, I've said some things I've cause tae regret. Among them was ma' attitude on marriage.

MARGARET—Lachie, you mustn't feel that—

LACHIE—Please dinnae interrupt me. I'm nae much of a man on the surface but I've a great and powerful will tae work. I've a wee butt-n-ben in Scotland—which ye know aboot. Ma' health is guid, regardless of the Colonel's spite. I've a fearful temper—but I dinna think I'll ever make ye suffer fur it. I'll dew ma' best. Until I get out of the army, I've ma' pay. Ye know wot it is and I'll sign it over tae ye. I'll gie ye all I can. Ye'll never want fur food and ye'll never worry aboot rent. I've wurked since I was seven. I've been a cabin boy, a seaman, a carpenter, a farmer, a miner, a stevedore, and a staff sergeant. I can always work fur ye. I'm twenty-one. I'm nae legitimate. Ma' mother was nae wed. I've good teeth. I'm nae tattooed. I hope ye'll nae be hasty in considering ma' proposal.

MARGARET (*sitting with hands over her eyes*)—Lachie, are you offering me your life, because you think you owe me something?

LACHIE—I offer ye ma' heart, because it does me nae guid wi' out ye.

MARGARET (*rising and turning away from him*)—Oh, Lachie— it isn't simple.

LACHIE—There's anoother in yur life?

MARGARET—It isn't that.

LACHIE—Ye dinna share ma' feeling? (*He waits. Drops down.*) I've made ye unhappy. I presumed too much. Can ye forgive me?

MARGARET (*turning on him as her confused emotions pour forth*)—Oh, you wretched, stubborn little man. *Why must I love you?*

LACHIE—Please—ye confuse me. Do ye—or don't ye?

MARGARET—God help us—I do.

LACHIE (*staring at her*)—I can nae believe it. (*Takes her hands.*) Ye'll marry me?

MARGARET—If you want me. Must I always kiss you first?

LACHIE (*cupping his hand around her face, kisses her gently— a little awkwardly, then seizes her in an embrace of emotional release. He breaks away and holds her at arm's length*)—Ah— ma' Bonnie Maggie.

MARGARET (*laughing*)—Oh, dear—not Maggie.

LACHIE (*both sitting at foot of* TOMMY's *bed*)—I'll dew naught to displease.

MARGARET—No need for promises.

LACHIE (*suddenly*)—But how can ye care fur me!

MARGARET—And no doubts.

LACHIE—Ah—nae. Just sae ye dew. Just sae ye dew.

Tommy, Kiwi and Digger have brought the bath-tub and taken it to the washroom. The matron is waiting for Margaret and she must go. "Lachie—there are many things I'd like to say to you, and I probably never shall," she is saying, as she kisses him. "We've suddenly crossed many rivers. Let's not waste time looking back."

Lachie is so happy, he tells Yank, he has a notion he'd like to play his bagpipe. He'll be wanting Yank to stand up with him when the date's set. And now he thinks he'll put his kilt away and rest a bit.

Lachie is back of the screen, changing, when the boys come back. Here's another chance to settle their bet. Craftily, quietly, they dispose themselves around Lachie's bed. Tommy has the best view through a crack of the screens. As he watches he pantomimes Lachie's movements. He mimics the Scot peeling off his shirt. He indicates that he is scratching his back. He reaches down—

At this moment the Colonel comes through the door. He watches for a second. "Just what is this all about?" he demands.

"We was just settling a bet, sir," explains Tommy, snapping to attention. The others take positions at the foot of their respective beds. "It's kilts—kilts, sir."

"Where is the orderly? Where is the sister?"

"I d-don't know. She just stepped out, sir."

"Well, where's Sgt. McLachlen?"

"He's in there, sir."

"Move the screen away. I want to talk to him."

As Yank and Kiwi move the screens, Lachie turns to face the Colonel. He has changed to his blues. Yes, he had taken the pills the Colonel sent over, but he is prepared, as a British soldier, to stand on his rights and not take any more.

"You men wait outside," the Colonel orders, turning to the others. They quickly disappear.

When they have gone, the Colonel resumes. He has been having a talk with the D.M.S. Before he had moved Lachie over to this ward he had asked G.H.Q. about the possibility of having him flown back to Scotland. He was told that his request was preposterous. There were too many priorities. Then he had decided to keep Lachie here.

"Ah—have you got along all right? Satisfied?" The Colonel is tugging nervously at his mustache.

"Aye. There's guid men here, sir," Lachie assures him.

"Well, I've just had a call from Army." The Colonel is sitting on the foot of Yank's bed. "Someone at G.H.Q. has decided you're more important than the waiting list."

LACHIE—Ye moost be joking, sir. I'm a sergeant. Of course, in the Camerons.

COLONEL—Sergeant or Brigadier, there's passage booked for you tomorrow, if I can get you to the Wing Commander. You're being given an A-1 priority. You can be in Scotland inside of three days. Do you want to go?

LACHIE—It's a great temptation. Whin cuid I return?

COLONEL (hesitating a beat)—You wouldn't return.

LACHIE—Ye mean I'd nae be permitted tae return tae ma' regiment?

COLONEL—Sergeant—I've been given a direct order. I disagree with that order, but I'm a soldier. I argued against it for an hour. Well, I have no choice. There seems to be a regulation somewhere—probably dates from the Boer War—anyhow the D.M.S. remembers it and says you must be given the full facts of your case.

LACHIE—But I've been gaen the facts.

COLONEL—When you came in here with the shrapnel in your kidney, there was a chance you'd recover.

LACHIE—Aye. I have.

COLONEL—You recovered from the operation—yes. But you've one kidney left—a bad one. I know you feel quite well but that one kidney is destined to—collapse.

LACHIE—Aye. Then wot dew ye dew?

COLONEL—Nothing. We can't give a man a new kidney. There's nothing that surgery or medicine can do to help. Do you understand?

LACHIE—Aye. And the mon?

COLONEL—Waits.

LACHIE—How long?

COLONEL—A week or two more.

LACHIE (*silent for a moment*)— That's nae much time.

COLONEL—I didn't tell you, Sergeant, because there seemed nothing to gain. Now—I've been ordered to tell you.

LACHIE—I thought ye had a spite on me.

COLONEL—Hardly. I wish I could give you a kidney of mine. I've damned little use for two. Would you like to go back?

LACHIE—Ma' brain is numb, and I must think.

COLONEL—G.H.Q. feels that you can do your country a further service. They'll make a hero of you. Fly you back with a great deal of fanfare. I know that part of it won't mean anything to you. But you'll see Scotland again. The alternative is to stay with us—stay here with your friends. (*At the word "friends" a bitter suspicion comes to* LACHIE. *He lifts his head slowly—and speaks—dreading to hear the answer to his question.*)

LACHIE (*slowly*)—Did the lads in the ward know aboot me, sir?

COLONEL—Yes. I wanted things made as pleasant as possible for you. I asked them to help you.

LACHIE—And the sister?

COLONEL—Naturally, she had to know.

LACHIE—I'd like tae go back tae Scotland, sir.

COLONEL (*rising*)—I can get you down to Calcutta in the morning in plenty of time—if that's your decision.

LACHIE (*rising with determination—facing window*)—That's ma' choice.

COLONEL (*rising*)—In the meantime—?

LACHIE—I'd like tae be left tae me'self.

COLONEL—Certainly—certainly. (*Takes a step towards* LACHIE's *unrelenting back.*) I wish I could say something wise and warm and reassuring.

LACHIE (*whirling on him*)—Ye can spare me that. I've had enough pity, thank ye!

COLONEL—If I can be of service to you, call on me—I'll take care of your papers and arrange for your transport.

The Colonel leaves. Lachie is pulling the screens back around his bed when the boys come back. They are curious to know what Old Cobwebs had on his mind. They're proud of the way Lachie stood up to him.

Yank has taken the roll of films from the camera. He will take it over to be developed. Before he can move Lachie has snatched the film out of his hand, unrolled it and thrown it on the floor. He has no answers to their astonished queries as to what's the matter. He steps inside the screens and closes them.

Margaret has come from her office. They turn for an explanation to her. She tells them what has happened. They are all a little stunned.

Now Lachie reappears. He is carrying the box with the kilt and all the presents in it. He leaves it on Yank's bed. "I'll return these tae ye," he says, bitterly. Turning to Margaret, he adds, "I'll be gaen away in the morning." There is pain in his eyes. "If ye've any decency in ye, will ye kindly nae speak tae me. Leave me in peace behind ma' screen. I'll nae wish tae see ye—any of ye."

"Now, wait a minute, Lachie." Yank is standing before him with his hand outstretched.

"I'll break yur face if ye poot a hand on me."

"You'll need us, Lachie. You'll need us," pleads Margaret.

"I'll need nae one," he says, turning to face the others. "I should hae known ye'd be like all the rest. Well, ye bought ma' friendship cheaply—fur the price of a kilt. I shuid hae poot a higher value on ma' pride. How righteous ye must hae felt in yur pity and guidness. I'll nae let you hurt me agaen."

He has gone back to the screen. The others stand silent and stunned as he closes himself in. The curtain falls.

It is the next morning. The screens have been put away. Lachie is finishing the packing of his duffle bag. His bagpipe, in its green case, lies near by. The men, subdued and quiet, are sitting on their beds.

Yank, collecting the breakfast plates and bowls, notices that Lachie has not touched his food. He knows the Scot is leaving in a few minutes.

"I was leaving myself this afternoon," says Yank, trying to be friendly; "but if you stayed, Lachie, I'd spend my two weeks' leave here with you. If you liked." There is no answer. "Well, I'm d-d-damned sorry to see you go." Still no answer. "I hope things won't be too bad." He is holding out his hand. "I'd like to say good-by now."

"Ye've said it," snaps Lachie.

Margaret brings Lachie's papers. They'll send him word as soon as his transport is ready.

"I'll hae ma' kit ready in a moment," says Lachie, without looking at her.

Yank is back. He asks if he can help with Lachie's bags. There is no answer. Kiwi, Digger and Tommy all offer to help. The silence is still heavy as the boys go out.

"May I stay and talk to you?" asks Margaret.

LACHIE—There's naught tae say.

MARGARET (*sitting on* YANK's *bed*)—Oh, my poor stubborn darling—please hear me. I'll never have another chance to talk to you.

LACHIE—There's naught tae say.

MARGARET—We wanted to save you all the unhappiness we could. Was that betrayal, Lachie?

LACHIE—Did ye forgit I was a soldier? Didn't ye know I'd faced dying before?

MARGARET—I can't let you walk out of here despising us.

LACHIE (*tying his bag*)—Ye can nae prevent me.

MARGARET—Do you think the way we feel about you less honest—less genuine—because we knew to begin with?

LACHIE (*looking at her for the first time*)—Dare ye answer that truthfully?

MARGARET—Of course we were more considerate because we knew. What kind of people would we be if we'd been indifferent?

LACHIE—The kind of people I shuid hae known ye wuid be. Ye're easy tae find the world over. The kind that will beat a mon, rob him, hound him, slander and betray him—and think it fair game unless he's dying. And then ye're frightened. Yur conscience drives ye tae guidness. Weel, I find yur sudden virtue nae worthy of an animal. I dinna thank ye fur wot ye did to me.

MARGARET—We're your friends, Lachie, no matter how you

acquired us. The only ones you have in the world. Don't value us lightly. Stay with us.

LACHIE—Ye made me think fur a little while I'd misjudged ma' fellowman. Ye gae me a fool's religion tae die on. If ye only knew the bitterness I moost thank ye fur.

MARGARET—Do you believe that the *only* reason we were kind to you was because we knew?

LACHIE—Do ye dare deny that it didna't help?—that it didna't goad ye on?

MARGARET—No—I can't deny that.

LACHIE—And was it easy tae like me?

MARGARET—No! It wasn't!

LACHIE (*almost shouting*)—And shuid I be proud that ye liked me only because I was tae die?

MARGARET—If that were the only reason—no.

LACHIE—I'll write a book, says I. I'll preach the wurd of God. I'll gae ma' hame tae ma' brothers, I says. Oh, how ye moost hae wanted tae laugh.

MARGARET—Lachie—Lachie—please listen to me. Forget everything but this: for a little while you learned the meaning of friendship. Didn't you say that you'd shared a moment with Kings?

LACHIE—If I moost die to learn tae love ma' fellowman—then I'll dew wi'out him. It's too high a price tae pay.

MARGARET—Oh, darling—what difference does it make why people are good?

LACHIE—I've done wi' ma' packing.

MARGARET—Would you hate it if I kissed you good-by? You did ask me to be your wife, you know.

LACHIE—Let me be, please.

Margaret goes to the door and calls Yank. As soon as she sees about the transport she will want him to help Lachie with his bags. The others drift in. Suddenly Blossom, noting bags and sensing Lachie's departure, takes a string of beads from around his neck and holds them out to the Scot. "Blossom," he mutters. "Bak-sheesh!" His gift ignored, the Basuto takes Lachie's hand and puts the beads in it.

"Leave me be!" shouts Lachie, throwing the beads against Blossom.

With this, Yank springs forward, blazing mad. Grabbing Lachie by the lapels of his coat he holds him fast. "I want to tell you something before you go," cries Yank. "There's just something mean in you that only a bullet can cure. You've been sore your whole life because things didn't come easy for you. So you took your spite out on every person you ever met. You don't want our friendship? Well—you didn't pay for it. You didn't *earn* it. You got it for *nothing*. So what are you kicking about? And now the pay-off! You're sore because you didn't know when you were going to die! Does anyone else know when he's going to die? No. But you had to know. You're the kind of hero that likes to bet on a sure thing. You don't know what courage is. You've been afraid to live since the day you were born. What do you think life is, Buster, a certified check?"

"Ye've tricked and cheated me! I risked your friendship, but ye didna gie me friendship—ye gae me pity."

"Did Blossom pity you? (*A pause.*) He didn't know you were going to die. He liked you. He wanted to give you something. And what do you do? You throw his friendship back in his face. *It's a good thing you're going to die.* A guy like you causes a lot of unhappiness in the world. I wouldn't save you if I could. That's the way I feel."

Yank has stormed back to his bed. He is struggling with the camera, putting in a new film, when Margaret, attracted by the shouting, comes to find out what is happening. Yank tells her. Lachie has gone back to his bed and sits there, moody and brooding.

"Lachie, your transport is here," announces Margaret. "Are you ready?" He does not answer. "Are you ready to go?"

"Aye."

"Yank—will you carry his kit for him?"

"No. He doesn't want any help. Let him manage alone."

"It's your last chance to help him."

"He doesn't have to go. He knows he's wrong but he's so d-d-damned stubborn he'll die alone rather than admit it. N-n-no."

Margaret turns to Digger. Digger does not move. She is about to appeal to Blossom when Lachie drags his bag off the bed, gets his bagpipe and starts for the door. "I need nae help. I'll go alone," he says. He is moving slowly with his head down.

Immediately Yank moves into action. Now that everything is clear, they can get some pictures! He presses the camera into Margaret's hands and calls to the others to get back into their picture pose.

In the excitement Lachie has stopped short. "I'd be willing to consider remaining if ye'd admit ye wronged me," he mutters.

"L-l-look—if you think we're going to beg you to stay—you're wasting your time. Get the picture, Sister."

"I'll nae gi' ye anoother chance," warns Lachie.

"We're ready if you are, Sister. Go ahead!" calls Yank.

Before Margaret can snap the camera Lachie has thrown down his bags and rushed over to her. They can't take a picture with his film. He paid for those films. They are his private property. Nor will he take his money back, even though Yank is quick to offer it. Which starts Yank off, excitedly reciting his Bible chapters—"Genesis, Exodus, Leviticus" . . .

"Oh, don't be spiteful, Lachie, please," pleads Margaret.

"Aw, let him take it!" Yank has reached for the camera and is starting to take out the film. "The hell with him! But I wish I could understand what makes a man want to die despised and friendless."

Lachie turns to look at them. He sees no sign of surrender in their eyes. Beaten, he sinks down on the foot of his bed. "I dinna want to die alone," he cries, with a smothered sob.

Margaret is kneeling beside him. "Lachlen, why don't you say what you want to say?" she says softly.

"It's nae easy fur me to say it." He has risen and walked across the room. His back is to them as he continues: "All my life I hated what I cuid nae have. It saved ma' pride. Boot now I've nae the time to squander on ma' pride. I want tae stay. If I moost beg ye tae take me back—then I beg ye. Cuid I hae ma' bed?"

"Why don't you get back into your blues, Buster?" asks Yank.

"Change in my office," suggests Margaret.

The blues are neatly folded on Lachie's pillow. He takes them and slowly disappears in Margaret's office.

"I wish I had a mother," explodes Yank. "I feel like kicking her in the teeth."

Perhaps Lachie would feel better if he could play his bagpipe, Digger suggests. Tommy doesn't think he would have enough wind left in him. Kiwi thinks perhaps Margaret should go in and see him. But Margaret doesn't agree—

"He's swallowed his pride," she says. "It will take him a moment or two to digest it."

They had better be finishing the picture, Yank thinks, before they grow long, gray beards. They have rushed back into position. Margaret is looking through the camera and urging them to get closer together.

"Are we very 'andsome looking, Sister?" Tommy wants to know.

"Not very handsome—but very wonderful," says Margaret, as she gets the focus. "One—two—"

Before she can say "Three!" Lachie has reappeared. He has put on his kilt and stands for a moment looking at them, obviously ill at ease—

"Wuid ye be sae guid as tae let me have ma' photo taken wi' ye?" he asks. No one speaks. "It *is* ma' film, tho' ye needn't consider that," he adds hastily.

"Your place is here," says Yank, pointing to the spot next to himself.

Lachie puts on his side-cap at a properly jaunty angle. Seeing Blossom's beads, he picks them up and joins the group.

"Ready . . ." Margaret is looking in the camera. Yank puts his arm around Lachie's shoulder. Lachie looks up and smiles. "It is a smile he has saved all his life." As Yank smiles back, Lachie sighs contentedly, crosses his arms for the picture and looks toward the camera—

"One . . . two . . . three . . . ! That's it!"

Lachie has turned to smile at Yank again. Suddenly he leaps into the air, holding his kilt down behind him with two hands.

"*Help!* Don't ye dew that!" he shouts. He turns quickly to face Tommy, kneeling on his bed.

"I found out! I peeked! I found out!" cries Tommy, laughing uproariously.

THE CURTAIN FALLS

THE GLASS MENAGERIE
A Drama in Seven Scenes

By Tennessee Williams

IT was while he was reading and seriously considering the script of a comedy that had the promise of being "sure-fire" box office, by title at least, that Tennessee Williams' "The Glass Menagerie" was brought to Eddie Dowling by a hopeful play broker. Being busy with one script, Mr. Dowling turned the Williams play over to Mrs. Dowling, whom older playgoers will remember as Ray Dooley, comedienne, and continued reading "The Passionate Congressman."

Shortly thereafter Mrs. Dowling appeared in the doorway of the Dowling study and announced that in her judgment Mr. Dowling should for the moment forget the affairs of the Congressman, however passionate, and pay heed to "The Glass Menagerie."

"You may not like it," quoth she, "and it may not make you any money, but if you don't read it now, and someone else should buy it, I'd never hear the last of it."

Having been previously well advised by Mrs. Dowling, Mr. Dowling did as she suggested. Immediately he found himself sharing her enthusiasm. Next day, in conference with Louis A. Singer, a Brooklynite eager to advance the production costs of the Congressman play, Mr. Dowling said, "Louis, I have a script here that I like. It is nothing that would appeal to you, and I don't believe it will make any money, but I want to do it."

"What's the name of it?" inquired Mr. Singer.

" 'The Glass Menagerie,' " answered Mr. Dowling.

"Doesn't sound like much," said Mr. Singer. "Let me read it."

He read it, and, for a backer, made a quick and definite decision. "It still doesn't sound like much, but if you want to do it, count me in."

Again Mr. Dowling pondered. Several people advised against his taking chances with a vague and slightly visionary "memory play," and an author practically unknown to Broadway, when he had another play that looked sure. But in the end he decided in favor of "The Glass Menagerie." It represented the sort of thing he wanted to do in the theatre, whether it made money or not.

The play was rehearsed in New York, produced in Chicago. The Western reviewers were enthused, but those playgoers who attended the early performances appeared cool, even indifferent, to the proceedings. At the end of the first week Mr. Singer put up the money to meet the payroll. Also at the end of the second week. And the third. Meantime, Chicago critics kept up a steady bombardment of praise for the play and for its performance, especially the performance of Laurette Taylor in the leading feminine role.

The fourth week about "broke even," as the showmen say. The fifth week turned a profit. And from that time until the play was withdrawn from Chicago, that it might be given an Easter week opening in New York, there were nothing but profitable weeks. A fortnight after the New York opening March 31 the New York Drama Critics' Circle voted "The Glass Menagerie" the best play written by an American and produced in New York during the season of 1944-45.

The New York drama critics were as ecstatic in their praise as their Chicago brethren had been and the immediate response of the playgoing public kept Mr. Williams' play entertaining capacity audiences for months on end.

"Being a 'memory play,' 'The Glass Menagerie' can be presented with unusual freedom of convention," Mr. Williams wrote in a descriptive preface to this exceptionally human comedy. "Expressionism and all other unconventional techniques in drama have only one valid aim, and that is a closer approach to truth. When a play employs unconventional techniques it is not, or certainly shouldn't be, trying to escape its responsibility of dealing with reality, or interpreting experience, but is actually, or should be, attempting to find a closer approach, a more penetrating and vivid expression, of things as they are. The straight realistic play, with its genuine frigid air and authentic ice cubes, its characters that speak exactly as its audience speaks, corresponds to the academic landscape, and has the same virtue of a photographic likeness."

And again: "Another extra-literary accent in this play is provided by the use of music. A single recurring tune, 'The Glass Menagerie,' is used to give emotional emphasis to suitable passages. This tune is like circus music, not when you are on the grounds, nor in the immediate vicinity of the parade, but when you are at some distance and very likely thinking of something else."

His description of his four characters is equally definite. Of Amanda he writes: "A little woman of great but confused vitality clinging frantically to another time and place. . . . She is not paranoic, but her life is paranoia. There is much to admire in Amanda, and as much to love and pity as there is to laugh at. Certainly she has endurance, and a kind of heroism, and though her foolishness makes her unwittingly cruel at times there is tenderness in her slight person."

"Amanda, having failed to establish contact with reality, continues to live vitally in her illusions, but Laura's situation is even graver. A childhood illness has left her crippled, one leg slightly shorter than the other, and held in a brace. . . . Stemming from this, Laura's separation increases until she is like a piece of her own glass collection, too exquisitely fragile to remove from the shelf."

"Tom, Amanda's son and the narrator of the play, a poet with a job in a warehouse. His nature is not remorseless, but to escape from a trap he has to act without pity."

Jim O'Connor, the caller, "is just a nice, ordinary young man."

Turning to the play we discover, when the gradually increased lighting permits, that the Wingfield apartment "is in the rear of the building; one of those vast hive-like conglomerations of cellular living units that flower as warty growths in overcrowded urban centers of lower middle-class population. . . ." . . . "The apartment faces an alley, and is entered by a fireescape, a structure whose name is an accidental poetic truth, for all these huge buildings are always burning with the slow and implacable fires of human desperation. . . . We view the landing in profile." . . .

Two rooms are visible: "The living room, which also serves as a sleeping room for Tom," and the dining room, "which is divided by a wide arch, or second proscenium, with faded rose-colored portieres, or second curtain."

There are bits of transparent glass on spidery shelves about the two rooms. Also a blown-up photograph of Tom and Laura's father—"The face of a very handsome young man in a doughboy's cap of the First World War. He is gallantly smiling, ineluctably smiling, as if to say—'I will be smiling forever.'"

As the play's action is begun, Tom, the narrator, dressed as a merchant sailor, leans casually against the ironwork of the fire-escape landing. "His presence is hardly observed until he strikes a match for a cigarette." From a night club across the alley come the strains of "St. Louis Blues." The music dies away as Tom begins to speak—

"Yes—I have tricks in my pocket, I have things up my sleeve," he is saying. "But I am the opposite of a stage magician. He gives you illusion that has the appearance of truth. I give you truth in the pleasant disguise of illusion. To begin with, I turn back time. I reverse it to that quaint period the thirties, when the huge middle-class of America was matriculating in a school for the blind. Their eyes had failed them, or they had failed their eyes, and so they were having their fingers pressed forcibly down on the fiery Braille alphabet of a dissolving economy. In Spain there was revolution. Here there was only shouting and confusion. In Spain there was Guernica. Here there were disturbances of labor, sometimes pretty violent, in otherwise peaceful cities such as Chicago, Cleveland—St. Louis. . . . This is the social background of the play."

From there Tom goes on to explain that the play is memory; that a memory play is dimly lighted; that it is sentimental and not realistic and that there is music because "in memory everything seems to happen to music." He introduces the characters of his mother, his sister and the gentleman caller who, Tom explains, is a symbol: "He is the long-delayed but always expected something that we live for."

There is also a fifth character who doesn't appear, except as a "larger-than-life-size photograph over the mantel." . . . "This is our father who left us a long time ago. He was a telephone man who fell in love with long distances—he gave up his job with the telephone company and skipped the light fantastic out of town. . . . The last we heard of him was a picture post-card from Mazatlan, on the Pacific coast of Mexico, containing a message of two words—'Hello—Good-by!' and no address. I think the rest of the play will explain itself. . . ."

As Tom steps into the scene and the lights brighten, Amanda and Laura are discovered sitting at a drop-leaf table, prepared to eat their dinner. They have been waiting for Tom to say grace. Amanda has also been waiting, apparently, for a chance to begin her correction of her son. She nags him about his table manners. He should chew his food more and he should not push it with his fingers. Food should be eaten leisurely and enjoyed.

The salivary glands should have a chance to function.

Tom is in no mood to accept correction. That is one reason he seldom enjoys a meal at home—he is always being told how to eat it. That's why he rushes through his meals—to get away from his mother's "hawk-like attention" to every bite he takes. Neither does he take kindly to her further suggestion that he smokes too much. When Amanda further insists that Laura should sit quiet at table, so she may "stay fresh and pretty—for gentlemen callers," Tom also knows well what that is leading up to—

"One Sunday afternoon in Blue Mountain," Amanda is saying, as she fetches a bowl of dessert from the kitchenette, "your mother received *seventeen!*—gentlemen callers! Why, sometimes there weren't chairs enough to accommodate them all. We had to send the nigger over to bring in folding chairs from the parish house."

"How did you entertain those gentlemen callers?" Tom wants to know.

"I understood the art of conversation!"

"I bet you could talk."

"Girls in those days *knew* how to talk, I can tell you."

"Yes?"

"They knew how to entertain their gentlemen callers. It wasn't enough for a girl to be possessed of a pretty face and a graceful figure—although I wasn't slighted in either respect—she also needed to have a nimble wit and a tongue to meet all occasions."

"What did you talk about?"

"Things of importance going on in the world! Never anything coarse or common or vulgar. My callers were gentlemen—all! Among my callers were some of the most prominent young planters of the Mississippi Delta—planters and sons of planters!"

As Amanda talks on "her face glows, her voice becomes rich and elegiac." There were, she remembers vividly, young Champ Laughlin, who later became vice president of the Delta Planters Bank; and Hadley Stevenson, who was drowned and left his widow a hundred and fifty thousand in government bonds. There were the Cutrere brothers, one of whom—Bates it was—was killed in a duel fought over her, and died with her picture in his pocket—

"And there was that boy that every girl in Delta had set her cap for! That beautiful, brilliant young Fitzhugh boy from Greene County!"

"What did he leave his widow?"

"He never married!—Gracious, you talk as though all my old admirers had turned up their toes to the daisies!"

"Isn't this the first you've mentioned that still survives?"

"That Fitzhugh boy went North and made a fortune—came to be known as the Wolf of Wall Street! He had the Midas touch, whatever he touched turned to gold! And I could have been Mrs. Duncan J. Fitzhugh, mind you! BUT—I picked your father!"

Laura has risen quickly. "Mother, let me clear the table."

"No, dear, you go in front and study your typewriter chart. Or practice your shorthand a little. Stay fresh and pretty!—It's almost time for our gentlemen callers to start arriving." . . . "How many do you suppose we're going to entertain this afternoon?"

This is too much for Tom. He has jumped to his feet with a groan, throwing down the paper he was trying to read.

"I don't believe we're going to receive any, Mother."

"What? No one—not one? You must be joking." Amanda is back at the table, laughing lightly. Laura nervously echoes the laugh as she slips between the portieres into the dining room. "Not one gentleman caller?" Amanda is repeating. "It can't be true! There must be a flood, there must be a tornado!"

"It isn't a flood, it's not a tornado, Mother. I'm just not popular like you were in Blue Mountain. . . ."

Tom utters another groan. Laura glances at him with a faint, apologetic smile. "Mother's afraid I'm going to be an old maid," she says. There is a catch in her voice.

The lights fade out.

SCENE II

A little later Laura is seated at a small table. In a bowl before her are several of her glass collection which she is washing and polishing. As she hears Amanda's step on the fireescape steps she thrusts the bowl of ornaments away and seats herself quickly before a diagram of a typewriter keyboard, "as though it held her spellbound."

Something has happened to Amanda. It is written in her face. "She has on one of those cheap or imitation velvety-looking cloth coats with imitation fur collar. Her hat is five or six years old, one of those dreadful cloche hats that were worn in the late twenties and she is clasping an enormous black patent leather pocketbook with nickel clasps and initials. This is her full-dress outfit, the one she usually wears to the D.A.R."

What has happened, it appears, was that Amanda, on her way to the D.A.R. meeting, had stopped in at Rubincam's Business College to find out how Laura was doing. And how shocked she was to find out that Laura had left the college some time ago! The college instructors barely remembered her—

" 'I wonder,' " one of them had said, " 'I wonder if you could be talking about that terribly shy little girl who dropped out of school after only a few days' attendance?' "

" 'No,' " I said, " 'Laura, my daughter, 's been going to school every day for the past six weeks!' "

" 'Excuse me,' " she said. "She took the attendance book out and there was your name, unmistakably printed, and all the dates you were absent until they decided that you had dropped out of the school."

"I still said: 'No, there must have been some mistake! There must have been some mix-up in the records!' And she said, 'No —I remember her perfectly now. Her hands shook so that she couldn't hit the right keys! The first time we gave a speed test, she broke down completely—was sick at the stomach and almost had to be carried into the wash-room! After that morning she never showed up any more. We phoned the house but never got any answer—while I was working at Famous and Barr, I suppose, demonstrating those— Oh! I felt so weak I could barely keep on my feet! I had to sit down while they got me a glass of water! Fifty dollars tuition, all of our plans—my hopes and ambitions for you—just gone up the spout, just gone up the spout like that."

It's true. Laura admits it. She has not been back to the business college since the humiliating experience of her illness. Those days her mother thought she was there she had gone walking. Even in Winter. Even with no more than her light coat to shield her. Mostly she had walked in the park. Occasionally she went where it was warm. Sometimes she did without lunch and went to a movie. Often she went to the art museum. And to the birdhouses at the Zoo. Every day she visited the penguins.

"You did all this to deceive me, just for deception?" demands Amanda. "Why?"

"Mother, when you're disappointed, you get that awful suffering look on your face, like the picture of Jesus' mother in the museum!"

"HUSH!"

"I couldn't face it."

Amanda is hopelessly fingering her huge pocketbook. "So

what are we going to do the rest of our lives? Stay home and watch the parades go by? Amuse ourselves with the glass menagerie, darling? Eternally play with those worn-out phonograph records your father left as a painful reminder of him? We won't have a business career—we've given that up because it gave us nervous indigestion!"

The picture is wearying to Amanda. She knows so well what becomes of unmarried women who are not prepared to occupy a position. She's seen such pitiful cases in the South—"little birdlike women without any nest—eating the crust of humility all their lives." . . . "Is that the future that we have mapped out for ourselves?" . . . "Of course some girls *do marry*. . . . Haven't you ever liked some boy?"

Yes. There was one boy. Laura had come across his picture a while ago, in her high school year book. Now she finds the heavy annual on the table and the boy's picture in it—

"His name was Jim," says Laura. "Here he is in 'The Pirates of Penzance.'"

"The what?"

LAURA—The operetta the senior class put on. He had a wonderful voice and we sat across the aisle from each other Mondays, Wednesdays and Fridays in the Aud. Here he is with the silver cup for debating! See his grin?

AMANDA (*absently*)—He must have had a jolly disposition . . .

LAURA—He used to call me—Blue Roses.

AMANDA—Why did he call you such a name as that?

LAURA—When I had that attack of pleurosis—he asked me what was the matter when I came back. I said pleurosis—he thought I said Blue Roses! So that's what he always called me after that. Whenever he saw me, he'd holler, "Hello, Blue Roses!" I didn't care for the girl that he went out with. Emily Meisenbach. Emily was the best-dressed girl at Soldan. She never struck me, though, as being sincere. . . . It says in the Personal Section—they're engaged. . . . That's six years ago!—they must be married by now.

AMANDA—Girls that aren't cut out for business careers usually wind up married to some nice man. Sister, that's what you'll do!

LAURA (*with a startled laugh*)—But, Mother—

AMANDA—Yes?

LAURA—I'm crippled!

AMANDA—Nonsense!—Laura.—I've told you never, never to

use that word. Why, you're not crippled, you just have a little defect—hardly noticeable, even! When people have some slight disadvantage like that, they cultivate other things to make up for it—develop charm—and vivacity—and—*charm!* That's all you have to do! (*She turns to the photograph.*) One thing your father had *plenty of*—was *charm!*

"The lights fade."

SCENE III

With the lights dimly up, Tom is speaking again from the fire-escape shadows. "After the fiasco at Rubicam's Business College," he is saying, "the idea of getting a gentleman caller for Laura began to play a more and more important part in Mother's calculations. It became an obsession. Like some archetype of the universal unconscious, the image of the gentleman caller haunted our small apartment. . . . An evening at home rarely passed without some allusion to this image, this specter, this hope. . . . Even when he wasn't mentioned, his presence hung in Mother's preoccupied look and in my sister's frightened, apologetic manner . . . hung like a sentence passed upon the Wingfields!"

Realizing the need of extra money that Winter, Tom explains, his mother had conducted a vigorous telephone campaign "roping in subscribers to one of those magazines for matrons called *The Home-maker's Companion.*" That is what Amanda is doing now, as the lights in the living room are raised. She has her friend, Ida Scott, also of the D.A.R., on the phone, and after she has inquired solicitously about Ida's sinus, she gets right down to business—

"Well, I just happened to notice that your subscription to the *Companion's* about to expire! Yes, it expires with the next issue, honey!—just when that wonderful new serial by Bessie Mae Hopper is getting off to such an exciting start. Oh, honey, it's something that you can't miss! You remember how 'Gone with the Wind' took everybody by storm? You simply couldn't go out if you hadn't read it. All everybody *talked* was Scarlett O'Hara. Well, this is a book that critics already compare to 'Gone with the Wind.' It's the 'Gone with the Wind' of the post-World War generation!—What?—Burning?—Oh, honey, don't let them burn, go take a look in the oven and I'll hold the wire! Heavens —I think she's hung up!"

Before the lights are on full the voices of Tom and Amanda are heard coming from the shadows back of the portieres, in front of which Laura is standing in a pool of light, her hands clenched and a panicky expression on her face.

Tom is protesting his disgust with his life at home. Amanda is trying to shut him up and to top his protests by assuring him with rough emphasis that he is a big idiot. No, she had not confiscated his books, as he claims. She had taken one terrible novel back to the library, yes— "That hideous book by that insane Mr. Lawrence. I cannot control the output of diseased minds or people who cater to them," she says, as Tom laughs wildly. "BUT I WON'T ALLOW SUCH FILTH BROUGHT INTO MY HOUSE! No, no, no, no, no!"

"House, house! Who pays the rent on it, who makes a slave of himself to—"

"Don't you dare to—!" Amanda is fairly screeching.

"No, no, *I* mustn't say things! *I've* got to just—"

"Let me tell you—!"

"I don't want to hear any more—!"

Tom has burst through the portieres. The lights now reveal "an upright typewriter and a wild disarray of manuscripts on the drop-leaf table. The quarrel was probably precipitated by Amanda's interruption of his creative labor."

Amanda has followed Tom into the living room, demanding shrilly that he WILL listen to her. Nor does she intend to let him escape by going out. She is convinced now that he has been doing things that he's ashamed of. She doesn't believe that he goes every night to the movies— "Nobody in their right minds goes to the movies as often as you pretend to," she sneers. Neither do they go at nearly midnight, and stay till 2 in the morning, and come home stumbling, "muttering to yourself like a maniac." And she is further convinced that, living as he does, doing the things he does, he is never in any fit condition to work—

"What right have you got to jeopardize your job?" demands Amanda. "Jeopardize the security of us all? How do you think we'd manage if you were—"

"Listen! You think I'm crazy *about* the warehouse?" He is bending fiercely toward the frail figure. "You think I'm in love with the Continental Shoemakers? You think I want to spend fifty-five *years* down there in that—*celotex interior* with *fluorescent* tubes? Look! I'd rather somebody picked up a crow-bar and battered out my brains—than go back mornings! I *GO!* Every time you come in yelling that God damn 'Rise and Shine! Rise and Shine!' I say to myself, 'How *lucky dead* people are!'

But I get up. I *go!* For sixty-five dollars a month I give up all that I dream of doing and being *ever!* And you say self—*self's* all I ever think of. Why, listen, if self is what I thought of, Mother, I'd be where *HE* is—*GONE!* (*Pointing to his father's picture.*) As far as the system of transportation reaches. Don't grab at me, Mother!"

"Where are you going?"

"I'm going to the *movies!*"

"I don't believe that lie!"

"I'm going to opium dens! Yes, opium dens, dens of vice and criminals' hang-outs, Mother. I've joined the Hogan gang, I'm a hired assassin, I carry a tommy-gun in a violin case! I run a string of cat-houses in the Valley! They call me Killer, Killer Wingfield. I'm leading a double-life, a simple, honest warehouse worker by day, by night a dynamic *czar* of the *Underworld,* Mother. I go to gambling casinos, I spin away fortunes on the roulette table! I wear a patch over one eye and a false mustache. Sometimes I put on green whiskers. On those occasions they call me—*El Diablo!* Oh, I could tell you things to make you sleepless! My enemies plan to dynamite this place. They're going to blow us all sky-high some night! I'll be glad, very happy, and so will you! You'll go up on a broomstick, over Blue Mountain with seventeen gentlemen callers! You ugly—babbling old—*witch.*"

Tom seizes his overcoat and lunges toward the door. At the door he is struggling into his coat as the women watch him, aghast. His arm catches in the sleeve. This infuriates him. Now he has torn the coat off and hurled it across the room. It strikes against Laura's collection. "There is a tinkle of shattered glass. Laura cries out as if wounded—"

"*My glass!*—menagerie . . ." She covers her face and turns away.

Amanda, still stunned and stupefied by the "ugly witch" has barely noticed what is happening. Now she recovers her speech—

"I won't speak to you—until you apologize!" she announces. Her voice is awful. She swings through the portieres and draws them together behind her.

Laura is clinging weakly to the mantel. Tom stares stupidly for a moment and then drops awkwardly on his knees beside the fallen glass. As he begins to pick it up he glances at Laura, "as if he would speak but couldn't."

The lights fade.

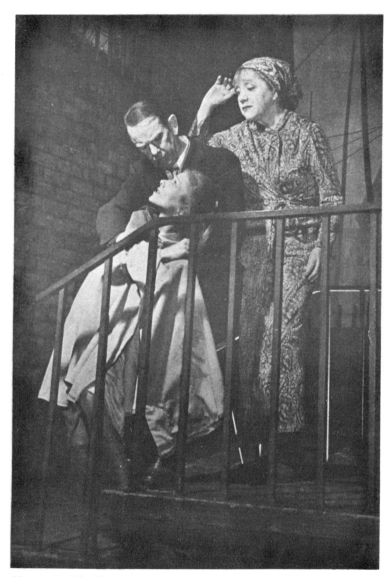

"THE GLASS MENAGERIE"

Amanda—If anyone breaks a leg on those fire-escape steps, the landlord ought to be sued for every cent he possesses!

(*Julie Haydon, Eddie Dowling, Laurette Taylor*)

SCENE IV

It is several hours later. The Wingfield house is dark. There is a faint light in the alley. A deep-tone church bell is tolling off the hour of five o'clock. At the head of the alley Tom appears, a little unsteadily. It is quite evident that he has been drinking. From his pockets he drags out a variety of souvenirs, including a noise-making rattle which he shakes after each solemn boom of the church bell, "as if to express the tiny spasm of man in contrast to the sustained power and dignity of the Almighty."

Presently Tom finds the key he has been searching for. As he tries to fit it in the lock it slips from his hand. He has struck a match and is searching for the key when Laura, in her night-dress, appears and opens the door.

Where has he been? He has been to the movies. It was a very long program, with a collection for the milk fund and an organ solo added.

"Did you have to stay through everything?" asks Laura, innocently.

"Of course! And oh, I forgot! There was a big stage show! The headliner on this stage show was Malvolio, the Magician. He performed wonderful tricks, many of them, such as pouring water back and forth between pitchers. First it turned to wine and then it turned to beer and then it turned to whiskey. I know it was whiskey it finally turned into because he needed somebody to come up out of the audience to help him, and I came up—both shows! It was Kentucky Straight Bourbon."

The magician was a very generous fellow, Tom reports. He did other tricks, too—such as letting them nail him up in a coffin and escaping without removing a single nail—

"There is a trick that would come handy for me," muses Tom. "Get me out of this 2 x 4 situation!"

Laura would shush him, but Tom resents that. What if he should wake up his mother— "Pay her back for all those 'Rise n' Shines,'" says Tom, as he lies down, groaning, on the couch. "You know it don't take much intelligence to get yourself into a nailed-up coffin, Laura— But who in hell ever got himself out of one without removing one nail?"

As if in answer to this, the photograph of the grinning father lights up.

A moment later the house is dark. When the lights come up the church bell is announcing the hour of six. Amanda can be heard calling from her room—"Rise and Shine! Rise and Shine! Laura, go tell your brother to rise and shine."

"I'll rise, but I won't shine!" announces Tom, sitting up on the couch, and staring stupidly at his sister.

Laura would plead with him. Won't he please speak to his mother this morning—speak to her and apologize? Tom doesn't see why he should. It was Amanda who started not speaking.

Again Amanda is calling from her room. Is Laura going to the store for butter, as she was told to do, or will Amanda have to get dressed and go for it herself? Laura is going—right away.

"Tell them to charge it," calls Amanda.

"Mother, they make such faces when I do that!"

"Sticks and stones can break our bones, but the expression on Mr. Garfinkel's face won't harm us!" carols Amanda. "Tell your brother his coffee is getting cold."

Laura has gone now, hurrying so fast that she slips on the fire-escape steps and cries out, greatly alarming her mother and brother until she calls again that she is all right.

"If anyone breaks a leg on those fire-escape steps the landlord should be sued for every cent he possesses," announces Amanda.

Tom has gone a little sheepishly to the table. His coffee is scalding hot and burns him with his first sip of it. Amanda, noting his distress, starts toward him, but quickly remembers her vow.

They are both unhappily conscious of their quarrel until Tom, watching Amanda intently over the rim of his coffee cup, finally reaches a decision. Rising slowly and awkwardly, he turns to Amanda—

"Mother. I—I apologize, Mother—"

Amanda draws a quick, shuddering breath and breaks into childlike tears—

"I'm sorry for what I said, for everything that I said, I didn't mean it—"

"My devotion has made me a witch and so I make myself hateful to my children," sobs Amanda.

It is hard for Tom to comfort his mother, but by degrees she gains control of her emotions. She is sure that if he will try, as he says he will, all will be well—

"Try and you will SUCCEED!" she declares, a little breathlessly. "Why, you—you're just FULL of natural endowments. Both of my children—they're UNUSUAL children! Don't you think I know it? I'm so—PROUD! Happy and—feel I've—so much to be thankful for—"

There is, however, one promise Amanda would exact from her son—that he will never be a drunkard. Tom is certainly willing to go that far. Then she would have him eat his cereal, and more cereal, that he may build himself up.

Also there is something she would like to discuss with Tom. It concerns Laura. Laura, Amanda thinks, is brooding too much. Brooding too much about Tom, because she thinks he is not happy in his home. Amanda admits she, too, has noted that Tom has acted queerly of late. She realizes that his ambitions do not lie in the warehouse, but like everybody in the whole world, he must expect to make sacrifices.

There is a confession Amanda would also like to make—she really had loved Tom's father. But when she sees Tom taking after his ways—drinking and staying out nights—it distresses her.

Tom's defense is simple. It isn't true that he goes out nights to get away from his home. If, as she says, there is much in her heart that she cannot tell him, there is also much in his heart that he can't tell her. True, he goes a lot to the movies. Why? Because he likes adventure. "Adventure is something I don't have much of at work, so I go to the movies."

"But, Tom, you go to the movies *entirely* too *much!*"

"I like a lot of adventure."

Amanda is a little baffled by this, but she is not ready to give up. "The world is full of young men employed in warehouses and offices and factories," she protests.

"Do all of them find adventure in their careers?"

"They do or they do without it! Not everybody has a craze for adventure."

"Man is by instinct a lover, a hunter, a fighter, and none of those instincts are given much play at the warehouse!"

"Man is by instinct! Don't quote instinct to me! Instinct is something that people have got away from! It belongs to animals! Christian adults don't want it!"

"What do Christian adults want, then, Mother?"

"Superior things! Things of the mind and the spirit! Only animals have to satisfy instincts! Surely your aims are somewhat higher than theirs! Than monkeys—pigs—"

"I reckon they're not."

Amanda is sure that Tom is joking, but in any event, to get back to Laura—

"We will have to be making some plans and provisions for Laura," Amanda has decided. "She's older than you, two years, and nothing has happened. She just drifts along doing nothing. It frightens me terribly how she just drifts along," sighs Amanda.

Tom—I guess she's the type that people call home-girls.

Amanda—There's no such type and if there is, it's a pity! That is useless, the home is hers, with a husband!

Tom—What?

Amanda—Oh, I can see the handwriting on the wall as plain as I see the nose in front of my face! It's terrifying! More and more you remind me of your father! He was out all hours without explanation!—Then *left! Good-by!* And me with the bag to hold. I saw that letter you got from the Merchant Marine. I know what you're dreaming of. I'm not standing here blindfolded. Very well, then. Then *do* it! But not till there's somebody to take your place.

Tom—What do you mean?

Amanda—I mean that as soon as Laura has got somebody to take care of her, married, a home of her own, independent— Why, then you'll be free to go wherever you please, on land, on sea, whichever way the wind blows you! But until that time you've got to look out for your sister. I don't say me because I'm old and don't matter!—I say for your sister because she's young and dependent. I put her in business college—a dismal failure! Frightened her so it made her sick at the stomach. I took her to the Young People's League at the church. Another fiasco. She spoke to nobody, nobody spoke to her. Now all she does is fool with those pieces of glass and play those worn-out records. What kind of a life is that for a girl to lead?

Tom—What can I do about it?

Amanda—Overcome selfishness! Self, self, self is all that you ever think of! (Tom *springs up to get his coat.*) Where is your muffler? Put your wool muffler on! (*He snatches it angrily from the closet and tosses it around his neck.*) Tom! I haven't said what I had in mind to ask you.

Tom—I'm too late to—

Amanda (*catching his arm*)—Down at the warehouse, aren't there some—nice young men?

Tom—No!

Amanda—There must be!—*some* . . .

Tom—Mother—

Amanda—Find out one that's clean-living—doesn't drink and —ask him out for Sister!

Tom—What?

AMANDA—For *Sister!* To *meet!* Get *acquainted!*
TOM (*stamping to door*)—Oh, my *go-osh!*
AMANDA—Will you? (*Imploringly.*) Will you? (*He starts down.*) Will you? *Will* you, dear?
TOM (*calling back*)—YES!

Amanda closes the door hesitantly and with a troubled but faintly hopeful expression. The curtain falls.

The lights have come up. Amanda is at the telephone trying to convince Ella Cartwright that she would be quite foolish to allow her subscription to the *Companion* to lapse—especially right now, just as Bessie Mae Hopper's new serial about the horsey set on Long Island is starting. What Ella's decision is we never learn.

SCENE V

The lights are down and up again. Now it is early dusk of a Spring evening. Amanda and Laura, in light-colored dresses, are removing the supper things from the table in the shadowed dining room. Tom, in white shirt and trousers, is moving toward the fire-escape.

As he passes Amanda she has a thing or two to say to Tom. She wishes, for one thing, that he would do her a favor and comb his hair. That is one respect in which she wishes he would emulate his father. Also, if he is going out to smoke, as he says, she is quite sure that he smokes too much.

A pack a day at fifteen cents a pack—if he would quit smoking he could save enough to give himself a night-school course in accounting in Washington U. "Just think what a wonderful thing that would be for you, son," Amanda concludes.

"I'd rather smoke," says Tom.

"I know. That's the tragedy of it. . . ."

Tom has gone through the screen door to the landing. Amanda turns to look at her husband's picture. It doesn't light up this time.

Tom again takes the audience into his confidence. "Across the alley from us was the Paradise Dance Hall," he is saying. "On evenings in Spring the windows and doors were open and the music came outdoors. Sometimes the lights were turned out except for a large glass sphere that hung from the ceiling. It would turn slowly about and filter the dusk with delicate rainbow colors. Then the orchestra played a waltz or a tango, something that had a slow and sensuous rhythm. Couples would come outside, to the relative privacy of the alley. You could see them kissing behind ash-pits and telephone poles. . . . This was the compensation for lives passed like mine, without any change or adventure. . . . Adventure and change were imminent in this year. They were waiting around the corner for all these kids. . . . Suspended in the mist over Berchtesgaden, caught in the folds of Chamberlain's umbrella. . . . In Spain there was Guernica! . . . But here there was only hot swing music and liquor, dance-halls, bars, and movies, and sex that hung in the gloom like a chandelier and flooded the world with brief, deceptive rainbows. . . . All the world was waiting for bombardments!"

Amanda has come outside. She spreads a newspaper on a step and sits down, "gracefully and demurely, as if she were settling into a swing on a Mississippi veranda."

There's a moon "rising over Garfinkel's Delicatessen." Amanda makes a wish on the moon—a wish for success and happiness for her precious children. She always wishes that when there is a moon.

If she had been wishing for a gentleman caller she would be getting her wish, Tom tells Amanda. The caller is coming. He is coming to dinner the next night!

That is lovely. Amanda is delighted. But tomorrow! It gives Amanda practically no time for preparations.

"Why didn't you phone me at once?" she demands. "As soon as you asked him, the minute that he accepted? Then, don't you see, I could have been getting ready!"

"You don't have to make any fuss!"

"Oh, Tom, Tom, Tom, of course I have to make fuss! I want things nice, not sloppy! Not thrown together. I'll certainly have to do some fast thinking, won't I?"

"I don't see why you have to think at all."

"You just don't know. We can't have a gentleman caller in a pigsty! All my wedding silver has to be polished, the monogrammed table linen ought to be laundered! The windows have to be washed and fresh curtains put up. And how about clothes? We have to *wear* something, don't we?"

"Mother, this boy is no one to make a fuss over!"

"Do you realize he's the first young man we've introduced to your sister? It's terrible, dreadful, disgraceful that poor little Sister has never received a single gentleman caller."

She is holding open the screen door. She would have Tom come inside and tell her more. Much more. Thank goodness she has the new sofa. She can have the floor lamp she has been making payments on sent out. And put the chintz covers on to brighten things up—

"What's the young man's name?" Amanda would know.

"His name is O'Connor."

"That, of course, means fish—tomorrow is Friday! I'll have that salmon loaf—with Durkee's dressing! What does he do? He works at the warehouse?"

"Of course! How else would I—?"

Another thing Amanda would like to know: Does the young man drink? Not that Tom knows of. That doesn't satisfy Amanda. The last thing she wants for her daughter is a boy who drinks! "Old maids are better off than the wives of drunkards!"

Tom would remind Amanda that lots of fellows meet girls they don't marry, but Amanda is quick to quiet him on that line. What is the prospective caller's position at the warehouse? He's a shipping-clerk. And what would be the salary of a shipping-clerk? Tom thinks it probably approximates $85 a month.

"For a family man, $85 a month is not much more than you can just get by on," ventures Amanda.

TOM—Yes, but Mr. O'Connor is not a family man.

AMANDA—He might be, mightn't he? Some time in the future?

TOM—I see. Plans and provisions.

AMANDA—You are the only young man that I know of who ignores the fact that the future becomes the present, the present the past, and the past turns into everlasting regret if you don't plan for it!

TOM—I will think that over and see what I can make of it.

AMANDA—Don't be supercilious with your mother! Tell me some more about this—what do you call him?

TOM—James D. O'Connor. The D is for Delaney.

AMANDA—Irish on both sides! Gracious! And doesn't drink?

TOM—Shall I call him up and ask him right this minute?

AMANDA—The only way to find out about those things is to make discreet inquiries at the proper moment. When I was a girl in Blue Mountain and it was suspected that a young man drank, the girl whose attentions he had been receiving, if any girl *was*, would sometimes speak to the minister of his church, or rather her father would if her father were living, and sort of feel him out on the young man's character. That is the way such things are discreetly handled to keep a young woman from making a tragic mistake!

Tom—Then how did you happen to make a tragic mistake?

Amanda—That innocent look of your father's had everyone fooled! He *smiled*—the world was *enchanted!* No girl can do worse than put herself at the mercy of a handsome appearance! I hope that Mr. O'Connor is not too good-looking.

Tom—No, he's not too good-looking. He's covered with freckles and hasn't much of a nose.

Amanda—He's not right-down homely, though?

Tom—Not right-down homely. Just medium homely, I'd say.

Amanda—Character's what to look for in a man.

Tom—That's what I've always said, Mother.

Amanda is further pleased to hear that Mr. O'Connor has gone in for self-improvement. He is studying radio engineering and public speaking at night school. That indicates that he is a forward-looking young man and one with an eye to the future.

There is one thing, however, about which Amanda should be warned, Tom thinks. O'Connor doesn't know about Laura. Nor will it be wise for his mother to expect too much of Laura. She is lovely and sweet and pretty to them, but there is no denying the fact that she is very different from other girls—

"I think the difference is all in her favor," snaps Amanda.

"Not quite all—in the eyes of others—strangers—she's terribly shy and lives in a world of her own and those things make her seem a little peculiar to people outside the house."

Such words as "crippled" and "peculiar" are never allowed in that house, Amanda warns him. And anyway, in what way is Laura peculiar?

"She lives in a world of her own—a world of little glass ornaments, Mother. . . . She plays old phonograph records—that's about all—"

He glances at himself in the mirror and starts for the door. Where is he going? He is going to the movies. Again Amanda would stop him if she could, but she can't. She looks after him worriedly and then turns to the door. Her vitality and optimism have returned. She calls gaily to Laura, "Let those dishes go and come in front."

Laura appears with a dish towel. "Laura, come here and make a wish on the moon! . . . A little silver slipper of a moon. . . . Look over your left shoulder, Laura, and make a wish!"

Laura looks faintly puzzled but she permits her mother to twist her around at an angle near the door. "Now, darling, wish!"

"What shall I wish for, Mother?"

"Happiness!—Good fortune!"

Amanda's voice is trembling. Her eyes fill with tears. The music rises, the lights dim. The curtain falls.

SCENE VI

Tom is again at the landing. "And so the following evening," he is saying, "I brought Jim home to dinner. I had known Jim slightly in high school. In high school Jim was a hero. He had tremendous Irish good nature and vitality with the scrubbed and polished look of white chinaware. He seemed to move in a continual spotlight. He was a star in basketball, captain of the debating club, president of the senior class and the glee club and he sang the male lead in the annual light operas. He was always running or bounding, never just walking. He seemed always at the point of defeating the law of gravity. He was shooting with such velocity through his adolescence that you would logically expect him to arrive at nothing short of the White House by the time he was thirty. But Jim apparently ran into more interference after his graduation from Soldan. His speed had definitely slowed. Six years after he left high school he was holding a job that wasn't much better than mine."

At the warehouse Tom and Jim were friends. Jim knew of Tom's secret passion for writing and used to kid him about it. Used to call him Shakespeare. And while the other boys were hostile and suspicious, Jim's attitude gradually brought them around to a friendlier attitude toward Tom.

Tom had known, too, that Jim had known Laura in school, but he wasn't at all sure that Jim remembered her. "If he did remember Laura, it was not as my sister," Tom confides. "When I asked him to dinner, he grinned and said, 'You know, Shakespeare, I never thought of you as having folks.' He was about to discover that I did. . . ."

The Wingfield apartment is all spruced up. Amanda "has worked like a Turk" in preparation for the gentleman caller. The new floor lamp, with a rose-colored shade, is in place. There are new white curtains at the windows, and chintz covers on the chairs and sofa.

As the lights come up Laura is discovered in the middle of the living room having a dress tried on. The arrangement of her hair has been changed. "A fragile, unearthly prettiness has come out in Laura: she is like a piece of translucent glass touched by light, given a momentary radiance, not actual, not lasting."

Amanda, adjusting the hem of Laura's dress, cannot understand why Laura should be trembling with nervousness. It is because Laura can't understand why Amanda should be making everything so important. She is even more disturbed when her mother, producing two powder puffs which she wraps in handkerchiefs, stuffs them in Laura's bosom. "They call them 'Gay Deceivers,' " explains Amanda.

"You make it seem like we were setting a trap," protests Laura, declaring that she will not wear them.

"All pretty girls are a trap, a pretty trap, and men expect them to be," answers Amanda, turning her daughter toward the mirror. "Now look at yourself, young lady. This is the prettiest you will ever be!"

And now Amanda must go and fix herself up. She is planning on a spectacular appearance. She will show them something! Something she has resurrected from an old trunk. "Styles haven't changed so terribly much after all," she calls while she is dressing.

Presently she appears through the portieres wearing a girlish frock of yellowed voile with a blue silk sash. "She carries a bunch of jonquils—the legend of her youth is nearly revived—"

"Now just look at your mother!" she bids them. "This is the dress in which I led the cotillion. Won the cakewalk twice at Sunset Hill, wore one Spring to the Governor's ball in Jackson! See how I sashayed around the ballroom, Laura?" She raises her skirt and does a mincing step around the room. "I wore it on Sundays for my gentlemen callers! I wore it the day I met your father."

As her memory quickens the memories come rushing in. "I had malaria fever all that Spring," she goes on. "The change of climate from East Tennessee to the Delta—weakened resistance —I had a little temperature all the time—not enough to be serious—just enough to make me restless and giddy! Invitations poured in—parties all over the Delta!—'Stay in bed,' said Mother, 'you have fever!' But I just wouldn't.—I took quinine but kept going, going, going!—Evenings, dances!—Afternoons, long, long rides! Picnics—lovely! So lovely, that country in May— All lacey with dogwood, literally flooded with jonquils!"

It was while she had her arms full of jonquils, Amanda remembers, that she met Laura's father. She stops for a moment now before his picture, and then quickly turns on the rose-colored lamp. She has begun to worry a little for fear Tom and the caller will not arrive before the rain that is threatening—

"What did you say his name was?" asks Laura.

"O'Connor."

"What is his first name?"

"I don't remember— Oh, yes, I do, it was Jim!"

Laura is seen to sway a little. She catches hold of a chair to steady herself. "Not Jim!" she mutters. "Are you sure his name is Jim O'Connor?"

"Yes. Why?"

"Is he the one that Tom used to know in high school?"

"He didn't say so. I think he just got to know him at the warehouse!"

"There was a Jim O'Connor we both knew in high school— (*Then with an effort.*) If that is the one that Tom is bringing to dinner—you'll have to excuse me, I won't come to the table."

"What sort of nonsense is this?"

"You asked me once if I'd ever liked a boy. Don't you remember I showed you this boy's picture?"

"You mean the boy you showed me in the year book?"

"Yes, that boy."

"Laura, Laura, were you in love with that boy?"

"I don't know, Mother. All I know is I couldn't sit at the table if he was him!"

"It won't be him! It isn't the least bit likely."

A sense of panic is beginning to control Laura. She begs her mother not to leave her there to let the boys in. That would be too much for her. If Tom has forgotten his key, let her mother—

Tom and Jim have appeared on the fire-escape. Tom rings the bell. Amanda calls to Laura to go to the door. But mounting panic has overcome Laura. She catches her breath and touches her throat. The bell rings again, Amanda calls again, but Laura is helpless. She pleads piteously with Amanda, who has come from the kitchen. Laura fears she is going to be sick. . . .

Amanda is firm. She will have no more of such silliness. Let Laura march to that door and open it. The order is imperative and Laura submits. But before she opens the door she has darted to the victrola and set a scratchy rendition of "Dardanella" playing.

At the door she responds timidly to Tom's introduction. Jim

is hearty and surprised. He had not known that Shakespeare had a sister. Why is her hand so cold? Maybe because she has been playing the victrola, suggests Laura—

"Must have been playing classical music on it," says Jim. "You ought to play a little hot swing music to warm you up!"

With the excuse that she has not finished playing the victrola, Laura leaves the boys rather abruptly and "darts through the portieres like a frightened deer."

"What was the matter?" Jim is grinning.

"Oh—Laura? Laura is—terribly shy," explains Tom.

"Shy, huh? It's unusual to meet a shy girl nowadays. I don't believe you ever mentioned you had a sister."

"Well, now you know."

They divide the *Post-Dispatch* between them, Jim taking the sports section, Tom sticking to the news. After a minute or two they move out to the terrace. Jim gives up reading. He wants to talk. Wants to sell Tom a bill of goods. Wants him to take a course in public speaking. Fits a fellow for executive positions—

"Ask yourself what is the difference between you an' me and men in the office down front? Brains? No! Ability? No! Then what? Just one little thing."

"What is that one little thing?"

"Primarily it amounts to—social poise! Being able to square up to people and hold your own on any social level."

Amanda calls from the kitchen to be sure that Tom and Mr. O'Connor have made themselves perfectly comfortable. Wouldn't Mr. O'Connor like to wash his hands? No, thanks! "I took care of that at the warehouse," Jim calls back.

Returning to the subject of their future at the warehouse, Jim has some rather disquieting news for Tom. "You're going to be out of a job if you don't wake up," warns Jim.

"I am waking up—"

"You show no signs."

"The signs are interior. I'm planning to change." Tom is leaning over the railing and the lights from the incandescent marquees of the movie houses across the alley light his face. "I'm right at the point of committing myself to a future that doesn't include the warehouse and Mr. Mendoza or even a night school course in public speaking."

"What are you gassing about?"

"I'm tired of the movies."

"Movies!"

"Yes, movies! Look at them— (*A wave toward the marvels of Grand Avenue.*) All of those glamorous people—having adventures—hogging it all, gobbling the whole thing up! You know what happens? People go to the *movies* instead of *moving!* Hollywood characters are supposed to have all the adventures for everybody in America, while everybody in America sits in a dark room and watches them have them! Yes, until there's a war. That's when adventure becomes available to the masses! *Everyone's* dish, not only Gable's!—Then the people in the dark room come out of the dark room to have some adventures themselves— Goody, goody!—It's our turn now, to go to the South Sea Island —to make a safari—to be exotic, far-off!—But I'm not patient. I don't want to wait till then. I'm tired of the *movies* and I am *about* to *move!*"

Future plans are still a bit vague in Tom's mind, but the change is coming soon. He is starting to boil inside. This month he joined the Union of Merchant Seamen—instead of paying the light bill. But what about his mother? Jim would know. What is going to happen when they turn off the lights—

"I won't be here," carols Tom. "I'm like my father. The bastard son of a bastard! See how he grins? And he's been absent going on sixteen years!"

When they hear Amanda coming Tom is quick to warn Jim that his mother is not acquainted with his plans. Now they have moved inside to meet Amanda. She greets them with almost excessive hospitality. "Tom is distinctly shocked at her appearance. Even Jim blinks a little."

"Well, well, well—so this is Mr. O'Connor," gurgles Amanda, coyly smiling and shaking her girlish ringlets. "Introductions entirely unnecessary. I've heard so much about you from my boy. I finally said to him, 'Tom—good gracious!—why don't you bring this paragon to supper?—I'd like to meet this nice young man at the warehouse!'—Instead of just hearing him sing your praises so much! I don't know why my son is so standoffish—that's not Southern behavior!"

Amanda gurgles on—now about the weather, which is unseasonably hot; now about the supper, which will be light—"Light clothes an' light food are what warm weather calls fo'—"

"It's come so quick this year. I wasn't prepared. All of a sudden—heavens! Already Summer!—I ran to the trunk an' pulled out this light dress— Terribly old! Historical almost! But feel so good—so good an' co-ol, y' know . . ."

Tom is getting a little anxious about supper. Of course that is all in Sister's hands, Amanda reminds him. Let him ask Laura about supper—

"It's rare for a girl as sweet and pretty as Laura to be domestic," Amanda assures Jim after Tom has left. "But Laura is, thank heavens, not only pretty but also very domestic. I'm not at all. I never was a bit. I never could make a thing but angelfood cake. Well, in the South we had so many servants. Gone, gone, gone! All vestige of gracious living! Gone completely! I wasn't prepared for what the future brought me. All of my gentlemen callers were sons of planters and so of course I assumed I would be married to one and raise my family on a large piece of land with plenty of servants. But man proposes—and woman accepts the proposal!—to vary that old, old saying a little bit— I married no planter! I married a man who worked for the telephone company!—That gallantly smiling gentleman over there! (*Points to the picture.*)—A telephone man who—fell in love with long-distance!—Now he travels and I don't even know where!"

Tom is back. Supper is on the table. But Laura isn't feeling well and will not come to table. Amanda will have none of that nonsense. Of course Laura will come to table. They will not be seated until she does—

"Laura? Laura Wingfield!" she calls. "You're keeping us waiting, honey! We can't say grace until you come to the table!"

Laura comes weakly through the back door and moves unsteadily toward the table. "She is obviously quite faint, her lips trembling, her eyes wide and staring." Suddenly she stumbles and catches at a chair with a faint moan.

Tom and Amanda both start toward her. "Why, Laura, you *are* sick, darling! Tom, help your sister into the living room, dear!" A despairing note creeps into Amanda's voice. She turns to the gentleman caller. "Standing over the hot stove made her ill," she explains. "I told her it was just too warm this evening, but—"

Tom has left his sister on the sofa and come back to the table. Laura is all right now. Outside it has started to rain. "What is that? Rain? A nice cool rain has come up." Amanda has given Jim a frightened look and turns to Tom—

"I think we may have grace—now. . . . Tom, honey—you say grace!"

For a second Tom stares stupidly at his mother. Then, with a half-frightened "Oh!" he begins—

"For these and all thy mercies—"

They bow their heads. Amanda steals a nervous glance at Jim.
In the living room Laura, stretched on the sofa, clenches her hand
to her lips to hold back a shuddering sob.

"God's Holy Name be praised—" concludes Tom. The lights
fade.

SCENE VII

It is a half hour later. Dinner is just being finished. The
portieres are drawn. In the living room Laura is still huddled on
the sofa, "her feet drawn under her, her head resting on a pale
blue pillow, her eyes wide and mysteriously watchful. The new
floor lamp with its shade of rose-colored silk gives a soft, becoming light to her face, bringing out the fragile, unearthly prettiness
which usually escapes attention."

Presently the rain stops. Then the lights go out. Amanda
would make a joke. "Where was Moses when the lights went
out?" If Jim doesn't know, he was in the dark. Fortunately
there are candles. And as soon as they can find the fuse box
in the kitchen, if Jim can tell a burned-out fuse when he sees
one—

But Jim finds the fuses are all right. Then it must have been
something else. Suddenly Amanda remembers the light bill. Had
Tom, by any chance, neglected to pay that—

"Shakespeare probably wrote a poem on that light bill, Mrs.
Wingfield," suggests Jim, with a grin.

Well, anyway, they got through dinner, Amanda reminds them,
cheerfully. It was very considerate of the light company to put
off plunging them into darkness that long. Now they will have
to "spend the rest of the evening in the nineteenth century, before Mr. Edison made the Mazda lamp!" announces Amanda.
And as a penalty for his carelessness Tom can help with the dishes.

Jim would like to help, too, but Amanda will not hear to that.
Jim has been quite wonderful, entertaining them the way he has.
And Sister is all by her lonesome in the parlor. It would be
wonderful if Mr. O'Connor would keep her company—

"I'll give you this lovely old candelabrum that used to be on
the altar at the Church of the Heavenly Rest. It was melted
a little out of shape when the church burned down. Lightning
struck it one Spring. Gypsy Jones was holding a revival at the
time and he intimated that the church was destroyed because the
Episcopalians gave card parties."

Amanda has put an apron on Tom and they disappear into
the kitchenette. With the candelabrum casting a flickering light

before him, Jim comes through the portieres into the living room.
Laura sits up nervously as he approaches. "Her speech at first is
low and breathless from the almost intolerable strain of being
alone with a stranger."

Jim's attitude is gently humorous. He greets Laura with a
hearty "Hello!" He is glad to find her feeling better. And
where would she suggest that he put the candles? On the floor,
perhaps? He'll spread papers to catch the drippings. He likes
to sit on the floor, too. Does Laura? She does? Then why
doesn't she? She does. Now, is she comfortable? She is. How
would she like some gum? "No, thank you," says Laura.

"I think that I will indulge, with your permission. (*Musingly
upwraps it and holds it up.*) Think of the fortune made by the
guy that invented the first piece of chewing gum. Amazing,
huh? The Wrigley Building is one of the sights of Chicago.—I
saw it Summer before last when I went to the Century of Progress.
—Did you take in the Century of Progress?"

"No, I didn't."

"Well, it was quite a wonderful exposition. What impressed
me most was the Hall of Science. Gives you an idea of what the
future will be in America, even more wonderful than the present
time is!"

Tom has told him, Jim reports, that Laura is shy? Is that
true? Laura wouldn't know.

"I judge you to be an old-fashioned type of girl. Well, I think
that's a pretty good type to be . Hope you don't think I'm being
too personal—do you?"

"I believe I *will* take a piece of gum, if you—don't mind," says
Laura, clearing her throat to cover her embarrassment.

"I—don't suppose—you remember me—at all?" Laura is saying a moment later.

JIM (*smiling doubtfully*)—You know I have an idea I've seen
you before. I had that idea soon as you opened the door. It
seemed almost like I was about to remember your name. But
the name that I started to call you—wasn't a name! And so I
stopped myself before I said it.

LAURA—Wasn't it—Blue Roses?

JIM (*springing up and grinning*)—Blue Roses! My gosh, yes
—Blue Roses! That's what I had on my tongue when you opened
the door! Isn't it funny what tricks your memory plays? I
didn't connect you with high school somehow or other. But
that's where it was, it was high school. I didn't even know you

were Shakespeare's sister!   Gosh, I'm sorry.

LAURA—I didn't expect you to. You—barely knew me!

JIM—But we did have a speaking acquaintance, huh?

LAURA—Yes, we—spoke to each other.

JIM—When did you recognize me?

LAURA—Oh, right away!

JIM—Soon as I came in the door?

LAURA—When I heard your name I thought it was probably you. I knew that Tom used to know you a little in high school. So when you came in the door— Well, then I was—sure.

JIM—Why didn't you *say* something, then?

LAURA (*breathlessly*)—I didn't know what to say, I was—too surprised!

JIM—For goodness' sakes! You know, this sure is funny.

LAURA— Yes! Yes, isn't it, though. . . .

JIM—Didn't we have a class in something together?

LAURA—Yes, we did.

JIM—What class was that?

LAURA—It was—singing—chorus!

JIM—Aw!

LAURA—I sat across the aisle from you in the Aud.

JIM—Aw.

LAURA—Mondays, Wednesdays, and Fridays.

JIM—Now I remember—you always came in late.

LAURA—Yes, it was so hard for me getting upstairs. I had that brace on my leg—it clumped so loud!

JIM—I never heard any clumping.

LAURA (*wincing at the recollection*)—To me it sounded like—thunder!

JIM—Well, well, well, I never even noticed.

LAURA—And everybody was seated before I came in. I had to walk in front of all those people. My seat was in the back row. I had to go clumping all the way up the aisle with everyone watching!

JIM—You shouldn't have been self-conscious.

LAURA—Oh, I know, but I was. It was always such a relief when the singing started.

JIM—Aw, yes, I've placed you now! I used to call you Blue Roses. How was it that I got started calling you that?

LAURA—I was out of school a little while with pleurosis. When I came back you asked me what was the matter. I said I had pleurosis—you thought I said Blue Roses. That's what you always called me after that!

JIM—I hope you didn't mind.

LAURA—Oh, no—I liked it.   You see, I wasn't acquainted with many—people . . .

JIM—As I remember, you sort of stuck by yourself.

LAURA—I—I—never had much luck at—making friends.

Jim can't understand why Laura should give way to her depressions the way she does. She should not let her physical handicaps or her shyness defeat her. True, shyness is something she will have to work out of gradually— But—

"People are not so dreadful when you know them," promises Jim. "That's what you have to remember! And everybody has problems, not just you but practically everybody has problems. You think of yourself as having the only problems, as being the only one who is disappointed. But just look around you and you will see lots of people as disappointed as you are."

Take his own case, for example. Jim can remember how sure he was when he was going to high school that he would be a lot further along at this time than he is. He can remember the wonderful write-up the school paper, *The Torch,* gave him—

"It said I was bound to succeed in anything I went into," recalls Jim. "Holy JEEZ! *THE TORCH!*"

Laura has picked up the high school annual from the table. They turn it through together, "Laura's shyness dissolving in his warmth."

There are pictures of Jim when he was the leading baritone in "The Pirates of Penzance." Laura remembers how beautifully he had sung in that. She had haunted all three performances, hoping to get him to autograph her book. He signs it now and with a flourish, impressed by her earnestness. She asks him whatever became of Emily Meisenbach—the girl Jim was said to be engaged to. That "kraut-head!" He was never engaged to her! Except "in Emily's optimistic opinion!"

What has Laura been doing since high school? Jim is interested. Laura hasn't been doing much. She had taken a course in business college, but she had to drop out—it gave her indigestion. Jim laughs at that.

And now? Well, she doesn't do much of anything now, except to look after her glass collection.

"You know what I judge to be the trouble with you?" Jim is saying, a little abruptly. "Inferiority complex! Know what that is? That's what they call it when someone low-rates himself! I understand it because I had it, too. Although my case was not so aggravated as yours seems to be. I had it until I took up public speaking, developed my voice, and learned that I had an aptitude for science. Before that time I never thought of myself as being outstanding in any way whatsoever! Now, I've never made a regular study of it, but I have a friend who says I can analyze people better than doctors that make a profession of it. I don't claim that to be necessarily true, but I can sure guess a person's psychology, Laura! . . . Yep, that's what I judge to be your principal trouble. A lack of confidence in yourself as a person. You don't have the proper amount of faith in yourself."

He reminds her of several of her own confessions—of the clumping she thought was so awful when she walked into class in high school. "You gave up an education because of the clump, which, so far as I know, was practically non-existent. A little physical defect is what you have. Hardly noticeable even! Magnified thousands of times by imagination! You know what my strong advice to you is? Think of yourself as *superior* in some way!"

"In what way would I think?"

"Why, man alive, Laura! Just look about you a little. What do you see? A world full of common people! All of 'em born and all of 'em going to die! Which of them has one-tenth of your good points! Or mine! Or anyone else's, as far as that goes— Gosh! Everybody excels in some one thing. Some in many! (*Unconsciously glances at himself in the mirror.*) All you've got to do is discover in *what!*"

As for himself, Jim's interest happens to lie in electro-dynamics. Hence his course in radio-engineering. And in public speaking. Television is also on the way, and Jim wants to be ready for it. His eyes are a little starry. "*Knowledge*— Zzzzzp! *Money*— Zzzzzp! *Power!* That's the cycle democracy is built on!"

Jim's attitude is convincingly dynamic. "Laura stares at him, even her shyness eclipsed in her absolute wonder."

"Now how about you?" His own enthusiasm has made Jim a bit self-conscious. "Isn't there something you take more interest in than anything else?"

But again her glass collection is the only absorbing interest Laura can think of. To meet his curiosity she shows a part of it to him. "They're ornaments mostly," she explains. "Most of them are little animals made out of glass, the tiniest little animals in the world. Mother calls them a glass menagerie!"

She picks out a piece—one of her oldest—to show him. It is a tiny glass unicorn that has to be handled very gently. But she will trust Jim with it. The unicorn is particularly beautiful when the light shines through him. And though he may feel sort of lonesome in this modern world, as Jim suggests, he has never complained. "He stays on a shelf with some horses that don't have horns and all of them seem to get along nicely together," reports Laura. At least she has never heard any arguments among them. Jim grins at this.

He has risen from the floor and started for the door, stretching as he goes and remarking the heroic size of his shadow on the ceiling. As he opens the door the music from the Paradise Dance Hall comes in plainly.

"How about cutting the rug a little, Miss Wingfield?" Jim asks gaily.

"Oh, I—"

"Or is your program filled up? Let me have a look at it." He grasps an imaginary card. "Why, every dance is taken! I'll just have to scratch some out." The music swells into "La Golondrina." "Ahhhh, a waltz!" exclaims Jim, holding his arms toward Laura.

"I—can't dance!" she says, a little breathlessly.

"There you go, that inferiority stuff!"

"I've never danced in my life!"

"Come on, try!"

"Oh, but I'd step on you!"

"I'm not made out of glass."

He has taken her in his arms and is carrying her a little clumsily through the steps of the waltz, Laura protesting that she can't, Jim insisting that she can—and proving it as he gets her to relax more and more.

Suddenly they bump into the table. The glass unicorn is knocked off. Its horn is broken off. Jim is distressed, but Laura accepts the accident philosophically.

"It doesn't matter," she insists. "Maybe it's a blessing in disguise. . . . I'll just imagine he had an operation. The horn was removed to make him feel less—freakish! Now he will feel more at home with the other horses, the ones that don't have horns . . ."

"Ha-ha, that's very funny," laughs Jim. "I'm glad to see that you have a sense of humor." Suddenly he is quite serious. "You know—you're—well—very different! Surprisingly different from anyone else I know." His voice has become soft and hesitant. "Do you mind me telling you that?" Laura is abashed beyond speech. "I mean it in a nice way . . . You make me feel sort of—I don't know how to put it! I'm usually pretty good at expressing things, but— This is something I don't know how to say."

Laura's hand is at her throat. Jim's voice becomes even softer—

"Has anyone ever told you that you were pretty." The music is drifting in softly from across the alley. Laura looks up slowly, with wonder, and shakes her head. "Well, you are!" Jim goes on, "in a very different way from anyone else. And all the nicer because of the difference, too." His voice has become low and husky. Laura has turned away, "nearly faint with the novelty of her emotions."

"I wish that you were my sister," Jim is saying. "I'd teach you to have some confidence in yourself. The different people are not like other people, but being different is nothing to be ashamed of. Because other people are not such wonderful people. They're one hundred times one thousand. You're one times one! They walk all over the earth. You just stay here. They're common as —weeds, but—you—well, you're—*Blue Roses!*"

"But blue is wrong for—roses . . ."

"It's right for you!—You're pretty!"

"In what respect am I pretty?"

"In all respects—believe me! Your eyes—your hair are pretty! your hands are pretty! (*He catches hold of her hand.*) You think I'm making this up because I'm invited to dinner and have to be nice. Oh, I could do that! I could put on an act for you, Laura, and say lots of things without being very sincere. But this time I am. I'm talking to you sincerely. I happened to notice you had this inferiority complex that keeps you from feeling comfortable with people. Somebody needs to build your confidence up and make you proud instead of shy and turning away and—blushing— Somebody—ought—ought to—kiss you, Laura."

Jim's hand has slipped up Laura's arm to her shoulder. Suddenly he turns her about and kisses her on the lips. When she is released she sinks to the sofa with a bright, dazed look.

Jim has backed away. He fishes nervously in his pocket for a cigarette. "Stumble-john!" he is muttering. There is a peal of girlish laughter from Amanda in the kitchen. "Stumble-john!" repeats Jim, accusingly. "I shouldn't have done that— That was way off the beam!"

Nervously he offers Laura a cigarette, but she doesn't smoke. Gingerly he sits on the sofa beside her. She is looking at him, speechlessly, waiting. He searches his pockets for a peppermint —a life-saver— Would she care for one? She doesn't seem to hear him. And then he tells her—

"Laura, you know, if I had a sister like you, I'd do the same thing as Tom. I'd bring out fellows and—introduce her to them. The right type of boys of a type to—appreciate her. Only—well —he made a mistake about me. Maybe I've got no call to be saying this. That may not have been the idea in having me over. But what if it was? There's nothing wrong about that.—The only trouble is that in my case—I'm not in a situation to—do the right thing. I can't take down your number and say I'll phone. I can't call up next week and—ask for a date. I thought I had better explain the situation in case you—misunderstood it and— hurt your feelings. . . ."

Very slowly Laura's look changes. She looks away from him and at the broken glass unicorn in her hand. There is another peal of laughter from Amanda in the kitchen.

"You—won't—call again?" Laura asks faintly.

"No, Laura, I can't." Jim has risen from the sofa. "As I was just explaining, I've—got strings on me. Laura, I've—been going steady! I go out all the time with a girl named Betty. She's a home-girl like you, and Catholic, and Irish, and in a great many ways we—get along fine. I met her last Summer on a moonlight boat trip up the river to Alton, on the *Majestic*. Well —right away from the start it was—love!"

Laura sways slightly and grips the arm of the sofa. Jim doesn't notice. He is again "enwrapt in his own comfortable being." Being in love, he explains, has made a new man of him, the power of love being pretty tremendous. The reason he happened to accept Tom's invitation to dinner was because Betty had been called to Centralia by a sick aunt.

The storm has abated a little. Laura is leaning back. Jim takes new notice of her, but he is still convinced that he is and has been a "Stumble-john!" Awkwardly he flops back on the sofa. "I wish that you would—say something!" He glances at her uneasily. "The holy candles in the altar of Laura's face have been snuffed out." In their place is a look of "almost infinite desolation."

Opening her hand on the broken glass ornament Laura gently takes Jim's hand, places the ornament in its palm and closes his fingers upon it. "A souvenir . . ." she mutters.

She has risen unsteadily and is crouching before the victrola to wind it up when Amanda comes briskly in from the kitchen.

She brings an old-fashioned cut-glass pitcher of fruit punch and a plate of macaroons. She is cheerfully enthused with the thought that Laura and Jim have been getting better acquainted, even if they do look very serious at the moment. Modern young people are much more serious than they were in Amanda's day. As a girl she was one of the gayest 'of the gay.

In the kitchen, Amanda reports, she and Tom have been having a lot of fun. She also has been chiding her son for not having brought his friend Jim over before. But, from now on they will have a lot of gay times. She will skip back to the kitchen now. "I know where my place is when young folks are having a serious conversation."

Jim would stop Amanda. In fact it is he who must be going, even though, as his hostess reminds him, it is only the shank of the evening. Amanda is ready to compromise—she will let him off this evening if he will promise to stay longer next time. Would Saturday night be a good night for him?

"I've a couple of time-clocks to punch, Mrs. Wingfield," Jim explains. "One at morning, another at night."

"My, but you ARE ambitious! You work at night, too?"

"No, ma'am, not work but—Betty." He has reached for his hat.

"Betty? Betty? Who's Betty?"

"Oh, just a girl. The girl I go steady with!" He smiles charmingly.

"Ohhhh . . . !" This with a long-drawn exhalation from Amanda. "Is it a serious romance, Mr. O'Connor?"

"We're going to be married the second Sunday in June."

There is a smothered "Ohhh—how nice!" from Amanda. Tom had not mentioned that his friend was engaged. That, explains Jim, was because the cat's not out of the bag at the warehouse yet. Again he would make his farewells. It has been a wonderful evening. "I guess this is what they mean by Southern hospitality," guesses Jim.

"Good-by, Laura." Jim has taken her hand. "I'm certainly going to treasure that souvenir. And don't you forget the good advice I gave you. Good-by, Shakespeare!" Jim has raised his voice in a cheery shout. "Thanks again, ladies— Good night!"

For a moment Amanda and Laura avoid looking at each other. Laura continues to fuss with the victrola, but Amanda doesn't think it is the time to play it. She calls lustily to Tom. When he comes she would congratulate him upon the wonderful joke he has played on them by not letting them know that his friend

O'Connor was engaged to be married.

Jim? Engaged? Tom didn't know either. Which may seem peculiar to Amanda, but it's the truth. "The warehouse is where I work, not where I know things about people!"

"You don't know things anywhere!" snaps Amanda. "You live in a dream; you manufacture'illusions." Tom is crossing to the door. "Where are you going?" Amanda demands.

"I'm going to the movies."

"That's right, now that you've had us make such fools of ourselves. The effort, the preparations, all the expense! The new floor lamp, the rug, the clothes for Laura! All for what? To entertain some other girl's fiancé! Go to the movies, go!—Don't think about us, a mother deserted, an unmarried sister who's crippled and has no job! Don't let anything interfere with your selfish pleasure! Just go, go, go—to the movies."

"All right, I will! The more you shout about my selfishness to me the quicker I'll go and I won't go to the movies!"

"Go, then! Then go to the moon!—you selfish dreamer."

Tom smashes his lemonade glass on the floor and bolts out the door, slamming it after him. Laura screams. The music from the dance hall grows louder.

On the fire-escape Tom stands gripping the handrail. Inside the house Amanda's and Laura's scene is played "as though viewed through soundproof glass," and is timed to synchronize with Tom's final narration. "Amanda appears to be making a comforting speech to Laura, who is huddled upon the sofa. Now that we cannot hear the mother's speech her silliness is gone and she has dignity and tragic beauty. Laura's dark hair hides her face until at the end she lifts it to smile at her mother—" . . .

"I didn't go to the moon," Tom is saying. "I went much further, for time is the longest distance between two places. . . . Not long after that I was fired for writing a poem on the lid of a shoe-box. I left St. Louis. I descended the steps of this fire-escape for a last time and followed, from then on, in my father's footsteps, attempting to find in motion what was lost in space . . . I traveled around a great deal. The cities swept about me like dead leaves, leaves that were brightly colored but torn away from the branches. I would have stopped, but I was pursued by something. It always came upon me unawares, taking me altogether by surprise. Perhaps it was a familiar bit of music. Perhaps it was only a piece of transparent glass. . . . Perhaps I am walking along a street at night, in some strange city, before I have found companions. I pass the lighted window of a shop where perfume is sold. The window is filled with pieces of colored glass, tiny transparent bottles in delicate colors, like bits of a shattered rainbow. Then all at once my sister touches my shoulder. I turn around and look into her eyes . . . Oh, Laura, Laura, I tried to leave you behind me, but I am more faithful than I intended to be! I reach for a cigarette, I cross the street, I run into the movies or a bar, I buy a drink, I speak to the nearest stranger—anything that can blow your candles out! (LAURA *bends over the candles.*) For nowadays the world is lit by lightning! Blow out your candles, Laura,—and so good-by. . . . (*She blows the candles out. The scene dissolves.*)

THE CURTAIN FALLS

HARVEY

A Comedy in Three Acts

By Mary Chase

(Digest by John Chapman)

WHEN the comedy about Dowd, Elwood P., and his rabbit friend arrived on November 1, 1944, the young season had already had more than the average number of hits. There had been "I Remember Mama," "Anna Lucasta," "Bloomer Girl," "Song of Norway" and "Soldier's Wife."

"Harvey" opened as a major triumph. It was obviously a box-office bonanza, and its qualities of whimsey were off the beaten Broadway path; and the casting of Frank Fay as Elwood was a "natural" such as seldom happens in an actor's lifetime. The history of Fay himself lent color and interest to the play—for here was a comeback story: the story of an actor who had once been rich on the stage, rich again on the screen; the story of an actor who had lost both fortune and fame through his own weakness, and who had reformed.

The public delight at Mr. Fay's success was heartwarming—to the public, at least. Mr. Fay was always a little puzzled at his having been "discovered" as an actor at this late date, since as a young man he had begun his long career in Shakespeare.

"Harvey" was also a triumph for its producer, Brock Pemberton—a triumph of persistence. Mary Coyle Chase, wife of Robert L. Chase, city editor of the Denver *Rocky Mountain News*, had written a play titled "Now You've Done It" in 1936, and Pemberton had produced it. The play was a rapid failure, but Mrs. Chase was not going to give up playwriting. When she finished another one, titled "The Pooka," she naturally sent it to Pemberton.

He liked it—although, as he has always said of a script, it needed work. It was the story of a mildly but permanently liquored fellow and his invisible rabbit companion. Pemberton's best friends didn't like it. His wife read the script and advised him not to do it. His director, Antoinette Perry, read it and came forth with the same advice. Pemberton doggedly insisted he was going to do the play anyway, and much correspondence and many revisions were mailed between him and the author in Denver.

There are many stories now about all the actors who read "The Pooka" and turned it down. Pemberton had not thought of Frank Fay until a friend in San Francisco suggested him. Purely on the basis of a few minutes' conversation Fay was engaged for the part, without having to go through the usual formality of "reading" for the manager. It was, everybody has agreed, perfect casting. So, too, was the selection of Josephine Hull for the role of Elwood's distraught sister.

When "The Pooka" reached its tryout date in Boston it had been renamed "Harvey"—that being the name of the pooka, or Celtic fairy spirit, which was Elwood Dowd's companion. Just to make sure, the careful Pemberton had one performance played in Boston in which Harvey was visible—an actor dressed in a $600 rabbit suit. It was not as funny that way, so Pemberton more or less cheerfully pocketed his $600 loss.

Mrs. Chase's play was awarded the Pulitzer prize as the best play of American authorship to be produced in New York in 1944. A reluctance on the part of the author's agent to permit much quoting from the script—because the entire play has not yet been published—makes it necessary to present "Harvey" herewith in story form.

When the late Marcella Pinney Dowd—a pioneer cultural leader who came West and founded the Wednesday Forum— passed on, she willed her estate to her son, Elwood. Perhaps Elwood was not as balmy then as he is now, at the age of 47. And so it is that Veta, a widow with a daughter who ought to be married by now, must live in Elwood's house.

This is a sore trial to Veta and Myrtle Mae—not because Elwood is mean or ungenerous, for he is sunny-tempered and generosity personified; it is a trial because of Elwood's bosom friend, Harvey. The women can't have much social life because Elwood insists upon introducing Harvey to everybody and people think it's rather queer and are apt not to come back any more.

However, Elwood is out somewhere and Veta has seized the opportunity to have a meeting of the Wednesday Forum. She is in the library of the old-hat Dowd mansion in what might be the author's own home city of Denver. She is on the phone, giving details of the Forum meeting to a society reporter, and the party is going on in the living room across the main hall. The most noticeable decoration in the library is a portrait of the late

Marcella Pinney Dowd, who must have been something of a dragon.

Myrtle Mae breaks up Veta's phone call by announcing the arrival of Mrs. Eugene Chauvenet Senior—also a dragon and Very Society. The Forum is going well indeed when such as she appears . . . and Veta cautions Myrtle Mae to be nice to her because she has a grandson about Myrtle Mae's age.

Myrtle Mae can't see what difference a grandson would make with Uncle Elwood in the offing—the biggest screwball in town. But Veta is determined to put Elwood out of mind for the present; he's playing pinochle at the firehouse, and Veta is going to make the best of her chance for a party. The embittered Myrtle, however, goes on; she passes from Elwood to Harvey and damns Harvey out loud. She also can't figure out why Grandmother left the house to Elwood.

Veta and her daughter join the Forum in the other room, and in a moment Elwood saunters into the library. He looks dignified, dreamy and benign. He is wearing a battered college-boy hat and is carrying another hat and a coat. As he comes in he bows an invisible someone else in with him, with the greatest affection and courtesy.

It is Harvey, of course, and he is invited to make himself comfortable. When the telephone rings Elwood takes the call and learns that a Miss Greenawalt would like him to join a club. Elwood, already a member of the University Club, the Country Club and the Fourth Avenue Firehouse Pinochle Club, is quite willing to join the new one. It is, Miss Greenawalt explains, a magazine subscription club. Elwood orders two memberships—for himself and for Harvey.

The rigors of pinochle at the firehouse indicate some freshening-up, so Elwood and his friend make for the bathroom just before Veta, Myrtle Mae and the important Mrs. Chauvenet come into the library for an intimate chat. Mrs. Chauvenet inquires about Elwood, who used to be one of her favorite people. Veta tries to change the subject, but before she can steer Mrs. Chauvenet back to the Forum Elwood reappears and there are affectionate greetings.

Then Elwood introduces Harvey—and a confused and bewildered look comes over Mrs. Chauvenet. Elwood, having begun the social amenities, takes Harvey into the other room to meet all the other people, and Mrs. Chauvenet suddenly decides she had better go home right now. It is another disaster for Veta and Myrtle Mae.

Just one too many disasters, in fact. Veta has determined upon action. She will take Elwood out to Chumley's Rest, a sanitarium for nuts like Elwood, operated by a pompous psychiatrist named Dr. Chumley.

Elwood is perfectly willing to go, for he wants Veta to have any little thing she might wish. He waits in a cab outside while his sister goes to the sanitarium office to make arrangements for having him retained.

There's a nurse in the office, Ruth Kelly, who notes names, facts and many of Veta's unconnected observations. The nurse buzzes for Wilson, the white-jacketed, not-too-bright strong-arm department, and asks him to get Mr. Dowd out of the cab and into Room 24.

Veta wants to see Dr. Chumley, but Dr. Chumley is the type who doesn't see anybody. All the seeing is done by his young assistant, Dr. Sanderson. Sanderson is summoned, and in the perfect psychiatrist's manner he begins to probe into Veta's worries about Elwood and what she wants done about him.

Veta wants Elwood committed permanently to Chumley's Rest because she can't stand another day of that Harvey. She's tired of setting a place at the table for him, and making room for him on the sofa, and calling him to the phone when Elwood is out somewhere and wants to talk to him.

Sanderson is interested in Harvey, of course, and asks who he is. Veta explains that he is a rabbit, six feet or six feet one-and-a-half high. He is always around the house, and it seems to Veta that if Elwood were lonesome he could at least bring somebody human to the house. Harvey is invisible—but every once in a while, Veta confesses, she sees him.

The young psychiatrist is certain now that he has an interesting case—but the case is Veta, not Elwood. When she goes down to the cab to get Elwood's things, Dr. Sanderson buzzes for Wilson and orders him to capture her. Her story about wanting Elwood committed is an old dodge employed by a cunning type of psychopath; she knew Elwood was about to have her committed, so she tried to discredit him.

Sanderson is horrified when he learns from Nurse Kelly that Wilson has already put Elwood in Room 24. He orders Elwood released, and decides that the situation is so serious that Dr. Chumley himself must be apprised of it.

Wilson captures Veta and carries her, struggling, to Room 13, and Elwood joins the nurse in the office. His adventures with Wilson and Room 24 have not disturbed him. Taking a chair for himself and another for Harvey, and laying the extra hat and coat on the table, he introduces himself to Miss Kelly and presents a card. When Sanderson comes back he presents another card and would like to present Harvey; but Sanderson is too upset about Veta to meet anybody else at the moment.

The young doctor suggests that Veta stay on at Chumley's Rest for a while on account of seeing a white rabbit six feet high. This, says Elwood, is up to Veta; if she wants to, all right. Perhaps he should consult the family lawyer, Judge Gaffney. Elwood wanders off on an unescorted tour of the sanitarium, and Dr. Chumley himself comes in. Chumley trusts that the difficulty about the woman with the rabbit has been smoothed over, and is assured it has.

He is about to go upstairs to see Veta when he notices the hat and coat on the table. Nobody seems to know whose they are. The hat is odd, because there are two holes cut in the crown; some new fad, no doubt.

Wilson arrives to report that he has got Veta's clothes off and has put her in a hydro tub. Chumley again is about to go see his new patient when Mrs. Chumley appears. They have a date for a cocktail party, so will he please give his patient a little quick diagnosis and get going?

At last the doctor goes to Veta—and Elwood wanders in. He introduces himself to Mrs. Chumley—and he seems to be looking for something. When she asks if there is something she can do for him a look of intense interest comes upon him and he asks what she had in mind. Well, he seemed to be looking for somebody, that's all.

Indeed he is looking for somebody. He is looking for Harvey. Harvey is Elwood's best friend, and is also a pooka. The last he saw of him he was in that chair and his hat and coat were on the table, but now they are gone. He does not know that the hat and coat have been hung in a closet, and presumes Harvey has them.

Mrs. Chumley offers to give Harvey a message if he should come in. She makes a note of it on Elwood's card—just a message for Harvey to meet Elwood downtown; he'll know where. Mrs. Chumley says that she and her husband are going to a cocktail party downtown at Dr. McClure's, and if Harvey turns up they can give him a lift in the car. Elwood wanders off downtown.

Dr. Chumley is quite irritated with Veta because she has kept insisting that the big white rabbit is her brother's, not hers. He orders some pills and another hydro tub for her, and now is ready

to go with his wife to the party. She reports that a man was here
—Elwood P. Dowd—and that he was looking for somebody he
came out with this afternoon.

Dr. Sanderson says he can't remember anybody else being
with Elwood, and neither can Nurse Kelly. But Mrs. Chumley
is positive Elwood was looking for a friend, because he mentioned
this friend sitting in the chair and having his hat and coat on the
table. The friend's name, she recalls, was Harvey, and Elwood
called him a pooka, whatever that meant.

Horrified realization creeps up on the nurse and Dr. Sanderson
—and on Dr. Chumley himself. The holes in the crown of the
hat were for a rabbit's ears, obviously! Sanderson has pulled the
boner of boners, for it is Elwood and not Veta who should be
upstairs in the hydro tub. Chumley confirms his suspicion by
telephoning Judge Gaffney and learning from the Judge that it
was Elwood who was to have been committed.

There's no cocktail party at Dr. McClure's for Chumley now.
He must capture Elwood—with the help of the powerful Wilson.

There is something on Mrs. Chumley's mind: What could a
pooka be? The encyclopedia might tell. She gets the right
volume out of the bookcase, but decides to go home and tell the
cook they'll be home for dinner after all. It is Wilson who looks
up "pooka," reading the definition syllable by syllable:

"From old Celtic mythology. A fairy spirit in animal form.
Always very large. The pooka appears here and there, now and
then, to this one and that one at his own caprice. A wise but
mischievous creature. Very fond of rum-pots, crack-pots, and
how are you, Mr. Wilson?"

A look of utter bewilderment comes over Wilson. He shakes
the book, examines it again, and queries:

"Who in the encyclopedia wants to know?"

Thus ends the first act.

ACT II

Back in the Dowd home, Myrtle Mae has been busy. Confident that Elwood now is safe in the booby-hatch, Myrtle has
already admitted a prospective purchaser for the house, and when
the doorbell rings again she admits Judge Gaffney, who seems
angry.

Veta Louise has phoned him at the club and got him out of a
golf game with a lot of hysterical talk, and is that Veta upstairs?

No, explains Myrtle Mae, that's a man upstairs who wants to

buy the house and cut it up into buffet apartments; her mother must be out at the sanitarium.

Judge Gaffney isn't happy about the setup. He always liked Elwood and he doesn't like the idea of his being locked up. And, besides, this house is his, and nobody else can sell it. While the Judge is talking affectionately of Elwood, Veta arrives—a shaking, gasping, disarranged Veta. They put her in and let Elwood out, she quavers, and she wants Judge Gaffney to sue Chumley's Rest. Her captor, Wilson, was a white slaver; she knows he was, because he had on one of those white suits and that's how they advertise.

Myrtle Mae is hopeful of hearing some tale of sex atrocity, and is obviously disappointed upon learning that all they did with Veta was put her in a tub of water. But Gaffney is aroused; he vows he will run Chumley out of the state.

Myrtle Mae's unhappiness is acute. There's a purchaser for the house, but Elwood has vanished—and certainly Elwood should be restrained. Why, the Judge ought to see what Elwood brought home six months ago—something that Myrtle and her mother hid in the garage . . . She goes to get it.

Wilson and Dr. Chumley arrive, still hunting for the crack-pot with the rabbit. They've been to seventeen bars, four firehouses and a grain elevator whose foreman is a friend of Elwood's, without finding their man.

The Judge and Dr. Chumley go upstairs to talk to Veta, who has been put to bed; Myrtle Mae, having brought a large, flat, paper-wrapped package from the garage, takes Wilson into the kitchen for a glass of milk and a sandwich.

In comes Elwood. He dials Chumley's Rest and Mrs. Chumley answers. Her husband is not there. No, she never did find Harvey. Elwood is sorry she couldn't make the McClure cocktail party. He went, looking for Harvey, and the people were all charming and he was able to leave quite a few of his cards.

Having completed his call, Elwood now notices the package Myrtle Mae has brought in. He unwraps it and admiringly reveals a painting of himself, seated on a chair, with a large white rabbit in a blue polka-dot collar and red necktie standing beside him. Elwood puts this work of art on the mantel, where it obscures the portrait of the late Marcella Pinney Dowd. Having arranged this decoration, he saunters out.

A ring of the phone brings Veta, with Dr. Chumley following. The phone call is a wrong number, but Veta thinks she has the right number when she suggests to Dr. Chumley that she is go-

Photo by Vandamm Studio.

"HARVEY"

"He (Elwood) . . . admiringly reveals a painting of himself with a large white rabbit in a blue polka-dot collar and red necktie. . . . Elwood puts this work of art on the mantel, where it obscures the portrait of the late Marcella Pinney Dowd."

(*Frank Fay*)

ing to sue him for $50,000. At the telephone, her back is to the
mantel, and Chumley is facing it. He is definitely interested in
the painting above it.

This portrait, says Veta, is the pride of the house. She knows
about art because she took a course in it last Winter. The difference between a fine oil painting and a mechanical thing like a
photograph is simply this: a photograph shows only the reality,
but a painting shows not only the reality but also the dream
behind it.

"It's our dreams that keep us going. That separates us from
the beasts. I wouldn't even want to live if I thought it was all
just eating and sleeping and taking off my clothes. Well—putting them on again—"

Veta turns to the mantel, screams, totters and falls back into
Chumley's arms. The old psychiatrist at work again, he soothes
her, assures her everything is all right, asks what is the matter.

Veta points wildly toward the painting of Elwood and Harvey.
"Doctor," she wails, "that is NOT my mother!"

The telephone, which is as convenient to dramatists as it is
to us ordinary householders, rings once more. It is Elwood on
the wire and Veta takes the call. Elwood won't say where he is,
but he wants to know if Harvey is there. Coached by Dr. Chumley, Veta says yes, Harvey is here, and why doesn't Elwood come
home now.

Elwood, cagey, wants Harvey to come to the phone. Again at
Chumley's suggestion, Veta reports that Harvey can't come to
the phone because he is upstairs taking a bath. She'll be glad to
send him over as soon as he is dry—if Elwood will tell where
he is.

But Elwood hangs up on her. Harvey, it seems, has just
walked in to join him, and Veta had better look in the bath tub
to see what stranger is there.

Veta knows, however, where Elwood is, because when he was
on the wire she heard the bartender answer the other phone and
it was Charlie's place, over at 12th and Main. Chumley immediately sets forth to make the capture.

Four hours later the office of Chumley's Rest is a scene of de-
jection. Young Dr. Sanderson, having been fired for his mistake of restraining Veta instead of Elwood, is packing his books
and belongings—and having a love spat with Nurse Kelly. These
two seem always to be demonstrating their mutual affection by
squabbling. Now it comes to the point where Sanderson, as is
the habit and privilege of all males, stalks out.

But Miss Kelly isn't alone for long, because Elwood strolls in, bringing her a bouquet of dahlias which he has just picked from Dr. Chumley's prize bed. He has come to take the nurse and Dr. Sanderson downtown for a drink, and he has a cab outside. He knocks on Sanderson's office door and when the young doctor sees him he presses the buzzer for Wilson. The object of a baffling manhunt has walked right in, all by himself.

Sanderson stalls, to keep Elwood on hand until Dr. Chumley arrives. Chumley, he explains, is Elwood's friend, and only wants to help him. Elwood thinks this is very nice and would like to help Dr. Chumley, too.

"If you'll begin by taking a co-operative attitude," counsels Sanderson, "that's half the battle. We all have to face reality, Dowd—sooner or later."

To which the ineffable Elwood replies, "I wrestled with reality for forty years, Doctor, and I am happy to state that I finally won out over it."

But, by the way, where is Dr. Chumley? Everybody would like to know, including Wilson, who has answered the buzzer and is now ready to escort Elwood back to Room 24. Elwood does not know where Chumley is now, but earlier, around dinnertime, he did see him at Charlie's place. They sat in a booth—the three of them: Elwood, Harvey and Chumley. They did some drinking, and Harvey thought Chumley should pick up part of the checks but the doctor couldn't see it that way; so Elwood paid for the whole party.

There was, continues Elwood, a beautiful blonde and her escort in the booth across from them, and Chumley went over and tried to explain to the blonde that they had once met in Chicago. The escort didn't like this, so he escorted Dr. Chumley back to Elwood's booth and advised him to mind his own affairs.

Next, the doctor wanted Harvey to go with him to Blondie's Chicken Inn, but Harvey wanted to go to Eddie's place. While Elwood was at the bar ordering another round of drinks the rabbit and the psychiatrist went out together—and that's all he knows about them.

At least some of Elwood's story checks. Nurse Kelly calls Charlie's and learns that Chumley was there—and, furthermore, he will not be welcome there again.

Elwood feels he must leave now. He has things to do. Miss Kelly would like to know just what it is that he does, and in explanation Elwood relates:

"Harvey and I sit in the bars and we have a drink or two and play the juke box. Soon the faces of the other people turn toward mine and smile. They are saying: We don't know your name, Mister, but you're a lovely fellow. Harvey and I warm ourselves in all these golden moments. We have entered as strangers—soon we have friends. They come over. They sit with us. They drink with us. They talk to us. They tell about the big terrible things they have done. The big wonderful things they will do. Their hopes, their regrets, their loves, their hates. All very large because nobody ever brings anything small into a bar. Then I introduce them to Harvey. And he is bigger and grander than anything they offer me. When they leave, they leave impressed. The same people seldom come back—but that's envy, my dear. There's a little bit of envy in the best of us—too bad, isn't it?"

This tale is superb research stuff for a rising young psychiatrist like Dr. Sanderson. He tries to probe Elwood's mind. How did Harvey get named Harvey? Because, replies Elwood quite simply, that is his name. He remembers when he first met him, several years ago. He had helped a friend who was a little drunk into a taxi, and then he heard somebody call his name.

Leaning against a lamp-post was this six-foot rabbit. Elwood did not regard this incident as remarkable, because when you have lived in a town as long as Elwood has you get used to the fact that everybody knows your name.

Elwood chatted with the rabbit a while and then asked his name. The rabbit wanted to know what name Elwood liked, and Elwood said Harvey. "What a coincidence," exclaimed the rabbit. "My name happens to be Harvey."

Dr. Sanderson gently suggests that Elwood come upstairs with him and the nurse, and Elwood pleasantly agrees—but says he can't visit very long because he has promised to take Harvey to the floor show at Charlie's. After they have left Dr. Chumley walks in, looking a little odd. He may be drunk, but if he is he is being very dignified about it.

Wilson wants to know if the doctor is all right. The doctor huffily replies that of course he is all right—but he is being followed. He orders Wilson to lock the entrance door. Then he goes to his private office, and locks the door behind him. Wilson is perplexed, but only momentarily; for problems of the mind do not remain long with Wilson. He shrugs, turns off the office lights and disappears into the sanitarium.

After a moment of darkness there is a rattle on the entrance door and the sound of a key turning. Slowly the door opens, and slowly it shuts. There is a pause, just long enough for somebody to cross the office, and then the door of Dr. Chumley's room opens and closes. Harvey has come in . . . and the curtain falls.

ACT III

In a few moments Chumley backs out of his office in an attitude of terror. He commands Harvey to go away, and at the same time advises the rabbit that he isn't there. He shouts for the faithful Wilson.

In come Judge Gaffney and Myrtle Mae. The Judge wants to know if it isn't possible that there might *be* something like this rabbit. He has, in fact, a sworn deposition from Veta Louise Simmons that she saw Harvey once, in her kitchen. He was staring at her, and she looked him right in the eye and said "To hell with you" and he left.

The effect of this information upon the shaken Chumley is visible. When Dr. Sanderson and the nurse come in he greets Sanderson complimentarily. Sanderson is not fired; he is a very astute man and Chumley wants him on his staff. This is good news for the young doctor and the nurse.

Myrtle Mae, however, doesn't care about Sandersons and nurses. What she wants is for Elwood to be put away in Chumley's Rest, just as had originally been planned. Elwood gets on one's nerves—particularly because he knows what is going to happen before it happens. Obviously, Harvey tells him.

Veta arrives, bringing Elwood's bathrobe. "Good," she observes as she surveys the gathering. "Nobody here but people."

Dr. Sanderson has an opinion on Elwood's case. Elwood is suffering from a third-degree hallucination, and Veta is the victim of autosuggestion. A rest in bed will fix Veta, but Elwood needs Shock Formula 977. A shot of 977 and Elwood won't see Harvey any more. This sounds reasonable to Veta. If Elwood can't see Harvey he won't let him in the house, and then when the rabbit comes to the door she, Veta, will deal with him firmly.

In comes the wandering Elwood again, humming pleasantly. He suggests that everybody come down to Charlie's for a drink—but Dr. Chumley, in a daze of discovery, would like to have a private conversation with him first.

Is it true, he asks, that Harvey gets advance notice of happenings? It is, indeed. Harvey can also stop clocks. He can look at your clock and stop it and you can go away as long as you like with whomever you like and go as far as you like. And when you come back not one minute will have ticked by.

"Einstein," explains Elwood, "has overcome time and space. Harvey has overcome not only time and space—but any objections."

This is completely fascinating to Dr. Chumley, and he indulges in some personal speculation. If Harvey would be good enough to stop *his* clock, the doctor would go to a cottage camp outside Akron with a pretty young woman—a stranger, and a quiet one. They'd lie under a maple tree and drink cold beer and he'd talk to her, for two weeks.

Elwood thinks maybe the woman would like a highball once in a while, instead of beer all the time. He thinks, too, that Dr. Chumley is making a mistake in not letting her talk. She might have picked up some interesting little news items.

Chumley eagerly wonders if Harvey would stop his clock for him and make this adventure in Akron possible, and Elwood sees no reason why not. He never heard Harvey say anything against Akron. The doctor, now on Elwood's side, warns him of Veta's plot to have him committed, and of her getting a power of attorney and the key to Elwood's safety box. Elwood takes the news calmly, merely observing that Veta is certainly a whirlwind to have done all this in one afternoon.

"God, man," exclaims Chumley, "haven't you any righteous indignation?"

"Dr. Chumley," replies Elwood, "my mother used to say to me, 'In this world, Elwood, you must be oh, oh, so smart or oh, so pleasant.' For years I was smart. I recommend pleasant. You may quote me."

Chumley even offers to commit Veta, but her brother doesn't think she would like it.

When the others come in again they have reached agreement. They have voted for Dr. Sanderson's shock treatment. It can't be given without Elwood's consent, but Veta is sure he will take it if she asks him to. The shock treatment is explained to him, and he is told that if he takes it he won't see Harvey any more. He will, instead, see his responsibilities.

Elwood agrees the shock treatment must be a nice thing for people who want it, and he'll be glad to recommend it to anybody who happens to need it; but for himself, he wouldn't care for it.

Veta pleads and weeps. She points out that she and Myrtle Mae never have any social life on account of the rabbit. Harvey has made them both miserable.

Gently and lovingly, Elwood says that if she feels that way

about Harvey he'll take the treatment, because he's always wanted his sister to have everything she wants. He goes with Dr. Sanderson into Sanderson's office.

A cab driver appears looking for Veta. She forgot to pay him $2.75. She digs in her purse, finally spills out its contents. Oddly—very oddly, and one feels that Harvey has had something to do with it—there is no money. Nobody else has any money, either; only Elwood, and he's inside getting an injection. The driver will have to wait.

But the driver, who knows about the injections they shoot into people out here, wants his money now; so there is nothing for Veta to do but interrupt the treatment and get Elwood out. Elwood has a pleasant chat with the driver, gives him a bill and tells him to keep the change, invites him to dinner. Then he goes back in for the Shock Formula.

Veta huffily remarks that the driver could just as well have waited, but he can't see it that way. "I've brought 'em out here to get that stuff," he observes, "and drove 'em back after they had it. It changes 'em. . . .

"On the way out here they sit back and enjoy the ride. They talk to me. Sometimes we stop and watch the sunsets and look at the birds flyin'. Sometimes we stop and watch the birds when there ain't no birds and look at the sunsets when it's rainin'. We have a swell time and I always get a big tip. But afterward—oh-oh!"

"What do you mean, afterwards oh-oh?" queries Veta.

"They crab, crab, crab. They yell at me to watch the lights, watch the brakes, watch the intersections. They scream at me to hurry. They got no faith—in me or my buggy—yet it's the same cab—the same driver—and we're goin' back over the very same road. It's no fun—and no tips—"

Veta is certain Elwood would have tipped, anyway, because he has always been generous.

"Not after this he won't be," warns the cabby. "Lady, after this he'll be a perfectly normal human being; and you know what bastards they are!"

This revelation, this gloomy prediction, is too much for Veta. Almost hysterically she pounds upon Dr. Sanderson's office door, demanding that the treatment be halted. She doesn't want Elwood to be the way the driver said he'd be.

When the others try to dissuade her she becomes more firm. What's wrong with Harvey, she would like to know. If she and Elwood and Myrtle Mae want to live with him, it's their business.

Elwood tenderly comforts her. "She's all tired out," he remarks. "She's done a lot today."

They leave Chumley's Rest. Elwood tarries to say good night to the doctor. He sees, emerging from Chumley's office, his invisible friend.

"Where've you been?" he asks. "I've been looking all over for you—"

And as Elwood and Harvey go forth together

THE CURTAIN FALLS

THE LATE GEORGE APLEY

A Comedy in Three Acts and Epilogue

By John P. Marquand and George S. Kaufman

IT was, by report, Max Gordon, the producer, who first suggested that there was a play to be extracted from "The Late George Apley." John Phillips Marquand had won a Pulitzer prize with this story when it was declared to be the best novel written by an American in 1937. But apparently neither play producers nor motion picture producers in general could see a play in it.

It was, also by report, Mr. Gordon who suggested that George Kaufman would be a perfect collaborator for Mr. Marquand. With this suggestion Mr. Marquand was quick to agree. "I know nothing about playwriting, and I understand Mr. Kaufman knows nothing about Boston," said the author. "We should get along famously." And they did.

One story born of this collaboration told of Mr. Marquand's suggestion to Leo G. Carroll, the actor who had been selected for the George Apley role, that he come with him one day for a brief visit to his Boston club. This would be the club, the author explained, which he had in mind in his book references to the Berkeley.

Mr. Carroll accepted the suggestion with enthusiasm and the visit was duly made. At the door of the club, as Mr. Marquand paused to register his guest, he casually informed the dignified ancient serving as receptionist that Mr. Carroll was a New Yorker. "In that case," quoth the ancient, "would you mind registering him in this book?" Saying which he produced the club register reserved for non-Boston, or "alien," guests. This adventure, Mr. Carroll admits, proved most helpful for an actor who was trying to acquire the "feel" of a Boston Brahmin.

"The Late George Apley" in play form was ready for mid-Summer rehearsal and was first tried in Wilmington, Del., in September, 1944. It was played for a week in Washington, and another week in Baltimore, before meeting its first severe test in Boston. The run of Bostonians loved the play, absorbing its gentle satire gracefully and with apparent delight. Here and there a captious citizen arose to question one minor exaggeration or another, and there were others who took delight in catching up the playwrights with such assertions as that Sigmund Freud was really not being discussed in Boston as early as 1912, or that Felix Frankfurter did not join the Harvard faculty until some months after the Messrs. Marquand and Kaufman have him doing so in their play. But in the main the current generation of Bostonians accepted the stage version of their immediate ancestors' lives as being true to tradition and the probabilities evoked.

"The Late George Apley" arrived in New York the evening of November 21. In the play list there were already scheduled four definite dramatic hits—"Anna Lucasta," "Soldier's Wife," "I Remember Mama," and "Harvey"—as well as two outstanding musicals, "Song of Norway" and "Bloomer Girl." But such was the temper and interest of wartime playgoers that it was perfectly simple for the "Apley" play to join the successes and add its bit to the record of this most unusual theatre year. The press reviews bordered the ecstatic, and the run continued through the season.

It is Thanksgiving Day, 1912, when we first meet the Apleys. The clan is gathering at the home of George Apley on Beacon Street. The living room into which we are ushered, is a large room, which "like many rooms in Boston," the authors point out, "is half sumptuously and half carelessly furnished, without any unity of decorations. This very lack of unity gives a comfortable sense of continuity, showing that the place has been occupied for many years by a family in comfortable circumstances."

This Thanksgiving morning George Apley, coming in from the street, smartly though conventionally appareled in black overcoat and high silk hat, finds Margaret, the maid, "a grim, austere woman of about seventy," engaged in a curious horticultural pursuit. She is attacking with an insecticide sprayer the green bugs that have appeared on the ivy in the bay window.

"I don't see why it is that something like this invariably happens on Thanksgiving Day," protests Mr. Apley, with a modest show of irritation. "Last year there was a blizzard, and the year before that the mince pie fermented. . . . Well, we can't do anything about it now, Margaret, just before Thanksgiving dinner. It's just another of those little things, Margaret—little things that interfere with our lives."

Emerson, Mr. Apley recalls, has something capital to say about that, if he can find Emerson. The Essays should be right next to Thoreau, but they're not. They are far over at the end of the shelf and, of all places, directly next to Hawthorne's "The Scarlet Letter." This second minor irritation is quickly relieved by Mr. Apley's locating the passage in Emerson for which he is looking—

" 'God reappears with all his Parts in every moss and every cobweb,' " he reads to a patient Margaret. " 'If the good is there, so is the evil; if the affinity, so the repulsion.' There you have it."

"Yes, sir," meekly agrees Margaret.

Mr. Apley is affectionately turning a page or two before he replaces Emerson in his rightful place, when Mrs. Apley comes into the room.

Catherine Apley, "in her middle years and still quite lovely," brings a bunch of snapdragons from the conservatory to put in a vase on the dresser. She has also put a mound of them, she reports, on the table between the pumpkins—a bit of a departure, she admits, but an inspiration of the moment.

Mr. Apley would locate his children. Where is John? John is on his way from Cambridge, but the trolleys are none too certain. John should be there, thinks his father, seeing that his cousin Agnes is coming. John will be a married man in no time now, though, of course, nothing has been said about it. Still, everyone seems to think—

And where is Eleanor? Eleanor is upstairs changing her dress. Eleanor, to her father, has not been quite her own self these last few weeks, but that is quite understandable to her mother.

The door slams and John bounds in. With a hearty "Hello, everybody!" he is on his way up the stairs before they can stop him. He must wash—

"Can't you wash at Harvard?" his impatient father calls after him.

Mrs. Apley has remembered that Agnes is to have her coming-out party a week from Thanksgiving and, according to her Phillips-Brooks calendar, that is going to give the Apleys a very complicated week—

"Now, tomorrow there is the Symphony," Catherine is saying. "We must go to that—we're sitting in the new seats."

Mr. Apley, who has been reading his paper, looks up, thoughtfully. "Oh, yes," he mutters, and adds, soberly: "I don't know why we ever changed."

CATHERINE— But you've been waiting for years, dear, till Mrs. Warren died, so we could move forward.

APLEY—I never knew it would put us next to the Hopkinses.

CATHERINE—The Bradley Hopkinses?

APLEY—Yes. You don't think, Catherine, that if we're sitting next to them, people may think our tastes verge on the radical?

CATHERINE—Why, George?

APLEY—You know what Bradley Hopkins said about that unfortunate Debussy selection, "Afternoon of a Faun." (*He lowers his voice.*) He said—he enjoyed it very much, and a great many people heard him say it. And if we were sitting next to them—

CATHERINE—I'm sure it will be all right. (*Returning to the calendar.*) Now, Saturday night is dinner at Major Higginsons, and Sunday we'll have to be at King's Chapel. I think, George, we ought to take the automobile. We never seem to use it.

APLEY—I wouldn't do that, Catherine. You know Patrick doesn't drive it very well. He's much more used to horses.

CATHERINE—I really don't see any use having an automobile—

APLEY—Catherine, Patrick has driven the family for forty years. He drove for father. I won't have anything done to hurt his feelings. We'll take the carriage.

CATHERINE—Of course, George.

APLEY (*looking at calendar over* CATHERINE'S *shoulder*)— Now— On Monday afternoon there is a trustees' meeting of the Sailors' Home, and Monday night is the Monday Night Club. Tuesday— Oh, yes! The Save Boston Society. It's about allowing an electric sign on the edge of the Common.

CATHERINE—Must you go to that, too, George?

APLEY—My dear, it's going to say Grape Nuts!

CATHERINE—I suppose we must stop that.

APLEY—Dear me! Tuesday—I completely forgot. The Blue Hill Bird Watchers Society is meeting.

CATHERINE—Is that more important, George?

APLEY—This particular meeting—I think it is, my dear. There has to be another President of the Bird Watchers—you remember old Dr. Beech died last week. And I have every reason to believe— (*He lets her guess his secret.*)

CATHERINE—Why, George, that's splendid.

APLEY—Mind you, I don't say I'm worthy of it. But—I've never missed a Sunday bird walk.

Mr. Apley has a feeling that it was his being the first to see a yellow-throated linnet in November on the Bird-Watchers' last walk that put him definitely in line for the presidency.

As for the week of crowded engagements, Mr. Apley doesn't

194   THE BEST PLAYS OF 1944-45

see how that can be avoided. After all they do have their obligations—

"*Someone* has to be a trustee of the Boston Waifs," George would remind his wife. "Someone has to look after the Sailors' Home. My grandfather . . . my father . . . These are things that have come down to me, Catherine. Last week alone, Catherine, I attended twelve meetings of different organizations—charitable, civic. Father was on most of them."

Eleanor has come down the stairs; "a nice looking girl unblemished by cosmetics." She is wearing a shirtwaist and low heels. She is, as they suspect, going for a walk after dinner. She is going for a walk with a very nice young man whom she is sure they will like. His name is Howard Boulder. No, he isn't Boston, as her father is quick to surmise. He is New York. But there is no reason for their being prejudiced.

Mr. Boulder, Eleanor informs them further, is giving a series of lectures at Harvard, in Emerson Hall, on American literature—

"It's one of those fellowships that are paid for out of somebody's will," explains Eleanor. "And he's done so well he's coming back in February."

"Why, that would be the Jonathan Smythe Fellowship!" her father suddenly recalls, with satisfaction. "That changes everything! Well, well! Catherine, Buzzy Loring is the chairman of the Jonathan Smythe Fellowship!" . . .

The family is beginning to arrive. George's sister, Amelia, and her husband, Roger Newcombe, are the first. Amelia is a bit on the aggressive side, and Roger is inclined to be cynically resigned to whatever happens.

Amelia is quick to notice Eleanor's odd choice of costume, but, as George explains, Eleanor is going walking after dinner, and with a very intelligent young man who gives lectures. "You know the Jonathan Smythe Foundation, Roger. Buzzy Loring is the trustee for it."

Roger knows. "I've worked out a way of remembering everything that Buzzy Loring is the trustee for," says he.

"Is that so? How do you do it?"

"Whatever it is, if you're not the trustee for it, he is," explains Roger.

The Willings are next to arrive—Horatio Willing and Jane, his wife. Horatio is a hearty, even ebullient, type. "Jane is a subdued woman, and you gather that it may have been Willing who subdued her." Again the greetings are cordially profuse and familiar.

"Sloppy Jane!" comments Amelia, facing her sister. "That's what they used to call you at Miss Hendrick's School. You've forgotten to take off your galoshes again." And so she has.

Shortly Agnes Willing a little timidly follows her parents into the room. "She is a rather pallid girl with a large bow in her hair, and she clutches a small package done up in tissue paper."

It is evident that there is considerable family expectancy concerned with the meeting of Agnes Willing and John Apley. It adds something to the apparent embarrassment of the young people when they do meet. Nor does Horace's calling Agnes' attention to the present she has brought for John, and forgotten to give him, lessen the tension of the moment.

Agnes' present is a tie—a knitted tie. "She's been knitting on it for two weeks," Horatio tells them. The tie isn't as good as it ought to be, Agnes insists, and she is going to knit a better one, with a lot more stripes.

After the family has deposed itself variously about the room, Horatio suddenly recalls something he has to tell them. That morning, just outside the Union League Club, Horatio had run into Walter Noble and Noble had practically assured him that George was going to be the next President of the Bird Watchers.

George is quite sure that nothing definite has been decided upon, but, with the slightest urging, he is perfectly willing to tell them how it all came about—

"It was in the Lawrences' pasture last Sunday—just where the path forks toward the brook. Not the big brook, the little brook . . . Anyhow, I don't know what first caught my attention. There was no sound. . . . Merely a flash of color in the juniper . . ."

There are interruptions, but George, save for reproving looks, tries to ignore them. John is pecking a little nervously at the piano and Wilson, the butler, has come quietly to warn Mrs. Apley that dinner is served—

". . . flash of color in the junipers—a bright flash of yellow, but I had time to raise my glasses, and there, on the lower limb of that big shag-bark hickory by the stone wall—"

Catherine has finally forced his attention. "Dinner is ready," she says, gesturing toward Amelia.

"Oh! . . . Well, we'll go in . . . Amelia."

"But WHAT was sitting there?" demands Roger. "You can't leave us dangling!"

"A yellow-throated linnet!"

By now the procession is forming and heading into the dining room.

"Well, I don't understand all this nonsense about birds," declares Amelia. "A bird is all right in its place, but why pry into its private life?"

At his father's suggestion, John has given Agnes his arm, and the exodus begins.

"It was right there on the lower limb," Apley is continuing, "and as I looked it burst into song. Like this . . ."

He has taken a small whistle out of his pocket and is blowing it as the curtain falls.

After dinner the women are the first to return to the living room. They file in slowly, heavily, "all giving evidence of that unwelcome repletion which so often follows a Thanksgiving dinner." Catherine has provided fans for them, and for a moment they sit fanning themselves in unison.

The men arrive, also heavily. Roger has brought a snifter brandy glass with a large portion of brandy in it. (AMELIA *does not like this, but* ROGER *does*.) George Apley shortly follows with a box of cigars.

When John and Agnes appear George motions them to a settee, an invitation they accept a little awkwardly. John doesn't take a cigar. "John is going to get a gold watch if he doesn't smoke before he is twenty-one," George explains. "We have a little agreement."

"What a beautiful relationship you and John have always had," beams Horatio. "I can't imagine anything ever coming between you."

Now Eleanor has come, and been motioned to her chair. "We've sat in these same seats for eighteen Thanksgivings," announces Jane, as though to herself.

"Why, what a peculiar thing to say, Jane. Why shouldn't we?" demands Horatio.

"What would Thanksgiving be without a family?" George would know.

"It is very good of you, George, to include Jane and me," says Horatio. "After all, Jane is only your third cousin."

"It is possible to be very fond of a cousin, Horatio," says George, and adds, significantly: "And your little Agnes is quite like our own daughter."

The talk has turned to Agnes' coming-out party. Her dress is nearly finished, and though it may have been cut a little low, it is always easy, as Catherine points out, to fill in with tulle.

"Thank goodness my party's all over." This from Eleanor. "I don't know anything more scaley than coming out."

"Scaley? Where did you hear that word, dear?" Her mother is interested.

"I don't know. I just heard it."

"Did you ever hear the word scaley, George?"

"No, I never did."

"I just happened to hear it," explains Eleanor, quickly. She turns to Agnes. "Are you excited about coming out, Agnes?"

"Oh, yes. I think coming out must be wonderful, except I'm a little bit afraid I'll be afraid."

"There's nothing to be afraid of. You just see the same old faces. No Yale boys. No Princeton boys. Just Harvard boys."

"And what is the matter with Harvard boys?" George Apley would know.

"Nothing, Father. They just go to Harvard." She has turned to Agnes: "And they've all got to dance with you, whether they want to or not, because it's your party."

"Oh, dear," sighs Agnes.

"Eleanor, you mustn't frighten your cousin," warns Catherine.

"It's just that I think coming-out parties are an outmoded folk custom," Eleanor goes on, with a suggestion of warmth. "It's the old idea of introducing the virgin to the tribes."

"Really, Eleanor!" Her mother is shocked.

"Why, Eleanor, there are some things that we simply don't mention!" Her father is serious.

"Why shouldn't we mention them?"

"Well, dear! Savage tribes!"

"Really, Father, if things exist I don't see why we shouldn't face them."

"Because we do not face virginity in the drawing room after a Thanksgiving dinner," declares George Apley, firmly. Eleanor gives up.

George is still firm when by open suggestion he maneuvers John and Agnes into the conservatory. Then he turns to the family with a problem. It concerns Cousin Hattie.

Cousin Hattie, it appears, has been dead a month. While she had lived she was never a problem, aside from the matter of sending a check now and then, to which George had attended, and a visit, perhaps once a year. But now that Cousin Hattie is dead—

"They buried her at Mt. Auburn, and to that I have no general objection," explains George. "The family plot at Mt. Auburn is completely democratic—any Apley connection, no matter how remote, is welcome to rest there if he chooses. Even you, Horatio."

Horatio is delighted.

No, it is not a question of Cousin Hattie's being buried in the Apley lot, George would explain. It is her location that is worrying him.

"Last week, when Catherine and I were motoring to Concord, we stopped for a moment at Mt. Auburn," continues George. "I was particularly anxious to see how the arborvitae border was doing back of Father's stone. Suddenly, to my astonishment, I saw a new headstone of pink granite with a recumbent figure upon it. There in *our* part of the lot was Cousin Hattie, large as life."

Amelia doesn't see how anything can be done about it now, but George has already written Henry Apley a letter explaining that he must move his mother somewhere else—preferably to the bottom of the slope.

Horatio is convinced that George is right, but he does regret the episode. It is pretty certain to create talk.

"It won't create any talk at all," snaps Roger. "Who gives a damn where the Apleys are buried."

This might easily have led to further discussion, but just then John and Agnes come back from the conservatory, evidently not with the friendliest feelings for one another. Sensing the situation, Catherine is quick to suggest that Agnes play something for them. Agnes had rather not, but, with much urging agrees finally to play her newest piece—a waltz from "The Quaker Girl" called "Come to the Ball."

At the piano, her confidence slowly increasing, Agnes sings a verse and a chorus of "Come to the Ball." Then they all join in the second chorus. They are singing quite lustily when the doorbell rings. Eleanor comes downstairs to answer it. Howard Boulder has called.

At Eleanor's bidding young Mr. Boulder comes into the room. "He is young—and perhaps a little carelessly dressed." He is not at all embarrassed, taking George Apley's introductions of the family quite casually. No, he will not have a cigar, but if Mr. Apley has any cigarettes—

"I'm sorry. I've never gone quite so far as cigarettes," confesses George, with a quick glance at Catherine.

"Mr. Boulder is giving the Jonathan Smythe lectures at Emerson Hall," George explains to the family. "That's quite an achievement at your age, Mr. Boulder."

BOULDER—I'm probably a year or two older than I look. Besides, I'm pretty used to it.

ELEANOR—He's been lecturing ever since he got his Ph.D.

APLEY—Indeed? And where was that, Mr. Boulder?

BOULDER—At Yale.

APLEY (*looking at* CATHERINE *then to* ROGER)—Yale!

ROGER (*nodding*)—That's what he said!

APLEY—What do you lecture on, Mr. Boulder?

BOULDER—It's a course on American literature. Particularly the Concord group.

APLEY (*with approval*)—The Concord group? (*To the room.*) Why, that would be all the great figures. Emerson, Thoreau, Alcott.

BOULDER (*with a smile*)—You should hear me read "Little Women."

APLEY—You must come to dinner some time, Mr. Boulder, so we can have a long talk about them. As a young man my father once met Thoreau. Emerson once came to breakfast with Dr. Oliver Wendell Holmes.

AMELIA (*clarifying the whole thing for* BOULDER)—That was in our grandfather's house on Louisburg Square.

BOULDER—I see.

APLEY—You make me anxious to hear your lecture, Mr. Boulder. What is it called?

BOULDER—The Concord-Myth.

APLEY (*slowly*)—The Concord-Myth? (ROGER *clears his throat, loudly, as though to say, "Well, Well, Well" indistinguishable.*)

APLEY (*slowly*)—I can't very well picture Emerson as being a myth.

BOULDER—Oh, Emerson's all right as far as he goes, sir. But there was a good deal of scaley writing up there in Concord. (*The* APLEYS *exchange looks—they have recognized the word.* ELEANOR, *of course, also realizes what has happened.*)

ELEANOR—Perhaps we'd better be starting. If we're going to walk all the way to Cambridge. (ELEANOR *rises on this speech,* BOULDER *rises, putting out his cigarette as he does so.*)

CATHERINE (*rising*)—Walk to Cambridge? But why, dear?

ELEANOR—Just for the walk. We're going to have tea at a friend of Howard's—Mr. Boulder's.

APLEY—You didn't tell us about that, dear. What friend?
ELEANOR—It's a Mr. Frankfurter. Mr. Felix Frankfurter.
APLEY—Frankfurter?
ELEANOR—He teaches at the Harvard Law School.
APLEY (*reluctantly*)—Oh! Well, if he's on the law school
faculty—
CATHERINE (*smoothing it over*)—Of course, George.

George is still firm in his belief that Emerson never wrote anything "scaley," but Mr. Boulder is equally firm in his conviction
that some of the Emerson poetry is pretty hard to take. Anyway, when he comes back in February the subject of his talks
will be "The Dead Hand of Emerson on American Creative
Thought—"
Eleanor takes her young man away before her father can give
his opinion of such a subject. To the family George rumbles on
quite seriously—
"I don't understand it. What can be the matter with the
Harvard Corporation to allow anyone, in Emerson Hall, mind
you, in Emerson Hall—"
"It's shocking," agrees Horatio.
Again Catherine would clear the situation by asking Agnes to
play. This reminds John that he really will have to be going.
He would love to hear Agnes play more, but there really is serious
studying to be done. He has dashed upstairs before they can
stop him.
Then the Willings decide that they had better be going, too,
so long as Agnes' cousins find that they cannot stay to entertain
her. Amelia, too, is ready to go, despite her brother's suggestion
that she should not hurry—
"What's there to stay for if everybody's gone?" Amelia wants
to know. "I did think that we might have at least one Thanksgiving without a family quarrel." And she is gone.
"The pilgrims had the Indians, George. We have Amelia,"
ventures Roger, following his wife into the hall.
John would sneak down the stairs and out the door without his
parents seeing him, but his father calls to him.
"John, I can't believe, I won't believe, that you intended what
you did just now," protests the elder Apley in a hurt tone. "I've
always been so proud of you, John. I don't think you understand how much you have hurt everyone's feelings. It isn't like
you, John. Now come. Tell your mother and me—what's the
matter?"

"Aren't you feeling well, dear?"   Catherine is anxious.

"Of course!"

"Have you got yourself in some sort of scrape at college?"

"No. Of course not."

"Then what is it?"

"I don't see why I should stand here and be questioned!" announces John, reaching for his books and papers. "If Eleanor can go out, why can't I? Why can't I lead my own life, like everybody else!"

John has bolted and the slam of the door is the only answer to his father's call. A moment later George detects a scent of violet perfume in the air. His nose leads him by degrees to an envelope lying on the chair where John had laid his books. The envelope, reeking of a cheap violet perfume, is addressed to John —and in a woman's handwriting.

"This explains his whole behavior," announces George.   He gives the envelope a closer inspection. "Oh, my God!"

"George, what is it?"

"It's postmarked Worcester!"

"Worcester—"

George's hand drops helplessly.   "The girl—is a foreigner, Catherine!"

The envelope flutters to the floor. The curtain falls.

ACT II

A week after Thanksgiving Catherine Apley is entertaining a small sewing group at home. In addition to Amelia and Jane two friendly neighbors are present—Lydia Leyton and Emily Southworth. "Voluminous petit points and knitting bags show that the afternoon has been spent in a useful pursuit. But now, sewing forgotten, the ladies are gathered cozily about a little tea table where Catherine presides before a heavy silver tea service."

So far the conversation has covered a variety of topics, ranging from Amelia's account of the time Father Apley had caught sight of a man in his shirt sleeves sitting on the front stoop of the house opposite the Apley place in the South End, and decided on the instant to move to Beacon Street, to the coming-out party of Jane's daughter, Agnes, to occur that evening.

Agnes' party dress is all ready, Jane reports.   Even if it should prove to be a little low in the bosom, Jane has some tulle handy. Yes, John has asked Agnes for the supper dance. Which recalls many other supper dances at other coming-out parties.

"Do you remember how George used to fill out your dance program, Jane?" asks Catherine.

"Yes, that was how I met Horatio. George wrote him in."

"With this new cutting in, I don't see how you can ever decide whom you like best. George and I danced and danced."

"Were you engaged then?" Jane would know.

"Oh, no. It was—quite a while after that."

"George was sent abroad for a year first," speaks up Amelia. "To forget."

"To forget what?"

"Never mind, Jane."

"I remember he went abroad, but I didn't know it was anything like that."

"It wasn't. It doesn't matter now." Amelia would dismiss the subject.

"It's all right, Amelia," says Catherine. "I don't know two people in Boston who are happier than George and I."

When the subject turns to husbands in general, and Boston husbands in particular, Catherine sticks to her guns. "George has always been thoughtful and kind, and a wonderful companion," she assures them.

"But wasn't he ever—you know what I mean?" "Romantic" is the word Jane had in mind. "Even on your honeymoon?"

"We had a perfect honeymoon," Catherine assures her. "We went to Rye Beach—the Farragut House. We rode every day, and in the evening we read Emerson."

"I think Boston men make the best husbands, don't you?" chips in Lydia Leyton. "I mean when you consider everything."

"Boston men are emotionally dependable—they're trained that way," announces Amelia. "But every once in a while something very strange does happen." In proof of which she recalls to them the case of Sonny Walker, who once led all the cotillions. Sonny, losing control of himself one day, had shot the tame squirrel that used to come to his window for crumbs. When that became known Sonny was not only dropped from the Bird Watchers, and the Berkeley Club, but he very shortly left Boston and was never heard of again.

All of which has caused Catherine to wonder a little if, after all, the Boston way is the right way. For her part Amelia has no doubts.

"I'm probably wrong," admits Catherine. "It's the children, I suppose. Realizing that they are growing up, and that they're at a point where . . ."

"Children don't know what they're doing, and they have to be told," asserts Amelia. "It's very simple—you just tell them."

"You haven't any children, Amelia," Catherine would remind her.

The arrival of George Apley breaks up the tea party. Soon they have all left, except Amelia. Amelia has lingered because she has something to tell George she thinks he should hear—

"George, do you know that at ten o'clock last night Eleanor and that young Boulder were seen standing on Commonwealth Avenue laughing at William Lloyd Garrison's statue?"

George, apparently, isn't concerned at the moment about Eleanor and Boulder. Nor does he think Amelia should be. So she flounces off to the attic to retrieve her mother's cuckoo clock.

There are other, and more serious, things on George's mind. For one thing, he has heard from Henry Apley in regard to the burying of Cousin Hattie in the Apley lot at Mt. Auburn. Cousin Hattie has been moved.

"I hope you didn't hurt his feelings," hopes Catherine.

APLEY—He has taken her out of Mt. Auburn entirely. He need hardly have done that. "In view of your astonishing attitude"—I don't think my attitude was astonishing—"It is my present plan to have her buried at sea. I trust you have no prior rights in the ocean." That seems an unnecessary remark.

CATHERINE (taking letter from him)—George, I wish you'd think about the children! Somehow I wish you hadn't gone quite so far as to send Horatio to Worcester. Do you think he was quite the person?

APLEY—Please, my dear. He's simply making some casual inquiries. He has a classmate in the Worcester Antiquarian Society.

CATHERINE—But so far as we know John and this girl may not even be—really serious.

APLEY—My dear, I think I know the signs of infatuation when I see them. I've been out to Harvard and asked some questions. And I find John has overdrawn his account at the Cambridge Trust Company, and now he is beginning to sell his clothes.

CATHERINE—His clothes? Oh, George!

APLEY—To a secondhand dealer named Max Keezer. I saw this myself. John's new blue serge is hanging in Mr. Keezer's window.

CATHERINE—His best suit?

APLEY—Mr. Keezer purchased it for a dollar and ninety-seven cents.

CATHERINE—Why, what does John need a dollar and ninety-seven cents for?

APLEY—To buy flowers, Catherine. I stopped in at the florist and inquired.

CATHERINE—I didn't know it had gone so far.

APLEY—Oh, not so far that it can't be managed, my dear. Has Eleanor come in yet?

CATHERINE—Not yet. Now, please don't be upset, George. I told her she could go to tea with Mr. Boulder.

APLEY—Why under the sun should that upset me, dear? Mr. Boulder is leaving for New York tomorrow.

CATHERINE (*watching him*)—But he's coming back in February.

APLEY—Oh, yes, yes.

CATHERINE—George, I think we may as well face it. I think that he and Eleanor are interested in each other.

APLEY (*unruffled*)—These things will all adjust themselves, given time, Catherine. You remember what Emerson said: "The mind—"

The voice of Eleanor in the hall interrupts George. "Hello, is anyone at home?" Eleanor's tone is a little high as to pitch, and when she and Mr. Boulder come into the room it is evident that they are both a little tight.

"I know what you've been doing, you two sweet old things," charges Eleanor, waving a playful finger at them. "You've been talking about me! And if you weren't talking about me, you were talking about John, weren't you?"

Both her father and mother ignore Eleanor and greet Mr. Boulder quite formally. Eleanor, however, is not to be ignored. She is quite sure that neither of them could ever guess where she and Mr. Boulder have been. They've been to the Copley-Plaza to a tea dansant—but they didn't take tea.

"What did you have, dear? Little cakes?" asks her mother innocently.

"We had cocktails," announces Eleanor, with a shake of her head. "I had two, and so did Howard."

"Well, that really sounds much worse than it was, sir," quickly protests Howard.

"And what do you think Howard said each time? He said 'When duty whispers low, thou must, the youth replies I can.'

Howard says it is one of Emerson's most nauseating lines."

"I don't think we should keep Mr. Boulder, Eleanor," says her father, icily. "I'm sure he has another engagement."

Eleanor would hold Howard if she could, but he insists that he has a lot of packing to do, seeing that he is leaving for New York next day. Eleanor follows him into the hall and presently, to the concern of the Apleys, there is a slight scuffling and Eleanor can be heard giggling nervously. When she comes back into the room she is carrying her hat.

"I think you had better go upstairs and lie down for a few minutes, dear," suggests Catherine.

"Can't I ever see *anyone* without being criticized?" demands Eleanor, protestingly.

"Eleanor, please!"

"I know what you'd like. You'd like to throw me at one of my cousins, like John. Well, I don't believe in inbreeding. I believe in natural selection."

Slowly, a little hysterically, Eleanor's defiance grows. Yes, the scuffling sound her father reports having heard was probably caused by Howard's trying to kiss her. He tried, and she let him. Didn't her father ever kiss her mother before they were engaged?

"You don't understand what I'm talking about because you haven't read Freud," declares Eleanor. "If you had, you'd know that emotion is healthy, Father."

"Catherine, take her out of here and give her some black coffee," thunders Apley.

"Just because he isn't in the social register, because he isn't exactly like everybody else. . . . Just because he's a Yale man. . . ." Eleanor is sobbing hysterically as her mother takes her upstairs.

For a moment Apley stands, statuesque and grim, clinching and unclinching his hands. He has gone to the bookcase and taken down Emerson. A ring at the door heralds the arrival of Horatio Willing.

Horatio has been to Worcester and is back with his report. Dole is the name of the family of the girl in whom John is interested. The girl's name is Myrtle. The father, Julian H. Dole, is President of the Dole Tool and Die Company. The Doles live in a yellowish brown house, with a lot of scrolls and things on it and there is an iron deer on the lawn. Also two iron dogs and a fountain—

The revelation is almost more than George can bear. He shuts his eyes to hide the pain of it. "John cannot have seen their house," he mutters.

To the contrary, John has been in the Dole house several times. Horatio had learned that from the maid, with whom he had struck up an acquaintance.

"You didn't just ring the door bell?" demands George, anxiously.

"Not until I had a plan," Horatio reassures him. "I thought at first I would say I was the man to read the gas meter, but I decided I was hardly the type. So I said I was a friend of John's, that I happened to be passing through Worcester, and he had asked me to stop and inquire if he had left his umbrella." He leans back, vastly pleased with himself.

APLEY—By Jove, I wouldn't have thought of that.

WILLING (*generously*)—Of course you would, George, if you'd put your mind to it. Anyway the maid said he hadn't left his umbrella.

APLEY—But then you had to leave.

WILLING—No! I happened to look down at her feet and saw she was wearing one shoe and one slipper, and it started me thinking. I asked her if she had a bunion.

APLEY—By Jove! And did she have?

WILLING—No. But she'd turned her ankle. I got her to tell me about it, and from that we fell into pleasant and easy conversation. As you know, I have a way with women.

APLEY (*impatiently*)—Yes, Horatio. What did you find out?

WILLING (*lowering his voice*)—John has been there several times. She said John was a nice young man, and it was cute to see him so sweet on Miss Myrtle when Miss Myrtle was so sweet on him. Those are her words, not mine.

APLEY—Obviously.

WILLING—Also, he telephones her every night from Harvard. The conversations are very lengthy. In addition, there are two letters daily. And flowers. All the time.

APLEY—The whole thing, of course, is nothing but sex. (HORATIO *nods, in full agreement.*) Personally, Horatio, it has always seemed to me that sex is largely nonsense.

WILLING—I know what you mean. I never heard it put quite that way.

Horatio is sure that George will know exactly how to handle the Dole situation. He certainly handled the Boulder matter well

That young man will not be coming back—

This is something of a surprise to Catherine, who has come downstairs to report that Eleanor is all right. Why won't Mr. Boulder be coming back?

"I felt it wise to write a letter about him to Buzzy Loring," George explains, pacing the room nervously. "I simply asked him if he knew what Boulder was saying about the late Ralph Waldo Emerson. He didn't, and he was deeply shocked."

Amelia has recovered the cuckoo clock. On the way from the attic she had seen Eleanor. There may be nothing the matter with Eleanor, as Catherine is quick to assure her, but to Amelia she acts as though she were intoxicated—

"I don't know how else to account for it," says Amelia. "She came out into the hall with her hair flying, looked right at me and said, 'Freud would certainly like to get at you!' What does she mean by that?" With this she disappears into the hall. The door slams after her when she leaves.

Agnes Willing runs in to show the Apleys her coming-out party dress. It is "a rather dowdy white ball gown, clearly constructed by a local seamstress," and Agnes is extremely self-conscious wearing it. The Apleys' inspection is sympathetic, particularly on Catherine's part, but George is convinced that something certainly is needed to set the gown off. He thereupon produces the Apley pearls, a string that had belonged to his mother, and puts them around Agnes' neck. They do give her more confidence. She is feeling quite cheerful when John bursts in with the announcement that he must see his father alone. Catherine and Agnes retire quickly to the sewing room upstairs.

John is plainly excited, and frankly resentful. Myrtle had called him from Cambridge. He has, he feels, been spied upon. Why should he not be treated as a grown-up? Why should Uncle Horatio have been sent sneaking into Worcester? If his father had reasons for such actions, why couldn't he talk to him, John, as he would to anyone else?

George Apley meets his son's resentment calmly. It is not easy for a father to talk of these things to his son. He knows more than John thinks. He knows what is the matter with John. John is in love—

"Yes! I'm in love and I'm proud of it!" shouts John.

"Of course you are. Of course you are. So was I at your age."

John is stunned by this revelation. It's true, insists his father. It may be that he was even more in love than John—quite drunk, quite mad with love—

"It was the most beautiful, the most impossible illusion I have ever known," says Apley.

JOHN—It isn't an illusion for me. It's the only thing that's real—the only time I've ever lived.

APLEY—Strange how life repeats itself. Strange and a little sad. I said those very words to my father, thirty years ago. It isn't an illusion, it's the only thing that's real.

JOHN—But it isn't the same! He listened to you! You and Mother got married!

APLEY—Yes. Your mother and I got married—later. (JOHN *looks at him.*) I was in love with quite a different girl, John.

JOHN—You were? You?

APLEY—Yes, John.

JOHN—Who was it?

APLEY—It makes no difference now. Her father was quite high up on the police force.

JOHN—Why didn't you marry her?

APLEY—Because it was impossible. She never could have lived on Beacon Street and I couldn't have lived in the South End.

JOHN—The South End? Was she Irish?

APLEY—That shocks you, doesn't it, John? That shows we're really a great deal alike. You can call it snobbish, if you want to use a snobbish term. We didn't have the same tastes, the same inclinations. It never would have worked, John.

JOHN—It's not like that with Myrtle and me. It'll last for-ever!

APLEY—No, John. You and I can't do this sort of thing. We can't escape what we are. Other people may be able to. But we can't.

JOHN—Why can't we?

APLEY—You may as well face it, John. You were born in Boston.

JOHN—What's that got to do with it?

APLEY—Boston is not just a city—it's an environment. And you and I are what we are because of what our environment has made us. We have a certain position, John, and you will inherit it just as I did. There is such a thing as duty, and you'll never be happy running away from it.

JOHN—If you call marrying Myrtle running away from it, I'll be happy.

APLEY—Happiness is a very rare commodity, John—especially in New England.

JOHN—All I know is I'm in love with Myrtle, and that's all that matters.

APLEY—No, John. Love is not all that matters. The little likes and dislikes that two people share in common, the small duties and activities that make up a day—these in the end are love. It's the little things that make for a satisfactory life.

Suddenly the Apley mood changes. George brightens perceptibly. It was just after he came back from abroad, he remembers, that he started his collection of Chinese bronzes. That had made a new man out of him, and it might be a good thing for John if he would start a collection of something—it doesn't much matter of what.

John is a little disgusted with the suggestion. His father has no idea of what he is going through—a statement that Father is quick to deny. And now there is one thing he would like to have John do for him—

"You've been very unkind to your Cousin Agnes lately," his father reminds John. "I want you to stay in this room for just a minute and say something agreeable to her. She's upstairs."

"What for? If you think—"

"No, no. I have no such idea, John. But tonight is her coming-out party, and it is the least you can do . . . I'll send her down . . . We have to go on living, John. . . ."

Agnes comes hesitantly down the stairs. When she notices that John doesn't see her she tiptoes to the piano and begins softly to play and sing "Come to the Ball." John listens for a moment and then greets her. His tone and manner are friendly and Agnes is happy. She naively attracts his attention to the pearls and is thrilled when he admits that they are beautiful.

But there is something that he must tell her. She waits expectantly to hear. If he has been rude or thoughtless lately, John begins, he is sorry. They have, he reminds her, known each other ever since they were children—

"We've played together in the Summer, and in the Winter we've always gone to dancing school together—for years and years. We've seen so much of each other that sometimes I've almost thought—"

"Thought what, John? Oh, go ahead!" Agnes has leaned a little closer toward him.

"Sometimes I've wondered if we don't know each other too well."

"Why—why— I don't see how two people—that is, a boy and a girl—*can* know each other too well, if—" She has stopped in confusion and is looking at her folded hands. "If—*you* ought to say it, John."

"Agnes—you don't understand. I don't love you. I'm in love with someone else."

It is a shock, but Agnes absorbs it bravely. "Who is it?" she asks, softly.

"It's no one you know, Agnes, but I'm in love with her. I just couldn't help it. The minute I saw her."

"All right, John."

"You're not—you don't mind, Agnes?"

"Of course I mind, John. I'm not going to pretend I don't. Of course I mind. But you can't help it."

"You're wonderful, Agnes."

"We can't help falling in love. Nobody can."

"I know you'll like her when you meet her. I hope we can all be friends."

Agnes has started for the hall. She stops and looks, first at John, and then away. "Everybody thinks—I'm going to have a rotten time at the party tonight," she says, her voice rising a little. "But I'm not. I'm going to have a wonderful time. A wonderful time!" And she runs into the hall.

When his mother comes down the stairs, John turns to her, expecting an endorsement of his father's stand. But Catherine Apley has no intention of interfering with her son's decision. If it will make him happy, if he loves the girl, and she loves him, let him marry her. John is shocked into a new happiness by this advice.

"Mother, I love you," he all but shouts, rushing to Catherine and kissing her impulsively. "I'm going right up there! I'm going to ask her tonight!" He has made a rush for the door, and all but upset his Uncle Roger, who is just coming in.

Roger has come to see George, who joins him presently. Roger has something to tell George that will certainly justify his brother-in-law taking a drink of Scotch, even if it is the first time he has drunk anything stronger than sherry for years. First, Roger brings word that the Bird Watchers had not elected George president. Why? Well, for one thing there was that cemetery business about Cousin Hattie. Henry Apley had been showing George's letter around. Then there was that Boulder business.

"They say you pushed him out of his job because he was seeing too much of Elly," reports Roger. "Did you?"

"That's a barefaced lie, Roger," answers George, with spirit.

ROGER—George, I wonder—I wonder if you see yourself the way other people see you. This Bird Watcher business—Cousin Hattie, Boulder—that's not important by itself, but it's symptomatic of everything else you're doing.

APLEY—Don't you think it's too late, Roger, to reconstruct my habits?

ROGER—Not in so far as they affect other people, George. I've seen Horatio, and that's really why I'm here. He told me he'd been to Worcester.

APLEY—Horatio always talks too much. What did he tell you?

ROGER—It wasn't so much what he told me as what I read between the lines. You're doing the same thing with John that you did with Cousin Hattie and Boulder. Raising objections about things that don't matter. Because you live in a narrow world, George.

APLEY—My world narrow?

ROGER—Yes! The man has an iron dog on his front lawn, so John can't marry his daughter. Is *that* being broad-minded, George?

APLEY—Have you realized what John will throw away if he marries this girl? Everything that Boston has to offer is his for the asking. You can't say that is nothing, Roger.

ROGER—I've watched John grow up. It seems to me he has the makings of a man.

APLEY—He can't help it, Roger, with his ancestry.

ROGER—Well, George, he's in love now, isn't he?

APLEY—Who isn't when he's twenty?

ROGER (*slowly*)—Yes. . . . You were in love yourself when you were twenty, George. Do you remember?

APLEY—It is not kind of you to bring that up, Roger.

ROGER—Have you forgotten how you felt, George? The day your father found out about it, the last time you ever saw *her*, the night you walked up the gangplank.

APLEY—I am not so forgetful as all that, Roger.

ROGER—And then you came back and you married Catherine. And then John was born. Do you remember what you said to me that day? You said, "I pray to God that he'll be happy."

APLEY—Yes, I remember, Roger. And then you and I went out and entered him for Groton.

ROGER—He isn't happy now, George. Think of how he must be feeling. Think of that, instead of worrying about iron dogs, and the Bird Watchers, and what people will say if you miss a meeting of the Tuesday Club. Be kind, George. You always have been to everyone in trouble. You've been generous. You've been understanding.

APLEY—Have I, Roger? I've always tried to understand.

ROGER—Then try—just once, George—to understand your children. Don't you want them to get just a little more out of life than you've had—somehow—somewhere?

APLEY—I'm not sure how much one has a right to expect of life, Roger. It has a strange way of escaping you. Before you know it, it has slipped out of your hands.

ROGER—Perhaps you've never stood up to it enough, George. God knows, I haven't either. All that you and I can do is to hope that others, those we love, do better. I guess that's all I'm trying to say.

APLEY—I have never meant to be unkind, Roger, I have never meant to be intolerant.

ROGER—I know you haven't, George. Why don't we leave it this way? We've had our chance, you and I. Let John and Eleanor have theirs.

For a long moment George stands, thinking heavily, after Roger has left him. The Scotch glass catches his eye. His mind rejects the drink, but he finally pours one out. Slowly he walks toward the bookcase and takes down his Emerson. He is standing by the table, the drink in one hand, Emerson in the other, when Catherine comes.

There is something that Catherine feels she must tell George. John has gone to Worcester. He has gone to ask that girl to marry him. And Catherine had told him to do it.

George turns slowly toward her. "We want him to be happy, Catherine," he says, quietly. "After all, he is in love."

It is hard for Catherine to believe her ears. "Have you been drinking, George?" she asks.

"Perhaps I've been wrong about the children— Perhaps they have a right to fall in love . . . Catherine?"

"Yes, George?" Catherine's voice is very low.

"I've been thinking . . . Worcester isn't Boston, but it is in Massachusetts."

"Of course, George."

The curtain falls.

ACT III

Next morning, about 9, everything in the Apley living room "is on a sprightly, cheerful note." There are fresh flowers on the table, a bright sun is streaming through the windows— "If there were a canary by the window, and indeed there might be, he would be singing loudly out of sheer joy at the beauty of the day."

George Apley is at his desk, "bright and spruce, each fiber of him tingling with a new sort of resolution which we have not observed in him before." George has been writing letters. The one he has just finished he is holding at arm's length and frankly admiring, "with the satisfaction of an artist who has achieved a masterpiece."

This, it shortly appears, is a letter to Henry Apley and it concerns the late Cousin Hattie. George would read it to Catherine, who comes from the dining room to join him.

"Is it a nice letter?" Catherine would know.

"I hope you'll think so, dear," says George. "I don't want to let myself go too far, because my position was basically just, but —well, this is just a rough beginning—"

" 'Dear Henry,' " he reads. " 'It occurred to me, in thinking things over last evening, that we can all die but once. As it happens, I still have a little time to consider where I wish to be placed in the family plot, and Cousin Hattie hasn't. That is why I suggest that we both, this morning, adopt the motto *Forgive and forget*, and join our efforts in endeavoring to activate another little motto, which is peculiarly our own: *Bring Cousin Hattie back.*' I think that's rather neatly put, don't you, dear?"

CATHERINE (*turning away a bit*)—Well—I see what you mean, George.

APLEY—And then I go on. (*He reads again.*) "I know that you are in delicate health, dear Henry, and that you will want to lie near her" . . . It's a hard letter to write.

CATHERINE—Yes—I think the idea is perfect, George, but there might be some other way of phrasing it. There'll be more time later. The children will be down any minute now.

APLEY (*putting the letter in his pocket*)—Well, perhaps you're right.

CATHERINE (*impulsively*)—George, the children are so happy. When you saw their faces this morning, when you heard them joking and singing, didn't it make you feel how worthwhile it's been—what you said to them—your whole new attitude.

APLEY—My attitude is not new, Catherine. I'm just the same as I always was.

CATHERINE (*kissing him*)—I know you are.

Eleanor, as happy as John, comes bounding down the stairs humming "My Hero!" The next moment she has given her somewhat startled father a great big kiss, just for being "such a sweet darling to John and me." Howard Boulder has just telephoned, Eleanor reports. He is coming over and she has planned a day for them. No, they will not sit in the conservatory, as Catherine suggests. First they will go skating on the river. Then they will go to Faneuil Hall Market, and have lunch in that place where all the butchers go.

But what if someone should see them—what if her grandfather's old butcher is still at Faneuil Hall? The thought worries Father. In that case, of course they could hide, Eleanor agrees.

It would be nice, Catherine thinks, if Eleanor were to bring Mr. Boulder home to dinner. Her father would like that, too. In celebration they could each have a Martini cocktail! Eleanor doesn't know that once upon a time her father was quite famous for his Martini cocktails.

"Isn't it wonderful—seeing her so happy?" exclaims Catherine, when Eleanor, still bursting with enthusiasm, has left them.

"What's she so happy about?" demands George. "I didn't know she was so fond of skating." . . .

Which reminds Catherine of something that has been puzzling her. It is about that book Eleanor had been reading—the Freud book. When she (Catherine) had looked for it in Eleanor's room she could not find it. Could it be that Eleanor had hidden it?

No. As a matter of fact George, too, had been interested in what Eleanor had said and he had himself taken the book—just to glance at it as a means of checking up. Yes, he confesses, that is why he had not got to bed until two in the morning the night before—

"It's really quite interesting, if you face it tolerantly," admits George. "It advances a theory that frankly never occurred to me."

"What's it about?"

"Why—it's about the mind, really. The mind and the way human relationships affect the mind."

"What sort of relationships?"

"THE LATE GEORGE APLEY"

Apley—It's postmarked Worcester.
Catherine—Worcester?
Apley—The girl—is a foreigner, Catherine.

(*Leo Carroll, Janet Beecher*)

"Well—I don't know exactly how to put it, Catherine."
"Please say what you mean, George. If Eleanor has been reading it—"

APLEY—Then I shall have to resort to a word that I have never used in your presence. It seems to be very largely a book about—sex.

CATHERINE—Oh! . . . But how can he write a whole book about—that?

APLEY—Dr. Freud does seem to pad it a little, here and there. For instance, he tells the story of a certain Mr. X. It seems that this Mr. X, when he was four years old, had an experience with his nurse that colored his entire life. Now I remember my own nurse very well. She was Hannah's sister, and I know that neither of us forgot ourselves even for a moment.

CATHERINE—But what happened between Mr. X and his nurse?

APLEY—That's what is so confusing. Nothing at all definite did happen, but after that he always dreamed of locomotives.

CATHERINE—George, the other night *I* had a strange dream too.

APLEY—Perhaps you'd better not tell me about it until you've looked this over, Catherine. It seems to be Dr. Freud's idea that sex very largely governs the lives of people, in other parts of the country. Of course he comes from Vienna.

CATHERINE—I see. (APLEY *is at his desk, putting the book back in its original place.*) There's no reason to hide the book, George.

APLEY—No. . . . No. I'll put it right here, next to Emerson. Come to think of it, Catherine, they have more than a little in common. Freud is trying to do the same thing with sex that Emerson did without it.

John, clattering down the stairs, disappears into the hall. His father calls him back. There are certain details about John's marriage plans that his father and mother would like to know. When, for instance, is John planning to bring Myrtle to see them? And when is John going to see Myrtle's father? Such things cannot be put off.

But John is too happy, too full of his memories of how pretty Myrtle looked when he asked her to marry him, to be worrying about details. Right now he must call Myrtle up. She's coming to town for dinner.

"Leave a message that you want to see Mr. Dole!" calls his father after him.

Amelia has sailed into the room just in time to hear this part of the conversation. But it is enough—

"It must be true, what I hear, then," says Amelia. "John is going to marry the daughter of a mechanic from Dorchester!"

"Who told you that, Amelia?"

"My dear, it is all over Boston. Her father collects old iron in his front yard."

Eleanor has heard the doorbell and run to welcome Howard Boulder. Amelia has heard of Howard, too. He's the one "who has been plying Eleanor with liquor." Nor does Howard's somewhat shaggy appearance, when Eleanor brings him in, reassure Amelia.

"Well, we might be able to explain Worcester," she snorts finally, looking Howard over appraisingly, "but this is the most terrible thing that has happened to the family since Uncle William married his trained nurse."

The effort of the Apleys to get better acquainted with their prospective son-in-law continues. They are interested in learning that in New York he lives in Greenwich Village, which sounds to Mr. Apley as though he were getting some fresh air at least. Apley is a little puzzled, however, when Howard informs them that his parents came originally from Staten Island. George can't seem to place Staten Island. Catherine reminds him that it is in the harbor, behind the Statue of Liberty. The fact that the elder Boulder was a dealer in canned goods is also a bit of a poser, until Howard explains that his father's business was wholesale rather than retail.

To strengthen their growing intimacy, Apley has written a letter to Buzzy Loring explaining the misunderstanding about Howard's Emerson lectures—a letter he is sure will straighten matters out most satisfactorily.

Horatio Willing, who has heard a part of this conversation, is naturally quite surprised at the turn affairs have taken—after what young Boulder had said about Emerson, but—

"There are other writers beside Emerson, Horatio," George is quick to assure him. "It is time you learned that."

Horatio is even more surprised when George insists upon ringing for Wilson and asking him to bring a Scotch and soda for Mr. Willing, and another for him—

"Are you ill, George?" Horatio asks, a little plaintively. "Your peculiar attitude at Agnes' dinner last night—"

"Horatio, have you ever heard of a man named Freud?"
George has the book in his hand.

"Why, no."

"It has just occurred to me, Horatio, that it is probably *you*
he is writing this whole book about."

It is, insists George, Horatio who has been directly responsible
for most of his major mistakes. It was Horatio who got him into
the Bird Watchers. It was Horatio who had come between him
and his son. It was Horatio who had gone sneaking up to
Worcester, to come back with all kinds of stories.

"But you asked me to go to Worcester, George. Don't you
remember?"

"Let us not split hairs, Horatio. Thank God your intrigues
were not successful. John is going to marry Myrtle Dole."

"Myrtle Dole? But—what about Agnes?"

"Agnes is a nice girl, Horatio. She has inherited a certain
charm from her mother. But John is not in love with Agnes."

"But, George, I've heard you say often that propinquity would
lead to love."

"Propinquity! Damn propinquity! I'm speaking of love, real
love, Horatio, something I do not believe you have ever known
in your sterile, pedestrian life."

"Yes, George . . ."

Evidently convinced that George had gone at least a little crazy,
Horatio goes to tell Agnes. In his excitement he leaves the door
wide open, and that lets Roger Newcombe in without the necessity of ringing.

In contrast to Horatio, Roger is well pleased with George's
news about John's plans. He is, however, measurably shocked
at George's suggestion that they drink to John this early in the
morning. If George has gone this far, it should be possible for
him to try and get a little pleasure out of life for himself. Why
shouldn't George join the poker game at the club this Friday
afternoon? There will be a lot of the old crowd playing. But
George doesn't feel that he could go that far. Besides, there is
to be a meeting of the Boston Waifs—

Wilson has announced that a Mr. Julian Dole is calling. Roger
decides he had better go out the back way. He disappears
through the dining room.

Julian H. Dole "is a man of about Apley's age, but his whole
air affords a sharp contrast to Apley. Mr. Dole might be described as a high-powered business executive in the better sense.

He is obviously used to dealing with people and used to being listened to."

George is delighted to see Mr. Dole—so delighted that he suggests that Wilson bring a bottle of the old Madeira from the cellar—not the Civil War, but the Mexican War Madeira. George is sure they will be wanting to drink a toast.

Mr. Dole is pleased to be so pleasantly welcomed. He also would very much like to meet Mrs. Apley—but perhaps if the men were to have a little talk first—

Before they can come to this John Apley appears. John has been wanting to meet Mr. Dole—Myrtle had probably told him —but everything had happened so suddenly—

"That's all right, my boy." Mr. Dole is very friendly and reassuring. But—

"I wonder if the young man could go into the other room and close the door for a moment?" he suggests to Apley. And then to John: "Do you mind? I'm talking to your father now."

Mr. Dole had seen John before; noticed him hanging around the Dole house. But there were a lot of other boys—

As for John's father, he had no idea of what was going on until a week ago. While he has never met Mr. Dole's charming daughter he feels that he knows her already. The Apleys are all quite delighted. For which Mr. Dole is truly thankful—

"Mr. Dole—of course I don't know what your ideas may be, yours and Mrs. Dole's," Apley is saying, "and I hope you won't mind my suggesting this—but I thought perhaps it might be better if the announcement of the engagement is made in Boston, rather than in Worcester."

DOLE—Well, isn't it customary for the bride's parents—

APLEY—Of course. The final decision rests entirely with the bride's parents. I was just thinking of the simplest way to explain matters here, from our point of view, and I thought if you and Mrs. Dole could go so far as to take an apartment in Boston, and then if the announcement were to come from *there*, I honestly see no reason why Worcester should be brought into it at all.

DOLE—I see.

APLEY—Tell me, Mr. Dole—er—(*Hopefully*.)—you weren't born in Worcester?

DOLE—No, I wasn't. Moved there ten years ago, when I bought the die works.

APLEY (*seeing a ray of hope*)—Ah! Where did you come from?

DOLE (*flatly*)—Kansas City.

APLEY (*swallowing hard*)—Oh!

DOLE (*beginning to enjoy himself*)—I take it you've never been to Kansas City!

APLEY (*not wishing to discuss it*)—No— As I was saying, the advantages of your living temporarily in Boston would be—well, several.

DOLE—Such as what?

APLEY—Well, for one thing, before any definite announcement was made, it would help for us to be seen together here and there —in the nature of preparation. For instance, I don't think it would be too difficult to get you a six months membership at one of my clubs—we could lunch there several times a week in the main dining room, where everyone would be sure to see us.

DOLE—The main dining room.

APLEY—And then I'm not sure, but it might be possible for Mrs. Dole to be invited for several weeks to my wife's sewing circle. And naturally there are the receptions and teas and the series of small dinners. We must be careful to have everyone prepared for the engagement before it is actually announced. I think it can be done. Of course, it isn't usual, but it's possible.

DOLE—It certainly sounds interesting.

APLEY—How's that?

DOLE (*putting out his cigar and rising*)—This is going to surprise you, Mr. Apley. I assure you I don't mean to offend you. But I don't think this would work out for my daughter!

APLEY (*rising*)—What is that, sir?

DOLE—The Apleys and the Doles just don't belong together—

APLEY—But that is exactly why I have suggested—

DOLE—Come now, Mr. Apley, you know it as well as I do. It's a mistake, a big mistake, to mix up different people.

APLEY—Are you serious about this, Mr. Dole?

DOLE—I'm dead serious, Mr. Apley. I came here thinking this would be all right, but I've learned better. We're not the same stripe, Mr. Apley. We've got nothing in common, and John and Myrtle wouldn't have, either. I felt it the minute I came in here. The butler, the house. You. And then the way you talked. You and I can't help it. It's the way we were born. (*He stops. APLEY turns his head away.*) There's no use quarreling about something we can't help. You know I'm right—don't you? . . . Don't you?

APLEY (*after a long pause; slowly pulling himself together and becoming the APLEY we have known; turning slowly to DOLE*)—

You have done me—a great favor, Mr. Dole. You have reminded me of something that I never should have forgotten.

Dole—Then we are agreed?

Apley—I am very grateful to you. I—I was not thinking on a straight line, Mr. Dole, but you have set me back upon the right track. Thank you.

Dole—Good for you. I've enjoyed meeting you, and I mean it. Good day, Mr. Apley. (*He starts for the door.*)

Apley (*following him and stopping him*)—There is just one point. (*An apprehensive glance toward the dining room.*) John is not likely to agree with us. He and your daughter might try to do something—foolish.

Dole—Well, I'll take care of that. Myrtle will be on a train for California before the day's over.

Apley—Splendid.

Dole—She has an aunt out there. She'll stay a year, if necessary. Two years—

Apley (*barely hearing him as he keeps his eyes on the dining room door*)—Yes—yes— And John shall go abroad, at once.

Dole—Well! Good-by, Mr. Apley! I'm sorry things didn't work out differently. (*They shake hands.*)

Apley—Good day, Mr. Dole.

Back from seeing Mr. Dole to the door, George calls his children. He has, he tells them, just been taught a lesson. Although Mr. Dole may not be a gentleman, George and he are in complete agreement. Mr. Dole does not approve of his daughter marrying John—

"It's a mistake to mix up different kinds of people—that's what he said, and he's right, John. I have been trying to believe that that is not so, but it is. We don't think the same thoughts, we don't share the same tastes, we don't live by the same loyalties."

"But aren't the thoughts and loyalties of all good people just about the same?" asks Eleanor.

"Eleanor, I have tried my best to do what I thought would make you and John happy. It is not your fault nor mine that it can't be. This may sound harsh to you, but I want you to promise me that you will put Howard Boulder entirely out of your mind."

"But what is wrong with Howard Boulder, Father?"

"There is nothing wrong with him. I even like him. But it would not work, Eleanor. You would not be happy."

"Father, have *you* been happy? Has the way *you* lived been so successful? Have you got so much out of life that you can tell us what *we* ought to do?"

"That has nothing to do with you, Eleanor."

Eleanor bursts into tears and rushes up the stairs. John, continuing his defiance, assures his father that no matter if he sends him away for ten years it will make no difference, and goes to tell Myrtle his decision.

Then Catherine comes. She has left Eleanor sobbing and feeling very alone. She sympathizes deeply with John—

"George, you feel that you've done right, don't you?" she asks. "Suppose you could look ahead ten years from now—"

"My dear, we can only hope."

George has turned to the ivy in the window. It is good that the green aphids have pretty well disappeared. Margaret had burned a cigar in a dustpan and blown the smoke on them, Catherine explains.

George has picked up Catherine's Phillips-Brooks calendar from the desk. What is it he has to do this afternoon? Oh, yes —the Boston Waifs— "He savors the word—it sounds all right to him now."

He is still looking at the calendar. "My! What with one thing and another we have a busy week," he reads. "The Symphony—Meeting of the Pew Holders of King's Chapel—Association for the Propagation of Wild Flowers in Franklin Park—Annual dinner of the Louisa May Alcott Admirers. . . ."

The curtain falls.

EPILOGUE

A dozen years later, in a corner of the Berkeley Club in Boston, a somewhat older Roger Newcombe is sitting in a red upholstered armchair. He is struggling with one of the club's newspapers, attached to a great wooden holder that makes reading it something of a gymnastic feat.

The woodwork of the club is dark oak, and the heavy furnishings are reminiscent of gentlemen's clubs at the turn of the century.

Rogers has just drained his Scotch and soda, and his sharp rap on the end table beside his chair immediately brings an elderly retainer with a new Scotch and soda. Evidently a familiar Berkeley custom.

Presently John Apley appears— "A John now in his early thirties—a new John, one who gives the impression of settled middle age, of assurance of inherited position. He wears a broad mourning band on his sleeve."

Yes, John admits to his Uncle Roger, he has been dropping in quite frequently of late. "You remember what Father used to say: The only way to get used to the Berkeley Club was to keep coming to it."

Yes, John will have a drink. He has had a tiring day. Let the faithful Henry open his father's locker and make him a Martini the way Father had taught him.

Mrs. Apley has telephoned, Henry reports, and left word that the car will not call for Mr. Apley today. It is bringing the children home from their Nature Walk. And will Mr. Apley kindly stop at the Pet Shop and bring the canary bird home with him?

"What was the matter with the canary bird?" Uncle Roger is curious.

"Its toe nails needed cutting," explains John.

"Couldn't Agnes cut them?"

"Agnes has been quite busy. She's been checking over Father's Chinese bronzes, before they go to the Art Museum. . . ." "By the way, I hope you and Aunt Amelia aren't doing anything next Wednesday," John asks a moment later. "We'd like you to come for dinner. It's our tenth anniversary."

ROGER—Tenth anniversary! Well, well!

JOHN—Naturally, we're keeping it very quiet. We don't want anyone to think, when we're all in mourning, that we're making an excuse to have a lot of fun.

ROGER—Just ask the family—then you won't have any fun. You know how I keep track of my wedding anniversaries, John? An extra drink each year. Took one drink on my first anniversary, two drinks on my second—I'll be married forty years in June! Yes, that's one way of getting out of Boston.

JOHN (*taking letter out of pocket*)—I invited Eleanor, of course, but she and Howard always make some excuse not to leave New York. I had rather a characteristic letter from her, this morning. You know the way Eleanor goes on. "Dear John: It seems impossible that you and Agnes have been married only ten years. Doesn't it seem like more?" I don't see why she always jokes about Agnes and me.

ROGER (*drily*)—I can't imagine.

JOHN—And then she says: "When Howard and I came back to Boston for the funeral, I could not help thinking a good deal about the old days. I think I understand things better now—

Father, Mother, you and Agnes. As Father used to say, 'There is nothing that makes you appreciate Boston more than getting away from it.'"

ROGER—Peculiar girl, isn't she?

JOHN—The funny thing is, she and Howard really seem to be so happy. I wonder if it's just a façade. Do you think they really *can* be happy, coming from such different backgrounds?

ROGER—No-o. They just *think* they're happy.

JOHN—It couldn't help but be a shock to Father, when she and Howard eloped. But he never gave the slightest sign.

ROGER—You know, I think I understood George a little better than you did. And I've got an idea, deep down at the bottom, he was rather pleased by Eleanor's courage.

JOHN (*surprised*)—Do you really think he was?

ROGER—That's what I do. You know, I miss George, miss him terribly. School, and games, and girls, and Beacon Street—We went through it all together. I always went to him when anything was wrong and I always came away feeling better. I could find him any afternoon sitting right there where you are sitting.

JOHN—I wish Father and I had never quarreled. I wonder what would have happened if I had married—

ROGER—Myrtle? You wouldn't have liked it, John—you wouldn't have liked it.

The Martini has arrived. It had taken Henry a little longer than he had planned. In trying to chill the glass the way Mr. Apley liked them Henry had broken one.

"There will never be another one like Father, will there, Henry? He was the best friend we ever had."

"Yes, sir. Indeed he was, sir."

"Here's to Father," says John, rising to his feet. "Oh, I wish you had something so you could drink, too, Henry."

"Oh, no, sir. Thank you, sir."

"Here's to George," says Roger, also rising. . . . "John, when your father took you to Paris, do you remember that painting by Titian in the Louvre? 'The Gentleman with a Glove?' Sargent should have painted your father that way."

"Yes, I wish he had."

"But there's one thing George would never have stood for. Not with one glove, John—not with one glove."

THE CURTAIN FALLS

SOLDIER'S WIFE

A Comedy in Three Acts

By Rose Franken

THERE is one advantage in scoring an early season hit on Broadway, and that is in getting a head start on the competition. Rose Franken's "Soldier's Wife" was an early October production. Late August and all September plays, with the exception of "Anna Lucasta," had proved pretty terrible samples of what the drama should not be. "Soldier's Wife" commanded not only a definite timeliness of subject, but boasted intelligent writing and a carefully selected company. The result greatly favored a continuing success, despite a press reception that was none too enthused.

Miss Franken was the first of our more thoughtful and observing dramatists working in the domestic field to accept, albeit with considerable misgiving, the challenge of those problems of readjustment that are certain to assail both the heads and the dependents of service men's families through the early post-war period.

How are demobilized soldiers and their young wives going to wrestle with and conquer these problems? "The coming back is almost as hard as the going away," says Kate Rogers, the heroine of "Soldier's Wife," when she is trying to adjust the thought in her mind. "A man's entitled to come back from the war and find his world the way he left it," advises her sister, a moment later.

Sometimes the returnee will find it so, and more times he will find it changed. The world doesn't stand still, even to accommodate a war-crazed population. And whatever the soldier finds will present a dramatist's problem of sorts.

In "Soldier's Wife" Miss Franken touches lightly, often amusingly, upon several of these problems, including one that may easily prove the most serious of all—the problem presented by an income-earning wife who comes suddenly upon a realization of a new financial independence. What is she going to do about that? And what is going to be the attitude of the surprised and somewhat startled husband?

Playgoers, however, were content to accept "Soldier's Wife"

largely as a stimulating addition to Broadway's theatre entertainment list. " 'Soldier's Wife' struck us as an unusually entertaining play," wrote Willella Waldorf in the *New York Evening
Post;* "simple, unpretentious, intelligent and full of a warm understanding of human nature and decent values, plus a con-
stantly diverting sense of humor. In short, a thoroughly civilized
comedy."

The John Rogers' apartment, in the upper Riverside Drive
district of Manhattan, overlooks the Palisades. The living room
"is a curious blend of sophistication and youth. The pair of love-
birds in the bay window and diapers spread out to dry over the
radiator give the tell-tale evidence of a young marriage on a limited income. . . . The floor plan is typical of a hundred similar
floor plans in the neighborhood, but the removal of an alcove
partition lends interest to what would have otherwise been a room
of box-like proportions. An air of comfort and ease is borrowed
from the spaciousness, and the furniture, conspicuously antique,
is placed with grace and purpose."

There are double doors leading into the dining room, a swing
door into the kitchen and a foyer hall with a house telephone.
There is also a passageway leading to the bedrooms.

As we enter the living room one evening in late Summer we find
Kate Rogers "seated on the floor amid a sea of newspapers, busily
wielding a large and professional paint brush over a kitchen step-
ladder chair." On the table nearby a small radio brings a news
commentator into the room. At the moment he is on the Italian
front. When he reaches the South Pacific Kate stops her painting to listen the more intently. The hoarse buzz of the house
telephone summons her. She scrambles to her feet, turns off the
radio and goes to answer.

"In her informal attire of long, loose house pajamas Kate might
be twenty or thirty, for her shoulder-length hair and slim figure
are of no determined age. One feels, however, that she would
be young at fifty and old at ten, and the chemical that so invades
her is sufficient to fill a room, even when she is alone in it."

It is Florence Lane, Kate's sister, who is downstairs and coming
up. Kate shrugs her surprise as she stirs about to recover the
baby's clothes from the radiator, "testing them for dampness
against her cheek in the eternal fashion of mothers." Now the
noise of the elevator and Florence comes in from the hall. She
"is a frank eight or ten years Kate's senior. Like Kate, she has
breeding and charm and a basic similarity of temperament con-

tributes to the deep rapport between them."

And why has Florence come? Just for a visit, Florence says. At 10 o'clock at night? In the rain? And why did she announce herself like company? If she had rung the bell, Florence explains, Kate might have thought she was a burglar. And, anyway, she didn't come to be put through a third degree.

Laying aside her things, Florence would like a few answers herself. Why the painting in the living room? Because the painters are finishing in the morning. Couldn't Kate have bought herself 10 cents' worth of enamel? No. That wouldn't have been the same as using the painters'. Still, why the living room? Because the kitchen isn't dry and the bathroom would have been too close to the baby's room.

Kate is worried about the baby. He hasn't a fever, but his cheeks are awfully red. Yes, baby *is* cutting a back tooth—

"You mean it's teething and not good looks?"

"I'm afraid so. My two used to get my hopes up the same way," says Florence.

"How are they?"

"Fine. Paul went to a basket-ball game. Dick's in bed with an apple and his algebra."

"Evenings are hard, aren't they?" Kate is somber.

"It begins as it's getting dark. The lights from other people's windows—"

"And the sound of a train whistle. It makes you homesick even when you're home. (*In a burst of confession.*) I'm glad you ran up tonight. I was awfully blue."

"No letter from John?" asks Florence, carefully.

"It's never been this long, even when he first went over."

"You'd have heard fast enough if anything were really wrong."

Kate admits that that is what John always wrote her. But something happened today. A man phoned—or at least his secretary did. A man named Martin—James Martin, the publisher. His son is in John's battalion. But as soon as Kate had told him that John was still overseas Martin had hung up. That seems funny to Kate.

"It sounds as if he thought John had come back," suggests Florence, trying desperately to seem nonchalant.

"Yes. And why?"

FLORENCE—They're sending men home, aren't they? After a certain length of time overseas?

KATE—Not so much from the South Pacific—unless they're sick or wounded. And then only after two years.

FLORENCE—John's been over almost two years—

KATE—Yes, but he's just gotten his captaincy. It's usually a promotion or leave—not both. (*Suddenly unable to hold her agony.*) Oh, God, how much longer is this going to last?— Sometimes I feel I just can't stand the waiting another minute—

FLORENCE—Maybe you won't have to.

KATE (*slowly*)—You've been trying to say something ever since you came—what is it?

FLORENCE—Put the paint brush down, that's a good girl—

KATE (*obeying in a trance, staring at her, whispering*)—What *is* it?

FLORENCE—John *is* back, Kate—

KATE (*stunned*)—John is—what?

FLORENCE—He's *here!*

KATE—In—in America?

FLORENCE—Not in America, in New York!

KATE (*in a panic*)—How do you know? Did you get a cable? Is he wounded?

FLORENCE (*lightly*)—He didn't sound wounded.

KATE (*wetting her dry lips*)—You talked to him?

FLORENCE—Certainly I talked to him. He phoned me from the airport.

KATE (*whispering*)—Why didn't he phone *me?*

FLORENCE—He wanted me to break the news to you first.

KATE (*bridling*)—What does he think I am—a milk-sop? (*Collapsing.*) Everything's going around. You don't think I'd be silly enough to faint—

FLORENCE—You dare—

KATE—Then I'm going to cry.

FLORENCE—You've got your emotions mixed, John's coming *home!*

KATE—That's why it's permissible— It's the only time it is permissible—when you're happy—

Kate has sunk to the sofa and is weeping bitterly. Florence lets her cry it out, dabbing furtively at her own eyes. Then, with brusque affection she calls a halt. Here, let Kate use her handkerchief—and let her be sure she gives it back.

Slowly Kate is able to control the daze into which she has fallen. There is no knowing whether it is only a leave, or whether

John will be sent back, or what. Meantime they must set the room to rights. The baby, Kate reports, is sleeping as if nothing had happened.

"What about the other bed, shall I make it up?"

"It's made. I always have it made up. I even put fresh sheets on every week."

"That's very touching."

"I don't put them in the laundry, I use them on my bed. John wanted a double bed, but I had to be smart and have twin beds. (*Bitterly.*) I kicked myself afterwards."

Now Florence is ready to go. Kate had rather she would stay —if just for a little while—

"The coming back is almost as hard as the going away," mutters Kate, inarticulately.

"That's natural. I remember once, when the boys were little, Phil had to go to South America without me. When he came back, we were strangers. We shook hands."

"How long did it last?"

"About twenty minutes."

There is another question they must decide. Shall they tell John about Phil, Florence's husband? John doesn't know that Phil died, and he was very devoted to Phil.

"Don't let's say anything about it tonight. A man's entitled to come back from the war and find his world the way he left it and everyone in it.—Even the husband of his wife's sister."

No, Florence has never thought of getting married again, even though she realizes that young boys need a man in their lives. Still, "There isn't a man in the world who'd interest me after Phil," insists Florence.

"Do you ever feel as if he's near to you?"

"For whole days at a time.—Then there's nothing."

For a moment they are silent. "It's ironic, isn't it," says Kate, "to think that John's been through one battle after another, while Phil stayed here, perfectly safe in his office—"

"I've thought of it so often.—Do you know I was ashamed to tell him how grateful I was when the Navy turned him down on account of his eyes?"

"It's enough to give you a philosophy even if you haven't any."

They have been putting in the time shelling peas for the baby's lunch next day, and chatting casually about many things when they suddenly become conscious of a noise in the hall. The elevator has stopped. The next moment a key sounds in the latch.

Kate hurriedly gathers up the pot of peas and the bowl and darts through the dining-room doors. The next moment John Rogers lets himself in.

"He is a few years older than Kate—vigorous, good to look at, and so essentially the gentleman that he doesn't have to act it. He is in army uniform, and carries overseas luggage. He takes a few steps toward the living room and whistles. The familiar, broken refrain releases Kate into action. She moves to meet him. They stare at each other for a moment before their lips meet in a kiss. They exchange no word, even after he has led her to the sofa. There is no youthful exuberance of home-coming, no easy camouflage of the profound emotions that have been stirred by their reunion."

KATE (*tremulously*)— Your latch key—just like you used it every night—

JOHN—That latch key was one of the few things I held on to.— I used to dream I was using it—this is pretty much like a dream— (*Touches her face almost timidly.*) You look just the same.

KATE—So do you.—Except for your eyes. They're changed.

JOHN—How?

KATE—I don't know.—They're the same color, the same size— but different.—John, you're all right, aren't you?—You're thinner, and you've got some gray hair! (*Proudly.*) I have too!

JOHN—Where?

KATE (*bending her head*)—Can't you see them?

JOHN (*holding her head between his hands*)—No. But I guess people who've lived through this war are entitled to a little gray hair— How's my son?

KATE—He's wonderful. (*Rises.*) He's asleep, but waiting for you—

JOHN (*holding onto her hand*)—In a minute. It's too much all at once. Florence told you I was coming, didn't she?

KATE (*nodding*)—Did you fly *all* the way?

JOHN—No. Transport. Four weeks.

KATE—That's why I haven't heard.—Why didn't you let me know you were coming?

JOHN—I didn't know, myself, until the last minute. Anyway, I wanted to come straight up from the airport—open the door and walk in—that's the way I'd always planned it— But I was afraid it might surprise you a little too much.

KATE—I think I'd have dropped dead of happiness—I almost
did, anyway.

JOHN (*low*)—Did you?

John finds the old place looking much the same. He's glad
she hadn't tried to find a smaller place, nearer to Florence and
Phil. That might have been the sensible thing to do, but then
he couldn't have used his latch key. And he wouldn't have had
any place to think of her in.

They are joking now—about the lovebirds, and about the dog
Kate might have gotten if a dog wasn't something two people
should pick out together—

"I got the baby to fill in," says Kate.

"That was a lot harder."

"I had your help to start off with."

"I hope he looks like you, though."

"He doesn't look like anybody. That's what I like about him,
he's independent."

"Good for him," says John, and adds, a little awkwardly, "I
guess I'll go in and see him. It's gotten to be a funny world
where men have never seen their sons."

He will find his son in the little room next to theirs, Kate tells
him—the little room she had written made such a nice nursery.
Which reminds him that those letters had made him pretty mad
—the idea of her taking chances with stepladders and things like
that when she was pregnant. It may be her competence has im-
proved, as she insists, but John is not entirely convinced, even if
the lamp socket she fixed does work, and the radio tube she
tightened is all right again—

And then Florence comes in from the kitchen and John has
greeted her happily. "He seems to be able to transfer to Florence all the freedom of emotion that was lacking in his meeting
with Kate."

"Is Phil with you?"

But Kate quickly shoos John into the bedroom. There is a
baby he has to be introduced to before he and Florence can begin
talking—

"You can turn on the light, he won't wake up," Kate tells
him, as she pushes him toward the bedroom.

"Go with him, the first time he sees his son," prompts Florence,
giving Kate a little push as well.

But Kate does not stir. "No," she says, as John disappears.
"If I'm there, he'll think he has to put his arms around me and

say things like—'the whole bloody war was worth this minute.' "

"He doesn't have to. It's all in his eyes."

"His eyes hurt me. They're all going to come home with that look of having been through things we don't know anything about. (*Desperately.*) How are we ever going to make it up to them! He came in here as if he didn't belong, as if he weren't sure. Florence, we were tongue-tied, we couldn't seem to say anything. And then I started to show off about that damn fool lamp. It was the worst thing I could have done—it gave him the feeling I didn't need him any more, I could get along without him. (*Passionately.*) It isn't true, but I don't know how to make him know it!"

"You'll get back to where you were. If it wasn't love to begin with, that's a different matter. But the war hasn't changed either of you, it's given you significance."

"I hope so."

John has come from the bedroom. Quickly they turn to him, curious and eager to hear what he thinks of his son.

"He's got an awful good pair of hands," says John, inarticulate with emotion.

"Is that the best you can say?" demands Florence.

"The rest was under the covers or asleep.—He's certainly got red cheeks for a city baby, though."

"That's his teeth," announces Kate flatly.

"Has he got teeth already?"

"His front ones. You'll hear the back ones coming in tonight."

Florence is going. John has gone into his duffle bag to find something he has brought for her. He lifts out several bundles of letters before he comes upon a small package containing a black opal.

Kate has gone to see that the baby is all right.

"How's she been, Florence?" John is quick to ask as Kate disappears.

"Just as you see her. Fine."

"A lot of youngness has gone out of her," John muses. "She's trying to put on an act for me."

"It's a habit we've gotten into."

Kate had a hard time when the baby came, she tells him. Septicemia. For a little while they were afraid neither of them would live.

"Thank God she had you and Phil," mutters John, an understatement of his gratitude.

But what about him, Florence would know. Is this to be a short leave? Will he be sent back overseas?

John doesn't know. He has been in a hospital in Sydney for two months. A belly wound he had got in a patrol skirmish. He doesn't want Kate to know. It isn't too serious, but they insist he'll not be fit for combat again and he's been sent home to recuperate. He will have to have another physical before they will let him go back.

"I've still got my job at the laboratory waiting for me," John is saying. "Six thousand a year and a future."

Kate has come from the bedroom and heard him. "A future where?" she wants to know. "In the Army?" And then she adds, in an agony of suspense: "I might as well get it said—how long will you be here? Will you have to go back again?"

"I don't know, dear. Maybe not. It'll be a couple of weeks, anyway, before I find out."

"Oh, God, be an angel, let him stay on this side of the ocean."

"We get kind of chummy with God in a war, don't we?—The toughest of us got so that we weren't ashamed of being sentimental."

Kate leaves them. Just before she goes John asks again how long Phil will be away, but the girls are quick to cover without a direct answer. John is a little mystified at that. "I saw tears in her eyes," he says.

"She's so terribly glad you're home," explains Kate.

"I wish I could cry—I'm numb," mutters John.

"So am I."

"I want to say 'I love you,' but I can't.—And I do love you, Kate, you know that."

"Maybe nature's kind to us in making us numb. Maybe if we were allowed to feel all the things we really did feel—we couldn't stand it. (*With deep honesty.*) Don't let's force it. It's a big thing when a husband comes home from war. It hasn't happened to any of us before. We have to be patient with ourselves."

"Perhaps you're right."

It's funny, thinks Kate, that it was so easy to write him everything. The fact that she did overlook telling him that she nearly died when the baby was born she doesn't consider a weakening admission. That's all over. And what about him? Has he told her everything?

Well, John may have overlooked a detail here and there, but he's all right. No, there had been no malaria. No, nor dengue fever either. Yes, there had been a gunshot wound. Little thing

—looks like a dimple now. No, he doesn't think he will let Dr. Wade go over him. The Government's taking care of him, and there's no cause for worry. Nor will he recede from this position—

"Kate. Promise me something."

"*Anything*—"

"Don't fuss over me."

"Not at all?" Her face falls.

"Not at all."

"Oh, my God!" There is a small wail of disappointment in her words. "All right, but just tell me one thing. Did they do anything about it?"

"Yes, ma'am."

"What?"

"Yes, ma'am—" And that is all she can get from him. All except the admission that forty-three members of his company were lost. And that Steve Martin was among them—

"Then it was his father who phoned today," Kate exclaims, fitting the pieces together. "But how did he know you were coming home?"

JOHN—One of the officers must have written him that I was bringing Steve's things.—Did he say anything about the letters, Kate?

KATE—What letters?

JOHN—Nothing—

KATE (*compassionately*)—Steve's letters?

JOHN—No, darling.—I hadn't meant to tell you any of it tonight. Not even about me. And certainly not about Steve.

KATE (*simply*)—It would have been wrong not to tell me. I'm your wife—I'm entitled to know the big things that have happened to you.

JOHN—By the same token, I suppose you're entitled to know about the letters. Because you wrote them. And big things happened to them.

KATE—I don't understand.

JOHN—I wonder if you will. It's such a crazy story, Kate. One of the thousand crazy stories that happen in a war— (*He is slow to begin, and then plunges on, jerky and inarticulate, his sentences punctuated alternately by quick nervous movement and spaces of long, slow reliving of the memories that are evoked. KATE does not stir from her place on the sofa. She asks no questions and is patient in the silences. She knows how to listen.*)

Steve and I— Well, they got us off the island pretty fast. In the hospital our beds were next to each other—it's a nice break when it happens that way. I wasn't so sick that I couldn't read, so I read all your old letters over— You know, Kate, some letters are only words strung together into news, and once you've gotten the news, the letter dies.—Yours weren't like that. There was a lot of living in them, a lot of gaiety. I guess I must have laughed out loud quite a lot, because Steve would say, "What's the joke?" and I got into the habit of reading things to him now and then. His own mail hadn't been forwarded down from the island yet, and it's tough when you don't hear from home.—One day, he asked me if he could read all your letters for himself. I was a little surprised because Steve was the most—well, what I mean, it wasn't just curiosity or anything of that sort. There was a kind of hungry look in his eyes when he asked me. I knew he wasn't going to get well by that time—I think he knew it too. . . . He wasn't very strong, but he'd read a little every day, and I'd watch his face, and every time he laughed or his expression changed, I felt cocky because my wife had written them. . . . And then all at once—I don't know whether I can explain it to you, Kate, so that you'll understand it. I stopped watching him. It was as if the letters weren't written by my wife, and they weren't written to me. They were written to him, by the wife he never had—and never would have.—It was just as if I gave you up to him so that he could know some fulfillment, some completion, that his body would never live to find. . . . That was the kind of look that was in his eyes when he tied the string around the package after he finished the last one, and put them on the table by his bed. He just lay there for a long time, not saying anything, but with a lot of peace and happiness in his face.—The next day he said, "These ought to be in a book. I'd like to write Dad about them—" I didn't take him seriously at the time, I told him it was just the publisher coming out in him. He said, "Could be, and I'd like this book to be my particular baby." . . . I told him he could write to his father, Kate. A letter went off that afternoon. Two days later, he died. (*His voice stops Neither of them speaks for a long moment. Then* JOHN *turns to her, almost appealingly.*) I guess it's crazy to bring that sense of sharing that the war gives you back to normal life?

KATE—It isn't. I know now how you felt when you watched Steve. We stop owning things, in war. I know—because after you sailed every man that went overseas was you, and belonged to me.

JOHN—Yes. (*Draws a cable out of his pocket.*) That's why I don't know what to say about this cable from Steve's father. It came just before I sailed for home.

KATE (*reading cable; incredulously*)—Oh, but he can't mean it. I don't know anything about writing! (*Studies cable again.*) He wants to publish it in the Fall.—John, I wouldn't know how to make them into a book!

JOHN—The funny thing is, you wouldn't have to do much to them. The one you wrote me for my birthday is a perfect ending.

KATE—But they're so intimate, I didn't stop at anything!

JOHN (*grinning an acknowledgment*)—Steve used to look at your picture. He said your outsides didn't match your insides.

KATE (*elliptically*)—Steve's father will be good and shocked.

JOHN—I don't think so. I think he'll see in them what Steve saw.

KATE (*with delayed impact*)—But, John, I'd hate people to read what was only meant for you.

JOHN (*drawing her to the sofa beside him*)—I know, darling. It's just that they don't seem to belong to either of us now. They've served their purpose as far as we're concerned.

In the end Kate agrees. Let Steve's father have the letters in the morning. Even if he publishes them, no one is going to read them. Who wants to read anybody's letters? Nobody.

"If I'm going to read anybody's letters I want to do it off their desk while they're not looking," says Kate.

The phone rings. It is Florence's youngest son, Dick. He is worried about his mother. But, as Kate explains, Mother probably had trouble getting a taxi. Of course Dick is excited about having a chance to talk to his Uncle John. And that's when the news of Phil's death reaches the returned soldier. John suddenly sits upright and tense. He hears Dick out in frozen silence. When he speaks his voice is gentle and muted—

"Yes, old boy, of course. That's the way he'd want it . . . You do that. I'll see you tomorrow, Dick." He puts the receiver down as if dazed. "He said that since his father died—and with Paul wanting to go in the Navy—he has to be the man of the house.—I can't seem to realize it. Why didn't you tell me?"

KATE—We didn't want to spoil things for you, darling.

JOHN—When did it happen?

KATE—March.

JOHN—What was it?

KATE—Pneumonia.

JOHN (*rising from the sofa, bitter and accusing*)—Both you and Florence let me rant on about what happened to me—and neither of you said a word about what happened over here. Just a couple of strong women.

KATE (*as a simple matter of fact*)—Women have to be strong these days.

JOHN—And it scares the bejesus out of a man. We're coming home to women who've gone through their own kind of hell and who can take it the same as we have. Suppose I don't go back to fight. What do you need me for? The war's made a man of you—

KATE (*battling his hysteria*)—John, it's sick for you to talk like that. I didn't want to learn to do without you, I *had* to!

JOHN (*after a brief struggle with himself*)—You're right, Kate. And the learning of it has been your quiet bloodshed. Please don't misunderstand me, darling. I'm awfully proud of you. The stuff I've just said—forget it—it doesn't mean a thing. I'm covered with the dust of two continents and the smell of war's still in me. I'll be human again after a hot bath.

KATE (*shaken*)—Everything's ready. I turned your bed down before, and got out your pajamas and robe—

JOHN—It sounds like heaven. (*Picks up his bag, goes to the door, and turns, uncertain.*)

KATE (*in answer to his unspoken question*)—In a minute. I have to cover the birds. (JOHN *exits.* KATE *looks after him, bereft of the power to regain their lost intimacy. She moves to low-boy in the bay-window and takes out a cretonne cover and puts it on the cage. As she does so, she sees the light go up in the bedroom, and, frozen, watches* JOHN *pull down the shade. Slowly, as though she were trying to put off the moment of joining him, she crosses room to switch off the lamp by the sofa, and in passing, notices the bundles of letters. Irresistibly drawn by the temptation of reading even her own mail, she slips a letter out at random, and begins to read it, turning the page upside down to follow a wayward postscript. It is as if, suddenly, she were plunged back into the rich and ribald camaraderie that was compounded of all the separate elements of their love.* JOHN'S *voice, rising in a commanding bellow from the direction of the bedroom, startles her abruptly.*)

JOHN—Kate!

KATE (*alarmed*)—What is it?

JOHN (*in a mounting blast of fury*)—This blasted thing is WET!
KATE (*stricken*)—Oh, my God, the bathroom stool—

"She drops the letter and rushes to the door, remembering to
dash back to switch the room to darkness. The glow from the
bedroom beckons" as the curtain falls.

ACT II

It is an early afternoon in early Fall. The Rogers' living room
is the same, "except that cretonne slip covers hide the lovely old
tapestry of the sofa. A small stack of additional covers is piled
on chair at rear of stage. The radiator still carries the insignia
of the baby's physiological development. A pair of miniature
panties, coupled with a fair-sized sheet drying in peaks, takes the
place of the didies."

Florence Lane is sitting on the sofa, working industriously at a
stack of mending. Presently the door opens and Kate appears,
loaded down with an assortment of bundles, a large paper bag
among them sprouting celery stalks. "It is at once apparent that
she is brimming with the joy of living."

Kate is full of chatter about many things—about Annie, who
is supposed to have stayed with the baby; about John—

"We went to the movies again last night, but I could tell he
didn't enjoy it. He'd rather stay home. He's sleeping better,
though, much better—"

And about the books. There are six brand new copies of "Soldier's Wife" standing conspicuously on the table. Compliments
of the publisher. Would Florence like one—autographed? Kate's
tongue is obviously in her cheek—

"No, but it's exciting, isn't it," bubbles Kate, "to think that
only a little while ago it was just a bunch of letters and now it's
got a title and everything. Like a baby. Something from
nothing."

"I wouldn't let John hear you say that."

And there is the story of the slip covers. Kate had bought
them, too, with her advance royalties. Imagine Mr. Martin's
insisting on her taking all that money! It may have been on
account of Steve, but she's sure they will never sell five hundred
dollars' worth of books.

Gradually the situation clears. There is still Florence's report
that she had to mix the baby's parsnips with the chocolate pudding to get him to eat it; and the further report that Annie

couldn't stay because her aunt got sick again and had a fainting
fit—

"Annie would be perfect if it wasn't for that damned aunt,"
interjects Kate, a little savagely. "I don't believe it's an aunt—"

"I've known for quite a while it was a sailor," says Florence.
"And her faints last exactly forty-eight hours."

There is a further report of shopping done with the royalties—
including the purchase of a new dress, hand-hemmed and everything, reduced from seventy-nine-fifty to— Let Florence guess.
No. Not twenty-five—

"You're out of your head," protests an outraged Kate. "You
couldn't buy the material for that! And look at all that embroidery— And hand-hemmed—"

"Twenty-five." Florence is obdurate.

"Twenty-two-fifty," Kate admits, demurely. "But that was
only because it was a small size. . . ."

A Mr. Craig has phoned—Mr. Alexander Craig. He is an interviewer. He is coming to interview Kate—at 4:30. It is
practically that now.

But, why an interview? When the book won't be published
until Monday?

"This is a fine how-do-you-do," wails Kate. "I don't know
the answers to anything. What's Mr. Craig going to ask me
about?"

"I didn't ask him."

"Do they always interview when a book is published?" Kate
is eyeing her sister accusingly.

"I wouldn't know."

"Even if it's only letters?"

"I wouldn't *know*." Florence is feeling a little ragged. "Are
you going to fix yourself up a little?"

Yes, Kate thinks she will wear her new dress. But she still
can't understand the interview. Nor why Mr. Craig is coming.
She has a feeling that he is probably old and stuffy, wears eye-
glasses and has pyorrhea— "Pyorrhea," she repeats. "Teeth
coming loose, like on the radio."

There is a ring at the door. Kate and Florence break into a
feverish rush to get the vegetables into the kitchen and the room
straightened. But when Florence goes to the door it is only
John. He's home early because, as Florence had telephoned
him, his wife is being interviewed. It is funny, he thinks, to
pretend that he is the expected Alexander Craig, but Kate recog-

nizes his voice and comes half dressed from the bedroom to put him in his place.

Now there is another ring at the door, and the excitement is repeated. This time John is pressed into service. Let him take care of the baby's things on the radiator.

Just another false alarm. This time it is only the hallboy with a box of long-stemmed roses for Kate. And who would be knowing Kate's favorite flower? Who would be rich enough to send the long-stemmed kind that go right through the box?

" 'In anticipation of our meeting. Alexander Craig.' " That's how the card reads. And is Kate astonished!

As it turns out, the roses are also a part of John's little joke. Yes, he had sent them. And what if they did cost as much as a big rib-roast? It doesn't mean he's crazy.

"Now you'll have to skimp on your lunches for a week," warns Kate. "What's the matter? Isn't the old man on the corner good enough for you?"

JOHN—His stems are too short.—Besides, these are from Steve—

KATE—I've been thinking of Steve too—wondering if I've any right to be so happy.

JOHN (*with a trace of bitterness*)—Why not? That's what he died for, so that people like us could lead happy, normal lives—having children, buying rib-roasts.

KATE—Take that look out of your eyes, darling.

JOHN—What look?

KATE—Of wanting to be back there with the rest of them, fighting mud and heat and Japs.

JOHN (*in an odd tone*)—How do you know I do?

KATE (*simply*)—Because I love you.

JOHN—It's a hell of a time for a man to poop out, I'll tell you that.

KATE—Getting an honorable discharge is not pooping out.

JOHN—For my money it is.

KATE—Well, for my money it isn't. (*Cheerfully.*) But as we haven't got any money, don't let's argue about it.—Anyway, you're doing an important job at the laboratory.

JOHN (*with an hysteria that has not been obvious*)—I like to kid myself I am. But dammit, while men are dying, I don't want to be lying in a soft bed, eating good food—I can't get used to being a civilian yet. They don't know what it's like over there, and I don't find myself sleeping well when I forget.—Don't listen to me, I'm nuts. What's more, it's damned unfair to you. Why don't you kick my tail and tell me to snap out of it?

KATE—Because I know how it is. I mean, I know you love your home and me and the baby, but when you've fought side by side with men, it's a relationship that has no parallel in any other relationship.

JOHN—That's it.

KATE (*with a kind of frustrated common sense*)—It won't do me any good to be jealous of it either. I'll just have to reckon with it, like a rival.—A lot of women will. It'll be part of their war work—after their men come home.

JOHN—You've got a pretty good bump of understanding, do you know it?

KATE—You kick *my* tail if I ever haven't.

JOHN—And you handle me like a wise old mother-hen. (*Warningly.*) But never let me know you're doing it.

KATE (*dropping a quick kiss on his nose*)—You think I'm a fool?

Kate has gone happily again to dress. "Only someone who's been unhappy could be as happy as that," observes John, as she disappears.

And Florence agrees. "She's been in heaven ever since she knew you weren't going back in the Army."

"I'm no picnic to live with these days," admits John, finding words a little difficult. "The first few weeks are the hardest, I suppose. That night I came home—that was the toughest half-hour of the war.—I guess we're afraid our women can do without us."

Fortunately John had found out that wasn't true of Kate. The paint job she did on the bathroom stool was enough to convince him that she was still the same old sweetly incompetent Kate.

The new dress finally appears with Kate in it, waiting to be hooked up. The dress doesn't make too big a hit with Florence, but it will pass. The left sleeve's put in crooked. That's probably the reason it was reduced.

The real arrival of Alexander Craig revives the scurrying for the third time. Now John dashes into the kitchen, and Kate makes for the bedroom, leaving Florence to do the honors.

Mr. Craig turns out to be the exact opposite of Kate's idea, but a good deal like the imitation John had given. "His counterpart is to be found lunching in any smart restaurant with any smart woman. He inflates the unrealness of himself with a degree of awareness which is rather engaging."

The conventional weather greetings over with, and the reasons for Mrs. Rogers' delay having been explained, the conversation turns to the interview and to Kate's book. No, Mr. Craig has not read it—

"I never read novels," says he. "And lady novelists particularly upset me."

"Then you must find interviewing rather trying."

"I do. I'm a playwright by profession."

"Oh. Would I have seen any of your plays?"

"I don't think you would. They don't run long enough."

"Oh."

"That goes back to the interviewing. When I can't pay my hotel bill, I do a piece for the Woman's Page of the *Herald*. I know the editor, I used to be married to her.—The whole thing leaves me acutely depressed, but it pays me a hundred dollars."

"It seems slightly unfair to your victim."

"On the contrary. I've perfected a system. Efficient, quick, and painless."

Kate has appeared and Florence has escaped, obviously avoiding her sister's pleading eye. Kate struggles for composure while Mr. Craig fills in an awkward pause selecting a place to sit. He picks up a Chippendale chair and is prepared to place it near the sofa when Kate is impelled to protest—

"Not that one, please," she says, hastily. "It broke again this morning, and I haven't had it fixed yet.—Do you know where I picked it up—?"

"No."

KATE—Columbus Avenue, of all places. It's a genuine Chippendale, except for one of the front legs and a little of the back.— Which shows it's a good piece, or they wouldn't have bothered.

CRAIG (*sitting beside her on the sofa*)—It's a point. (*Prepares to write.*) Do you go in for antiques?

KATE—It's so much cheaper than new stuff, and looks twice as expensive.—Must you write everything down? It makes me nervous.

CRAIG (*with unction*)—Just a few notes. I won't keep you long.—Have you a regular schedule for working?

KATE—That is something that's impossible with a young baby. —If it doesn't rain, I don't get the silver polished for weeks on end.

CRAIG (*momentarily baffled*)—Do you put the silver out in the rain?

KATE—No. The baby can stay *in* when it rains.

CRAIG (*writing busily*)—I see.—If the weather's nice, you have to join the perambulator parade. If it isn't, you can clean the silver. In short, a very good housekeeper. (*Pencil poised.*) And an excellent cook, I daresay.

KATE (*tersely*)—Excellent.

CRAIG—Any favorite recipes?

KATE—No. John hates fancy entrées and desserts that wobble.

CRAIG—The strong silent type that favors corn-beef and cabbage.

KATE—I have it in self-defense; the people downstairs seem to live on it. I don't mind the smell of my own cabbage, but I can't stand theirs.

CRAIG—Sheer Fascism.—Tell me more about yourself. Baby a girl?

KATE—John and I have boys.

CRAIG—How do you know?

KATE—We've proved it.

CRAIG—Oh.—Of course one swallow doesn't make a Summer. (*Clears his throat.*) What about sports?

KATE (*subtly reversing their positions*)—The baby? Too young.

CRAIG—No, you.

KATE—No time.

CRAIG (*recovering his poise*)—Splendid. I have no time for outdoor sports either.—Now about your husband— What is he? A doctor, lawyer, business man?

KATE—Chemist. And very brilliant.

CRAIG (*writing as he talks*)—And you adore him. You take out his pajamas every night and open his eggs every morning—

KATE—How'd you know?

CRAIG (*smoothly*)—How does a physician recognize measles?

KATE (*as* CRAIG *smiles and rises*)—Is that all?—

CRAIG—Efficient, quick and painless.

KATE—I thought an interview would be entirely different.

CRAIG—Some are.

As he is about to leave, Mr. Craig suddenly recalls that it was Mrs. Rogers' writing schedule that he really intended to ask her about. "Some writers begin to write at midnight," he explains, "others get up at dawn, take long walks around the reservoir, square themselves before the typewriter—and boom—they're off—"

Kate tries to explain that she isn't a writer at all, really. Her book is no more than a collection of letters—yes, just letters that begin with "Dear" and end with "Sincerely," as Craig describes them. But of course they are real letters; she didn't make them up, as he suspects.

"You can't make up a love letter," protests Kate.

"You should read some of mine," counters Mr. Craig.

The house phone rings. It is someone for Mr. Craig—a Peter Gray. That name is familiar to Kate, too, and it turns out that Peter Gray is the editor of the paper that is printing the interview. Also, when Peter decides to come up and Kate opens the door for her, it is discovered that Peter Gray is a woman and extremely attractive in her middle thirties. "She is slightly on the Amazon side, but with a very potent charm when she cares to exert it. She is smartly groomed and carries the breezy assurance of competence and achievement."

Peter Gray has come because she, too, wanted to meet Mrs. Rogers. Now that she has met her, she insists that Mr. Craig ("Sandy" she calls him) shall do a lovely piece about her.

Kate, a little embarrassed, thinks she hears the baby and excuses herself. The Craig curiosity breaks with Kate's departure. Peter was to meet him at Linda's, if she remembers. Why here?

Peter has her reasons. In any event, she wants a good interview. She will send a photographer for pictures—

"Why not add a couple of years to your life and pretend the whole thing never happened," suggests Craig, a little bitterly. "As for myself, I'm going to get out of this cretonne rabbit hutch. I refuse to be bored. That's one thing I will not sell—my right to be bored."

With that he drops a "light and tantalizing kiss on Peter's lips. It means nothing, yet it seems to touch in her some chord of response. Her arms slip around his neck."

They might have dinner and go to a show, Peter suggests. Craig is perfectly agreeable—if she will get the tickets. She will. But she will not come with him right now. She has important business to transact. Suddenly Craig is suspicious—

"Look here, what's up?" he demands. "You're too good an editor to waste your time on a little nonentity."

PETER—Change that, darling—I'm not too good an editor—I'm the best goddam editor in the business. I'm on my toes and I've got my nose to the ground.

CRAIG—A very involved posture. I've seen you take it before. But this time I'm afraid you're going to trip and get it in the neck. Nobody loves a housewife—but a house.

PETER—But everybody loves success, including you and me. The smell of it lures us like human bloodhounds.

CRAIG—Don't tell me little Mrs. Whosis has written a best seller. I can't take it.

PETER—You'll have to take it.

CRAIG—It's the war. Anything sells now.

PETER—I know. Some of us get rich and some of us die. But little Mrs. Whosis is a slightly special case of war profiteering.— Have you read the book?

CRAIG—I write. I don't read.

PETER—It's beautiful.

CRAIG—Beautiful like in beauty, or beautiful my way?

PETER—Beautiful your way too.

CRAIG (*distrustfully*)—When did you read it?

PETER—I haven't got time to read. I saw the reviews.

CRAIG—What reviews?

PETER (*aiming her barbs*)—On the front page of every book-section next Sunday.

CRAIG—There's no justice in the world.—Wait a minute. How'd you get hold of them this early?

PETER (*using her compact*)—I have ways and means. Darling, even the publisher hasn't seen them yet.

CRAIG—So that's why you sent me to do this interview.

PETER—Certainly. I want to beat the other papers to a Sunday spread.

CRAIG (*shrewdly*)—That's not all you want—

PETER (*pleasantly*)—Of course not. Every editor in town will be after her but they'll be too late.

CRAIG—You're going to sign her up today, I suppose.

PETER (*nodding*)—She's going to write me a daily column— "Letters to Soldiers."—How does the idea strike you?

CRAIG—Stinking.

PETER—That's why it might be good.

CRAIG—But she's not a writer. She admits it.

PETER—Wait till she sees her first check. She'll think she's the Great American Author. They all do.—Only I don't want her to get a swelled head until I have her signed up. One word out of you and I'll wring your neck.

Craig having a second interview to do, is preparing to leave, but first he must telephone for the theatre seats Peter is getting. Kate and Peter have gone to have a look at the baby. Florence, passing through from the kitchen with the yellow roses, notes

Craig standing at the phone. Casually she tosses at him the information that she has saved his card. "How did you know yellow roses were Kate's favorite?" she adds, putting the card on the table. "She loved them—"

Craig, glancing at the card and seeing his name on it, spends a confused moment reorienting himself. Then with a satisfied smile he slips the card in his pocket. When Peter comes from the bedroom to borrow a cigarette and to tell him she is going to wait and see the baby get his bath, he confesses to a change of mind. Now he is sure he can begin again from scratch and do a handsome interview. Why the change? Well, Craig is convinced he has discovered just a tiny little serpent in this garden of domestic bliss. He shows her the card: " 'In anticipation of our meeting. Alexander Craig.' "

No, Sandy had not blown himself. Let Peter remember that she had failed to give him an expense account. The roses, and the card, must mean that Kate had sent the flowers to herself. And that, in turn, would indicate that little Mrs. Rogers must be a lonely woman—

Florence is on her way out. Peter has gone to see the baby bathed. Craig would help Florence on with her coat.

"There's quite a lot about your sister I'd like to ask you," Craig is saying. "What's going to happen to her when something really big hits her?"

"Kate's been hit by something really big."

"What?"

"She didn't know if her husband was coming back, you know. No woman does."

"I didn't mean that sort of thing. I meant the book going over, and making a lot of money."

"I'm afraid you have the dramatist's approach to life."

"I'm afraid you have the idealist's approach."

"Not quite—" There are overtones of her own bereavement in Florence's voice.

John Rogers lets himself in. Florence introduces him to Alexander Craig and the situation is explained. Florence is just leaving. Kate is bathing the baby. Peter Gray is with her. Peter is the woman editor of the— Craig is getting sick of saying that.

"I hear great things about your wife's book," ventures Craig, when he and John are alone. "I predict that it will be the beginning of a very important career."

"Be damned ironic if it were."

"She's very clever, though," suggests Craig, with the suggestion of innuendo.

"Actually, no. Clever is about the last word I'd use to describe Kate. She's a very simple person."

"Of course, simple is as simple does, as the saying goes."

The talk turns to the war. John sees by the paper that the Yanks have taken another island in the Pacific. He is sorry that he wasn't with his old regiment if it had had a hand in that particular operation.

"Must seem pretty good to be home. All in one piece," ventures Craig.

"Yes." John's answer is short. "I was over-age when the big rush was on."

"That's a tough break."

"Said the old lady as she kissed the cow.—(*Adds with his peculiar detachment.*) I'm a yellow bastard."

"What can you do with a man who admits it?" John is amused.

"That's what I mean. Some men are soldiers, and some aren't. I'd be a hell of a pain in the Army.—It's a relief you don't want to knock my block off. Most veterans do. I'm getting so I hate to meet a veteran. (*Soberly.*) I know they've been through hell—"

"Damn bores, most of us."

"You see, I couldn't say that."

John is about to serve a drink when Peter Gray joins them. The drink idea is one Peter can endorse with enthusiasm. It is evident her first impressions of John are more favorable than she had anticipated.

"He's too nice for this sort of thing," she says, when John has gone to fetch the drinks. She is glancing at the card that came with the roses. "Why does she want to make him jealous? Good God, he's as much in love with her as if they weren't married."

"There goes the expert again."

"She ought to have her little bottom spanked."

"Frankly, her little bottom interests me at this point. And I think, as I said before, that if I had a little more time I could do a very good interview. But my price will now be a hundred and fifty dollars."

"It's a deal."

John has brought the drinks and Peter takes pleasure in helping him serve them. It is while they are having the drinks that the prospects of Kate's book proving something of a sensation are broached to John. Peter would like to have his help in getting

"SOLDIER'S WIFE"

John—The funny thing is, you wouldn't have to do much to them. The one you wrote me for my birthday is a perfect ending.

Kate—But they're so intimate. 1 didn't stop at anything.

John (grinning)—Steve used to look at your picture. He said your outsides didn't match your insides.

(*Myron McCormick, Martha Scott*)

his wife to write a column.

John is considerably flustered by the news. When they show him an advance feature review from next Sunday's *Times*, with Kate's picture boldly displayed, he is even more astonished. " '. . . it takes its place among the gayer chronicles of the war' " . . . he reads, wonderingly. Perhaps, he thinks, the review owes something to Publisher Martin's influence. They assure him that good reviews are the one thing you can't buy. Craig knows.

"And once the ball starts rolling, there's nothing you can do to stop it," Peter tells him. "Shall I tell you something? Metropolitan is going to put in a bid of forty thousand for the picture rights."

"How do you know?"

"I know because I'm the best goddam edi—" Peter catches Craig's taunting grin. "Anyway I'm one of the best business men. If you sit tight you'll probably get twice that."

"It's a little terrifying."

"I wish someone would frighten me."

"Tell me, have you got a literary agent?" asks Peter. "You'll need one," she adds, as he shakes his head. "You'd better use me."

"It won't cost you anything but ten percent of your reputation," warns Craig.

Kate, having finished with the baby, is back with them. The phone rings. It is another message for Mr. Craig. Peter's secretary has got the theatre seats and will send them to the box office in Peter's name.

Suddenly an idea is born in Peter's mind. Why shouldn't Mrs. Rogers go to the theatre with Mr. Craig?

It's a splendid idea, agrees Kate, but there would be no one to stay with the baby. John offers to take on that chore. Then who will stay with John?

"He's a big boy now—" Peter suggests, lightly, dragging John to the window to show her the view.

Craig renews his pleading. If Kate will go to the theatre with him they could finish the interview. He had the wrong attack before. He thinks now he will change the title from "Marriage Can Be Like That" to "Around the Clock with Kate—"

"Isn't that awfully familiar, a newspaper calling me by my first name?"

"Wait'll you get out to Hollywood. They'll shorten it to Katie. Or lengthen it to Kit."

"Hollywood!"

"You talk too much, Sandy."

"It's just a figure of speech," Craig adds, hastily. "Everybody goes to Hollywood sooner or later. Actor, writer, beggarman, thief— Remember when you were a little girl? And took castor-oil?"

Kate is not satisfied with that explanation. Finally John shows her the review. Her astonishment is profound, especially when she discovers the picture of herself, and later when she comes upon " '. . . has managed to harness in letters written to her husband a chronicle of marriage so gay, so lusty and so knowing' "—

"I wish I could write like that," she says, fervently, and a little wistfully.

"They apparently think you can," says Peter.

The next minute Kate thinks she has heard the baby. All thought of the review excitement slips out of her mind as she dashes for the bedroom.

"His cheeks are red as can be again," she reports a moment later. "I bet anything he is cutting another molar."

JOHN—He's all right—don't worry about him.

CRAIG—I'll call back for you at eight-thirty, hm?

KATE—I wouldn't dream of leaving the baby if he's teething.

JOHN—Nonsense.

PETER—It's one of the things he has to do for himself, you know.

KATE—I wouldn't leave John.

JOHN—That's ridiculous, dear. I want you to go. You haven't been to the theatre in God knows when.

PETER—I'll stay and keep him company, if that's what's bothering you—

CRAIG (*sotto-voce*)—Ah, now we're beginning to see daylight—

PETER—Why not take Mrs. Rogers *out* for dinner, Sandy, instead of calling back?

JOHN—Go ahead, darling. It'd be a nice change for you.

KATE—I wouldn't think of it. (*Puts review aside and glances at her watch.*) I didn't dream it was so late. (*Polite but unenthusiastic.*) Wouldn't you both like to stay here?

PETER—Of course not. It's too much for you—

CRAIG (*brightly*)—It wouldn't be if I help her fix the supper— and you two can do the dishes after we leave.

PETER—Do you know, I think it would be fun!

KATE (*suddenly*)—So do I!

CRAIG (*to* KATE)—Have you got any herbs?

KATE—All kinds.

CRAIG—I like a woman with herbs in her kitchen—

KATE (*with an edge*)—But I haven't got any eggs.

JOHN (*trying to enter into the spirit of festivity*)—I'll go out and get some, dear.

KATE (*with a wicked glance at* CRAIG)—Don't be silly, I've got corn-beef and cabbage.

CRAIG—My favorite dish.

PETER (*softly*)—Now may I have a drink?   Straight.

JOHN (*pouring drinks*)—Of course—

PETER (*lifting her drink and locking* JOHN'S *eyes with her own*) —To the Soldier—   (JOHN *does not respond.*)

CRAIG (*lifting his own glass*)—To the Soldier's Wife.

JOHN (*lovelly*)—I'll drink to that—

The curtain falls.

ACT III

Several days later John lets himself into the Rogers' living room to find it empty. The baby's perambulator has been moved up to face the windows, but the baby isn't in it. Florence, emerging from the bedroom, explains that she has just given the baby his supper and put him back in his room.

Where's Kate? She is having her final fitting so she can wear her new clothes to dinner and to the theatre with Alexander Craig, in celebration of the publication of "Soldier's Wife." And at six John and Peter are to meet the story editor of Metropolitan.

"It looks as though you two were going to lead a pretty exciting life from now on," says Florence.

"It looks that way," admits John. "They not only want to buy 'Soldier's Wife' but they want Kate to go out to Hollywood and do the script.—At seven hundred and fifty a week."

"But she doesn't know how to write."

"That seems to be of minor importance. Peter wants her to do a column, too. Daily letters to men overseas."

"It does hurt, doesn't it, John?"

"Sure it hurts. Last week we were just an ordinary married couple. Now Kate's got an earning capacity that makes mine look sick.—We're not the only ones it's happening to, though. There's a chap down at the lab who's got a punctured ear-drum and his wife is a Captain in the Marines.—A little far-fetched, but the same principle."

"Kate's been through too much to let a little success throw her."

"That's what I'm betting on—at pretty good odds, too," says John.

The bell rings and when John opens the door Kate and Peter fairly sweep into the room. "Kate is transformed into the height of sophisticated fashion. She minces into the room like a wax doll, her eyes unblinking and straight ahead."

Peter is proud of the exhibit. She has made Kate over. "I took a day off from the office and a year off my life, but it was worth it," she says. John and Florence look on wonderingly, as Peter parades Kate through the poses that Karena, the modiste, has shown her. Kate would, if she could, also give charm, as Peter directs, but she can't. The lipstick, the perilously poised hat, the mascara, the girdle, even the heels of her shoes, hold her "frozen with discomfort."

When Kate does find her voice it is to protest the cost of all this extravagance. "Everybody knows Karena never touches anything under two-nine-five," Peter has said.

"Well, I didn't know it, and I think she has a big nerve," explodes Kate. "That's four times more than the sofa cover cost!"

"And you're not a fourth as big as the sofa," points out John.

Kate and Peter had stopped in to see Linda Rivers on the way home. Peter had wanted to get the reaction of a stranger. Linda had raved over Kate. "I call her Linda already, and she calls me My Pet," reports Kate. "She thought I was just 'marvelous my dear'—so young, so chic, to write a book that everybody's talking about."

If she should go to Hollywood, Kate could, if she wanted to, rent one of Linda's houses—the one with the swimming pool and the projection room. Or, if she didn't go to Hollywood, they could rent Linda's penthouse facing the East River, "with an enormous terrace, full of trees in pots, and white rugs, and all the furniture very modern."

"It sounds homey," says John, sourly.

"It's gorgeous, really. And what a bargain for these days. If we lived there, I'd never have to take the baby out, I'd just put him on the terrace—"

At Peter's bidding, Kate has gone to put on a negligee that has also been added to her wardrobe. John is listening to Peter's recital of those charming frailties Kate has displayed on the shopping tour.

"Couldn't she stay the way she was?" John asks.

"No, darling, she couldn't. She didn't have a rag to her name. And there'll be luncheons and radio broadcasts and Heaven knows what not."

"It sounds pretty rugged. I hope I don't have to tag along."

"You won't. It'll be all Kate's party—"

"I feel my jaw setting in the concrete of chronic disapproval," says Florence, after Peter leaves them to make sure Kate doesn't get into the negligee "backside front."

JOHN (*his lips tightening*)—I know. Before the month is over we'll be living in a penthouse with white rugs.

FLORENCE—You're bound not to stand in her way, aren't you, John?

JOHN—I've gone over the whole thing with myself. What right have I? I can't put my foot down and say, "You'll live on what I earn, young lady, and like it."

FLORENCE—She should.

JOHN—Whose in-law are you, anyway? (*Soberly.*) No, but why should she, Florence?

FLORENCE—Because your marriage is more important than all the success in the world. . . . I know.

JOHN—I know you do. But I can't expect Kate to know that.

FLORENCE—I'd like to think you could.—John, have you talked to her?

JOHN—Between the book and the baby, I haven't had a minute alone with her. Besides, I couldn't say those things to her. If I did, she'd go on the way we were to protect my pride. Out of pity, maybe, because I'd been in the war.

FLORENCE—That wouldn't be good.

JOHN (*pacing the floor*)—Damn right it wouldn't be good. I don't know, maybe the war's done something to me. Maybe I should be a little more of a man or a little less of a man. Where does Craig come in taking Kate out to celebrate the publication of the book? That's my department!

FLORENCE—Why didn't you ask her?

JOHN (*comically*)—I didn't think she wanted to go.—Anyway, I have to keep reminding myself that I'm only married to her, I don't own her.

There is something that has been bothering John, he tells Peter Gray, when they are alone a moment later. Why has she (Peter) been so nice to Kate and him? Running her legs off to get Kate outfitted. Helping him with the movie deal. Why does she take all this interest?

"It's part of my job," answers Peter. "All good editors are promoters.—You see, I've been busy promoting myself, too. (*Abruptly.*) Tell me, John, you've never met my kind of woman before, have you?"

"No. Both you and Craig seem to be out of a different world."

"Don't you like our world?" asks Peter. She might be making love to him obliquely.

"It's a pretty small one. From the little I've seen of it, everybody kisses everybody else, everybody gets married to everybody else's husband and everybody says everything stinks."

"At least we keep moving."

"Where?"

"That, I haven't found out yet."

Alexander Craig has come for Kate. John and Peter are ready to start for their engagement with the movie people. Kate, re-appearing in an elaborate white chiffon house-gown, stops them all in their tracks.

"I'll have to learn to kiss your hand from now on," says John, saying good-by to Kate at the door. Kate doesn't care for the implication.

"Good-by, darling. Have fun with Sandy," Peter calls to Kate. John takes her masterfully by the shoulders and starts her in the direction of the elevator.

When Kate and Craig are left alone, his eyes lock her eyes "in a kind of wordless challenge." Deliberately she answers him by walking toward him. "It seems, for an instant, as if she is about to go into his arms, but her real objective is the baby carriage. She catches it by the handle, trundles it around and wheels it into the hall," calling to Florence to catch as she pushes the carriage out of sight.

"Don't take it so hard," advises Craig, sensing her thought. "Have you forgotten that if a married woman is attractive to other men, she becomes more attractive to her husband?—Or divorced, as the case may be."

"It's an interesting alternative."

The hallboy has brought Kate another box of yellow roses with long stems. Whom are they from? Craig would know. Nobody Craig knows, Kate answers, happily. Nor is she interested in the card. A glance at it shows that it is the same card that came with the first roses. That, to Kate, means that John had sent them. But this time he had sent them for Steve Martin.

Craig will not accept this easy explanation. As a matter of fact the roses are from him. It was he who had crossed out the "In Anticipation of Our Meeting" and substituted "In Celebration." How did he get hold of the card? Florence had brought it in the first day he had come.

"In all the excitement we must have forgotten to tell her that they weren't from you."

"You must have."

KATE—You must have thought you were crazy!

CRAIG (*with unction*)—No, dear, I thought *you* were crazy. You see, it's all right for a woman to send flowers to herself, but not when she's married to a decent guy like John, just to make him jealous.

KATE—Is *that* what you thought?

CRAIG—But that's only half of it. Now I send them, and you try to make me jealous by saying that a boy named Steve sent them—

KATE (*holding her ears*)—Oh, stop it, for heaven's sake, Sandy —you're making it so complicated, and it's not.—Listen what happened— John sent me the first batch as a joke—and because he loves me—and when I scolded him for being extravagant, he said they were really from Steve—

CRAIG—Who's Steve?

KATE (*reluctantly*)—We haven't wanted this to be bandied about, but Steve was James Martin's son. He was in John's company. He was killed.—They were awfully good friends. The book was really Steve's idea, and when these flowers came I thought John had saved the card and sent some more because the book was being published today.

CRAIG—I see.

KATE—I didn't have the least idea that you'd gotten hold of the card and sent them— They're lovely. Thank you ever so much.

CRAIG (*bitterly*)—Thank *you*.

KATE—I'm sorry it turned out to be so simple.

CRAIG—Do you know what it feels like to feel like the rear end of a horse?

KATE (*affably*)—Do you feel that way?

CRAIG—Acutely. The only consolation I have is that Peter's going to feel like the same end.

KATE—Did Peter think I sent the roses to myself too? To make John jealous?

CRAIG—What else was she to think?

KATE—Well, why didn't either of you say so? I'd have cleared it right up!

CRAIG—I only hope it's not too late—

KATE (*slowly*)—You mean—Peter decided to make *me* jealous—

CRAIG—Peter is no altruist. I'm afraid it was much more fundamental than that.

Florence, going from the bedroom to the kitchen, stops to admire the flowers. Kate goes to dress. These sisters, Craig observes, enjoy an unusually harmonious closeness.

"You seem to have the sort of attunement that begins before you are born and goes on after you die," he suggests, and adds: "Don't mind me, I wrote an article on reincarnation once and then got interested in it. When a boy, I used to be the same way. I'd read books on medicine and get all the diseases."

Craig is curious, too. He would like to know why Florence doesn't like him. Of course that may be his guilty conscience. Florence thinks it very well might be. Still, he knows that he is not the type of man either she or Kate really admires. But he would like to be. At least, he would like to be a man with a future—

"Haven't you?" asks Florence.

"I can't seem to keep one. You know, I'm even borrowing on what I get paid for this interview to take Kate out to dinner to-night. Something metaphysical about that. Self-eater, so to speak. (*As* FLORENCE *smiles.*) I like to see you smile. I'd like to see you laugh— Couldn't I make you laugh?"

"You make me want to cry."

"Peter told me that. What's the matter with you women? I think I'm funny."

"Not really. You're just an unhappy imitation of yourself."

"That could almost be a compliment."

"I think I meant it to be," says Florence, gravely.

"I bet your husband was a swell sort."

"That could almost be a compliment to me."

"I wanted it to be.—You pass it on without knowing it.— That's one of the things that's wrong with me. Too many unhappy marriages in my life. (*There is a catharsis beneath his flippancy.* FLORENCE *listens quietly as he goes on, a little jerkily.*) I was married once before. When I was much younger. To someone much older. That didn't work out either. When I finally met Peter, we were both pretty ragged, neither of us wanted any more responsibility or obligations.—It should have worked out beautifully. Just a pair of civilized bums."

"Strange how little of your life you carry in your face."

"Lady, it's an art. If you live hard enough and fast enough, Life never touches you."

"Perhaps it passes you by."

"You pass *it* by. There's a big difference."

Kate has come to be buttoned up. Florence attends to this little job and then, gathering up the flowers, slips quietly into the kitchen. Kate is ready to go now, She is not wearing her new green dress. She thought she would be much more comfortable in the twenty-two-fifty item.

Craig isn't particularly pleased. Even if people are not likely to notice what she is wearing in the darkened theatre, they will notice during intermissions. Also in the night-club they would be going to later. But Kate has decided she isn't going to a night club. She doesn't want to keep John up late.

Craig has brought the interview with him. Kate would like to read it, but he prefers reading it to her. He does so, hurdling her interruptions as successfully as possible—

As Craig has written it, the interview is a little on the florid side. " 'High above the roof-tops of New York, overlooking the river,' " reads Craig; " 'With the island like a little green toy' "—

"What island?"

"Welfare."

"That's not in the Hudson river—" Kate's composure is disarming.

" 'Katherine Putnam Rogers lives like a fairy princess of old, in the choicest of modern settings' "—

"Nobody in his right mind could call this place modern—"

"Will you be quiet?" Craig shifts his position and goes on. " 'Only a shade whiter than the white velvet rugs that cover the floor, is the giant white cockatoo that swings from his perch in the great glass bay window of Kate's study. Nobody but Kate touches that cage.' That's true, isn't it?"

"Put those love-birds back where they belong," firmly orders Kate. "And put the Hudson river back where *it* belongs. And put me back where I belong, in my nice, old-fashioned apartment"—

"Are you going to let me finish?"

"No, I am not! I won't have white rugs on my floor."

Nor will she be moved into Linda Rivers' apartment right over her head. Crazy about Linda's apartment she may be—for Linda. But not for Kate—

"And another thing: Do you think I'd move from this place when I've only just got the kitchen painted?"

Craig is staring at her incredulously as he crumples the interview in his hand and throws it in the wastebasket.

Kate is sorry. She knows it is hard for Sandy to understand the way she feels about it. She doesn't want to hurt him, but, someway, the war does change people. No, she doesn't want to forget the war—

"You can't forget any great experience you've lived through," she says. "It's happened to you and suddenly you discover it's part of you, and at moments you feel very rich and privileged because you've been a part of it."

Craig is right, Kate admits, when he suspects that she doesn't really care much about going out with him tonight. She's only going because she doesn't want John to think he should take her. Perhaps, Craig suggests, she is trying to make marriage a little subtle—

KATE—All marriage is subtle. You mightn't know you're doing it, but you have to work at it. The war's helped me quite a lot. It's been a short-cut—I might have stumbled around looking for the right road, if I'd taken the long way around.

CRAIG (*humbly*)—I don't see what you mean, exactly.

KATE—When John joined up, I let him go. I had to. Just the way Florence had to let Phil go. And in the beginning it was like learning to live without any insides at all. Even after I knew the baby was coming, I was just as empty. And then gradually, the emptiness turned into competence, and efficiency. Like widowhood. (*She pauses, finding it hard to put in words, but as* CRAIG's *silence commands her, she goes on undramatically.*) A woman learns to be a widow, in war-time. Until, suddenly, her husband comes back from the grave. And that's going to happen all over the world when peace comes. And there are going to be heartaches, and strangeness, because there's going to be a lot of money and success and independence in women that there's never been before. . . . Maybe a lot of marriages won't be put together again. And everything those men thought they were fighting for, they weren't fighting for at all. A little like John saving his latch-key to use in Linda Rivers' apartment— It just couldn't open that door.

CRAIG—I guess it couldn't.

KATE—I know what this place seems like to you—it's dreary and commonplace. And people who love each other aren't interesting. And a happy marriage with children adds up to a very little story against the glittering kind of life you lead. It's so easy to pull things down—if you don't know what it's all about.

CRAIG—You're right. I don't know what it's all about. The nearest thing I'll ever get to a baby is the Stork Club.

There is a phone call for Florence. It is from New London. Paul, her 18-year-old, has lied about his age and enlisted at the submarine school. It means that Paul won't get home again— not for a long time. It isn't an easy shock for Florence to take, but she masters it.

They would help her if they could. Certainly she is not to be permitted to go home to her empty apartment. Dick, her younger boy, is away at a birthday party. He won't be home for all hours.

Suddenly Craig has an idea. Why shouldn't he and Florence double-cross Kate and the two of them go out to dinner?

That, Kate agrees enthusiastically, is a wonderful idea. But it takes a lot of urging before Florence will submit. One by one they batter down her objections, and finally she agrees. That makes Craig quite happy. As it has worked out, it was almost worth losing the hundred and fifty dollars he would have got for the interview—plus the six he spent for the flowers.

Kate moves mechanically about the room after Florence and Craig have gone. She is still plunged in Florence's grief. Glancing at her watch she turns on the radio. The communiqué is direct from Australia, through Washington. The commentator is relating details of the taking of a new airstrip. When the report is finished she turns it off, pausing for a second to lean her cheek against the radio—

"Thanks, God, for sending him back to me," she says, softly.

Kate is hidden by the back of the sofa when John lets himself in. He goes quietly on a search of the apartment, calling to Florence. Then Kate gives a little whistle that is peculiarly their own and he finds her.

But why? Why is she home? Where is Sandy? Where's Florence? Why didn't she go with Sandy?

As for that, what about him? Where's Peter? How did the radio deal turn out? Where's he been?

The radio meeting was postponed and John and Peter had gone to a Linda Rivers' cocktail party. Certainly they urged him to stay, but why should he? He had only gone to see the apartment. It's wonderful.

Suddenly John notices Kate's dress. Is that another new one? He likes it—likes it a lot better than the fancier one she had on before. Better color. Fits better, too.

"What's the matter you're noticing all of a sudden?" demands an amused Kate.

"I guess I always saw you, but I never looked at you," says John.

"Now Sandy *looked* at me, but he never saw me. That must be the fundamental difference between a husband and a lover."

She tells him about Florence's telephone message from Paul. And of the look in Florence's eyes. Kate had that look once, John remembers. But it is almost gone now.

Was John ever in love with Peter, Kate suddenly wants to know. No, John wasn't. He might have been, he admits, or thought he was. Incidentally, he reports, Peter is going to China, after she covers an assignment in Washington interviewing some Congresswoman.

Now they have decided, or at least Kate has decided, that they can have a little supper at home at their own private Stork Club. Which reminds her, for one reason or another, that she has decided to have another baby—

"I always plan my babies ahead," she explains. "I think a baby that's an accident is an insult to the child."

"And a severe shock to the parents."

Having a baby might cramp her literary career, John points out.

"Do I have to have a literary career?" she demands. "I don't like to write—"

"You don't? And you could support me in such fine style."

"Get yourself another wife. I didn't get married for that."

John has taken her in his arms. "Oh, Kate, you're such a fool," he mutters. "And so wise, so terribly wise. You put your nickel in the slot and hit the jack-pot and all you want back is your nickel."

"And my husband, if you don't mind."

Now she is reminded of the Newfoundland pup she had seen in a pet shop. She had given up the idea of having him then. But things have changed—

"Say, John, I *would* like you to look at that Newfoundland," she says. "He could eat a few spare royalties now and then, couldn't he?"

JOHN—Yes, they're not very choosey.

KATE—The man in the store said he thought it was too big for an apartment. Do you?

SOLDIER'S WIFE 259

JOHN—Not if we move out.

KATE—The man in the store said a Newfoundland really ought to be in the country, near water. How'd you feel about living in the country near water, John?

JOHN (*at length*)—I'd feel pretty good about it.—How would you?

KATE—The country is the only place I'd consider moving to from this apartment. What do you say we start looking tomorrow?

JOHN—I've got your movie people to see tomorrow.

KATE—Oh, let that go, this is more important. (*As he searches table and book-shelves.*) What are you looking for?

JOHN—That book on economics you were showing off with.

KATE—It's on the top shelf among the reds.

JOHN (*getting book*)—It belongs down there—among the greens.

KATE (*getting the delayed impact*)—Are you going to *read?*

JOHN—It's too early to go to bed.

KATE (*resigned to wait*)—Oh, all right, I'll mend. (JOHN *sets the clock ahead, and settles on the sofa with his pipe and book, very pleased with himself.* KATE *gets her basket of mending, and the nursery lamp, now minus the plug.*) God, how I hate to mend.

JOHN—You do it very badly.

KATE (*cheerfully*)—Don't I though?

JOHN—I feel like I'm walking on pebbles.

KATE (*giving him the lamp*)—Would you like to fix this?

JOHN (*examining it*)—The two little businesses came out again, hm?

KATE—I guess so.

JOHN (*digging into his pocket for his knife.* KATE *catches sight of the clock. She is surprised and gratified at the speedy passing of time, and sets her watch accordingly. She settles herself at the other end of the sofa.* JOHN *looks at her out of the corner of his eye as he starts to scrape the tips of the lamp cord. The yellow roses on the table behind the sofa brush against him. He turns to move the vase. Surprised and gratified*)—Funny, isn't it, how those roses picked up again?

KATE (*squinting to thread her needle*)—Isn't it—?

THE CURTAIN FALLS

ANNA LUCASTA

A Drama in Three Acts

By Philip Yordan

PHILIP YORDAN, who wrote "Anna Lucasta," will doubtless one day write the full and complete story of how Anna came
to Broadway and won a season's success. It probably will be a
different story from any so far released. Not different in essential particulars, but different in its evaluation of the factors that
most greatly contributed to "Anna's" success.

Mr. Yordan wrote the play originally as the story of a Polish
family's adventure in a small Pennsylvania town. He brought
it, together with several other of his early playwriting efforts,
from Chicago to New York, and peddled it with his other plays
among the Broadway producers. Many producers liked it, but
no one of them was ready to buy it.

In due time Mr. Yordan also acquired a sales agent, Claire
Leonard, and it was she who took the Lucasta script to Abram
Hill, the founder of the American Negro Theatre in New York's
suburb of Harlem, suggesting that it be rewritten, or at least
readapted, as the story of a Negro family. It took Mr. Hill the
better part of a year to decide that there might be something in
Miss Leonard's suggestion, by which time Harry Wagstaffe
Gribble, a Broadway director, had become interested in the
drama's possibilities. It was tried first, in its Negro family version, in a small basement theatre in Harlem. Those newspaper
reviewers who saw it did a bit of raving over its outstanding
dramatic virtues, and especially over the opportunities it afforded
a company of Negro actors to prove that, given proper material,
they were to be numbered among the most convincing of American character actors. John Wildberg, a Broadway producer who
had had recent success with a revival of the all-Negro "Porgy and
Bess," decided to bring the Negro version of "Anna" to Broadway.
Mr. Gribble thereupon undertook to do a bit more adapting during the Summer. When "Anna" reached the Mansfield Theatre
in late August it had become not only a drama of social significance, but also a drama of social significance with comedy overtones added. It was to the comedy that the Negro players re-

sponded most successfully. "Anna" was an overnight hit. A few of the reviewers who had approved the Harlem version, which was more tragic than comic, resented the liberties taken. They insisted that when the heroine was permitted to live with some promise of happiness in place of taking her own life as a victim of social and racial injustices she could not dominate, the play was definitely cheapened. In the main, however, the reviews were a little wildly enthusiastic and the playgoing public frankly approved the drama as adapted.

In early 1941, as the play opens, the Lucastas are living in a small Pennsylvania town. The living room of their cottage, in which we meet them, is cheaply furnished, but not altogether on the shabby side. There is a new piece of furniture here and there, obviously of the installment store type.

At the moment the living room is occupied by two members of the family, Katie and Stella, fairly prepossessing young women who evidently take some pride in their appearance. Stella is the conscious one just now. She is engaged in letting out a dress while she bitterly questions the wisdom of starting to have a kid at this time. Katie would comfort her, if she could, with the suggestion that however hard the times, education is still free. But Stella is far from comforted—

"Education my foot!" she snaps. "What did education get you—Stanley? And all the learnin' in the world wouldn't help me with Frank. What he don't know he won't listen to. For six years he kept yellin' that I was cheatin' him out of 'Man's greatest experience—fatherhood!' Now I'm pregnant he calls me careless. I think I'll let out the full seam instead of fussin' with it every month. Might as well look like a barrel from the start."

Theresa Lucasta, the mother of the brood, is in from the kitchen with a tray of dishes and food for the table. She is a kindly person, ample of girth and of a pleasing expression. Like most mothers she quickly finds something to worry about. Where are the boys? They should be there. Stanley was there, they tell her, but had gone for the mail. There's a letter at the postoffice for Pa, and " 'tain't no love letter," Stella is willing to bet.

No, 'tain't. Theresa is confident of that. She had cured Pa of his interest in love letters thirty years ago. She had come upon a "passion letter" from a girl down in Bessemer which Pa had tried to hide from her. And did she fix Pa! She tore the letter into bits and fed it to him in his stew. "If he ever got another passion note he tore it up before I could cook it," says Theresa.

Nor is she prepared to accept Stella's theory that "scarin' Pa out of all them little tid-bits is what cracked him up." She knows what's wrong with Joe. It's those "cozy things" the doctor talks about; "a psychosis," maybe, according to Katie.

"That's when a person has a secret that gets too heavy to carry—he can't get rid of it, so he breaks down under the load." And Katie doesn't mean the kind of "load" Stella does. Pa ain't had a drink since he took his first spell. Theresa knows what caused that.

"Joe did a great wrong two years ago, and he won't be happy until he makes it right."

The boys have arrived—Stanley and Frank. Stanley is Katie's husband, and Frank belongs to Stella. Stanley is small and on the cautious side. Frank is big and gruff, hearty and cynical and pretty proud of himself as a man and a charmer. An "overgrown tom-cat" Stella calls him.

The letter Stanley brings for Pa is from Otis Slocum of Bessemer, Alabama. Theresa can read enough to make that out on the envelope. Otis Slocum ain't no gal, but a fine man. So Theresa is willing to let Joe have this letter without gravy on it.

There is a good deal of speculation about Pa's letter before Theresa comes back to get the dinner on. Stella suspects it is somebody tryin' to put the bite on Pa. "They still think the streets are paved with gold up North."

"You all can let Paw talk you into sendin' money to those Alabam hicks," says Stanley. "He ain't goin' to get any of mine."

"How much you got?" Frank is suspicious.

"As much as you, I'll bet."

"Then you ain't got a dime and you owe Ma five bucks," chortles Frank.

"Stanley's all squared up and he's got twenty dollars put away," boasts Katie.

"Even if we had a lot of dough, it wouldn't be right to send any of it down South," insists Stanley. "Do you know why?"

"I'm following you, boy—carry on." This from Frank.

"It's the principle of the thing. Everybody's gotta make their own way. That's democracy. Everyone for himself."

"That ain't democracy," says Frank. "Democracy's all for all and one for one."

"And you're the one." Stella isn't fooled.

"I was until you had to go and make it two," snaps Frank.

Anyway, it ain't a question of democracy; it's a question of pamperin' people, Frank tells them. Just like this here Lend-lease. That ain't right, neither. Does anybody think we're ever goin' to get paid for all that stuff? Frank had heard a fellow sayin' just the other day that so long as we kept sendin' stuff to those fightin' guys in Europe the longer they were goin' to go on fightin'—

"What we ought to do is to let them fight till they're fit out," says Frank. "And when they're all fit out they'll get hongry. And when they're hongry they'll find a way to eat. And the only way to eat is to work. And the only people who eat without working is the politicians. And just as soon as this country gets back on its feet again, that's what I'm goin' to be—a politician."

Joe Lucasta comes down the stairs in his dressing gown. He is feelin' terrible—terrible headache— "like a thousand little devils dancin'—" He can't even read Otis Slocum's letter. Katie will have to read it for him—

"I want everyone to hear it because it's from Otis Slocum, my oldest friend, and it's sure to be good. Ma remembers Otis." . . .

"If he wants us to send him our old clothes he's out of luck—we got 'em on," offers Frank.

"Hush! Let Katie read the letter."

KATIE (reading)—"My dear friend, Joe Lucasta. I hope you are fine and rich up North."

STELLA—Here it comes.

KATIE—"We're havin' bad days down here and I ain't got the strength I used to have. Doctor says I worked too hard and got to take it slow from here on. All my boys and girls got married —all except Rudolf. Rudolf's gettin' painfully restless for a woman."

STANLEY—Tell him to take a shower! (FRANK and STELLA laugh.)

JOE—Shut up! Read more, Katie.

KATIE—"Good healthy women are scarce in these parts owin' to hard times and a lot of loose livin'. So I sold half my land and gave Rudolf the money so he can get himself a good wife when he come up North. He's bringing eight hundred dollars, Joe. (STANLEY whistles.) And I want you to pick him a good strong woman, clean and God-fearin'. I know you will do this for old times' sake. So bless you, Joe, and be good to my boy Rudolf. Otis Slocum."

STELLA—What does that farmer think—you can buy a woman like you buy pigs?

FRANK—Sometimes pigs is a better buy. (*Belches.*) When the hell we goin' to eat?

THERESA—I'll bring you yours in a trough!

STELLA—Eight hundred dollars!

FRANK—That's a lot of money for a jerk to be carryin' around.

STANLEY—Yeah—really *too* much.

STELLA—For twenty-nine dollars I could get that swell coat down in Simon's window.

FRANK—We gotta get a new bed for Stella and me. I'm getting tired o' nailin' them goddamed things together in the middle of the night.

STELLA—What are you going to do, Pa?

JOE—Huh?

STELLA—About Rudolf?

JOE—I'll look after him. There's plenty of good women would be glad to get Otis Slocum's son for nothing.

FRANK—You got the right idea, Pa. We gotta get him a woman for free. Eight hundred bucks is real money. We need it bad.

JOE—What you mean "we need it"? What's the money got to do with us?

FRANK—Well, if he's willin' to pay for a wife and we get him one we ain't cheatin' him, are we?

STANLEY—It's business—that's what it's like.

KATIE—Stanley! You can't stoop that low!

STANLEY—Katie, don't give me the big eye with all that Hell fire!

JOE—That's just where you'd go if you try to steal Otis Slocum's money!

The Lucastas are divided as to what should be done to get hold of Otis Slocum's eight hundred dollars—legitimately if possible, illegitimately if necessary. Stanley would look upon it as a business deal. Stella is already turning the eight hundred dollars into a new car, a fur coat, etc. Frank is for any deal that will work. When their father protests, the young people assure him that he need to have no part in the enterprise. They will find a girl for Rudolf, and plenty of use for Otis' money.

The family is well through their meal when Theresa is struck with an idea. Her Anna is the girl for Rudolf! It is an idea with the explosive effect of a bomb.

"Have you gone plumb out of your mind?" demands an outraged Joe.

"No, Joe. It come to me like a big light. Here's our chance to give Anna a fresh start."

JOE—I made a rule in this house that we don't talk no more about her!

THERESA—And I keep that rule, Joe. We don't talk no bad about Anna, but this is good for her. This is good we can do Anna.

STELLA—She ain't no good, but she'd do for him.

KATIE—You're speaking of your own sister!

STELLA—So what? She's a class A slut!

THERESA—Don't you say that, Stella. No one got a right to call her that!

KATIE—She couldn't have been worse than some of us.

STELLA—What are you looking at me for?

THERESA—Anna was good, Katie. But no one saw into her. And my love wasn't strong enough to hold her in this house.

STELLA—She wouldn't have stayed anyway. But Pa had the guts to kick her out.

FRANK—That's the last time he ever showed he had any guts.

THERESA—Pa wouldn't give her a chance to explain. He never saw into her.

STELLA—He saw enough when he caught her rollin' in the hay with—

JOE—You shut your mouth or I'll slap you down.

FRANK—You just try it! Nobody's goin' to slap my wife down but me!

STELLA—You and who else?

FRANK—Now let's settle this thing. And let's all keep our heads. Here's our chance to look at this thing from the human angle.

STANLEY—What?

FRANK—We've all got different angles on this thing, so let's put 'em all together and do as I say. Anybody can see that Ma's right! She's absolutely right. She's hit the nail right on the haid. Anna is the girl we ought to get for Rudolf. So we'll just git her!

JOE—Never! Never in this—

FRANK—Must you talk all the time! Are you going to be the only one that won't look at it from the human angle? All right! Let's take it from Anna's angle. She's got everything Rudolf's lookin' for—plenty of good looks and a lot of experience.

STELLA—Two years is a long time . . . Maybe she's changed.

STANLEY—Henry Ledbelly met her in a Brooklyn bar and she gave him her picture. She looks just the same as the day Pa caught her in—

THERESA—Stanley!

STANLEY—She don't look a day older, Ma.

STELLA—What if she won't have Rudolf?

JOE—Stop that talk! Didn't you hear Katie read the letter? Didn't you hear Otis tell me to find his boy a clean, God-fearin' woman?

FRANK—How do you know she ain't God-fearin'? You sure put the fear of God into her. Besides, all women are built the same and if we don't tell him, that hick will never know the difference. Let's stick to the human angle!

THERESA—Joe, you've got to give Anna this chance!

JOE—No! . . . No! . . . No! Theresa, have you gone crazy? She never comes back to this house! Nothin' any of you say can make me take her back. I swore that two years ago and I'm swearin' it now! She don't come back in this house! She don't come back in this house!

With Joe gone the scheming of the others goes on—Frank, Stanley and Stella trying to think of ways to get the money; Theresa and Katie holding out for Anna and a new chance for her with Rudolf and his money.

Theresa knows what's the matter with Joe. He wants Anna back, too, but his bull-headed pride won't let him admit he'd wronged her. Theresa is going to have another talk with Joe.

"You don't realize what you're doing, Ma," says Katie. "They only want her back to sell her like a slave."

"Slave!" Theresa resents the suggestion. "I don't know what you're talkin' about, child. I just want to have Anna back home —that's all. I'll make Joe go fetch her. I'll break him down. You'll see, you'll see." And she has gone quickly up the stairs.

Presently Theresa's voice can be heard. She is pleading desperately with Joe, begging him on her knees, to go bring Anna home. But Joe stands firm—hysterically firm.

"Guess we'll just have to beat the hell out of him, Stanley." Frank can think of no other way.

Now Theresa and Joe have argued their way downstairs. When Theresa throws herself in Joe's way he pushes her roughly aside and she falls, still pleading— "Frank, Stanley—make him give

Anna another chance! Make him!"

"Sure, Ma—you leave him to me." Frank is ready to take charge. Let all the rest of them get out. They go, but not until Stanley has told Joe that they gotta get some sense into him—and been slapped for his advice. Joe and Stanley are lunging wildly at each other when Frank separates them—

"Cut that out!" Frank shoves Stanley away, but keeps hold of Joe. Stanley sneaks out. "Gee! I hate to see anything like that. Your own son raising his hand to you. That's bad, Joe. That's bad upbringing. You ain't done so good by Stella, either. It's been a hard job housebreaking that woman. No. Looks like the only one you gave any lovin' care to was Anna. You was real fond of her, wasn't you, Joe?"

"I was."

"And she turned out to be your prize mistake. Well, that's the pity of it all. But as the sayin' goes, it's an ill wind that don't carry a silver linin', and we can still make some good out of all this bad, you and me."

Joe has been lying, and Joe knows he's lying. That's Frank's conclusion. He didn't kick Anna out just because he caught her "wallowin' like a pig." He didn't turn against Anna because the Hymn Book told him to, because he (Joe) ain't a religious man. Never has been. And it ain't because he's protecting Otis Slocum's money that he don't want to bring Anna back—

"You just heard from Otis today, yet you kept Anna out of this house for two whole years," charges Frank, threateningly. "Now I'm goin' to give you one last chance to say the truth, Joe. Come on out with it! It'll save you a whole lot of sweat!"

"I don't know what you're talkin' about. There ain't no truth but what I've said!"

"Oh, yes, there is! You're afraid of her! That's what's eatin' your guts! You're scared of her!"

"Afraid? What can she do to me?"

"I dunno! What does she do to you?"

"Nothin'! Nothin'!"

"Nothin' but the mere mention of her name turns you into a tremblin' old fool . . . scared!"

"You're a devil! You're a mean, wicked devil to say such things to me. They're lies! They're lies!"

"Then prove it by bringing her back, showing all of us that you can act like a father to her. A nice, kind father, Joe!"

"No! No!"

"Yellow, eh? Well, I'll just have to give you a little courage.

This is where you need it, Joe!" . . .

Frank has given his father-in-law a vicious pummel in the gut.
And slapped his face, as he straightens up.

"You're out of condition, Joe.   We'll have to do this more often
when you get back.   You've just got time to make the evenin'
train for New York."

"I *can't!* I *can't do it!*" wails Joe.

But he decides that he can, with a little more shaking up.
Frank calls lustily to Stanley to come back.   From Stanley he
has the address in Brooklyn where the Ledbelly boy had seen
Anna.   And he also sends Stanley to get the twenty dollars he and
Katie have saved.   Now he's ready to escort Joe to the train.
They might stop on the way and have a drink, if it wasn't that
Joe can't handle the stuff any more.   Maybe he'd better just take
a cup of hot tea, with plenty of lemon to settle his nerves.

"Is he going, Frank?   Is he really goin'?" calls Theresa.

"Yeah, Ma.   He had a change of heart."

"That's my good Joe."

"Come on, Joe.   You're holding up the parade.   When you
gotta go—ya gotta go."

"I knew you'd do it, Joe," calls Theresa.   "God bless you.
We're gonna have our Anna back again."

"Yeah, we're goin' to have our Anna back again," echoes Frank.

Stanley has come downstairs with his piggy bank.   "Let's go!"
he calls.

Frank grabs the bank, holds it up and shakes it.   "Ain't that a
lovely sound?" he says.

The curtain falls.

Noah's Bar, in Brooklyn, is typical of its kind.   A dulled
flashiness outside; a grimy and dark interior, with a heavy ma-
hogany bar, replete with damp bar towel, mirror, an array of dusty
bottles and Noah, the proprietor, serving as his own barkeep.
Noah is of a reasonable corpulence and friendly with friends.
Outsiders, would-be grafters and tight spenders better watch out.

Noah's visitor just now is Eddy, a competitor from a place
known as the Towers.   Eddy is having a drink and his competitor's soul is filled with satisfaction when he discovers a speck
of dirt in it.   It's only something that came off the ice, Noah
assures him as he flips it out with a stirring rod.   During the
operation he also dips a finger in the glass.

"If my bartender did that at the Towers, I'd have both his legs
broken," observes Eddy.

"That ought to fill your nights with sweet dreams," cracks Noah, and goes back to swabbing the bar. Presently he is attracted to the window. There's something going on down at Uncle Ben's place.

A moment later Blanche, a saucy, flashy, street-walker type, dashes through the door and makes straight for Eddy. She's looking for protection. She would have Eddy pretend that he brought her into Noah's. Not that she wants anything from Eddy, as he suspects, but just a little help in an emergency—

"Someone just pitched a rock through Uncle Ben's window and I think the cop's lookin' for me," hurriedly explains Blanche. Before she can explain further the cop walks in. "Oh, you're so right, Eddy," Blanche is saying as the officer approaches. "The class of municipal employees is getting lower and lower. I hear half the cops is recruited from the criminal types."

The officer is not impressed. "C'mon, let's have those binoculars!" he growls.

"Are you addressing me?" Blanche is indignant.

"All right!" He has grabbed Blanche's purse. "Let's take a look." He turns to the others. "I want to warn you guys—if anyone tries to sell you a pair of binoculars—they're hot!"

"Me being a close friend of Eddy's should be sufficient indication that I don't have to stoop to pickin' things out of no pawn-shop window," says Blanche, following Eddy from the table to the bar. "Thanks, Edward. I think you was offering me a rum-cola when we was so rudely interrupted."

The door opens and Anna Lucasta comes in. She is a pretty, light-complexioned young woman, flashily dressed but with considerable taste. She ignores Noah's "Hello, baby!" and goes straight to the bar. A double gin is what Anna wants. Nor is she interested in the cop's story about the rock someone had thrown through Uncle Ben's window. She knows nothing about that and she pushes the cop away. She wants more air. Also she thinks Blanche should give the man back his binoculars.

"Of all the backhanded remarks!" Blanche is fighting mad. "That's what I'm always telling you about her, Eddy. You never know where you stand with her."

"He knows where *he* stands!" Anna is quick to assure them.

It's a dull night on the street, Anna reports. Everything's slowed down to a stop.

"When your train's going too fast God puts the brakes on to give you a chance to think," philosophizes Noah.

"I don't wanna think. I wanna drink." Anna pushes her glass

toward him. "Do it again."

"You ain't paid for the first one, baby," Noah reminds her.

Eddy has thrown a bill on the bar. Let Noah take out for Anna's first drink and leave the bottle. But Anna will have none of Eddy's money, nor his gin, either. She wants nothing to do with Eddy. Nor any of his propositions. Eddy's a louse, if you ask Anna.

"You don't make sense, Kid," protests the persistent Eddy. "Last year I offered you a room at the Towers, and you go slinging hash for twelve bucks a week. Now I'm here to offer you *first* room on the first floor. What do you say to that?"

"Go crawl into the woodwork," says Anna.

"This ain't no time for jokes."

"And I ain't got no time for jerks."

"You're too fresh for your age," growls Eddy, moving threateningly toward Anna. "What you need is a couple of years softening up in the workhouse."

"You're scairin' me to death, louse."

With that the enraged Eddy makes a grab for Anna. She beats him off as best she can. When he refuses to take his dirty hands off her she burns him with her cigarette. With a yell of pain Eddy collapses in a chair.

Blanche has rushed in, full of sympathy, which Eddy spurns. For the present he is through with them both. For Anna he has a parting shot— "You'd better change your mind and quit being so particular. Someday you'll need a pal."

"I'd sooner pal with rats," says Anna.

"Keep it up and you soon will."

With this Eddy leaves them. Blanche can't understand Anna's attitude. "You can't treat a big shot that way," she warns.

"He turns my stomach."

"So what? He can bring you right to the top. The Towers . . . that's a career. What if he does nauseate you—give him a smile and a laugh and get him where you want him, and then use the knife. That's my system."

It's getting late. Noah is still doing a little business in the front room, but not much. Blanche is ready to go, but first she would do a little business with Noah. She stops him on his next trip to the bar.

"Noah, how'd you like to buy a nice pair of binoculars?" she queries, reaching into her dress and producing them. "Take a look through them. See what you can see."

"Without lookin' through 'em I can see from one to ten at

hard labor. Give 'em back to Uncle Ben."

"Why? Didn't he rob me? Didn't I pay him interest for four years on my joolry and my Persian lamb cap and muff—not to mention all my electrical appliances? And then when the tickets was a trifling 60 days overdue, didn't he sell 'em so now I ain't got a thing to wear in case any important social function crops up."

"Break the law and the law'll break you!"

"I didn't break that window. And I didn't steal no binoculars, either. I was walking down the street, mindin' my own business, and there was that hole in the window and these binoculars was sitting right on the sill—they fell in my hand—I *found* 'em!"

"You take those things and you ain't any different from those hoodlums in Europe who's stealing countries."

"I get a pair of binoculars and right away I'm Hitler! Such an ignorant comparison."

Blanche has left. Noah is ready to close up. He has brought Anna a couple of sandwiches wrapped in paper. It is getting mean outside. He thinks she had better be going. He hands her a dime instead of the drink she suggests.

"Do you know where a lady can sleep for a dime?" she asks, with a wry smile.

There is a rattling of the door. "Open up for a hot sailor on a cold night," calls a cheery voice.

"Hey, Noah," Anna calls from the window. "It's Danny Johnson. Let him in!"

The door is opened and Danny literally breezes in. He is carrying a sea-bag which he sets down at the end of the bar.

"Hello, Noah!" he calls. "Hija, baby. Goddam, it sure is cold. Don't close the door. There's a stingy gob out there." He is back at the door now. "Hey, Lester, pay the taxi man—quit arguin' about the change. Come on in. You're lettin' in the breeze—" He has caught sight of Anna, now, and that is cause for greater excitement—

"Anna, baby!"

"Danny, boy!"

DANNY (*grabbing her*)—I've been looking all over for you. Gee, it's certainly good to see you.

ANNA—Take it easy, I'm not a sack of potatoes.

DANNY—You lost weight, baby.

ANNA—Yeah, among other things.

DANNY—But you're still a fine chick. (LESTER *enters.*) Hey,

Lester, look what I found!

LESTER—You sure don't lose no time.

DANNY—No, this is the gal I've been ravin' about.

LESTER—Oh, pardon me.

NOAH (*starting to close the door*)—And pardon me—is this the last of the convoy?

DANNY—Oh, sure, Noah—no more! I want you to meet Lester, he's the treasurer.

NOAH—Hello, Lester. What'll it be?

DANNY—Lester, I want you to know Anna Lucasta—and when you've met Anna, then you've really met someone.

LESTER—How are you?

ANNA—I think you've really met someone in Lester.

DANNY—I don't know nothing but the best people.

NOAH—If you'll excuse me, Mr. Treasurer, I'll lock up in here —and you'll let me know when the social hour is over.

DANNY—The night is young, Noah!

NOAH—That's what I'm afraid of!

DANNY—Why didn't you write me? We been diggin' up the whole town for you. Only came down here on a last hunch, didn't we, Lester?

LESTER—That's right. Last hunches are usually the best.

ANNA (*laughing*)—Your friend got the makins.

DANNY—Yeah, I'm totin' him around to bring out my finer qualities. He says I'm a gentleman in the rough. I sure am rough, ain't I, baby? And don't you love it? (*He kisses her and she laughs.*)

LESTER—Maybe I better go and write myself a letter.

DANNY—No, no, you stay right here and enjoy yourself.

LESTER—Enjoy myself! (ANNA *laughs.*) Well, we could be more sociable if we offered the lady a drink.

ANNA—Couldn't you think of that?

DANNY—My mind's racin' way ahead of that.

ANNA (*sliding off his knee*)—Yes, take it easy, but we got company, remember.

Lester has bought them a drink and Danny has opened up his sea-bag. They have had a time finding her, Danny tells Anna, but everything is shipshape now. "I found you and you ain't never goin' to slip away from me again—you can bet your boots on that."

Danny has taken a heavy chain necklace from his bag and slipped it around Anna's neck. That pleases Anna. She thinks perhaps it brings out her better qualities, as Lester would say. There's a bracelet to go with the necklace. That probably came off an ankle, Anna thinks, and Danny isn't the fellow to deny it.

Further deep digging in the bag brings out a statuette. That would be Papa Agoué, and Anna better be nice to Papa.

"Don't get him mad," warns Danny. "You treat him with respect and he'll do you favors. Right now he's planning something pretty big for you."

"Do you know what he's talking about, Lester?"

"Oh, it's a mighty big plan."

"Tell her who Papa Agoué is," Danny suggests.

"That's a model of Agoué, the Haitian Deity of the Sea. It seems he's good to sailors."

"Papa and me got something in common," says Anna.

"Be serious, will you?" Danny is in no triflin' mood. "My cruise is up in a few days and I'm not signing up for another four years' hitch."

"What's the matter—they givin' you the rush?"

"Givin' me the rush? Do you hear that, Papa? Why the Admiral hisself got down on his knees and begged me not to quit, didn't he, Lester?"

"Cried like a baby."

"What are you goin' to do now?" Anna's interest is only casual.

"Gonna buy me a '38 Buick an' go back to hackin', and Papa's goin' to ride the radiator cap."

"Where does Lester ride?"

"He still rides the billows."

Danny's plan, it now appears, is concerned with his settlin' down. He needs an anchor. Naturally, he thought of Anna. What Anna thinks is that he is lookin' for a cook. But she is willing to listen. "What are you leading up to?" she asks.

"The plan. I'll give it to you straight, baby. A home without a woman in it is just a pile of cold bricks. Let's you and me get together—whaddaya say, baby?"

"Are you asking me to marry you, Danny?"

"Marry! Great character! You ain't serious, are you?"

"What do you think?"

"You said it so funny you gave me goose pimples." Anna is laughing wildly. "You shouldn't scare me like that." Anna's laughter grows even wilder. "What's the matter? Have you gone nuts?"

"Sure, I'm nuts! So are you—the whole world is nuts tonight, isn't it, Lester?" She dances toward Lester and puts out her arms. "Come on, Lester. Let's dance."

Lester can't dance—or thinks he can't—but Anna manages to get some sort of action from him. They are hard at it when Noah comes back to shout an order that they stop. Don't sailors believe in signs—like "No dancin' allowed!"

Suddenly Joe Lucasta appears in the doorway. He stands for a minute, doubtful as to what his reception is to be. Anna stops dancing and stares back at him—

"Will you look what the storm's blown in!" she says, finally. And to Joe: "What do you want?"

"I—I came up to find you—and—to talk to you, Anna!"

"You handed me enough to last a lifetime. I don't have to take anything from you here. So, stay off my territory! Beat it!"

"Who is the old guy?" Danny is ready to take a hand.

"Boys! You've got strong nerves—meet my old man."

"What's on your mind, Pop?"

"I want to talk to my daughter, alone."

Lester is for going, but Anna wants them to stick around. She doesn't have to talk to her father. It's a free country. "He told me what he thought of me two years ago—and kicked me out."

"He kicked you out?" That's news to Danny.

"Sure, and carried on like a maniac—said I'd broke his heart and smashed his life because I'd sinned once—or maybe twice."

Joe tries to explain. He is there to ask Anna to forget what happened and come home. He's not the only one that's askin'. It's the whole family. No, there's nothin' wrong with her mother. Ma wants to see her real bad. Will she come?

"What are you plaguin' the kid for—gettin' her all upset—" Danny wants to know.

JOE—You stay out of this, sailor. This isn't your business.

DANNY—Who says so? I know what she's thinkin' and so would you if you used a little sense. She don't belong at home no more and you should have thought of that before you kicked her out.

LESTER—What right have you to talk that way, Danny? Of course she belongs at home, if they want her. Have you got anything better to offer?

DANNY—Why don't you pipe down! Who's askin' for your opinion?

NOAH—I thought you were for free speech.

ANNA—Well, at least, Lester ain't depending on Papa Agoué.

DANNY—No—he's still prayin' at his mammy's knee.

NOAH—That still has its points. If you want the advice of your number one gin peddler, Anna, you'll go. At least it'll give you time to think.

DANNY—To think! Who the hell wants to spend their life thinkin'?

ANNA—You might try it for five minutes.

JOE—I've got a railroad ticket for you in my pocket, Anna. Won't you please come?

ANNA—The family? Stanley married one of those Foster girls from Scranton, didn't he?

JOE—Catherine—an awful nice girl—you'd like her, Anna.

ANNA—I suppose Ma still makes a spoon bread and peach cobbler. And she sure keeps the linens clean and fresh.

JOE—Will you come?

ANNA—O.K., what can I lose?

DANNY—Nothing, but your mind—from boredom.

ANNA—At least it's three squares and a place to flop.

DANNY—You can have them with me.

ANNA—I've been many a month without 'em, kid, while you were bringing rain.

JOE—We'll go and get your things now.

ANNA—Take it easy, I've got 'em all on. I'll remember you, Noah, whenever I'm thirsty.

DANNY—Send me a postcard—"X marks my window."

ANNA—Will you frame it, Danny?

DANNY—I'll tear it up.

ANNA—Good hackin', Kid. (*She kisses him.*) And be nice to Lester, will you? Let him bring out your finer qualities.

DANNY—He'll sure never send me home to peach cobbler.

ANNA—He might find you a good cook. Well, I'll be thinkin' of you all.

Anna and Joe go out the door. The curtain falls.

ACT II

Four days later the Lucasta living room is lighted. Theresa is laying the table for the evening meal. Singing as she works, Theresa's choice of song is "You Better Mind." Stanley is helping, in Stanley's way. He has brought in an armful of logs. Stanley hasn't been warm in months, he explains, when Theresa protests his being too generous with expensive wood. So long as the family is putting on the dog for Rudolf, Stanley means to take advantage of the situation.

Katie is the first to arrive. She has been out hunting a job—and found one in the library. Katie is determined to earn her own money and be independent. Especially she wants to be independent of a family that will let itself in for the kind of trick they are trying to play on Anna and Rudolf.

"You talkin' to me, Katie?" Theresa is of a mind to resent her daughter's suspicions.

"No, she slammin' me," says Stanley, "because I think, like Frank and Stella, that if we make Anna respectable by marrying her to this dirt jedey—we certainly rate a few of the potatoes he's carryin'."

"Who says he's bringing potatoes?"

"He means the eight hundred dollars," explains Katie.

"Oh! Well, if they git married, Katie, I'm sure they'd both want to help out."

"You ain't suggested that to her, have you, Ma?"

"Of course not. I'm waiting to see if Rudolf's good enough for Anna."

"You just live in the clouds, don't you, Ma?"

"I feel like I was in heaven ever since Anna come home. It's so good just to hear her voice again—even though she do say frisky things. She made me laugh fit to bust last night in bed, tellin' me about some of the funny folks she had to wait on in that restaurant in Brooklyn."

"So that's what she was slingin', eh—hash!"

"Yeah, Stanley—that's how she lived. I always knew that Anna was good at heart, and wouldn't end in the gutter because she made one *slip*."

"Do you think she only slipped once, Ma?"

"I know Anna's good—and no one can tell me different. I knew that the first night she was home, when she cuddled up in my arms and cried herself to sleep. I knew her heart was just as good and sweet as when she was a little baby in that same bed at my breast. Once she wake up and just say: 'Is it snowin'?' And I say: 'Yes, honey, it's snowin'.' And she say: 'That's nice,' and went off to sleep again, just like a little baby."

"Ma—you're a dear. Let's go and fix the dinner."

Joe, it appears, did not go with Stella and Frank to the station to meet Rudolf. Joe preferred to stop off and wait in Mike's saloon. There, he informs Theresa, he was among friends at least.

He's home now and a little ugly. He is ready to fight Stanley at the drop of a kidding remark when Anna appears.

Anna is looking rested and freshly groomed. Her dress is simple but clean, and becoming. She has brought Joe's hymn book, which she has been reading. "Ma said it was your gospel and your guide, so I dug it up last night. It put me to sleep and gave me nightmares. Beats me why people want to sing about dying and going to Hell."

"There's plenty in here about Heaven, too, and how to git there," protests Joe. " 'Beulah Land!' My pappy and my grandpappy used to sing, and sing, and sing 'Dwellin' in Beulah Land.' They'd sing and sing until they didn't have another bit of breath left."

"And no more gin!" adds Stanley.

Now Joe is ready to fight again. Anna has a time quieting him. All right, if he wants to sing "Beulah Land," let him give out. She pulls him out of his chair and puts her arms around him. If he'll sing they'll swing it. She tries to force her father into a dance, but the minute her body touches his he draws away. "Something akin to terror seizes him."

"Let go of me!" yells Joe. "Don't do that to me! Have you gone crazy?" With this he grabs his hat and dashes out of the house.

"Well, what's wrong now? Can't you even dance in this house?" demands a startled Anna.

Stella is back from the train. Yes, Rudolf had arrived. Frank's getting him a room at Meriwether's. What's Rudolf like? Well, Stella thinks they may be surprised. Anna's curiosity is mounting. "You mean he's even too dumb for—for—for me?"

A moment later another cat's out of the bag. Katie warns Anna again that Frank and Stella are not out to make Anna respectable. They're just hoping to get Rudolf's money. So! The "sucker" has money! That interests Anna. How much? "Eight hundred dollars!" pipes Katie, to Stella's disgust.

"Eight hundred! Not bad!" admits Anna.

"Well, you can forget it," sneers Stella. "He won't fall for you. He ain't your type, either."

"Almost anybody could be the type with eight hundred dollars. Can he talk?"

"Never stops."

"Well, as long as he can say 'yes' I should be able to bring him to the point."

Now Frank is back with his report. "Did you get him settled?"

Stella wants to know. Her anxiety is plainly apparent.

Frank is very secure and self-possessed. "Sure! I took him out and bought him a couple of beers. He got real drowsy. Then I took him back to Meriwether's and watched him unpack. He's all set for a long night's sleep. You and me will go down early tomorrow, buy him his breakfast and take him to church."

Ma will be terribly disappointed that Rudolf isn't coming to dinner. Frank suggests that perhaps Anna will tell her. That takes Anna out of the room, and gives him and Stella a chance to talk over the situation with Stanley.

"We've got to get a whole new approach to this thing, Stanley," says Frank. "Rudolf ain't all that we bargained for."

STANLEY—Has he got a ring through his nose?

FRANK—No, but he's got one on his finger that ought to bring about ten bucks in hock.

STELLA—His father gave it to him when he graduated from Agricultural College.

STANLEY (*gaping*)—Graduated from College!!

STELLA—With honors!

FRANK—Otis has sure done us a dirty trick.

STANLEY—We're still goin' to marry him to Anna, aren't we?

FRANK—Not a chance. He's too clean-cut. He'd see through her in a minute.

STANLEY—How are we goin' to get his dough?

FRANK—That's the problem.

STANLEY—Are you sure he's got it?

FRANK—Oh, hell, yeah. He's got a wallet in his breast-pocket that makes him walk lopsided—

STANLEY—If only we hadn't listened to Ma about gettin' Anna. We should have got Tom's daughter for him like I said. She's homely as sin, but she's a virgin.

STELLA—Listen, brainstorm, Frank *mentioned* to Rudolf that Otis said he was anxious to git married, and what do you think he said?

STANLEY—What?

STELLA—"Aw, that was Paw's idea. I'm goin' to take my time and find me the right woman. And I know just the kind of wife I want."

FRANK—We've got to prevent him from meeting Anna. Can't have her disgracing us.

STANLEY—You'll have your work cut out. She's hot after the dough!

Photo by George Karger, Pix Inc.

"ANNA LUCASTA"

Danny—I told you to lay off her if you didn't want to be put in the Brig. Wasn't your liberty up this morning?
Lester—That's my affair.

(*Canada Lee, John Tate, Hilda Simms*)

FRANK—Who told her about the dough?

STELLA—Stanley!

STANLEY—I did not—it was Katie. She gave the whole thing away!

STELLA—It was you said his middle name was "greenback"!

STANLEY—Only after Katie had spilled—

FRANK—Goddam it! Can't I leave you two alone a minute? Moment my back's turned, some one of you gums up the works! Well, there's only one thing to do. I've got to get him out of town. I'll make some excuse to run him over to Scranton. I'll do it tomorrow right after church.

STELLA—Now listen—we ain't going to get mixed up with no police. You ain't going to take no one for a ride.

FRANK—What are you trying to say—that I'd knock him over the head and take his dough?

STELLA—You don't get into no car with him unless I'm along.

FRANK—Sometimes I wonder if you Lucastas have got a decent thought in your haids.

STANLEY—Never mind the decent stuff—let's think of something practical.

Frank would be better pleased if Stanley just didn't try to think of anything. Frank'll do the thinking. And it will have to be along new lines. An investment line, probably. A new hoe or something.

Theresa, as Frank predicted, is terribly upset by Rudolf's failure to appear for the old-fashioned Southern meal she has cooked for him. But in the middle of her lamentations Rudolf appears. He hadn't felt just right about not coming to pay his respects, even though Frank evidently had advised against it. Family introductions follow, and that is when Rudolf meets Anna.

At first Rudolf takes Anna for a neighbor. Stella had forgotten to mention that she had a sister. And, as Anna explains, she has been away for so long the family's hardly got accustomed to having her back.

"Shouldn't take long to get accustomed to you," says Rudolf, pleasantly.

"It don't as a rule," admits Anna.

This isn't the way Frank would like to have the conversation go. Twice he tries to break it up, but without success. Before they know it Anna has Rudolf taking off his coat so's he will be more comfortable. When she takes the coat from him she discovers the roll of money. That's something he ought to keep on him, she advises. "You never can tell about people these days."

It is a huge roll Rudolf is carrying. His father had given it to him mostly in small bills. It is a good-lookin' "hunk o' pay dirt" he is wearing on his finger, too, Anna notes. Keepsake from some girl, probably. No, that is a ring his father gave him when he graduated from Agricultural College.

"Go on!" chides Anna. "I bet.you can read and write!"

"Sure. I can even add two and two together and make it four."

It is Frank's advice that Rudolf put his money in the bank first thing in the morning. That's Rudolf's idea, too. By the way —what particular thing was it that interested Rudolf most in Agricultural College, Frank would know. Well, Rudolf can't remember anything in particular. He was interested in everything that went into and came out of the ground. The thing he ma-→ jored in, however, was fertilizer.

"Fertilizer! Why, that's just plain ordinary—manure." Frank can hardly imagine.

"You ought to know someone in that, Frank," suggests Stella.

Joe Lucasta has come home. He evidently has been spending even more time at Mike's bar than Theresa suspected. He is staggering drunk. He has some difficulty recognizing Rudolf and placing him properly in his mind. After that he is free with his advice. Rudolf had better watch out for women—and wine— "If one don't get you the other will."

Now Joe has confused Rudolf with his father—Joe's old friend Otis. Frank thinks it is probably time to take Joe out. Joe doesn't want to go. He'd rather stay and fight. One swing at Frank and Joe falls flat on his face. Frank and Stanley carry him to his room. "Get Ma," Frank calls back. "She's the only one he'll let take his clothes off."

Anna and Rudolf are alone. They try, at first, to cover a slight mutual embarrassment by "jiving," as Anna calls it. Gradually their talk becomes more serious. Rudolf's confession is frank. He liked Anna from the first, and he's trying to be friends. He likes her taste—her simple dress—and the way she fills it out.

"Stella said you'd be a shock. I didn't think she meant a fast worker," says Anna, with her guard still up.

"No one ever called me that before—except on harvestin' a crop."

"Well, get wise. I'm not a field of spinach."

"It isn't necessary to tell me that."

"It isn't necessary to tell a girl she fills out her dress."

"Oh, a bit of a prude."

"Prude! Well, that's certainly a new one." Anna is amused.
"I didn't tell you anything I wouldn't tell my own sisters. They never took offense."
"Probably just my dirty mind."
Presently they have decided to quit this pecking at each other and start all over. Anna agrees to brush the chip off her shoulder, and Rudolf is bent on re-establishing himself in her good graces.
"You're swell, Anna. I like you a lot." Rudolf's voice is warm and sincere.
"Then go ahead—pay your compliment."

RUDOLF—Isn't it enough—that I like you?
ANNA—Well, now, come to think of it, perhaps it is.
RUDOLF (offering his hand)—Then we can be friends?
ANNA (putting her hand in his)—Sure. That shouldn't be difficult.
RUDOLF—Gee, your hands are soft! Soft and cool like— like top-soil. I love to take it and let it trickle through my hand like this. Now I know what it feels like—like soft finger-tips.
ANNA—Say, they'll be setting *your* words to music next.
RUDOLF—What's wrong with your voice?
ANNA—I don't know. Does it jar you?
RUDOLF—No, it's music—like the mocking-bird, harsh at times, but mostly awful sweet.
ANNA—Rudolf, what's your line? Are you just the college cut-up?
RUDOLF—If that's how I strike you—sure. I'm just a college cut-up.
ANNA—Well, you can't be serious, telling me my voice is like a mocking-bird, and my hands like top-soil.
RUDOLF—When you say it like that it sounds silly and makes me a plain ass.
ANNA—No, I don't mean it like that, but you're such a funny kid; I never met anyone like you.
RUDOLF—I sure never met anyone like you. I sure never did —so pretty, and so high-spirited, and yet so understanding. All the time you're "jiving" as you call it, you seem to be looking right through people and reading their thoughts.
ANNA—According to you, I don't always read them right.
RUDOLF—I think that's because you don't trust people. Some-one must have hurt you.
ANNA—More than one, brother.

RUDOLF—Why should anyone hurt you? You're sweet like—like some little young animal with big tender eyes. Sure—that's who you are—you're Tandy.

ANNA—Tandy?

RUDOLF—A little filly Paw raised. I loved Tandy more than anything or any person in the world.

ANNA—Don't you still love her?

RUDOLF—She died. And did I cry! I cried for a whole week.

ANNA—Say, what are you trying to do to me? That's a hell of a thing to tell me—that I'm like something that died.

RUDOLF—Aw, honey—I'm sorry. I wasn't trying to make *you* cry.

ANNA—Well, you have—give me your handkerchief.

RUDOLF—Here, let me. My! You're pretty when you cry. You're sweet, Anna—you're sweet!

ANNA—No, I'm just a fool.

RUDOLF—The kind of fool that makes a lot of sense.

As Anna looks at him wonderingly, Rudolf takes her in his arms and kisses her passionately.

Theresa walks in on that kiss and is ready to shout "Hallelujah!" So far as Theresa is concerned that kiss settles everything. But Anna will not have it that way. The kiss meant nothing. She learned how to kiss long ago. She kissed Rudolf like he was her big brother, and that is what he is going to stay.

"Don't you love him, honey? How can you help it? He's the finest boy I ever did see."

"Sure, he's fine. Fine as silk, but silk isn't for me, and no one knows it better than you."

Rudolf would deny the soft impeachment. He's coarse as hell, and Anna knows it, if Theresa will excuse him for swearin'.

"Go ahead and cuss all you want," advises Theresa. "Give *her* a good cussin' out. No one ever whopped her when she was little. That's all that's wrong with her. Go on!"

Sure, Anna likes Rudolf. Likes him more than a little. But not enough to marry him. The whole thing's crazy. "A guy walks into a house to say 'hello,' and ten minutes later you're marryin' him off to your daughter," she says to her mother.

"No one's marryin' me to anyone I don't want," puts in Rudolf. "And it don't take ten minutes to fall in love. It only takes ten seconds. I knew that the minute I saw your face."

"Rudolf, you're just a kid! You don't know nothin'. A face!

Everyone isn't like you, with nothing but goodness in them to show in their faces."

"You thought I was bad at first."

"Yeah, and I found out different. You think I'm good!"

"I know you're good, Anna. Well, suppose we tell each other all our crimes, and then decide if we love each other."

"I don't expect to know you that long," counters Anna.

"Anna, honey, don't you see what's happenin'?" Theresa's tone is pleading. "God has sent this lovely boy into our house just for you. He's sent him in answer to prayer—my prayers—and Katie's, because you never had a fair chance. And the boy done fell in love with you right from the start. That's God's doin', too. God's givin' you your chance for love and happiness. You ain't goin' to break his heart and Rudolf's, too, is you?"

"God can stand anything, Ma. Rudolf ain't so husky."

Anna continues to protest, and Rudolf to plead until finally Rudolf has his way—

"Come on— Knock that last little sliver off your shoulder. Say you'll marry me," pleads Rudolf.

"At your own risk, Rudolf."

"I'll take it."

"O.K., sucker!"

"I'll make you happy, Anna."

The family's excitement, coupled with its congratulations, is pretty exciting. Stella, Frank and Stanley are good at covering their disappointment. They'll still stick pretty close to Rudolf and they hope Anna will be happy.

Theresa is so full of joy she is ready to burst. The fact that Joe is in her bed with his shoes on doesn't worry her at all. She's going to get something to make them all happy for a celebration. And she does—a bottle of reasonably ancient brandy, which she had had hidden near the sink—where she knew Frank seldom went. It's good, too—

"Man who gave me this was way up in the bootleggin' business," boasts Theresa.

"And now he's way down in Leavenworth," adds Frank.

Now they have all raised their glasses— "To Anna and Rudolf."

"Now get up, Anna. Put your arms around me. Now— On behalf of myself and my bride-to-be I thank you all, and together we thank Thee, dear God."

As Rudolf and Anna drink there is a terrible thump on the ceiling.

"What's that?" demands Rudolf.

"That's God falling out of bed," ventures Frank.

The curtain falls.

ACT III

Three days later, in the Lucasta living room, Frank is doing his part to prepare for Anna's wedding. He is pouring the contents of a jug into a pinch bottle.

Theresa, in the kitchen, is putting the finishing touches to a cake. She is still lacking a bride and groom that she has been keeping in a box under her bed. Katie will get them.

Joe Lucasta is feeling a little better after his last spell, but he refuses to have anything to do with the wedding. He won't play the heathen by taking Anna up the aisle. But, Frank warns him, if he does any little thing to interfere with the ceremony he'll get his head dunked in the horse trough.

Stanley is the missing one at the moment. Rudolf, who has just come in, reports that he had waited an hour for Stanley at the Meriwethers'. Stanley was going to bring up the Chevy that Rudolf has bought for his honeymoon. Frank thinks Stanley has probably succumbed to a temptation to take a little joy ride on his own first.

Frank has gone into the kitchen, which gives Rudolf a chance to ask Theresa to take charge of the present he has got for Anna. It's an attractive overnight bag, and inside is "something she has set her heart on," in addition to Otis Slocum's wedding present and the eight hundred dollars. Theresa will find a safe place for that—right under her bed.

Rudolf's getting nervous. It may be they'll all have to walk to the church if Stanley fails to show up with the car. Theresa thinks perhaps he needs a little sneaker to settle his nerves—but not out of the pinch bottle. That is one of Frank's refills. Theresa's got something that she squeezed the grapes for herself.

Theresa has seen Anna in Stella's wedding gown and she looks lovely. She is also prepared to report that Anna certainly loves Rudolf. "Katie tells me she never heard a person talk about anyone the way Anna talks about you," says Theresa. "Katie say Anna say, 'Katie, if Jesus Himself was to come back on earth He couldn't act sweeter and kinder than Rudolf.'"

"Don't tell me that, Ma. It's easy to be good to Anna. It's so easy to be good when you're first in love. But I'm goin' to see that we keep it this way."

"You've got to be patient with her. She do get frisky at times."

"Don't I know it! She's got a mind of her own, as I've found out in only three days."

For one thing Anna had refused to spend any part of her honeymoon in New York. "I guess she wasn't very happy there," guesses Rudolf. So he had got the loan of a cabin in the mountains from one of the professors at the Agricultural College.

Katie and Stella are yellin' for Ma to come and get dressed. Ma isn't worried. It won't take her long to get into her finery —all except the hat. She'll need help with that. There ain't no way of tellin' which is the back or the front.

Frank has come in, prepared to take over any job the others fall down on. He will represent Mr. Lucasta and give the bride away. He will, if necessary, represent Stanley and act as best man. Rudolf gives him the ring and the license, just in case.

Frank is glad to note, from the size of Rudolf's wallet, that he had banked his money. But he isn't quite happy when Rudolf admits that he had banked it with Anna.

Stanley has showed up finally with the Chevy. Everything's about ready. Stella and Katie shoo Rudolf out of the room, lest he see Anna when she comes downstairs. That would mean awful bad luck.

Frank is anxious to find out where Anna has hidden Rudolf's eight hundred. Katie must know. She's been sleepin' with Anna. But if Katie knows she refuses to tell. Nor will she be bullied. Not by Frank, nor Stella, either. If they get too nasty about it Katie will get a policeman to see that they don't steal it.

"Who's stealing?" shouts Stella. "She offered to split it fifty-fifty with us."

KATIE (*holding her own*)—She hadn't met Rudolf then. She was just talking your language—kidding you along.

FRANK—She'd better not kid about anything so serious! Four hundred dollars belongs to us. It's part of the deal. . . .

KATIE—There is no deal! This is a love-match. Those two kids are in love, if you've ever heard of the word!

FRANK—Aw, muck! She's just takin' him for a ride.

STELLA—You don't think anyone that's been what she has, could really fall in love, do you?

KATIE (*becoming a little hysterical*)—God! How I wish I'd never met you two! Sometimes you almost make me ashamed of my blood! There are people who *want* to think we're all like you, and that it's not just the few that have let inhuman treatment make them hard and rotten and crooked.

FRANK—Crap! No one's treated me inhuman! I'd like to see 'em try it! I'm what I am of my own free will and observation, because I observe and I see who gits on in this world! It's the hard ones, the strong ones; and they git on because they take what the other fellow ain't fit to hold, and they don't listen to no soft women's talk.

ANNA (*coming in on the speech*)—Gosh, Frank, you're in the groove, Kid! The preacher ought to let you say a few words in church!

STELLA—Come here!

FRANK—God damn! Ain't that some bride! Who would think two people could look so different in the same dress?

STELLA—When I wore it you looked different yourself. There was some sort of line to show where your chest started.

FRANK—Wait a couple of months and look at yourself in the mirror!

STELLA—Shut up!

ANNA—Hey! Quit scrapping on my wedding morn, kids! What's the matter, Katie? Have you been crying?

KATIE—No, dear, of course not. I'll get your bouquet.

Frank is still fussing with Anna's handbag. And he is going to catch hell if he puts dirty finger marks all over it, Stella warns him. A moment later Anna has taken the bag from him and is surprised to find it locked. Frank admits that he had been trying to open it, but couldn't.

Theresa has come, her hat on upside down, as expected. They're ready to start for the church now, after Ma has kissed her "little baby" and had a bit of a cry, and Anna has assured Mom that she loves her.

Frank is pretending to blubber, too, and for a moment Stella is fooled into thinking that he is also "going soft on them." But Katie knows. "Soft like a crocodile!" says she, with a contemptuous look at her big brother-in-law.

This sets Theresa laughing. "Now I know what he's always reminded me of," she chortles, turning to Anna. "Honey, I got to apologize to you for sending you up the aisle with a crocodile —but it's the best we can do."

"Now don't upset him, Ma—he just hates to give me away," answers a broadly grinning Anna.

"This family will never get a sense of dignity," mutters Frank, offering his arm to Anna.

Theresa remembers the bag with the wedding present. "Thank

God! Here's one thing the crocodile won't get," she says, picking it up.

The curtain falls.

The wedding is over. The front door at the Lucastas is suddenly thrown open and in comes Rudolf, joyfully carrying his bride across the doorstep. "How's that, Mrs. Slocum?"

"Fine, except that you left my shoe on the front porch." Anna sticks her stockinged foot out before him.

"Starting to kick things around already, eh?"

The shoe is recovered. There is a piece of rough paper inside. Looks like a note. Rudolf has some difficulty making out the writing—

" 'We got cold waiting outside, so we gone to warm up inside,' " laboriously reads Rudolf. " 'Me and Papa—Papa—A-g-o—' What's this word?"

" 'Agoué,' " reads Anna in a shocked voice.

" 'Agoué. P.S. Will be back later.' Wedding guests, I suppose."

"Yes—yes—wedding guests." Anna is trembling. Now she is anxious that she and Rudolf should get away as quickly as possible. Even without waiting for Rudolf to bring the folks back from the church. Let them get away right now!

Rudolf can't understand this sudden eagerness? "What's come over you, honey? You're actin' awful strange. It's bad enough that your pa's behaved the way he has. I don't want my pa to know that I ran off without sayin' good-by to your ma and Katie and all."

"Oh, sure—sure—by all means let's not offend Otis Slocum!"

The incipient quarrel is over almost as quickly as it was begun. It is the house that has unnerved Anna. "I hate everything about it. I want to get away and never come back."

A moment later the bride is in her husband's arms, pleading desperately not to be left alone. "Oh, darling Rudolf, hold me tight!" Anna pleads. "Hold me tight enough to kill me, will you?"

"Kill you! Honey, we're just starting to live!"

"Thank you, Rudolf. Thank you for everything."

"I'll be back before you miss me," calls Rudolf, as he disappears through the door.

Anna has picked up her bouquet and wedding veil and gone upstairs. Outside there is the sound of a motor car starting, and the greetings of two men. "Morning, friend!" "Morning!"

A moment later Danny Johnson is standing in the doorway. Anna appears on the stairs. "Hello, sugar!" Danny calls. "Did you get my note?"

"Yes, Danny."

DANNY—Well, I'm here.

ANNA—Don't take off your coat!

DANNY—Why?

ANNA—You've got to get out of here.

DANNY—What goes on here? How come? What are you all dolled up for—a fancy dress ball?

ANNA—I've just been married.

DANNY—Always kiddin'—what are you trying to do—give me goose pimples? (*Looking at wedding decorations.*) It looks as if someone were getting married. But it couldn't be you.

ANNA—Why not?

DANNY—Because I only got your letter yesterday when I went for my papers and I beat it right down here like you asked me to.

ANNA—Look, Danny, I thought after two days I couldn't stand it here, so I sent for you to come and get me. I didn't think you'd show up for another week.

DANNY—Now wait a minute—you ain't married—hey, who was that guy with the Chevy and the monkey suit?

ANNA—My husband. We just came from the church. (*She shows her ring.*)

DANNY—Well, what do you know? How did you get in this jam, Kid? That funny old father of yours put something over on you?

ANNA—No. This is on the level, Danny, and it's my own doing.

DANNY—Who is this guy, and what's his racket? He looked like a parlor punk to me.

ANNA—He's the swellest guy I ever met, Danny.

DANNY—When did you meet the sonofabitch?

ANNA—Since I came home.

DANNY—What did he do—put something in your drink?

ANNA—I don't know, but I'm sure floating.

DANNY—Aw, come on. You're talking to Danny Johnson. Remember?

ANNA—Yes. You're swell, too, Danny.

DANNY (*pouring himself a drink*)—You don't have to con me. What's the catch? Is this heel loaded?

ANNA—I wouldn't care if he didn't have a nickel.

DANNY—Oh, then he *has* got dough. Well, I'm beginning to get your angle. Why couldn't you say that in the first place?

Danny is ready to go. What are they waiting for? Anna isn't going. Not if she can help it. If Danny's a good sport he will go away before anyone sees him and let her work out her problem alone.

"I think I can make good if I can just get away from everything and everybody soon enough," says Anna. "I'm in love with him, Danny."

"You used to tell me that, baby."

"In love with you? I couldn't have because I never knew what it was until now."

Danny is willing to take his chances and he hasn't any idea of leaving. He thinks perhaps he'll wait and beat the bejeezis outa Rudolf—

"He ain't your kind!" says Danny. "You'd go crazy in a month without the lights and the swing and a guy that can get you there in the groove. That's what I'm going to give you, Kid. That's what I'm here for."

"I'm through with that, Danny. I don't want it anymore."

"You ain't never through, once you've had the taste of it. And you've got it in your blood. You took to it like a duck to water. I should know. I got you at the start."

"I tell you I'm through. I'm never going back to it!"

"You can't get away from it. Anyone looking for it can see it in your eyes like I did, the first flash I got of you. You don't belong to one guy. You'll never stick to one guy. You can't."

"I can. I will, damn you! I know you, you're only trying to scare me."

"I'm trying to save you a lot of grief, baby. Go on with this hick you've married and bury yourself on some farm. But one day some guy will *drive* by and spot you in the field and all he'll have to do is touch you—and you'll turn weak as water. It's no use fighting, Anna. You're one of us—we're the real stuff—people like you and me. Many's the time we've set the earth on fire together. Stick to me and we'll burn it up."

Danny is finished. Yes, he'll go, but it ain't good-by. He knows that Anna will come crawlin' back, and when she does he'll probably take her in. He's weak that way, too.

But before Danny can get away Joe Lucasta arrives. A calm and vengeful Joe who recognizes Danny as the sailor he had seen Anna kissing at that bar in Brooklyn. Perhaps, says Joe, it is good that Danny has found Anna again. He can be taking her away when Rudolf drops her. And Rudolf will drop her as soon as he knows what her father knows about her, about the times he has caught her and about her sendin' for Danny now to come and sleep with her—

"Hey! Not so quick on the trigger, Pop." Danny is ready to take a hand in this argument. "And anyway, what's the percentage for you in bustin' up your little daughter's wedding?"

"He's made that his life's work—messing mine up," interrupts Anna. "But I've got happiness right in my hand, Pa, and if you spoil it—if you so much as open your mouth to Rudolf, I swear to God I'll kill you, and I won't give a damn what happens because there wouldn't be anything left to live for."

Danny is ready to take care of that little matter for her and fix Joe so he won't be telling anybody anything. But Anna stops him. Joe explains that he didn't have to tell Rudolf. He isn't counting on Rudolf, but on Otis, his father. Otis knows. Joe had written him and Otis is on his way North. He'd be in now if his train were on time. Joe produces the telegram to prove that.

"Do you know what you're doing, baby?" Danny's sympathy is still keen. "Swimming between a barracuda and a shark. This old bastard and his side kick are going to chew you up bit by bit. And this Rudolf of yours is a goddam jellyfish, just floating by while they do it."

"Rudolf isn't weak," persists Anna. "He's as fine as they come. He loves me and he'd go through hell for me. But no man could take the hell they're going to give him—to come back on his wedding day and be told that his wife's been a prostitute."

"Why did you leave it till his wedding day?" sneers Joe. "Why didn't you tell him yourself right at the start?"

"Because he took me on his own level. And I have a right to make good on that level. I didn't fool him, Pa—I fought him. Ma must have told you how I tried to stop him but he cut me off every time with his belief—his faith that I'm good. It's his religion, Pa, and he makes me good. I know it's hard for you to believe that because you despise me for what I've been. But it's true. Can I tell you something? I'm—I'm just waiting to be alone with him—as if—as if he was the first guy I'd ever known. Won't you please—you and Otis—won't you give me a chance to go away and make good? If I make a mess of it—if I eve slip back—I promise you one thing—I'll never bother anyone again. No one will ever see me. I'll know where to go and what to do."

JOE—Too bad you didn't come out with all that before, Daughter. And you ain't convinced me by your tearful story—and because I ain't convinced I wrote a letter to a certain other party and mailed it just now. Even if you were with Rudolf when he hears from that party he'll have to get rid of you—or else let you drag him down to your level.

DANNY—So there's a third man eating fish, eh? Before he gets through, Kid, you'll be swimming in a school of them.

JOE—It's funny you should mention that, sailor, because that's just where I wrote to—a school. My wife told me that Rudolf was lookin' to his college to get him a teacher's post. So my letter was to the fellow that has charge of appointment there. He won't recommend anyone whose wife might teach young folks things they can't get out of books.

ANNA—You crazy old fool! You're not protecting him—you're just destroying him.

DANNY—If you want to hang around here and let them chew up this Papa's boy you've married and use you for sauce—go to it. But I came down here to take you back where you fit in—make up your mind.

ANNA—Well, Pa—you've made another good job of it. Something told me not to come home with you—that I'd only get it in the neck again. You twisted old fool! Your brains are so jazzed up you don't see what you're doing! Weren't you satisfied to make a mess of me—did you have to mess up the kid, too? Poor Rudolf—poor kid!

JOE—Oh, don't make out you're crying for him. You don't care what man's making love to you, just so long as it is a man! You're going back to your Danny—to your three square meals, a place to sleep—with Danny!

DANNY—I don't like the look of his eyes, Kid. You'd better get out of here quick!

ANNA—Ah, to hell with him—I'd just as soon take a sock at him myself.

DANNY—Do as I tell you—get your coat!

ANNA—Disgusting old psalm-singing idiot!

JOE—Get out of my house, sailor—and take her with you!

DANNY—Open the door and beat it down to the car!

Joe—Take her in your damn car and drive her to Hell.

Anna—Don't hit him, Danny!

Danny (*taking the poker away from* Joe—*turns him away and sends him sprawling across the room*)—Aw, go and kiss Otis!

Joe picks up a chair and throws it after Danny as the curtain falls.

It is eight days later and we're again in Noah's Bar. Noah is back of the bar talking to Rudolf, who is just finishing a note and sealing it in an envelope. Rudolf is going back to Alabama. His search for Anna has so far proved fruitless.

Noah would cheer Rudolf if he could. This much he knows— that Anna don't love Danny, and never has. She was just kiddin' Danny along. "You can take that from someone who sees a lot of lovin' from behind this here bar."

"I didn't come to spy. I only came to find her. I knew all the facts before I started," says Rudolf.

"Anna'll come back," Noah is saying. "I wish you didn't have to go home. Anna'll walk in here one day soon. I know. I watch people. I know how they act. I know Anna ain't in love with that Danny and she'll come back here."

"That's what I'm afraid of. She'll come back here—she won't come back to me."

"Well—if you're here—and *she* comes here—then she comes to you, don't she? That's mathematics."

"At college they call that logic, Noah. But it would have to be something they don't teach in college, Noah, to bring us back together again."

"Goin' to college won't keep you from gettin' in a mess with a woman—and nothin' they teach you there can get you out of one. When life hits you one on the jaw, you've got to hit back."

Rudolf is ready to do that, but just now it seems to him that all life doesn't seem as important as a girl's voice saying: "Hold me tight! Hold me tight enough to kill me!"

Katie Lucasta has come to Noah's Bar in search of Rudolf. Rudolf had written that he was leaving for Alabama if he had not found Anna by this date, and Katie, having had a note from Anna, had run up with it to catch him.

From the note Rudolf makes out that Anna is with a sailor named Danny Johnson somewhere in Harlem. The note doesn't give any address, but it is the opinion of Blanche that if Anna is anywhere in Harlem she will be spending a lot of her time at the Savoy. Anna had rather dance than eat. So Rudolf, taking Katie with him, is off for the Savoy.

They have been gone but a few minutes when the door is flung open and in bursts Anna and the sailor Lester, who was Danny's friend. Anna has been drinking. Her spirits are high, her speech tough, her thirst mounting. Double gin is what Anna wants, and Lester will pay. Lester pays for everything—and Anna means everything.

Noah would be paternally protective if Anna would let him. She's already had enough to drink, he tells her, and it is plain that she stands in need of sleep. Anna can, if she wants to, sleep at Blanche's house tonight, but Anna doesn't care for that idea—

"Nothin' doin'," says she. "I know that old gag—'pitch in together.' I'm pitchin' in with Lester. Ain't that right, Lester? Didn't I promise to love you forever and ever? Well, go on— tell me! You're among friends. Speak up! You ain't afraid Danny will hear you, are you?"

"You know I'm not afraid of Danny."

"How can you be when he ain't here—or is he? Say, where did we leave Danny? I can't remember when I saw him last."

"We left him last night at his garage."

"Oh, sure—he was under his goddamed old Buick—wasn't he? Didn't he look a sight? Grease from head to foot. Ever see Danny with grease on him, Noah?"

"No, I never did."

"Well, you should. He's awful pretty! Don't you think Danny's pretty, Lester?"

"No, I don't; and I don't think you are either, like this."

Noah and Blanche are in a half-whispered consultation. Anna catches the word Savoy. So that's where they think Danny is? He ain't. Danny's gone back to hackin' in Hackensack. And if she can't have another double gin it is Anna who is going to the Savoy. She hasn't got any use for a couple of psalm-singers.

"You ain't goin' to the Savoy. You ain't goin' nowhere," says Noah, laying hands on Anna and holding her where she is. "You're staying here. I want to talk to you alone."

" 'I want to talk to you alone, Anna—I want to talk to you alone.' Are you going to ask me to go home with you?"

"No. I'm goin' to straighten you out right here."

"Hear him! The guy that fills me up with double rotguts! That's a hot one! You old stinker! Lemme go!"

She is still cursing and struggling when Danny Johnson comes through the door. He goes directly to Lester, who has moved down beside Anna—

DANNY—So here you are. If you're tryin' to duck you shouldn't leave a trail of double gins behind you.

ANNA—I've got a very important plan for you. Guess what?

DANNY—Forget me, baby. You'll need all your nerve for your own plan! Did she take you for your dough . . . Lester?

LESTER—No, and what's more she didn't try.

DANNY—That's like her. Sparin' the saps and putting her pals through the wringer.

ANNA—I didn't ask you for nothin'.

DANNY—But you sure took me for plenty—clothes and hats and presents—and booze by the case—not to mention putting my Buick on the blink trying to drive it when you were drunk. (ANNA *laughs*.) Yeah—laugh—go on and laugh—laugh at this too. (*He takes something out of his pocket*.) See what this is? It's Papa Agoué's head. You busted it clean off—and busted my luck with it. If you had to try suicide, did you have to use my Buick? Where did you two sleep last night?

LESTER—None of your goddamed business!

DANNY—You silly lunkheads!

ANNA—What's that to you?

DANNY—I told you to lay off her if you didn't want to get put in the brig! Wasn't your liberty up this morning?

LESTER—That's my affair.

DANNY—And you're lucky to get off with thirty days foolin' with her. This babe's going batty. She's heading for the rocks. She'll sink and take all hands down with her. I saw a girl in Haiti get this way from Religion. She went around knifing her friends and wound up jumping into Shark Bay.

NOAH—Well, this ain't Haiti, sailor—and there's always been a touch of voodoo about you that don't go in a respectable Christian bar. If she broke your luck, what did you follow her for?

DANNY—Whaddya think? To take her back and have her sittin' up in joints all night laughing like a maniac—and takin' her home and havin' her callin' me a greaseball. I ain't aimin' to go to the chair for knocking her block off—that's what I'd do with another night of her.

All Danny wants is what's left of the money he gave Anna— and the wrist watch he gave her. She won't be needin' dough where she's headin', and she wouldn't expect him to go on making payments on the watch for someone else to steal.

As for Lester— His ship is still in drydock. Danny has his flivver outside. He'll take Lester back to the ship and put in a good word for him against his having gone AWOL. "I've done plenty of favors for Cokey Joe. Maybe he'll go easy on you if I tell him the tale!"

"Well," says Blanche, as the sailors disappear, "as I always say, 'If you lie down with dogs you'll get up with fleas.' I'll take a rum-cola, Noah, double."

But Noah isn't doing any more business that evening. He's closin'. Whatever time it is, he's closin'.

Before she goes Blanche suggests a way out for Anna. Eddy is still lookin' for a girl at the Towers. "Now, Gawd knows you've never given me no reason to do you a favor, but when I see anyone throwin' themselves away like you are it's my instink to try and save them. Now, whatever you say, Eddy's a swell guy, and if you go and tell him you'll stand by him, you can have his shirt. In fact you can move right into the room he threw the bitch out of."

"Thanks, Blanche. Thanks for tryin' to save me."

"Don't mention it! Funny how all the wrong people get all the right breaks."

Noah also has plans for Anna. He didn't believe she would be serious about the Towers and Eddy. "I'd rather go jump in the river!" That's how Anna feels.

She will never have to do that, Noah promises. Now it is his idea that they should have some black coffee, and then they will go lookin' for some good people Noah knows about—"people who are goin' to take care of you and see that you never go wanderin' again."

Anna is suspicious of any such talk as that. She'll fight her way out of Noah's place if she has to. But she is startled into staying for a little when Noah calls her "Mrs. Slocum." Who's been telling him things? Rudolf has; "Alabam" Noah and Blanche call him.

"Where has he gone?" Anna is interested now.

"Up to the Savoy with your sister-in-law. These are the good people I want to take you to."

ANNA—He wants to see me?

NOAH—Well, if he's there and you go there he'll have to see you, won't he? That's logic.

ANNA—But didn't they tell him anything? Didn't anything *happen* after I left?

NOAH—Accordin' to Alabam everything happened except earthquake and flood. It was a new kind of family party because no one could sit down. Your father had broke all the furniture. The first thing that happened when he said you had left with Danny was a battle royal over your money, in which your sister gave her husband a black eye and punched your brother on the nose. But your ma had hid the money under her bed so the poor dogs got none. Then your father gave Alabam his picture of you as a woman of sin and in the middle of it had a spell and passed out. I don't know how you're going to take this, Anna, but you haven't got a father no more.

ANNA—Pa—dead!

NOAH—That same night. His last request was to be buried in Bessemer—so your father-in-law took him there.

ANNA—Ma—what's happened to Ma?

NOAH—Well, I don't suppose she's jumpin' around for joy. Of the two people closest to her, one's dead and the other one might be, for all she knows. You want to think of others sometimes—not only of yourself.

ANNA—Whaddya mean? Do you think I left Rudolf because I wanted to? I was only thinking of him. I bet he didn't tell you my pa wrote to his college and told them that he'd married a—

NOAH—Sure—sure—he knows that. I'd just like to see some old poop hintin' things to Alabam about his wife. It wouldn't be Alabam that'd lose out—it would be that old poop, because Alabam would chase his ass right into Mississippi. You know it might not be a bad thing for you to meet Alabam some time. He's a hell of a guy when you get to know him.

ANNA—Well, who's married to him—me or you?

NOAH—You'd better find out if you are—still.

ANNA (*opening the letter and reading*)—It isn't a letter—it's just a sentence.

NOAH—What does he say?

ANNA—"Darling—isn't it enough that I love you?"

NOAH—God, ain't that wonderful. That ought to make you happy. (ANNA *cries*.) I said happy, baby—don't cry. What are you crying for? Listen, honey, he told me the most wonderful things about his love for you—things I never did hear a man say before about a woman. He said that all life wasn't as important as hearin' a girl say—"hold me tight—hold me tight enough to kill me." (*Knock on the door.*) I'm closed!

RUDOLF'S VOICE—It's me, Noah.

NOAH—Alabam?

RUDOLF'S VOICE—I left my grip. I guess I'll need it.

NOAH—He wants his grip.

ANNA—What can you do with a guy like that?

RUDOLF'S VOICE—Let me in . . . It's snowing.

ANNA (NOAH *takes* RUDOLF'S *bag and places it at the door.* ANNA *picks up bag.*)—I'm bringing you your grip, Snowman!

Noah opens the door and Anna goes out.

THE CURTAIN FALLS

FOOLISH NOTION

A Comedy in Three Acts

By Philip Barry

(Digest by John Chapman)

THE arrival of Philip Barry's "Foolish Notion" on March 13, 1945, under Theatre Guild auspices, caused a divergence of opinion among reviewers—and a similar divergence among subscribers whom the Guild polled after they saw the play. Undoubtedly the presence of Tallulah Bankhead in the role of Sophie Wing was a great help at the box-office, and the comedy still was doing sturdy business when it was taken off at the beginning of Summer.

Critic Howard Barnes called Mr. Barry's script "murky." Lewis Nichols felt that the play had a good idea but that most scenes were overwritten. Said Burton Rascoe: "It is so smart, so brilliant, so clever that I haven't the slightest idea what it is about and I was bored stiff by it." Ward Morehouse found that the blend of realism and fantasy was not particularly successful. John Chapman took it for a good time in a frankly, highly theatrical manner—and had a good time. The majority of subscribers polled said they had enjoyed the comedy, but some did not and some others had some qualifying reservations. Press and subscribers were practically unanimous in stating that Miss Bankhead had given a brilliant and enjoyable performance—as Tallulah Bankhead.

Mr. Barry, last represented by "Without Love," had come forth in "Foolish Notion" with a comedy of rather involved structure—partly the familiar drawing-room triangle, partly a series of dream scenes in which characters imagine how they will react to a situation which is shortly to confront them. In their dreams they get a lot off their minds—dead wood, one of them calls it—and in the final reality their reactions are not what they had thought they were going to be. It was felt by some that this final reality was a sort of desperation on the part of the playwright; that he had thought himself into a jam from which he could not extricate himself to everybody's satisfaction—including, perhaps, his own.

Matching Mr. Barry's imaginativeness, which included such maneuvers as having all dream-characters make their entrances backward, was the setting of Jim Hapgood's (Henry Hull's) library. The focal decoration was a portrait of Jim. As conceived by the playwright and executed by Designer Jo Mielziner, the portrait hung on the "fourth wall"—the invisible wall between players and audience. Thus, as lights rose or grew dim over the painting, the actors faced the audience when seeming to look directly at it. Yet the picture was visible in reality to the audience, which saw it as it was reflected from a mirror over a fireplace. This was accomplished by making the mirror of scrim and placing the painting behind it, so that it became visible when—and only when—the lights over it were turned up.

Jim Hapgood has been away at the war a long time and may be dead; but his house in New York still stands and is occupied by his wife—or widow—and their adopted daughter, an intense and imaginative little person aged 12.

The library of Jim Hapgood's house is a high-ceilinged, old-fashioned, made-over room, furnished with good pieces of mixed style and period, including a harp beside a grand piano. The most important decoration, so far as the story is concerned, is a full-length portrait of Jim which can be viewed direct or in reflection from a big mirror over the fireplace. The audience sees the picture—a $10,000 job by Augustus John—by reflection.

It is 9 o'clock of a late-August evening and in the library are Happy Hapgood, the adopted child; Jim's wife, known on the stage as Sophie Wing; Gordon Roark, a handsome and sophisticated actor about Sophie's age who is given to such bright remarks as, "I'm so bored I could spit"; and, finally, a girl of 22 named Florence Denny who has now given up her desire to become an actress and wants to be a teacher.

Sophie is urging little Happy to do something and Happy is balking. "It isn't that you don't want to?" "No, Mother." "It isn't that you can't?" "No, Mother." "You *would* like Miss Denny to know how you've come along, wouldn't you?" "Yes, Mother." "Then give, Happy, give!"

Miserably, haltingly, Happy tries to give. She sings, "A wand'ring minstrel I, a thing of shreds and patches"—but breaks off at the "dreamy lullaby" line. "You know," she says, "that whenever I do anything—paint or draw or sing or anything—it's got to be *for* someone!"

Not even Miss Denny, apparently, will serve as the recipient of Happy's song . . . and now it develops that Miss Denny has been brought to the house to be a companion and instructor to

Happy while her mother and Gordon Roark make a tour in a play. Sophie explains that Florence is going to stay with Happy and teach her things "out of sheer kindness and a very old friendship."

There is some talk about the tour, and a "story" that broke, and interviews, broadcasts and photographs—when Happy interrupts and says she knows whom she will sing her song to. She is looking at the reflection of Jim Hapgood's portrait in the mirror above the fireplace. "Well, he's my father, isn't he? He adopted me just as much as she did, didn't he?"

"Yes," Gordon Roark agrees, "he did—and was."

"How do you mean 'was'? Just because he's been away for a while—"

" 'A while'—dear God, have mercy!"

"And what do you mean by that, may I ask? 'Missing' means missing—and that's all it means!"

Sophie gently urges Happy to let them have the song, and Happy turns again to the mirror. While the child is gazing a maid comes in with "another batch of telegrams" for Sophie and is told to put them on the desk. Miss Denny, interested in Happy's behavior, asks, "But why at the mirror? Is that part of the method? Do they teach them to watch themselves all the time?"

It is apparent that Happy is enrolled in an acting school for children, but the mirror business isn't part of the curriculum. Sophie explains to Florence Denny by pressing a switch; the light over the portrait comes on and the reflection in the mirror becomes brighter. Finally Happy goes into her song—this time Gilbert and Sullivan's "Poor wandering one . . ." At the end she repeats the couplet, "Take heart, fair days will shine—Take any heart— take mine," and makes a gesture of giving her heart as she does so. Sophie thinks the gesture is a little too much, because in acting an excess of sentiment only defeats itself. "Tell her about the art of acting, Gordon."

"Me? You know I'm an actor for three reasons and three only: I like to show off and get paid for it, I hate to get up in the morning and I like you around in my evenings."

This chatter among play-actors is interrupted by the arrival of Horatio Wing, Sophie's father, who is possibly more stage-struck than anyone else present. Horatio is a spry, wiry little man in his late 70's—a Professor Emeritus of Dramatic Literature who will quote any scene from anything provided it is a Classic. He has also kept up on his playgoing, because when Florence Denny is introduced he remembers her as the girl with the freckles in a play called "A Month in the Country."

Horatio turns his attention to Happy, asks how things are going at the dramatic school, and suggests "a little recitation of sorts, brief, but full of fire." Happy gives forth with—Robert Burns' "To a Louse."

> "O wad some Pow'r the Giftie gie us
> To see oursels as ithers see us.
> It wad frae mony a blunder free us
> An' foolish notion."

GORDON—"Foolish Notion" is right. It's impossible. It's tough enough seeing others straight, without expecting to—

SOPHIE—He's in one of his pretties, Father.

HORATIO—I detected that.

GORDON—Look, O holy father of the great star: I am about at the end of my rope. For years you've obstructed Sophie and me in our quite honorable intention of—

SOPHIE—Gordon! Careful, will you?

GORDON—Oh, all right, all right.

HAPPY—Why, what don't I know? What is it I'm supposed not to?

SOPHIE—It's past your bedtime.

HAPPY—Things are going on here.

SOPHIE—Say good night now, there's a dear.

HAPPY—I've felt them all week. I feel things, you know. And either someone gives me the information I want or I'll do something I wouldn't normally.

FLORENCE—What's that, Happy?

HAPPY—I'll go to the newspapers for it!

This is a highly practical idea for a child of 12—or for anybody, for that matter, because the romance of Sophie Wing and Gordon Roark has been quite an item in the public prints. Happy knows that secret things are being kept from her and they have something to do with Father, whom she loves so much. When Horatio expresses surprise that the child has not been told Sophie lamely explains she was waiting for the proper time. The time definitely seems to be now, and as Gordon remarks, "Act One, Scene One. Exposition," the explanation begins:

SOPHIE—A few years ago—in the Summer of 1939, it was—your father went to Europe on a little so-called trip—

GORDON—Or pleasure-jaunt, so-called.

SOPHIE—Would you prefer to take over?

GORDON—Oh, no—you're going fine.

SOPHIE—Suddenly the war came. Many Americans tumbled over themselves to get out in time. But your father cabled me, "This is our fight too. Have enlisted—have enlisted in—" (*She cannot go on.*)

HORATIO—In a Scottish regiment, he enlisted. One of the finest —in fact, the Gordon Highlanders.

GORDON—Complete with kilts and bagpipes. Known affectionately in the last war as The Ladies from Hell.—Only I wonder if he did. I wonder if he went to war at all.

SOPHIE—You know he did. (*To* HAPPY.)—And he did mention the kilts and the bagpipes in his cable. He was forever joking.

HAPPY—I know. We used to have some lovely ones together.

GORDON—Go on: twist my arm: make me laugh.

HAPPY—And riddles, lots of funny riddles.

SOPHIE—Some rather naughty ones, as I remember.

HAPPY—He said he wanted me to grow up uninhabited.

SOPHIE—And—I mean in the cable—he told me not to worry— and to wish him well—and to tell his publishers no more humorous books for a while, but real life at last and—and much love.

HAPPY—And then what?

SOPHIE—That was all, Happy. I never heard from him again. Months I waited. Like many writers, he rarely wrote letters, so at first I didn't worry—at least not too much. Then suddenly one night I woke in a panic and got through to our embassy in London—you remember, Gordon? We were rehearsing "A Man of Taste."

GORDON—I prefer to forget that one.

SOPHIE—A few days later came the sad message—he was missing in action—near a place in France called Etretat. Of course I continued to hope—

GORDON—And to hope.

SOPHIE—But it was no use. Never anything more: just "missing." So you see—

HAPPY—But I know all that. What I want to know is—

SOPHIE—So all I could do was to work harder than ever.—I was lucky in finding a superb natural actor right under my nose—

GORDON—And a very charming place to be found, too.

SOPHIE—And Gordon Roark and Sophie Wing became quite well liked—

GORDON—Sophie Wing and Gordon Roark did. Mind your billing, while cooing, my dear.

SOPHIE—By quite a large public—and this and that and ups and downs and successes and failures—

GORDON—But mostly successes. Only the Lunts can stand up to us, really.

SOPHIE (*with fine scorn*)—The Lunts! . . . And now we're asked to go to Mexico and South America on a government-sponsored good-will tour and naturally it's most terribly exciting.

But Happy has known all this already. She knows that the company is going on ahead of Sophie and Gordon, and that they are to leave tomorrow—but what she wants to know is, what is *new* that has been happening. All this excitement, and the telegrams and the phone and the newspaper people . . .

"Is it—have they—oh, is Father coming back?" No, it's not that. Then what is it? Gordon takes things in hand and, speaking deliberately, explains:

"In Mexico City one day next week—I should say about Thursday—in a simple but becoming dress—with a small bouquet of native orchids and, I've no doubt, a rudimentary Spanish mantilla, your mother is going to make me her husband."

This is not understandable, even monstrous, to Happy. She cannot understand how this can be when there still is Father. Has there been a divorce? No. Then what, and why? Gently Sophie explains that when a man has been missing a certain amount of time one goes to a court and the court decides that the man is no longer living—or legally dead.

"But he's not! I just absolutely know he's not!" says the little girl. Gordon tries to make it easier by saying, "For some strange reason, or lack of it, I love your mother dearly, and she loves me—and we've waited a long time to be married—and now that we can be we're going to be . . ."

The unhappy child is finally packed off to bed. Old Horatio, upon learning that his daughter is nearly packed for her tour, advises that she and Gordon take a reservation he has happened to make for himself for a drawing room to Washington at midnight—and that they should get married as soon as ever they can. Why?

"You're both aware of the fact that I still believe James to be alive somewhere."

Horatio pursues his hunch. Hasn't Sophie received any messages lately? Of course—many; mostly congratulations.

"If I were you," says the Professor Emeritus of Dramatic Literature, "I would open no further telegrams, nor mail, nor messages. I would take no more telephone calls." There has been too much fuss in the papers about the Sophie Wing-Gordon Roark romance, and if Jim is alive anywhere his humor and his curiosity won't be able to withstand it. As a matter of fact, Jim might be here. The rescue ship *Gripsholm* docked the other day and among the passengers listed was one Hamish Dun. Since Jim was always assuming other identities, like calling himself Young Lord Bastard of Bath, this well might be he. For Hamish is the Scotch for James, and Dunne was Jim's mother's maiden name.

"I warn you," says Horatio, "I urge you: move rapidly."

The argument convinces Gordon and he is all for taking the midnight to Washington, but Sophie hesitates momentarily. It could be . . . But in a while she decides to make the break and when Florence Denny asks if there is anything she can do to help make ready, Sophie lets her read some of the telegrams which the maid has been piling up on the desk. Some publishers want an article. A movie studio wants to know if Sophie wants to reconsider. A stage producer offers any inducement. A perfumer offers a fee for endorsement.

There is one odd-sounding wire which Florence puzzles over. "Be at telephone at half-past nine for a message from Tang—I guess it's Tanglefoot."

The import of the message does not strike Sophie immediately, but in a moment she gets it. The telegram must be from Jim—because nobody but she and Gordon could have known that name—the name they called Jim when his feet got mixed up from drinking.

Florence thinks it's some kind of joke. Horatio believes it no joke at all, and again urges Sophie to depart immediately. "There is very little else I can tell you, Daughter. The rest is in your hands—and Gordon's. I'm sure Jim will do the civilized thing."

Sophie hesitates, despite Gordon's insistence upon leaving immediately. "You don't know," she says, "what it does to a woman to be torn for years between the memory of one man and the living presence of another." Suppose Jim should be broken —crippled . . . "I can't run out on things . . . Gordon, he did love me so dearly."

Florence, having put Happy in bed, with her grandfather reciting passages of "Cyrano" at her, puts in her opinion. She is sure Jim has been dead for a long, long time—and he was too nice ever to have pulled a trick like this. True, she was such a kid when she first knew Jim, but . . .

The telephone rings, and it's almost 9:30, and everybody freezes. Gordon answers in a strained voice, finds the caller is a woman asking for Florence Denny. Sounds like a phone operator. Florence, puzzled how anybody could know where she is, goes to the phone—and hears only the dial tone. Whoever called has hung up.

A clock chimes 9:30. Sophie and Gordon tense again, and Florence laughs uncertainly and says, "It does seem to me that for people of the great imaginative powers you two are supposed to have, you aren't using them at all properly."

To which Sophie replies, " 'O wad some Power the Giftie gie us . . .' "

"You both," continues Florence, "claim to know him so well. Then it ought to be pie for you to figure out in advance how— if he should turn up—he'll act, you'll act, we'll all act, and be perfectly prepared for any or everything. Act it out in your minds, darlings—rehearse it!"

Horatio wanders in, followed by Happy wearing a thin little gray wrapper much too small for her—something she has clung to because Jim had given it to her. Happy walks in backward "to see myself as others see me." Horatio explains he is looking for a certain edition of "Cyrano." It is now 9:40 and Gordon insists that Sophie go pack. She agrees to, and when the maid brings some more telegrams she tears them in two. She has reached the hall doorway when the phone rings again. Horatio takes it. It's a strange message and hard to get, but he finally masters it.

The call is for Sophie. It is from the operator at the Plaza Hotel. "She says a gentleman who didn't give his name asked her to say that he would be here about 10 o'clock with Flora—or Flora may precede him."

"Well, I guess you were right," declares Gordon. "I guess it's real, my friends."

Horatio confesses he doesn't understand the Flora business, but Gordon is positive that Gordon does. "Look here, all of you: One thing understood: I see him first, and I see him alone."

"Him!" excitedly declares Happy. "You mean my father?"

"That's what I mean.—Absolutely alone; I insist on it."

Happy, ecstatic, imagines Jim's arrival. He will call her Pickle. She will ask him riddles, like the one about a garbage wagon being the thing that has four wheels and flies. Sophie can't understand the Flora business, though; now, if it had been an actress named Lily Spring, she could . . . But the Flora business is simple to Gordon: Jim often called flowers flora. And Gordon wants to meet Jim alone, first.

GORDON—You get the hell out of here, Sophie.

SOPHIE—Yes, sir, darling . . . You know, I feel cool as a cucumber now. What sort of lighting do you want?

GORDON—Medium.

SOPHIE (*extinguishes wall brackets*)—This way?

GORDON—Now dim the baby spots and pull in the bastard-ambers.

SOPHIE—It *is* exciting.

GORDON—I liked him, you know. And he liked me. We had a very good exchange. He was an absolute scoundrel, and I've missed him very much. (*She turns and gazes at the portrait.*) I—I wonder how he'll seem to us—

SOPHIE—I wonder how we'll seem to him.

GORDON—I can't imagine either way. I simply can't imagine.

SOPHIE—You and Florence—without an ounce of it—you're lucky, you're really— (*Suddenly she stops and gasps.*)

GORDON—Why? What is it?

SOPHIE—I swear to you I saw him wink.

GORDON—*Get* out. *Get out!*

SOPHIE—Be thinking, Gordon—oh, do be thinking! We've got to know in advance—we've got to use our heads—we've got to be prepared for him—we've just simply got to!

Alone now, Gordon lights a cigarette, slumps in a chair and starts thinking. "Figure something, Roark—come on—figure it!" As he lifts his cigarette to his lips he becomes transfixed as there is a distant sound of music—a weird blend of harp and bagpipe. Slowly the light on the portrait, as reflected in the mirror, comes up by itself. . . .

The curtain falls.

ACT II

Gordon has been having quite a session with himself. He is still alone, now coatless, with an almost-empty highball glass in front of him. The music still hovers about, and, speaking to nobody, he tries out various greetings to the imminent Jim.

"Hello, old boy. Just dropped in from nowhere, eh?" This doesn't seem to go so well, so he essays another approach: "Well, well! If it's not the Tanglefoot himself! And a sight for sore eyes . . ."

Next he tries studied nonchalance, standing against the fireplace. "So it's you, you happy bastard. Seems only yesterday. Boy—what a treat! . . . So just you turn around and get right back where you came from, or else—or else—" By now he is delivering his threat into the mirror, and as the music and the light fade Jim Hapgood himself enters the room.

Jim is wearing a worn suit. He is slight, wan, bespectacled, a trifle stooped, half-smiling; and he carries a box of flowers.

GORDON—May I—and may I ask to what we are indebted for this charming visit?

JIM—Don't be pompous, Gordon. In an actor it causes the attention to wander.

GORDON—I am simply demanding politely to know why the living bejesus you turn up at this point!

JIM (sitting down)—Honey, I just couldn't resist. When as close a relative as a wife makes a public ass of herself— (He indicates another chair.) Sit down. You know you're always welcome in any house of mine.

GORDON—I happen to be here for very definite reasons.

JIM—All the same, it shall never be said of me that I wouldn't give you house-room.

GORDON—Four years, eleven months, two days.

JIM—Not yet. I didn't sail till midnight that night.

GORDON—I'm glad to see you've got rid of some of your puppy-fat.

JIM—You don't look too well yourself. Worry?

GORDON—Possibly.

JIM—Not over me?

GORDON—Possibly.

JIM—To say that I am touched is to put it very—

GORDON—But not any more!

JIM—No? How so?

GORDON—You're dead.

JIM—You're kidding.

The colloquy between Gordon and Jim continues. Gordon says he's got the papers to prove that Jim is dead and Jim replies that here he is. When Gordon remarks that, at the time of his departure, Jim was drinking like a fish, Jim sunnily counters with the observation that Gordon was acting like a ham. "Ham Fish!" they chorus, in remembrance of their old times of bad joke-making together.

But Gordon pulls himself back from this sudden mood of friendliness. He and Jim have a serious situation. Jim was a care and a weight and a drain on Sophie for years, and he was drunk half the time. "And hung-over the other half," Jim admits. Gordon, pressing his advantage, points out that Sophie has done well since his departure.

Jim agrees: "The front pages, the columns, the six o'clock broadcasts. No, with me that never could have happened. I had, and imparted, a certain dignity you lack."

"I remember that dignity. I remember the way you'd sweep into a room on all fours."

"That was to amuse Happy. That was my trained-seal act."

Gordon and Jim—as Gordon imagines Jim—continue to box around in bright conversation. Yes, Happy is fine—quite an extraordinary youngster. And between the school and Florence she should be all right.

"Florence?"

"You remember Florence Denny. Sophie's understudy . . ."

Jim remembers. "The little 17-year-old. Oh, sure. She had nice legs."

Just as Jim wants to know about Happy and Sophie and Gordon, so does Gordon wants to know about Jim. Did he do what he did because he intended to?

"I got out," replies Jim, "because I was mortally sick of myself, sick of my life here, sick to death of what I was doing to Sophie. I wanted to be somewhere else, someone else, no ties, no bonds, nothing expected of me."

"How did you swing it?"

"It was easy. I was knocking around London then with a fiery young Irish poet I'd run into in Dublin. Came the war and O'Malley was hot to partake of it, to enlist, but O'Malley had only the sight of one eye and had been turned down flat. He was going crazy. So one night, somewhat in—my, I'm glad I drink."

"It's a good thing, at times."

"Anyhow, inspired with it, I had an idea. I offered to take the boy's physical for him if, when my orders came, he'd go as me."

And that, according to the present story, is how one "Jim Hapgood" went to war with the Ladies from Hell. All Jim himself did was loaf, and read, and invite his soul—and his soul invariably sent regrets. He wrote some verse and some nature studies.

"But," objects Gordon, "you can't escape your own times that way!"

"Watch me. And for that matter I don't seem to detect any service stripes on you."

Gordon demands that Jim give it to him straight—what is he after? He can't be in love with Sophie or he never would have done what he did. "She was wonderful in 'Sunset Gun,'" says Jim. ". . . I saw the last night. I thought you stank."

This is a facer for Gordon, because "Sunset Gun" closed three weeks ago and the *Gripsholm* with its crowd of rescued folk had docked much later. "You mean to say you've been here since then?"

"Oh, long before."

The two men drink and talk, mostly about Sophie. Jim believes Gordon adores her, but Gordon says it's nothing of the sort —he is simply on to her . . . and trapped. Jim is lucky to be free and he should clear out while the clearing is good. Sometimes Gordon wishes he could quit acting and run a factory or a truck farm. Jim points out that farming means getting up early. "I'd go to California," says Gordon. "Noon here is only 9 o'clock there."

They are pouring another drink when Sophie, in a negligee and with her hair down, comes in—walking backward. Her greeting is "Hi, kids. How's tricks?" She would like Gordon to leave so that she and Jim can talk alone, but Gordon refuses.

GORDON—I would mind very much. I'm staying right here.
JIM (*to* SOPHIE)—Then perhaps you and I might—
GORDON—And so are you two! And kindly make it brief.
SOPHIE—Well, you've heard him.
GORDON—And now listen to our ghostly visitor: a real voice from the tomb.
JIM—It's so dark, where you've put me. It's so very lonely, Sophie.
SOPHIE—I'm sorry it had to be so, but it had to be.
JIM—You haven't the memory I once thought you had.
SOPHIE—I have a memory all right, but— Oh, such a daze—
JIM—Do you remember One-Twenty West Tenth?
SOPHIE—It would be odd if I didn't.
JIM—The window-boxes in the Spring, full of petunias?
GORDON—Oh, my God!

Gordon is forced to listen, most unhappily, while Sophie and Jim run through memories of lunching on milk and crackers, the Siamese cat, the cockroaches and mice in the apartment . . .

Gordon groans, "Oh, Heaven protect me from this drizzle of youthful drool."

Suddenly Jim looks at him. "Who's this?"

"You remember our friend Gordon Roark," says Sophie.

"Oh, sure—sure! Sit down, old boy."

The drinking continues and by now Jim is showing it. He yearns for his poor days. He got some good work done on West Tenth. Even sold some to *The New Yorker, Harper's, The Atlantic*. Sophie had a great chance then with Jim to live a life of the spirit, "full of changes, and excesses and strange excursions . . .

"But you were also bitten with ambition and worshipful of the little gods of order, neatness, exactitude, respectability." Jim rises clumsily, remarking that they both bore him, and stumbles against Sophie, who puts her arms about him and holds him up.

"Tanglefoot! There! See? You've been a bad boy again."

"Sophie—oh, my lovely—"

Things are going badly for Gordon because Jim has aroused his wife's protective instinct. The light comes up in the mirror again and the trio are joined by Horatio, also entering backward. When he turns to view the scene of liquored husband and sustaining wife he remarks that it's a sad sight.

"Come to bed, Jim," Sophie urges.

"No! No!" protests Gordon.

But Sophie wins. Talking comfortingly, invitingly to Jim, she leads him toward the bedroom—backward; and Gordon sinks groaning into his chair. Horatio, too, backs out, and the light dims.

In an instant Horatio reappears, walking forward, remarking that it is sad, leaving Happy with only that pretty little Miss Denny . . .

Gordon springs up, blinks, almost shouts as he seizes Horatio's hands. The light is normal now, and Gordon, profoundly mixed-up, notices that Jim's box of flowers is no longer on the table and there is only Gordon's one whiskey glass. To Horatio's puzzlement, Gordon seems to be talking riddles. "It's not going to happen that way . . . Oh, he's wily."

Abruptly, Gordon asks Horatio if he will mind waiting for Jim while Gordon goes across the street to his own place to close his bags. "Watch him. Don't let him fool you," he warns.

Horatio settles into a chair. "Jim fool me? Not likely." The light in the mirror comes up again, and Horatio, looking at the

"FOOLISH NOTION"

"The call is for Sophie. It is from the operator at the Plaza Hotel. She says a gentleman who didn't give his name asked her to say that he would be here about 10 o'clock with Flora—or Flora may precede him."

(Donald Cook, Tallulah Bankhead, Joan Shepherd, Aubrey Mather)

portrait, addresses it: "Jim—Jim—you and I understand each other. Don't make it too hard for me, son . . ."

Again the eerie harp and bagpipe music is heard, with the bagpipe predominating. The mirror light dims and someone comes in—but it is not Jim. It is a woman, walking backward; as she turns Horatio sees a young, pretty, pale individual who looks quite a lot like Elsie, the housemaid—surprisingly like Elsie. She is shabbily but becomingly clad in a shirtwaist, a pleated plaid skirt, a beret.

"Excuse me, sir—I'm Flora."

Horatio chuckles. "That's no surprise. He said you might precede him." He invites her to a seat.

"Hamish, he—that's to say, Captain Dun, he told me to—"

"Dun? Hamish?"

"Why, yes, he said--"

"By George, I was right!" exclaims Horatio. And he finds in interviewing Flora that he was right all the way through. She and "Hamish" had met on the *Gripsholm* . . . Yes, she is his mistress. And how about Horatio? Hasn't he ever—

"And why not? Why not, indeed? When one is my age, even though a veritable flowering of New England, one attains to quite a different attitude toward—but listen to me! One would think I was 90."

"*I* never would," invites Flora, coyly.

The old boy finds Flora charming, and he becomes almost kittenish as he talks about sex and himself. He admires Sophie very much, but finds himself more comfortable with his new visitor. "All my life," he explains, "I have been ruled by clever women. I simply wish to make the point that clever men like James and me do not need clever women about. In fact, they're apt to be constricted by them . . . What the clever man needs is—well, someone like you: the simple solace, the companion of the flesh . . ."

As Horatio rambles on he mentions that James—that is, Hamish—is married to his daughter, Sophie; whereupon Flora is convulsed with laughter.

Horatio fears it is hysterics at the girl's learning her lover is already married—but it isn't hysteria, it's mirth. Flora explains that she doesn't think Hamish knows he has a wife, or even knows about Horatio. "You see, he's been through quite a lot. There's a lot of them don't rightly remember things as they were.

"They take humoring, you know—" Flora breaks off, exclaims, "It's Hamish! He's here!"

A figure backs in, and she greets him: "Hello again, Hamish."
He turns—and it is Jim again . . . but a different Jim: erect,
healthy, ruddy, dashing in the uniform of the Gordon Highlanders.
Flora performs an introduction:

"This is—is my friend, Mr. Horatio Wing.—Meet Captain
Dun, of the Gordon Highlanders."

"How do you do, sir?" says Jim—and from now on he speaks
with a Scottish burr. When Flora drapes herself over his chair
he orders her to "take a bit daunder there the whiles and be still.
This is between men . . . Mr. Wing, did she say?"

"That is correct."

"Then happen you're some kind of blood-relation to the
woman, Sophie Wing."

"I am her father."

"Speak up, man! I have not a great deal of time."

"Her father, I said."

"There, now!—Do you forgive me: 'twas uncivil."

"Not at all."

"I say 'twas uncivil!"

"Very well, so it was."

Obviously Jim is under a mental strain, and obviously he is
trying to remember something. "Professor" and "Wing" seem
to mean something to him, but he cannot grasp it, bang his fist
against his brow though he does. His memory, he confesses, is
gone. The only reason he knows he is Captain Lord Hamish Dun
is that the papers and the tag they found on him said so.

Flora, off in a corner, is singing "Embraceable You" to herself.
Horatio suggests that perhaps Jim isn't Lord Dun at all, and Jim
agrees that it's a common superstitious practice among troops to
exchange dog-tags.

"A Lady from Hell—and in such a predicament," sympathizes
Horatio. Then he queries, "Where are your kilties?"

Jim stares at his trousered legs, and when Horatio observes
that he is rather partial to kilts Jim says it is easily set right. He
had lent his kilts to Flora—and he now orders her to give them
back. Shucking his trousers, he gives them to her; then dons her
skirt and pulls his plaid socks high on his legs.

Horatio, still trying to restore Jim's memory, is throwing out
hints when Gordon climbs quietly in through a window and starts
to cross the room backward. When Gordon sees Flora about to
step into Jim's trousers he goes directly to her and begins making
wolfish passes while Jim and Horatio continue boxing around on
the fringes of memory.

"Tell me what brought you here."

"They found a note in my wallet. At the top was 'Sophie Wing, New York,' and this address. It said, 'Dear Tanglefoot: Just a reminder to count ten before you take the tenth one. Come home soon.' And it was signed, 'Fondly, Sophie.' "

Jim is now mixing up the pronunciations of "home" and the Scottish "hame." Could he, he wonders, be an American?

Flora by now is forced to run from Gordon's advances, and he pursues her out of the room as Horatio challenges Jim's self-wondering.

"What do you think?"

"Father," says Jim—now in his own voice—"I'm asking you."

Horatio is vastly pleased. He always knew Jim would do the civilized thing. Gordon is an obstacle, yes; but Sophie will be his who proves he loves her most. "Now I'll go fetch her."

But as he moves to do so Sophie enters, backward. She is in a resplendent evening dress. Taking her aside, Horatio warns, "Gently, my dear, gently. He does not know us. Shock . . . Among his effects a note from you to Tanglefoot . . . Play up." Then he makes an introduction:

"Captain, this is my daughter, Miss Sophie Wing, the actress. Captain Lord Hamish Dun, dear. The Dun of Dundee—(*To Jim.*)—or Mrs. James Hapgood, if you prefer."

"It's hard to choose," remarks Jim. "Enchanted to meet them both."

Sophie plays up, making humorous small-talk. His name, Hamish—it sounds like something to eat. Or is she thinking of haggis?

"I loathe the stuff," says Jim.

"You order, won't you?—For me, just any little thing out of season."

Jim explains he has a little note for her signed "Fondly," so it seems they once were friends. Sophie agrees. Being in New York just for the night, Jim thought he'd drop in. Sophie observes that this was sweet of him.

If perhaps she could give him some idea of his original identity—

"Why bother with it? . . . Particularly when your present one is so charming?"

"I know it isn't given to many men to be completely reborn at —I suppose I must be close to 40."

"You'll be 42 on March the tenth."

"The tenth. I must remember that, and give myself a present."

Jim now begins to advance his campaign a little. He remarks that Sophie is a dashed attractive woman. He works up to the question, "You're sure that I didn't have—well, for instance—a wife?"

Indeed he did. She and Sophie were inseparable. But as to the wife— "She thought you dead. She found someone else and went off with him."

"And is happy, I trust."

"Gives every indication, they say."

"What was she like?"

"She was an incredible little fool. But all the same, a dashed attractive woman! . . . Well?"

"I do hope that somehow, somewhere, we shall—"

"Do you? Why—"

"Because I don't know ever when I've met a lovelier, more engaging person. So full of wisdom and understanding—and yet so fresh and gentle—and so young." He will remember her as she is now, standing like an angel against the harp.

Sophie plucks a string and asks if Jim plays. He can't say that he does. But she leads him to the instrument, presses him down upon the little chair, and begins to sing. "Embrace me, my sweet embraceable you . . . Come! With me—*with* me!"

As she continues the song Jim begins to accompany her on the harp; haltingly at first, then fluently. When the song is ended he continues with Debussy's arpeggio for harp—then stops in amazement at himself. "Well, I'm damned!"

Happy, in her too-snug wrapper, backs silently in as Sophie turns on the light over the portrait and shows it to Jim. "Rather like someone you know, don't you think?"

"What's a great, huge portrait of me doing here?"

Happy, directed by Horatio, has come behind Jim and suddenly she claps her hands over his eyes. "Who is it? Name me who it is?"

Jim gathers the child in his arms. "Happy! Oh, Happy, you blessed child."

Suddenly Jim checks himself, thrusts Happy away from him and says, coldly, "Your child, Miss Wing—Mrs. Hapgood? Very happy to meet her. Very happy indeed. Happy, happy, happy—" As the child backs silently out of the room and the mirror light comes up, Sophie confronts her husband.

"So! It didn't come back—it was always there. All the time you were putting it on—acting—acting!"

Jim insists he must go now; he has an appointment. "But

why?" demands Sophie.

"Need you ask, my dear?" queries the wise Horatio. And as he bars Jim's exit Sophie exclaims, "Now I know—oh, now I know!"

Jim's "Please—please let me pass" to Horatio is brusque.

Sophie, realization full upon her now, exults, "It was to set me free! What greater love has any man—with pain, with purpose, to cut his loved one free—free from every claim—even from her most secret memory, her most fond desire?—That she may truly know, may truly choose?" Then, dryly, "Very well, I choose."

Over Jim's protest she says, "Give it up, Jim. You did your best, out of your own best heat."

From Horatio she gets the Washington tickets, tells him to have Gordon telephone the Shoreham, drags Jim to the doorway. As the two back swiftly out Sophie calls, "Dear Father, all that we are—all that we hope to be, we owe to—"

Horatio raises a hand in benediction. "Good-by! Good luck! God bless!" The light dims, and Horatio sinks back into his chair, alone for a moment. Happy, in her same wrapper but walking forward now, comes behind Horatio and claps her hands over his eyes. "Who is it? Name me who?"

Horatio knows.

"What have you been doing?" asks Happy.

"Clearing my mind of a lot of useless lumber. People read too much."

Sophie, in a dressing gown, comes in brushing her hair and Happy hides behind Horatio's chair. Sophie is looking for Gordon and her father explains he has gone across to get his bags. No, Jim hasn't come yet. Well, will Horatio hold the fort, and let her know the minute Jim arrives?

"Yes, dear."

"Pray for me, Father."

Sophie goes out and Happy pops up. Could she stay here in the library? Miss Denny popped off to sleep.

Horatio, suddenly feeling like popping off to sleep himself, turns the fort over to Happy. "Call me promptly when he comes" —and he goes to his room to lie down.

Now it is Happy's turn. As she slips into Horatio's chair and gazes yearningly at the portrait the light comes up and in the distance there is the music of a harp. Into the room backs a girl of 17—a girl who looks very much as Florence Denny must have looked a few years ago. She is laden with packages, and as she arranges them on the table she sings to herself.

She breaks off the melody. "Hello you, hiding there some-where. Can't fool me, Pickle." Happy is now discovered to be crouching behind the harp, and as she comes forth, she says, "Why, it's Flor—Flore—it's Miss—"

" 'Flora' it is! Florence is a hideous name."

If it's Flora, then she must know where Jim is. The excited child is assured that he will be along any minute. This is every-thing Happy has hoped for—but, all the same, she is scared.

"Flora" moves toward the kitchen to make Happy some choco-late, and there enters, backward, a man wearing a sealskin cape over the uniform of a sergeant in the U. S. Marines. He has a revolver in its holster. He is muttering and kicking at some in-visible thing on the floor and he speaks with a guttural accent.

"Not so fast, not so fast! Easy, Esgimo, easy. Bick up dose flippers, you are in a brivate home."

It is Jim, putting on Happy's favorite seal act. He wears a false walrus mustache and gold-rimmed glasses. When Happy makes a dash for him he warns, "Qu-viet! Qu-viet! Not zo glose!" So the delighted youngster goes instead to Flora, who has not left the room, and holds her hand.

The seal-trainer makes his spiel. His rare animal can answer questions. Two vlaps for yes, one vlap for no.

"When's my father coming home?"

Jim gets down on the floor, bristles his mustache, points his nose. When Happy queries, "Is my father glad he's home?" Jim flaps his hands twice, like flippers.

The act continues a moment, until Happy says she's too old for this now; she's 12. So Jim becomes Jim, and they hug. Flora welcomes him, too, with a couple of kisses on the cheeks before she takes up her packages and backs out, humming her song.

JIM—How's your mother?
HAPPY—I knew you'd ask that.
JIM—Well, how is she?
HAPPY—Just the same.
JIM—And Gordon?
HAPPY—Even more so.
JIM—Dear, dear, what shall we do?
HAPPY—We've got to be very careful, Father.
JIM—You think?
HAPPY—I know. I know lots of things.

JIM (*taking a small flat case from a pocket*)—Such as—
HAPPY (*voice sinking*)—Don't do anything they ask you.
JIM—But why, Happy?
HAPPY—It isn't safe.—And never turn your back to them.

The small flat case contains a string of pearls for Happy. Father and daughter, still in the ecstasy of reunion, pay slight attention to the backing-in of Horatio, who is wearing a large false nose and reciting from "Cyrano." He's just on his way to the bathroom again. But their attention is caught by the rearward entrance of Sophie and Gordon.

Their greetings are cool. They try to send Happy away, but Jim commands that she stay.

"You do look a wee bit peaked, dear," observes Sophie to her husband. "I have the most marvelous little pills. I'll get one for you."

Happy, onto the plot, whispers a warning and Jim declines the pills. He refuses a drink offered by Gordon; tells him he can go right to hell. But Gordon fixes a drink anyway and Jim is about to drink when Happy interrupts:

"Hip-dominigo-honiga-zunk."

To which Jim replies: "Da-bunk, da-hip, da-labar-zoo." But again he is about to drink and again the desperate Happy breaks in with a routine about Al—Al who?—Alcohol. Jim puts down his glass untasted and one crisis has passed.

Horatio comes in and out again, still working on "Cyrano," and Gordon finds on the table what he has been looking for—a paper knife. But sharp-eyed Happy catches him picking it up and attacks him with a couple of riddles. He drops the knife and she maneuvers it into the waste-basket.

Again the evil pair tries to send Happy away and again Jim orders that she stay. Sophie tries another gambit—sympathy. Jim looks very tired. And why shouldn't he be? Jim bites. All day long he's been on planes and boats and submarines just to get here.

Sophie coaxes him to a sofa, bends over him and kisses him lightly to cover the stealthy approach of Gordon with a pillow. Again the doughty Happy foils the dastards. "Father—quick! They're going to smother you!"

Father leaps up, and Happy explains that Sophie and Gordon want to kill him so they can get married. As Gordon makes a lunge for him Jim pulls his revolver, makes Gordon drop the pillow. But Sophie still has a devilish influence over her husband.

She makes him give her the gun and hands it to Gordon.

"Always in the way," remarks Gordon—and he shoots Jim. Dying, Jim sings to Happy like a phonograph running down, "You're my everything underneath the—underneath the—underneath the—"

Happy wildly denounces the murderers, who put the gun by Jim's hand to make it look like suicide and swiftly back out, leaving the heartbroken child standing over her father's corpse and singing, "Poor wand'ring one . . ." When she gets to the repeat of the last couplet—"Take heart, fair days will shine— Take any heart—take mine," the mirror light has come up full and dimmed again.

Now Happy is in her chair, her arm across her eyes, sobbing. The corpse and the gun are gone and the room is in order as Florence Denny runs in, followed by Sophie, who is now dressed for traveling.

"You killed him!" accuses Happy.

It takes some moments to calm her, persuade her she's been dreaming. At last she confesses that she did think bad things about Sophie, but she doesn't any more. "I—I think I've thought them out of me." Florence leads her up to a bath and bed, and Sophie, alone, slumps into the dream-chair and gazes in front of her.

"Dear God, have mercy on us all, is—is the prayer of—yours fondly, Sophie Wing."

She sits, waiting, staring; there is violin music far away. The curtain falls.

ACT III

Sophie's own turn for imagining how she will receive Jim has now come. She is in the chair which Gordon, Horatio and Happy had occupied. Nervous, chain-smoking, fussing with the arrangement of her blouse, she goes to the windows and closes the one Gordon had opened. Again she looks at the portrait and then at herself in the mirror, and murmurs, her head sunk, "I am of ladies most dejected and wretched."

The violin music comes up, and so does the light in the mirror and backward, as always, a figure enters. It is a woman who seems to be gesturing thanks to a servant who has shown her the way. When the woman and Sophie confront one another, Sophie discovers the visitor is in comfortable middle life, distinguished in dress and appearance, and still somewhat beautiful. She looks quite a lot like Rose, who brought in all those telegrams.

"I know I ought to remember you," ventures Sophie.

"Indeed you ought, my dear."

"I'm afraid I'm famously bad at it—why—why, it *is!* It's Lily Spring!" An actress out of times gone by—but not Lily Spring any more. She is known now, over there, as Flora—the title of a song she has sung for the Tommies, the Aussies and the Yanks. This new edition of "Flora" speaks:

"You did get word that I would be here?"

"Why, yes—there was a sort of message. But naturally, not having been in Europe, 'Flora' meant less than nothing to me."

"My trademark there, my incognito here."

"Convenient."

"Still the same pretty chip on the same pretty shoulder."

"Not at all," says Sophie. "I'd simply like to know—"

"But why? *We* never seriously competed. I am an actress, while you are—what do they call it?—a personality."

"That's what they call it."

"And what you would like to know is what brought me. Naturally. Well, I thought it wise to come a little ahead of—of James, and talk to you a bit about him. Does that seem logical?"

"Not particularly. I don't know that husband and wife have any special need of an interpreter. And you'll forgive me for being impatient, I hope."

"I'll forgive you for nothing."

"There! Now we know where we're at! All right; let's go."

"Must you be vulgar?"

"In such a rarefied atmosphere, yes. Spill it, sister."

The two women have at one another in a poisonous verbal battle. Sophie presumes "Flora" is Jim's mistress. Flora thinks this would be handy for Sophie because it might relieve her sense of guilt about Gordon Roark. And Sophie was, Flora continues, wrong about James from the beginning. He needed mothering. And he should have had a child, or children.

Sophie says they'd wanted children but none had arrived, so they adopted one. And what has Sophie done about her? Her level best.

Flora continues her taunts: A man doesn't drink unless his wife's at fault somehow. Jim had a true creative gift which Sophie failed to foster. And as for herself, Sophie, too, could have been a fine creative artist if it hadn't been for her vanity and love of pleasure and attention.

Sophie, thus goaded, finally lets go. "Listen, Madame Flora, Dame Lily Spring and Mrs. Siddons! There's no such thing as a creative artist. Writers, sculptors, painters, actors—we're all the same—interpreters—and all of the same thing—of life! And if, while you're actually being Lady Macbeth—Phedre—Roxanne —what you will—I'm still just Sophie Wing, the personality again. Maybe I'm a spot or two closer to life than you are.—Which is where I'm beginning most awfully to want to be—closer, no matter what it's like—closer, closer!"

"Very well delivered," comments Flora dryly.

Sophie switches to the subject of Jim. Is he coming, and is he still Flora's? He's coming, and he's Flora's in a way—but she may be returning him to Sophie, "such as he is."

This phrase is alarming, and Sophie learns that Jim has been both wounded and ill. "It's possible I may not want him back," she hedges.

"Oh, you'll find him much more manageable now, much easier to handle."

"I don't like this. I don't like it at all. Where *is* he? What's delaying him? It's late."

"He'll be along directly. A friend and I brought him together —the two of us, on a boat."

" 'Brought' him? Why? What's wrong? Isn't he able to—?"

Sophie, frightened, calls out for Gordon and her father. "There's something hideous that's going to happen; I know it, I can feel it! Oh, you evil, evil woman—why can't you come straight out with it—tell me how badly hurt he is—or how sick in his mind or heart?"

"I doubt he's ever been happier in his life."

Sophie has begun a raging tirade against Flora when, in response to her call, Gordon and Horatio back into the room. Horatio immediately recognizes the newest version of Flora. "Why, I do believe it's Lily Spring herself!" He promptly goes into some chatter about show business. After a while Gordon introduces himself and recalls the first time he saw Lily Spring in "The Tempest" at New Haven. And when he met her afterward all he could do was stutter and blush.

The conversation is beginning once more to edge around to the subject of Jim when Elsie, the maid, comes in backward with a sealed package in her hand. She gives it to Sophie, saying a gentleman who wouldn't give his name had left it. A funny sort of gentleman. Dressed funny, too.

"Another going-away present," hazards Sophie.

"Aren't you going to open it?" asks Flora.

"It can wait . . ."

"I'd open it, if I were you. It won't bite you."

Gordon steps in to help. He breaks the seal, unwraps the package. "Who, for heaven's sake," queries Sophie, "would be sending me a silver vase? People are sweet but ridiculous. Such an odd shape. What possible use—?"

"But isn't it in lovely taste?" pursues Flora. "Read what it says."

Horatio has guessed what the inscription will be and murmurs sympathetically before Sophie reads the inscription:

"Captain James Dunne Hapgood. Eighth Gordon Highlanders. March 10, 1902—August 12, 1944. 'This was a Man.' "

Yes, they are Jim's ashes in a silver urn.

Flora, smiling, backs out, accompanied by the gallant Horatio. Gordon doesn't know what to say in comfort as Sophie stands with the urn cupped in her hands, her head bent over it.

"Oh, my poor sweet," she apostrophizes. ". . . a small heap of gray dust closed in a silver urn. Dear eyes, that saw so much pain and sorrow—dear lips that spoke such kind, humorous wisdom—gentle hands that strewed blessings and laughter like seed in the earth—that you are come to this!"

This sort of stuff, and more of it, is the crusher to Gordon. Abruptly he bids Sophie good-by. "I thought that with this, you at last would be free. Now I see that his hold is even stronger upon you." Despite Sophie's protests, her wondering what shall be done now with the tour, Gordon backs out, leaving her miserably alone.

Sophie now contemplates the urn. Shreds rose petals before it. Loosens her hair, bends her head and lets her tresses fall over it. Straightening, she begins with a decorator's eye to look for a place to put it. Not the mantelpiece. She tries it on top of the harp, and this time is satisfied. Sadly she declaims:

" 'His life was gentle, and the elements
        So mixed in him, that Nature might stand up
        And say to all the world "This was a Man"!' "

A brash run of the harp-strings is heard, followed by Jim's voice:

"And at last just where you wanted me—eh, old girl? All tucked up for the night. Isn't it cozy?"

Sophie, sobbing, calls, "Somebody! Somebody!" The light in the mirror comes up, goes down—and now the urn is no longer on the harp and the strewn petals are gone from the table. Florence Denny runs in, full of comfort, just as she was in Happy's crisis.

"Oh," exclaims Sophie, "I've been having such horrible thoughts! Is that really me? Oh—shameful! Is that the way I really am?—No, no—not 'am'—I couldn't stand it. 'Was'— *was!*—Because I've been done over—you hear me? I've been dipped and bathed and scrubbed and scoured—I've been skinned alive and I deserve it."

"Didn't I tell you," soothes Florence, "the anticipation was bound to be twice as bad as—? But why doesn't he come, if he's coming?"

Rose has come in to announce that there's a gentleman downstairs to see Sophie—himself—the spit an' image!

Sophie telephones Gordon across the street, gives the news of Jim's arrival, asks Rose to show Jim up. Florence starts to go, but Sophie begs her to stay—to stay and hold the fort while she freshens up.

Florence is alone when Jim enters and puts a small box of flowers on the table. He is in civilian clothes and seems more youthful than he did in the preceding encounters. Her greeting to him is, "You louse!"

His attitude is one of amazement at her good looks; hers is one of bitterness toward him for having run out on Sophie without ever trying to get word to her—and for returning just in time to do the most damage to Sophie and Gordon. He knows about them, doesn't he? Oh, yes, he's been reading the papers. And why did he make them wait two hours tonight?

"What I did was to sound an alert. The moments before the bomb falls are very valuable for thinking things out—clearly, quickly and definitely."

Florence, too, has been thinking things out—and has things on her mind. Making Jim promise not to interrupt—a promise he doesn't always keep—she pours out her heart. At 17 she was crazy mad in love with Jim. Once she flung herself at him, and for the next week he scarcely spoke to her and the week after he sailed away. Later, she believed him dead—but she could not forget him. A few affairs were exciting, yes; but really they were no good because Jim also was always there. "Three *is* a crowd, you know, in such things." And she has come back now to take care of Happy because she knew Jim loved the child.

"Anyhow, there it is. And now you can forget it. And by crikey, I feel free at last—and oh, oh, oh, it's good!" She moves away from him as Sophie comes in. Their greetings are light, friendly. Each looks five years younger, instead of older. Jim is out of the war, honorably, the only damage being one ear that won't work. He has learned to drink moderately. He has brought a present for Happy which is on its way. Florence goes to bring the child down. Jim gives Sophie the box of camellias he has brought.

"The 'Flora' you said you were bringing?"

"No. That's a bull-mastiff bitch."

"A—"

"A puppy I got for Happy . . . Let's settle other things."

"I—I'm not allowing myself to take this big, Jim."

"I more or less noticed you weren't."

"I did my big take when your wire arrived—and the telephone call—and afterward."

"All to the good."

"Now tell me you intended I should—"

"In a way. I didn't want—"

"Hysterics?"

"Or histrionics."

"Calculating devil, aren't you?"

The waiting, the imagining, have been hard on both of them, but now it's over and things can be settled. "Do you still care for me?" asks Sophie.

"I care about you, and enormously."

"There's a difference."

"Is there?"

"I think there is.—Look: What do you want of us—for us?"

Jim thinks this is up to Sophie, because, after all, he was the one who ran out—but now he is willing to reassume his responsibilities if she wants him to. She wonders if he does; does he love her?

"Well, I've always enormously loved the idea of you . . ."

When Gordon comes in the salutations of the two men are light, bantering—but Gordon, too, has something on his mind:

"Just what gives you the idea you can barge in here after years and disrupt everything?" And how would Jim like to have that portrait staring down at him day after day for years?

The preliminary discussion of the triangle is lightly facetious. When Sophie queries, "Oh, my dears, what am I to do . . . ?" Jim admiringly comments, "Isn't she wonderful?" "You ought," replies Gordon, "to hear her in her tub with only a sponge and a cake of soap for props."

"Now how would you possibly know that?"

Gordon's is the first definite move toward clearing the atmosphere. He announces that he is withdrawing from the competition. He is fed up with humble pie. As for the tour, there are three prominent leading men eager to go with Sophie. As he starts to walk out Sophie calls him back.

"Gordon, what on earth's come over you?"

"The innate dignity of man." He denounces Jim for his desertion, wonders if he really was in the war. Did he change his name to Hamish Dun? What *has* he been doing?

Jim never heard of Hamish Dun. In June of 1940 he went on a raid to Etretat, and it was a slaughter which few escaped. Jim hid out with Norman peasants, went via underground to Paris and remained a member of the underground until the Liberation. He did not try to get messages out because he was pretty certain he had been reported killed in the raid and that is the way he wanted it to be.

Sophie knows now why Jim returned. "You came because you knew I'd never be free of you until—you *have* freed me, Jim. How have you done it?"

"By freeing myself first, I guess."

But Gordon is not yet sure about why Jim left in the first place. It was simple. In the first place, he knew about Gordon and Sophie—even before they did themselves; and in the second place he was hopelessly in love with someone else—hopelessly, because of a great disparity in ages. There was only one answer —to get out.

Florence and Horatio have come in, Happy is on her way and Sophie is set for action.

SOPHIE (*to* GORDON)—I think it's time we left, don't you?

HORATIO—Left?

SOPHIE—If we're to make the train.

GORDON—Sophie, I told you I've decided I can live without you.

SOPHIE—Maybe—but without you, I can't. And I do so cling to life.

HORATIO—What's this, what's this? Your husband returns and you—

SOPHIE—I suppose I may have to divorce him, now. But if I do, I'll get the meanest, cheapest, most Mexican one I can—to show my thorough disapproval of the practice! . . . Take care of yourself, Father.—Tell Happy good-by for us, Florence. I think it's better if I—

FLORENCE—She loves you, Sophie. She just doesn't know it yet.

SOPHIE—Bless you. It takes a long time sometimes, doesn't it?—Good-by, Jim.

JIM—You know what I think of you.

SOPHIE—I'll treasure it.—He loves the idea of me, Gordon. You love me. And a person needs to be loved with a whole heart. And whether you like it or not, that's the way you are by me.

GORDON—I'm not averse to it.

SOPHIE—. . . And how Jim is by Florence.

HORATIO—What's this? What's this?

SOPHIE—Or is that only my imagination, too?

JIM—Sophie, you're a fearful and wonderful woman.

SOPHIE—No, darling—just a personality! So now you can complete that telephone call—regardless of the "disparity," can't you?

FLORENCE—Sophie, this is the most—

SOPHIE—My dear, you've always been old for your age. In wisdom I put you at about 28. And Jim is easily five years younger than he was five years ago. That makes him a neat 32. Four years' difference is just right.—When I think of the awful three months a Winter when I'm a year older than Gordon! Good-by, angelic ones. Good-by. Good luck. God bless!

Gordon and Sophie leave, and Horatio, although a bit staggered by developments, is game. He asks Florence and Jim to dine with him tomorrow, and makes his departure.

Was that really Jim on the telephone, as Sophie hinted? Florence wants to know. It really was. He just had to know she'd be there.

"I—I'm not sure I can stand it."

"You'll have to. You're stuck with me now.—Willing?"

"Willing."

In her prettiest dress, Happy comes in, and her reunion with her father is pretty much as she had dreamed it—a greeting in gibberish, an embrace, some childish riddles . . . but no foul plot to worry about.

There is the bark of a young dog downstairs. That's Flora, for Happy.

"Go get her, Happy. Let's have all our good things together." The child moves toward the hall, Jim and Florence look at each other.

THE CURTAIN FALLS

DEAR RUTH

A Comedy in Two Acts

By Norman Krasna

THE Norman Krasna Broadway adventures have not all been happy ones, but they have been interestingly varied. He was well started on a career that was to land him among the highest-salaried writers of screen plays in Hollywood when he submitted a first play to the Eastern market. It was called "Louder, Please." It lampooned his fellow screen workers, and was a failure.

He came again with a second play, a fairly lurid but very tense melodrama called "Small Miracle," and this was a success. Some years later, when he had grown rich but not indolent, he brought in an exciting item having to do with an escaping German war prisoner called "The Man with Blond Hair." But Broadway even then (1941) was in no mood to sympathize with German heroes, however un-Nazi-like they might be, and the blond one went down to a quick defeat.

The signs indicate that Mr. Krasna accepted that particular defeat with a mental reservation. If Broadway would not take what he considered good for it, he would trick it into taking what Broadway was silly enough to insist a play-doctor should order. "Dear Ruth" was and is the result. So sure were the sponsors of this comedy's success that they deliberately kept its promotion "in the family," as it were. Mr. Krasna turned the script over to Moss Hart, his friend, with the plea that Mr. Hart stage it with the same skill he had employed in staging another sweeping popular success, "Junior Miss." Mr. Hart accepted the assignment with enthusiasm. He induced his brother, Bernard, to join with his good friend, Joseph Hyman, in the formation of a new producing unit for the presentation of the play.

It is not often that dreams so deliberately inspired come true, but they did in this instance. "Dear Ruth" was produced in early December, 1944. The reviewers were enthusiastic in their praise. Audience reaction was both immediate and favorable, and the comedy ran easily through the season.

On a Saturday morning, in the late Summer of 1944, the sun is beating into the living room of the Wilkins' home on Columbia

Heights, New York. "It's not a new house, and it's not old, either. Four active people and a servant live in it, and two children grew up right here, so it can't be too shiny."

There are French windows at the back of the room, looking out upon a part of the yard, into which juts the end of a ping-pong table. There is also an alcove fitted with a gate-leg table and a built-in seat which is used for breakfast, to take advantage of the early sun.

"Mrs. Wilkins subscribes to the *American Home,* and there are knick-knacks accumulated for twenty years." The room is also pleasantly and comfortably furnished.

Presently Dora, a colored maid, backs her way through a door leading to the dining room and kitchen. She is carrying a tray of breakfast furnishings, including glasses filled with orange juice, a basket of rolls and such silver and dishes as will be needed. The table set, Dora goes to the door to recover a bottle of milk, a bottle of cream and the morning newspaper.

Mrs. Wilkins (Edith) is the first one down. She "is in her early forties, a generous, sentimental woman suspiciously like the backbone of the country." She is wearing a pretty, flowered quilted robe. Knowing the Judge's dislike of paper napkins she would replace, if she could, the Kleenex substitutes Dora is using. But, as Dora explains, the laundry just keeps promisin' and never shows up. (And that's the last box of Kleenex, too.)

Miriam Wilkins is the next to appear. "Miriam lacks one week of sweet sixteen, and is a high school senior. This, you may not readily grasp, is one full year ahead of the average student. Miriam's nature is such that she is always—in one way or another—a year ahead of the average anything. She wears the shirt and full skirt of the current vogue, and a beret."

Mrs. Wilkins does not care for the beret on Miriam, seeing her face is anything but small, but Miriam is quick to explain that she is wearing it as a symbol of protest. "Our political science class does not agree with the State Department as regards to their French policy," Miriam explains. "We have decided to wear the beret, the National hat of France, as our protest. We hope to interest *Life Magazine.*"

Judge Wilkins (Harry being his given name) "is forty-five, easy-going, and a fit companion for his nice wife. He's a Municipal Judge, so he wears a blue suit."

This morning the Judge is in a fairly agreeable mood, but he doesn't think he will eat the baked apple and cream Dora has fixed for him. This distresses Miriam—

"Your stomach has to have something to work on, Dad," she protests. "In the morning you have an empty thirty feet of small intestine."

"Hasn't everybody?"

"I'm in charge of your father's small intestine," interjects Mrs. Wilkins. "All thirty feet, if you don't mind. And I don't care for such talk at breakfast."

Miriam's concern over her father's diet, it now appears, is caused by her anxiety over her ability to meet the test of the blood bank contribution for which she has signed him. And when her resentful parents insist she had no right to sign her name to such a promise, Miriam blandly explains that she had not signed her name, but her father's.

"As a Judge I felt that you had an additional responsibility, to set an example," says she.

"I'm a traffic court Judge," snaps Harry. "Let Frankfurter give blood."

Now Ruth Wilkins has appeared on the stairs. "Ruth is twenty-two, very beautiful, and charming, and intelligent too. She is dressed for business, but being intelligent she does not wear tailored suits. She has her hat on."

Two honks of an automobile horn call Miriam to her car pool and she is on her way. It now being Ruth's turn to report, she admits that she was home rather early the night before. Yes, there had been a small quarrel, which would account for the hour. It was about her using tobacco—

"You know Albert," says Ruth. "He's kind of a health bug. Always ordering milk for me, when I want coffee, and this cigarette thing's his latest." . . . "At the pictures, I promised him I'd give up smoking. Well, I was going to—gradually. Unfortunately, my purse spilled open, and Albert got down on his knees to gather up the contents. Suddenly he shouted 'Cigarettes!' Half the Music Hall turned around."

A continuous horn honk announces the arrival of Ruth's car pool. She has no sooner left the house than Mrs. Wilkins again brings the young man of the quarrel into the conversation. "Harry, what do you think of that Kummer boy?"

"Thirty-four's no boy."

"Besides being thirty-four?"

"He can support an old father-in-law. Easy."

"Do you think she likes him?"

"Can't tell about our Ruthie. She doesn't talk much."

"No, she doesn't."

"Don't know where she gets that clam-like quality. Not from us."

"My grandfather was like that. Like a clam."

"I've seen his picture."

"Do you know why that Kummer boy isn't in the Army? He says it's a bad back."

"It's not enough to disqualify him as a husband. I've got a bad back."

"You didn't have it the first ten years."

"Complaint department's right here."

"A girl's entitled to ten years without a bad back."

A ring at the door brings Dora from the kitchen, and later back to the living room with the announcement that a Mister William Seawright has called to see Miss Ruth. The Wilkinses are a little mystified, but decide to see the young man.

Bill Seawright "is twenty-four, an Air Corps Lieutenant, and we like him, right off."

Bill is disappointed to find that he has missed Ruth by only a few minutes. He could have been earlier, but he had stopped to change his clothes and freshen up. "I was in Italy thirty hours ago," he tells them, to their surprise. "I've been terribly rude in intruding like this, interrupting your breakfast, and not calling on the phone first."

Yes, he will have a cup of coffee. But nothing more. He had had breakfast on the plane.

"Was Ruth expecting you?" asks Edith. "I mean this morning."

"No, she wasn't. She wasn't expecting me for quite a while."

EDITH—She'll be at the bank in another ten minutes. You can call her from here.

BILL—I wasn't counting on the phone. You know how it is. I've gotten this far without telling her. What time does she usually come home?

EDITH—About 5:30.

BILL—You're not going to warn her?

EDITH—Well—

BILL (accusingly)—Yes, you were!

EDITH—Girls aren't crazy about surprises. I notice you freshened up before you came here.

BILL—She'll look good to me just the way she is. (He sees RUTH's picture.) Excuse me. I hope you don't mind. (He takes a picture from his wallet.) This is all I've had.

EDITH—It's not a very good picture of her.

HARRY (*leaning over*)—It's very good. I took it.

BILL—This picture's been on twenty-five missions. I used to take it out, for luck, and prop it up on my ammunition belt.

HARRY—You're a gunner?

BILL—Yes, sir. On a B-26.

HARRY—I guess you've got some stories to tell.

BILL (*lost in the picture*)—I beg your pardon.

HARRY—Go right ahead. That's more important.

BILL—You think if I showed up at the bank, they'd give her the day off?

HARRY—They might.

EDITH—Why don't you?

BILL (*thinking it over*)—I've been going over that first minute I'd see her, for so many months. I kind of don't like the setting. All those people around.

HARRY—Well, she's a teller at Accounts Receivable, there'd be people. And she's in a cage, with bars in front of her.

BILL (*smiling*)—The bars wouldn't stop me, sir.

HARRY—Tell me, how did you happen to be a gunner? Or are you given any choice?

BILL—Yes, you are. I was in Engineers when I got to England. But I had an idea the war wouldn't be over too quickly. And there was Ruth and her letters. She's quite a letter writer. Well, I was there, and she was here. And a war in between. So, I applied for gunnery school. You see, twenty-five missions and you come home.

HARRY (*impressed*)—They must've been some letters.

BILL—They were.

Bill goes on his way. He'll be back at 5:30. He'll wander down to the bank—and—if he gets his nerve up, he may—

Edith kisses him on the cheek as he leaves them. He's a nice boy, she announces to Harry. And Bill Seawright is a nice name. She should warn Ruth, she thinks. "She ought to have her hair done, and a facial." But the Judge is against all that.

"He calls her 'Baby!' Think of that!" muses Edith.

The curtain falls.

It is 5:15 o'clock the same afternoon. Miriam is at the telephone, making notes on a writing pad. Apparently someone would like to know how you address the Secretary of War. Miriam suggests "Dear Henry L. Stimson, Secretary of War—" She has another idea: ". . . Talk to the Committee, and, if they approve, let's send it along. We haven't even started in China."

There are still other and more serious matters to be discussed. "Laura, did it ever occur to you that Mr. Gromitt might be a Fascist?" Miriam demands of her phone listener. "Why not? What would be cleverer than for Fascists to put their mouth-pieces into High Schools as treachery? You're reaching a genera-tion of prospective voters right at the source. . . . I would do it, if I were a Fascist. . . ." The click of the front door is heard. It is Miriam's father. "Good-by, dear," continues Miriam in the phone, "a prominent member of the last generation just walked in."

"Thank you." The Judge has gone quickly to the couch.

"Dad, I'm disappointed in you," announces Miriam, leaving the phone and turning to the Judge.

"I'm sorry, honey."

"How can you stay aloof from the exciting world maelstrom around you? Not watching, not caring, not hearing?"

"I listen to Kaltenborn."

"Kaltenborn! The world's on fire, you're occupied with a cigarette lighter. (*He looks at her.*) Your impulses are right, I know you well enough for that."

"Thank you."

"But you're not throwing yourself into the fight. We need you. We can use you."

"Thank you."

"We can use anybody we can get."

It now develops that Judge Wilkins has been to the blood bank and made his contribution. But not without some little difficulty. He already has had four glasses of orange juice—

"There were twenty women in the room, and I was the only person that had to lie down and have a blanket. I hope the kid that gets my blood doesn't need it bad. I haven't got much con-fidence in it."

The appearance of Mrs. Wilkins calls for an exchange of signals between her father and Miriam. Nothing of his adventure is to be passed on. Which, as it turns out, is an unnecessary precau-tion. Edith had been at the blood bank, too. Miriam, it seems, had also arranged that.

A squab dinner has been ordered for Lieut. Seawright. The family will make an impression if possible. And, thinks the Judge, he and Edith had better be ready to make a quick decision. "That Lieutenant didn't strike me as exactly the patient type. And he's got that overseas look in his eyes."

"We don't know much about him. We ought to get acquainted with him first."

Edith does not favor hasty war marriages. Neither does Harry, for that matter. But he hopes somebody asks them.

Ruth is home from the bank, "bright and shiny." She goes straight to her mother and kisses her. And then to her father. She has news! Great news! She is going to be married! And right away!

The Wilkinses are measurably excited until they discover that it isn't Lieut. Seawright but Albert Kummer that Ruth is talking about. Her Albert had suddenly come to the point of proposing—

"He was very cute," reports Ruth. "He called up all the others in the car pool, and told them he couldn't pick them up. And when I got in, there he was, alone, with a big box of candy on my seat."

"The car pool?"

"I didn't bring the candy home, I gave it to the girls. But that wasn't the touching part. He was smoking a cigarette. He said he'd rather take up smoking opium before he'd lose me. You know that's sweet. And he kept coughing. He's not used to cigarettes."

But what about the Lieutenant? Doesn't Ruth know that he has come home—"to roost," as Harry puts it. Ruth doesn't even know what they are talking about.

"Ruth, Bill's home!" announces Edith solemnly. "He was here. And we thought he's the one you were marrying. He was going to the bank just to get a look at you. We took it for granted you meant him."

"Bill who?"

"Bill Seawright. Don't you even remember him?"

"I don't know who or what you're talking about. Not the faintest notion."

"Lieutenant William Seawright, Ruth."

"The one who calls you Baby!" adds Harry.

Ruth is still groping for an answer. Miriam knows. She has come in from the dining room just in time to catch the name. "Bill!" she ejaculates, excitedly. The Wilkinses begin to catch a glimmer of what has happened.

"What have you done?" Harry demands and when Miriam

doesn't answer he quickly adds: "I want the whole story out of you! From the beginning. Every word of it!"

MIRIAM (*after a long pause*)—I didn't know he was coming back.

RUTH—Who was coming back? What is all this?

MIRIAM—He said he wouldn't fly any more! I didn't see how he *could* come back!

EDITH—How did this whole thing start?

HARRY—From the beginning!

MIRIAM—It all started with our Bundles for Britain.

HARRY—Go on!

MIRIAM—We decided on a Bundles for America! You remember I was President!

HARRY—You're always President! Go on!

MIRIAM—We knitted things for our boys overseas. And we sent letters with our gifts. To encourage them, to keep up their morale. To tell them America was behind them, that they could count on us for sweaters, and socks, and knitted ties.

HARRY—Get to this Lieutenant!

MIRIAM—They answered us. And they asked for pictures.

RUTH—You sent my picture to some Lieutenant? (*To her parents.*) That's it, isn't it?

HARRY—She sent more than a picture! You should've heard him!

MIRIAM (*quietly*)—Yes, I sent him more than a picture. I sent him hope, and faith, and a will to go on. I made him a soldier, from a lonely, frightened youngster.

HARRY—He's a grown man!

MIRIAM—Not in spirit.

HARRY—In sex he is!

EDITH—Harry!

HARRY—That's what it comes down to! That poor sucker's home to see his sweetheart. He's entitled to something, and he's come home to get it.

RUTH—Did he say that?

HARRY—What do you think a fellow who's nervous in a plane and flown twenty-five missions expects? He wants to see his girl! He's had your picture on his gun! He's in love with you!

RUTH—You're exaggerating it. There's a limit to how much you can do with a letter. Or letters. How many have there been?

MIRIAM (*after a moment*)—Sixty.

ALL—SIXTY!

RUTH—You—I—wrote him sixty letters?

MIRIAM—They weren't all letters. Most of them were poems.

EDITH—Since when do you write poems? You can't rhyme two lines.

MIRIAM—They weren't my poems. Wordsworth, Byron, Shelley. I'd send him a poem, V-mail, and he'd send one in answer. V-mail. We didn't put one personal word in those letters, we felt it was sacrilege to intrude.

RUTH—Sixty letters!

MIRIAM—Only thirty actually, the rest were poems.

RUTH—What did you write in those letters? You don't mind telling me?

MIRIAM—I wrote him what he wanted to hear. He was lonely, and frightened, and he poured his heart out to me. (*No one says anything.*)

HARRY—Who's going to pour it back?

MIRIAM—I'm not sorry for what I've done. I've given a soldier to the war.

EDITH—His mother'll be happy to hear that.

Miriam's mother is not too excited, but her father is all but purple with anger. Of all the foolhardy things that Miriam has done, this is the first time she has done anything at the expense of others. And she needn't think she can get out of it, as she says she will, by making a clean breast of the entire thing—

"If you're asking me do I think that's kind, no," Miriam admits. "He'll suffer, but in years to come he'll be grateful that I gave him the opportunity to contribute as much as he was capable of, in this struggle of our new generation against the old."

There is a moment's silence. When the Judge answers, his manner is repressed and his tone deliberate: "You are not to leave this house after school for six months! You are to have no allowance, either in money or clothes, for one year! You are not to participate in any of your French, China, Dutch, or political science freedom movements ever again while you're under my roof! And that's final and irrevocable! I take an oath on it!"

"You're another generation, Father."

"Don't you address me again this evening! This child's perverted. And you're to blame, Edith! You're the keeper of my home, the molder of my children! And I'm not satisfied with the molding!"

When Bill Seawright does arrive the family greetings are a little strained, but most cordial. Judge Wilkins brings the Lieutenant in and introduces him. Of course he knows them all—from Ruth's letters, he explains. Especially Miriam. Ruth had written freely of Miriam—of her work for the French, and China, her political science class and so on. "And I agree with you that it's our generation against the last," he says to Miriam. She thanks him throatily, and sits down quickly.

He had promised, Bill recalls, to bring Ruth lilacs for this first meeting, but lilacs are out of season.

Judge Wilkins thinks perhaps Bill is feeling the need of a drink as much as he is. Bill, having considered the matter before he came, had decided that artificial fortifying was really cowardly. A moment later he changes his mind. He will have a drink.

Another ring of the doorbell sets them all fluttering and exchanging worried glances. When Dora comes, Ruth sends her back to the kitchen. "That's someone calling for me," she explains to Bill.

"I shouldn't have surprised you," agrees Bill.

"Well—" Ruth is thinking fast. "Would you mind our slipping out the back way?"

"I wouldn't mind at all," exclaims Bill, gratefully, and with a happy "Good night! Good night, all," he vanishes.

"I couldn't humiliate him here in front of you," Ruth hurriedly explains to her parents. "I just couldn't. I'll tell him alone."

There is another ring at the front door. Ruth has recovered her hat and coat. "Tell Albert exactly how it happened," she tells them. "He'll understand and I'll call him tomorrow." Under her breath, as she passes Miriam, she adds: "You little louse!"

Albert Kummer "is thirty-four, a few pounds heavier than prescribed on the insurance table and, to get the point, not deserving of Ruth. He's a go-getter."

Albert greets them with a "Hello, Mother! Hello, Dad!" He has brought a second box of candy to take the place of the one Ruth had given away at the bank. He looks upstairs anxiously.

"Albert, have a seat," invites Harry.

"What is it?" asks Albert. He senses something.

"To start from the beginning. Do you remember an organization called 'Bundles for Britain?'" Harry is pacing the floor as he talks.

"Yes, I do."

"There was also something called 'Bundles for America.'"

"I was President," announces Miriam.

"You keep out of this!" snaps her father.

The curtain is down.

It is one-thirty the next morning. The curtains are drawn in the living room. The Judge and Mrs. Wilkins are sitting on the couch and Albert in the easy chair. They are waiting. A coffee pot and cups attest the vigil. It has got to the point where sustaining conversation is a little trying.

"The way I figure it, she didn't want to spoil his dinner," Edith is saying. "So she didn't tell him during dinner. Then, since he'd already bought tickets to a show, there was no reason spoiling that. And that's where they went."

"After that she didn't want to spoil his supper," suggests Albert, none too kindly.

Albert has been trying to reserve the church for a fortnight from then. He may be able to advance the date, but he isn't sure. He prefers a church wedding. There is something substantial about it. Which reminds the Judge that he and Edith were married by a Justice of the Peace in New Haven—a ball-playing Justice who kept his spiked shoes on during the ceremony.

There is the sound of a taxi outside. From the window Edith sees Ruth getting out, followed by the Lieutenant. The Lieutenant stops to pay the fare and then starts in with Ruth.

It wouldn't do, thinks Edith, for them to be seen. That would be too embarrassing. Let them all go upstairs quickly. Albert doesn't care much for the idea, but he follows the Judge. Edith flicks off the lights.

When Ruth comes in Bill is right behind her. As she turns on the lights and takes off her hat she notices the coffee pot and cups. When she turns around she finds herself in Bill's arms. He kisses her. (She really couldn't get out of it. It's quite a kiss.)

Bill would repeat the kiss, but she puts him off, gently but firmly. He is still holding hands as she leads him to the couch. When they are seated she disengages his grip. "And we keep our hands in our laps," she says, clasping her own. "Now, we talk. Witty, if possible." Bill can do no more than look at her adoringly. "Cat got your tongue?" she asks, playfully. He smiles but does not answer. "You said you wanted to talk," Ruth goes on. "If you haven't anything to say, it's time to leave."

In answer Bill begins to recite poetry—

> "There is a Lady sweet and kind,
> Was never face so pleased my mind;

I did but see her passing by,
And yet I love her till I die.

Her gesture, motion, and her smiles,
Her wit, her voice, my heart beguiles,
Beguiles my heart, I know not why,
And yet I love her till I die."

"From Thomas Ford's 'Music of Sundry Kinds,' " concludes Bill, assuming the tone of a radio announcer. "Written in sixteen hundred and seven. I don't know the month."

"Very nice, William," admits Ruth.

BILL—From your letters I thought you'd be quoting poetry all the time.

RUTH—We're not to mention the letters. We've made a rule about that.

BILL (*affectionately*)—Why shouldn't we?

RUTH—This is a new phase of our relationship. It's to stand on its own, without benefit of Shelley and Swinburne.

BILL—We never exchanged any Swinburne!

RUTH (*after a moment*)—My last letter was Swinburne. You didn't get it. And we're not to mention letters! Stick to that rule! (*To change the subject.*) Did you have a nice time to-night?

BILL (*another tone*)—Yes, I had a nice time tonight. I'll remember it as long as I live.

RUTH—I didn't think the play was that memorable.

BILL—I didn't look twice at the stage all evening.

RUTH—I know you didn't.

BILL—That's because I'm crazy about the way you crinkle your nose.

RUTH—It's caused by a malformation of the bone structure making an unequal stress of the skin.

BILL—I'm crazy about the malformation of your bone structure.

RUTH—I wonder how doctors and nurses make love at that. They certainly must reduce everything to fundamentals.

BILL—To hell with fundamentals! (*He leans forward to kiss her. She holds him off.*)

RUTH—Bill!

BILL—I can't help it, Ruth.

RUTH—Then you'll have to go. It's late, anyway.

BILL—No, no, we'll just talk! I'll keep my hands in my
pockets! (*He does.*) There you are. You're as safe as if you
were in your own home. Now, what do you think of the political
scene? In your own words, two or three thousand of them.

RUTH—Dandy.

BILL—Dandy, eh? I see what you mean. (*He looks at her for
a long moment.*) Ruth, are you disappointed in me?

RUTH—In what way?

BILL—Did you picture me differently?

RUTH—I didn't picture you anyway.

BILL—You had my photograph.

RUTH (*only a second's delay*)—Oh, I mean your character,
your manner. I had no hint of that. Except that you liked
poetry.

BILL—I thought my letters were pretty revealing. (*An accu-
sation.*) More than yours. You jumped around so. I never
knew what subject you'd take up next. Let's free India, let's
expose capitalism, let's print a different colored money.

RUTH (*groping*)—I thought you'd be interested.

BILL—That piece on sex life in the Soviet. That interested me.

RUTH—You're not to say one more word about those letters!

BILL (*changing his position*)—Crinkle your nose a little.

RUTH—Put your hands back in your pockets! (*He's trying to
kiss her.*) Lieutenant, you're an officer and a gentleman!

BILL (*struggling*)—It's only a temporary appointment.

There is the sound of coughing from the head of the stairs.
Presently Judge Wilkins appears, coming down. He is wearing a
robe, under which his trousers and shoes are showing. He is trying to make it appear that he has been asleep. He has come, he
says, for some baking soda.

"There was a man here from the bank," he tells Ruth.

Ruth understands. "What did he have to say?" she asks.

"There's some work you have to do," says Harry, meaningly.
"It's upstairs."

"It is?"

"You've work to do tonight!"

"I guess I have."

Bill is sympathetic. If he can't help Ruth with the work, he'll
go. But he will be back in eight and a half hours. He kisses
Ruth sweetly.

"Don't mind me. I'm an innocent bystander!" calls Judge
Wilkins from the stairs. A moment later, as the front door clicks

behind Bill, the Judge calls up to the others, right merrily—
" 'Come down, come down, wherever you are!' "
Albert is not at all pleased that Ruth found it impossible to
tell Lieut. Seawright exactly what the situation is. It may have
been she was too busy kissing. No, Albert is not jealous; just
envious."
"I haven't been out with a boy that age since high school,"
declares Ruth. "He's a baby."
"Babies are usually kissed good night!" pouts Albert.
"He's the sweetest, most touching, most romantic kid I've ever
seen. Albert, I'd like to have a son like him."
"How old is he?"
"Twenty-four."
"You're twenty-two! Won't that be a little difficult?"
"He's only here one more day, and then his group's off to the
Pacific. The least I can do is keep him happy tomorrow. And
then, when he's left, I'll write him, and break our relationship off
gently. Certainly he deserves that."
After a bit of heavy thinking, Albert agrees that Ruth may be
right, though he is not very happy about it. "How do you intend
to entertain him tomorrow, my little one-woman canteen?" he
asks.
"He wants to ride in the subway. And on the 5th Avenue bus.
And he wants to eat breakfast in the Automat. It's kind of
young, but please understand, he's been away two years, Albert.
Promise me, Albert, that you'll trust me for 24 hours. I want
you to say that you want me to do it. Please, Albert!"
"Anything you say, dear. I'm so sleepy now I'm numb."
"You're a sweet man, and I love you," agrees Ruth, kissing
him good-by.
Miriam is discovered listening on the stairs. She is wearing a
robe and slippers. Ruth calls her down for further explanation
about the letters. "Your Lieutenant is charming!" Ruth assures
her. "A little impulsive, but charming!"
"Ruth, my estimation of you is increased a thousand fold,"
declares Miriam, solemnly.

RUTH—Do you mind giving me a hint of your letters? I'm
finding it a little difficult to keep up a conversation, not knowing
what I wrote him.
HARRY—Yeah, since when are you an authority on sex life
in the Soviet?
MIRIAM—I only quoted an article in *The New Freedom*.

Harry—And what is *The New Freedom?*

Miriam—It's a magazine our political science group subscribed to.

Harry—I'd like to see a copy.

Miriam—We canceled our subscription when it turned reactionary. We burned our copies.

Edith—Miriam, Hitler started by burning books that didn't agree with him. You should be tolerant of every opinion.

Miriam—I don't want to appear rude, Mother. I know this action of mine has distressed the family and I've made a resolution to be more careful in the future—

Edith (*interrupting*)—I'm glad to hear it, dear—

Harry (*agreeing*)—And about time!

Miriam (*finishing her sentence*)—But in world affairs and political science, I consider you as simple as a child. Well-meaning, but a child.

Harry—Miriam, I have never laid a hand on you in my life. Certainly not in anger. But you're begging for a tanning that's going to break my record wide open. Get upstairs to bed! This instant!

Miriam (*starting to go*)—I'm sorry I've upset you, Father.

Ruth—Before you go, Miriam. Have you, by any chance, the letters Bill, the Lieutenant, sent you?

Miriam (*taking a shoe box from under a sofa cushion*)—Excuse me, Mother. . . . You'll find them in chronological order. (*She turns to the stairs.*) Good night.

Edith and Ruth—Good night.

Ruth (*as Miriam disappears*)—I wonder if we ought to have Miriam psychoanalyzed?

A moment later the family is rummaging through the letters with enthusiasm. From time to time one stops to read an excerpt aloud. " 'Tell me, my Heart. . . . If This Be Love,' by George Lyttleton, seventeen-hundred nine—seventeen ninety-three.' " Judge Wilkins is investigating. "This is all a poem," he reports.

" 'Dear Ruth: The first paragraph of your last letter I found very touching. You wrote "I consider myself quite adult, yet I find traces of my childhood clinging to me. Occasionally, secretly, I buy a box of crackerjack—just for the prize. Crackerjacks, at my age! And then I dream I'm a queen, with a royal lover sending me presents—every hour on the hour. Sometimes I fear my body's ahead of my mind." ' " Edith folds and replaces a second letter. "Sometimes I think we don't know Miriam very well," she says.

The Judge has found one in which Bill tells of an adventure with an English girl. He would greatly like to read the one that followed. He finds it. When he has finished that he is convinced that Bill certainly favors large families.

Now Ruth, come upon something that excites her sympathy in the letter she is reading, decides that they are to read no more of Bill's correspondence. Quickly she recovers the letters her father and mother are reading. She will read them, she announces, because they were written to her. If she finds anything that should affect their action toward Bill she will let them know.

"As the legal authority in this house, may I point out a discrepancy in your reasoning?" asks the Judge.

"I have to read them," repeats Ruth. "You know that's true. And I'm surprised that you'd descend to the level of a peeping Tom."

"I'm only interested in his reactions to being abroad. I skipped the personal things." Edith is quite indignant.

"How did you know they were personal until you read them?"

"I could sense it."

The Judge and Mrs. Wilkins have started upstairs to bed. "Pst! Tell me how he comes out with that English girl," Harry calls back to Ruth.

"You're not old enough."

With the family gone, Ruth takes the shoe box and finds herself a comfortable seat. As she starts the first letter, "her expression changes from interest to compassion. She is visibly touched. She bites her underlip. She sighs."

The curtain falls.

ACT II

It is ten o'clock Sunday morning. The radio is playing softly. There are lilacs everywhere, in every conceivable sort of vase, bowl, etc. Judge Wilkins and Miriam are reading parts of the comic sections of the Sunday papers. When the phone rings Miriam is quick to answer it. Quick to explain, too, that she can't come over. She has been confined to quarters. Her father soon changes that—

"I've decided to suspend your punishment on Sundays," he tells her. "You can go to Clara's."

"I'd just as soon stay here," announces Miriam, with a loud sigh.

"There's no reason for me to be punished. Go to Clara's."

Ruth, Mrs. Wilkins announces when she comes downstairs, is still locked in her room. "She read those letters until four in the morning. Then she slept awhile, and Dora brought her coffee and a roll for breakfast. Dora thinks she was crying."

Albert appears, "practically trilling." He carries a roll of plans and a tiny bunch of flowers. He is struck with the display of lilacs. Dora is just bringing in another load.

"How much are they paying Lieutenants in this war?" demands Albert. "How did they get here?"

"In a horse and wagon," Edith explains. "A little old man drove up and said: 'Tell Her Highness it's 9 o'clock,' and he unloaded them."

Albert is a little disgusted to hear that Ruth had sacrificed her sleep to finish the letters. It's ridiculous!

When Ruth comes downstairs she is dressed for the street. She is still "immersed in the mood." She dutifully kisses Albert, but he is not pleased. To their cautious queries as to what she found in the letters she answers that she found many beautiful things—

"He's idealistic. That's the word," she tells them. "If the world disillusions him, they'll have a lot to answer for."

"Oh, he admitted it?" There is the trace of a sneer in Albert's tone.

"You're not laughing at him. Only at me, because I'm not able to explain him. And I wish I'd never gotten into this. I'm very uncomfortable."

"You're not any more uncomfortable than I am!" says Albert.

Albert's discomfort is increased considerably when Dora appears with a huge pack of crackerjack boxes tied together with twine. There are two hundred boxes altogether, she reports. The same little old man had brought them—

" 'Your Highness, it is 10 o'clock,' " he had said. " 'Sign here!' "

"That was in the letters . . . that I liked crackerjacks," Ruth would explain to Albert. "Now, you know, that's cute."

Albert has become firm. He would appreciate it very much if Ruth would break her date with the Lieutenant. It might be unkind, as Ruth insists, but in some things it is kinder to be cruel. No, Albert is not taking the affair seriously, but he is convinced the Lieutenant is—

"Albert, I didn't know you could be jealous," coos Ruth, coming close to him. "And I love you for it. I wouldn't want you otherwise. No woman wants a man who's never jealous!"

"DEAR RUTH"

Bill—May I take this opportunity to announce the engagement of Miss Ruth Wilkins to Lt. William Seawright, Serial Number 0917573.

(Bartlett Robinson, Virginia Gilmore, John Dall)

"If that does it, I can make you pretty happy."

"I promise you, the Lieutenant won't get on any subject that's remotely personal. We'll ride on the bus, in the subway and visit the Automat. And they're not secluded places. I can manage him, believe me, my worry is—can I manage you."

Albert's humor improves a little as Ruth kisses him. He is reminded of the plans he has brought. The plans for their house! The most beautiful house in the whole world, Ruth tells them. A little expensive, as Albert admits, but he is confident he can make a good deal. He has brought the plans to show them because he is a little puzzled—

"Can you tell a bathroom from a closet?" he asks the Judge.

"I've never had much trouble before," the Judge boasts.

Albert has gone to raise the window so that some of the smoke from the Judge's pipe can find an exit. As he looks out he notices a girl staring at the house. She was there when he came in.

From the open window he calls to ask if he can be of assistance. A moment later he has brought the girl in. She is Lieut. Seawright's sister, Martha, and she is waiting for Bill.

"He was considering sending me your picture," Martha explains to Ruth. "I was to return it, but he changed his mind. He didn't think the mail was safe enough."

Martha wouldn't like the Wilkinses to get the impression that the Seawrights are an eccentric family, meeting that way, and all. But the truth is, she had been engaged to a Sergeant who is with Bill at the hotel, and it would be embarrassing if they had met. What Martha would like to know now is the hour Bill and Ruth have selected for their wedding. She will have to leave right after the ceremony, and—

The query has the effect of a small bombshell. "You mean—do we know what time—Bill and I—are going to be married?"

"Yes."

"No, we don't."

The situation is still a little foggy when Bill arrives. He comes in with a breezy "Good morning!" assures them all without even looking at them that they are looking fine, goes straight to Ruth and kisses her. Again she is at some trouble to master the situation—

"Thank you for the flowers," she says; "they're beautiful."

"Honey, that was all they had."

"Some other fellow might want to buy lilacs for a girl. What is he going to do?"

"I can't help him. Everything's fair in love and war. I'm in both."

Then, for the first time, Bill sees Martha. Their greeting is affectionate, but it is plain that Bill isn't going to have much time for sister—

"I don't know how my kid sister got in here uninvited—but she's always been like that," he explains to the others.

"She was very entertaining," Albert assures him.

"Yes, she's pretty cute." Bill is looking fondly at Martha. "But I'm going to have to leave you for a while, Sis. Ruth and I have some personal business."

But Ruth is quick to put a damper on this plan. She is not going to let Bill, who hasn't seen his sister for two years, treat her that way. Why can't they all go for a bus ride together, as Edith suggests? Albert will come along and that will make a foursome. Bill is not for that at all, but he is quickly outvoted. Nor is Albert pleased. He has an idea that Bill is planning to propose to Ruth on that ride—

"He'll be mauling her on that bus! And I don't intend to sit there and watch!"

"But you'll be up front," Edith reminds him. (That is the way Bill had arranged it.)

"Damn it, what about *my* morale? Aren't civilians human too?" With that last protest Albert leaves to join the party and slams the door on the way out.

Edith is worried for fear Albert and the Lieutenant might fight, but Harry isn't worried. He has a feeling that if they do, the Lieutenant will knock Albert's block off. Edith hadn't thought of that.

There is a phone call from Bill's hotel. That would be the Sergeant, and he is in a quandary. Either he has to check out before 11 o'clock or pay for another day. The only solution to that situation that Judge Wilkins can think of is to invite the Sergeant out for lunch. It is only after he has done so that Edith remembers that the Sergeant and Bill's sister aren't supposed to meet. But there is nothing to do about that now.

"Sit calmly and be engulfed. That's my motto," says Harry.

From the kitchen Dora carries in a small, gaily painted phonograph. "The man said this was for 11 o'clock, but he had to deliver it sooner because he is on a route," she explains.

"I don't intend to even turn around. I'm ignoring the whole thing," announces the Judge.

Dora puts the needle to the record. It blares forth "I Love You Truly."

The Judge is relieved. "I was afraid he'd sent Frank Sinatra," he confesses.

Dora giggles. The curtain falls.

It is noon. Sergeant Chuck Vincent, a presentable young non-com, has arrived for lunch. He has brought both his and Lieut. Seawright's B-4 bags and they are stacked against the wall. Where the phonograph had stood there is now a beribboned magnum of champagne. The Judge and Mrs. Wilkins have evidently been having a little trouble entertaining the Sergeant.

At the moment Chuck is telling them of how their bomber (his and Lieut. Seawright's) happened to get its name. The crew had been asked to vote. Every fellow suggested the name of his girl, but, because he (Chuck) had sort of lost his girl at the time, he voted for "Ruth." This at Lieut. Seawright's suggestion. Still, they lost. The rear gunner won with "Helen."

However, it didn't stay "Helen," as Chuck explains. "After our fifth mission he got an engraved invitation to her wedding."

"Did you change the name of the plane?"

"He added one word—and that's how our plane got to be called 'Helen Gone.' "

Chuck calls headquarters to learn whether or not his own and Lieut. Seawright's orders have arrived. They haven't, but they may get in at any minute. No, he doesn't know where they will be going. Somewhere in the Pacific.

"I think that's very inconsiderate of them, not telling you," sympathizes Mrs. Wilkins.

"Mrs. Wilkins, I think you've hit on the best definition of war I've ever heard," agrees Chuck. "Just one inconsideration after another."

No, Chuck has not made up his mind about what he is going to do after the war. Not, at least, after the first minute. That minute he is going to devote to punching Lieutenant Seawright in the nose. And why? Because that morning, as early as six o'clock, the Lieutenant had his Sergeant walking up and down Madison Avenue looking in jewelers' windows for an engagement ring. Finding one, Lieut. Seawright had hunted out the jeweler's name and phone number (the store being closed on Sunday) and talked with him for half an hour before he got him to agree to come down and open his shop—

"Then I had to wait an hour in front of the store for Mr.

Cooper to appear," concludes Chuck. "Still without breakfast,
while Bill looked for lilacs in Long Island. Which is why, as I
started to say, the first item on my post-war agenda is to punch
ex-Lieutenant Seawright on his civilian nose!"

They try to think of something they can get for Chuck, even
though he has had his breakfast. Maybe he'd like some crackerjack. No, he wouldn't, but that reminds him that he had promised Lieut. Seawright to fashion some of the crackerjack into
a bride and groom! Can he do that in the kitchen? He can.

"I wonder if the jeweler will take that ring back," wonders
Edith, when Chuck has left.

"You're lucky if you get your daughter back," submits the
Judge.

"That Lieutenant just charges through every obstacle. He certainly is impulsive." Edith is secretly admiring.

"I don't see how the war's lasted this long," adds Harry.

Now Albert Kummer appears. "His hair is mussed. His tie
is awry. The pocket of his coat is hanging free." And he is
awful mad.

"Is Ruth back?" demands Albert.

"Not yet. Why, what's happened to you, Albert?" Edith is
alarmed.

ALBERT—I was arrested by the Interborough Rapid Transit
Company!

EDITH—Oh, no!

ALBERT—Oh, yes! And I have a summons to prove it. (*He
plunges his hand in the pocket that is torn free, and that makes
him madder, if possible. He finds the summons in his other
pocket.*) I'm to appear in court next Friday at two o'clock!
And I don't intend to! (*To* HARRY *who reads the summons.*)
You got me into this, and you can damn well get me out!

HARRY—This isn't my court, Albert, but I'll go down with you.
We can probably explain it. What happened?

ALBERT (*almost too mad to talk*)—We were standing on the
platform of the damn train enjoying ourselves . . . riding on the
subway! How I got hooked into this whole thing, I don't know.
How can anyone want to ride on the subway for amusement?

EDITH—I don't know.

HARRY—Start from the beginning, Albert!

EDITH—Well, let him!

HARRY—I'm only trying to get the whole picture.

ALBERT—The four of us were standing on this platform, jammed against the door! We pulled into a station! The door opened! Then it started to close! Just as it was about to close someone pushed me! I know who pushed me! The door shut! I was on the station, they were on the train! Off it went! I'M SO DAMN MAD I CAN SPIT! (*Quietly.*) I have to sit down. I'm not supposed to get excited.

HARRY—How did you get arrested?

EDITH—Speak quietly, Albert, your face is blue.

ALBERT—Thank you. I ran upstairs and got a taxi! We raced two stations ahead! I was going to catch that train!

EDITH—That was very clever.

ALBERT—I got to the turnstile, just as the train was pulling in. I DIDN'T HAVE A NICKEL!

HARRY—Better speak lower, Albert.

ALBERT (*mopping his brow*)—So I WENT UNDER THE TURN-STILE! I'm not supposed to get excited. (*Quieter now.*) A guard grabbed me by the collar. I tried to explain it to him, to let go of me, I had to get in that train. The whole thing became confused. Another guard came over and jumped on me! They called a policeman; there's the summons. For stealing a nickel. Prominent bank executive arrested for stealing a nickel!

EDITH—This hasn't turned out well at all.

ALBERT—No, it hasn't, Mrs. Wilkins. And I'd be very grateful if you wouldn't say nothing can possibly happen.

EDITH—But nothing can, Albert. It's daytime, and all he can do is—propose to her. That's just words.

ALBERT—It's how a man proposes! You don't just ask a girl, you kiss her! And if she objects you keep kissing her. (*On a rising crescendo.*) And she'll keep objecting, and he'll keep kissing her, and I hope you don't think I'm eccentric, if I tell you, I damn well don't like it!

Albert is trying desperately to control himself when Martha arrives. She had not only become separated from Albert, she explains, but from Ruth and Bill, too. Albert is not interested in that part of her story. What he wants to know is did she, or did she not, push him out of the subway? Martha doesn't think she did, but Albert is positive. She pushed him out because Bill told her to—

"You thought they were entitled to a little privacy! You said that to me on the bus." Albert is fairly explosive.

"Well, I must say, Mister Kummer, that doesn't seem unreasonable," protests Martha. "After all, they love each other, and couldn't very well propose with you pointing out the tall buildings."

"She pushed me all right," Albert assures the Wilkinses.

Chuck has just come from the kitchen with his crackerjack bride and groom when Bill and Ruth appear. Bill has his arm around Ruth's shoulder. They have an announcement to make. At least Bill has—

"May I take this opportunity to announce the engagement of Miss Ruth Wilkins to Lieutenant William Seawright. Serial Number 0917573."

Chuck is the first to offer his heartiest congratulations. Judge Wilkins adds his. "I know you wouldn't do anything you didn't think was right—and necessary," he says, with a hurried and worried glance at Albert.

Martha and Edith add their felicitations and finally Albert decides that it might as well be unanimous. That pleases Bill—

"Thank you, Mr. Kummer! I know you're an old friend of the family, and I was afraid—what with the subway—"

"No, no! I'm very sympathetic to people getting married! You see I'm engaged to be married myself!"

"Really? (*He offers his hand.*) Well, congratulations!"

"Thank you! Thank you very much! That is, I'm supposed to be engaged! There's a little confusion about it at the moment!"

"That's too bad. I hope it works out."

"I hope so too, but I can't see how."

"It'll work out, Albert, believe me," announces Ruth, with all the decision she can muster.

Bill has taken the engagement ring from Chuck, and put it on Ruth's finger. "Baby, let me look at you. I'm not going to see you for a long, long time," he says, gazing lovingly into her eyes. Then he kisses her, slowly and long. "Remember that!" he admonishes, as he comes out of the kiss. They start out on the terrace for lunch.

"You have to understand why Ruth did that," the Judge tries to assure Albert, as Ruth and Bill disappear through the door. "There must be a reason. I'm sure there is."

"Understand!" snaps Albert. "I've got a deposit on the house, a minister and church reserved, and I have to shake hands with a man who's engaged to my fiancée! There's a limit to how much flesh and blood can understand!"

Miriam has come from the kitchen munching an apple. She is sitting on the stairs when Ruth and Bill reappear. They have their plates of food, this being a buffet luncheon. Neither o them sees Miriam. They are no more than seated, side by side, than Bill begins—

"The future Mrs. Seawright! Honey, I'll never completely forgive you for that act in the taxi!"

"Act?"

BILL—I understand a girl doesn't say "Yes" as soon as she's asked, but you overdid the reluctance. You certainly did!

RUTH (*hoping to keep it light*)—I wanted to be sure you were serious.

BILL (*solemnly*)—I'll tell you how serious I was. (*Simply.*) If you hadn't promised to marry me, Ruth, I don't think I'd've been any good out there at all. That's on the level!

RUTH (*evidently understanding*)—I believe you.

BILL—And out there is no place for a someone not to care what happens to him.

RUTH—Well, you're all right now, so fly good.

BILL—Ruth, how about getting married after all? We've got the time!

RUTH—Now, Bill—

BILL (*eagerly*)—It'd really be the way to do it.

RUTH (*apprehensively*)—You're not being a good sport!

BILL—Awful romantic!

RUTH (*being strong*)—Bill, we agreed it'd be different if you had more time! But you're leaving in a few hours. Now let's be practical! People don't get married after knowing each other one day!

BILL (*eyeing her lovingly*)—You're always reading about it.

RUTH—You never read about what happened to them later!

BILL (*sweetly*)—You're a dirty coward!

RUTH—Yes, I am.

Martha has come rushing from the yard. She is plainly agitated. Evidently her first contact with Chuck Vincent has been a little embarrassing. "Both of us—just standing there—afraid to look at each other!" She is trying to explain.

Ruth is sympathetic. She puts an arm around Martha. "You go right upstairs and fix your face!" Ruth advises. "First door to the right."

The Judge has come to report that Albert is so nervous he has spilled spaghetti sauce on Chuck's uniform. Catching sight of Miriam, he sends her to the back porch. But not before Miriam has a chance to assure Bill solemnly that "God moves in a mysterious way his wonders to perform." A sentiment with which Bill is in enthusiastic agreement.

Albert, Edith and Chuck come from the terrace. Chuck is industriously trying to rub out the stain of the spaghetti sauce. Fortunately, he assures the apologetic Albert, it almost matches.

"Use some cleaning fluid," suggests Edith. "You'll find it in a cabinet upstairs. First door to the right."

Before anybody can stop him Chuck has bounded up the stairs. Ruth looks helplessly to Bill. But Bill is not worried—

"Let them have it out," he says. "There's no reason they shouldn't be speaking to each other."

The phone is ringing. The call is for Bill, as he expected. It is also travel orders, but not those he expected. He seems a little dazed as he hangs up—

"We're staying in America," he says, quietly. "We're going to be instructors at Eglin Field, Florida!"

There is a breathless "No!" from Edith, Harry and Ruth in unison. And an exchange of worried glances. Bill has walked quickly over to Ruth. "This sure is my lucky day," he says, throatily. "Honey, I don't know what my expression is like, but you ought to see yours."

He has bent down to kiss her solemnly. Edith all but chokes on her food.

"Very nice of the Army," stutters Albert.

"Isn't it?" Bill turns to Harry and Edith. "Do you trust me on the train with your daughter, just being engaged?"

The Wilkinses are plainly disturbed. Ruth is quick to take over. She doesn't think she could do that. There's the bank, which is awfully short of help. Albert will tell him that. And Albert does. But that doesn't convince Bill—

"Oh, come now, you're not going to keep two people in love apart, on account of a measly bank! Are you, Albert?"

Chuck and Martha come joyfully downstairs. They are holding hands. "We finally agreed it was my fault," announces Chuck.

"Bill, we want to get married," says Martha, freeing herself from Chuck's impulsive embrace.

"Even if it's just for today?"

"Even if it's just for today."

"Sis!" He has his hands on his sister's shoulders. "Sis! Your first wedding present! Chuck and I are staying here as instructors! In Florida!"

Now the excitement mounts. Especially with Bill and Chuck.

It is Bill's idea that the Judge should marry them—all of them. But Ruth feels that they should talk things over first, she and Bill. Still Bill isn't discouraged. Let Chuck wangle a three-day waiver. He (Bill) will pick up their orders and the tickets. Now he is ready to listen to Ruth's explanation of why she can't leave for Florida right now—which he promises to ignore.

The others have left them. Bill would hold Ruth close as she explains why she can't start for Florida, but she fends him off. With some effort she begins—

"Now, listen to me! The plain truth is . . . I promised to marry you, never intending to go through with it."

"You'll have to make that a little clearer, Ruth."

"I thought you'd be leaving. You promised me you would . . ." Bill says nothing and she goes on: "Try to see my side of it. You thought you loved me, you were going away to face something terribly hazardous. I had no other choice."

"I do love you."

"Not really. You couldn't."

"I'm going to get leaves in Florida. I'm going to come and see you."

"No, Bill, no!"

"I know you like me, Ruth. I couldn't be wrong about that . . ."

Ruth hesitates, but this is something she has to do and she does it. "There are other factors."

"Ruth."

"I'm not really interested—" It isn't easy for her to say this. "And it wouldn't be right to waste your time." It is as though she had slapped him, but he says nothing. "I'm sorry it's turned out this way. It's entirely my fault. I think it best if we don't let on—with your sister getting married. We could say I'm coming to Florida later, and let—it go at that!"

"That's very kind of you."

Ruth slowly takes off Bill's ring and hands it to him. She will go now, she says, and see if she can find a little gift for Martha and Chuck. He does not watch her go. He has thrust his hands in his pockets and is kicking at the carpet when Miriam appears.

Miriam had passed Ruth on the porch, she reports, and from her expression she was about to burst into tears. What's happened? Had Ruth told him? How?

"Straight from the shoulder," says Bill. "They're using it a lot this year. It's called the 'It's kinder to be cruel' method. It stinks."

No, Bill is not angry with Miriam. Nor does he quite understand when she reminds him of the poet Burns' conviction that "the best laid plans of mice and men aft gang agley." Even when she remembers that they had exchanged a lot of Burns at first it means nothing to Bill.

"It must have been hard on you to find time to type all those letters," Miriam continues. "I did mine in school, as part of typing practice." By then it is coming to him. "I didn't let anyone know what I was typing," Miriam goes on. "I must say it of myself, I can keep a secret. No one has ever gotten anything out of me. I could probably be of use to the Government, in a way."

Now the mist is lifting. A full-size turmoil is beating inside Bill. He has leaned forward and is gazing intently at Miriam as he tries to piece everything together.

"I wouldn't feel too badly about Ruth," Miriam is saying. "I know you're attracted to her. On the surface. She's pretty bourgeoise. You know what that means? (*He nods.*) To be able to marry Albert, a reactionary of the first water. I don't understand it. She isn't even the last generation. . . . Sometimes I lose faith."

BILL—Holy H— Harry!

MIRIAM—What's the matter?

BILL (*for himself*)—You wrote those letters! Didn't you? Byron—Shelley—lilacs—crackerjacks! Every hour on the hour! Holy H—! What must she think of me? And your parents? Why, I'm the biggest sap that ever— Oh, my God! Albert! Why, she's engaged to be married to Albert! Of course! Holy H—!

MIRIAM (*accusingly*)—You didn't know! You tricked me into telling you!

BILL (*recalling, in agony*)—"I did but see her passing by, and yet I'll love her till I die."

MIRIAM (*suddenly a little girl*)—I didn't mean to tell you. I've only made it worse!

BILL—No, you didn't. It was bad as it could get before.

MIRIAM—How can you ever forgive me?

BILL—There's only one thing we can both do that's the right thing.

MIRIAM—I'll do anything you say! I'll tell any lie you like!

BILL—This'll be harder for you. Do nothing. Don't let Ruth know I know! Don't let anyone know! She did all this for me. She could've told 'em, but she didn't. She wanted me to have these two days. Let's keep it that way, Miriam. Promise?

MIRIAM—I promise.

BILL—Cross your heart?

MIRIAM—I'm not a child!

DORA (*coming in with a huge baby panda*)—This one just came. Every hour on the hour.

BILL (*wrought up on his own*)—I better go for those tickets.

DORA—Where shall I put it?

MIRIAM—Just any place, Dora. (DORA *places it on chair.* MIRIAM *is looking after* BILL)—Good-by. (*She starts to the stairs, but stops at the liquor tray. She pours a stiff drink of Scotch. She drinks.*) Don't feel a thing. (*She sits alongside the panda.*) A fool there was, and he made his prayer, To a rag, a bone, and a hank of hair. What does he see in my sister? (*She drinks again.*) Still don't feel anything. (*To* PANDA.) What did you say?

The curtain falls.

At four o'clock that afternoon Judge Wilkins has filled out the marriage license form and given it to Chuck to sign. He follows with a few light instructions as to how a groom is expected to act and what questions he is expected to answer.

Then Bill arrives. He has done a good job composing himself. He has been held up waiting for a bedroom cancellation. He glances a little nervously at Ruth; for a moment their eyes meet.

"Can't understand your not being able to talk Ruth into Florida," Chuck is saying. "What's happened to you, Bill? Combat fatigue?"

"Could be."

"I had confidence in you. It's all gone." Bill and Ruth look at each other. Chuck turns to Ruth. "When exactly are you coming down? We ought to know, because he's not going to be fit to live with until you do!"

"I couldn't say right now," Ruth answers; "but—when I can—Bill understands."

Chuck has turned to Bill. "You're starting out wrong with this gal! You're going to be understanding one thing after another!"

"I tried."

Albert has come from upstairs. Now they're all ready and the Judge arranges their positions. "You stand there, Chuck, beside her. Bill, Ruth, Edith, Albert—"

When they are quiet he begins the service: "Friends, we are gathered together here in the presence of this company. . . ."

"Sergeant Charles Vincent, will you have this woman as your wedded wife? . . ."

"Martha Seawright, will you have this man as your wedded husband? . . ."

Chuck produces the ring and puts it on Martha's finger . . . "And thereto I plight thee my troth . . ."

"Join your right hands . . . In accordance with the authority vested in me by the law of the State of New York, I pronounce you man and wife."

Judge Wilkins pauses briefly and then reads on: " 'Then may follow such additional remarks as the official may deem advisable.' " He looks at his watch. "It is advisable you hurry!"

There are congratulations and kissing. "The first one'll be called Bill," announces an excited Chuck, shaking hands with his Lieutenant. "If it's a girl, the second one. If not the second, the third. One of 'em'll eventually be called Bill."

"I hope I don't put you to too much trouble."

Chuck and Martha have gone upstairs to complete their going-away plans. Miriam has reappeared. She giggles a little, and is not altogether certain on her feet. Ruth and her mother go quickly to Miriam. They are quick to notice the smell of liquor. The Judge, too. But Miriam is not particularly flustered. Leaning against the sofa she begins to recite—

> "My candle burns at both ends,
>   It will not last the night,
>   But, oh, my foes, and oh, my friends,
>   It gives a lovely light."

The next minute Miriam is threatening to collapse. She does not feel good. Not at all. The Judge and Mrs. Wilkins quickly take hold of her arms and pilot her toward the stairs—

Ruth has turned apologetically to Bill. "I don't know what to say! You must realize it's some dreadful mistake."

"All kids take a drink as a joke," says Bill. "It happened to me. Often." With this thirsty reminder Bill thinks he needs a drink right now. He pours two—one for Albert. Then he tells them that he knows all. Miriam had let the story slip.

"I'm sorry, Bill. I was hoping you wouldn't find out," says Ruth.

"I know. Thank you."

"You realize how it happened? I only meant to help. I never thought it would go so far. But you were so impetuous—and one step led to another—there just didn't seem to be any point where I could stop it."

"Of course."

"Well, it's over now, what'll we drink to?" Albert, at least, is happy.

"To your happy marriage, if I may." Bill is game.

"You bet."

Albert would go farther. Come midnight, he and Ruth will drive Bill to the station. Bill doesn't care for the plan. He'll go alone, if they don't mind.

"You know," beams Albert, "what kills me about the whole thing? All that poetry flying back and forth across the Atlantic! That kills me! Well, will you excuse me for a minute? This is the first time I've felt it safe to leave you two alone."

Judge Wilkins has brought Miriam to apologize, which Miriam does with some elaboration. "My behavior was inexcusable. I'm going to devise a punishment for myself . . . besides what you do to me. And I hope you're not going to be lenient."

"A lady's entitled to take a drink once in a while," submits the Judge, putting his arm about her.

A quick glance at his watch warns Bill that the newly-weds must hurry. He is ready, too, with his good-bys.

"I hope there are no hard feelings," says Ruth, as their eyes meet.

"Why, of course not! What right would I have to feel that way?" There is a slight squeak in Bill's voice, and he is talking a bit too rapidly. "If anything, the obligation is the other way. You couldn't have been more considerate—you certainly couldn't. (*Little trouble with his throat here.*) The whole thing's really funny—the more you think of it. My coming here, the way I did—and how you acted—and the subway—and the rest— You were very considerate— (*To* HARRY.) All of you. And your wife— And Albert, Mister Kummer!—That was very kind of him, after all, he's all right! (*He is smiling desperately again.*) There won't be room in the car for all of us, and our bags—I'll get a taxi. Would you tell them I've gone ahead, and I'll meet them at the train?"

"Of course."

With a couple more nervous good-bys, and a last look at Ruth, Bill is out of the door and gone.

"Well, that's that," says Ruth, with the click of the door.

"I owe you two dollars," announces the Judge, casting an anxious glance toward the stairs. Ruth is glaring at him.

"Did you think I was going to run off with him?" she demands, hotly.

"No, no! Not at all! It was just such big odds. I only bet two dollars."

"A Lieutenant I've met for one day—that's all it's been—one day of his being amusing and touching—and you expect me to exchange that for a man I've known for years—who loves me—who offers me security—(*Louder than necessary.*)—and whom I love?"

"I only lost two dollars!"

But Ruth does not stop. She knows her father thought she would marry Bill and she suspects he really hoped she would.

"I'm a Judge. I never take sides."

"You wanted me to marry him!"

"The question's irrelevant!"

The Judge does admit, however, that he thought Fate was pushing Ruth. Well, as for that—

"I'm a fatalist, too!" Ruth all but shouts, pointing toward the door. "And he's gone! Damn! Damn! Damn! Damn!" she cries, defiantly. "Oh, I liked him! I admit it! And if he'd've kept on for another minute, just now, I don't know what I'd've done. But he didn't. And that's Fate too! (*She stops.*) I'm going to have a drink! (*She walks to the liquor, talking through the pouring.*) I'm over him already! And tomorrow I'll be over him still more! And the next day he'll be even fainter! And the day I'm married I won't even be able to remember what he looked like! (*She holds the glass up, as a toast.*) That's my answer to Fate!"

Just as she is about to drink, there is a noise in back of her and in rushes Bill. He had forgotten to leave Chuck's railroad tickets. Ruth does not turn around.

"Just a minute! Photo finish!" exclaims the Judge, with another glance upward. Ruth has turned slowly around as Bill is taking the tickets from his pocket. He looks up to see an expression in her eyes he has never seen there before.

"I've always wanted to see Florida." Ruth has not moved.

"What do you mean?" Bill is afraid to put the right interpretation on that speech.

RUTH—Just crazy about it!
BILL (*not moving*)—Are you sure?

RUTH (*pleading for acceptance*)—I've never been so sure about anything in my life!

HARRY (*looking at the stairs. Simply*)—I hear them.

BILL (*putting down the envelope*)—It's one bedroom.

RUTH—My father hasn't brought it up! Who asked you?

HARRY (*as* BILL *looks to him for reassurance*)—Do you take this woman to be your lawful wedded wife?

BILL (*startled*)—Yes, sir, I mean, I do!

HARRY (*low and quick*)—Do you take this man—?

RUTH (*grabbing* BILL *by the arm*)—I do.

HARRY (*following after them*)—Power invested in me . . .

RUTH (*over her shoulder*)—I'll send you a wire where to send my clothes. Tell Albert there's insanity in the family!

HARRY (*nodding*)—I pronounce you . . . (*Louder.*) MAN AND WIFE! That's not very legal, but it'll save 'em from the Mann Act!

EDITH (*preceded down the stairs by* CHUCK *carrying two suitcases,* MARTHA *and* ALBERT)—"Off we go—into the wild blue yonder—"

ALBERT (*happily*)—I called Dr. Hardwick and I've got the church for next Sunday at ten o'clock.

CHUCK—We all set? (*The cab heard starting off.*)

HARRY (*not knowing exactly how to begin*)—If you'll all be seated, this'll only take a minute . . .

EDITH—Harry, we can just make it!

CHUCK—We'll miss the train!

HARRY—Don't worry about the train. To come to the point— (*From right, a lanky blond, open-faced* SAILOR *appears, clutching his hat. All look at him.*)

SAILOR—Excuse me, the door was open. Is Miss Ruth Wilkins at home?

MIRIAM (*from the depths*)—Harold! Harold Klobbermeyer!

HARRY (*wailing*)—No! No!

EDITH (*screeching*)—Oh! Noooo!

THE CURTAIN FALLS

THE PLAYS AND THEIR AUTHORS

"A Bell for Adano," a comedy in three acts by Paul Osborn, based on a novel by John Hersey of the same title. Copyright, 1944, by the authors. Copyright and published, 1945, by Alfred A. Knopf, New York.

Paul Osborn has made several previous appearances in the distinguished company of Best Play authors—with "On Borrowed Time," with "The Vinegar Tree" and last season with "The Innocent Voyage," an adaptation of "A High Wind in Jamaica." He is an Evansville, Indiana, boy, is approaching his middle forties, is a graduate of the University of Michigan and learned a lot about playwriting studying with George Pierce Baker at Harvard.

John Hersey, the wartime author of this best of wartime comedies, served as a correspondent at the front and wrote "A Bell for Adano" in the heat of his resentment at certain occurrences on the Italian front following the Sicily invasion. He was born, the year being 1914, in Tientsin, China, his American parents being established there at the time. He attended school there. Later he was sent to Hotchkiss, to Yale and finally to Clare College, Cambridge. The Summer of 1937 he worked as private secretary to Sinclair Lewis. Since then he has been an editor on the staff of *Time* magazine, being sent to the Orient as correspondent for *Time* and *Life* in 1940. His war books have included "Men on Bataan" and "Into the Valley," relating his adventures in the Philippines and on Guadalcanal, when he went into action with the Marines. His story of the invasion of Sicily, as told in "A Bell for Adano," won him the Pulitzer award for the best novel of the year.

"I Remember Mama," a comedy in two acts by John Van Druten, adapted from a volume of short stories by Kathryn Forbes. Copyright, 1944, by the authors. Copyright and published, 1945, by Harcourt, Brace and Co., Inc., New York.

John Van Druten first joined the Best Plays group twenty years ago, when his "Young Woodley," barred in London because the English censor insisted it reflected discreditably upon the English
358

public school system, was given sanctuary by Producer George C. Tyler in New York and proved one of the successes of the season. Mr. Van Druten was at the time a lecturer at a Welsh university and hopeful of becoming a playwright. The success of "Woodley" (which afterward had a London run also) helped him to realize that ambition. In recent seasons his "Voice of the Turtle" and "There's Always Juliet" have been included in this yearbook list. He was born in London in 1902 and has long been an American citizen. He does most of his writing at his ranch in California. Near Hollywood, of course.

"The Hasty Heart," comedy in three acts by John Patrick. Copyright, 1944, by the author. Copyright and published, 1945, by Random House, Inc., New York.

John Patrick was born in Kentucky, but he never feels quite easy about proclaiming that fact, seeing that he left the state at the age of two months. His writing career began in San Francisco. So good were his radio scripts the National Broadcasting Company brought him to New York. He has written radio scripts for Helen Hayes, his dramatizations including "Arrowsmith" and "Kitty Foyle." In Hollywood he worked, usually with collaborators, on twenty-four different pictures. One was a Charlie Chan, another a Mr. Moto number. Early in 1942, hoping to see early front-line action, he joined the American Field Service and was assigned to a British ambulance unit. He saw action with Montgomery's Eighth Army in Egypt, and with the Ninth Army in Syria. He was in South America, South Africa, Suez, Cairo, Jerusalem, Lebanon, the Syrian desert, and finally on the Assam-Burma front. It was while he was in Syria that he met the Scot who is the prototype of his "Hasty Heart" hero. He wrote the play about him while he was en route home aboard an Army transport. Mr. Patrick's schools have included Holy Cross in New Orleans, Columbia University in New York and Harvard Summer school. He is in his middle thirties and hopeful of continuing successfully in his playwriting career. His produced plays have included "The Willow and I" and "Hell Freezes Over." He also has one called "The Gentle Ghost," which he is holding.

"The Glass Menagerie," a "memory play" in seven scenes, by Tennessee Williams. Copyright, 1944, by the author. Copyright and published, 1945, by Random House, Inc., New York.

Tennessee Williams is 31 years old. He was born in Columbus, Mississippi, and his folks named him Thomas Lanier. When he was asked how come the Tennessee he answered that he did not like Thomas Lanier. Sounded too much like "William Lyons Phelps." Young Mr. Williams took naturally to writing, and has done a lot of it, in college and out. But there were years after he graduated from the State University of Iowa when he made his living in a variety of other pursuits. He has been, his biographers relate, a clerk for a shoe company, an elevator pilot, a bellhop, a movie usher, a waiter, and a teletyper. There is also a story that for a time he read verse in a Greenwich Village nightclub, much to the delight of the customers. He has written perhaps a dozen plays, short and long, but mostly short. He is well known to Little Theatre groups. His one long play to reach production before "The Glass Menagerie" was called "Battle of the Angels." It was produced by the Theatre Guild in 1943, tried out in Boston, with Miriam Hopkins as the star, and withdrawn before reaching New York. Tennessee Williams will, of course, go on writing plays, but he warns his admirers that not many of them will be pleasant plays.

"Harvey," a comedy in three acts by Mary Coyle Chase.

Mary Coyle Chase, Denver-born thirty-seven years ago, did her bit of newspaper work as a reporter and special writer. She married in the profession, as it were, her husband, Robert L. Chase, being the current city editor of the *Rocky Mountain News*. The care of a house and three young sons forced her to confine her writing chores to the home, so she turned to plays. She has had one other play produced, a comedy called "Now You've Done It," which Brock Pemberton and Antoinette Perry staged in 1937. It did not last long. She finished "Harvey" upwards of a year ago and has done a lot of tinkering with it since then. She has sold several short stories and is now at work on a novel.

"The Late George Apley," a comedy in three acts by John P. Marquand and George S. Kaufman, based on Mr. Marquand's novel of the same name. Copyright, 1944, by the authors.

John Phillips Marquand has devoted most of his literary years to the writing of novels, several of which attained the best seller lists and one of which, this same "The Late George Apley," won the Pulitzer prize in 1938. His adaptation of "Apley" in play form, with George S. Kaufman acting as guide, counselor and friend, is Mr. Marquand's first adventure with the theatre. He was born in Wilmington, Delaware, in November, 1893. His prep school and high school years were spent in Newburyport, Massachusetts, and from there he went to Harvard, graduating in 1915. He has a Litt.D. degree from the University of Maine. For two years after he left Harvard he was assistant managing editor of the *Boston Transcript* and was later on the Sunday staff of the *New York Herald Tribune*. He saw service with the A.E.F. in the First World War.

George S. Kaufman is an old hand at writing Best Plays, having made his debut in this series as a collaborator with Marc Connelly the season of 1921-22, when their "Dulcy" was one of the comedy hits. They followed with "Beggar on Horseback," "Merton of the Movies" and other successes. Mr. Kaufman's first single entry was "The Butter and Egg Man." He wrote, among other notable contributions, "The Royal Family" and "Dinner at 8" with Edna Ferber, "Once in a Lifetime" and "You Can't Take It with You" with Moss Hart, "First Lady" with Katherine Dayton and "Of Thee I Sing" with Morrie Ryskind and the Gershwins, George and Ira. He has been the Great Collaborator of the American theatre the last quarter century.

"Soldier's Wife," a comedy in three acts by Rose Franken Meloney. Copyright, 1944, by the author. Copyright and published, 1945, by Samuel French, Inc., New York.

This is Rose Franken's fourth appearance as a Best Play author. In the issue of 1931-32 she was represented by her first produced play, "Another Language." She returned with "Claudia" the season of 1940-41 and with "Outrageous Fortune" in 1943-44. Miss Franken is the mother of three children. Her oldest son spent three years in the jungles of New Guinea. Recently, it has been written of her, "she has lived with the firm conviction that men will return from this war with the better qualities of their natures enriched and fortified; the weaklings will be destroyed, as they would be in any of the emergencies of life." Hence her urge to translate into the stuff of the theatre

the story of the hero of "Soldier's Wife." "He is a normal male
returning to a wife who, if their marriage is to survive, must find
herself equally matured, and her values equally stabilized, by the
experience through which she has passed." Born in Dallas, Texas,
Miss Franken has done a good deal of writing for the magazines.
Her "Claudia" was for many months one of the most popular
radio serials.

"Anna Lucasta," a drama in three acts by Philip Yordan. Copy-
     right, 1944, by the author. Copyright and published, 1945,
     by Random House, Inc., New York.

     Philip Yordan is Chicago-born, thirty-one years old, a lawyer
by profession, or at least by schooling, and a writer—in particular a writer of plays—by choice. Being wise when he began
writing plays, he did not stop with the first one and wait for its
sale. He wrote several and brought them to the Broadway market to see what would happen. They were read with great interest by several producers, but none was sold. These included plays
entitled "Any Day Now," "Get Off the Earth" and "Joe Macbeth," as well as "Anna Lucasta." Among his readers was William Dieterle, Hollywood director. Following a breakfast meeting in Chicago Mr. Dieterle decided to engage Mr. Yordan as a
sort of personal playwright. He took him to Hollywood, where he
worked for upwards of two years on such scripts as "All That
Money Can Buy," "Syncopation," etc. He was inducted into the
Army, but later granted an honorable discharge. Mr. Yordan
is still fussing with the cinema, but plans to devote a lot of time
to the legitimate theatre.

"Foolish Notion," a comedy in three acts by Philip Barry. Copy-
     right, 1944, by the author.

     Philip Barry's last previous appearance in these pages was in
the volume representing the season of 1938-39. Then two of his
plays were included—"The Philadelphia Story," which Katharine
Hepburn played so successfully and so long, and "Here Come the
Clowns," a minor success staged and played by Eddie Dowling.
Previous to 1938-39, however, Mr. Barry was a frequent con-
tributor, beginning as far back as 1922-23, when his Harvard
prize play, "You and I," was included. "Holiday," "Paris
Bound," "Tomorrow and Tomorrow" and "The Animal Kingdom" have been some of the other Barry best sellers at the box

offices. He was born in Rochester, New York, graduated from Yale and studied drama with George Pierce Baker at Harvard. He tried being an embassy attaché in London for a time, and after that wrote advertising copy until his success with "You and I" delivered him to the theatre.

"Dear Ruth," a comedy in three acts by Norman Krasna. Copyright, 1944, by the author. Copyright and published, 1945, by Random House, Inc., New York.

Probably the life of Norman Krasna will one day be written to illustrate a from-rags-to-riches theme in a literary history of America. Mr. Krasna made that romantic journey in less than ten years. He went from an $18-a-week clerkship (neckties in the basement was his line) to a $1,200-a-week scenario-writing job in Hollywood in seven years. It is told of him that, being shown the door by a Warners' executive during a heated debate, Mr. Krasna saved time by jumping out the window. A ground floor window, naturally. A few years later he came back through the door and signed a contract with Warners to write and produce four motion pictures for the satisfying sum of $500,000. In his early days he had been a copy boy on the *New York Morning World*, running errands for the late Alexander Woollcott, Heywood Broun, Herbert Bayard Swope and others. He wrote, as a first play, a comedy called "Louder, Please" that failed. He followed with "Small Miracle," a melodrama that ran the better part of a season. He failed again with "The Man with Blond Hair" and this season hit the jackpot a second time with "Dear Ruth." He is still in Hollywood, still rich and, presumably, still happily ambitious to add to his fame and his dividends.

PLAYS PRODUCED IN NEW YORK

June 15, 1944—June 16, 1945

LOVE ON LEAVE

(7 performances)

A comedy in three acts by A. B. Shiffrin. Produced by Charles Stewart and Martin Goodman at the Hudson Theatre, New York, June 20, 1944.

Cast of characters—

Sam Wilson	Millard Mitchell
Mary	Mary Sargent
Paula	June Wilson
Lucy	Rosemary Rice
Larry Draper	James Dobson
Robert Lewis	Stanley Bell
Flo	Joann Dolan
Hoagy	Bert Freed
Nick Hardy	John Conway
Slim	Ramsay Williams
Dr. Graham	Ross Matthew
Mrs. Lewis	Eleanor Gordon
A Policeman	Roderick Maybee
Sergeant	John Farrell

Act I.—Scenes 1 and 3—The Studio-Living-Room of the Wilsons'. 2—Approach to the Times Square Subway Station. Act II.—Scene 1—Room in the Hotel Esquire. 2—Studio-Living-Room. Act III.—Studio-Living-Room.

Staged by Eugene S. Bryden; settings by Paul Morrison.

Sam Wilson, being an expert on child psychology, suffers the illuminating experience of having his own 14-year-old daughter project herself into an adventure with a sailor who turns out to be decently clean-minded and helpful in an emergency. The Wilson daughter, Lucy, tags after a loose girl of the neighborhood. They find themselves in a hotel room with a couple of sailors. Lucy's choice, realizing that she is lying about her age, and having a young sister of his own, promptly takes Lucy home. There Lucy, to cover her shame, swears she has been plied with liquor and "seducted." A doctor is called and the truth comes out.

(Closed June 24, 1944)

364

HATS OFF TO ICE

(46 performances)

(Continuing)

A musical icetravaganza in two acts; lyrics and music by James Littlefield and John Fortis; musical arrangements by Paul Van Loan. Produced by Sonja Henie and Arthur M. Wirtz at the Center Theatre, New York, June 22, 1944.

Principals engaged—

Freddie Trenkler	Carol Lynne
Geoffe Stevens	Lucille Page
Rudy Richards	Claire Wilkins
Bob Ballard	Peggy Whight
James Caesar	Elouise Christine
Paul Castle	Jean Sturgeon
Culey Sisters	Brandt Sisters
Robert Uksila	Gretle Uksila
Pat Marshall	Andrei Kristopher
John Patterson	Everett Anderson
Don Loring Rogers	

Act I.—1—Overture. 2—Hats Off to Ice. 3—Little Red Riding Hood. 4—Double Vision. 5—Love Will Always Be the Same. 6—Sophisticated Lady. 7—Goddess of the Hunt. 8—Shore Leave. 9—The Boogie Woogie Bachelor. 10—They've Got What It Takes. 11—Bouncing Ball of Ice. 12—Isle of the Midnight Rainbow. Act II.—1—Entr'acte. 2—A Persian Legend. 3—Russian Rhythm. 4—The Skating Rileys. 5—The Lazy Q. 6—Pathway to the Stars. 7—Out of the Blue. 8—Cocktail Time in Rio. 9—Over the Jumps. 10—Nautical Nonsense. 11—Slavic Rhapsody. 12—G. I. Nuisance. 13—Here's Luck.

Staged by William H. Burke and Catherine Littlefield; skating directed by May Judels; music directed by David Mendoza; choreography by Catherine and Dorothie Littlefield; settings by Bruno Maine; costumes by Grace Houston; lighting by Eugene Braun.

TEN LITTLE INDIANS

(410 performances)

(Continuing)

A melodrama in three acts by Agatha Christie. Produced by Messrs. Shubert and Albert de Courville at the Broadhurst Theatre, New York, June 27, 1944.

Cast of characters—

Rogers	Neil Fitzgerald
Mrs. Rogers	Georgia Harvey
Fred Narracott	Patrick O'Connor
Vera Claythorne	Claudia Morgan
Philip Lombard	Michael Whalen
Anthony Marston	Anthony Kemble Cooper
William Blore	J. Pat O'Malley
General Mackenzie	Nicholas Joy
Emily Brent	Estelle Winwood
Sir Lawrence Wargrave	Halliwell Hobbes

Dr. Armstrong..................................Harry Worth
    Acts I, II and III.—Living Room of House on Indian Island, Off
the Coast of Devon, England.
    Staged by Albert de Courville; settings by Howard Bay.

Ten people are a little mysteriously summoned to a small
island off the coast of Devonshire, England. When they have
gathered together an equally mysterious phonograph is heard to
blare forth the news that each of them is known to have been
associated with the death of one or more persons at some previous
time, and are here to meet their proper fate. There is no escape.
A storm has isolated the island and put the telephone out of com-
mission. One by one they are shuffled off. As each death occurs
an Indian figurine topples off a mantelpiece. The last two selected victims, however, manage to solve the mystery and effect
their own escape. They are the romantic interest.

SCHOOL FOR BRIDES

(367 performances)

(Continuing)

A farce comedy in three acts by Frank Gill, Jr., and George
Carleton Brown. Produced by Howard Lang at the Royale
Theatre, New York, August 1, 1944.

Cast of characters—

    Charlie..John Sheehan
    Stephen Garrett...................................Charles Gary
    Julie ....Yolande Donlan
    Diane...Frances Charles
    Alice..Mary Best
    Joanne...Olivia Russell
    Leslie....................................Elizabeth Worthington
    Grace ....Darby Moore
    Jeff Connors ....Warren Ashe
    Stephanie ....Lucia Carroll
    Ronnie ....Joan Webster
    Suzan ....Kay Lawrence
    Vicki...Shirley Whitney
    Frederick M. Hasty...............................Roscoe Karns
    Dean Baxter (Constance King) ....Bernadene Hayes
    Mary...Ann Turner
    Acts I and III.—Drawing-Room of Stephen Garrett's Summer
Home on Long Island Sound. Act II.—Upstairs Bedroom of Garrett's Home.
    Staged by Harold Morton; settings by Ernest Glover.

Jeff Connors, promoter of an agency for models, sees a chance
to take money from a much-married-and-divorced playboy by
setting up his models as pupils in a school for brides and making
the playboy one of the professors. Bedroom jokes until curtain-
time. Then the playboy falls in love with a woman who promises to make a real good wife, instead of with one of his pupils.

CATHERINE WAS GREAT

(191 performances)

A comedy in a prologue and three acts by Mae West. Produced by Michael Todd at the Shubert Theatre, New York, August 2, 1944.

Cast of characters—

IN THE PROLOGUE

Jim	Hubert Long
Mike	Robert Strauss
Greg	Philip Huston
Roy	Mischa Tonken
Corporal Joe	Joel Ashley

Soldiers: Milton Gordon, Carl Bensen, Jack Burke, John Colby, Boyd de Brossard, Antony Fortune, Eddy Grove, William Skelton, Carl Specht.

IN THE PLAY

Count Nikolai Mirovich	Coburn Goodwin
Captain Dronsky	Philip Cary Jones
English Ambassador	Henry Vincent
Ambassador Choiseul	Owen Coll
Ambassador Murad Pasha	Don de Leo
Captain Danilov	Don Gibson
Alexis Orloff	Hubert Long
Count Panin	Charles Gerrard
Chief Chamberlain	John Stephen
Gregory Orloff	Philip Huston
Catherine II	Mae West
Prince Potemkin	Joel Ashley
Varvara	Elinor Counts
Florian	Ray Bourbon
Lieutenant Bunin	Gene Barry
Marshal Suvorov	John Parrish
Ivan VI	Michael Bey
Pugacheff	Bernard Hoffman
Innkeeper	Harry Bodin
Maurice	Leon Hamilton
Admiral Semechkin	William Malone
Semyonev	Victor Finney
Vanya	Frank Baxter
Chimneysweep	Lester "Red" Towne
Chechkofski	Dayton Lummis
Page Boys	Buddy and Dickie Millard

Ladies-in-Waiting: Edna Eckert, Michael Mauree, Mila Niemi, Gloria Pierre, Mary Reid, Gloria Brent.

Councillors: William C. Tubbs, Frank Stevens, Albert Bayne, Joseph Mann, Charles Hart, Robert Morse.

Chamberlains: Michael Spreder, Victor Finney.

Ushers: Dick Ellis, Reginald Allen.

Guards: George Anderson, Eden Burrows, Jerry Lucas, Richard Spohr, Raymond Stenzi, John Frederick.

Prologue.—A USO Recreation Room in U.S.A. Act I.—Scenes 1 and 3—Council Chamber in Winter Palace, St. Petersburg, Russia, 1762. 2—Royal Suite of Empress Catherine II. Act II.—Scenes 1 and 4—Royal Suite. 2—Inn Several Miles Outside St. Petersburg. 3—Court-Martial Room in Winter Palace. Act III.—Scenes 1 and 3—Royal Suite. 2—Fireplace in Room of Count Mirovich. 4—Secret Room of Ivan VI. 5—Council Chamber.

Staged by Roy Hargrave; settings by Howard Bay; costumes by Mary Percy Schenck and Ernest Schrapps; choreography by Margaret Sande.

In a USO recreation room somewhere in these United States
several of the boys are discussing history; the history of Russia
mostly and the part Catherine the Great played in it. They see
Catherine as a Diamond Lil in queenly costumes and lofty head-
dresses, moving through a gold-leafed Palace and picking handsome male companions wherever she finds them. As they let
their imaginations play on Catherine's possibilities as an aid to
the Army's entertainment the scene shifts to match their imaginations. Catherine does her bit for Russia and her best for the
Army—and Mae West.

(Closed January 13, 1945)

SPOOK SCANDALS

(2 performances)

The Michael Todd Midnight Players, members of the casts
of "Catherine Was Great," "Mexican Hayride" and "Pick-Up
Girl," presented "Spook Scandals," at the President Theatre,
New York, December 8, 1944. Songs and comic acts were added
to the program between three one-act plays: "The Gobi Curse"
by Arthur Gondra, "The Coffin Room" by Al Henderson and
"The Blind Monster" by Jerry Sylvon. Original music was by
Sergio De Karlo. The entertainment was conceived and directed
by Jerry Sylvon; choreography by Paul Haakon, Marta Nita and
Paul Reyes; lighting by Sammy Lambert. The cast included
Don de Leo, Gedda Petry, Al Henderson, Dean Myles, Mila
Niemi, Eva Reyes and Kendal Bryson.

(Closed December 9, 1944)

GOOD MORNING CORPORAL

(13 performances)

A comedy in three acts by Milton Herbert Gropper and Joseph
Shalleck. Produced by William B. Friedlander at the Playhouse,
August 8, 1944.

Cast of characters—

Corporal Rourke.....................................Joel Marston
Dottie Carson...................................Charita Bauer
Helen Moore...................................Frances Tannehill
O'Banion Broderick..............................Russell Hardie
A Man...Donald Foster
Alvin Stacey.......................................Lionel Wilson
   Acts I, II and III.—Dottie Carson's Apartment, New York City.
   Staged by William B. Friedlander; setting by Robert Barnhart.

Dottie Carson was service mad. She wanted to provide comfort and contentment for every fighting man she met. Her enthusiasm and misdirected patriotism got her married to a marine, a sailor and an army corporal. She met each of them in a gin mill and all three ceremonies were performed when the low contracting parties were tight. The marine and the sailor had their leaves canceled the day they discovered they were married, and were shortly thereafter reported missing. Before the corporal can settle down to married bliss with Dottie both his predecessors reappear. The question of marital priorities is freely discussed for three acts.

(Closed August 18, 1944)

THE TWO MRS. CARROLLS

(585 performances)

A drama in two acts by Martin Vale. Returned by Robert Reud and Paul Czinner to the Booth Theatre, New York (after six weeks' vacation), August 14, 1944.

Cast of characters—

Clemence	Michelette Burani
Pennington	Stiano Braggiotti
Sally	Elisabeth Bergner
Geoffrey	Onslow Stevens
Mrs. Latham	Margery Maude
Cecily Harden	Joan Wetmore
Dr. Tuttle	Leslie Barrie
Harriet	Grace Coppin

Act I.—Living Room in the Villa La Vista in the South of France.
Act II.—Scene 1—Living Room. 2—Sally's Bedroom.
Staged by Reginald Denham; settings by Frederick Fox; costumes by Grace Houston.

Produced originally at the Booth Theatre, New York, August 3, 1943, "The Two Mrs. Carrolls" ran all Summer and all Winter, being withdrawn July 1, 1944, so the company and Elisabeth Bergner, the star, could have a six-week rest. The engagement was resumed August 14, 1944.

(Closed February 3, 1945)

SONG OF NORWAY

(346 performances)
(Continuing)

An operetta in two acts by Milton Lazarus from a play by Homer Curran based on the life and music of Edvard Grieg;

music and lyrics adapted by Robert Wright and George Forrest;
orchestral and choral arrangements by Arthur Kay. Produced
by Edwin Lester at the Imperial Theatre, New York, August 21,
1944.

Cast of characters—

Sigrid	Janet Hamer
Einar	Kent Edwards
Eric	Robert Antoine
Gunnar	William Carroll
Grima	Patti Brady
Helga	Jackie Lee
Rikard Nordraak	Robert Shafer
Nina Hagerup	Helena Bliss
Edvard Grieg	Lawrence Brooks
Father Grieg	Walter Kingsford
Father Nordraak	Philip White
Mother Grieg	Ivy Scott
Freddy	Frederic Franklin
Count Peppi Le Loup	Sig Arno
Louisa Giovanni	Irra Petina
Members of the Faculty	Ewing Mitchell, Audrey Guard, Paul De Poyster
Inn Keeper	Lewis Bolvard
Frau Professor Norden	Doreen Wilson
Elvera	Sharon Randall
Hedwig	Karen Lund
Greta	Gwen Jones
Marghareta	Ann Andre
Hilda	Elizabeth Bockoven
Miss Anders	Sonia Orlova
Henrik Ibsen	Dudley Clements
Tito	Frederic Franklin
Maestro Pisoni	Robert Bernard
Butler	Cameron Grant
Adelina	Alexandra Danilova
Maid	Nora White
Signora Eleanora	Barbara Boudwin
Children	Sylvia Allen, Grace Carroll, Pat O'Rourke, Shannon Randolph

Dancing Peasants, Employees at Tito's, The Ballet of the Teatro
Reale, and Characters of the Fantasy by the Artist Personnel of The
Ballet Russe de Monte Carlo, Sergei J. Denham, Director, Alexandra
Danilova, Frederic Franklin, Nathalie Krassovska, Leon Daniellan,
Maria Tallchief, Ruthanna Boris, Alexander Goudovitch, Mary Ellen
Moylan, Serge Ismailoff, Anna Istomina, Nicholas Magallanes,
Michael Katcharoff, Julia Horvath, Peter Deign, Allan Banks, Her-
bert Bliss, Vida Brown, Alfredo Corvino, Pauline Goddard, Helen
Kramarr, Karel Shook, Gertruda Swobodina, Nikita Talin, Nora
White.

Singing Peasants, Guests and Faculty at Copenhagen and Guests
at the Villa Pincio.

By the Singing Ensemble of the Los Angeles and San Francisco
Civic Light Opera.

Act I.—Scene 1—Troldhaugen—Just Outside Bergen, Norway,
1860.   2—A Square on outskirts of Bergen.   Act II.—Scene 1—
Reception Room of Royal Conservatory, Copenhagen.   2—Tito's
Chocolate Shop, Rome.   3—Ballroom of Villa Pincio, Rome.   4—
Interior of Grieg Home, Troldhaugen.   5—The Song of Norway.

Staged by Charles K. Freeman; choreography by George Balanchine; music directed by Arthur Kay; production designed by
Lemuel Ayers; settings by Carl Kent; costumes by Robert Davison.

Edvard Grieg, the Norwegian composer, was a bit on the un-
ruly side, especially after he met Louisa Giovanni, a famous

prima donna from Rome, Italy. Edvard's wife, to whom he strove mightily to remain loyal, and his best friend, Rikard Nordraak, worked strenuously to keep him in line and in the end they were successful. Edvard remained true to his lady and to his country.

LOWER NORTH

(11 performances)

A comedy in three acts by Martin Bidwell. Produced by Max J. Jelin at the Belasco Theatre, New York, August 25, 1944.

Cast of characters—

Hank	Jerry Rand
Peterson	Frank Bradley
Sobieschyk	David Graham
Cochran	Dort Clark
Heath	Douglas Jones
Johnson	Dean King
Curley	Arthur Hunnicutt
Bruce	Robert Breton
Karnes	Eddie Waglin
Spadoni	Robert Myers
Jim	Kim Spalding
Pratzell	Rusty Lane
Phillips	Bob Lackaye
Barton	Charles Clancy
Mary	Sara Anderson
Johnny	John Farrell
Marine (Dress Blues)	Royal Rompel
Andy	Don Grusso
Frank	Phil Pine
Ruby	Blanche Faye
Pearl	Blanche Gladstone
Burks	Paul Ford
The Marine Sergeant	John Conway
Mr. Hines (Traveling Salesman)	Watson White
Phyllis	Cora Smith
Dorothy	Flora Knight
Messenger	Mitchell Ahrons

Act I.—Upper Deck of Group 1 School Building in a Naval Training Station. Act II.—The Rendezvous Bar. Act III.—The Cubicle Called Lower North.

Staged by David Burton; settings by Raymond Sovey.

Curley and Jim, Bruce, Spadoni and a bunch of the boys in training at a Naval Station have various adventures developing what it takes to become an honor to the service and a satisfaction to themselves. Jim "goes over the hill" to be with his wife, and would stay over the hill when he learns that she is going to make him a papa. The wife, Mary, talks him out of his rebellion and his pals at the station cover for him when he arrives late next day. Anyway, he didn't have to worry. Pratzell, the tough sergeant, really had a heart of gold. He wouldn't report a guy like Jim.

(Closed September 2, 1944)

ANNA LUCASTA

(343 performances)
(Continuing)

A drama in three acts by Philip Yordan. Presented by John Wildberg at the Mansfield Theatre, New York, August 30, 1944.

Cast of characters—

Katie	Theodora Smith
Stella	Rosetta LeNoire
Theresa	Georgia Burke
Stanley	John Proctor
Frank	Frederick O'Neal
Joe	George Randol
Eddie	Hubert Henry
Noah	Alvin Childress
Blanche	Alice Childress
Officer	Emory Richardson
Anna	Hilda Simms
Danny	Canada Lee
Lester	John Tate
Rudolf	Earle Hyman

Act I.—Scene 1—Lucasta Living Room, Pennsylvania, 1941. 2—Noah's Bar, Brooklyn. Act II.—Lucasta Living Room. Act III.—Scene 1—Lucasta Living Room. 2—Noah's Bar.

Staged by Harry Wagstaff Gribble; settings by Frederick Fox.

See page 260.

SLEEP NO MORE

(7 performances)

A farce in three acts by Lee Loeb and Arthur Strawn. Produced by Clyde Elliott at the Cort Theatre, New York, August 31, 1944.

Cast of characters—

George Slater	Raymond Bramley
Smithers	John "Skins" Miller
Harry Foster	John Kane
Diana Clark	Patricia Ryan
Millie Jenkins	Louise Larabee
H. Clifford Gates	Robert Armstrong
Mr. Riley	Len Hollister
William Jennings Brown	George Offerman, Jr.
Detective Sergeant Krump	G. Swayne Gordon
Mrs. Ridgeway	Doris Underwood
Oscar Ridgeway	Gerard Martin
Mr. McClellan	Horace Cooper
John B. Timmons	Ed Latimer

Act I.—George's Barber Shop. Acts II and III.—The "New" Offices of H. Clifford Gates and Associates.

Staged by Cledge Roberts; settings by A. A. Ostrander.

H. Clifford Gates, a crooked promoter of goofy inventions, takes on the exploitation of a pill that banishes sleep. This is the discovery of William Jennings Brown of Indiana, who, to demonstrate that his no-sleep pellet is effective, takes one a day for six days and remains wide awake and noisy. When nature finally rebels, and Brown falls asleep in the midst of an important sale, the jig's up and the curtain's down.

(Closed September 4, 1944)

LAST STOP

(23 performances)

A comedy in two acts by Irving Kaye Davis. Produced by Victor Hugo-Vidal at the Barrymore Theatre, New York, September 5, 1944.

Cast of characters—

Mrs. Sheppard	Frederica Going
Mrs. Chubb	Enid Markey
Rev. Mr. Cummings	William Hughes
Mrs. Manning	Mary Gildea
Mrs. Hollister	Nell Harrison
Mrs. Miller	Daisy Belmore
Mrs. Smith	Laurie McVicker
Mrs. Dingman	Mary Perry
Mrs. Fitzpatrick	Grace Valentine
Mrs. Baldwin	Augusta French
Mrs. Mabledoor	Eda Heineman
Walter	Seth Arnold
Catherine Chandler	Catharine Doucet
Mr. Cook	Gregory Robins
Mrs. Anna Haines	Minnie Dupree
Howard Haines	Raymond Bailey
Isabel Haines	Mavis Freeman
Mary Stevens	Effie Afton
Mr. White	Robert Stewart
State Trooper	Clark Poth
Reporter	Alan Brock

Acts I and II.—Parlor of an Old Ladies' Home.
Staged by Irwin Piscator; setting by Sam Leve; costumes by Rose Bogdanoff.

Catherine Chandler, proprietress of an Old Ladies' Home, would add to her ill-gotten profits by selling the property to a night club promoter and moving her charges to a firetrap location previously prepared. Mrs. Anna Haines, suspecting the worst, organizes her fellow inmates in rebellion against the conspirator, digs up various nefarious acts with which to confront the Chandler woman, and finally takes charge of the home in the interest of her supporters.

(Closed September 23, 1944)

THE DAY WILL COME

(20 performances)

A drama in three acts by Leo Birinski. Produced by Harry Green at the National Theatre, New York, September 7, 1944.

Cast of characters—

Baranova	D. J. Thompson
Shura	James Dobson
Artamon	Bruce Halsey
Fyodor Semionitch	John Paul
Marpha	Jan Sherwood
Parasha	Camila Ashland
Nikita	John F. Hamilton
Moshko	Sterling Mace
Kolya	Ronnie Jacoby
Anushka	Lenore Thomas
Avrum Dovid	Harry Green
Karl	Frederick Coe
Franz	Richard Bolton
General Von Bruck	Arthur Vinton
Captain Birkenbach	Ronald Alexander
Sergeant	William Forrest
General Gensler	Stephen Roberts
General Ziemsen	Bernard Pate
General Von Hoff	William Pringle
Adolf Hitler	Brandon Peters

Peasants and Villagers: The Misses Agnes McCarthy, Inez Spear, Chiquita Gomez, Lizzie Cubitt, Barbara Brooks, Doris Deane, Joan Lovinger, Renee Renay, Helene Fenwick, Olga Alexander, Vera Alexander and Alma Larsen. Messrs. Francis Ballard, David L. Green, Roland Green, John Alexanderson, Arthur Villars, Peter Barbier, Harold Wagenheim, Mike Carter, Frederic Faber, Martin Pierce, John Hewitt, John Zack, Steve Borris.

Acts I, II and III.—A Russian Isba.

Staged by Lee Elmore; setting by Frederick Fox.

Avrum Dovid, who might be the legendary Wandering Jew, is the patriarch of a Russian village who stays behind when everyone else flees before the advancing Hitler and his destroyers. Assuming, by inference, the virtues of a reincarnated Nostradamus, the old Jew advises Hitler to beware the snows of Moscow. There is a debate, in which Hitler explains his hatred of the Jews as being due to their having given birth to Christianity, and the patriarch speaks eloquently for the claims of humanity. The patriarch is executed by the Germans, only to reappear as an apparition before which Hitler succumbs to madness.

(Closed September 23, 1944)

NEW YORK CITY CENTER OF MUSIC AND DRAMA

HARRIET

(11 performances)

A comedy in three acts by Florence Ryerson and Colin Clements. Revived by Gilbert Miller at City Center, New York, September 27, 1944.

Cast of characters—

Auntie Zeb	Alberta Perkins
Henry Ward Beecher	Richard Wilder
Catherine Beecher	Jane Seymour
Harriet Beecher Stowe	Helen Hayes
Calvin Stowe	Robert Emhardt
William Beecher	John Hayes
Edward Beecher	Ralph Stantley
Mary Beecher Perkins	Martha Jones
Thomas Beecher	Archie Smith
Isabella Beecher	Ethel Craft
James Beecher	Val Wrenne
Dr. Lyman Beecher	Robert Harrison
Mr. Tuttle	Henry Craig Neslo
Mr. Wycherly	Elmer Lehr
Celestine	Mildred Taswell
Freddie Stowe (as a child)	Peter Griffith
Mrs. Hobbs	Virginia Dyer
Freddie Stowe (as a young man)	Ralph Douglas
Georgie Stowe	Jean Lewis
Hatty Stowe	Phyllis Rene Campbell
Eliza Stowe	Lenore Wade
Jerusha Pantry	John O'Connor
Lowell Denton	Robert North
Sukey	Edna Thomas
Haley	Benedict MacQuarrie
Jane	Philippa Bevans

Act I.—The Stowe Cottage, Cincinnati, Ohio, 1830. Act II.—The Stowe House, New Brunswick, Maine, 1850. Act III.—The Stowe Mansion, Andover, Massachusetts, 1861.

Staged by Elia Kazan; settings by Lemuel Ayers; costumes by Aline Bernstein.

"Harriet" ran for 377 performances, starting March 3, 1943, at the Henry Miller Theatre, New York.

(Closed October 5, 1944)

THE MERRY WIDOW

(32 performances)

An operetta in three acts, adapted by Sidney Sheldon and Ben Roberts, with new musical version by Robert Stoltz and lyrics by Adrian Ross, from the original by Victor Leon and Leo Stein, with music by Franz Lehar. Presented by Yolanda Mero-Irion and the New Opera Company at City Center, New York, October 7, 1944.

Cast of characters—

The King	John Harrold
Popoff	Karl Farkas
Jolidon	Nils Landin
Natalie	Xenia Bank
Olga Bardini	Lucy Hillary
General Bardini	Gordon Dilworth
Novakovich	Alan Vaughan
Cascada	Dennis Dengate
Khadja	Alfred Porter
Guests	Connie Clark, Ward Richard
Nish	Norman Budd
Sonia Sadoya	Marta Eggerth
Prince Danilo	Jan Kiepura
Clo-Clo	Lisette Verea
Lo-Lo	Annette Norman
Frou-Frou	Mary Broussard
Do-Do	Babs Heath
Margot	Alice Borbus
Jou-Jou	Annette Norman
Première Danseuses	Babs Heath, Nina Popova
Premier Dancer	Jack Gansert
Gaston	John Harrold

Act I.—Scene 1—Prologue. 2—The Marsovian Embassy in Paris, 1906. Act II.—Grounds of Sonia's House, near Paris. Act III.—Maxim's Restaurant, Paris.

Staged by Felix Brentano; music directed by Fritz Zweig; choreography by George Balanchine; settings by Howard Bay; costumes by Walter Florell.

A revival of "The Merry Widow" was staged at Carnegie Hall the Summer of 1942, with Wilbur Evans the Danilo and Helen Gleason the Sonia. Before that there had been revivals in 1929, with Beppe de Vries and Evan Thomas, and in 1931, with Alice McKenzie and Donald Brian.

(Closed November 4, 1944)

THE NEW YORK CITY SYMPHONY

The New York City Symphony under the direction of Leopold Stokowski began the season at the City Center October 9, 1944. "Children's Christmas Story," a production conceived by Stokowski, including a narration of biblical events by Augustun Duncan, a Collegiate Chorale of sixty voices under the direction of Robert Shaw and a pantomime enacted by 55 New York City school children, was presented December 21, 23 and 24, 1944. The production was designed by Robert Edmond Jones and lighted by Hans Sondheimer. The children were directed by Anita Zahn. At Easter Stokowski offered Bach's "St. Matthew Passion." The Collegiate Chorale intoned the concerted numbers and the Narrator was Joseph Laderoute.

The New York City Center Opera Company, founded and organized by Laszlo Halasz, started its Fall season November 9, 1944, and continued for three weeks.

MANON LESCAUT

(2 performances)

An opera in four acts, after the book by Marcel Prevost; music by G. Puccini. Presented by The New York Center Opera Company at City Center, New York, November 9 and 16, 1944.

Cast of characters—

```
Manon Lescaut....................................Dorothy Kirsten
Lescaut, Sergeant of the King's Guards...........John DeSurra
The Chevalier Des Grieux..........Norbert Ardelli, William Horne
Geronte De Ravoir, Treasurer-General................Ralph Telasko
Edmondo, a Student...........................Thomas Hayward
The Innkeeper..................................Rudy Trautman
A Singer.......................................Helen LeClaire
The Dancing-Master................Eduardo Rael, Arthur Ulisse
A Lamplighter...................Emanuel Kazaras, Edward Visca
    Act I.—Amiens.  Act II.—Paris.  Act III.—Havre.  Act IV.—
America.
    Staged by Jose Ruben; music directed by Laszlo Halasz.
```

LA BOHEME

(4 performances)

An opera in four acts by Puccini. Presented at City Center, November 10, 17, 21 and 24, 1944.

Cast of characters—

```
Mimi..........................Dorothy Kirsten, Irma Gonzalez
Musetta.......................Marguerita Piazza, Natalie Bodanya
Rodolfo.........................William Horne, Mario Berini
Marcello.......................................John DeSurra
Schaunard........................Edward Rael, Emile Renan
Colline.........................Carleton Gauld, Ralph Telasko
Benoit    )
Alcindoro )  ·····································Paul Dennis
    Acts I and IV.—Attic Studio on Montmartre.  Act II.—Café
Momus.  Act III.—At the Gate of Paris.
    Staged by Jose Ruben; music directed by Laszlo Halasz.
```

CAVALLERIA RUSTICANA

(3 performances)

A melodrama in one act by G. Targioni-Tozetti and G. Menasci; music by P. Mascagni. Presented at City Center, New York, November 11, 19 and 25, 1944.

Cast of characters—

```
Santuzza..................................Mobley Lushanya
Turiddu........................Eric Rowton, Thomas Hayward
Alfio...........................................Francis Row
Lola..........................................Alice Howland
Mamma Lucia....................Mary Kreste, Carroll Taussig
    Scene—A Sicilian Village.
    Staged by William Wymetal; music directed by Jean Morel.
```

PAGLIACCI

(3 performances)

A drama in two acts by R. Leoncavallo. Presented at City
Center, November 11, 19 and 25, 1944.

Cast of characters—

Nedda......................Irma Gonzalez, Natalie Bodanya
Canio......................Eric Rowton, Norbert Ardelli
Tonio......................John de Surra, Jess Walters
Silvio......................Eduardo Rael
Beppo......................Romolo de Spirito, Arthur Ulisse
    Acts I and II.—A Calabrian Village.
    Staged by William Wymetal; music by Jean Morel.

LA TRAVIATA

(3 performances)

An opera in four acts by Giuseppe Verdi. Presented at City
Center, New York, November 12, 19 and 25, 1944.

Cast of characters—

Violetta Valery......................Dorothy Kirsten
Alfred Germont......................Mario Berini
George Germont......................Jess Walters, George Czaplicki
Flora Bervoix......................Marjorie King
Annina......................Blanche Archembault, Harriet Greene
Gaston de Letorieres......................Arthur Ulisse
Baron Douphol......................Emanuel Kazaras
Marquis D'Orgibny......................Edward Visca
Doctor Grenville......................Alexander Lorber, Paul Dennis
Solo Dancers......................Pilar Gomez and Giovanni Rozzino
    Act I.—Terrace of Violetta's Mansion, Paris, 1850. Act II.—A
Villa Near Paris. Act III.—Ballroom in Flora's Mansion. Act
IV.—Violetta's Bedroom.
    Staged by Jose Ruben; music directed by Jean Morel; choreog-
raphy, Helene Platova.

TOSCA

(3 performances)

An opera in three acts by V. Sardou, L. Illica and G. Giacosa
music by G. Puccini. Presented at City Center, November 15
19 and 26, 1944.

Cast of characters—

Floria Tosca......................Frances Cassard
Mario Cavaradossi......................Mario Berini
Baron Scarpia......................George Czaplicki
Cesare Angelotti......................Ralph Telasko
Spoletta......................Paul Dennis
A Sacristan......................Emil Renan, Stanley Carlson
Sciarrone......................Emanuel Kazaras
Gaoler......................Alexander Lorber

A Shepherd-Boy, Roberti, Executioner, a Cardinal, a Judge, a
Scribe, an Officer, a Sergeant, Soldiers, Police Agents, Ladies,
Nobles, Citizens, Artisans, etc.
Act I.—Interior of a Church in Rome. Act II.—Scarpia's Study.
Act III.—Citadel of San Angelo.
Staged by William Wymetal; music directed by Laszlo Halasz.

THE GYPSY BARON

(11 performances)

An opera in three acts and prologue revised and adapted to
English by George Mead; music by Johann Strauss. Presented
at City Center, New York, November 14, 18, 22, 25 and from
November 28 to December 3, 1944.

Cast of characters—

Barinkay...William Horne
Saffi...Polyna Stoska
Czipra.........................Alice Howland, Elizabeth Wysor
Arsena....................Marjorie King, Marguerite Piazza
Zsupan...Stanley Carlson
Ottokar.........................Arthur Ulisse, Thomas Hayward
Carnero..............................Paul Dennis, Emile Renan
Count Homonnay...................................Carlton Gauld
Solo Dancers.................{ Ruth Harris (Czardas and Waltz)
                            { Tashamira (Gypsy dances)
    Villagers, Gypsies, Hussars, Vivandieres, Soldiers, Citizens,
Town-folk, etc.
    Prologue.—Ballroom in Royal Palace in Budapest. Act I.—
Transylvanian Countryside. Act II.—Gypsy Encampment Near
Ruins of Barinkay's Castle. Act III.—Public Square in Vienna.
    Staged by William Wymetal; music directed by Thomas Martin.

The first anniversary of the New York City Center, celebrated
December 11, 1944, included a piano program by Jose Iturbi.

LITTLE WOMEN

(23 performances)

A play in three acts by Marian de Forest, based on Louisa
May Alcott's novel. Revived by Eddie Dowling at City Center,
New York, December 12, 1944.

Cast of characters—

Jo...Mary Welch
Meg..Margot Stevenson
Amy...Susana Garnett
Beth...Frances Reid
Mrs. March.......................................Velma Royton
Hannah..Valerie Valaire
John Brooke.......................................Clark Williams
Laurie...John Ruth
Mr. Laurence.....................................Harrison Dowd
Aunt March..Grace Mills
Mr. March...David Lewis
Professor Bhaer..................................Herbert Berghof

Acts I, II and III.—Sitting Room of the March Home in Concord, Massachusetts.
Staged by Jessie Royce Landis assisted by Gus Shirmer Jr.

(Closed December 30, 1944)

THE CHERRY ORCHARD

(8 performances)

A comedy in four acts by Anton Chekov; translated by Irina Skariatina. Revived by Carly Wharton and Margaret Webster at the City Center, New York, January 1, 1945.

Cast of characters—

Lopahin (Yermolay Alexeyevitch).....................John Bleifer
Dunyasha (a maid)................................Fiona O'Shiel
Epihodov...A. P. Kaye
Firs (an old valet)................................Horace Sinclair
Anya (daughter of Lyubov Andreyevna)................Lois Hall
Varya (adopted daughter of Lyubov Andreyevna)..Carmen Mathews
Lyubov Andreyevna (the owner of the Cherry Orchard)
                                                    Eva LeGallienne
Leonid Andreyevitch (her brother).............Joseph Schildkraut
Charlotta Ivanovna (a governess)..................Leona Roberts
Her Dog...Touche
Semyonov-Pistchik (a landowner)...............Samuel Goldenberg
Yasha (a young footman)..........................Kenneth Tobey
Petya Trofimov (a student).....................Hugh Franklin
A Tramp...Bruce Adams
The Station Master..............................Robert Hartung
A Post Office Clerk.................................Jack Lynds
                                             ⎰ Madeleine L'Engle
Servants and Guests......................... ⎨ Cavada Humphrey
                                             ⎪ Anne Jackson
                                             ⎱ Howard Patnode

Staged by Eva LeGallienne; settings by Motley.
Acts I and IV.—The Old Nursery. Estate of Lyubov Andreyevna.
Act II.—The Open Country. Act III.—Living Room.

"The Cherry Orchard" was produced by Carly Wharton and Margaret Webster at the National Theatre, New York, January 1, 1944, and played 96 performances before beginning an extensive road tour.

(Closed January 6, 1945)

LA VIE PARISIENNE

(37 performances)

An operetta in three acts by Jacques Offenbach with English libretto by Felix Brentano and Louis Verneuil; musical version by Antal Dorati; lyrics by Marian Farquhar. Revived by Yolanda Mero Irion for the New Opera Company at City Center, New York, January 12, 1945.

Cast of characters—

Stationmaster....................................Phillip George
Policeman..Roy Ballard
Newsboy.....................................Irene E. Sherrock
Flower-Girl.....................................Loretta Schere
Comte Raoul de Gardefeu, a rich nobleman........Brian Lawrence
Baron Bobinet, his friend.......................Edward Roecker
Metella, a famous opera singer...................Marion Carter
Gontran, a man about town.......................Lee Edwards
Jackson, trainer of Mr. Hutchinson's race horses....David Morris
Evelyn, Mr. Hutchinson's daughter...............Lillian Andersen
Mr. Hutchinson, an American millionaire..........Arthur Newman
Première Danseuses...........................{ Anna Istomina
                                             { Elena Kramarr
Premier Dancer.................................James Lyons
Custom Inspectors...........................{ Nicholas J. Insardi
                                            { Sylvan Evans
Gabrielle, a modiste...........................Frances Watkins
Alphonse, Gardefeu's butler........................Lee Edwards
Delivery People: George Bakos, Doris M. Sward, Bonnie Murray,
    Jeannette Weise.
Chorus: Louise Barnhart, Charlotte Cheney, June Dunn, Patricia
    Glennon, Rosalind Guest, Jean Mary Lawrence, Millicent Lewis,
    Bonnie Murray, Flora Previn, Loretta Schere, Irene E. Sher-
    rock, Doris M. Sward, Jeannette Weise, Mary Lou Wallace,
    George Bakos, Roy Ballard, Salvatore Cosentino, William Peen
    Bradford, Sylvan Evans, Nicholas J. Insardi, John J. Girt,
    William G. Schwarz, Barkev Vartanyan, Phillip George.
Ballet: Jeanne Reeves, Jane Kiser, Irene Larson, Aline Dubois,
    Gloria Morgan, Jane Rattinger, Kirra LeHachova, Deanne Ben-
    more, Elmer Maddox, Julian Mitchell, Stephen Billings, Rex
    Harrower.
Railroad Employees, Travelers, Tradespeople, Servants, Waiters,
    Guests at the Cafe Anglais, etc.
Act I.—A railway Station, Paris. Act II.—Scene 1—Salon at
Gardefeu's House. 2—Banquet Room at Café Anglais. Act III.—
Gardefeu's Salon.
    Staged by Ralph Herbert; choreography by Leonide Massine;
music directed by Antal Dorati; choral direction by Irving Landau;
settings by Richard Rychtarik; costumes by Ladislas Czettel.

Arthur Mahoney and Thalia Mara gave a dance recital at City
Center, New York, February 11, 1945. They danced "La Valse
Viennoise—Preview," "Gonna See My Gal," "Jota Aragonesa"
and "Love Song." The lighting was by Frederick Kiesler and
costumes were by Marco Monetdoro.

Paul Draper, tap dancer, and Larry Adler, harmonica virtuoso,
gave nine performances at City Center between Christmas and
New Year's. Mr. Adler presented one première performance,
the "Sailor's Song," written for the occasion by Darius Milhaud.

YOU CAN'T TAKE IT WITH YOU

(17 performances)

A farcical comedy in three acts by Moss Hart and George S.
Kaufman. Revived by Frank McCoy at City Center, March 26,
1945.

Cast of characters—

Penelope Sycamore	Daisy Atherton
Essie	Dorothy Stone
Rheba	Eula Belle Moore
Paul Sycamore	John Souther
Mr. De Pinna	Donald Keyes
Ed	Lance Cunard
Donald	Charles Benjamin
Martin Vanderhof	Fred Stone
Alice	Lucille Marsh
Henderson	Edward Kreisler
Tony Kirby	Richard Maloy
Boris Kolenkhov	Charles Collins
Gay Wellington	Emma Bunting
Mr. Kirby	John Clubley
Mrs. Kirby	Dorothy Scott
Three Men	Spencer Sawyer / Charles Foley / George McLain
Olga	Ulla Kazanova

Acts I, II and III.—Home of Martin Vanderhof, New York.
Staged by Frank McCoy; setting by Harry Gordon Bennett.

"You Can't Take It with You" opened at the Booth Theatre, New York, December 14, 1936, and ran for 837 performances. The original cast included Josephine Hull as Penelope Sycamore, Henry Travers as Martin Vanderhof and Paula Trueman as Essie.

(Closed April 7, 1945)

CARMEN JONES

(21 performances)

A musical comedy in two acts and five scenes based on Meilhac and Halévy's adaptation of Prosper Merimée's "Carmen"; music by George Bizet with new orchestral arrangements by Robert Russell Bennett. Revived by Billy Rose at City Center, New York, May 2, 1945.

Cast of characters—

Corporal Morrell	Robert Clarke
Foreman	George Willis
Cindy Lou	Elton J. Warren or Carlotta Franzell
Sergeant Brown	Jack Carr
Joe	LeVern Hutcherson or Napoleon Reed
Carmen	Muriel Smith or Inez Matthews
Sally	Sibol Cain
T-Bone	Edward Roche
Tough Kid	Carlos Van Putten
Drummer	Cosy Cole
Bartender	Maithe Marshall
Waiter	Edward Christopher
Myrt	June Hawkins
Frankie	Theresa Merritte
Rum	John Bubbles
Dink	Ford Buck
Boy	Bill O'Neil
Girl	Erona Harris

```
Husky  Miller.....................................Glenn  Bryant
Dancing  Girl....................................Ruth  Crumpton
Poncho..........................................Elijah  Hodges
Bullet  Head.......................................Lee  Allen
    Act  I.—Scene  1—Outside  Parachute  Factory  Near  Southern
Town.  2—Roadside.  3—Billy  Pastor's  Café.  Act  II.—Scene  1—
Terrace,  Meadowland  Country  Club,  Chicago.  2—Outside  Sport
Stadium.
    Staged  by  Hassard  Short;  libretto  directed  by  Charles  Friedman;
choreography  by  Eugene  Loring;  choral  direction  by  Robert  Shaw;
music  directed  by  David  Mordecai;  setting  by  Howard  Bay;  cos-
tumes  by  Raoul  Pene  DuBois.
```

The original production opened December 2, 1943, and ran for 503 performances.

OTHELLO

(24 performances)

A tragedy by William Shakespeare adapted to two acts and eight scenes by Margaret Webster with music by Tom Bennett. Revived by The Theatre Guild in association with John Haggott at City Center, New York, May 22, 1945.

Cast of characters—

```
Roderigo.........................................Don  Keefer
Iago.............................................Jose  Ferrer
Brabantio.....................................Francis  Compton
Othello..........................................Paul  Robeson
Cassio..........................................Ralph  Clanton
Duke............................................Louis  Lytton
Lodovico........................................Philip  Huston
1st  Senator....................................Ronald  Bishop
2d  Senator.......................................Ted  Yaryan
3d  Senator....................................Francis  Letton
A  Messenger...................................Stockman  Barner
Desdemona.........................................Uta  Hagen
Montano........................................Angus  Cairns
1st  Soldier  at  Cyprus.........................Jay  Brassfield
2d  Soldier  at  Cyprus.........................Ronald  Bishop
3d  Soldier  at  Cyprus........................William  Browder
Emilia...........................................Edith  King
Bianca.........................................Nan  McFarland
Gratiano.......................................Louis  Lytton
    Senators,  soldiers,  servants  and  citizens—Barbara  Anderson,  Vir-
ginia  Mattis,  John  Granger,  Leonard  Klein,  Robert  Leser,  Robinson
Stone,  William  Sandy,  Daniel  Cullitan.
    Act  I.—Scene  1—Venice  Street.  2—Council  Chamber.  3—Cyprus
Seaport.  4—Castle  in  Cyprus.  Act  II.—Scene  1—Castle  in  Cyprus.
2—Room  in  Castle.  3—Street  in  Cyprus.  4—Bedroom  in  Cyprus.
    Staged  by  Margaret  Webster;  setting  and  lighting  by  Robert
Edmond  Jones.
```

The Theatre Guild-Margaret Webster production of "Othello" closed at the Shubert Theatre, New York, July 1, 1945, after a run of 296 performances. The above cast is practically the same as the original.

(Closed June 10, 1945)

DOWN TO MIAMI

(8 performances)

A comedy in three acts by Conrad Westervelt. Produced by Edgar MacGregor at the Ambassador Theatre, New York, September 11, 1944.

Cast of characters—

Torrence Applegate	Herbert Heyes
Mrs. Applegate	Merle Maddern
Rufus Applegate	Charles Lang
Helen Gunston	Lyn Logan
Stella	Anna Franklin
Morris Mandel	Robert Leonard
Mrs. Mandel	Dora Weissman
Harry Katz	John Gould
Gloria Mandel	Elaine Ellis
Lois	Robert Strauss
Waiter	Zac Caully
Michael O'Hara	Brian O'Mara

Act I.—The Terrace Breakfast Room, Rooney Square Hotel, Miami Beach, Florida. Act II.—Lounging Room of a Private Bathing Suite. Act III.—The Mandel Suite.

Staged by J. B. Daniels; settings by Stewart Chaney; production supervised by Macurdy Hilliard.

The Applegates and the Mandels, vacationing in Miami, continue a racial and business feud until the Mandel girl gets the Applegate boy, whereupon everybody makes up.

(Closed September 16, 1944)

STAR TIME

(120 performances)

A vaudeville show assembled and presented by Paul Small at the Majestic Theatre, New York, September 12, 1944.

Principals engaged—

Lou Holtz	Benny Fields
Tony de Marco	Sally de Marco
Berry Brothers	Whitson Brothers
Armand Cortez	Shirley Dennis
Jimmy Mulcay	Mildred Mulcay
George Prospery	Francine Bordeau

(Closed December 9, 1944)

WHILE THE SUN SHINES

(39 performances)

A comedy in three acts by Terence Rattigan. Produced by Max Gordon at the Lyceum Theatre, New York, September 19, 1944.

Cast of characters—

Horton...J. P. Wilson
The Earl of Harpenden...........................Stanley Bell
Lieutenant Mulvaney...............................Lewis Howard
Lady Elizabeth Randall...............................Anne Burr
The Duke of Ayr and Stirling...................Melville Cooper
Lieutenant Colbert...............................Alexander Ivo
Mabel Crum.......................................Cathleen Cordell
   Acts I, II and III.—Sitting Room of Lord Harpenden's Chambers
in The Albany, London, England.
   Staged by George S. Kaufman; setting by Edward Gilbert.

The Earl of Harpenden, about to marry Lady Elizabeth Randall, would turn his former mistress, Mabel Crum, over to Lieutenant Mulvaney, a Yank in Britain he had met at a night club. The Lieutenant is willing, but mistakes Lady Elizabeth for the proffered Mabel and immediately makes such desperate love to her that her Ladyship begins to doubt if she really loves the Earl. The doubt is sustained until Mabel magnanimously resolves the issue.

(Closed October 21, 1944)

THE ODDS ON MRS. OAKLEY

(24 performances)

A farce in two acts by Harry Segall. Produced by Robert Reud at the Cort Theatre, New York, October 2, 1944.

Cast of characters—

Oliver Oakley......................................John Archer
Susan Oakley..Joy Hodges
The Professor...............................Morton L. Stevens
Eddie..Ben Laughlin
Dennie.......................................Hildegarde Halliday
Gladys...Virginia Reed
Sam..Allen Kearns
Louie..John Effrat
La Verne..Betty E. Haynes
Jim..Don Darcy
Jim's Wife..Sally Gabler
Howard Stickney..............................Bruce MacFarlane
   Act I.—Scenes 1 and 3—The Oakleys' Apartment, New York
City.   2—Turf Club Cocktail Lounge at Race Track.   Act II.—
Turf Club Cocktail Lounge.
   Staged by Arthur Sircom; settings by Frederick Fox.

When Oliver and Susan Oakley decide to separate and divide their household accumulations they agree that Fanny, a race horse they had won at a raffle, shall belong alternately to each of them, running three months for Oliver and then three months for Susan. Fanny, a sensitive and loyal animal of feminist leanings, proceeds to win for Susan and lose consistently for Oliver. Race track conspirators attempt to capitalize on Fanny's changing moods. Susan wagers her chastity on Fanny and loses, but her would-be seducer proves a good sport. The Oakleys are reconciled.

(Closed October 21, 1944)

MEN TO THE SEA

(23 performances)

A drama in three acts by Herbert Kubly. Produced by Dave Wolper at the National Theatre, New York, October 3, 1944.

Cast of characters—

Hazel	Maggie Gould
Christabel	Toni Gilman
Nic	Joe Verdi
Madame Mosh	Grace Mills
Julie	Joyce Mathews
Bonnie	Susana Garnett
Joe Foster	Tom Noonan
Duckworth	Randolph Echols
Brophy	Richard Camp
Chauncey	Michael Strong
Reuben	Maurice Ellis
Howard Moore	James Alexander
Hyacinth	Mildred Smith
French Sailor	James Elliott
Dick Graham	Frank Etherton
Hughes	Bill Hunt
Tall Girl	Mary Jean Copeland
Red	Marguerite Clifton
Harry	Paul Crabtree

Act I.—Scenes 1, 2 and 4—Christabel's Room on First Floor of Rooming House, Brooklyn, in September of a War Year. 3—Hazel's Room. Act II.—Scene 1—Hazel's Room, Christmas Eve. 2—Gun Tub on Deck of Destroyer *Christabel*. Act III.—Christabel's Room, the following June.

Staged by Eddie Dowling; settings and lighting by Howard Bay; costumes by Grace Houston.

Duckworth, a youthful philosopher in command of a gun crew in the Navy, and his young wife, Christabel, are living in a loosely run boarding house hard by the Brooklyn Navy Yard. In the same house four other sailors' wives are quartered. While their men are at sea the wives revert to type. Christabel bears her mate a child, and temporarily loses her reason when news of his death reaches her. Two of the wives defend their right to a limited promiscuity in trying to conquer their devastating loneliness. One, a colored girl, remains steadfast to her vows. Another, whose husband left her at the altar to run for his ship, flirts innocently with a nerve-shocked Britisher. While a drunken drinking party is staged on Christmas Eve in Brooklyn, the husbands are being shot up on their destroyer at sea. Pretty confusing, and pretty sad.

(Closed October 21, 1944)

SOLDIER'S WIFE

(253 performances)

A play in three acts by Rose Franken. Produced by William Brown Meloney at the Golden Theatre, New York, October 4, 1944.

Cast of characters—

Katherine Rogers.................................Martha Scott
Florence Lane....................................Frieda Inescort
John Rogers......................................Myron McCormick
Alexander Craig..................................Glenn Anders
Peter Gray.......................................Lili Darvas
Acts I, II and III.—Rogers Apartment, Manhattan.
Staged by Rose Franken; setting by Raymond Sovey.

See page 224.

(Closed May 12, 1945)

BLOOMER GIRL

(294 performances)
(Continuing)

A musical comedy in two acts, adapted by Sig Herzig and Fred Saidy from a play by Lilith and Dan James; music by Harold Arlen; lyrics by E. Y. Harburg; orchestrations by Russell Bennett. Produced by John C. Wilson in association with Nat Goldstone at the Shubert Theatre, New York, October 5, 1944.

Cast of characters—

Serena...Mabel Taliaferro
Octavia..Pamela Randell
Lydia..Claudia Jordan
Julia..Toni Hart
Phoebe...Carol MacFarlane
Delia..Nancy Douglass
Daisy..Joan McCracken
Horatio..Matt Briggs
Gus..John Call
Evelina..Celeste Holm
Joshua Dingle....................................Robert Lyon
Herman Brasher...................................William Bender
Ebenezer Mimms...................................Joe E. Marks
Wilfred Thrush...................................Vaughn Trinnier
Hiram Crump......................................Dan Gallagher
Dolly..Margaret Douglass
Jeff Calhoun.....................................David Brooks
Paula..Lee Barrie
Prudence...Eleanor Jones
Hetty..Arlene Anderson
Betty..Eleanor Winter
Hamilton Calhoun.................................Blaine Cordner
Pompey...Dooley Wilson
Sheriff Quimby...................................Charles Howard
1st Deputy.......................................John Byrd
2nd Deputy.......................................Joseph Florestano

```
3rd  Deput y......................................Ralph  Sassano
Augustus.........................................Hubert  Dilworth
Alexander.........................................Richard  Huey
State  Official.........................................John  Byrd
Governor  Newton..................................Butler  Hixon
```
Act I.—Scene 1—Conservatory, Applegate Mansion, Cicero Falls,
New York, a Small Manufacturing Town, 1861. 2—Bathroom.
3—The Lily. 4—Hedge Outside Applegate Estate. 5—The Yellow
Pavilion. 6—Applegate Garden. Act II.—Scene 1—Village Green.
2—Corridor of Town Jail. 3—Stage of Cicero Falls Opera House.
4—Conservatory.
Staged by E. Y. Harburg; book directed by William Schorr;
music directed by Leon Leonardi; choreography by Agnes de Mille;
settings and lighting by Lemuel Ayers; costumes by Miles White.

Evelina, sixth daughter of Horatio Applegate, manufacturer of
ladies' hoopskirts in Cicero Falls, New York, rebels against her
father's decree that she shall marry a hoopskirt salesman, as her
five sisters have obediently done before her. To make her rebellion complete Evelina joins her aunt, Dolly Bloomer, in a
campaign to put pantalettes on all women, even before they get
the vote. Evelina also supports her radical aunt as an abolition-
ist, which complicates matters when she (Evi) falls in love with
a handsome young Southern slaveholder, Jefferson Calhoun. Love
and duets win the day.

MEET A BODY

(24 performances)

A murder-mystery comedy in three acts by Jane Hinton.
Produced by H. Clay Blaney at the Forrest Theatre, New York,
October 16, 1944.

Cast of characters—

```
Margaret  MacGregor..............................Ruth  McDevitt
Officer  McVey.....................................John  Boyd
John  MacGregor.................................Whitford  Kane
Manny  Siegelmann....................................Al  Shean
Everett  T.  George.................................Le  Roi  Operti
Tim  MacGregor....................................Paul  Potter
Norman  Clark...................................John  McQuade
Horace  Craig.......................................Forrest  Orr
Ellen  Thorne.......................................Nan  Butler
Carla  Thorne..................................Helene  Ambrose
Doctor  Hester.....................................Dann  Malloy
Detective  Sergeant  Corey........................Harry  Gribbon
The  Dancer....................................Stephen  Morrow
```
Acts I, II and III.—Living Room of MacGregor's Mortuary on
the Lower East Side of New York.
Staged by William Castle; setting by Willis Knighton.

Everett T. George, famous publisher, arrives at the John
MacGregor Mortuary Parlors with $10,000, a sealed envelope to
be opened after he is murdered and several carefully worked-out

plans for his funeral. Within the hour he is a deader. The MacGregors accept the assignment of carrying out the dead man's instructions. Three suspected intimates who would profit by his passing are also done in. "Murder, murder, everywhere, and not a cop to think," was Louis Kronenberger's explanation in New York's *P.M.*

(Closed November 4, 1944)

THE VISITOR

(23 performances)

A drama in three acts by Kenneth White, adapted from a novel by Carl Randau and Leane Zugsmith. Produced by Herman Shumlin at the Henry Miller Theatre, New York, October 17, 1944.

Cast of characters—

Elizabeth	Dorrit Kelton
Walter Dawson	Ralph Forbes
Judith Cunningham	Frances Carson
Ellen Wood	Anna Minot
David Cunningham	Walter N. Greaza
Mack Burrell	Thomas Chalmers
Bud Owen	Richard Hylton
Joe Willard	Will Hare

Acts I, II and III.—Living Room of David Cunningham's House.
Staged by Herman Shumlin; setting by Howard Bay.

Bud Owen, presumably drowned when he was 14, turns up when he is 17 at the home of his mother, Judith Cunningham, and his stepfather, David. There is at least a shadow of doubt as to Bud's identity, which he succeeds in quieting for two acts and a half. In the final exposure the plan of a family member to make way with both Bud and his mother, so that an inheritance can be collected, is revealed.

(Closed November 4, 1944)

I REMEMBER MAMA

(278 performances)
(Continuing)

A comedy in two acts, adapted by John Van Druten from Kathryn Forbes's book, "Mama's Bank Account." Produced by Richard Rodgers and Oscar Hammerstein 2nd, at the Music Box, New York, October 19, 1944.

Cast of characters—

Katrin...Joan Tetzel
Mama...Mady Christians
Papa..Richard Bishop
Dagmar..Carolyn Hummel
Christine...Frances Heflin
Nels...Marlon Brando
Mr. Hyde.......................................Oswald Marshall
Aunt Trina.....................................Adrienne Gessner
Aunt Sigrid...Ellen Mahar
Aunt Jenny..Ruth Gates
Uncle Chris......................................Oscar Homolka
A Woman.......................................Louise Lorimer
Mr. Thorkelson.....................................Bruno Wick
Dr. Johnson.....................................William Pringle
Arne..Robert Antoine
A Nurse...Marie Gale
Another Nurse...................................Dorothy Elder
Soda Clerk......................................Frank Babcock
Madeline..Cora Smith
Dorothy Schiller.................................Ottilie Kruger
Florence Dana Moorhead.....................Josephine Brown
Bellboy..Herbert Kenwith

Acts I and II.—In and around the Forbes Home on Telegraph Hill, San Francisco, California.

Staged by John Van Druten; settings and lighting by George Jenkins; costumes by Lucinda Ballard.

See page 67.

VIOLET

(23 performances)

A comedy in three acts by Whitfield Cook. Produced by Albert Margolies at the Belasco Theatre, New York, October 24, 1944.

Cast of characters—

Clarence...John Cherry
Pete Granden.................................Harvey Stephens
Mrs. Elfie Tunison.............................Doro Merande
Elisha Bly...Len Hollister
Lily Foster..Helen Claire
Esther...Paula Trueman
Bruce) Batch 1 .... (Billy Nevard
Violet) (Pat Hitchcock
Evelyn) (Fuzzy McQuade
Arthur) Batch 2 .... (Martin David
Susie (Jimsey Somers
Sidney Watrous...................................Carlo Robinson
Walter Meeker...................................Mason Adams
Crystal..Fay Baker
Charlotte Watrous.................................Joan Vitez
Henry Watrous...................................Leslie Litomy
W. W. Upthegrove...............................Russell Gaige

Acts I, II and III.—Living Room of Pete Granden's Remodeled Farmhouse in Vermont.

Staged by Whitfield Cook; setting by Howard Bay; costumes by Grace Houston.

Pete Granden, twice married and twice divorced, is thinking of taking an old love, Lily Foster, as a third wife. He invites Lily to spend a week-end at his Vermont farm, where he plans to propose marriage. Pete's plans become considerably complicated when both his former wives and his five children appear on the scene. Those who remained for the last act reported a happy ending of a sort.

(Closed November 11, 1944)

SNAFU

(158 performances)

A comedy in three acts by Louis Solomon and Harold Buchman. Produced by George Abbott at the Hudson Theatre, New York, October 25, 1944.

Cast of characters—

Josephina	Eugenia Delarova
Madge Stevens	Elspeth Eric
Laura Jessup	Patricia Kirkland
Ben Stevens	Russell Hardie
Mr. Taylor	John Souther
Kate Hereford	Bethel Leslie
Aunt Emily	Enid Markey
Senator Phil Ford	Ralph W. Chambers
1st Legionnaire	Edwin Cooper
2nd Legionnaire	Ernest Rowan
3rd Legionnaire	Stephen Gierasch
Ronald Stevens	Billy Redfield
Pfc. Danny Baker	Dort Clark
Mrs. Garrett	Ann Dere
Detective	Cliff Dunstan
Martha	Eve McVeagh
Col. West	Winfield Smith

Acts I, II and III.—Living Room of Stevens Home 'n Southern California.

Staged by George Abbott; setting by John Root.

Ronald Stevens, a Sergeant in the South Pacific, has been called to headquarters by his military superior and informed that "his mama wants him." Ronald had lied about his age, and is sent home. Arriving home Ronald is angered and humiliated. For a little he tries to continue an army routine at home. When a pal from the front, on furlough, is accused of having broken into a girls' school, Ronald is mistaken for the real culprit and has some difficulty proving his innocence. Adjustments are gradually achieved and Ronald, belatedly decorated with the Purple Heart for valor at the front, accepts his fate.

(Closed March 10, 1945)

THE PERFECT MARRIAGE

(92 performances)

A comedy in three acts by Samson Raphaelson. Produced by Cheryl Crawford at the Barrymore Theatre, New York, October 26, 1944.

Cast of characters—

Rosa	Evelyn Davis
Dale Williams	Victor Jory
Jenny Williams	Miriam Hopkins
Mabel Manning	Helen Flint
Addison Manning	James Todd
Gloria Endicott	Martha Sleeper
Helen Williams	Joyce Van Patten

Acts I, II and III.—Upstairs Sitting Room and Bedroom of Mr. and Mrs. Dale Williams in New York City.

Staged by Samson Raphaelson; setting by Oliver Smith.

Celebrating their tenth wedding anniversary, Dale and Jenny Williams decide that the magic has gone out of their married life and that neither has retained the sex appeal for the other that they feel marriage should develop and sustain. They agree upon a divorce. During preliminary preparations, however, they discover a new love, or succeed in reviving their old love, and all is well.

(Closed January 13, 1945)

NO WAY OUT

(8 performances)

A drama in three acts by Owen Davis. Produced by Robert Keith at the Cort Theatre, New York, October 30, 1944.

Cast of characters—

Cora Hilliard	Viola Frayne
Dr. Enid Karley	Irene Hervey
Bob Karley	Jerome P. Thor
Barbara Trent	Nancy Marquand
Napoleon	John Marriott
Molly Levenseller	Viola Roache
Dr. Walter Levenseller	Donald Foster
Hesther Darrow	Jean Casto
Dr. Niles Hilliard	Robert Keith
Jim Slade	Maurice Burke

Acts I, II and III.—Living Room of the Old Trent Mansion in a Large City in Northern New York.

Staged by Robert Keith and Owen Davis; setting by Edward Gilbert.

Dr. Hilliard, having permitted the husband of his mistress to die for the want of curative medication, marries the widow.

After squandering her fortune on Wall Street he turns to her daughter, also an heiress, and is letting her die as a victim of the mysterious Addison's disease, also by denying her proper treatment, when a visiting physician, Dr. Enid Karley, suspects what is happening. For a time she refuses to violate the ethics of the medical profession by exposing Dr. Hilliard, but the villain is finally undone.

(Closed November 4, 1944)

EMBEZZLED HEAVEN

(52 performances)

A drama in three acts by L. Bush-Fekete and Mary Helen Fay, based on a novel by Franz Werfel. Produced by The Theatre Guild at the National Theatre, New York, October 31, 1944.

Cast of characters—

Teta	Ethel Barrymore
Bichler	Sanford Meisner
Countess Argan	Bettina Cerf
Mojmir (The Child)	Edward Fernandez
Mila	Wauna Paul
Zdenka	Madeline Lee
George	Val Witherill
Jarmila	Peggy Meredith
Franziska	Augusta Roeland
Mail Carrier	Don Valentine
Mrs. Schultz	Else Basserman
Pastor	Martin Blaine
Kovalsky	Frank Richards
Prossnitzer	Wolfe Barzell
Mojmir	Eduard Franz
Masha	Sheila Trent
Sottomaestro	Marcel Dill
Kompert	Harry Neville
Monsignore	John McKee
Pope	Albert Basserman
Maestro Di Camera	Edward Kilcullen
Papal Valet	Julian Benjamin
Swiss Guards	Paige Edwards, Robert Fletcher
Sediaris	David Barnaby, Robert O'Brien
Physician	Graham Velsey

Prologue—Teta's Room, Argan Castle, Near Prague, 1913. Act I.—Kitchen, Argan Castle, 1938. Act II.—The Church Garden, Detva, Moravia. Act III.—Reception Hall. The Vatican.
Staged by B. Iden Payne; settings by Stewart Chaney; production supervision by Theresa Helburn and Lawrence Langner.

Teta, a cook in the castle of the Count and Countess Argan, worries a little about her future, especially after she dies. A good Catholic, she still has a feeling that a bit of special pleading would do her no harm. When she is asked to help in the education of a nephew she agrees on condition that the boy will study for the priesthood. For twenty-five years she contributes to the support and education of the nephew, without ever having contact with him. When she does go to visit him in what he claims is his first pastorate, Teta discovers that her nephew is a crook and had long since run away from the theological seminary. A pilgrimage to Rome gives her an audience with the Pope, including the Pontiff's understanding forgiveness and blessing.

(Closed January 13, 1945)

HARVEY

(265 performances)

(Continuing)

A comedy in three acts by Mary Chase. Produced by Brock Pemberton at the 48th Street Theatre, New York, November 1, 1944.

Cast of characters—

Myrtle Mae Simmons	Jane Van Duser
Veta Louise Simmons	Josephine Hull
Elwood P. Dowd	Frank Fay
Miss Johnson	Eloise Sheldon
Mrs. Ethel Chauvenet	Frederica Going
Ruth Kelly, R.N.	Janet Tyler
Marvin Wilson	Jesse White
Lyman Sanderson, M.D.	Tom Seidel
William R. Chumley, M.D.	Fred Irving Lewis
Betty Chumley	Dora Clement
Mr. Peeples	Lawrence Hayes
Judge Omar Gaffney	John Kirk
E. J. Lofgren	Robert Gist

Acts I and II.—Scene 1—The Library of the Old Dowd Family Mansion in a City in the Far West. 2—Reception Room of Chumley's Rest. Act III.—Chumley's Rest.

Staged by Antoinette Perry; settings by John Root.

See page 176.

BLACKFRIARS' GUILD

DON'T GEORGE

(22 performances)

A comedy in three acts by Katharine Laure from her own short story, "Winner Take Paul." Produced by the Blackfriars' Guild at the Blackfriars' Theatre, New York, November 2, 1944.

Cast of characters—

Adelaide Averson	Carol Dunning
George Averson	Hal Hershey
Laura Carwood	Romola Robb

Paul Leland.....................................Arthur Allen
David Averson...................................Jack O'Neil
Edythe Averson...............................Eleanor Stafford
    Staged by Dennis Gurney; setting by Viola Kruener.

The second play produced by Blackfriars' Guild during the
1944-45 season was "Home Is the Hero" which opened January
18, 1945, and closed February 11 after 23 performances. The
cast included Ella Playwin, Kate Gibbons, David Bell, Laura
McClure, Miriam Galley, Virginia Dwyer, Dorothy Buquo, Harold Heagy, Beth Shea, Richard Corby, and Robert Echlin.

"Simons's Wife," a drama in three acts by Francis Alwaise,
was produced March 8, 1945, and continued until March 27.
The cast included Ruth Fischer, James Kearney, W. Hussung,
Helen Purcell, Wilson Brooks, Fran Lee, Joseph Boley, David
Knight, Robert Hawkins, Joseph Fox and Frank P. Soden.

The fourth and final production of the season was "Slice It
Thin," a farce in three acts by Lieutenant Edward N. Heghinian
with songs by Al Moritz and settings by Jerry Boxhorn. The
play opened May 10, 1945, and closed May 27. The cast included Miriam Craig, Neal Miller, Joan Field, Sudie Bond, Sidney Welch, Wilson Brooks, Joan Emslie, Delmar Nuetzman,
Dorothy Morrison and John Rosene.

SLEEP, MY PRETTY ONE

(12 performances)

A drama in three acts by Charlie and Oliver Garrett. Produced by Richard W. Krakeur in association with Roger Clark
at the Playhouse, New York, November 2, 1944.

Cast of characters—

Edward...J. Colville Dunn
Kathryn (Kitty) Sturdevant...................Norma Chambers
Emily Groat.....................................Theresa Dale
Eleanor Coates...............................Audrey Ridgewell
Winifred Agate..................................Julie Stevens
Donald Sturdevant..............................Harry Ellerbe
Mrs. Alicia Sturdevant........................Pauline Lord
Lt. ("Hank") Williams...........................Don Gibson
Dr. Ogden Pomfret..............................Ivan Simpson
    Acts I and II.—Living Room in a House on Gramercy Park,
New York. Act III.—Scenes 1 and 2—A Sitting Room at the Top
of the House, 1944.
    Staged by Roy Hargrave; settings by Raymond Sovey.

Alicia Sturdevant suffered a nervous collapse when her husband
was lost on the *Titanic*. Later she achieves a pathological attachment for her bachelor son, Donald, and is willing to commit
murder to prevent his being taken from her by marriage. She

craftily manages the elimination of two fiancées, and comes within
an ace of putting a third out of the way.

(Closed November 11, 1944)

ROBIN HOOD

(15 performances)

A comic opera in three acts by Reginald de Koven and Harry
B. Smith. Produced by R. H. Burnside at the Adelphi Theatre,
New York, November 7, 1944.

Cast of characters—

Robert of Huntington (Afterwards Robin Hood)......Robert Field
Sheriff of Nottingham............................George Lipton
Sir Guy of Gisborne..............................Frank Farrell
Little John......................................Harold Patrick
Will Scarlett....................................Wilfred Glenn
Friar Tuck.......................................Jerry Robbins
Allan-a-Dale.....................................Edith Herlick
Lady Marian Fitzwalter (A Ward of the Crown,
    Afterwards Maid Marian)....................Barbara Scully
Dame Durden..............................Zamah Cunningham
Annabel..................................Margaret Spencer
Milkmaids, Sheriff's Men, King's Men, Villagers, Archers, and
Outlaws.
    Act I.—A Market Place in Nottingham, England, at the time of
Richard I. Act II.—Sherwood Forest. Act III.—Courtyard of the
Sheriff's Castle.
    Staged by R. H. Burnside; settings by United Studios; costumes
by Veronica.

"Robin Hood" was sung originally by the Bostonians in New
York at the Standard Theatre, September, 1891, after having
opened in Chicago the previous season, where it was listed a
failure. The tide in the opera's favor turned in Detroit during
the following road tour. By the time New York was reached the
country was talking about the new hit. The Bostonians kept it
popularly in their repertory for sixteen years. Henry Clay
Barnabee sang the role of the Sheriff, W. H. McDonald was the
Little John, George Frothingham the Friar Tuck, Eugene Cowles
the Will Scarlett and Jessie Bartlett Davis the Allan-a-Dale for
years. They were a definite part of the operetta's success through
its stage life.

(Closed November 18, 1944)

IN BED WE CRY

(47 performances)

A comedy in three acts by Ilka Chase, dramatized from novel with same title by Miss Chase. Produced by John C. Wilson at the Belasco Theatre, New York, November 14, 1944.

Cast of characters—

Jasper Doolittle	Paul McGrath
Bruce Morely	John Kane
Devon Elliott Wainwright	Ilka Chase
Suzanne	Virginia Kaye
Tim Wainwright	Francis DeSales
Hilda	Gynia Gray
Miriam Doyle	Claudia Walden
Barbara Horlick	Helen Marcy
Nick Van Alston	Maury Tuckerman
Dick Hadley	Douglas Gregory
Jennie Moore	Ruth Matteson
Claire Dangerfield	Eleanor Audley
Fairweather	Harold Crane
Kurt Fabri	Frederic Tozere
Delivery Boy	Milton Spelvin
Maria Sellner	Elena Karam

Act I.—Scene 1—Devon Elliott's Office in Devonshire House, January, 1941. 2—Devon's Drawing Room. Act II.—Scenes 1 and 3—The Drawing Room. 2—Kurt's Apartment. Act III.—The Office.

Staged by John C. Wilson; settings by Joseph B. Platt.

Devon Elliott Wainwright, beauty specialist, loses the husband, Tim Wainwright, who had helped her build up the business of Devonshire House cosmetics. Tim is a scientist and he tires of concocting formulas for perfumes, face creams, and such. Devon takes Kurt Fabri, a fascinating refugee, as a lover, but the hurt of her heart is not healed. Tim goes to war and is killed. His death cures Devon of her fascination for Kurt and she marries her manager, Jasper Doolittle, who has loved her ever since the play began.

(Closed December 23, 1944)

SADIE THOMPSON

(60 performances)

A play with music in two acts by Howard Dietz and Rouben Mamoulian, adapted from "Rain," a drama by John Colton and Clemence Randolph, based on a story by Somerset Maugham; music by Vernon Duke. Produced by A. P. Waxman at the Alvin Theatre, New York, November 16, 1944.

Cast of characters—

Joe Horn...Ralph Dumke
Corporal Hodgson.................................Daniel Cobb
Private Griggs...............................Norman Lawrence
Sergeant Tim O'Hara............................James Newill
Ameena...Grazia Narciso
Honeypie..Beatrice Kraft
Mrs. Alfred Davidson.............................Zolya Talma
Cicely St. Clair.................................Doris Patston
Lao Lao.....................................Remington Olmsted
Sadie Thompson.....................................June Havoc
Quartermaster Bates..............................Walter Burke
Reverend Alfred Davidson......................Lansing Hatfield
Polynesian Girl..............................Milada Mladova
Polynesian Boy...................................Chris Volkoff

    Act I.—Scene 1—Trader Joe Horn's Hotel-Store in Pago Pago,
on the Island of Tutulia in the South Seas. 2—The Jungle. Act
II.—Trader Horn's Hotel-Store.
    Staged by Rouben Mamoulian; dances directed by Edward Caton;
music by Charles G. Sanford; chorus by Millard Gibson; settings by
Boris Aronson; costumes by Motley and Azadia Newman.

A musicalized version of the drama "Rain," in which the original story is preserved and melded a little awkwardly with a
series of songs and South Seas ballets.

(Closed January 6, 1945)

THE STREETS ARE GUARDED

(24 performances)

A drama in prologue, epilogue and two acts by Laurence
Stallings; music by Tom Bennett. Produced by John C. Wilson
at the Henry Miller Theatre, New York, November 20, 1944.

Cast of characters—

Admiral Overhold, U.S.N...........................Len Doyle
Colonel White, U.S.M.C.........................Gordon Nelson
Tom Jelks, Ch. Phar. Mate, U.S.N.............Morton L. Stevens
The Marine...Phil Brown
Memphis Jones, Ch. B'sun's Mate, U.S.N........George Matthews
Master Sergeant Winters, U.S.A.A.F...........Robertson White
Corporal Beaseley, U.S.A.A.F.....................Paul Crabtree
Corporal Crofton, U.S.A.A.F......................Joel Marston
Choppy, Musician 2nd Class, U.S.N................Jack Manning
Angelika...Jeanne Cagney
Naval Aide, Lieut. Comdr., U.S.N.................John Effrat
Seaman, U.S.N....................................Byron Griffith
Seaman, U.S.N......................................Terry Little
Hanson, Ch. Yeoman, U.S.N.......................Lewis Charles
A Colonel of Marines.........................Roderick Maybee
    Prologue and epilogue.—U.S. Naval Hospital at Washington. Acts
I and II.—An Island in the Pacific.
    Staged by John Haggott; settings by Lee Simonson.

The Marine escapes Bataan and makes his way in an open
boat several hundred miles southward. Landing on a small island
he finds two airmen, three Navy men and a Dutch nurse. Tom

Jelks, pharmacist's mate, delirious with fever, has prayed for a miracle. Let the Lord send quinine and a savior. He accepts the Marine as an answer to his prayer. The others are sufficiently effected to insist that the Marine, who is wearing his dead Captain's helmet, shall become their leader. With Memphis Jones's help, the Marine invades a neighboring island and steals medicines and a walkie-talkie radio from the Japs. With the medicines the pharmacist's mate is cured; with the radio help is summoned. The Marine disappears. Miracle or not? Who knows?

(Closed December 9, 1944)

THE LATE GEORGE APLEY

(240 performances)
(Continuing)

A comedy in three acts and epilogue by John P. Marquand and George S. Kaufman, based on Mr. Marquand's Pulitzer Prize novel. Produced by Max Gordon at the Lyceum Theatre, New York, November 23, 1944.

Cast of characters—

Margaret............................Mrs. Priestly Morrison
George Apley.......................................Leo G. Carroll
Catherine Apley.......................................Janet Beecher
John Apley...David McKay
Eleanor Apley......................................Joan Chandler
Wilson...Byron Russell
Amelia Newcombe................................Margaret Dale
Roger Newcombe...................................Percy Waram
Horatio Willing..................................Reynolds Evans
Jane Willing....................................Catherine Proctor
Agnes Willing..................................Margaret Phillips
Howard Boulder....................................John Conway
Lydia Leyton......................................Ivy Troutman
Emily Southworth..................................Mabel Acker
Julian H. Dole.................................Howard St. John
Henry...Sayre Crawley

Acts I, II and III.—George Apley's House in Beacon Street, Boston, 1912. Epilogue.—Corner of the Berkeley Club, 1924.
Staged by George S. Kaufman; settings and costumes by Stewart Chaney.

See page 190.

RHAPSODY

(13 performances)

An operetta in two acts by Leonard Louis Levinson and Arnold Sundgaard, based on an original story by A. N. Nagler; lyrics by John Latouche, Russell Bennett and Blevins Davis;

music by Fritz Kreisler; music adaptations and arrangements by Russell Bennett. Produced by Blevins Davis in association with Lorraine Manville Dresselhuys at the Century Theatre, New York, November 22, 1944.

Cast of characters—

Lotzi Hugenhaugen	John Cherry
Lili Hugenhaugen	Gloria Storey
Charles Eckert	John Hamill
Frau Tina Hugenhaugen	Bertha Belmore
Ilse Bonen	Patricia Bowman
Greta	Mildred Jocelyn
Casanova	Eddie Mayehoff
Madame Boticini	Rosemarie Brancato
Demi-Tasse	Mister Johnson
Ivan	George Zoritch
Sonya	Alexandra Denisova
Emperor Francis I	George Young
Empress Maria Theresa	Annamary Dickey
Captain of the Palace Guard	Randolph Symonette
Jailer	Gar Moore
Specialty Dancer	Jerry Ross

Act I.—Scene 1—Music Room of Hugenhaugen Home, Vienna, during reign of Maria Theresa. 2—Gardens at Schoenbrunn Palace. 3—Room in Palace. 4—Mayvine Pavilion Outside Vienna. Act II.—Scene 1—The Jail. 2—Anteroom of the Empress' Chambers. 3—Apartment of Casanova in the Palace. 4—Hall in the Palace. 5—Ballroom in Schoenbrunn Palace.

Staged by David Lichine; music directed by Fritz Mahler; settings by Oliver Smith; lighting by Stanley McCandless; costumes by Frank Bevan.

A story of court intrigue involving a lyrical Empress Maria Theresa, and a not so lyrical Emperor Francis I, in association with a befuddled Casanova and a gorgeously dressed stageful of attendants floundering in a sea of expensive scenery.

(Closed December 3, 1944)

THE MAN WHO HAD ALL THE LUCK

(4 performances)

A play in three acts by Arthur Miller. Produced by Herbert H. Harris at the Forrest Theatre, New York, November 23, 1944.

Cast of characters—

Shory	Grover Burgess
J. B. Feller	Forrest Orr
Hester Falk	Eugenia Rawls
David Beeves	Karl Swenson
Aunt Belle	Agnes Scott Yost
Patterson Beeves	Jack Sheehan
Amos Beeves	Dudley Sadler
Dan Dibble	Sydney Grant
Gustav Eberson	Herbert Berghof
Harry Bucks	James MacDonald
Augie Belfast	Lawrence Fletcher

Act I.—David Beeves's Repair Shop in a Small Mid-Western Town.

Act II.—Scene 1—Living Room of David's House. 2—Spare Bedroom in David's House. Act III.—David's Living Room.
Staged by Joseph Fields; settings by Frederick Fox.

David Beeves is a lucky fellow. He gets the girl he wants to
marry when her father, who hated him, dies suddenly. He earns
success in his garage business when a wandering mechanic helps
him with a tough job. He becomes a father when he longs for
children, and he runs a mink farm successfully through a threatened mink epidemic. His brother, Amos, who wanted to be a big
league baseball pitcher, spends his life training and fails in the
end because he didn't learn to use his mind as well as his arm.
David doesn't understand why he has all the luck until he figures
that it was because he worked hard and honestly with such gifts
as the Lord had given him.

(Closed November 25, 1944)

HAND IN GLOVE

(40 performances)

A drama in prologue and three acts by Charles K. Freeman
and Gerald Savory, based on the novel, "Hughie Roddis," by
Gerald Savory. Produced by Arthur Edison at the Playhouse,
New York, December 4, 1944.

Cast of characters—

Jenny	Jean Bellows
Mr. Ramskill	George Lloyd
Auntie B	Isobel Elsom
Hughie	Skelton Knaggs
Mr. Forsythe	St. Clair Bayfield
Mrs. Willis	Viola Roache
Lily Willis	Islay Benson
Curly Latham	Victor Beecroft
Purple Cap	Almon Bruce
Bowler Hat	Todd Stanton
Sergeant	Robin Craven
Chief Constable	Wallace Widdecombe
Man from London	Aubrey Mather

Prologue.—A Deserted Narrow Street Near Old Queens Dock,
Halsey, Yorkshire, England. Winter, 1944. Acts I, II and III.—
Kitchen in Auntie B's House.
Staged by James Whale; settings by Sam Leve; costumes by Bob
Davison.

Mr. Ramskill is a strange young man who boards with Auntie
B. Between times he strangles young women and mutilates their
bodies with sharp pieces of tin or broken crockery. Being crafty
as well as abnormal, Mr. Ramskill throws suspicion of his murders on Hughie Roddis, who is Auntie B's idiot nephew. From
8:30 till 10:30 the drooling Hughie looks pretty guilty. Then

Scotland Yard steps in in the person of a Man from London and the whole thing is cleared up.

(Closed January 6, 1945)

A BELL FOR ADANO

(217 performances)

(Continuing)

A drama in three acts by Paul Osborn, based on a novel by John Hersey. Produced by Leland Hayward at the Cort Theatre, New York, December 6, 1944.

Cast of characters—

Major Victor Joppolo	Fredric March
Sergeant Leonard Borth, M.P.	Everett Sloane
Giovanni Zito	Gilbert Mack
Giuseppe Ribaudo	Tito Vuolo
Cacopardo	Silvio Minciotti
Craxi	Joe Verdi
Father Pensovecchio	Leon Rothier
Marguerita	Miriam Goldine
Carmelina	Alma Ross
Laura Sofia	Florence Aquino
Gargano	Harold J. Stone
Tina	Margo
Captain Purvis	Bruce MacFarlane
Sergeant Frank Trapani, M.P.	Jack Arnold
Corporal Chuck Schultz, M.P.	Fred Barton
Colonel George Middleton	Harry Selby
Bellanco	Michael Vallon
D'Arpa	Mario Badolati
Spinnato	Doreen McLean
Pietro Afronti	Albert Raymo
Carlo Erba	Charles Mayer
Basile Giovanni	J. Scott Smart
Mayor Nasta	Rolfe Sedan
Joe Pollock, M.P.	Clark Poth
Tomasino	Alexander Granach
Lt. Livingston, U.S.S. Navy	Phil Arthur
Bill Munroe, M.P.	Rex King

Acts I, II and III.—Office of Mayor in City Hall of Adano, Sicily.

Staged by H. C. Potter; setting and costumes by Motley; lighting supervised by William Richardson.

See page 30.

SEVEN LIVELY ARTS

(183 performances)

A musical revue in two acts assembled by Billy Rose; lyrics and music by Cole Porter; music for ballet by Igor Stravinsky; sketches by Moss Hart, George S. Kaufman, Robert Pirosh, Joseph Schrank and Charles Sherman; Doc Rockwell's comments by Ben Hecht. Produced by Billy Rose at the Ziegfeld Theatre, New York, December 7, 1944.

Principals engaged—

Beatrice Lillie
Bert Lahr
Benny Goodman
Alicia Markova
Anton Dolin
Doc Rockwell
Nan Wynn
Jere McMahon
Paula Bane
Billy Worth
Bill Tabbert
Dolores Gray

Mary Roche
Albert Carroll
Michael Barrett
Dennie Moore
Thomas Kenny
Edward Hackett
King Ross
Teddy Wilson
Red Norvo
Morey Feld
Sid Weiss
Robert Austin

Corps de Ballet: Franca Baldwin, Virginia Barnes, John Begg, Angelina Buttignol, Phyllis Brown, Evangeline Collis, Margarita de Valera, Bettye Durrence, Adriana Favaloro, Louise Ferrand, Jerry Florio, Nina Frenkin, Helen Gallagher, Arlene Carver, Mimi Gomber, Edward Hackett, Jean Harris, Ray Johnson, Harriet Katzman, Thomas Kenny, Lee Lauterbur, Constance Love, Richard Martini, Paul Olson, Michael Pober, Lester Russon.

Singers: Robert Austin, Johnsie Bason, Charlotte Bruce, Irene Carroll, Nina Dean, Rose Marie Elliott, Paul Fairleagh, Vincent Henry, Bob Herring, Raynor Howell, Stella Hughes, Jimmy Kane, Robert Kimberly, Mary Ann Krejci, Ethel Madson, John Mathews, Helen Molveau, Louise Uewton, Richmond Page, Allen Sharp, Gordon Taylor, William Utely, Martha Emma Watson.

Page Boys: Charles Franklin Beck, Sonny Cavell, Alan Grossman, Barry Laffin, Buddy Millard, Dickie Millard, Donald Rose.

Ladies of Fashion: Savona King, Jean Colleran, Alma Holt, Cissy Smith, Truly Barbara, Viki Maulsby, Gwen Shirey, Susan Blanchard, Adrian Storms, Paddy Ellerton, Gayle Mellott, Temple Texas.

Staged and lighted by Hazzard Short; dances and songs directed by Jack Donohue; choral group trained by Robert Shaw; music directed by Maurice Abravanel; sketches directed by Philip Loeb; choreography by Anton Dolin; settings by Norman Bel Geddes; costumes by Mary Shaw and Valentina.

(Closed May 12, 1945)

DARK HAMMOCK

(2 performances)

A drama in three acts by Mary Orr and Reginald Denham. Produced by Meyer Davis and Sam H. Grisman at the Forrest Theatre, New York, December 11, 1944.

Cast of characters—

Coral Platt..Mary Orr
Marvin Platt..............................Charles McClelland
Doc Bunnell...................................Scott Moore
Carlos Antuna..................................James Ganon
Belle....................................Mabel D. Bergen
Goldie..Alonzo Bosan
Andrew Jackson Sparks.....................Arthur Hunnicutt
Florence McDavid................................Elissa Landi

```
Amelia Coop.......................................Mary Wickes
Butch Smith.......................................Alan Dreeben
       Acts I, II and III.—Marvin Platt's Farmstead, Known as "Dark
Hammock," on the Kissimee Prairie, Florida.
       Staged by Reginald Denham; setting by Sam Leve; costumes by
Kermit Love; lighting by Jack Daniels.
```

The Platts, Coral and Marvin, are living on the Platt place in deeper Florida. Coral, being years the younger, and viciously ambitious, decides to get rid of Marvin as soon as he fixes his will in her favor. To accomplish this end she feeds the poor innocent the heads of sulphur matches in his milk. She would have succeeded if it had not been for the accidental visit of Dr. Florence McDavid, and Amelia Coop, her assistant. They become suspicious and shortly have the case against Coral all tied up.

(Closed December 12, 1944)

DEAR RUTH

(216 performances)
(Continuing)

A comedy in two acts by Norman Krasna. Produced by Joseph M. Hyman and Bernard Hart at the Henry Miller Theatre, New York, December 13, 1944.

Cast of characters—

```
Dora..............................................Pauline Myers
Mrs. Edith Wilkins...............................Phyllis Povah
Miriam Wilkins..................................Lenore Lonergan
Judge Harry Wilkins.............................Howard Smith
Ruth Wilkins...................................Virginia Gilmore
Lt. William Seawright...............................John Dall
Albert Kummer................................Bartlett Robinson
Martha Seawright..................................Kay Coulter
Sgt. Chuck Vincent..........................Richard McCracken
Harold Kobbermeyer...................................Peter Dunn
       Acts I and II.—Living Room of the Wilkins Home, New York
City, 1944.
       Staged by Moss Hart; setting by Frederick Fox.
```

See page 326.

LAFFING ROOM ONLY

(201 performances)
(Continuing)

A musical revue in two acts by Ole Olsen, Chic Johnson and Eugene Conrad; music and lyrics by Burton Lane. Produced by the Messrs. Shubert, Olsen and Johnson at the Winter Garden, New York, December 23, 1944.

Principals engaged—

Ole Olsen
Frank Libuse
William Archibald
Robert Breton
Harry Burns
Charles Senna
Fred Peters
Bruce Evans
Pat Brewst
Kenny Buffett
Charles O'Donnell
Joe Young
J. C. McCord
Lou Wills, Jr.
Jack Lierce
Ronnie Chetwood
Forrest Bonshire
Ken Patterson
Stanley Stevens
Herbert Ross
O'Donnell Blair
Mata and Hari
Willie West & McGinty

Chic Johnson
Betty Garrett
Kathryn Lee
Ethel Owen
Catherine Johnson
Mary La Roche
Frances Henderson
Margot Brander
Ida James
Penny Edwards
Jean Moorhead
Shannon Dean
Lee Joyce
June Walker
Eleanor Leaman
Penny Holt
Marcia Maier
Gretchen Hauser
Virginia Barrett
Billy Young
Ernest D'Amato
McKee and Kramer
Fred Waring's Glee Club

Staged by John Murray Anderson; comedy directed by Edward Cline; music directed by John McManus; dances by Robert Alton; settings by Stewart Chaney; costumes by Billy Livingston.

SOPHIE

(9 performances)

A comedy in three acts by George Ross and Rose C. Feld, based on "Sophie Halenczik, American," stories by Rose Feld. Produced by Meyer Davis and George Ross at the Playhouse, New York, December 25, 1944.

Cast of characters—

Annie Halenczik...........................Ann Shepherd
Ernest Hopkins................................Will Geer
Tom Blanchard..............................Richard Deane
Chet Blanchard.............................John McGovern
Frankie Halenczik.............................Donald Buka
Sophie Halenczik...........................Katina Paxinou
George Odanos...............................John Harmon
Mr. Parker.................................Kurt Richards
Irene Halenczik..............................Donna Keath
Mrs. Scudder...................................Doris Rich
Capt. Thornton Scudder....................Ronald Alexander
Marge Nelson..........................Marguerite Clifton
Anton Halenczik..............................Louis Sorin
Elsie....................................Eda Reiss Merin
Joey..Jerry Boyar

Acts I, II and III.—The Home of Sophie Halenczik, R.F.D. 4, Ridgetown, Connecticut.

Staged by Michael Gordon; setting by Samuel Leve; costumes by Rose Bogondoff.

Sophie Halenczik is a Connecticut boardinghouse keeper who has a son in the Army. When the son is to become a father Sophie takes in his unwed wife. Attracting the attention of some of her more intolerant neighbors, to whom she represents Communism in the raw, she manages, before the evening is over, to convince them that she is not only a better citizen of Connecticut than they, but also a better American.

(Closed December 31, 1944)

SING OUT SWEET LAND

102 performances)

A "Salute to American Folk and Popular Music" by Walter Kerr; special music by Elie Siegmeister. Produced by The Theatre Guild at the International Theatre, New York, December 27, 1944.

Principals engaged—

Alfred Drake	Bibi Osterwald
Burl Ives	Alma Kaye
Philip Coolidge	Ellen Love
Jack McCauley	Ethel Mann
Peter Hamilton	Irene Hawthorne
James Westerfield	Juanita Hall
Robert Penn	Christine Karner
Ted Tiller	Irene Jordan
Jules Racine	Adrienne Gray
Charles Hart	Peggy Campbell
William Sharon	Dorothy Baxter
Lawrence Gilbert	Ruth Tyler
Sam Green	Pat Newman
Morty Halpern	Calvin Harris
George Cassidy	

Staged by Leon Leonidoff; book directed by Walter Kerr; music directed by Elie Siegmeister; dances by Doris Humphrey and Charles Weidman; chorus directed by Arthur Lessac; settings by Albert Johnson; costumes by Lucinda Ballard; production under supervision of Lawrence Langner and Theresa Helburn.

A cavalcade of America through a selection of her folk songs. Starts with a Puritan hymn, "Who Is the Man?", and works its way melodiously and with many changes of scenery down through the periods that produced "Frankie and Johnny" and "Casey Jones" to the jazz and jive songs of the present.

(Closed March 24, 1945)

ON THE TOWN

(197 performances)
(Continuing)

A musical comedy in two acts by Betty Comden and Adolph Green, based on idea by Jerome Robbins; music by Leonard

Bernstein. Produced by Oliver Smith and Paul Feigay at the Adelphi Theatre, New York, December 28, 1944.

Cast of characters—

```
Workman..........................................Marten Sameth
2nd Workman......................................Frank  Milton
3rd Workman......................................Herbert Greene
Ozzie............................................Adolph Green
Chip.............................................Cris  Alexander
Sailor...........................................Lyle Clark
Gabey............................................John Battles
Andy.............................................Frank Westbrook
Tom..............................................Richard D'Arcy
Flossie..........................................Florence MacMichael
Flossie's Friend.................................Marion Kohler
Bill Poster......................................Larry Bolton
Little Old Lady..................................Maxine Arnold
Policeman........................................Lonny Jackson
S. Uperman.......................................Milton Taubman
Hildy............................................Nancy Walker
Policeman........................................Roger Treat
Figment..........................................Remo Bufano
Claire...........................................Betty Comden
Highschool Girl..................................Nellie Fisher
Sailor in Blue...................................Richard D'Arcy
Maude P. Dilly...................................Susan Steell
Ivy..............................................Sono Osato
Lucy Schmeeler...................................Alice Pearce
Pitkin...........................................Robert Chisholm
Master of Ceremonies.............................Frank Milton
Singer...........................................Frances Cassard
Waiter...........................................Herbert Greene
Spanish Singer...................................Jeanne Gordon
The Great Lover..................................Ray Harrison
Conductor........................................Herbert Greene
Bimmy............................................Robert Lorenz
```

Act I.—Scene 1—Brooklyn Navy Yard. 2—Subway. 3—Street. 4—Miss Turnstiles. 5—A Taxi. 6—Museum. 7—Outside the Park. 8—Corridor of Carnegie Hall. 9—Madame Dilly's Studio. 10—Claire's Apartment. 11—Hildy's Apartment. 12—Times Square. Act II.—Scene 1—Night Clubs. 2—Gabey in Playground of the Rich. 3—The Subway. 4—Coney Island. 5—Coney Island.

Staged by George Abbott; musical numbers and choreography directed by Jerome Robbins; music directed by Max Goberman; settings by Oliver Smith; costumes by Alvin Colt.

Three young gobs in training at Brooklyn Navy Yard get their first chance to see New York the day they are issued 24-hour passes. In the first subway they ride in they read the legend of Miss Subways, the beauty of the month, on a display card. They decide to run the beauty down and take her, and maybe a couple of her friends, on their own excursion of the big town. Which they do.

TRIO

(67 performances)

A drama in three acts by Dorothy and Howard Baker, adapted from a novel by Dorothy Baker. Produced by Lee Sabinson at the Belasco Theatre, New York, December 29, 1944.

Cast of characters—

Janet Logan..Lois Wheeler
Pauline Maury..................................Lydia St. Clair
Ray Mackenzie................................Richard Widmark
Ted Gordon....................................Kenneth Williams
Miss Hawley..............................Mary Alan Hokanson
Ralph Hackett.......................................Ken Tower
Mrs. Girard..Sara Perry
Dean Harry Kennedy...............................Harry Irvine
House Boy...Henry Goon
    Acts I and III.—Pauline Maury's Apartment. Act II.—Ray
Mackenzie's Apartment.
    Staged by Bretaigne Windust; settings by Stewart Chaney.

Ray Mackenzie is determined to break up what he considers an unholy and unhealthy attachment possessed by Pauline Maury for her young friend, Janet Logan. Miss Maury fights desperately to hold her control over Miss Logan, but is finally defeated. The young people are married. Miss Maury kills herself.

(Closed February 24, 1945)

THE HASTY HEART

(191 performances)

(Continuing)

A drama in three acts by John Patrick. Produced by Howard Lindsay and Russell Crouse at the Hudson Theatre, New York, January 3, 1945.

Cast of characters—

Orderly...Francis Neilsen
Yank..John Lund
Digger...John Campbell
Kiwi..Victor Chapin
Blossom...Earl Jones
Tommy..Douglas Chandler
Margaret..Anne Burr
Colonel...Edward Cooper
Lachlen..Richard Basehart
    Acts I, II and III.—Convalescent Ward of British General Hos-
pital Behind the Assam-Burma Front.
    Staged by Bretaigne Windust; setting by Raymond Sovey.

See page 103.

MANY HAPPY RETURNS

(3 performances)

A comedy in three acts by Clare Kummer. Produced by Harry Bloomfield at the Playhouse, New York, January 5, 1945.

Cast of characters—

```
Ethel.............................................Nan Butler
Jo Barnett....................................Michael Dreyfuss
Henry Burton..................................Neil Hamilton
Albert .......................................Leonard Carey
Fay...............................................Nell O'Day
Eddie...........................................Don Gibson
Charles Barrows...............................Rex O'Malley
Jane............................................Jayne Cotter
Cynthia Laceby..................................Mary Astor
Tom Carruthers............................Vincent Gardner
```
Acts I and III.—Living Room of Henry Burton's House in New York City. Act II.—Mrs. Laceby's Apartment.
Staged by Peter Berneis; settings by Stewart Chaney.

Henry Burton, aware that his son is about to leave home and break up his marriage, tries to avert that catastrophe by visiting the Cynthia Laceby who has fascinated the boy. As it turns out, Cynthia had only flirted with the son because she wanted to be near the father, for whom she had long acknowledged a great fondness.

(Closed January 6, 1945)

A LADY SAYS YES

(87 performances)

A musical comedy in prologue and two acts by Clayton Ashley and Stanley Adams; music by Fred Spielman and Arthur Gershwin. Produced by J. J. Shubert in association with Clayton Ashley at the Broadhurst Theatre, New York, January 10, 1945.

Cast of characters—

1945
```
First Nurse...............................Helene Le Berthon
Licetta.........................................Sue Ryan
Second Nurse..............................Jackson Jordan
Third Nurse...............................Blanche Grady
Doctor.......................................Jack Albertson
Scapino.......................................Bobby Morris
Ghisella......................................Carole Landis
Christine....................................Christine Ayres
Hildegarde................................Jacqueline Susann
Lt. Anthony Caufield, U.S.N.R.................Arthur Maxwell
Dr. Gaspare..................................Earl McDonald
Isabella.......................................Martha King
Captain Gordon.............................Pittman Corry
```
1545
```
Captain Desiri.............................Pittman Corry
Francesca.................................Helene Le Berthon
Rosa........................................Blanche Grady
Carmela...................................Jackson Jordan
Dr. Bartoli..................................Jack Albertson
Isabella.......................................Martha King
Scapino.......................................Bobby Morris
Anthony Gaspare.............................Arthur Maxwell
Christine....................................Christine Ayres
Hildegarde................................Jacqueline Susann
```

Licetta..Sue Ryan
Gaspare...Earl McDonald
Killer Pepoli...Fred Catania
Second...Al Klein
Pantaloon..Steve Mills
Ghisella....................................Carole Landis
Page Boy...Francelia Schmidt
    Prologue.—Scene 1—Waiting Room of a Hospital, 1945. 2—The
Operating Room. Act I.—Scene 1—A Street in Venice, 1545. 2—
Ghisella's Bedroom. Act II.—Scene 1—Street in Venice, 1545. 2—
Garden of the Emperor of China. 3—Hospital Laboratory, 1945.
4—Cannibal Club. 5—Garden Party, Washington, D. C.
    Musical ensembles and dances staged by Boots McKenna; ballets
by Natalie Kamarova; music directed by Ving Merlin; settings by
Watson Barratt; costumes by Lou Eisele; lighting by William
Thomas.

His potency as a prospective bridegroom having been questioned, Lieutenant Anthony Caufield dreams that he goes back to
Venice and to China in 1545 to prove the validity of his asser-
tion that he is okay. This he does to the satisfaction of the heroine, a blonde and handsome Ghisella.

(Closed March 25, 1945)

GOOD NIGHT, LADIES

(78 performances)

A farce in three acts by Cyrus Wood adapted from "Ladies'
Night" by Avery Hopwood and Charlton Andrews. Produced
by Howard Lang and Al Rosen at the Royale Theatre, New York,
January 17, 1945.

Cast of characters—

Marie.................................Rosemary Bertrand
Dodie Tarleton.................................Randee Sanford
Kittie Bonner.....................................Sunnie O'Dea
Mike Bonner......................................Skeets Gallagher
Mrs. Theresa Tarleton...........................Kathryn Givney
Alicia Blake......................................Marlo Dwyer
Fred Blake......................................Max Hofmann, Jr.
Prof. John Matthews..............................James Ellison
Mrs. Blanche O'Brien..............................Ann Fortney
Anna...Lucille Benson
Myrtle Shea. ....Louise Jarvis
Eve La Bouche....................................Lana Holmes
Policewoman.....................................Beatrice Newport
Fireman..Wendell Ates
    Acts I and III.—The Bonner Apartment. Act II.—The Cos-
metrian.
    Staged by Edward Clarke Lilley; settings and lighting by Freder-
ick Fox; costumes by Billy Livingston.

Known originally as "Ladies' Night," the farce "Good Night,
Ladies" was produced in August, 1920, and had some Broadway
success. Afterward it was revived and lightly revised and, under
its current title, ran for over a year in Chicago. The story is of a

timid college professor whose friends take him to a costume ball to break down his embarrassment in the company of the opposite sex. The ball is raided and the professor and his friends escape to a Turkish bath next door on ladies' night.

(Closed March 24, 1945)

REBECCA

(20 performances)

A drama in three acts by Daphne Du Maurier. Produced by Victor Payne-Jennings at the Ethel Barrymore Theatre, New York, January 18, 1945.

Cast of characters—

Frith...Richard Temple
Beatrice Lacy..............................Margaret Bannerman
Major Giles Lacy................................Franklyn Fox
Frank Crawley...................................Claude Horton
Maxim de Winter...........................Bramwell Fletcher
Mrs. de Winter.............................Diana Barrymore
Maid...Jacqueline Max
Robert.......................................Kenneth Treseder
Mrs. Danvers...................................Florence Reed
Jack Favell.....................................George Baxter
Col. Julyan...................................Reginald Mason
William Tabb.....................................Edgar Kent
    Acts I, II and III.—Southern End of Hall at Manderley, the Home of Maxim de Winter, Cornwall, England.
    Staged by Clarence Derwent; setting by Watson Barratt; assisting producer, Gilda Dahlberg.

The stage version of "Rebecca" followed both a movie and a radio version. In many sections of the country it was tremendously popular, but not in New York, where its success was no better than moderate. The story of the uncovering of Maxim de Winter as the murderer of his first wife, whom he had discovered in an infidelity, is dramatically accomplished, with the fanatical Mrs. Danvers, housekeeper, continuing as the chief menace.

(Closed February 3, 1945)

A GOOSE FOR THE GANDER

(15 performances)

A comedy in three acts by Harold J. Kennedy. Produced by Jules J. Leventhal and Frank McCoy at the Playhouse, New York, January 23, 1945.

Cast of characters—

David	Conrad Nagel
Suzy	Maxine Stuart
Lorraine	Choo Choo Johnson
Benson	Joyce Sirola
Tony	Harold J. Kennedy
Katherine	Gloria Swanson
Jonathan	John Clubley
Chauffeur	George Margolis
Wally	David Tyrrell

Acts I, II and III.—Living Room of Dave Richardson's Home in Greenwich, Conn.

Staged by Tommy Ward; setting by Frederick Fox.

Katherine, returning home unexpectedly, discovers her husband, David, having breakfast with an attractive young Suzy in negligee. How long this has been going on not even David can remember, he having been fuzzy with liquor when it started. Katherine, to be even, induces Suzy the siren to stay on and help her entertain three of her own former suitors, whom she invites to the house. Getting even doesn't work out very satisfactorily.

(Closed February 3, 1945)

THE TEMPEST

(100 performances)

A comedy in prologue and two acts by William Shakespeare; interpreted by Margaret Webster, based on a production idea by Eva La Gallienne; music by David Diamond. Produced by Cheryl Crawford at the Alvin Theatre, New York, January 25, 1945.

Cast of characters—

Ship-master	Joseph Hardy
Boatswain	Steven Elliott
Alonso, King of Naples	Philip Huston
Gonzalo	Paul Leyssac
Antonio	Berry Kroeger
Sebastian	Eugene Stuckmann
Prospero	Arnold Moss
Miranda	Frances Heflin
Ariel	Vera Zorina
Caliban	Canada Lee
Ferdinand, Prince of Naples	Vito Christi
Adrian	Jack Bostick
Trinculo	George Voskovec
Stephano	Jan Werich
Master of Ceremonies } Spirits	{ Larry Evers
Dancer }	{ Diana Sinclair

Mariners, Shapes and Spirits: Steven Elliott, Larry Evers, Joseph Hardy, Norman Peck, Charlotte Keane, Diana Sinclair, Patricia Wheel.

Prologue.—On a Ship at Sea. Acts I and II—On an Island.

Staged by Margaret Webster; music directed by David Diamond; settings and costumes by Motley; lighting by Moe Hack.

This is a stream-lined version of the next to last play Shakespeare wrote. Margaret Webster has reduced it from five to two acts and a prologue. The prologue reveals a heaving shipwreck scene and the two acts are played on a revolving stage that reveals various angles of Prospero's and Caliban's living quarters. In this pictorial and imaginative version the "We are such stuff as dreams are made on" speech has been lifted from the fifth act to serve as the play's tag.

(Closed April 21, 1945)

UP IN CENTRAL PARK

(163 performances)
(Continuing)

A musical play in two acts by Herbert and Dorothy Fields; music by Sigmund Romberg. Produced by Michael Todd at the Century Theatre, New York, January 27, 1945.

Cast of characters—

Clara Manning	Martha Burnett
James Fisk, Jr.	Watson White
Daniel	Daniel Nagrin
Governess	Louise Holden
1st Child	Ann Hermann
2nd Child	Joan Lally
3rd Child	Janet Lally
4th Child	Mary Alice Evans
Headwaiter	John Quigg
Page Boy	Henry Capri
Arthur Finch	Wally Coyle
Ellen Lawrence	Elaine Barry
Bicycle Rider	Stanley Schimmel
George Jones	Guy Standing, Jr.
Bagpipe Players	Isobel Glasgow, James McFadden, Thomas Lorimer
Newsboys	Kenneth Casey, Teddy Casey
Organ Grinders	William Nuss, Charles Wood
A Laborer	Bruce Lord
Danny O'Cahane	Walter Burke
Timothy Moore	Charles Irwin
Bessie O'Cahane	Betty Bruce
Rosie Moore	Maureen Cannon
John Matthews, of the *New York Times*	Wilbur Evans
Thomas Nast, of *Harper's Weekly*	Maurice Burke
William Dutton	John Quigg
Andrew Munroe	Robert Field
Vincent Peters	Paul Reed
Mayor A. Oakey Hall	Rowan Tudor
Richard Connolly, Comptroller of the City of New York	George Lane
Peter Sweeney, Park Commissioner	Harry Meehan
William Marcey Tweed, Grand Sachem of Tammany Hall	Noah Beery, Sr.
Butler	Herman Glazer
Mildred Wincor	Lydia Fredericks
Joe Stewart	Fred Barry
Porter	Harry Matlock

Lotta Stevens...Delma Byron
Fanny Morris..Kay Griffith
  Act I.—Scene 1—A Site in Central Park (June, 1870). 2—The
Park Commissioner's Temporary Office in Central Park (July, 1870).
3—The Lounge of the Stetson Hotel (Formerly McGowan's Pass
Tavern), (Christmas Eve, 1870). 4—The Bird House in the Central
Park Zoo. 5—The Central Park Gardens (February, 1871). Act
II.—Scene 1—The Annual Tammany Hall Outing (July, 1871).
2—Office of George Jones (Owner of the *New York Times*). 3—
Central Park West. 4—The Stetson Hotel. 5—The Mall in Central
Park (July 4, 1872). 6—The Bandstand in the Mall.
  Staged by John Kennedy; dances by Helen Tamaris; music di-
rected by Max Meth; orchestrations by Don Walker; settings and
lighting by Howard Bay; costumes by Grace Houston and Ernest
Schraps.

In the days of the Currier and Ives lithographs and the Boss
Tweed gang of city grafters a *New York Times* reporter, John
Matthews, and a *Harper's Weekly* cartoonist, Thomas Nast, expose Tweed and save the City of New York thousands and thousands of dollars. Then John marries Rosie Moore, pretty daughter of a minor Tammany politician.

ALICE IN ARMS

(5 performances)

A comedy in three acts by Ladislaus Bush-Fekete, Sidney
Shelton and Mary Helen Fay. Produced by Edward Choate and
Marie Louise Elkins at the National Theatre, New York, Janu-
ary 31, 1945.

Cast of characters—

Mike..Johnnie Venn
Willis..James O'Neil
Daisy...Florence Shirley
Alice..Peggy Conklin
Helen..Judith Abbott
Florence..Darthy Hinkley
Walter..Roger Clark
Collins...Tom McElhany
1st Private..Jerry Vincent
2nd Private.......................................Richard Coogan
Steve..Kirk Douglas
Beeker...George Ives
Henry...Mickey Stewart
Colonel Benson...................................G. Albert Smith
  Acts I, II and III.—Daisy Madison's House in Linwood, Penn-
sylvania.
  Staged by Jack Daniels; setting by Frederick Fox.

Alice, three years a WAC in Europe, is home with a medical
discharge trying to take up her life again in Linwood, Pennsylvania. She plans to marry Walter, the local industrialist to whom
she was engaged when she went away, and probably would have
done so if Sergeant Steve Grant hadn't turned up. It was with
Sergeant Steve that Alice had had a wonderfully romantic time

in Paris. Also the Colonel Benson whom she had served as a secretary in Europe comes home with a heart full of love and a proposal of marriage. Alice is pretty confused until late evening. Then she decides on the Sergeant.

(Closed February 3, 1945)

THE OVERTONS

(151 performances)

(Continuing)

A comedy in three acts by Vincent Lawrence. Produced by Paul Czinner at the Booth Theatre, New York, February 6, 1945.

Cast of characters—

```
Cora  Overton...................................Arlene  Francis
Julia.............................................Mary  Lawrence
Judith  Bancroft.................................Glenda  Farrell
Jack Overton.......................................Jack  Whiting
Tommy...........................................Donald  Kohler
Minot..............................................Charles  Lang
James Lawson..................................Walter N. Greaza
     Acts I and II.—Living Room of the Overtons' Home near New
York.    Act III.—Bedroom.
     Staged by Elisabeth Bergner; settings by Edward Gilbert; cos-
tumes by Hattie Carnegie.
```

Cora and Jack Overton, having been married for eight years, have complete faith and trust in each other until Judith Bancroft, who wouldn't mind having an affair with Jack, is seen disrobing in his boathouse. Thereupon Cora forgets all eight years of trusting Jack and packs her valise for a trip. Jack, his pride hurt, refuses to deny or explain. Cora, impressed by this defiance, decides finally to take another chance and is back home for the final curtain.

HOPE FOR THE BEST

(117 performances)

A comedy in three acts by William McCleery. Produced by Jean Dalrymple and Marc Connelly at the Fulton Theatre, New York, February 7, 1945.

Cast of characters—

```
Howard  Hilton......................................Jack  Hartley
Mrs.  Bassett.....................................Doro  Merande
Margaret  Hicks  Harwood..........................Joan  Wetmore
Professor  Wechsler................................Leo  Bulgakov
Sgt.  Joe  Jordan..................................Paul  Potter
```

Lucille Daly...Jane Wyatt
Michael Jordan....................................Franchot Tone
    Acts I, II and III.—Living Room of Michael Jordan's House in Connecticut.

Michael Jordan is a popular columnist of the small-town, wholesome type. His fiancée, Margaret Harwood, is a sophisticated political writer. Michael becomes conscious of his insignificance as an influence, whatever his popularity, and wants to take up political columning. His fiancée would sneer him out of his ambition, but a visiting Lucille Daly, realizing Michael's potentialities, helps him screw his determination to the sticking point. After which it is absurdly easy for them to fall in love.

(Closed May 19, 1945)

ONE-MAN SHOW

(36 performances)

A drama in three acts by Ruth Goodman and Augustus Goetz. Produced by Jed Harris at the Barrymore Theatre, New York, February 8, 1945.

Cast of characters—

Lucian Gardner..................................Frank Conroy
A Woman.......................................Elizabeth Brew
Tom...Mitchell Harris
James Dockerel...............................Hugh Franklin
Racine Gardner............................Constance Cummings
Emory Jelliffe....................................James Rennie
Blanche.......................................Kasia Orzazewski
Francis Kearny..................................John Archer
    Acts I, II and III.—Gardner Gallery, New York City.
    Staged by Jed Harris; setting by Stewart Chaney.

Lucian and Racine Gardner, father and daughter, together run the Gardner Gallery in New York. Their mutual affection for, and dependence upon, each other develops a kind of possessiveness that impels Racine to decide against marriage with a poor but honest artist and also against selling herself for the good of the gallery to a wealthy admirer. Along comes Francis Kearny, a young member of the State Department staff, who not only falls in love with Racine but discovers the unhealthy hold her father has upon her. In the end he is able to break the father's influence and he and Racine are married.

(Closed March 10, 1945)

THE STRANGER

(16 performances)

A drama in three acts by Leslie Reade. Produced by Shepard Traube at the Playhouse, New York, February 12, 1945.

Cast of characters—

Napoleon Mickalieff	Eugene Sigaloff
Jean Prunier	Alfred Hesse
Bill Humphreys	Kim Spalding
Police Constable Hood	Stanley Bell
Christina Thomson	Perry Wilson
Liz	Stella Todd
Mrs. Gregory	Eva Leonard-Boyne
Maggie MacAndrews	Wendy Atkin
David Mendelsohn	Eduard Franz
A Gentleman	Morton L. Stevens

Acts I, II and III.—Meeting Room of the International Workmen's Educational Club in London. 1888.

Staged by Shepard Traube; setting and lighting by Boris Aronson; costumes by Rose Bogdanoff.

Members of a workers' club in London's Whitechapel, 1888, are generally and severally suspect in a series of Jack the Ripper murders occurring off stage with great frequency. A traveling cobbler, carrying a long, sharp knife and a generally suspicious air, is chief suspect and, as it turns out, likewise chief innocent.

(Closed February 24, 1945)

SIGNATURE

(2 performances)

A drama in three acts by Elizabeth McFadden, based on a short story by Melville Davisson Post entitled "Naboth's Vineyard." Produced by Richard Skinner and Dorothy Willard at the Forrest Theatre, New York, February 14, 1945.

Cast of characters—

Judge Simon Kilrail	Frederic Tozere
Zeke	Morris McKenney
Charles Borse	Lawrence Fletcher
Thadeus Braxton	Charles Francis
John Cartwright	Donald Murphy
Randolph	Lyster Chambers
Abner Davisson	Judson Laire
Nora Davisson	Marjorie Lord
Lance Moor	Charles Keane
1st Guard	William Forester
William Taylor	Bob Stevenson
Fendler	Charles S. Dubin
Alice Steuart	Anne Jackson
2nd Guard	Lew Herbert
Nathaniel Madison	George Lessey
Aunt Sophie Gide	Nell Harrison

```
Dr. Martin Storm...................................John McKee
Hon. Thomas Fargon............................Gregory Robins
Diccon............................................Page Spencer
Morrey............................................Bruce Halsey
Rev. Rockford........................................Peter Pann
Henry.............................................Coby Neal
Arnold...........................................Harry Kadison
Dayton............................................Charles Kuhn
Rev. Adam Rider...................................Cyrus Staehle
Alkiri...........................................Frederic Faber
Donovan.........................................Edwin Cushman
Elnathan Stone....................................Glenn Regent
Ward...............................William McMillen
```
      Acts I, II and III.—Conference Room in the Courthouse of a
Hill Town of Virginia, 1856.
      Staged by Roy Hargrave; setting by Stewart Chaney.

A wealthy farmer has been murdered. His hired hand is accused of the crime, which, to save him, is thereupon confessed
by the hired hand's sweetheart. John Cartwright, a forthright and
young attorney, does not believe in the guilt of either of the young
people accused. In their defense he proves that the trial judge,
Simon Kilrail, is the guilty party and, after considerable maneu-
vering, is able to unmask and convict his honor.

(Closed February 15, 1945)

AND BE MY LOVE

(14 performances)

A comedy in three acts by Edward Caulfield. Produced by
Arthur J. Beckhard in association with Victor Hugo-Vidal at the
National Theatre, New York, February 21, 1945.

Cast of characters—
```
Sarah Fenton......................................Lotus Robb
Henry............................................Walter Hampden
Martha Webster...................................Esther Dale
Mrs. Spence...................................Edmonia Nolley
Mr. Spence........................................Sydney Grant
Phyllis...........................................Ruth Homond
Allen.............................................Charles Colby
Mr. Fillmore........................................Jed Prouty
Ada Bennett......................................Violet Heming
Lizzie.............................................Viola Dean
No. 2527..........................................Graham Velsey
```
      Acts I, II and III.—Sitting Room of Sarah Fenton's House in
Riverhead, Connecticut.
      Staged by Arthur J. Beckhard; setting by Raymond Sovey.

Henry Smith, actor, flees his matinee idol's life. Meeting
Sarah Fenton, a Connecticut widow scientist who is also trying
to get away from her family complications, they agree to a trial
marriage period at Sarah's place in the country. In the end their

respective subterfuges are exposed, and they decide to make their home life legal.

(Closed March 3, 1945)

CALICO WEDDING

(5 performances)

A comedy in three acts by Sheridan Gibney. Produced by Lester Meyer and Richard Myers at the National Theatre, New York, March 7, 1945.

Cast of characters—

Captain George Gaylord	William Post
Lieutenant Jensen	Roderick Winchell
Nora	Eva Condon
Mary Gaylord	Grete Mosheim
Herbert Abercrombie	Forrest Orr
Mrs. Abercrombie	Mary Sargent
Frederick Boynton	Louis Jean Heydt
Betty Marlowe	Patricia White
Peg Hall	Barbara Joyce
Alma Biddle	Joy Geffen
Hendrik Van Delden	Jerome P. Thor
"Cap" Wilson	Henry Richards
Lotus Wilder	Jane Hoffman
Alan Packard	Vincent Gardner
Bob Willard	John Kane

Act I.—Scene 1—A Radio Listening Post, Alaska, Spring, 1944. 2—Bedroom of the Gaylords' Apartment, New York City, Spring, 1937. 3—The Living Room. Acts II and III.—The Living Room. Staged by Sheridan Gibney; settings by Frederick Fox.

Captain George Gaylord gives most of his time and his thought to the advertising business, which irks his wife, Mary, terribly. To bring George to book, Mary decides to flirt freely with Frederick Boynton, a returned explorer from the Antarctic, which she does. They drink together and retire to an adjoining bedroom. The question as to whether they went farther than that is continued as an open one in a prologue confession.

(Closed March 10, 1945)

IT'S A GIFT

(47 performances)

A comedy in three acts by Curt Goetz and Dorian Otvos. Produced by Goval Corporation at the Playhouse, New York, March 12, 1945.

Cast of characters—

Prof. Theodore W. Herrmann	Curt Goetz
Matilda Herrmann	Valerie Van Martens

```
Atlanta, 17...........................................Julie  Harris
Thomas,  15.........................................Robert  Muscat
Peter, 14...........................................David  Green
Lewis,  13..........................................Roland  Green
Ursula, 12..........................................Sally  Ferguson
Otto, 11............................................William  Kinney
Evelyn, 10..........................................Yvonne  Pothen
Dan, 9..............................................Victor  Vraz
Sophie, 8...........................................Winnie Mae Martin
Elsie, 7............................................Joan  Gordon
Sandy,  6...........................................Kevin  Mathews
Finnie, 4...........................................Evelyn  Daly
Emily...............................................Hilda  Laufkoetter
Rev.  Endicott......................................Whitford  Kane
Herbert  Kraft......................................Michael  Strong
Mayor  Doubleday....................................G.  Swayne  Gordon
Belinda.............................................Marjorie  Peterson
Madame  De  La  Jardinerre..........................Suzanne  Caubaye
Rosita..............................................Elaine  Carter
Chiquita............................................Hope  Miller
Lupe................................................Doris  Brent
Dolores.............................................Elsa  Johnson
Mr.  Flynn..........................................Morton  DaCosta
```
Acts I and III.—Home of Professor Herrmann in Hazelton, Pennsylvania. Act II.—A House in Montevideo, Uruguay.

Staged by Robert Henderson; settings by Samuel Leve; costumes by Rose Bogdanoff.

Prof. Theodore Herrmann, married and the father of twelve children, learns that his sister in South America has left a considerable inheritance to his oldest daughter. On investigation the Professor discovers that the sister, having been cast out of his house for a moral lapse when she was young, has stipulated that before the money goes to the daughter some member of the family must also be guilty of a carnal sin. The Professor thereupon decides that he would not mind too much if his daughter did bear a child before she was legally a wife.

(Closed April 21, 1945)

FOOLISH NOTION

(104 performances)

A comedy in three acts by Philip Barry. Produced by The Theatre Guild at the Martin Beck Theatre, New York, March 13, 1945.

Cast of characters—

```
Sophie  Wing........................................Tallulah  Bankhead
Happy  Hapgood......................................Joan H. Shepard
Florence  Denny.....................................Barbara  Kent
Gordon  Roark.......................................Donald  Cook
Rose................................................Mildred  Dunnock
Horatio  Wing.......................................Aubrey  Mather
Elsie...............................................Maria  Manton
Jim  Hapgood........................................Henry  Hull
Flora...............................................Maria  Manton
```

Flora..Barbara Kent
Flora...Mildred Dunnock
   Acts I, II and III.—Library on Second Floor of Jim Hapgood's
House in New York, November, 1944.
   Staged by John C. Wilson; production under supervision of
Armina Marshall; designed and lighted by Jo Mielziner; costumes
by Mainbocher.

See page 298.

(Closed June 9, 1945)

DARK OF THE MOON

(111 performances)
(Continuing)

A legend with music in two acts by Howard Richardson and
William Berney; music by Walter Hendl. Produced by the
Messrs. Shubert at the 46th Street Theatre, New York, March
14, 1945.

Cast of characters—

John...Richard Hart
Conjur Man......................................Ross Matthew
The Dark Witch..................................Iris Whitney
The Fair Witch................................Marjorie Belle
Conjur Woman.................................Georgia Simmons
Hank Gudger.....................................John Gerstad
Miss Metcalf..................................Frances Goforth
Mr. Jenkins..Gar Moore
Uncle Smelique.......................................Roy Fant
Mrs. Summey.................................Kathryn Cameron
Mr. Atkins....................................James Lanphier
Mrs. Bergen.................................Agnes Scott Yost
Edna Summey.................................Millicent Coleman
Burt Dinwitty...................................Robert Pryor
Hattie Heffner.............................Peggy Ann Holmes
Mr. Bergen.....................................Allan Tower
Mr. Summey....................................Stanley Nelson
Marvin Hudgens..................................John Gifford
Barbara Allen......................................Carol Stone
Floyd Allen.....................................Conrad Janis
Mrs. Allen......................................Maidel Turner
Mr. Allen......................................Sherod Collins
Preacher Haggler.............................Winfield Hoeny
Greeny Gorman.............................Dorothy I. Lambert
Dancing Witches.........Marguerite de Anguera, Jinx Heffelfinger
                          Peggy Ann Holmes, Lil Liandre
   Act I.—Scene 1—Peak of Ridge in Smoky Mountains. 2—Central
Square of Buck Creek. 3—The Allen Cabin on Chunky Gal
Mountain. 4—The General Store of Buck Creek. Act II.—Scene
1—Clearing in Woods near Barbara's and John's Cabin. 2—
Barbara's and John's Cabin. 3 and 5—Peak of Ridge in Smoky
Mountains. 4—The Church of God, Buck Creek.
   Staged by Robert E. Perry; dances directed by Esther Junger;
settings and lighting by George Jenkins; production supervised by
John Huntington.

John is a witch boy. His mother was a witch, his father a
buzzard. He lives high in the Smoky Mountains and consorts
freely with witch girls. When he spies pretty Barbara Allen in

the valley he makes a compact with the Conjur Woman. She is to make him human so he can marry Barbara, but if Barbara should prove untrue to him within a year he is to renounce his humanness and return to the witch tribe forever and ever. The marriage is consummated and Barbara gives birth to a witch child, which is burned by the midwives. At a religious revival Barbara is induced by her Christian kin to surrender herself to Marvin Hudgens to break the spell. After which Barbara dies and John goes back to the witches.

HAPPILY EVER AFTER

(12 performances)

A comedy in three acts by Donald Kirkley and Howard Burman. Produced by Bernard Klawans and Victor Payne-Jennings at the Biltmore Theatre, New York, March 15, 1945.

Cast of characters—

Charlie Porter	Parker Fennelly
Martha Whatcoat	Kathleen Lockhart
Sam Jarvis	George Calvert
Rev. Homer Whatcoat	Gene Lockhart
Alec Dixon	Warren Douglas
Rita Collins	Margaret Hayes
David Macdonald	Barry Macollum
Beulah Robinson	Dulcie Cooper
Mack	William Thomson
Dinty	William C. Tubbs
H. A. Stillwater	Herbert Heyes
Stubbs	Nicholas Saunders
Stan	Charles Wallis
Lil	Melba Rae
Sheriff	Hans Robert

Acts I, II and III.—Living Room of Parson Homer Whatcoat in a Small Marrying Town in Maryland.
Staged by Crane Wilbur; setting by Watson Barratt.

The Rev. Whatcoat has been a marrying parson in Maryland for enough years to have tied the knot for 9,999 couples, now the parents of thousands of children. As he is about to publicize his 10,000th wedding he is exposed by a couple of bright young newspaper reporters. He had never been ordained, say they, and all his marriages are illegal. The Rev. Whatcoat, however, proves them wrong.

(Closed March 24, 1945)

THE DEEP MRS. SYKES

(72 performances)

A comedy in two acts by George Kelly. Produced by Stanley Gilkey and Barbara Payne at the Booth Theatre, New York, March 19, 1945.

Cast of characters—

Mr. Sykes	Neil Hamilton
Mrs. Sykes	Catherine Willard
Ada	Myra Forbes
May	Charlotte Keane
Cyril	Romney Brent
Myrtle Weaver	Margaret Bannerman
Mrs. Fentriss	Jean Dixon
Ralph	Richard Martin
Adeline	Mary Gildea
Roy	Ralph Glover
Ethel	Gwen Anderson
Mrs. Taylor	Katherine Anderson
Mr. Manzoni	Tom McElhany
Mr. Taylor	Grandon Rhodes

Act I.—Living Room in the Home of Mr. Sykes. Act II.—Drawing Room at Mrs. Taylor's.
Staged by George Kelly; settings by Eleanor Farrington.

Mrs. Sykes is convinced that her woman's intuition is a gift. It helps her to the conviction that her husband has been sending white lilacs to Mrs. Taylor, a pianist who lives across the way. Mrs. Sykes doesn't like this idea and would shift the suspicion to the wives of other husbands in her social group. In the end the Sykes intuition is proved all wrong. It is her married son who loves the pianist, though her intuition still prompts her to reject his own confession.

(Closed May 19, 1945)

KISS THEM FOR ME

(103 performances)
(Continuing)

A comedy in three acts by Luther Davis, based on the novel "Shore Leave" by Frederic Wakeman. Produced by John Moses and Mark Hanna at the Belasco Theatre, New York, March 20, 1945.

Cast of characters—

F. Neilson	John McGovern
Lt. Comdr. Wallace	Edward Crandall
Mississip	Dennis King, Jr.
Mac	Richard Davis

```
Ensign.................................................Douglas Jones
Crewson...........................................Richard Widmark
Turnbill...............................................Robert Allen
Wac..............................................Sonya Stokowski
Alice...................................................Judy Holliday
Gwynneth............................................Jayne Cotter
Tailor................................................Harold Grau
Chief...................................................George Cory
Nurse Wilinski......................................Virginia Kaye
Chief Nurse.........................................Amy Douglass
Gunner...........................................George Mathews
Hedrick.............................................Dudley Sadler
Charlie................................................Daniel Petrie
Mr. Hardy..............................................Paul Ford
Mrs. Hardy...............................Patricia Quinn O'Hara
```
Acts I and III.—Living Room of Suite in the St. Mark Hotel, San Francisco. Act II.—Officers' Solarium in a Naval Hospital.
Staged by Herman Shumlin; setting by Frederick Fox.

Crewson, Mac and Mississip a little miraculously find themselves in San Francisco with a four-day leave from the airplane carrier with which they have been fighting for three years in the South Pacific. They get themselves a swell suite in the St. Mark Hotel, and let it be known that they want to have nothing to do with anything but liquor, women and a juke box for the term of their stay. Interruptions, planned and accidental, interfere with their scheme. They are hounded by munitions manufacturers, Navy red tape and a variety of romantic adventures. When Crewson is grounded and Mississip transferred, the boys decide to break leave and get back to their ship any way they can.

THE FIREBRAND OF FLORENCE

(43 performances)

A musical comedy in two acts by Edwin Justus Mayer and Ira Gershwin, based on "The Firebrand" by Mr. Mayer; music by Kurt Weill. Produced by Max Gordon at the Alvin Theatre, New York, March 22, 1945.

Cast of characters—
```
Hangman.....................................Randolph Symonette
Tartman...........................................Don Marshall
Souvenir Man.........................................Bert Freed
Maffio.............................................Boyd Heathen
Court Clerk...........................................Allen Noel
Magistrate.........................................Marion Green
Cellini...........................................Earl Wrightson
Ottaviano.........................................Ferdi Hoffman
Ascanio............................................James Dobson
Emelia..............................................Gloria Story
Angela............................................Beverly Tyler
Marquis...............................................Paul Best
Captain of the Guard...........................Charles Sheldon
Duke.............................................Melville Cooper
Page.............................................Billy Williams
Duchess.............................................Lotte Lenya
Major-Domo........................................Walter Graf
```

Harlequin..Jean Guelis
Colombina..Norma Gentner
    Apprentices: John Cassidy, Lynn Alden, Walter Rinner, Frank
Stevens.

Models:

The "Leonardo da Vinci" Model....................Yvette Heap
The "Titian" Model...............................Doris Blake
The "Botticelli" Model...........................Marya Iversen
The "Raphael" Model..............................Gedda Petry
The "Veronese" Model.........................Rose Marie Elliot
The "Bronzino" Model.........................Perdita Chandler

    Act I.—Scene 1—Public Square in Florence, Italy. 1535. 2—Be-
fore the Standards of Florence. 3—Cellini's Workshop. 4—The
City Gates. 5—The Garden of the Summer Palace. Act II.—
Scene 1—Cellini's Workshop. 2—The Palace Gates. 3—A Loggia in
the City Palace. 4—The Standards of Florence. 5—Grand Council
Chamber of the Palace. 6—Before the Standards of France. 7—
The Palace of the King of France.
    Staged by John Murray Anderson; book directed by John Haggott;
music by Maurice Abravanel; dancing by Catherine Littlefield; settings and lighting by Jo Mielziner; costumes by Raoul Pene DuBois.

Edwin Justus Mayer's "The Firebrand" was originally produced in New York, October 15, 1924, with Frank Morgan as
the Duke, Joseph Schildkraut as Cellini and Eden Gray as
Angela. It ran for 261 performances. A digest was included
in "The Best Plays of 1924-25."

(Closed April 28, 1945)

THE BARRETTS OF WIMPOLE STREET

(88 performances)

A drama in three acts by Rudolf Besier. Revived by Katharine
Cornell at the Ethel Barrymore Theatre, New York, March 26,
1945.

Cast of characters—

Doctor Chambers.................................Russell Gaige
Elizabeth Barrett Moulton-Barrett..............Katharine Cornell
Wilson..Brenda Forbes
Henrietta Moulton-Barrett.......................Emily Lawrence
Arabel Moulton-Barrett..........................Patricia Calvert
Octavius Moulton-Barrett............................Erik Martin
Alfred Moulton-Barrett..........................Stanley Parlan
Charles Moulton-Barrett..........................Howard Otway
Henry Moulton-Barrett...........................Roger Stearns
George Moulton-Barrett...........................Keinert Wolff
Edward Moulton-Barrett..........................McKay Morris
Bella Hedley.....................................Betty Brewer
Henry Bevan......................................Roger Stearns
Robert Browning..................................Brian Aherne
Doctor Ford-Waterlow.............................Ivan Simpson
Captain Surtees Cook..........................Chester Stratton
Flush...Himself
    Acts I, II and III.—Elizabeth Barrett's Bed-Sitting Room at
50 Wimpole Street, London, England, 1845.
    Staged by Guthrie McClintic; setting and costumes by Jo
Mielziner.

"The Barretts of Wimpole Street" was first produced and played by Miss Cornell in New York, February 9, 1931, with Brian Aherne and Brenda Forbes of the above revival in the cast. The play ran for 370 performances. A 17,000-mile American tour followed. A revival was staged in New York in February, 1935. In 1944 Miss Cornell (again with Mr. Aherne) took the play to Europe for a tour of the soldier camps of the American army, during which 140 performances were given.

(Closed June 9, 1945)

LADY IN DANGER

(12 performances)

A comedy-mystery in three acts by Max Afford and Alexander Kirkland. Produced by Pat Allen and Dan Fisher at the Broadhurst Theatre, New York, March 29, 1945.

Cast of characters—

Bill Sefton	James Gannon
Monica Sefton	Helen Claire
Miss Hodges	Elfrida Derwent
Dr. Francis Gresham	Alexander Kirkland
Sylvia Meade	Vicki Cummings
Andrew Meade	Rodney McLennan
Karl Kurt	Paul Fairleigh
Chief Inspector Burke	Clarence Derwent
Detective Dennis Marsh	Ronald Alexander
Constable Pogson	Hudson Faussett
Frederick Smith	Gary Blivers

Acts I, II and III.—The Sefton Apartments, Villa Flats, Melbourne, Australia.

Staged by Clarence Derwent; setting by Harry Gordon Bennett.

Monica Sefton was the wife of an American newspaper correspondent in Australia and a bit of an author on her own. She wrote detective stories mostly, and knew a lot about poisons. Naturally, when someone opened the Seftons' apartment closet and a poisoned chauffeur fell out, dead as a mackerel, Monica was suspect. It didn't take Inspector Burke long to pin the murder on Monica, but he was wrong. The chauffeur had been scratched by a black cat with curare on its toenails. It was all a Japanese plot.

(Closed April 7, 1945)

THE GLASS MENAGERIE

(88 performances)

(Continuing)

A drama in two parts by Tennessee Williams; incidental music by Paul Bowles. Produced by Eddie Dowling and Louis J. Singer at the Playhouse, New York, March 31, 1945.

Cast of characters—

The Mother....................................Laurette Taylor
Her Son......................................Eddie Dowling
Her Daughter.................................Julie Haydon
The Gentleman Caller.........................Anthony Ross
    Parts I and II.—An Alley in St. Louis.
    Staged by Eddie Dowling and Margo Jones; setting and lighting by Jo Mielziner.

See page 140.

A PLACE OF OUR OWN

(8 performances)

A comedy in three acts by Elliott Nugent. Produced by John Golden in association with Elliott Nugent and Robert Montgomery at the Royale Theatre, New York, April 2, 1945.

Cast of characters—

Margie Johns.................................Toni Favor
Pete Reis...................................John Howes
Nancy Monroe...............................Jeanne Cagney
Charles Reddy..............................Robert Keith
Jesse Ward.................................Seth Arnold
David Monroe...............................John Archer
Sam Reddy..................................J. C. Nugent
Mary Lorimer..............................Mercedes McCambridge
Augusta....................................Lotta Palfi
Henry Barfuss.............................Jack Howard
Mike McGroarty............................Anthony Blair
Joe Kaplan................................Wolfe Barzell
Mrs. Brandt...............................Helen Carew
    Acts I, II and III.—Living Room in the Reddy Home, Calais, Ohio, 1919.
    Staged by Elliott Nugent; setting by Raymond Sovey; costumes by Lucinda Ballard.

David Monroe, home from the First World War, marries Nancy Monroe. Nancy's father, Charles Reddy, wanting to hold her as a housekeeper, buys the local paper and turns it over to David as a wedding present. David is a liberal, a disciple of Woodrow Wilson and a worker for the League of Nations. Reddy is a reactionary and an anti-everything progressive. Reddy tries to dictate David's editorial policy. David rebels and runs away with his cousin, Mary Lorimer, but is brought back shortly to patch up his affairs at home. Peace at last.

(Closed April 4, 1945)

STAR SPANGLED FAMILY

(5 performances)

A comedy in three acts by B. Harrison Orkow. Produced by Philip Waxman and Joseph Kipness at the Biltmore Theatre, New York, April 10, 1945.

Cast of characters—

```
Gwen  Purchase...................................Dennie  Moore
Messenger..........................................Byron  Griffith
Sally  Jones.........................................Frances  Reid
Paul................................................Harlan  Stone
Harold.............................................Franklin  Allen
Mervin  Mitchell...................................Lewis  Charles
Dr.  Richard  Morley............................Edward  Nugent
"Bud"  Jones......................................Donald  Devlin
Margaret  Jones......................................Jean  Adair
Harry  Lupinsky.................................Stephen  Morrow
Victor  Gunther....................................Leon  Charles
Glen..............................................Jimmy  Sommer
Nurse  Craig.........................................Mary  Best
Dr.  Newton.......................................Bram  Nossen
     Acts  I,  II  and  III.—Sally  Jones's  Living  Room  in  a  Mid-Man-
hattan  Apartment.
     Staged  by  William  Castle;  setting  by  Edward  Gilbert;  costumes
by  Lou  Eisele.
```

Sally Jones, widow of the war hero, Mac Jones, marries Dr. Richard Morley, who was in the war but not a hero. Hero Mac's mother considers the marriage an insult to the memory of her son. She works to poison the mind of Mac's son, her grandson, Bud, against his stepfather. She nearly succeeds. But not quite.

(Closed April 13, 1945)

CAROUSEL

(68 performances)
(Continuing)

A musical play in prelude and two acts adapted by Benjamin F. Glazer from Ferenc Molnar's play, "Liliom"; music by Richard Rodgers; book and lyrics by Oscar Hammerstein II; orchestrations by Don Walker. Produced by The Theatre Guild at the Majestic Theatre, New York, April 19, 1945.

Cast of characters—

Carrie Pipperidge.....................................Jean Darling
Julie Jordan..Jan Clayton
Mrs. Mullin...Jean Casto
Billy Bigelow...John Raitt
1st Policeman...Robert Byrn
David Bascome...Franklyn Fox
Nettie Fowler...Christine Johnson
Enoch Snow..Eric Mattson
Hannah..Annabelle Lyon
Boatswain...Peter Birch
Jigger Craigin..Murvyn Vye
Arminy..Connie Baxter
Penny...Marilyn Merkt
Jennie...   Joan Keenan
Virginia..Ginna Moise
Susan...Suzanne Tafel
Jonathan..Richard H. Gordon
2nd Policeman...Larry Evers
Captain...Blake Ritter
1st Heavenly Friend...................................Jay Velie
2nd Heavenly Friend...................................Tom McDuffie
He..Russell Collins
She...Kathleen Comegys
Enoch Snow, Jr..Ralph Linn
Louise..Bambi Linn
Jimmy...Robert Pagent
Principal...Lester Freedman
Minister..Russell Collins

Prelude—An Amusement Park on the New England Coast. 1873. Act I.—Scene 1—Tree-lined Path Along the Shore. 2—Nettie Fowler's Spa on the Ocean Front. Act II.—Scene 1—An Island Across the Bay. 2—Waterfront. 3—Up There. 4—Down Here. On a Beach. 1888. 5—Outside Julie's Cottage. 6—Outside a Schoolhouse.

Staged by Rouben Mamoulian; supervised by Lawrence Langner and Theresa Helburn; choreography by Agnes De Mille; music directed by Joseph Littau; settings by Jo Mielziner; costumes by Miles White.

Molnar's "Liliom" had its first production in New York at the Garrick Theatre, under Theatre Guild auspices, April 20, 1921. Eva LeGallienne and Joseph Schildkraut played the leads. It was revived by Miss LeGallienne at the Civic Repertory Theatre October 26, 1932, again with Mr. Schildkraut, and by Vinton Freedley, with Burgess Meredith and Ingrid Bergman, at the 44th St. Theatre, March 25, 1940. In the "Carousel" adaptation the locale is changed to New England in 1873. Liliom becomes Billy Bigelow and Julie is Julie Jordan. Billy, a tough Summer park barker, marries Julie and bullies her until he learns he is to become a father. To get money to rear his child he helps with a holdup and kills himself when he is about to be arrested. At the gates of heaven, after fifteen years in Purgatory, Billy is given a chance to return to earth and redeem his soul by doing one good deed. On earth he meets his daughter, is angered by her refusal to accept a star he has brought her, slaps her and goes back to Purgatory.

COMMON GROUND

(61 performances)

(Continuing)

A drama in three acts by Edward Chodorov. Produced by Edward Choate at the Fulton Theatre, New York, April 25, 1945.

Cast of characters—

```
Aide..............................................Arthur   Gondra
Buzz  Bernard.......................................Philip  Loeb
Kate  DeRosa.......................................Nancy  Noland
Geegee  (Genevieve  Gilman)...........................Mary  Healy
Nick  DeRosa........................................Joseph  Vitale
Alan  Spencer....................................Donald  Murphy
1st  Italian  Soldier...........................J.  Anthony  Selba
2nd  Italian  Soldier..................................Lou  Gilbert
3rd  Italian  Soldier..................................Rupert  Pole
Ted  Williamson...................................Paul  McGrath
Captain  Angelini..................................Luther  Adler
Colonel  Hofer...............................Peter  Von  Zerneck
        Acts  I,  II  and  III.—Music  Room  of  Old  Italian  Castle,  Just
    Preceding  the  Capture  of  Naples.
        Staged  by  Edward  Chodorov  and  Jerome  Robbins;  setting  and
    lighting  by  George  Jenkins.
```

Buzz Bernard, "Geegee" Gilman, the DeRosas, Nick and Kate, and Alan Spencer are members of a U.S.O.-Camp Shows group touring the military camps on the Italian front. Their plane is forced down near Naples some weeks before the liberation of that city. The Nazi commandant, Colonel Hofer, gives them their choice of continuing their tour as propagandists of the Nazi cause or being shot—all except Bernard. He, being a Jew, is to be sent to a concentration camp in any case. After an hour's debate the show folk, representing five nationalities but all Americans at heart and in fact, decide to die as patriots rather than live as traitors.

TOO HOT FOR MANEUVERS

(5 performances)

A comedy in three acts by Les White and Bud Pearson. Produced by James S. Elliott at the Broadhurst Theatre, New York, May 2, 1945.

Cast of characters—

```
Sergeant  Walter  Burrows......................Dickie  Van  Patten
Sergeant  Reggie  Winthrop.......................Michael  Dreyfuss
Captain  Hamilton...................................Ronald  Telfer
Corporal  "Einstein"  Smetts.........................Alastair  Kyle
Colonel  Steve  Hadley..............................Richard  Arlen
Amy  Burrows....................................Helene  Reynolds
```

```
Cadet "Wimpy" Worthington........................Billy Nevard
Alex..............................................Arthur Hunnicutt
Major Peters......................................Jed Prouty
Colonel Bedloe...............................Lawrence Fletcher
Major Stanley.....................................Harry Antrim
Mr. Winthrop......................................Fleming Ward
Mrs. Winthrop............................Agnes Heron Miller
Mr. Perkle........................................Harry Koler
Patsy Laverne.....................................Eve McVeagh
Countess Rosini.................................Ellen Andrews
Veronica........................................Sheila O'Malley
Hilda.............................................Edith Leslie
Cadet No. 1.......................................Roy Robson
Cadet No. 2.......................................Marty Miller
Cadet No. 3.......................................Pat O'Rourke
```
Acts I and III.—Headmaster's Office, Hadley's Military Academy,
New York. Act II.—Scene 1—Headmaster's Office. 2—Reception
Room at Countess Rosini's.
Staged by Les White and Bud Pearson; settings by Wolfgang
Roth; costumes by Lou Eisele.

Colonel Steve Hadley, headmaster of Hadley's Military Academy in upstate New York, becomes suspicious of a reducing salon and massage parlor up the road from his academy, run by a Countess Rosini. When two of the upper classmen are seen coming out of the Countess Rosini's place the Colonel and other faculty members start an investigation that uncovers a bathtub of innuendoes and double meanings. After which the salon, the Countess and all her girls are proved legitimate. The boys were merely trying to reduce for the basketball team.

(Closed May 6, 1945)

BLUE HOLIDAY

(8 performances)

A Negro variety show with music and lyrics by Al Moritz; songs by Duke Ellington, E. Y. Harburg and Earl Robinson. Produced by Irvin Shapiro and Doris Cole at the Belasco Theatre, New York, May 21, 1945.

Principals engaged—

Ethel Waters	Josh White
Mary Lou Williams	Timmie Rogers
Josephine Premice	Willie Bryant
Lillian Fitzgerald	Muriel Gaines
Lavinia Williams	Talley Beatty
Evelyn Ellis	Mildred Smith
The Three Poms	The Chocolateers
Hall Johnson Choir	Katherine Dunham Dancers

Staged by Moe Hack; choreography by Katherine Dunham; music directed by Hall Johnson; settings by Perry Watkins.

(Closed May 21, 1945)

FOXHOLE IN THE PARLOR

(29 performances)
(Continuing)

A play in two acts by Elsa Shelley. Produced by Harry Bloomfield at the Booth Theatre, New York, May 23, 1945.

Cast of characters—

Leroy...Reginald Beane
Tom Austen.....................................Russell Hardie
Vicki King.......................................Ann Lincoln
Ann Austen......................................Flora Campbell
Senator Bowen..................................Raymond Greenleaf
Dennis Patterson...............................Montgomery Clift
Kate Mitchell....................................Grace Coppin
 Acts I and II.—A Little Street in Lower Manhattan, Mid-April, 1945.
 Staged by John Haggott; setting by Lee Simonson.

Dennis Patterson, sensitive young artist, is home from the wars emotionally upset by his experiences with death and dying at the front. Two Greenwich Village friends, the Austens, try desperately to aid in his rehabilitation but a tough-minded sister, Kate Mitchell, insists he should go home with her. Failing in this, the sister seeks to have Dennis committed to a sanitarium. He is rescued by a retired U. S. Senator on his way to the San Francisco peace conference. The Senator takes Dennis along as an aide in stimulating interest in the world-security plans of the conference delegates.

MEMPHIS BOUND!

(28 performances)
(Continuing)

A musical comedy in two acts by Albert Barker and Sally Benton; lyrics and music by Don Walker and Clay Warnick. Produced by John Wildberg at the Broadway Theatre, New York, May 24, 1945.

Cast of characters—

Hector...William C. Smith
Melissa Carter (Aunt Mel).....................Edith Wilson
Chloe..Ann Robinson
Roy Baggott.....................................Billy Daniels
Mrs. Paradise...................................Ada Brown
Lily Valentine...................................Sheila Guys
Penny Paradise..................................Ida James
Henny Paradise.................................Thelma Carpenter
Mr. Finch..Frank Wilson
Winfield Carter (Windy)........................Avon Long
Pilot Meriwether (Pops).......................Bill Robinson

Timmy..Timothy Grace
Sheriff McDaniels...............................Oscar Plante
Eulalia..Joy Merrimore
Sarabelle.......................................Harriet Jackson
Bill...Charles Welch
Gabriel...William Dillard
   Cherubs: Georgia Ann Timmons, Marliene Strong.
   Delta Rhythm Boys: Traverse Crawford, Rene De Knight, Carl
  Jones, Kelsey Pharr, Lee Gaines.
   Act I.—Scene 1—Deck of the *Calliboga Queen*, Near Calliboga,
Tennessee. 2—A Street. 3—A Cell in Calliboga Jail. 4—"H.M.S.
Pinafore" aboard the *Calliboga Queen*. Act II.—Scene 1—The
Village Square. 2 and 6—The Street. 3 and 5—The Cell. 4—
The Trial. 7—"Pops" Meriwether in the rest of "Pinafore."
   Production under supervision of Vinton Freedley; staged by
Robert Ross assisted by Eva Jessye; dances directed by Al White,
Jr.; music by Charles Sanford; settings and lighting by George
Jenkins; costumes by Lucinda Ballard.

Aunt Mel Carter organizes a troupe of colored singers and dancers for a trip down the Mississippi. They leave on the showboat *Calliboga Queen* for a performance of "H.M.S. Pinafore" in Memphis. The *Calliboga* gets suck on a sandbar and the troupe has to give a performance of "Pinafore" to raise money to get her off. Complications follow.

ROUND TRIP

(7 performances)

A comedy in three acts by Mary Orr and Reginald Denham. Produced by Clifford Hayman at the Biltmore Theatre, New York, May 29, 1945.

Cast of characters—

Edgar Albright..............................Sidney Blackmer
Virginia Albright...........................Patricia Kirkland
Donald McDermott...........................Paul Marlin
Sarah Albright..............................June Walker
Jane Daniels................................Edith Meiser
Clive Delafield.............................Eddie Nugent
Griselda....................................Angela Jaye
Tommy Rolls.................................Robert Woodburn
Linda Marble................................Phyllis Brooks
Hortense....................................Viola Dean
Jack Admirall...............................Edward Rowley
Lloyd Wilde.................................Morton L. Stevens
   Acts I and III.—The Den of the Albrights' Home, Ironville,
Ohio. Act II.—Clive Delafield's Apartment, Woodrow Hotel, New
York City.
   Staged by Reginald Denham; settings by Samuel Leve; costumes
by Bianca Stroock.

Sarah Albright, of Ironville, Ohio, finds herself fascinated by the attractive personality of Clive Delafield, a Broadway actor in search of a backer for his play. When Clive goes back to New York Sarah follows after, only to discover the actor living with a dizzy blonde in a side street. Edgar Albright, Sarah's husband,

organizing a tour of investigation on his own, takes a fancy to the
actor's blonde and takes her back to Ironville as his secretary.
The Albright daughter finally brings about a parental recon-
ciliation.

(Closed June 2, 1945)

HOLLYWOOD PINAFORE

(20 performances)
(Continuing)

A modernized version of Gilbert and Sullivan's "H.M.S. Pinafore"; book and lyrics revised by George S. Kaufman. Sullivan
score retained. Produced by Max Gordon in association with
Meyer Davis at the Alvin Theatre, New York, May 31, 1945.

Cast of characters—

Joseph W. Porter....................................Victor Moore
Mike Corcoran......................................George Rasely
Ralph Rackstraw...................................Gilbert Russell
Dick Live-Eye.................................William Gaxton
Brenda Blossom.............................Annamary Dickey
Louhedda Hopsons.............................Shirley Booth
Bob Beckett..Russ Brown
Miss Hebe...Mary Wickes
Miss Gloria Mundi.............................Diana Corday
Miss Beverly Wilshire............................Pamela Randell
Little Miss Peggy....................................Ella Mayer
Doorman..Dan De Paolo
Secretaries.......Jackson Jordan, Eleanor Prentiss, Drucilla Strain
Guard...Ernest Taylor
Other Little Maids..............Barbara Heath, Helene Constantine
Talent Scout.......................................Regis Powers
Her True Love..............................Ronny Chetwood
Two More Boys.....................Shaun O'Brien, Jack Purcell
Armand, the Movie Hero............................John Butler
Director...Stanley Herbertt
Studio Assistants....Eleanor Boleyn, Ann Newland, Virginia Meyer
   Acts I and II.—Pinafore Pictures Studios, Hollywood, includ-
ing Antony Tudor's ballet interlude "Success Story" with Viola
Essen.
   Staged by George S. Kaufman; production supervised by Arnold
Saint Subber; music directed by George Hirst; ballet by Antony
Tudor; ensemble dances by Douglas Coudy; settings and lighting by
Jo Mielziner; costumes by Kathryn Kuhn and Mary Percy Schenck.

For half its length, "Hollywood Pinafore" successfully satirizes
the Gilbert-Sullivan classic. Joseph W. Porter serves as the head
of a huge motion picture producing unit. Ralph Rackstraw
represents a group of wage slaves, mostly writers, who wear prison
garb as their work-a-day uniforms. Dick Live-Eye, with patch,
is an actor's agent, on the prowl for his 10 per cent. And the
Bumboat Woman becomes Louhedda Hopsons, Little Miss Butter-
cup, a Hollywood columnist. The second half of "Hollywood

Pinafore" is devoted to an effort to recapture the spirit of the first half.

CONCERT VARIETIES

(19 performances)

(Continuing)

A vaudeville entertainment in two acts assembled by Billy Rose. Produced by Billy Rose at the Ziegfeld Theatre, New York, June 1, 1945.

Principals engaged—

Katherine Dunham & Co.	Jerome Robbins & Co.
Imogene Coca	Zero Mostel
Deems Taylor	Rosario & Antonio
Eddie Mayehoff	Nestor Chayres
Salici Puppets	Sidney Catlett
William Archibald	Albert Ammons
Pete Johnson	Talley Beatty
Janet Reed	John Krise

Technical director—Carlton Winckler; music directed by Pembroke Davenport.

EQUITY-LIBRARY THEATRE

The most ambitious—and to date the most successful—of Experimental Theatre enterprises in the Broadway sector is that of the Equity-Library Theatre. This organization, inspired, directed and sustained largely by the enthusiasm of the actors themselves, began functioning seriously the season of 1943-44. In three months six Public Library productions were staged in various library neighborhoods. Last season an additional thirty-seven productions were added to this list, making a total of forty-three productions in sixty-six weeks.

John Golden started the Equity-Library Theatre off with a subscription of $1,000, to which he has added from time to time. Sam Jaffe, representing Equity, and George Freedley, curator of the Theatrical section of the New York Public Library, representing the Library Associations, were assisted in the organization and conduct of the shows by an Actors' Committee including Margaret Webster, Aline MacMahon, Dudley Digges, Ruth Hammond, John Kennedy, Philip Loeb, Alexander Clark, Clarence Derwent and Walter Greaza.

Admission to the shows is free. Actor and directional services are volunteered. Equity permits a 20 per cent non-Equity, or amateur, cast. The 1944-45 selection of plays included "Squaring the Circle," a "program of youth" consisting of "The Shy and Lonely," "Hello Out There," an excerpt of "These Endearing Young Charms," "Mary Rose," "The Importance of Being Ernest," "Mary Stuart," scenes from "The Merchant of Venice," "The Happy Journey," "As You Desire Me," "Holiday," "No More Ladies," "The Shining Hour," "Co-Respondent Unknown," "Maedchen in Uniform," "Come of Age," "Winterset," "Death Takes a Holiday," "The Sea-Gull," "Front Page" (Act II), "My Sister Eileen" (Act I), "Smilin' Through," "Twelfth Night," "Rocket to the Moon," "Ladies in Retirement," "When We Dead Awaken," "Letters to Lucerne," "The Animal Kingdom," "Hamlet," "The Late Christopher Bean," "The Moon in Yellow River," "The Tragedy of Nan," "The Children's Hour," "The Bourgeois Gentleman," "The Wild Duck," "Escape Me Never," "Measure for Measure," "The White Steed" and "Golden Boy."

DANCE DRAMA

An unusual number of productions on Broadway included ballets and elaborate dance programs during the season of 1944-45. Among them were "Song of Norway," "Bloomer Girl," "Sadie Thompson," "Seven Lively Arts," "Laffing Room Only," "Sing Out Sweet Land," "On the Town," "Up in Central Park," "Dark of the Moon," "The Firebrand of Florence," "Carousel," "Memphis Bound!", "Hollywood Pinafore," "Blue Holiday," and "A Lady Says Yes."

At the Lewisohn Stadium, July 17, 1944, Anton Dorati directed "Blue Bird," "Grand Pas de Deux—The Sleeping Beauty," and "Les Sylphides." Alicia Markova danced "The Dying Swan" and Anton Dolin the Ravel "Bolero." August 7 and 8, 1944, Mia Slavenska, Leonide Massine, Igor Youskevitch, Yura Lazovski, Audrey Keane and Norma Vaslavina were the principal dancers. The program included "Salome" set to a Glazounov symphonic poem; Anton Dvorak's "Carneval Overture," "La Farucca," "Spectre de la Rose" by C. M. von Weber, Rimsky-Korsakoff's "Capriccio Espanol," Moussorgsky's Hopak from "The Fair at Sorochinsk," Yogoslav Pageant including "Symphonic Kolo" by Jakov Gotovac and "Balkan Sketches" by Marko Taitchevitch and Tchaikovsky's "Grand Pas de Deux." Music was directed by Franz Allers.

The Ballet Russe de Monte Carlo officially opened the Fall season at City Center, September 10, 1944, continuing for two weeks and reappearing for a Spring season in February, closing March 25, 1945.

Among the premières presented were a choreographic setting of Richard Strauss music for the Turkish ballet in Molière's "Le Bourgeois Gentilhomme" and "Danses Concertantes" with music by Stravinsky, both created by George Balanchine and Eugene Berman; "Imperial Ballet" with music by Tchaikovsky, choreography by Balanchine and settings and costumes by Doboujinsky; "Frankie and Johnny" by Ruth Page and Bentley Stone with music by Jerome Moross and setting by Clive Rickabaugh; "Mozartiana" set to Tchaikovsky's fourth suite of Mozart arrangements with choreography by Balanchine and setting by Christian Berand; "Pas de Deux" created by Balanchine to entr'acte music from Tchaikovsky's "Sleeping Beauty."

The dancers in principal roles included Nathalie Krassovska, Alexandra Danilova, Dorothy Etheridge, Ruthania Boris, Leon Danielian, Yurek Lazowski, Frederic Franklin, Marie Tallchief, Mary Ellen Moylan, Jean Yazvinsky, Alexandra Goudovitch, Nicolas Magallanes, James Starbuck, Michel Katcharoff, Nakita Talinn, George Verdak, Robert Lindgren, Julia Horvath, Ruth Page, Bentley Stone, Pauline Giddard, Nora White, Gertrude Svobodina and Corvino.

Le Meri and the Natya Dancers presented programs of dances from Java, Burma, India, Syria, Morocco, North Africa, Spain, Italy, etc., at the Ethnologic Theatre, from July 18 until the middle of January.

Pearl Primus, under the management of Max J. Jelin, assisted by a group of Negro dancers and musicians, appeared at the Belasco Theatre, New York, October 4 through October 14, 1944. Gordon Heath was narrator and Josh White accompanied Miss White as singer-guitarist. The dancers included Randolph Scott, Joe Comadore, Albert Popwell, James Alexander and Thomas Bell. On the program were "African Ague," "Mischievous Interlude," "Slave Market," "Haitian Play Dance," "African Ceremonial," "Yanvalao," "The Negro Speaks of Rivers" by Langston Hughes with music by Sarah Malament, "Strange Fruit" set to poem by Lewis Allen, "Study in Nothing" with music by Mary Lou Williams, "Rock Daniel" with music by Lucky Millinder, "Hard Times Blues" by Joah White and "Our Spring Will Come" set to music by John Cage from a poem by Langston Hughes. At Times Hall, January 11 and 12, 1945, Pearl Primus, Josephine Premice and Hadassah presented a program of Hindu and African dances including voodoo and carnival dance dramas and songs of Haiti.

The Ballet Theatre, at the Metropolitan Opera House, under the management of S. Hurok, began its Fall season October 8 and continued through November 5, 1944. Guest stars included Tamara Toumanova, Tatania Riabouchinska, Anton Dolin, Argentinita, Pilar Lopez, Leonide Massine, David Lichine, Michael Kidd, Jose Greco, Manolo Vargas, Andre Eglevsky and Igor Youskevitch. The regular company included Nana Gollner, Nora Kaye, Rex Cooper, Margaret Banks, John Kriza, Muriel Bentley, Shirley Eckl, Hugh Laing, Lucia Chase, Rosella Hightower, Paul Petroff, Alicia Alonzo, Miriam Golden, Diana Adams, Jerome Robbins, Dick Beard, Maria Karnilova, Dimitri Romanoff, Janet Reed and Antony Tudor.

Premières included George Balanchine's new version of "Waltz Academy" with music by Vittorio Rieti, décor by Oliver Smith and costumes by Alvin Colt and "Graduation Ball" by David Lichine with Johann Strauss music and décor by Mstislav Doboujinsky. The four-week Spring season began April 1, 1945. The new productions were "Undertow" by Antony Tudor with music by William Schuman and décor by Raymond Breinin; "Moonlight Sonata" by Leonide Massine, set to the Beethoven classic with décor and costumes by Sergei Soudeikine; a revised version of Agnes de Mille's "Tally-Ho"; "Harvest Time" by Bronislava Nijinska, set to music of Henri Wieniawski in an arrangement by Antal Dorati and costumes by Enid Gilbert and "Rendezvous" by Mme. Nijinska to music by Rachmaninoff. Guest artists for the Spring season included Alicia Markova, Nicolas Orloff, Albis Kavan, Agnes de Mille and Argentinita. Antal Dorati was musical director, assisted by Mois-Zlatin.

The Ballet International, Inc., with the Marquis de Cuevas as president and director, opened its first season at the International Theatre, New York, October 30, 1944. Alexander Smallens was musical director and George Schick assisted by Boris Kogan were conductors. Among the designers for the revivals were Sergei Soudeikine, Horace Armistead, Grace Houseton, Ignatiev, Doboujinsky, Dunkel and Mitrouk. The company numbering 54 dancers was headed by André Eglevsky and William Dollar. The principals included the ballerinas Viola Essen and Marie-Jeanne, Constance Garfield, Katia Geleznova, Elise Reiman, Lisa Maslova, Yvonne Patterson, Nina Golovina, Zoya Leporsky, Edward Caton, Jean Guélis, Kari Karnakowski, Alexander Iolas, Simon Semenoff, Sergei Ismailoff, Francisco Moncion, and Toni Worth. The premières included "Brahms Varieties" by Bronislava Nijinska with sets and costumes by Marcel Vertès; "Sentimental Colloquy" by André Eglevsky to music of Paul Boeles with décor by Salvador Dali; "The Last Flower" based on the Thurber story by William Dollar with music by Nicolas Nabokoff and décor by Stewart Chaney; "Mad Tristan" choreographed from Richard Wagner music by Mme. Nijinska with story and settings by Dali; "Memories" by Simon Semenoff to Brahms music and story by Winthrop Palmer with sets by Dubois; "The Mute Wife" by Antonia Cobos to Paganini music arranged by Vittorio Rieti with décor by Rico LeBrun; "Pictures at an Exhibition" by Mme. Nijinska to Moussorgsky music with setting by Boris Aronson; "Sebastian" by Edward Caton to music by Gian-Carlo Menotti with costumes by Milena and setting by Oliver Smith; "Prince Goudal's Festival" by Boris Romanoff with music from

Rubinstein's opera, "The Demon," and sets by Mstislav Doboujinsky. The season closed December 24, 1944.

Regina Devi, Hindu dancer, assisted by Indrani and Namora, gave a series of dance programs at Carnegie Music Hall under the auspices of Theatre of All Nations, December 8 and 9, 1945.

Katherine Dunham and her troupe of singers and dancers were presented by S. Hurok in a program called "Tropical Revue" for a three-week engagement at the Century Theatre starting December 26, 1944. In the company were Lucille Ellis, Lavinia Williams, Sylvia Fort, Roger Ohardieno, Vanoye Aikens, Bobby Capo and the Dowdy Quartette. The dances were "L'Ar'ya" dealing with voodoo in Martinique with music by Robert Sanders; "Flaming Youth 1927" with motif sung by Helen Dowdy and a new version of "Havana Promenade."

Argentinita and her company of Spanish dancers and musicians opened the Spring season February 18, 1945, at Carnegie Hall, New York. Among the new dance dramas executed by Argentinita, Pilar Lopez, José Greco and Manolo Vargas a new version of "Ruta de Sevilla," and three choreographies to music by Pittaluga; "Danza del Chivato" by Vargas, "Dance No. 4" by Miss Lopez and two dances from "La Romeria de los Cornades."

The African Academy of Arts and Research gave an inaugural festival in the Spring of 1944 and two programs in early April of 1945, at Carnegie Hall, New York, presenting Asadata Dafore, Alma Sutton, Abdul Assen, Norman Koker and Josephine Premice dancing African dances and Princess Orelia and Pedro presenting dances of Brazil and Cuba. Also at Carnegie Hall in the Spring of 1945, Ruth St. Denis and Ted Shawn with 16 other dancers under the management of Jacob's Pillow Dance Festival, Inc., appeared in "Rajput Nautch," "Brahms' Waltz," "Tillers of the Soil," etc.

Martha Graham appeared at the National Theatre, New York, in 7 performances from May 14 through May 19, 1945. The new dance dramas presented were "Appalachian Spring" with choreography by Miss Graham and music by Aaron Copland (recipient of last season's Pulitzer award), "Mirror Before Me," from a Mellarme poem with music by Paul Hindesmith, and "John Brown" with music by Charles Mills. Louis Horst conducted the music, décor was by Isamu Noguchi, lighting by Jan Rosenthal and costumes by Edythe Gifond. In the supporting company were May O'Donnell, Nina Fonaroff, Margery Mazia, Yuriko, Ethel Winters, Erick Hawkins, Merce Cunningham, Richard Hylton, Jane Dudley, Jean Erdman and Pearl Lang.

OFF BROADWAY

"Stars of Tomorrow" opened at the Malin Theatre, New York, July 19, 1944, sponsored by Jules Denes. A variety bill was performed with a cast which included Rose Mortel, Gea Gianni, Roy and Gladyce Royce, H. Warren Hyer, Maria Karolyi, Susanne Pierre and Jimmy McGarry.

"Korb'n," by David Blum, was produced at the Provincetown Theatre, New York, September 26, closing October 10, 1944, after 24 performances.

"Abraham," written, produced and directed by Tom Donahue, was presented at the Cherry Lane Theatre by The Little Theatre of St. Therese, November 28, 1944. Leonida Moser and Eugene Diserio headed the cast.

Modern Play Productions presented "Design for Laughter" by William Mishkin and John Francis with music by Private Alexander Maissel at the Provincetown Theatre, New York, November 29, 1944. Appearing in the cast were Robert Feyti, Josephine Lombardo and Millicent Lewis.

"Mom's Boy," by Ruth Woodward, was presented at the Barbizon-Plaza Theatre under the sponsorship of Josh Binney, December 16, 1944. Helen Hayne, Jed Allison and Billee Ward were in the cast.

The Lighthouse Players under the direction of Jane Rose appeared in "Ladies in Retirement" at the Lighthouse Little Theatre, December 15 and 16, 1944. The players were Lillian Hillman, Peggy Foley, Sarah Rae, Ruth Askenas, Mayme Teitelbaum, Ida Scotti and Helen Zivan.

THE HEDGEROW THEATRE

The Hedgerow Theatre of Moylan, Pennsylvania, started a season of repertoire at the Cherry Lane Theatre, New York, January 16, 1945, with "The Emperor Jones" by Eugene O'Neill. Other plays presented were "Tomorrow's Yesterday" by Jack Kinnard; "Thunder on the Left" by Jean Ferguson Black, from Christopher Morley's novel; "Quintin Quintana" by Ramon Naya. Jasper Deeter staged the productions and the lighting was done by Mahlon Naill. Miriam Philips assisted Mr. Deeter

in the direction of "The Emperor Jones." The settings were by
Mahlon Naill and Eleanor Plaisted Abbott. "Tomorrow's Yesterday" was directed by Rose Schulmann. The settings were
by Dolores Tanner and the costumes by Helen Alexander.
"Quintin Quintana" was designed by Joseph Gistirak.

In the several casts were Jasper Deeter, Catherine Rieser,
Mahlon Naill, Elsie Winacour, Robert Councill, Anne Follman,
Joseph Leberman, Helen Alexander, Miriam Philips, Rose Schulmann, Irving Weiss, Audrey Ward, Ruth Esherick, Dan Christ-
man, Arthur Hanson, Wanda Donn, Kenneth Carter, Arthur
Rich, Thomas Meigs, Alfonso Morriconi and Harold Hays. The
engagement ended February 11, 1945.

HENIE ICE SHOW

Sonja Henie presented her 1945 version of "Hollywood Ice
Revue" for 18 performances at Madison Square Garden, begin-
ning January 17, 1945. The principals included Fritz Dietl,
Gene Theslof, Dorothy and Hazel Caley, Freddie Trenkler, Bruce
Clark, Bud Moore and Charles Storey. The choreography and
staging were by Catherine Littlefield and the costumes by Billy
Livingston.

"Sweet Genevieve," by M. G. and Marchette Chute, was pro-
duced by M. G., Marchette and Joy Chute and Mina Cole at the
President Theatre, New York, March 20, 1945. The cast in-
cluded Grace Kleine, Sam Benham, Rosilyn Weiss, Jay Davis,
Ruth Manning, Ruth Grubbs, Nolia Trammel, Hal Hershey and
Paul Rapport.

"Eternal Cage," by Jules Denes, was produced by C. Sherman
Hoyt at the Barbizon-Plaza for 10 performances starting March
21, 1945. The author staged the play and Harry Bennet de-
signed the setting. The cast included Frank Gibney, Sheila
Bromley, George Blackwood, Frances Dale, Joanna Douglas and
William Forrest.

"If Five Years Pass," adapted by Richard O'Connell and
James Graham from the Spanish of Federico Garcia Lorca, was
produced by the Jane Street co-operative organization at the
Provincetown Playhouse, April 6, 1945. Joann Strauss directed a
large cast. Among the players were Les Mahoney, Rudolph
Watson, Ellen Deming, Marie de Wolfe and Paz Davila. Incidental music was composed by Lorainne Henderson.

SAN CARLO OPERA COMPANY

Fortune Gallo's San Carlo Opera Company opened its twelve-day Spring season at the Rockefeller Center Theatre, May 16, 1945, with Bizet's "Carmen." A ballet of 200 was headed by Lucien Prideaux and Lydia Arlova and the music was directed by Nicholas Rescigno. "Aïda," "Cavalleria Rusticana," "Pagliacci" and other operas were produced. In the company were Margery Mayer, Sydney Rayner, Mary Henderson, Louis Decesare, William Wilderman, Clelia Venditti, Olympia Di Napoli, Richard Vivaldi, Carlo Morelli, Elda Ercole, Marie Powers, Betty Stone, Mario Palermo, Stefan Ballerini, Mostyn Thomas, and Tandy Mackenzie.

The Theatre of All Nations produced "The Private Life of the Master Race," a documentary play in three acts by Bertold Brecht in English version by Eric Russel Bentley with music by Hans Eisler, at the Pauline Edwards Theatre, New York, June 11, 1945. The large cast was headed by Albert and Else Basserman and the principal players were Clarence Derwent, Paul Andor, Vilma Kurer and Hester Sondergard. The play was staged by Bertold Viertel and George George, the settings and lighting were by Leo Kerz and the music was directed by Josef Schmid. Maurice Ellis was narrator and Robert Penn was a ballad singer.

FOREIGN LANGUAGE PLAYS

The Yiddish Theatre of New York opened the 1944-45 season with "Good News," a two act musical by Isador Lillian and Joseph Rumshinsky, at the Second Avenue Theatre, New York, September 27, 1944. The musical was staged by Menasha Skulnik, the settings were by Michael Saltzman and the dances were directed by Valentina Belova. The principal players were Menasha Skulnik, Miriam Kressyn, Max Kletter, Esther Saltzman, Anna Thomashefsky, Yetta Zwerling, Paula Klida and Morris Tarlovsky. The run was concluded February 27, 1945, with 200 performances.

"They All Want to Get Married," by Julie Berns with music by Alexander Olshanetsky, opened the season at the Public Theatre, New York, October 8, 1944, and ran until April 15, 1945, with 245 performances. The play was produced and directed by Judah Bleich, choreographed by Benjamin Zemach, and the settings were by Leo Kerz. In the cast were Aaron Lebedeff, Lucy and Mischa Gehrman, Diana Goldberg, Irving Grossman, Nina Rochelle and Luba Kadison.

"The Miracle of the Warsaw Ghetto," a drama in three acts by H. Leivick with music by Sholem Secunda, was presented in Yiddish at the New Jewish Folk Theatre, New York, by Joseph Green, October 10, 1944. The drama was staged by Jacob Ben-Ami, choreography was by Benjamin Zemach, and settings by H. A. Condell. Among the players were Jacob Ben-Ami, Berta Gersten, Dina Halpern, Isidor Cashier, Dora Weissman, Menachem Rubin, Muriel Gruber and Mark Topel. Closed December 18, 1944.

"We Will Live," written by David Bergelson and directed by Jacob Ben-Ami, had its première at the Jewish Folk Theatre, New York, December 20, 1944. Jacob Ben-Ami and Michael Gibson headed the cast.

"My Friend Yossel," a musical comedy, was produced by Menasha Skulnik at the Second Avenue Theatre, New York, March 3, 1944. Sholem Secunda wrote the music and Michael Saltzman designed the settings.

The Theatre of All Nations presented an all-French festival of music and drama dedicated to General De Gaulle at the Barbizon-Plaza Theatre, New York, November 11, 1944. Among the artists featured in the program were Annabella, Joseph Rogatchewsky, Cecile Jahiel, Robert Franc, Mildah Polia, Penny Caldwell and Pierre de Cailleux. "The Man Who Never Gave Up" by Jacques Ferrand was produced.

The Austrian Theatre Guild presented in German Carl Lindau's two-act operetta "Vienna at Night" (with music by Johann Strauss) at Carnegie Hall, April 29, 1945. The book and lyrics were revised by Karl Farkas who also staged the production and acted the leading role of Jean. Margit Bokor, Hungarian soprano, John Hendrik, Eleanor Lansing, Licci Balla, Herman Leopoldi, Ralf Telasko and Ella Bleyer were in the cast. Herbert Winkler directed the music. A ballet "Valse Viennoise" was danced by Arthur Mahoney and Thalia Mara and a half dozen young women of the original "Viennese Schrammeln d'Grinzinger."

The East and West Association presented a program representing the type of modern theatre developed in war-time China with three one-act plays translated by Wang Yung at the Barbizon-Plaza Theatre, New York, May 4, 1945.

"The Quiet Don," an opera in four acts by Ivan Dzerzhinsky from the novel by M. Sholokhoff, was sung in Russian by the Russian Grand Opera Company at Carnegie Hall, New York, May 27, 1945. The principals in the cast were Arsen Tarpoff, Nadia Ray, Maria Maximovitch and George Doubrowsky. The music was directed by Michael Fiveisky and the chorus by Dmitri Chutro.

STATISTICAL SUMMARY

Plays	Number Performances	
Angel Street	1,295	(Closed December 30, 1944)
Carmen Jones	503	(Closed February 10, 1945)
Chicken Every Sunday	318	(Closed January 6, 1945)
For Keeps	29	(Closed July 8, 1944)
Helen Goes to Troy	97	(Closed July 15, 1944)
Jacobowsky and the Colonel	417	(Closed March 10, 1945)
Mexican Hayride	481	(Closed March 17, 1945)
One Touch of Venus	567	(Closed February 10, 1945)
Othello	296	(Closed July 1, 1944)
Over 21	221	(Closed July 8, 1944)
Pick-up Girl	198	(Closed October 21, 1944)
Ramshackle Inn	216	(Closed July 8, 1944)
Take a Bow	12	(Closed June 24, 1944)
Doughgirls, The	671	(Closed July 29, 1944)
New Moon, The	53	(Closed June 24, 1944)
Searching Wind, The	318	(Closed January 20, 1945)
Two Mrs. Carrolls, The	585	(Closed February 3, 1945)
Three's a Family	497	(Closed July 8, 1944)
Wallflower	192	(Closed July 8, 1944)
Ziegfeld Follies	553	(Closed July 22, 1944)

LONG RUNS ON BROADWAY

To June 17, 1945

(Plays marked with asterisk were still playing June 17, 1945)

Plays	Number Performances	Plays	Number Performances
Tobacco Road	3,182	Boy Meets Girl	669
*Life with Father	2,362	Blithe Spirit	657
Abie's Irish Rose	2,327	The Women	657
Arsenic and Old Lace	1,444	A Trip to Chinatown	657
Hellzapoppin	1,404	Rain	648
Angel Street	1,295	Janie	642
Lightnin'	1,291	The Green Pastures	640
Pins and Needles	1,108	Is Zat So	618
*Oklahoma!	952	Separate Rooms	613
*Kiss and Tell	948	Star and Garter	609
The Bat	867	Student Prince	608
My Sister Eileen	865	Broadway	603
White Cargo	864	Adonis	603
You Can't Take It with You	837	Street Scene	601
Three Men on a Horse	835	Kiki	600
Stars on Ice	830	Blossom Time	592
The Ladder	789	The Two Mrs. Carrolls	585
The First Year	760	Brother Rat	577
Sons o' Fun	742	Show Boat	572
The Man Who Came to Dinner	739	The Show-Off	571
Claudia	722	*The Voice of the Turtle	570
Junior Miss	710	Sally	570
Seventh Heaven	704	One Touch of Venus	567
Peg o' My Heart	692	Rose Marie	557
The Children's Hour	691	Strictly Dishonorable	557
Dead End	687	Ziegfeld Follies	553
East Is West	680	Good News	551
Chauve Souris	673	Let's Face It	547
The Doughgirls	671	Within the Law	541
Irene	670	The Music Master	540
		What a Life	538
		The Boomerang	522

447

Plays	*Number Performances*	*Plays*	*Number Performances*
Rosalinda	521	Carmen Jones	503
Blackbirds	518	Personal Appearance	501
Sunny	517	Panama Hattie	501
Victoria Regina	517	Bird in Hand	500
The Vagabond King	511	Sailor, Beware!	500
The New Moon	509	Room Service	500
Shuffle Along	504	Tomorrow the World	500

NEW YORK DRAMA CRITICS' CIRCLE AWARD

The New York Drama Critics' Circle did not even hesitate in its choice of a prize play to represent the theatre season of 1944-45. Tennessee Williams' "memory play," "The Glass Menagerie," was the winner on both the first, or trial balloon, ballot, and the final, or signed, ballot, which now represents the Circle's voting plan. Mr. Williams' play was given a clear majority of eight of the fourteen votes on the first ballot, and nine on the second. Mary Coyle Chase's fantastic comedy, "Harvey," Paul Osborn's "A Bell for Adano," and Dorothy and Howard Baker's "Trio" were also mentioned.

Previous to its arrival in New York for a production the night of March 31, "The Glass Menagerie" had had an exciting experience in Chicago. The critical reviews were enthusiastic, but the apathetic reaction of the public was depressing. For three weeks the play languished. After that it was enthusiastically, even a little wildly, supported.

Knowing that both the Critics' Circle and the Pulitzer Prize Committee voted in New York early in April; that, in fact, the Pulitzer judges did not consider until the following season any play produced after the first of April, the producers of "The Glass Menagerie" abruptly broke off the Chicago engagement of their play while it was still a favorite and brought it to Broadway. Thus they played for two prizes and won one. The Pulitzer award went to "Harvey."

Other Critics' Circle awards have been:

1935-36—Winterset, by Maxwell Anderson
1936-37—High Tor, by Maxwell Anderson
1937-38—Of Mice and Men, by John Steinbeck
1938-39—No award. ("The Little Foxes" and "Abe Lincoln in Illinois" led the voting.)
1939-40—The Time of Your Life, by William Saroyan
1940-41—Watch on the Rhine, by Lillian Hellman
1941-42—No award.
1942-43—The Patriots, by Sidney Kingsley
1943-44—No award.
1944-45—The Glass Menagerie, by Tennessee Williams

PULITZER PRIZE WINNERS

"For the original American play performed in New York which shall best represent the educational value and power of the stage in raising the standard of good morals, good taste and good manners."—The Will of Joseph Pulitzer, dated April 16, 1904.

In 1929 the advisory board, which, according to the terms of the will, "shall have the power in its discretion to suspend or to change any subject or subjects . . . if in the judgment of the board such suspension, changes or substitutions shall be conducive to the public good," decided to eliminate from the above paragraph relating to the prize-winning play the words "in raising the standard of good morals, good taste and good manners."

The present terms of the Pulitzer award are "for an original American play performed in New York, which shall represent in marked fashion the educational value and power of the stage, preferably dealing with American life."

The Pulitzer selection of a play of American authorship that consistently meets the terms of the award as stated above was Mary Coyle Chase's fantastic comedy called "Harvey." There being no record of a vote, it is assumed the choice was unanimous. The Pulitzer committee had, like the Drama Critics' Circle, been unable to find an American play worthy its award to represent the season of 1943-44.

Previous Pulitzer prize play awards have been—

1917-18—Why Marry? by Jesse Lynch Williams
1918-19—No award.
1919-20—Beyond the Horizon, by Eugene O'Neill
1920-21—Miss Lulu Bett, by Zona Gale
1921-22—Anna Christie, by Eugene O'Neill
1922-23—Icebound, by Owen Davis
1923-24—Hell-bent fer Heaven, by Hatcher Hughes
1924-25—They Knew What They Wanted, by Sidney Howard
1925-26—Craig's Wife, by George Kelly
1926-27—In Abraham's Bosom, by Paul Green
1927-28—Strange Interlude, by Eugene O'Neill
1928-29—Street Scene, by Elmer Rice
1929-30—The Green Pastures, by Marc Connelly

1930-31—Alison's House, by Susan Glaspell
1931-32—Of Thee I Sing, by George S. Kaufman, Morrie
            Ryskind, Ira and George Gershwin
1932-33—Both Your Houses, by Maxwell Anderson
1933-34—Men in White, by Sidney Kingsley
1934-35—The Old Maid, by Zoe Akins
1935-36—Idiot's Delight, by Robert E. Sherwood
1936-37—You Can't Take It with You, by Moss Hart and
            George S. Kaufman
1937-38—Our Town, by Thornton Wilder
1938-39—Abe Lincoln in Illinois, by Robert E. Sherwood
1939-40—The Time of Your Life, by William Saroyan
1940-41—There Shall Be No Night, by Robert E. Sherwood
1941-42—No award.
1942-43—The Skin of Our Teeth, by Thornton Wilder
1943-44—No award.
1944-45—Harvey, by Mary Coyle Chase

PREVIOUS VOLUMES OF BEST PLAYS

Plays chosen to represent the theatre seasons from 1899 to 1944 are as follows:

1899-1909

"Barbara Frietchie," by Clyde Fitch. Published by Life Publishing Company, New York.

"The Climbers," by Clyde Fitch. Published by the Macmillan Co., New York.

"If I Were King," by Justin Huntly McCarthy. Published by Samuel French, New York and London.

"The Darling of the Gods," by David Belasco. Published by Little, Brown & Co., Boston, Mass.

"The County Chairman," by George Ade. Published by Samuel French, New York and London.

"Leah Kleschna," by C. M. S. McLellan. Published by Samuel French, New York.

"The Squaw Man," by Edwin Milton Royle.

"The Great Divide," by William Vaughn Moody. Published by Samuel French, New York, London and Canada.

"The Witching Hour," by Augustus Thomas. Published by Samuel French, New York and London.

"The Man from Home," by Booth Tarkington and Harry Leon Wilson. Published by Samuel French, New York, London and Canada.

1909-1919

"The Easiest Way," by Eugene Walter. Published by G. W. Dillingham, New York; Houghton Mifflin Co., Boston.

"Mrs. Bumpstead-Leigh," by Harry James Smith. Published by Samuel French, New York.

"Disraeli," by Louis N. Parker. Published by Dodd, Mead and Co., New York.

"Romance," by Edward Sheldon. Published by the Macmillan Co., New York.

"Seven Keys to Baldpate," by George M. Cohan. Published by Bobbs-Merrill Co., Indianapolis, as a novel by Earl Derr Biggers; as a play by Samuel French, New York.

"On Trial," by Elmer Reizenstein. Published by Samuel French, New York.

"The Unchastened Woman," by Louis Kaufman Anspacher. Published by Harcourt, Brace and Howe, Inc., New York.

"Good Gracious Annabelle," by Clare Kummer. Published by Samuel French, New York.

"Why Marry?" by Jesse Lynch Williams. Published by Charles Scribner's Sons, New York.

"John Ferguson," by St. John Ervine. Published by the Macmillan Co., New York.

1919-1920

"Abraham Lincoln," by John Drinkwater. Published by Houghton Mifflin Co., Boston.

"Clarence," by Booth Tarkington. Published by Samuel French, New York.

"Beyond the Horizon," by Eugene G. O'Neill. Published by Boni & Liveright, Inc., New York.

"Déclassée," by Zoe Akins. Published by Liveright, Inc., New York.

"The Famous Mrs. Fair," by James Forbes. Published by Samuel French, New York.

"The Jest," by Sem Benelli. (American adaptation by Edward Sheldon.)

"Jane Clegg," by St. John Ervine. Published by Henry Holt & Co., New York.

"Mamma's Affair," by Rachel Barton Butler. Published by Samuel French, New York.

"Wedding Bells," by Salisbury Field. Published by Samuel French, New York.

"Adam and Eva," by George Middleton and Guy Bolton. Published by Samuel French, New York.

1920-1921

"Deburau," adapted from the French of Sacha Guitry by H. Granville Barker. Published by G. P. Putnam's Sons, New York.

"The First Year," by Frank Craven. Published by Samuel French, New York.

"Enter Madame," by Gilda Varesi and Dolly Byrne. Published by G. P. Putnam's Sons, New York.

"The Green Goddess," by William Archer. Published by Alfred A. Knopf, New York.

"Liliom," by Ferenc Molnar. Published by Boni & Liveright, New York.

"Mary Rose," by James M. Barrie. Published by Charles Scribner's Sons, New York.

"Nice People," by Rachel Crothers. Published by Charles Scribner's Sons, New York.

"The Bad Man," by Porter Emerson Browne. Published by G. P. Putnam's Sons, New York.

"The Emperor Jones," by Eugene G. O'Neill. Published by Boni & Liveright, New York.

"The Skin Game," by John Galsworthy. Published by Charles Scribner's Sons, New York.

1921-1922

"Anna Christie," by Eugene G. O'Neill. Published by Boni & Liveright, New York.

"A Bill of Divorcement," by Clemence Dane. Published by the Macmillan Company, New York.

"Dulcy," by George S. Kaufman and Marc Connelly. Published by G. P. Putnam's Sons, New York.

"He Who Gets Slapped," adapted from the Russian of Leonid Andreyev by Gregory Zilboorg. Published by Brentano's, New York.

"Six Cylinder Love," by William Anthony McGuire.

"The Hero," by Gilbert Emery.

"The Dover Road," by Alan Aelxander Milne. Published by Samuel French, New York.

"Ambush," by Arthur Richman.

"The Circle," by William Somerset Maugham.

"The Nest," by Paul Geraldy and Grace George.

1922-1923

"Rain," by John Colton and Clemence Randolph. Published by Liveright, Inc., New York.

"Loyalties," by John Galsworthy. Published by Charles Scribner's Sons, New York.

"Icebound," by Owen Davis. Published by Little, Brown & Company, Boston.

"You and I," by Philip Barry. Published by Brentano's, New York.

"The Fool," by Channing Pollock. Published by Brentano's, New York.

"Merton of the Movies," by George Kaufman and Marc Connelly, based on the novel of the same name by Harry Leon Wilson.

"Why Not?" by Jesse Lynch Williams. Published by Walter H. Baker Co., Boston.

"The Old Soak," by Don Marquis. Published by Doubleday, Page & Company, New York.

"R.U.R.," by Karel Capek. Translated by Paul Selver. Published by Doubleday, Page & Company.

"Mary the 3d," by Rachel Crothers. Published by Brentano's, New York.

1923-1924

"The Swan," translated from the Hungarian of Ferenc Molnar by Melville Baker. Published by Boni & Liveright, New York.

"Outward Bound," by Sutton Vane. Published by Boni & Liveright, New York.

"The Show-Off," by George Kelly. Published by Little, Brown & Company, Boston.

"The Changelings," by Lee Wilson Dodd. Published by E. P. Dutton & Company, New York.

"Chicken Feed," by Guy Bolton. Published by Samuel French, New York and London.

"Sun-Up," by Lula Vollmer. Published by Brentano's, New York.

"Beggar on Horseback," by George Kaufman and Marc Connelly. Published by Boni & Liveright, New York.

"Tarnish," by Gilbert Emery. Published by Brentano's, New York.

"The Goose Hangs High," by Lewis Beach. Published by Little, Brown & Company, Boston.

"Hell-bent fer Heaven," by Hatcher Hughes. Published by Harper Bros., New York.

1924-1925

"What Price Glory?" by Laurence Stallings and Maxwell Anderson. Published by Harcourt, Brace & Co., New York.

"They Knew What They Wanted," by Sidney Howard. Published by Doubleday, Page & Company, New York.

"Desire Under the Elms," by Eugene G. O'Neill. Published by Boni & Liveright, New York.

"The Firebrand," by Edwin Justus Mayer. Published by Boni & Liveright, New York.

"Dancing Mothers," by Edgar Selwyn and Edmund Goulding.

"Mrs. Partridge Presents," by Mary Kennedy and Ruth Warren. Published by Samuel French, New York.

"The Fall Guy," by James Gleason and George Abbott. Published by Samuel French, New York.

"The Youngest," by Philip Barry. Published by Samuel French, New York.

"Minick," by Edna Ferber and George S. Kaufman. Published by Doubleday, Page & Company, New York.

"Wild Birds," by Dan Totheroh. Published by Doubleday, Page & Company, New York.

1925-1926

"Craig's Wife," by George Kelly. Published by Little, Brown & Company, Boston.

"The Great God Brown," by Eugene G. O'Neill. Published by Boni & Liveright, New York.

"The Green Hat," by Michael Arlen.

"The Dybbuk," by S. Ansky, Henry G. Alsberg-Winifred Katzin translation. Published by Boni & Liveright, New York.

"The Enemy," by Channing Pollock. Published by Brentano's, New York.

"The Last of Mrs. Cheyney," by Frederick Lonsdale. Published by Samuel French, New York.

"Bride of the Lamb," by William Hurlbut. Published by Boni & Liveright, New York.

"The Wisdom Tooth," by Marc Connelly. Published by George H. Doran & Company, New York.

"The Butter and Egg Man," by George Kaufman. Published by Boni & Liveright, New York.

"Young Woodley," by John Van Druten. Published by Simon and Schuster, New York.

1926-1927

"Broadway," by Philip Dunning and George Abbott. Published by George H. Doran Company, New York.

"Saturday's Children," by Maxwell Anderson. Published by Longmans, Green & Company, New York.

"Chicago," by Maurine Watkins. Published by Alfred A. Knopf, Inc., New York.

"The Constant Wife," by William Somerset Maugham. Published by George H. Doran Company, New York.

"The Play's the Thing," by Ferenc Molnar and P. G. Wodehouse. Published by Brentano's, New York.

"The Road to Rome," by Robert Emmet Sherwood. Published by Charles Scribner's Sons, New York.

"The Silver Cord," by Sidney Howard. Published by Charles Scribner's Sons, New York.

"The Cradle Song," translated from the Spanish of G. Martinez Sierra by John Garrett Underhill. Published by E. P. Dutton & Company, New York.

"Daisy Mayme," by George Kelly. Published by Little, Brown & Company, Boston.

"In Abraham's Bosom," by Paul Green. Published by Robert M. McBride & Company, New York.

1927-1928

"Strange Interlude," by Eugene G. O'Neill. Published by Boni & Liveright, New York.

"The Royal Family," by Edna Ferber and George Kaufman. Published by Doubleday, Doran & Company, New York.

"Burlesque," by George Manker Watters. Published by Doubleday, Doran & Company, New York.

"Coquette," by George Abbott and Ann Bridgers. Published by Longmans, Green & Company, New York, London, Toronto.

"Behold the Bridegroom," by George Kelly. Published by Little, Brown & Company, Boston.

"Porgy," by DuBose Heyward. Published by Doubleday, Doran & Company, New York.

"Paris Bound," by Philip Barry. Published by Samuel French, New York.

"Escape," by John Galsworthy. Published by Charles Scribner's Sons, New York.

"The Racket," by Bartlett Cormack. Published by Samuel French, New York.

"The Plough and the Stars," by Sean O'Casey. Published by the Macmillan Company, New York.

1928-1929

"Street Scene," by Elmer Rice. Published by Samuel French, New York.

"Journey's End," by R. C. Sherriff. Published by Brentano's, New York.

"Wings Over Europe," by Robert Nichols and Maurice Browne. Published by Covici-Friede, New York.

"Holiday," by Philip Barry. Published by Samuel French, New York.

"The Front Page," by Ben Hecht and Charles MacArthur. Published by Covici-Friede, New York.

"Let Us Be Gay," by Rachel Crothers. Published by Samuel French, New York.

"Machinal," by Sophie Treadwell.

"Little Accident," by Floyd Dell and Thomas Mitchell.

"Gypsy," by Maxwell Anderson.

"The Kingdom of God," by G. Martinez Sierra; English version by Helen and Harley Granville-Barker. Published by E. P. Dutton & Company, New York.

1929-1930

"The Green Pastures," by Marc Connelly (adapted from "Ol' Man Adam and His Chillun," by Roark Bradford). Published by Farrar & Rinehart, Inc., New York.

"The Criminal Code," by Martin Flavin. Published by Horace Liveright, New York.

"Berkeley Square," by John Balderston. Published by the Macmillan Company, New York.

"Strictly Dishonorable," by Preston Sturges. Published by Horace Liveright, New York.

"The First Mrs. Fraser," by St. John Ervine. Published by the Macmillan Company, New York.

"The Last Mile," by John Wexley. Published by Samuel French, New York.

"June Moon," by Ring W. Lardner and George S. Kaufman. Published by Charles Scribner's Sons, New York.

"Michael and Mary," by A. A. Milne. Published by Chatto & Windus, London.

"Death Takes a Holiday," by Walter Ferris (adapted from the Italian of Alberto Casella). Published by Samuel French, New York.

"Rebound," by Donald Ogden Stewart. Published by Samuel French, New York.

1930-1931

"Elizabeth the Queen," by Maxwell Anderson. Published by Longmans, Green & Co., New York.

"Tomorrow and Tomorrow," by Philip Barry. Published by Samuel French, New York.

"Once in a Lifetime," by George S. Kaufman and Moss Hart. Published by Farrar and Rinehart, New York.

"Green Grow the Lilacs," by Lynn Riggs. Published by Samuel French, New York and London.

"As Husbands Go," by Rachel Crothers. Published by Samuel French, New York.

"Alison's House," by Susan Glaspell. Published by Samuel French, New York.

"Five-Star Final," by Louis Weitzenkorn. Published by Samuel French, New York.

"Overture," by William Bolitho. Published by Simon & Schuster, New York.

"The Barretts of Wimpole Street," by Rudolf Besier. Published by Little, Brown & Company, Boston.

"Grand Hotel," adapted from the German of Vicki Baum by W. A. Drake.

1931-1932

"Of Thee I Sing," by George S. Kaufman and Morrie Ryskind; music and lyrics by George and Ira Gershwin. Published by Alfred Knopf, New York.

"Mourning Becomes Electra," by Eugene G. O'Neill. Published by Horace Liveright, Inc., New York.

"Reunion in Vienna," by Robert Emmet Sherwood. Published by Charles Scribner's Sons, New York.

"The House of Connelly," by Paul Green. Published by Samuel French, New York.

"The Animal Kingdom," by Philip Barry. Published by Samuel French, New York.

"The Left Bank," by Elmer Rice. Published by Samuel French, New York.

"Another Language," by Rose Franken. Published by Samuel French, New York.

"Brief Moment," by S. N. Behrman. Published by Farrar & Rinehart, New York.

"The Devil Passes," by Benn W. Levy. Published by Martin Secker, London.

"Cynara," by H. M. Harwood and R. F. Gore-Browne. Published by Samuel French, New York.

1932-1933

"Both Your Houses," by Maxwell Anderson. Published by Samuel French, New York.

"Dinner at Eight," by George S. Kaufman and Edna Ferber. Published by Doubleday, Doran & Co., Inc., Garden City, New York.

"When Ladies Meet," by Rachel Crothers. Published by Samuel French, New York.

"Design for Living," by Noel Coward. Published by Doubleday, Doran & Co., Inc., Garden City, New York.

"Biography," by S. N. Behrman. Published by Farrar & Rinehart, Inc., New York.

"Alien Corn," by Sidney Howard. Published by Charles Scribner's Sons, New York.

"The Late Christopher Bean," adapted from the French of René Fauchois by Sidney Howard. Published by Samuel French, New York.

"We, the People," by Elmer Rice. Published by Coward-McCann, Inc., New York.

"Pigeons and People," by George M. Cohan.

"One Sunday Afternoon," by James Hagan. Published by Samuel French, New York.

1933-1934

"Mary of Scotland," by Maxwell Anderson. Published by Doubleday, Doran & Co., Inc., Garden City, N. Y.

"Men in White," by Sidney Kingsley. Published by Covici, Friede, Inc., New York.

"Dodsworth," by Sinclair Lewis and Sidney Howard. Published by Harcourt, Brace & Co., New York.

"Ah, Wilderness," by Eugene O'Neill. Published by Random House, New York.

"They Shall Not Die," by John Wexley. Published by Alfred A. Knopf, New York.

"Her Master's Voice," by Clare Kummer. Published by Samuel French, New York.

"No More Ladies," by A. E. Thomas.

"Wednesday's Child," by Leopold Atlas. Published by Samuel French, New York.

"The Shining Hour," by Keith Winter. Published by Doubleday, Doran & Co., Inc., Garden City, New York.

"The Green Bay Tree," by Mordaunt Shairp. Published by Baker International Play Bureau, Boston, Mass.

1934-1935

"The Children's Hour," by Lillian Hellman. Published by Alfred Knopf, New York.

"Valley Forge," by Maxwell Anderson. Published by Anderson House, Washington, D. C. Distributed by Dodd, Mead & Co., New York.

"The Petrified Forest," by Robert Sherwood. Published by Charles Scribner's Sons, New York.

"The Old Maid," by Zoe Akins. Published by D. Appleton-Century Co., New York.

"Accent on Youth," by Samson Raphaelson. Published by Samuel French, New York.

"Merrily We Roll Along," by George S. Kaufman and Moss Hart. Published by Random House, New York.

"Awake and Sing," by Clifford Odets. Published by Random House, New York.

"The Farmer Takes a Wife," by Frank B. Elser and Marc Connelly.

"Lost Horizons," by John Hayden.

"The Distaff Side," by John Van Druten. Published by Alfred Knopf, New York.

1935-1936

"Winterset," by Maxwell Anderson. Published by Anderson House, Washington, D. C.

"Idiot's Delight," by Robert Emmet Sherwood. Published by Charles Scribner's Sons, New York.

"End of Summer," by S. N. Behrman. Published by Random House, New York.

"First Lady," by Katharine Dayton and George S. Kaufman. Published by Random House, New York.

"Victoria Regina," by Laurence Housman. Published by Samuel French, Inc., New York and London.

"Boy Meets Girl," by Bella and Samuel Spewack. Published by Random House, New York.

"Dead End," by Sidney Kingsley. Published by Random House, New York.

"Call It a Day," by Dodie Smith. Published by Samuel French, Inc., New York and London.

"Ethan Frome," by Owen Davis and Donald Davis. Published by Charles Scribner's Sons, New York.

"Pride and Prejudice," by Helen Jerome. Published by Doubleday, Doran & Co., Garden City, New York.

1936-1937

"High Tor," by Maxwell Anderson. Published by Anderson House, Washington, D. C.

"You Can't Take It with You," by Moss Hart and George S. Kaufman. Published by Farrar & Rinehart, Inc., New York.

"Johnny Johnson," by Paul Green. Published by Samuel French, Inc., New York.

"Daughters of Atreus," by Robert Turney. Published by Alfred A. Knopf, New York.

"Stage Door," by Edna Ferber and George S. Kaufman. Published by Doubleday, Doran & Co., Garden City, New York.

"The Women," by Clare Boothe. Published by Random House, Inc., New York.

"St. Helena," by R. C. Sherriff and Jeanne de Casalis. Published by Samuel French, Inc., New York and London.

"Yes, My Darling Daughter," by Mark Reed. Published by Samuel French, Inc., New York.

"Excursion," by Victor Wolfson. Published by Random House, New York.

"Tovarich," by Jacques Deval and Robert E. Sherwood. Published by Random House, New York.

1937-1938

"Of Mice and Men," by John Steinbeck. Published by Covici-Friede, New York.

"Our Town," by Thornton Wilder. Published by Coward-McCann, Inc., New York.

"Shadow and Substance," by Paul Vincent Carroll. Published by Random House, Inc., New York.

"On Borrowed Time," by Paul Osborn. Published by Alfred A. Knopf, New York.

"The Star-Wagon," by Maxwell Anderson. Published by Anderson House, Washington, D. C. Distributed by Dodd, Mead & Co., New York.

"Susan and God," by Rachel Crothers. Published by Random House, Inc., New York.

"Prologue to Glory," by E. P. Conkle. Published by Random House, Inc., New York.

"Amphitryon 38," by S. N. Behrman. Published by Random House, Inc., New York.

"Golden Boy," by Clifford Odets. Published by Random House, Inc., New York.

"What a Life," by Clifford Goldsmith. Published by Dramatists' Play Service, Inc., New York.

1938-1939

"Abe Lincoln in Illinois," by Robert E. Sherwood. Published by Charles Scribner's Sons, New York and Charles Scribner's Sons, Ltd., London.

"The Little Foxes," by Lillian Hellman. Published by Random House, Inc., New York.

"Rocket to the Moon," by Clifford Odets. Published by Random House, Inc., New York.

"The American Way," by George S. Kaufman and Moss Hart. Published by Random House, Inc., New York.

"No Time for Comedy," by S. N. Behrman. Published by Random House, Inc., New York.

"The Philadelphia Story," by Philip Barry. Published by Coward-McCann, Inc., New York.

"The White Steed," by Paul Vincent Carroll. Published by Random House, Inc., New York.

"Here Come the Clowns," by Philip Barry. Published by Coward-McCann, Inc., New York.

"Family Portrait," by Lenore Coffee and William Joyce Cowen. Published by Random House, Inc., New York.

"Kiss the Boys Good-bye," by Clare Boothe. Published by Random House, Inc., New York.

1939-1940

"There Shall Be No Night," by Robert E. Sherwood. Published by Charles Scribner's Sons, New York.

"Key Largo," by Maxwell Anderson. Published by Anderson House, Washington, D. C.

"The World We Make," by Sidney Kingsley.

"Life with Father," by Howard Lindsay and Russel Crouse. Published by Alfred A. Knopf, New York.

"The Man Who Came to Dinner," by George S. Kaufman and Moss Hart. Published by Random House, Inc., New York.

"The Male Animal," by James Thurber and Elliott Nugent. Published by Random House, Inc., New York, and MacMillan Co., Canada.

"The Time of Your Life," by William Saroyan. Published by Harcourt, Brace and Company, Inc., New York.

"Skylark," by Samson Raphaelson. Published by Random House, Inc., New York.

"Margin for Error," by Clare Boothe. Published by Random House, Inc., New York.

"Morning's at Seven," by Paul Osborn. Published by Samuel French, New York.

1940-1941

"Native Son," by Paul Green and Richard Wright. Published by Harper & Bros., New York.

"Watch on the Rhine," by Lillian Hellman. Published by Random House, Inc., New York.

"The Corn Is Green," by Emlyn Williams. Published by Random House, Inc., New York.

"Lady in the Dark," by Moss Hart. Published by Random House, Inc., New York.

"Arsenic and Old Lace," by Joseph Kesselring. Published by Random House, Inc., New York.

"My Sister Eileen," by Joseph Fields and Jerome Chodorov. Published by Random House, Inc., New York.

"Flight to the West," by Elmer Rice. Published by Coward, McCann, Inc., New York.

"Claudia," by Rose Franken Maloney. Published by Farrar & Rinehart, Inc., New York and Toronto.

"Mr. and Mrs. North," by Owen Davis. Published by Samuel French, New York.

"George Washington Slept Here," by George S. Kaufman and Moss Hart. Published by Random House, Inc., New York.

1941-1942

"In Time to Come," by Howard Koch. Published by Dramatists' Play Service, Inc., New York.

"The Moon Is Down," by John Steinbeck. Published by The Viking Press, New York.

"Blithe Spirit," by Noel Coward. Published by Doubleday, Doran & Co., Garden City, New York.

"Junior Miss," by Jerome Chodorov and Joseph Fields. Published by Random House, Inc., New York.

"Candle in the Wind," by Maxwell Anderson. Published by Anderson House, Washington, D. C.

"Letters to Lucerne," by Fritz Rotter and Allen Vincent. Published by Samuel French, Inc., New York.

"Jason," by Samson Raphaelson. Published by Random House, Inc., New York.

"Angel Street," by Patrick Hamilton. Published by Constable & Co., Ltd., London, under the title "Gaslight."

"Uncle Harry," by Thomas Job. Published by Samuel French, Inc., New York.

"Hope for a Harvest," by Sophie Treadwell. Published by Samuel French, Inc., New York.

1942-1943

"The Patriots," by Sidney Kingsley. Published by Random House, Inc., New York.

"The Eve of St. Mark," by Maxwell Anderson. Published by Anderson House, Washington, D. C.

"The Skin of Our Teeth," by Thornton Wilder. Published by Harper & Brothers, New York and London.

"Winter Soldiers," by Dan James.

"Tomorrow the World," by James Gow and Arnaud d'Usseau. Published by Charles Scribner's Sons, New York.

"Harriet," by Florence Ryerson and Colin Clements. Published by Charles Scribner's Sons, New York.

"The Doughgirls," by Joseph Fields. Published by Random House, Inc., New York.

"The Damask Cheek," by John Van Druten and Lloyd Morris. Published by Random House, Inc., New York.

"Kiss and Tell," by F. Hugh Herbert. Published by Coward-McCann, Inc., New York.

"Oklahoma!", by Oscar Hammerstein 2nd and Richard Rodgers. Published by Random House, Inc., New York.

1943-1944

"Winged Victory," by Moss Hart. Published by Random House, Inc., New York.

"The Searching Wind," by Lillian Hellman. Published by Viking Press, Inc., New York.

"The Voice of the Turtle," by John Van Druten. Published by Random House, Inc., New York.

"Decision," by Edward Chodorov.

"Over 21," by Ruth Gordon. Published by Random House, Inc., New York.

"Outrageous Fortune," by Rose Franken. Published by Samuel French, New York.

"Jacobowsky and the Colonel," by S. N. Behrman. Published by Random House, Inc., New York.

"Storm Operation," by Maxwell Anderson. Published by Anderson House, Washington, D. C.

"Pick-up Girl," by Elsa Shelley.

"The Innocent Voyage," by Paul Osborn.

WHERE AND WHEN THEY WERE BORN

(Compiled from the most authentic records available.)

Abbott, George ....Hamburg, N. Y. 1895
Abel, Walter ....St. Paul, Minn. 1898
Adams, Maude ....Salt Lake City, Utah 1872
Addy, Wesley ....Omaha, Neb. 1912
Adler, Luther ....New York City 1903
Adler, Stella ....New York City 1904
Aherne, Brian ....King's Norton, England ..1902
Akins, Zoe ....Humansville, Mo. 1886
Allgood, Sara ....Dublin, Ireland 1883
Ames, Florenz ....Rochester, N. Y. 1884
Anders, Glenn ....Los Angeles, Cal. 1890
Anderson, Gwen ....Holland, Ia. 1921
Anderson, Judith ....Australia 1898
Anderson, Mary ....Trussville, Ala. 1917
Anderson, Maxwell ....Atlantic City, Pa. 1888
Andrews, A. G. ....Buffalo, N. Y. 1861
Andrews, Ann ....Los Angeles, Cal. 1895
Angel, Heather ....Oxford, England 1909
Anglin, Margaret ....Ottawa, Canada 1876
Arden, Eve ....San Francisco, Cal. 1912
Arling, Joyce ....Memphis, Tenn. 1911
Arliss, George ....London, England 1868
Ashcroft, Peggy ....Croydon, England 1907
Astaire, Fred ....Omaha, Neb. 1899
Astor, Mary ....Quincy, Ill. 1906
Atwater, Edith ....Chicago, Ill. 1912
Atwell, Roy ....Syracuse, N. Y. 1880
Atwill, Lionel ....London, England 1885

Bainter, Fay ....Los Angeles, Cal. 1892
Baker, Lee ....Michigan 1880
Bankhead, Tallulah ....Huntsville, Ala. 1902
Banks, Leslie J. ....West Derby, England 1890
Barbee, Richard ....Lafayette, Ind. 1887
Barrett, Edith ....Roxbury, Mass. 1904
Barry, Philip ....Rochester, N. Y. 1896

Barrymore, Diana ....New York City 1921
Barrymore, Ethel ....Philadelphia, Pa. 1879
Barrymore, John ....Philadelphia, Pa. 1882
Barrymore, Lionel ....Philadelphia, Pa. 1878
Barton, James ....Gloucester, N. J. 1890
Basehart, Richard ....Zanesville, Ohio 1919
Baxter, Lora ....New York 1907
Beecher, Janet ....Jefferson City, Mo. 1887
Behrman, S. N. ....Worcester, Mass. 1893
Bell, James ....Suffolk, Va. 1891
Bellamy, Ralph ....Chicago, Ill. 1905
Bennett, Richard ....Cass County, Ind. 1873
Berghof, Herbert ....Vienna, Austria 1909
Bergner, Elisabeth ....Vienna 1901
Berlin, Irving ....Russia 1888
Best, Edna ....Sussex, England 1900
Binney, Constance ....Philadelphia, Pa. 1900
Blackmer, Sydney ....Salisbury, N. C. 1898
Boland, Mary ....Detroit, Mich. 1880
Bolger, Ray ....Dorchester, Mass. 1906
Bondi, Beulah ....Chicago, Ill. 1892
Bordoni, Irene ....Paris, France 1895
Bourneuf, Philip ....Boston, Mass. 1912
Bowman, Patricia ....Washington, D. C. 1912
Brady, William A. ....San Francisco, Cal. 1863
Braham, Horace ....London, England 1896
Brent, Romney ....Saltillo, Mex. 1902
Brian, Donald ....St. Johns, N. F. 1877
Brice, Fannie ....Brooklyn, N. Y. 1891
Broderick, Helen ....New York 1891
Bromberg, J. Edward ....Hungary 1903
Brotherson, Eric ....Chicago, Ill. 1911
Brown, Anne Wiggins ....Baltimore, Md. 1916
Bruce, Nigel ....San Diego, Cal. 1895
Bryant, Charles ....England 1879
Buchanan, Jack ....England 1892
Burke, Billie ....Washington, D. C. 1885
Burr, Ann ....Boston, Mass. 1920
Byington, Spring ....Colorado Springs, Colo. ..1898

Cabot, Eliot ....Boston, Mass. 1899
Cagney, James ....New York 1904
Cagney, Jeanne ....New York 1920

Corthell, Herbert ....Boston, Mass. 1875
Cossart, Ernest ....Cheltenham, England 1876
Coulouris, George ....Manchester, England 1906
Courtleigh, Stephen ....New York City 1912
Coward, Noel ....Teddington, England 1899
Cowl, Jane ....Boston, Mass. 1887
Craig, Helen ....Mexico City 1914
Craven, Frank ....Boston, Mass. 1880
Cronyn, Hume ....Canada 1912
Crosman, Henrietta ....Wheeling, W. Va. 1865
Crothers, Rachel ....Bloomington, Ill. 1878
Cummings, Constance ....Seattle, Wash. 1911

Dale, Margaret ....Philadelphia, Pa. 1880
Davis, Owen ....Portland, Me. 1874
Davis, Owen, Jr. ....New York 1910
De Cordoba, Pedro ....New York 1881
Digges, Dudley ....Dublin, Ireland 1880
Dixon, Jean ....Waterbury, Conn. 1905
Dowling, Eddie ....Woonsocket, R. I. 1895
Drake, Alfred ....New York City 1914
Dressler, Eric ....Brooklyn, N. Y. 1900
Duncan, Augustin ....San Francisco 1873
Duncan, Todd ....Danville, Ky. 1900
Dunn, Emma ....England 1875
Dunning, Philip ....Meriden, Conn. 1890
Dupree, Minnie ....San Francisco, Cal. 1875
Durante, Jimmy ....New York City 1893

Edney, Florence ....London, England 1879
Eggerth, Marta ....Budapest, Hungary 1915
Eldridge, Florence ....Brooklyn, N. Y. 1901
Ellerbe, Harry ....Georgia 1905
Emery, Gilbert ....Naples, New York 1875
Emery, Katherine ....Birmingham, Ala. 1908
Erickson, Leif ....California 1917
Errol, Leon ....Sydney, Australia 1881
Ervine, St. John Greer ....Belfast, Ireland 1883
Evans, Edith ....London, England 1888
Evans, Madge ....New York City 1909
Evans, Maurice ....Dorchester, England 1901
Evans, Wilbur ....Philadelphia, Pa. 1908

Fabray, Nanette ....New Orleans, La. 1921
Fassett, Jay ....Elmira, N. Y. 1889
Fay, Frank ....San Francisco 1897
Ferber, Edna ....Kalamazoo, Mich. 1887
Ferguson, Elsie ....New York 1883
Ferrer, Jose ....Puerto Rico 1909
Field, Sylvia ....Allston, Mass. 1902
Fields, W. C. ....Philadelphia, Pa. 1883
Fischer, Alice ....Indiana 1869
Fitzgerald, Barry ....Dublin, Ireland 1888
Fitzgerald, Geraldine ....Dublin, Ireland 1914
Fletcher, Bramwell ....Bradford, Yorkshire, Eng. ..1904
Fontanne, Lynn ....London, England 1887
Forbes, Brenda ....London, England 1909
Forbes, Ralph ....London, England 1905
Foster, Phœbe ....New Hampshire 1897
Foy, Eddie, Jr. ....New Rochelle, N. Y. 1906
Francis, Arlene ....Boston, Mass. 1908
Fraser, Elizabeth ....Brooklyn, N. Y. 1920
Friganza, Trixie ....Cincinnati, Ohio 1870

Gahagan, Helen ....Boonton, N. J. 1902
Gaxton, William ....San Francisco, Cal. 1893
Geddes, Barbara Bel ....Cleveland, Ohio 1912
Geddes, Norman Bel ....Adrian, Mich. 1893
George, Grace ....New York 1879
Gerald, Ara ....New South Wales 1902
Gershwin, Ira ....New York 1896
Gielgud, John ....London, England 1904
Gillmore, Margalo ....England 1901
Gilmore, Virginia ....El Monte, Cal. 1919
Gish, Dorothy ....Dayton, Ohio 1898
Gish, Lillian ....Springfield, Ohio 1896
Gleason, James ....New York 1885
Golden, John ....New York 1874
Goodner, Carol ....New York City 1904
Gordon, Ruth ....Wollaston, Mass. 1896
Gough, Lloyd ....New York City 1906
Granville, Charlotte ....London 1863
Granville, Sydney ....Bolton, England 1885
Grant, Sydney ....Boston, Mass. 1873
Greaza, Walter ....St. Paul, Minn. 1900

Green, Mitzi ....New York City 1920
Greenstreet, Sydney ....England 1880
Groody, Louise ....Waco, Texas 1897
Gwenn, Edmund ....Glamorgan, Wales 1875

Hall, Bettina ....North Easton, Mass. 1906
Hall, Natalie ....North Easton, Mass. 1904
Hall, Thurston ....Boston, Mass. 1882
Halliday, John ....Brooklyn, N. Y. 1880
Halliday, Robert ....Loch Lomond, Scotland ..1893
Hampden, Walter ....Brooklyn, N. Y. 1879
Hannen, Nicholas ....London, England 1881
Hardie, Russell ....Griffin Mills, N. Y. 1906
Hardwicke, Sir Cedric ....Lye, Stourbridge, England.1893
Hargrave, Roy ....New York City 1908
Harrigan, William ....New York 1893
Hart, Richard ....Providence, R. I. 1915
Havoc, June ....Seattle, Wash. 1916
Haydon, Julie ....Oak Park, Ill. 1910
Hayes, Helen ....Washington, D. C. 1900
Hector, Louis ....England 1882
Heflin, Frances ....Oklahoma City, Okla. 1924
Heflin, Van ....Walters, Okla. 1909
Heineman, Eda ....Japan 1891
Heming, Violet ....Leeds, England 1893
Henie, Sonja ....Oslo, Norway 1912
Hepburn, Katharine ....Hartford, Conn. 1907
Henreid, Paul ....Trieste, Italy 1905
Hobart, Rose ....New York 1906
Hobbes, Halliwell ....Stratford, England 1877
Hoey, Dennis ....London, England 1893
Holm, Celeste ....New York City 1919
Hopkins, Arthur ....Cleveland, Ohio 1878
Hopkins, Miriam ....Bainbridge, Ga. 1904
Holmes, Taylor ....Newark, N. J. 1872
Homeier, Skippy ....Chicago, Ill. 1930
Huber, Paul ....Wilkes-Barre, Pa. 1895
Hull, Henry ....Louisville, Ky. 1888
Humphreys, Cecil ....Cheltenham, England 1880
Hunter, Glenn ....Highland Mills, N. Y. 1896
Huston, Walter ....Toronto 1884
Hutchinson, Josephine ....Seattle, Wash. 1898

Inescort, Frieda ....Hitchin, Scotland 1905
Ingram, Rex ....Dublin, Ireland 1892
Ives, Burl ....Hunt Township, Ill. 1909

Jagger, Dean ....Columbus Grove, Ohio....1904
Jameson, House ....Austin, Texas 1902
Joel, Clara ....Jersey City, N. J. 1890
Johann, Zita ....Hungary 1904
Jolson, Al ....Washington, D. C. 1883
Johnson, Harold J. (Chic) ....Chicago, Ill. 1891
Johnson, Raymond Edward ...Kenosha, Wis. 1912
Joslyn, Allyn ....Milford, Pa. 1905
Joy, Nicholas ....Paris, France 1892

Kane, Whitford ....Larne, Ireland 1882
Karloff, Boris ....Dulwich, England 1887
Kaufman, George S. ....Pittsburgh, Pa. 1889
Kaye, A. P. ....Ringwood, England 1885
Kaye, Danny ....New York City 1914
Keith, Ian ....Boston, Mass. 1899
Keith, Robert ....Scotland 1899
Kelly, Gene ....Pittsburgh, Pa. 1912
Kerrigan, J. M. ....Dublin, Ireland 1885
Kiepura, Jan ....Warsaw, Poland 1902
Kilbride, Percy ....San Francisco, Cal. 1880
King, Dennis ....Coventry, England 1897
Kingsford, Walter ....England 1876
Kingsley, Sidney ....New York 1906
Kirkland, Alexander ....Mexico City 1904
Kirkland, Muriel ....Yonkers, N. Y. 1904
Kirkland, Patricia ....New York 1926
Kruger, Alma ....Pittsburgh, Pa. 1880
Kruger, Otto ....Toledo, Ohio 1895

Landi, Elissa ....Venice, Italy 1904
Landis, Jessie Royce ....Chicago, Ill. 1904
Lane, Rosemary ....Indianola, Ia. 1916
Larimore, Earl ....Portland, Oregon 1899
Larrimore, Francine ....Russia 1898
Lauder, Harry ....Portobello, Scotland 1870
Laughton, Charles ....Scarborough, England 1899
Lawford, Betty ....London, England 1904
Lawrence, Gertrude ....London 1898

Miller, Gilbert ....New York 1884
Miller, Marilyn ....Findlay, Ohio 1898
Miramova, Elena ....Tsaritsyn, Russia 1907
Miranda, Carmen ....Portugal 1912
Mitchell, Grant ....Columbus, Ohio 1874
Mitchell, Thomas ....Elizabeth, N. J. 1892
Mitzi (Hajos) ....Budapest 1891
Moore, Grace ....Del Rio, Tenn. 1901
Moore, Victor ....Hammondton, N. J. 1876
Morley, Robert ....Semley, Wiltshire, England.1908
Morgan, Claudia ....New York 1912
Morgan, Helen ....Danville, Ill. 1900
Morgan, Ralph ....New York City 1889
Morris, Mary ....Boston 1894
Morris, McKay ....San Antonio, Texas 1890
Moss, Arnold ....Brooklyn, N. Y. 1910
Muni, Paul ....Lemberg, Austria 1895

Nagel, Conrad ....Keokuk, Iowa 1897
Natwick, Mildred ....Baltimore, Md. 1908
Nazimova, Alla ....Crimea, Russia 1879
Nolan, Lloyd ....San Francisco, Cal. 1903
Nugent, J. C. ....Miles, Ohio 1875
Nugent, Elliott ....Dover, Ohio 1900

O'Brien-Moore, Erin ....Los Angeles, Cal. 1908
Odets, Clifford ....Philadelphia 1906
Oldham, Derek ....Accrington, England 1892
Olivier, Laurence ....Dorking, Surrey, England..1907
Olsen, John Siguard (Ole) ...Peru, Ind. 1892
O'Malley, Rex ....London, England 1906
O'Neal, Frederick ....Brookville, Miss. 1905
O'Neill, Eugene Gladstone ...New York 1888
Ouspenskaya, Maria ....Tula, Russia 1876
Overman, Lynne ....Maryville, Mo. 1887

Patterson, Elizabeth ....Savannah, Tenn. 1898
Pemberton, Brock ....Leavenworth, Kansas 1885
Pennington, Ann ....Philadelphia, Pa. 1898
Petina, Irra ....Leningrad, Russia 1900
Philips, Mary ....New London, Conn. 1901
Pickford, Mary ....Toronto 1893
Picon, Molly ....New York City 1898
Pollock, Channing ....Washington, D. C. 1880

Powers, Leona ....Salida, Colo. 1900
Powers, Tom ....Owensburg, Ky. 1890
Price, Vincent ....St. Louis, Mo. 1914
Pryor, Roger ....New York City 1901

Rains, Claude ....London, England 1889
Raitt, John ....Santa Ana, Cal. 1917
Rambeau, Marjorie ....San Francisco, Cal. 1889
Rathbone, Basil ....Johannesburg 1892
Raye, Martha ....Butte, Mont. 1916
Reed, Florence ....Philadelphia, Pa. 1883
Rennie, James ....Toronto, Canada 1890
Ridges, Stanley ....Southampton, England ...1891
Ring, Blanche ....Boston, Mass. 1876
Roberts, Joan ....New York City 1918
Robinson, Bill ....Richmond, Va. 1878
Robinson, Edward G. ....Bucharest, Roumania 1893
Robson, Flora ....South Shields, Durham, Eng.1902
Roos, Joanna ....Brooklyn, N. Y. 1901
Ross, Anthony ....New York 1906
Ross, Thomas W. ....Boston, Mass. 1875
Royle, Selena ....New York 1905
Ruben, José ....Belgium 1886

Sands, Dorothy ....Cambridge, Mass. 1900
Sarnoff, Dorothy ....Brooklyn, N. Y. 1919
Savo, Jimmy ....New York City 1895
Scheff, Fritzi ....Vienna, Austria 1879
Schildkraut, Joseph ....Bucharest, Roumania 1896
Scott, Cyril ....Ireland 1866
Scott, Martha ....Jamesport, Mo. 1914
Scully, Barbara ....Detroit, Mich. 1924
Segal, Vivienne ....Philadelphia, Pa. 1897
Selwart, Tonio ....Munich, Germany 1906
Shannon, Effie ....Cambridge, Mass. 1867
Shean, Al ....Dornum, Germany 1868
Sherman, Hiram ....Boston, Mass. 1908
Sherwood, Robert Emmet ....New Rochelle, N. Y. 1896
Sidney, Sylvia ....New York 1910
Simms, Hilda ....Minneapolis, Minn. 1920
Simpson, Ivan ....England 1881
Skinner, Cornelia Otis ......Chicago 1902
Skinner, Otis ....Cambridgeport, Mass. 1858

Varden, Evelyn .... Venita, Okla. 1893
Venuta, Benay .... San Francisco, Cal. 1912

Walker, Nancy .... Philadelphia, Pa. 1922
Walker, June .... New York 1904
Walsh, Mary Jane .... Davenport, Ia. 1915
Warfield, David .... San Francisco, Cal. 1866
Waring, Richard .... Buckinghamshire, England. 1912
Warwick, Robert .... Sacramento, Cal. 1878
Waters, Ethel .... Chester, Pa. 1900
Watkins, Linda .... Boston, Mass. 1908
Watson, Lucile .... Quebec, Canada 1879
Watson, Minor .... Marianna, Ark. 1889
Webb, Clifton .... Indiana 1891
Webster, Margaret .... New York City 1905
Welles, Orson .... Kenosha, Wis. 1915
West, Mae .... Brooklyn, N. Y. 1892
Westley, Helen .... Brooklyn, N. Y. 1879
Weston, Ruth .... Boston, Mass. 1911
White, George .... Toronto, Canada 1890
Whiting, Jack .... Philadelphia, Pa. 1901
Whorf, Richard .... Winthrop, Mass. 1908
Widmark, Richard .... Sunrise, Minn. 1914
Willard, Catherine .... Dayton, Ohio 1895
William, Warren .... Aitkin, Minn. 1896
Williams, Emlyn .... Mostyn, Wales 1905
Williams, Rhys .... Wales 1903
Wiman, Dwight Deere .... Moline, Ill. 1895
Winwood, Estelle .... England 1883
Witherspoon, Cora .... New Orleans, La. 1891
Wood, Peggy .... Brooklyn, N. Y. 1894
Worlock, Frederick .... London, England 1885
Wright, Haidee .... London, England 1868
Wyatt, Jane .... Campgaw, N. J. 1912
Wycherly, Margaret .... England 1883
Wynn, Ed. .... Philadelphia, Pa. 1886
Wynn, Keenan .... New York City 1917
Wynyard, Diana .... London, England 1906

Young, Roland .... London, England 1887
Yurka, Blanche .... Bohemia 1893

Zorina, Vera .... Berlin, Germany 1917

NECROLOGY

June 18, 1944—June 18, 1945

Bennett, Richard, actor, 72. Famous actor of stage and screen; first appearance in "The Limited Mail" (1891); associated with Charles Frohman Company from 1896 for 17 years; popular in "Charley's Aunt," "What Every Woman Knows," "Beyond the Horizon," "They Knew What They Wanted," "Damaged Goods," "He Who Gets Slapped," etc.; last Broadway appearance in "Winterset" (1935); played in many screen plays. Born Bennet's Switch, Ind.; died Los Angeles, Calif., October 22, 1944.

Beresford, Harry, actor, 77. Almost 60 years in American theatre; debut in "Little Jack Sheppard" (1885) in London; with Henry E. Dixey to America (1886); played in stock and touring companies for thirty years; made hit on Broadway in "Boys Will Be Boys" (1919); other plays "The Old Soak," "The Perfect Alibi," "Michael and Mary," etc.; screen career included "The Sign of the Cross," "Seven Keys to Baldpate," etc. Born London, England; died Los Angeles, Calif., October 4, 1944.

Blaney, Charles E., author, producer, 78. Started at 21 as actor and author of "A Railroad Ticket"; was producer of many plays on Stair and Havlin's Circuit; operated chain of theatres in New York, Newark, Brooklyn, Baltimore, Philadelphia and New Orleans; authored and produced long list of melodramas including "More To Be Pitied Than Scorned," "King of the Opium Ring," etc. Born Columbus, Ohio; died New Canaan, Conn., October 21, 1944.

Brown, Albert O., producer, 73. Theatrical manager; associated with William A. Brady as manager of The Playhouse in New York and press agent for Brady productions; was shepherd of The Lambs from 1922 to 1932; president of Percy Williams Home and trustee of Actors Fund of America. Born New York City; died New York City, March 6, 1945.

Cherry, Effie, vaudeville actress and singer, 66. One of the original Cherry Sisters of vaudeville fame; debut in New York (1896) at Hammerstein's Olympia Music Hall; last

appearance (1935) in "The Gay Nineties" night club. Born
on farm near Indian Creek, Iowa; died Cedar Rapids, Iowa,
August 5, 1944.

Clarke, Wilfred, actor, author, producer, 71. Nephew of Edwin
Booth; first appeared on stage with his father, John Sleeper
Clarke, in London, Eng., in "Nicholas Nickleby" (1885);
leading comedian with Barry Sullivan, Edwin Booth, Laurence Barrett, Julia Marlowe and Ada Rehan; vaudeville
headliner over Keith-Orpheum Circuits. Born Philadelphia,
Pa.; died New York City, April 27, 1945.

Cregar, Samuel Laird, actor, 28. Stage and screen actor famous
for character parts; first appeared at 11 with Stratford-on-
Avon Players in England; played one year with Jasper
Deeter's Hedgerow Theatre and another with Pasadena Community Playhouse; starred in "Oscar Wilde" in California;
featured in films "Blood and Sand," "Heaven Can Wait,"
etc. Born Philadelphia, Pa.; died Hollywood, Calif., December 9, 1944.

Crosman, Henrietta Foster (Mrs. Maurice Campbell), actress,
79. Famous star of the 1900s; debut on Broadway in "The
White Slave" (1883); toured with Robert Downing in
classical repertoire; starred in "Mistress Nell" (1900); with
Augustin Daly, Daniel Frohman and many other stock companies; in 1902 acclaimed foremost Rosalind of her time,
playing 100 nights on Broadway; last Broadway show
"Thunder in the Air" (1929); played in vaudeville and motion pictures; retired in 1936. Born Wheeling, West Virginia; died Pelham Manor, New York, October 31, 1944.

Dayne, Blanche (Mrs. Will Cressy), actress, 73. Debut at 5
with Emma Abbott in Troy, New York; played Eva and
Topsy in "Uncle Tom's Cabin" at 7; with Howard's Minstrels at 10; teamed in vaudeville as Cressy and Dayne who
became top-flight headliners in U. S. and abroad; during
World War I entertained in France; retired in 1930. Born
Troy, New York; died Hackensack, New Jersey, June 27,
1944.

Dinehart, Alan, actor, director and author, 54. Stage, vaudeville
and screen star; won recognition first in "The Meanest
Man in the World," playing from Coast to Coast in vaudeville (1913); co-author of "The Alley Cat," "In Love with
Love," "Applesauce," "The Patsy," etc.; screen actor since
1931. Born St. Paul, Minn.; died Hollywood, Calif., July
17, 1944.

Downing, Robert L., actor, 86. Noted tragedian of the 80s and 90s; began stage career with National Stock Co., Washington, D. C. (1877), supporting Edwin Booth, John McCullough, Joseph Jefferson, Thomas Keene, etc.; leading man for Mary Anderson; starred in "The Gladiator" (1886); retired (1908) to become Evangelist; pastor of Christian Church, Portsmouth, R. I., until 1918. Born Washington, D. C.; died Middletown, Md., October 1, 1944.

Evans, Charles Evan, actor, producer and impresario, 88. Dean of American comedians; started stage career at 13 in "Streets of New York"; did character parts with Henry Duffy Players in California; played 3,600 times in "A Parlor Match" (1884 to 1894); last remembered as Judge Townsend in "Lightnin'." Born Rochester, New York; died Santa Monica, Calif., April 16, 1945.

Fielding, Edward (Edward B. Elkins), actor, 70. Debut on stage in England in "The Great Ruby" (1899); with Herbert Beerbohm Tree's Company in London; with Olga Nethersole in "Sapho"; last appearance on Broadway in "The Brown Danube" (1939). Born Brooklyn, New York; died Beverly Hills, Calif., January 10, 1945.

Gottschalk, Ferdinand, actor and playwright, 75. Fifty-seven years on American stage; professional debut in Toronto, Canada, with Rosina Vokes in "Which Is Which?" (1887); for many years prominent in Empire and Lyceum Theatre Stock Companies; film career started in 1933 and included "The Sign of the Cross," "Grand Hotel," "Marco Polo," etc. Born London, England; died London, England, November 17, 1944.

Grey, Jane (Mary E. Tyrrell), actress, 61. Stage debut in Los Angeles with Belasco company in "Rose of the Rancho"; several years with stock in Los Angeles, Columbus, Providence, Cleveland and Elitch's Gardens, Denver; Broadway debut in "Is Matrimony a Failure?" (1909); last play on Broadway "A Lady Detained" (1935). Born Middlebury, Vermont; died New York City, November 9, 1944.

Haswell, Percy (Mrs. George Fawcett), actress, 74. Started Broadway career as a child actress in "A Night Off" (1885); toured with Otis Skinner in "The Honor of the Family" and other plays; leading lady for William Crane for three seasons and toured with E. H. Sothern; star of her own stock company in Baltimore; last appearance with Fawcett

Players in Nantucket, Mass., in 1943. Born Austin, Texas; died Nantucket, Mass., June 13, 1945.

Irving, Isabel (Mrs. William Thompson), actress, 73. On stage 48 years; first appearance with Rosina Vokes in "The Schoolmistress" (1887); last New York appearance in all-star revival of "Three Wise Fools" (1936); prominent member of Augustin Daly's company for five seasons; with Daniel Frohman's company and later leading lady for John Drew. Born Bridgeport, Conn.; died Nantucket, Mass., September 1, 1944.

La Verne, Lucille, actress, 76. First appearance on Broadway with Fanny Davenport in "La Tosca" (1888); gained fame in "Sun-up" as Widow Cagle; last appearance on Broadway in "Mulatto" (1935); La Verne Theatre in Richmond, Va., was named for her. Born Memphis, Tenn.; died Culver City, Calif., March 4, 1945.

Locke, Edward, playwright and actor, 75. First success "The Climax" produced in 1909; started career writing vaudeville sketches; plays included "The Case of Becky," "The Dancer," "The Love Call" and others; as actor appeared with David Warfield and Cecil Spooner in early 1900s; was vice-president of Actors' Society of America. Born Stourbridge, Worcester, Eng.; died East Islip, New York, April 1, 1945.

McNamara, Edward J., actor, 57. First theatrical engagement with Field's Minstrels (1908); protégé of Enrico Caruso; sang on tour with Mme. Schumann-Heink for six years; among Broadway plays popular in "Strictly Dishonorable," "Parnell" and "Margin for Error." Born Paterson, New Jersey; died on train near Boston, Mass., November 10, 1944.

Moore, Percy, actor, 67. First with E. H. Sothern repertory; remembered in "The Traveling Salesman, "The Cat and the Canary," "Adam and Eva" and "The Man Who Came to Dinner"; executive secretary of Episcopal Actors' Guild; director of The Players. Born Montreal, Canada; died New York City, April 8, 1945.

Mordkin, Mikhail M., dancer and ballet master, 63. Organizer of Mordkin Ballet (later Ballet Theatre of New York); first appearance in America as partner of Pavlova in 1910 at the Metropolitan; ballet master and choreographer at Imperial Theatre in Russia; later ballet manager at the Soviet Opera.

Born Moscow, Russia; died Millbrook, New Jersey, July 15, 1944.

Nash, George Frederick, actor, 71. Known on stage for more than 50 years; debut in "The Rivals" with Joseph Jefferson (1888); remembered in "East Is West," "The Witching Hour," "Officer 666," etc.; last New York appearance in "The Old Maid" (1935); also appeared in many film plays. Born Philadelphia, Pa.; died Amityville, New York, December 31, 1944.

Parker, Louis Napoleon, dramatist and composer, 91. Great grandson of Isaac Parker, Chief Justice of Massachusetts from 1814 to 1830; music instructor in London for 19 years; started to write plays at forty; first play "A Buried Talent" (1890); first New York play, "Rosemary" (1896); others, adaptations of "L'Aiglon," "Cyrano de Bergerac" and "Chanticler"; wrote "Disraeli," "Pomander Walk," "Joseph and His Brethren," etc. Born Calvados, France; died Devonshire, England, September 21, 1944.

Richman, Arthur, dramatist, 58. First play "Not So Long Ago" (1920); others "Ambush," "The Awful Truth" and "A Serpent's Tooth"; director of American Theatre Wing War Services; honorary president of Authors' League of America and head of Society of American Dramatists and Composers. Born New York City; died New York City, September 10, 1944.

Rives, Amelie (Princess Troubetzkoy), dramatist and novelist, 81. Wrote "The Quick and the Dead" and "Herod and Miriamne"; dramas included "The Fear Market," "Allegiance" (with Prince Troubetzkoy) and "Love in a Mist" (with Gilbert Emery). Born Richmond, Va.; died Charlottesville, Va., June 15, 1945.

Roselle, William, actor, 67. First stage appearance with Ada Rehan and Otis Skinner in "The Taming of the Shrew" (1902); played in "On Borrowed Time," "The Connecticut Yankee," "The Man Who Came to Dinner" and several editions of "Ziegfeld Follies"; recently toured in "The Doughgirls." Born New York City; died New York City, June 1, 1945.

Sidney, George, actor, 68. Musical comedy comedian; began career in music halls and vaudeville at 12; associated with Harry von Tilzer in comedy skits; with Ward and Vokes for three seasons, making "Busy Izzy" famous; appeared in "Potash and Perlmutter" and played 600 times in "Welcome Stranger." Born Hungary; died Hollywood, Calif., April 29, 1945.

Tully, Richard, playwright and producer, 67. Greatest success "The Bird of Paradise" (over which a famous plagiarism suit was fought); other plays were "Rose of the Rancho," "Omar the Tentmaker," "The Flame," etc. Born Nevada City, Calif.; died New York City, January 31, 1945.

Velez, Lupe (Guadeloupe Velez de Villabos), actress and dancer, 36. Started dancing in Mexico City at 13; Broadway career included "Strike Me Pink," "Hot Cha," "You Never Know," etc.; remembered in London in "Transatlantic Rhythm" (1936); well known for colorful films, especially "The Gaucho" and "Mexican Spitfire"; married Johnny Weismuller. Born San Luis de Potosi, Mexico; died Beverly Hills, Calif., December 14, 1944.

Warwick, Robert (Robert Taylor Bien), actor, 66. Started Broadway career in 1903 in "Glad of It"; supported Wilton Lackaye, Digby Bell, Virginia Harned, Grace George, Mrs. Leslie Carter, Jeanne Eagels, etc.; last appearance on Broadway in "Primer for Lovers" (1929); appeared in many silent films and "talkies"; was Major in American Air Force in World War I. Born Sacramento, Calif.; died Hollywood, Calif., December 3, 1944.

Watson, Billy (Isaac Levie), actor-producer, 78. Known as "King of Burlesque"; producer-star of "Krausmeyer's Alley" and "Watson's Beef Trust"; debut as singer at Chatham Square Museum (1881); built several theatres, including Watson's Cozy Corner in Brooklyn and the Orpheum in Paterson, New Jersey. Born New York City; died Asbury Park, New Jersey, January 14, 1945.

THE DECADES' TOLL

(Persons of Outstanding Prominence in the Theatre
Who Have Died in Recent Years)

	Born	Died
Aborn, Milton	1864	1933
Ames, Winthrop	1871	1937
Anderson, Mary (Navarro)	1860	1940
Baker, George Pierce	1866	1935
Barrymore, John	1882	1942
Belasco, David	1856	1931
Benson, Sir Frank	1859	1939
Bernhardt, Sarah	1845	1923
Campbell, Mrs. Patrick	1865	1940
Cohan, George Michael	1878	1942
Crabtree, Charlotte (Lotta)	1847	1924
De Koven, Reginald	1861	1920
De Reszke, Jean	1850	1925
Drew, John	1853	1927
Drinkwater, John	1883	1937
Du Maurier, Sir Gerald	1873	1934
Duse, Eleanora	1859	1924
Fiske, Minnie Maddern	1865	1932
Frohman, Daniel	1851	1940
Galsworthy, John	1867	1933
Gorky, Maxim	1868	1936
Greet, Sir Philip (Ben)	1858	1936
Herbert, Victor	1859	1924
Patti, Adelina	1843	1919
Pinero, Sir Arthur Wing	1855	1934
Pirandello, Luigi	1867	1936
Rejane, Gabrielle	1857	1920
Rogers, Will	1879	1935
Russell, Annie	1864	1936
Schumann-Heink, Ernestine	1861	1936
Sembrich, Marcella	1859	1935
Shaw, Mary	1860	1929

	Born	Died
Skinner, Otis	1858	1942
Sothern, Edwin Hugh	1859	1933
Terry, Ellen	1848	1928
Thomas, Augustus	1857	1934
Yeats, William Butler	1865	1939

INDEX OF AUTHORS

487

INDEX OF PLAYS AND CASTS

INDEX OF PRODUCERS, DIRECTORS AND DESIGNERS